Bayesian Optimization

Bayesian optimization is a methodology for optimizing expensive objective functions that has proven success in the sciences, engineering, and beyond. This timely text provides a self-contained and comprehensive introduction to the subject, starting from scratch and carefully developing all the key ideas along the way. This bottom-up approach illuminates unifying themes in the design of Bayesian optimization algorithms and builds a solid theoretical foundation for approaching novel situations.

The core of the book is divided into three main parts, covering theoretical and practical aspects of Gaussian process modeling, the Bayesian approach to sequential decision making, and the realization and computation of practical and effective optimization policies.

Following this foundational material, the book provides an overview of theoretical convergence results, a survey of notable extensions, a comprehensive history of Bayesian optimization, and an extensive annotated bibliography of applications.

Roman Garnett is Associate Professor in Computer Science and Engineering at Washington University in St. Louis. He has been a leader in the Bayesian optimization community since 2011, when he cofounded a long-running workshop on the subject at the NeurIPS conference. His research focus is developing Bayesian methods – including Bayesian optimization – for automating scientific discovery.

T0324901

ROMAN GARNETT
Washington University in St Louis

BAYESIAN OPTIMIZATION

CAMBRIDGE
UNIVERSITY PRESS

Shaftesbury Road, Cambridge CB2 8EA, United Kingdom

One Liberty Plaza, 20th Floor, New York, NY 10006, USA

477 Williamstown Road, Port Melbourne, VIC 3207, Australia

314–321, 3rd Floor, Plot 3, Splendor Forum, Jasola District Centre, New Delhi – 110025, India

103 Penang Road, #05–06/07, Visioncrest Commercial, Singapore 238467

Cambridge University Press is part of Cambridge University Press & Assessment,
a department of the University of Cambridge.

We share the University's mission to contribute to society through the pursuit of
education, learning and research at the highest international levels of excellence.

www.cambridge.org
Information on this title: www.cambridge.org/9781108425780

DOI: 10.1017/9781108348973

First published 2023

A catalogue record for this publication is available from the British Library.

ISBN 978-1-108-42578-0 Hardback

CONTENTS

PREFACE

My interest in Bayesian optimization began in 2007 at the start of my doctoral studies. I was frustrated that there seemed to be a Bayesian approach to every task I cared about, *except* optimization. Of course, as was often the case at that time (not to mention now!), I was mistaken in this belief, but one should never let ignorance impede inspiration.

Meanwhile, my labmate and soon-to-be frequent collaborator Mike Osborne had a fresh copy of RASMUSSEN and WILLIAMS's *Gaussian Processes for Machine Learning* and just would *not* stop talking about GPs at our lab meetings. Through sheer brute force of repetition, I slowly built a hand-wavy intuition for Gaussian processes – my mental model was the "sausage plot" – without even being sure about their precise definition. However, I was pretty sure that marginals were Gaussian (what else?), and one day it occurred to me that one could achieve Bayesian optimization by maximizing the probability of improvement. This was the algorithm I was looking for! In my excitement I shot off an email to Mike that kicked off years of fruitful collaboration:

> Can I ask a dumb question about GPs? Let's say that I'm doing function approximation on an interval with a GP. So I've got this mean function $m(x)$ and a variance function $v(x)$. Is it true that if I pick a particular point x, then $p\big(f(x)\big) \sim \mathcal{N}\big(m(x), v(x)\big)$? Please say yes.
>
> If this is true, then I think the idea of doing Bayesian optimization using GPs is, dare I say, trivial.

The hubris of youth!

Well, it turned out I was 45 years too late in proposing this algorithm,[1] and that it only seemed "trivial" because I had no appreciation for its theoretical foundation. However, truly great ideas are rediscovered many times, and my excitement did not fade. Once I developed a deeper understanding of Gaussian processes and Bayesian decision theory, I came to see them as a "Bayesian crank" I could turn to realize adaptive algorithms for *any* task. I have been repeatedly astonished to find that the resulting algorithms – seemingly by magic – *automatically* display intuitive emergent behavior as a result of their careful design. My goal with this book is to paint this grand picture. In effect, it is a gift to my former self: the book I wish I had in the early years of my career.

In the context of machine learning, Bayesian optimization is an ancient idea – KUSHNER's paper appeared only three years after the term "machine learning" was coined! Despite its advanced age, Bayesian optimization has been enjoying a period of revitalization and rapid progress over the past ten years. The primary driver of this renaissance has been advances in computation, which have enabled increasingly sophisticated tools for Bayesian modeling and inference.

Ironically, however, perhaps the most critical development was not Bayesian at all, but the rise of deep neural networks, another old idea

The first of many "sausage plots" to come.

1 H. J. KUSHNER (1962). A Versatile Stochastic Model of a Function of Unknown and Time Varying Form. *Journal of Mathematical Analysis and Applications* 5(1):150–167.

2 J. SNOEK et al. (2012). Practical Bayesian Optimization of Machine Learning Algorithms. *NeurIPS 2012*.

granted new life by modern computation. The extreme cost of training these models demands efficient routines for hyperparameter tuning, and in a timely and influential paper, SNOEK et al. demonstrated (dramatically!) that Bayesian optimization was up to the task.[2] Hyperparameter tuning proved to be a "killer app" for Bayesian optimization, and the ensuing surge of interest has yielded a mountain of publications developing new algorithms and improving old ones, exploring countless variations on the basic setup, establishing theoretical guarantees on performance, and applying the framework to a huge range of domains.

Due to the nature of the computer science publication model, these recent developments are scattered across dozens of brief papers, and the pressure to establish novelty in a limited space can obscure the big picture in favor of minute details. This book aims to provide a self-contained and comprehensive introduction to Bayesian optimization, starting "from scratch" and carefully developing all the key ideas along the way. This bottom-up approach allows us to identify unifying themes in Bayesian optimization algorithms that may be lost when surveying the literature.

intended audience

The intended audience is graduate students and researchers in machine learning, statistics, and related fields. However, it is also my sincere hope that practitioners from more distant fields wishing to harness the power of Bayesian optimization will also find some utility here.

prerequisites

For the bulk of the text, I assume the reader is comfortable with differential and integral calculus, probability, and linear algebra. On occasion the discussion will meander to more esoteric areas of mathematics, and these passages can be safely ignored and returned to later if desired. A good working knowledge of the Gaussian distribution is also essential, and I provide an abbreviated but sufficient introduction in Appendix A.

Chapters 2–4: modeling the objective function with Gaussian processes

The book is divided into three main parts. Chapters 2–4 cover theoretical and practical aspects of modeling with Gaussian processes. This class of models is the overwhelming favorite in the Bayesian optimization literature, and the material contained within is critical for several following chapters. It was daunting to write this material in light of the many excellent references already available, in particular the aforementioned *Gaussian Processes for Machine Learning*. However, I heavily biased the presentation in light of the needs of optimization, and even experts may find something new.

Chapters 5–7: sequential decision making and policy building

Chapters 5–7 develop the theory of sequential decision making and its application to optimization. Although this theory requires a model of the objective function and our observations of it, the presentation is agnostic to the choice of model and may be read independently from the preceding chapters on Gaussian processes.

Chapters 8–10: Bayesian optimization with Gaussian processes

These threads are unified in Chapters 8–10, which discuss the particulars of Bayesian optimization with Gaussian process models. Chapters 8–9 cover details of computation and implementation, and Chapter 10 discusses theoretical performance bounds on Bayesian optimization algorithms, where most results depend intimately on a Gaussian process model of the objective function or the associated reproducing kernel Hilbert space.

The nuances of some applications require modifications to the basic sequential optimization scheme that is the focus of the bulk of the book, and Chapter 11 introduces several notable extensions to this basic setup. Each is systematically presented through the unifying lens of Bayesian decision theory to illustrate how one might proceed when facing a novel situation.

Chapter 11: extensions

Finally, Chapter 12 provides a brief and standalone history of Bayesian optimization. This was perhaps the most fun chapter for me to write, if only because it forced me to plod through old Soviet literature (in an actual library! What a novelty these days!). To my surprise I was able to antedate many Bayesian optimization policies beyond their commonly attested origin, including expected improvement, knowledge gradient, probability of improvement, and upper confidence bound. (A reader familiar with the literature may be surprised to learn the last of these was actually the first policy discussed by KUSHNER in his 1962 paper.) Despite my best efforts, there may still be stones left to be overturned before the complete history is revealed.

Chapter 12: brief history of Bayesian optimization

Dependencies between the main chapters are illustrated in the margin. There are two natural linearizations of the material. The first is the one I adopted and personally prefer, which covers modeling prior to decision making. However, one could also proceed in the other order, reading Chapters 5–7 first, then looping back to Chapter 2. After covering the material in these chapters (in either order), the remainder of the book can be perused at will. Logical partial paths through the book include:

- a minimal but self-contained introduction: Chapters 1–2, 5–7
- a shorter introduction requiring leaps of faith: Chapters 1 and 7
- a crash course on the underlying theory: Chapters 1–2, 5–7, 10
- a head start on implementing a software package: Chapters 1–9

A reader already quite comfortable with Gaussian processes might wish to skip over Chapters 2–4 entirely.

I struggled for some time over whether to include a chapter on applications. On the one hand, Bayesian optimization ultimately owes its popularity to its success in optimizing a growing and diverse set of difficult objectives. However, these applications often require extensive technical background to appreciate, and an adequate coverage would be tedious to write and tedious to read. As a compromise, I provide an annotated bibliography outlining the optimization challenges involved in notable domains of interest and pointing to studies where these challenges were successfully overcome with the aid of Bayesian optimization.

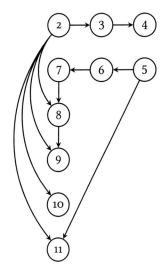

A dependency graph for Chapters 2–11. Chapter 1 is a universal dependency.

Annotated Bibliography of Applications: Appendix D, p. 313

The sheer size of the Bayesian optimization literature – especially the output of the previous decade – makes it impossible to provide a complete survey of every recent development. This is especially true for the extensions discussed in Chapter 11 and even more so for the bibliography on applications, where work has proliferated in myriad branching directions. Instead I settled for presenting what I considered to be the most important ideas and providing pointers to entry points for the relevant literature. The reader should not read anything into any omissions; there is simply too much high-quality work to go around.

Additional information about the book, including a list of errata as they are discovered, may be found at the companion webpage:

bayesoptbook.com

I encourage the reader to report any errata or other issues to the companion GitHub repository for discussion and resolution:

github.com/bayesoptbook/bayesoptbook.github.io

Thank you!

Preparation of this manuscript was facilitated tremendously by numerous free and open source projects, and the creators, developers, and maintainers of these projects have my sincere gratitude. The manuscript was typeset in LaTeX using the excellent and extremely flexible memoir class. The typeface is Linux Libertine. Figures were laid out in MATLAB and converted to TikZ/PGF/PGFPLOTS for further tweaking and typesetting via the matlab2tikz script. The colors used in figures were based on www.colorbrewer.org by Cynthia A. Brewer, and I endeavored to the best of my ability to ensure that the figures are colorblind friendly. The colormap used in heat maps is a slight modification of the Matplotlib viridis colormap where the "bright" end is pure white.

I would like to thank Eric Brochu, Nando de Freitas, Matt Hoffman, Frank Hutter, Mike Osborne, Bobak Shahriari, Jasper Snoek, Kevin Swersky, and Ziyu Wang, who jointly provided the activation energy for this undertaking. I would also like to thank Eytan Bakshy, Ivan Barrientos, George De Ath, Neil Dhir, Peter Frazier, Lukas Fröhlich, Ashok Gautam, Jake Gardner, Javier González, Ryan-Rhys Griffiths, Philipp Hennig, Eugen Hotaj, Jungtaek Kim, Simon Kruse, Jack Liu, Bryan Low, Ruben Martinez-Cantin, Keita Mori, Kevin Murphy, Matthias Poloczeck, Jon Scarlett, Sebastian Tay, Sattar Vakili, Jiangyan Zhao, Qiuyi Zhang, Xiaowei Zhang, and GitHub users cgoble001 and chaos-and-patterns for their suggestions, corrections, and valuable discussions along the way, as well as everyone at Cambridge University Press for their support and patience as I continually missed deadlines. Finally, special thanks are due to the students of two seminars run at Washington University reading, discussing, and ultimately improving the book.

Funding support was provided by the United States National Science Foundation (NSF) under award number 1845434. Any opinions, findings, and conclusions or recommendations expressed in this book are those of the author and do not necessarily reflect the views of the NSF.

This book took far more time than I initially anticipated, and I would especially like to thank my wife Marion, my son Max (arg Max?), and my daughter Matilda (who escaped being named Minnie!) for their understanding and support during this long journey.

Roman Garnett
St. Louis, Missouri, November 2022

NOTATION

All vectors are column vectors and are denoted in lowercase bold: $\mathbf{x} \in \mathbb{R}^d$. vectors and matrices
Matrices are denoted in uppercase bold: $\mathbf{A}$.

We adopt the "numerator layout" convention for matrix calculus: matrix calculus convention
the derivative of a vector by a scalar is a (column) vector, whereas the
derivative of a scalar by a vector is a row vector. This results in the chain
rule proceeding from left-to-right; for example, if a vector $\mathbf{x}(\theta)$ depends chain rule
on a scalar parameter θ, then for a function $f(\mathbf{x})$, we have:

$$\frac{\partial f}{\partial \theta} = \frac{\partial f}{\partial \mathbf{x}} \frac{\partial \mathbf{x}}{\partial \theta}.$$

When an indicator function is required, we use the Iverson bracket indicator functions
notation. For a statement s, we have:

$$[s] = \begin{cases} 1 & \text{if } s \text{ is true;} \\ 0 & \text{otherwise.} \end{cases}$$

The statement may depend on a parameter: $[x \in A]$, $[x \geq 0]$, etc.

Logarithms are taken with respect to their natural base, e. Quantities logarithms
in log units such as log likelihoods or entropy thus have units of *nats*, nats
the base-e analogue of the more familiar base-2 bits.

SYMBOLS WITH IMPLICIT DEPENDENCE ON LOCATION

There is one notational innovation in this book compared with the
Gaussian process and Bayesian optimization literature at large: we make
heavy use of symbols for quantities that depend *implicitly* on a putative
(and arbitrary) input location x. Most importantly, to refer to the value
of an objective function f at a given location x, we introduce the symbol
$\phi = f(x)$. This avoids clash with the name of the function itself, f, while
avoiding an extra layer of brackets. We use this scheme throughout the
book, including variations such as:

$$\phi' = f(x'); \qquad \boldsymbol{\phi} = f(\mathbf{x}); \qquad \gamma = g(x); \qquad \text{etc.}$$

To refer to the outcome of a (possibly inexact) measurement at x, we use
the symbol y; the distribution of y presumably depends on ϕ.

We also allocate symbols to describe properties of the marginal predictive distributions for the objective function value ϕ and observed
value y, all of which also have implicit dependence on x. These appear
in the following table.

COMPREHENSIVE LIST OF SYMBOLS

A list of important symbols appears on the following pages, arranged
roughly in alphabetical order.

symbol	description
$\equiv$	identical equality of functions; for a constant c, $f \equiv c$ is a constant function
∇	gradient operator
$\varnothing$	termination option: the action of immediately terminating optimization
$\prec$	either Pareto dominance or the Löwner order: for symmetric $\mathbf{A}, \mathbf{B}$, $\mathbf{A} \prec \mathbf{B}$ if and only if $\mathbf{B} - \mathbf{A}$ is positive definite
$\omega \sim p(\omega)$	is sampled according to: ω is a realization of a random variable with probability density $p(\omega)$
$\bigsqcup_i \mathcal{X}_i$	disjoint union of $\{\mathcal{X}_i\}$: $\bigsqcup_i \mathcal{X}_i = \bigcup_i \{(x, i) \mid x \in \mathcal{X}_i\}$
$\lvert\mathbf{A}\rvert$	determinant of square matrix $\mathbf{A}$
$\lvert\mathbf{x}\rvert$	Euclidean norm of vector $\mathbf{x}$; $\lvert\mathbf{x} - \mathbf{y}\rvert$ is thus the Euclidean distance between vectors $\mathbf{x}$ and $\mathbf{y}$
$\lVert f \rVert_{\mathcal{H}_K}$	norm of function f in reproducing kernel Hilbert space $\mathcal{H}_K$
$\mathbf{A}^{-1}$	inverse of square matrix $\mathbf{A}$
$\mathbf{x}^\top$	transpose of vector $\mathbf{x}$
$\mathbf{0}$	vector or matrix of zeros
$\mathcal{A}$	action space for a decision
$\alpha(x; \mathcal{D})$	acquisition function evaluating x given data $\mathcal{D}$
$\alpha_\tau(x; \mathcal{D})$	expected marginal gain in $u(\mathcal{D})$ after observing at x then making $\tau - 1$ additional optimal observations given the outcome
$\alpha_\tau^*(\mathcal{D})$	value of $\mathcal{D}$ with horizon τ: expected marginal gain in $u(\mathcal{D})$ from τ additional optimal observations
α_{EI}	expected improvement
α_{f^*}	mutual information between y and f^*
α_{KG}	knowledge gradient
α_{PI}	probability of improvement
α_{x^*}	mutual information between y and x^*
α_{UCB}	upper confidence bound
α_{TS}	Thompson sampling "acquisition function:" a draw $f \sim p(f \mid \mathcal{D})$
β	confidence parameter in Gaussian process upper confidence bound policy
$\beta(\mathbf{x}; \mathcal{D})$	batch acquisition function evaluating $\mathbf{x}$ given data $\mathcal{D}$; may have modifiers analogous to α
$\mathbf{C}$	prior covariance matrix of observed values $\mathbf{y}$: $\mathbf{C} = \mathrm{cov}[\mathbf{y}]$
$c(\mathcal{D})$	cost of acquiring data $\mathcal{D}$
$\mathrm{chol}\,\mathbf{A}$	Cholesky decomposition of positive definite matrix $\mathbf{A}$: if $\mathbf{\Lambda} = \mathrm{chol}\,\mathbf{A}$, then $\mathbf{A} = \mathbf{\Lambda}\mathbf{\Lambda}^\top$
$\mathrm{corr}[\omega, \psi]$	correlation of random variables ω and ψ; with a single argument, $\mathrm{corr}[\omega] = \mathrm{corr}[\omega, \omega]$
$\mathrm{cov}[\omega, \psi]$	covariance of random variables ω and ψ; with a single argument, $\mathrm{cov}[\omega] = \mathrm{cov}[\omega, \omega]$
$\mathcal{D}$	set of observed data, $\mathcal{D} = (\mathbf{x}, \mathbf{y})$
$\mathcal{D}', \mathcal{D}_1$	set of observed data after observing at x: $\mathcal{D}' = \mathcal{D} \cup \{(x, y)\} = (\mathbf{x}', \mathbf{y}')$
$\mathcal{D}_\tau$	set of observed data after τ observations
$D_{\mathrm{KL}}[p \parallel q]$	Kullback–Leibler divergence between distributions with probability densities p and q
$\Delta(x, y)$	marginal gain in utility after acquiring observation (x, y): $\Delta(x, y) = u(\mathcal{D}') - u(\mathcal{D})$
$\delta(\omega - a)$	Dirac delta distribution on ω with point mass at a
$\mathrm{diag}\,\mathbf{x}$	diagonal matrix with diagonal $\mathbf{x}$
$\mathbb{E}, \mathbb{E}_\omega$	expectation, expectation with respect to ω
ε	measurement error associated with an observation at x: $\varepsilon = y - \phi$
f	objective function; $f : \mathcal{X} \to \mathbb{R}$
$f\vert_\mathcal{Y}$	the restriction of f onto the subdomain $\mathcal{Y} \subset \mathcal{X}$
f^*	globally maximal value of the objective function: $f^* = \max f$
γ_τ	information capacity of an observation process given τ iterations

symbol	description
$\mathcal{GP}(f; \mu, K)$	Gaussian process on f with mean function μ and covariance function K
$\mathcal{H}_K$	reproducing kernel Hilbert space associated with kernel K
$\mathcal{H}_K[B]$	ball of radius B in $\mathcal{H}_K$: $\{f \mid \|f\|_{\mathcal{H}_K} \leq B\}$
$H[\omega]$	discrete or differential entropy of random variable ω
$H[\omega \mid \mathcal{D}]$	discrete or differential of random variable ω after conditioning on $\mathcal{D}$
$I(\omega; \psi)$	mutual information between random variables ω and ψ
$I(\omega; \psi \mid \mathcal{D})$	mutual information between random variables ω and ψ after conditioning on $\mathcal{D}$
$\mathbf{I}$	identity matrix
K	prior covariance function: $K = \text{cov}[f]$
$K_{\mathcal{D}}$	posterior covariance function given data $\mathcal{D}$: $K_{\mathcal{D}} = \text{cov}[f \mid \mathcal{D}]$
K_{M}	Matérn covariance function
K_{SE}	squared exponential covariance function
κ	cross-covariance between f and observed values $\mathbf{y}$: $\kappa(x) = \text{cov}[\mathbf{y}, \phi \mid x]$
ℓ	either a length-scale parameter or the lookahead horizon
λ	output-scale parameter
$\mathcal{M}$	space of models indexed by the hyperparameter vector $\boldsymbol{\theta}$
$\mathbf{m}$	prior expected value of observed values $\mathbf{y}$, $\mathbf{m} = \mathbb{E}[\mathbf{y}]$
μ	either the prior mean function, $\mu = \mathbb{E}[f]$, or the predictive mean of ϕ: $\mu = \mathbb{E}[\phi \mid x, \mathcal{D}] = \mu_{\mathcal{D}}(x)$
$\mu_{\mathcal{D}}$	posterior mean function given data $\mathcal{D}$: $\mu_{\mathcal{D}} = \mathbb{E}[f \mid \mathcal{D}]$
$\mathcal{N}(\boldsymbol{\phi}; \boldsymbol{\mu}, \Sigma)$	multivariate normal distribution on $\boldsymbol{\phi}$ with mean vector $\boldsymbol{\mu}$ and covariance matrix Σ
$\mathbf{N}$	measurement error covariance corresponding to observed values $\mathbf{y}$
$\mathcal{O}$	is asymptotically bounded above by: for nonnegative functions f, g of τ, $f = \mathcal{O}(g)$ if f/g is asymptotically bounded by a constant as $\tau \to \infty$
$\mathcal{O}^*$	as above with logarithmic factors suppressed: $f = \mathcal{O}^*(g)$ if $f(\tau)(\log \tau)^k = \mathcal{O}(g)$ for some k
Ω	is asymptotically bounded below by: $f = \Omega(g)$ if $g = \mathcal{O}(f)$
p	probability density
q	either an approximation to probability density p or a quantile function
$\Phi(z)$	standard normal cumulative density function: $\Phi(z) = \int_{-\infty}^{z} \phi(z') \, dz'$
ϕ	value of the objective function at x: $\phi = f(x)$
$\phi(z)$	standard normal probability density function: $\phi(z) = (\sqrt{2\pi})^{-1} \exp(-\frac{1}{2}z^2)$
Pr	probability
$\mathbb{R}$	set of real numbers
R_{τ}	cumulative regret after τ iterations
$\bar{R}_{\tau}[B]$	worst-case cumulative regret after τ iterations on the RKHS ball $\mathcal{H}_K[B]$
r_{τ}	simple regret after τ iterations
$\bar{r}_{\tau}[B]$	worst-case simple regret after τ iterations on the RKHS ball $\mathcal{H}_K[B]$
$\mathbf{P}$	a correlation matrix
ρ	a scalar correlation
ρ_{τ}	instantaneous regret on iteration τ
s^2	predictive variance of y; for additive Gaussian noise, $s^2 = \text{var}[y \mid x, \mathcal{D}] = \sigma^2 + \sigma_n^2$
Σ	a covariance matrix, usually the Gram matrix associated with $\mathbf{x}$: $\Sigma = K_{\mathcal{D}}(\mathbf{x}, \mathbf{x})$
σ^2	predictive variance of ϕ: $\sigma^2 = K_{\mathcal{D}}(x, x)$
σ_n^2	variance of measurement error at x: $\sigma_n^2 = \text{var}[\varepsilon \mid x]$
$\text{std}[\omega]$	standard deviation of random variable ω
$\mathcal{T}(\phi; \mu, \sigma^2, \nu)$	Student-t distribution on ϕ with ν degrees of freedom, mean μ, and variance σ^2
$\mathcal{TN}(\phi; \mu, \sigma^2, I)$	truncated normal distribution, $\mathcal{N}(\phi; \mu, \sigma^2)$ truncated to interval I

symbol	description
τ	either decision horizon (in the context of decision making) or number of optimization iterations passed (in the context of asymptotic analysis)
Θ	is asymptotically bounded above and below by: $f = \Theta(g)$ if $f = \mathcal{O}(g)$ and $f = \Omega(g)$
θ	vector of hyperparameters indexing a model space $\mathcal{M}$
$\operatorname{tr} \mathbf{A}$	trace of square matrix $\mathbf{A}$
$u(\mathcal{D})$	utility of data $\mathcal{D}$
$\operatorname{var}[\omega]$	variance of random variable ω
x	putative input location of the objective function
$\mathbf{x}$	either a sequence of observed locations $\mathbf{x} = \{x_i\}$ or (when the distinction is important) a vector-valued input location
x^*	a location attaining the globally maximal value of f: $x^* \in \arg\max f$; $f(x^*) = f^*$
$\mathcal{X}$	domain of objective function
y	value resulting from an observation at x
$\mathbf{y}$	observed values resulting from observations at locations $\mathbf{x}$
z	z-score of measurement y at x: $z = (y - \mu)/s$

INTRODUCTION

Optimization is an innate human behavior. On an individual level, we all strive to better ourselves and our surroundings. On a collective level, societies struggle to allocate limited resources seeking to improve the welfare of their members, and optimization has been an engine of societal progress since the domestication of crops through selective breeding over 12 000 years ago – an effort that continues to this day.

Given its pervasiveness, it should perhaps not be surprising that optimization is also *difficult*. While searching for an optimal design, we must spend – sometimes quite significant – resources evaluating suboptimal alternatives along the way. This observation compels us to seek methods of optimization that, when necessary, can carefully allocate resources to identify optimal parameters as efficiently as possible. This is the goal of mathematical optimization.

Since the 1960s, the statistics and machine learning communities have refined a *Bayesian* approach to optimization that we will develop and explore in this book. Bayesian optimization routines rely on a statistical model of the objective function, whose beliefs guide the algorithm in making the most fruitful decisions. These models can be quite sophisticated, and maintaining them throughout optimization may entail significant cost of its own. However, the reward for this effort is unparalleled sample efficiency. For this reason, Bayesian optimization has found a niche in optimizing objectives that:

- are costly to compute, precluding exhaustive evaluation,
- lack a useful expression, causing them to function as "black boxes,"
- cannot be evaluated exactly, but only through some indirect or noisy mechanism, and/or
- offer no efficient mechanism for estimating their gradient.

Let us consider an example setting motivating the machine learning community's recent interest in Bayesian optimization. Consider a data scientist crafting a complex machine learning model – say a deep neural network – from training data. To ensure success, the scientist must carefully tune the model's hyperparameters, including the network architecture and details of the training procedure, which have massive influence on performance. Unfortunately, effective settings can only be identified via trial-and-error: by training several networks with different settings and evaluating their performance on a validation dataset.

The search for the best hyperparameters is of course an exercise in optimization. Mathematical optimization has been under continual development for centuries, and numerous off-the-shelf procedures are available. However, these procedures usually make assumptions about the objective function that may not always be valid. For example, we might assume that the objective is cheap to evaluate, that we can easily compute its gradient, or that it is convex, allowing us to reduce from global to local optimization.

In hyperparameter tuning, all of these assumptions are invalid. Training a deep neural network can be extremely expensive in terms of both time and energy. When some hyperparameters are discrete – as many features of network architecture naturally are – the gradient does not even *exist*. Finally, the mapping from hyperparameters to performance may be highly complex and multimodal, so local refinement may not yield an acceptable result.

The Bayesian approach to optimization allows us to relax all of these assumptions when necessary, and Bayesian optimization algorithms can deliver impressive performance even when optimizing complex "black box" objectives under severely limited observation budgets. Bayesian optimization has proven successful in settings spanning science, engineering, and beyond, including of course hyperparameter tuning.[1] In light of this broad success, GELMAN and VEHTARI identified adaptive decision analysis – and Bayesian optimization in particular – as one of the eight most important statistical ideas of the past 50 years.[2]

Covering all these applications and their nuances could easily fill a separate volume (although we do provide an overview of some important application domains in an annotated bibliography), so in this book we will settle for developing the mathematical foundation of Bayesian optimization underlying its success. In the remainder of this chapter we will lay important groundwork for this discussion. We will first establish the precise formulation of optimization we will consider and important conventions of our presentation, then outline and illustrate the key aspects of the Bayesian approach. The reader may find an outline of and reading guide for the chapters to come in the Preface.

1.1 FORMALIZATION OF OPTIMIZATION

Throughout this book we will consider a simple but flexible formulation of sequential global optimization outlined below. There is nothing inherently Bayesian about this model, and countless solutions are possible.

We begin with a real-valued objective function defined on some domain $\mathcal{X}$; $f\colon \mathcal{X} \to \mathbb{R}$. We make no assumptions regarding the nature of the domain. In particular, it need not be Euclidean but might instead, for example, comprise a space of complex structured objects. The goal of optimization is to systematically search the domain for a point x^* attaining the globally maximal value f^*:[3]

$$x^* \in \arg\max_{x \in \mathcal{X}} f(x); \qquad f^* = \max_{x \in \mathcal{X}} f(x) = f(x^*). \qquad (1.1)$$

Before we proceed, we note that our focus on maximization rather than minimization is entirely arbitrary; the author simply judges maximization to be the more optimistic choice. If desired, we can freely transform one problem to the other by negating the objective function. We caution the reader that some translation may be required when comparing expressions derived here to what may appear in parallel texts focusing on minimization.

1 R. TURNER et al. (2021). Bayesian Optimization Is Superior to Random Search for Machine Learning Hyperparameter Tuning: Analysis of the Black-Box Optimization Challenge 2020. *Proceedings of the NeurIPS 2020 Competition and Demonstration Track.*

2 A. GELMAN and A. VEHTARI (2021). What Are the Most Important Statistical Ideas of the Past 50 Years? *Journal of the American Statistical Association* 116(536):2087–2097.

Annotated Bibliography of Applications: Appendix D, p. 313

outline and reading guide: p. x

objective function, f

domain of objective function, $\mathcal{X}$

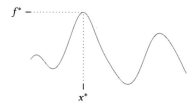

An objective function with the location, x^*, and value, f^*, of the global optimum marked.

3 A skeptical reader may object that, without further assumptions, a global maximum may not exist at all! We will sidestep this issue for now and pick it up again in § 2.7, p. 34.

---

input: initial dataset $\mathcal{D}$ ▸ can be empty
repeat
     $x \leftarrow$ POLICY($\mathcal{D}$)   ▸ select the next observation location
     $y \leftarrow$ OBSERVE(x)   ▸ observe at the chosen location
     $\mathcal{D} \leftarrow \mathcal{D} \cup \{(x, y)\}$ ▸ update dataset
until termination condition reached   ▸ e.g., budget exhausted
return $\mathcal{D}$

Algorithm 1.1: Sequential optimization.

In a significant departure from classical mathematical optimization, we do not require that the objective function have a known functional form or even be computable directly. Rather, we only require access to a mechanism revealing *some* information about the objective function at identified points on demand. By amassing sufficient information from this mechanism, we may hope to infer the solution to (1.1). Avoiding the need for an explicit expression for f allows us to consider so-called "black box" optimization, where a system is optimized through indirect measurements of its quality. This is one of the greatest strengths of Bayesian optimization.[4]

4 Of course, we do not *require* but merely *allow* that the objective function act as a black box. Access to a closed-form expression does not preclude a Bayesian approach!

Optimization policy

Directly solving for the location of global optima is infeasible except in exceptional circumstances. The tools of traditional calculus are virtually powerless in this setting; for example, enumerating and classifying every stationary point in the domain would be tedious at best and perhaps even impossible. Mathematical optimization instead takes an indirect approach: we design a sequence of experiments to probe the objective function for information that, we hope, will reveal the solution to (1.1).

The iterative procedure in Algorithm 1.1 formalizes this process. We begin with an initial (possibly empty) dataset $\mathcal{D}$ that we grow incrementally through a sequence of observations of our design. In each iteration, an *optimization policy* inspects the available data and selects a point $x \in \mathcal{X}$ where we make our next observation.[5] This action in turn reveals a corresponding value y provided by the system under study. We append the newly observed information to our dataset and finally decide whether to continue with another observation or terminate and return the current data. When we inevitably do choose to terminate, the returned data can be used by an external consumer as desired, for example to inform a subsequent decision.

5 Here "policy" has the same meaning as in other decision-making contexts: it maps our state (indexed by our data, $\mathcal{D}$) to an action (the location of our next observation, x).

terminal recommendations: § 5.1, p. 90

We place no restrictions on how an optimization policy is implemented beyond mapping an arbitrary dataset to some point in the domain for evaluation. A policy may be deterministic or stochastic, as demonstrated respectively by the prototypical examples of grid search and random search. In fact, these popular policies are *nonadaptive* and completely ignore the observed data. However, when observations only come at significant cost, we will naturally prefer policies that adapt their behavior in light of evolving information. The primary challenge in optimization is designing policies that can *rapidly* optimize a broad class of objective functions, and intelligent policy design will be our focus for the majority of this book.

Observation model

For optimization to be feasible, the observations we obtain must provide information about the objective function that can guide our search and in aggregate determine the solution to (1.1). A near-universal assumption in mathematical optimization is that observations yield *exact* evaluations of the objective function at our chosen locations. However, this assumption is unduly restrictive: many settings feature inexact measurements due to noisy sensors, imperfect simulation, or statistical approximation. A typical example featuring additive observation noise is shown in the margin. Although the objective function is not observed directly, the noisy measurements nonetheless constrain the plausible options due to strong dependence on the objective.

Inexact observations of an objective function corrupted by additive noise.

We thus relax the assumption of exact observation and instead assume that observations are realized by a stochastic mechanism depending on the objective function. Namely, we assume that the value y resulting from an observation at some point x is distributed according to an observation model depending on the underlying objective function value $\phi = f(x)$:

measured value, y

observation location, x

objective function value, $\phi = f(x)$

$$p(y \mid x, \phi). \tag{1.2}$$

Through judicious design of the observation model, we may consider a wide range of observation mechanisms.

As with the optimization policy, we do not make any assumptions about the nature of the observation model, save one. Unless otherwise mentioned, we assume that a set of *multiple* measurements $\mathbf{y}$ are conditionally independent given the corresponding observation locations $\mathbf{x}$ and objective function values $\boldsymbol{\phi} = f(\mathbf{x})$:

conditional independence of observations given objective values

$$p(\mathbf{y} \mid \mathbf{x}, \boldsymbol{\phi}) = \prod_i p(y_i \mid x_i, \phi_i). \tag{1.3}$$

This is not strictly necessary but is overwhelmingly common in practice and will simplify our presentation considerably.

One particular observation model will enjoy most of our attention in this book: *additive Gaussian noise.* Here we model the value y observed at x as

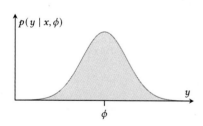

Additive Gaussian noise: the distribution of the value y observed at x is Gaussian, centered on the objective function value ϕ.

$$y = \phi + \varepsilon,$$

where ε represents measurement error. Errors are assumed to be Gaussian distributed with mean zero, implying a Gaussian observation model:

$$p(y \mid x, \phi, \sigma_n) = \mathcal{N}(y; \phi, \sigma_n^2). \tag{1.4}$$

observation noise scale, σ_n

heteroskedastic noise: § 2.2, p. 25

Here the observation noise scale σ_n may optionally depend on x, allowing us to model both homoskedastic or heteroskedastic errors.

If we take the noise scale to be identically zero, we recover the special case of exact observation, where we simply have $y = \phi$ and the observation model collapses to a Dirac delta distribution:

$$p(y \mid \phi) = \delta(y - \phi).$$

Although not universally applicable, many settings do feature exact observations such as optimizing the output of a deterministic computer simulation. We will sometimes consider the exact case separately as some results simplify considerably in the absence of measurement error.

We will focus on additive Gaussian noise as it is a reasonably faithful model for many systems and offers considerable mathematical convenience. This observation model will be most prevalent in our discussion on Gaussian processes in the next three chapters and on the explicit computation of Bayesian optimization policies with this model class in Chapter 8. However, the general methodology we will build in the remainder of this book is not contingent on this choice, and we will occasionally address alternative observation mechanisms.

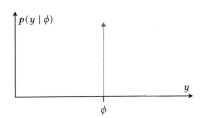

Exact observations: every value measured equals the corresponding function value, yielding a Dirac delta observation model.

inference with non-Gaussian observations: § 2.8, p. 35

optimization with non-Gaussian observations: § 11.11, p. 282

Termination

The final decision we make in each iteration of optimization is whether to terminate immediately or continue with another observation. As with the optimization policy, we do not assume any particular mechanism by which this decision is made. Termination may be deterministic – such as stopping after reaching a certain optimization goal or exhausting a preallocated observation budget – or stochastic, and may optionally depend on the observed data. In many cases, the time of termination may in fact not be under the control of the optimization routine at all but instead decided by an external agent. However, we will also consider scenarios where the optimization procedure can dynamically choose when to return based upon inspection of the available data.

optimal termination: § 5.4, p. 103

practical termination: § 9.3, p. 210

1.2   THE BAYESIAN APPROACH

Bayesian optimization does not refer to one particular algorithm but rather to a philosophical approach to optimization grounded in Bayesian inference from which an extensive family of algorithms have been derived. Although these algorithms display significant diversity in their details, they are bound by common themes in their design.

Optimization is fundamentally a sequence of decisions: in each iteration, we must choose where to make our next observation and then whether to terminate depending on the outcome. As the outcomes of these decisions are governed by the system under study and outside our control, the success of optimization rests entirely on effective decision making.

Increasing the difficulty of these decisions is that they must be made under *uncertainty,* as it is impossible to know the outcome of an observation before making it. The optimization policy must therefore design each observation with some measure of faith that the outcome will ultimately prove beneficial and justify the cost of obtaining it. The sequential nature of optimization further compounds the weight of this uncertainty, as the outcome of each observation not only has an immediate impact, but also forms the basis on which all future decisions are made. Developing an effective policy requires somehow addressing this uncertainty.

The Bayesian approach systematically relies on probability and Bayesian inference to reason about the uncertain quantities arising during optimization. This critically includes the objective function itself, which is treated as a random variable to be inferred in light of our prior expectations and any available data. In Bayesian optimization, this belief then takes an active role in decision making by guiding the optimization policy, which may evaluate the merit of a proposed observation location according to our belief about the value we might observe. We introduce the key ideas of this process with examples below, starting with a refresher on Bayesian inference.

Bayesian inference

To frame the following discussion, we offer a quick overview of Bayesian inference as a reminder to the reader. This introduction is far from complete, but there are numerous excellent references available.[6]

Bayesian inference is a framework for inferring uncertain features of a system of interest from observations grounded in the laws of probability. To illustrate the basic ideas, we may begin by identifying some unknown feature of a given system that we wish to reason about. In the context of optimization, this might represent, for example, the value of the objective function at a given location, or the location x^* or value f^* of the global optimum (1.1). We will take the first of these as a running example: inferring about the value of an objective function at some arbitrary point x, $\phi = f(x)$. We will shortly extend this example to inference about the *entire* objective function.

In the Bayesian approach to inference, *all* unknown quantities are treated as random variables. This is a powerful convention as it allows us to represent beliefs about these quantities with probability distributions reflecting their plausible values. Inference then takes the form of an inductive process where these beliefs are iteratively refined in light of observed data by appealing to probabilistic identities.

As with any induction, we must start somewhere. Here we begin with a so-called *prior distribution* (or simply *prior*) $p(\phi \mid x)$, which encodes what we consider to be plausible values for ϕ before observing any data.[7] The prior distribution allows us to inject our knowledge about and experience with the system of interest into the inferential process, saving us from having to begin "from scratch" or entertain patently absurd possibilities. The left panel of Figure 1.1 illustrates a prior distribution for our example, indicating support over a range of values.

Once a prior has been established, the next stage of inference is to refine our initial beliefs in light of observed data. Suppose in our

---

6 The literature is vast. The following references are excellent, but no list can be complete:

D. J. C. MACKAY (2003). *Information Theory, Inference, and Learning Algorithms.* Cambridge University Press.

A. O'HAGAN and J. FORSTER (2004). *Kendall's Advanced Theory of Statistics.* Vol. 2B: Bayesian Inference. Arnold.

J. O. BERGER (1985). *Statistical Decision Theory and Bayesian Analysis.* Springer–Verlag.

prior distribution, $p(\phi \mid x)$

7 Here we assume the location of interest x is known, hence our conditioning the prior on its value.

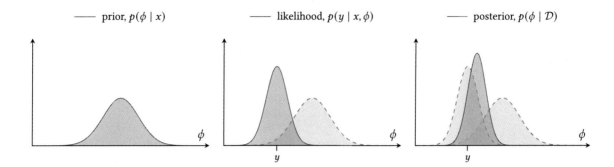

Figure 1.1: Bayesian inference for an unknown function value $\phi = f(x)$. Left: a prior distribution over ϕ; middle: the likelihood of the marked observation y according to an additive Gaussian noise observation model (1.4) (prior shown for reference); right: the posterior distribution in light of the observation and the prior (prior and likelihood shown for reference).

example we make an observation of the objective function at x, revealing a measurement y. In our model of optimization, the distribution of this measurement is assumed to be determined by the value of interest ϕ through the observation model $p(y \mid x, \phi)$ (1.2). In the context of Bayesian inference, a distribution explaining the observed values (here y) in terms of the values of interest (here ϕ) is known as a *likelihood function* or simply a *likelihood*. The middle panel of Figure 1.1 shows the likelihood – as a function of ϕ – for a given measurement y, here assumed to be generated by additive Gaussian noise (1.4).

likelihood function (observation model), $p(y \mid x, \phi)$

Finally, given the observed value y, we may derive the updated *posterior distribution* (or simply *posterior*) of ϕ by appealing to Bayes' theorem:

posterior distribution, $p(\phi \mid x, y)$

$$p(\phi \mid x, y) = \frac{p(\phi \mid x)\, p(y \mid x, \phi)}{p(y \mid x)}. \tag{1.5}$$

The posterior is proportional to the prior weighted by the likelihood of the observed value. The denominator is a constant with respect to ϕ that ensures normalization:

$$p(y \mid x) = \int p(y \mid x, \phi)\, p(\phi \mid x)\, \mathrm{d}\phi. \tag{1.6}$$

The right panel of Figure 1.1 shows the posterior resulting from the measurement in the middle panel. The posterior represents a compromise between our experience (encoded in the prior) and the information contained in the data (encoded in the likelihood).

Throughout this book we will use the catchall notation $\mathcal{D}$ to represent all the information influencing a posterior belief; here the relevant information is $\mathcal{D} = (x, y)$, and the posterior distribution is then $p(\phi \mid \mathcal{D})$.

data informing posterior belief, $\mathcal{D}$

As mentioned previously, Bayesian inference is an inductive process whereby we can continue to refine our beliefs through additional observation. At this point, the induction is trivial: to incorporate a new

— posterior predictive, $p(y' \mid x, \mathcal{D})$

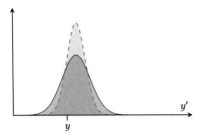

Posterior predictive distribution for a repeated measurement at x for our running example. The location of our first measurement y and the posterior distribution of ϕ are shown for reference. There is more uncertainty in y' than ϕ due to the effect of observation noise.

8 This expression takes the same form as (1.6), which is simply the (prior) predictive distribution evaluated at the actual observed value.

stochastic process

objective function prior, $p(f)$

differentiability: § 2.6, p. 30

characteristic length scales: § 3.4, p. 56

stationarity: § 3.2, p. 50

observation, what was our posterior serves as the prior in the context of the new information, and multiplying by the likelihood and renormalizing yields a new posterior. We may continue in this manner as desired.

The posterior distribution is not usually the end result of Bayesian inference but rather a springboard enabling follow-on tasks such as prediction or decision making, both of which are integral to Bayesian optimization. To address the former, suppose that after deriving the posterior (1.5), we wish to predict the result of an independent, *repeated* noisy observation at x, y'. Treating the outcome as a random variable, we may derive its distribution by integrating our posterior belief about ϕ against the observation model (1.2):[8]

$$p(y' \mid x, \mathcal{D}) = \int p(y' \mid x, \phi)\, p(\phi \mid x, \mathcal{D})\, d\phi; \qquad (1.7)$$

this is known as the *posterior predictive distribution* for y'. By integrating over all possible values of ϕ weighted by their plausibility, the posterior predictive distribution naturally accounts for uncertainty in the unknown objective function value; see the figure in the margin.

The Bayesian approach to decision making also relies on a posterior belief about unknown features affecting the outcomes of our decisions, as we will discuss shortly.

Bayesian inference of the objective function

At the heart of any Bayesian optimization routine is a probabilistic belief over the objective function. This takes the form of a *stochastic process,* a probability distribution over an infinite collection of random variables – here the objective function value at every point. The reasoning behind this inference is, in essence, the same as our single-point example above.

We begin by encoding any assumptions we may have about the objective function, such as smoothness or other features, in a *prior process* $p(f)$. Conveniently, we can specify a stochastic process via the distribution of the function values $\boldsymbol{\phi}$ corresponding to an arbitrary *finite* set of locations $\mathbf{x}$:

$$p(\boldsymbol{\phi} \mid \mathbf{x}). \qquad (1.8)$$

The family of *Gaussian processes* – where these finite-dimensional distributions are multivariate Gaussian – is especially convenient and widely used in Bayesian optimization. We will explore this model class in depth in the following three chapters; here we provide a motivating illustration.

Figure 1.2 shows a Gaussian process prior on a one-dimensional objective function, constructed to reflect a minimal set of assumptions we will elaborate on later in the book:

- that the objective function is smooth (that is, infinitely differentiable),
- that correlations among function values have a characteristic scale, and
- that the function's expected behavior does not depend on location (that is, the prior process is *stationary*).

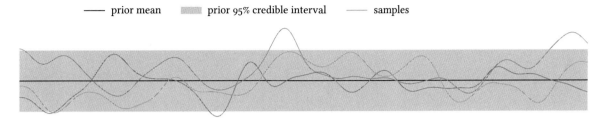

——— prior mean ▨ prior 95% credible interval ——— samples

Figure 1.2: An example prior process for an objective defined on an interval. We illustrate the marginal belief at every location with its mean and a 95% credible interval and also show three example functions sampled from the prior process.

We summarize the marginal belief of the model, for each point in the domain showing the prior mean and a 95% credible interval for the corresponding function value. We also show three functions sampled from the prior process, each exhibiting the assumed behavior. We encourage the reader to become comfortable with this plotting convention, as we will use it throughout this book. In particular we eschew axis labels, as they are always the same: the horizontal axis represents the domain $\mathcal{X}$ and the vertical axis the function value. Further, we do not mark units on axes to stress relative rather than absolute behavior, as scale is arbitrary in this illustration.

plotting conventions

We can encode a vast array of information into the prior process and can model significantly more complex structure than in this simple example. We will explore the world of possibilities in Chapter 3, including interaction at different scales, nonstationarity, low intrinsic dimensionality, and more.

nonstationarity, warping: § 3.4, p. 56
low intrinsic dimensionality: § 3.5, p. 61

With the prior process in hand, suppose we now make a set of observations at some locations $\mathbf{x}$, revealing corresponding values $\mathbf{y}$; we aggregate this information into a dataset $\mathcal{D} = (\mathbf{x}, \mathbf{y})$. Bayesian inference accounts for these observations by forming the *posterior process* $p(f \mid \mathcal{D})$.

observed data, $\mathcal{D} = (\mathbf{x}, \mathbf{y})$
objective function posterior, $p(f \mid \mathcal{D})$

The derivation of the posterior process can be understood as a two-stage process. First we consider the impact of the data on the corresponding function values $\boldsymbol{\phi}$ alone (1.5):

$$p(\boldsymbol{\phi} \mid \mathcal{D}) \propto p(\boldsymbol{\phi} \mid \mathbf{x}) \, p(\mathbf{y} \mid \mathbf{x}, \boldsymbol{\phi}). \tag{1.9}$$

The quantities on the right-hand side are known: the first term is given by the prior process (1.8), and the second by the observation model (1.3), which serves the role of a likelihood. We now extend the posterior on $\boldsymbol{\phi}$ to all of f:[9]

$$p(f \mid \mathcal{D}) = \int p(f \mid \mathbf{x}, \boldsymbol{\phi}) \, p(\boldsymbol{\phi} \mid \mathcal{D}) \, \mathrm{d}\boldsymbol{\phi}. \tag{1.10}$$

The posterior encapsulates our belief regarding the objective in light of the data, incorporating both the assumptions of the prior process and the information contained in the observations.

We illustrate an example posterior in Figure 1.3, where we have conditioned our prior from Figure 1.2 on three exact observations. As the

9 The given expression sweeps some details under the rug. A careful derivation of the posterior process proceeds by finding the posterior of an arbitrary *finite*-dimensional vector $\boldsymbol{\phi}_* = f(\mathbf{x}_*)$:

$$p(\boldsymbol{\phi}_* \mid \mathbf{x}_*, \mathcal{D}) =$$
$$\int p(\boldsymbol{\phi}_* \mid \mathbf{x}_*, \mathbf{x}, \boldsymbol{\phi}) \, p(\boldsymbol{\phi} \mid \mathcal{D}) \, \mathrm{d}\boldsymbol{\phi},$$

which specifies the process. The distributions on the right-hand side are known: the posterior on $\boldsymbol{\phi}$ is in (1.9), and the posterior on $\boldsymbol{\phi}_*$ given the *exact* function values $\boldsymbol{\phi}$ can be found by computing their joint prior (1.8) and conditioning.

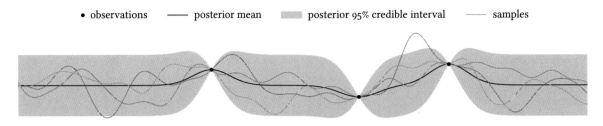

observations ——— posterior mean ▨ posterior 95% credible interval ——— samples

Figure 1.3: The posterior process for our example scenario in Figure 2.1 conditioned on three exact observations.

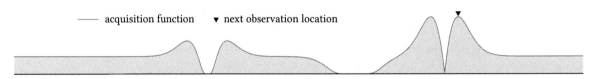

——— acquisition function   ▼ next observation location

Figure 1.4: A prototypical acquisition function corresponding to our example posterior from Figure 1.3.

observations are assumed to be exact, the objective function posterior collapses onto the observed values. The posterior mean interpolates through the data, and the posterior credible intervals reflect increased certainty regarding the function near the observed locations. Further, the posterior continues to reflect the structural assumptions encoded in the prior, demonstrated by comparing the behavior of the samples drawn from the posterior process to those drawn from the prior.

Uncertainty-aware optimization policies

Bayesian inference provides an elegant means of reasoning about an uncertain objective function, but the success of optimization is measured not by the fidelity of our beliefs but by the outcomes of our actions. These actions are determined by the optimization policy, which examines available data to design each successive observation location. Each of these decisions is fraught with uncertainty, as we must commit to each observation before knowing its result, which will form the context of all following decisions. Bayesian inference enables us to express this uncertainty, but effective decision making additionally requires us to establish preferences over outcomes and act to maximize those preferences.

Chapter 5: Decision Theory for Optimization, p. 87

Chapter 6: Utility Functions for Optimization, p. 109

Chapter 7: Common Bayesian Optimization Policies, p. 123

To proceed we need to establish a framework for decision making under uncertainty, an expansive subject with a world of possibilities. A natural and common choice is *Bayesian decision theory*, the subject of Chapters 5–6. We will discuss this and other approaches to policy construction at length in Chapter 7 and derive popular optimization policies from first principles.

Ignoring details in policy design, a thread running through all Bayesian optimization policies is a uniform handling of uncertainty in the objective function and the outcomes of observations via Bayesian inference. Instrumental in connecting our beliefs about the objective function to decision making is the posterior predictive distribution (1.7), representing our belief about the outcomes of proposed observations. Bayesian optimization policies are designed with reference to this distribution, which guides the policy in discriminating between potential actions.

In practice, Bayesian optimization policies are defined indirectly by optimizing a so-called *acquisition function* assigning a score to potential observation locations commensurate with their perceived ability to benefit the optimization process. Acquisition functions tend to be cheap to evaluate with analytically tractable gradients, allowing the use of off-the-shelf optimizers to efficiently design each observation. Numerous acquisition functions have been proposed for Bayesian optimization, each derived from different considerations. However, all notable acquisition functions address the classic tension between *exploitation* – sampling where the objective function is expected to be high – and *exploration* – sampling where we are uncertain about the objective function to inform future decisions. These opposing concerns must be carefully balanced for effective global optimization.

acquisition functions: § 5, p. 88

An example acquisition function is shown in Figure 1.4, corresponding to the posterior from Figure 1.3. Consideration of the exploitation–exploration tradeoff is apparent: this example acquisition function attains relatively large values both near local maxima of the posterior mean and in regions with significant marginal uncertainty. Local maxima of the acquisition function represent optimal compromises between these concerns. Note that the acquisition function vanishes at the location of the current observations: the objective function values at these locations are already known, so observing there would be pointless. Maximizing the acquisition function determines the policy; here the policy chooses to search around the local optimum on the right-hand side.

example and discussion

Figure 1.5 demonstrates an entire session of Bayesian optimization, beginning from the belief and initial decision from Figure 1.4 and progressing iteratively following Algorithm 1.1. The true (unknown) objective function is also shown for reference; its maximum is near the center of the domain. The running marks below each posterior show the locations of each measurement made, progressing in sequence from top to bottom, and we show the objective function posterior at four waypoints.

Dynamic consideration of the exploitation–exploration tradeoff is evident in the algorithm's behavior. The first two observations map out the neighborhood of the initially best-seen point, exhibiting exploitation. Once sufficiently explored, the policy continues exploitation around the second best-seen point, discovering and refining the global optimum in iterations 7–8. Finally, the policy switches to exploration in iterations 13–19, systematically covering the domain to ensure nothing has been missed. At termination, there is clear bias in the collected data toward higher objective values, and all remaining uncertainty is in regions where the credible intervals indicate the optimum is unlikely to reside.

The "magic" of Bayesian optimization is that the intuitive behavior of this optimization policy is not the result of ad hoc design, but rather

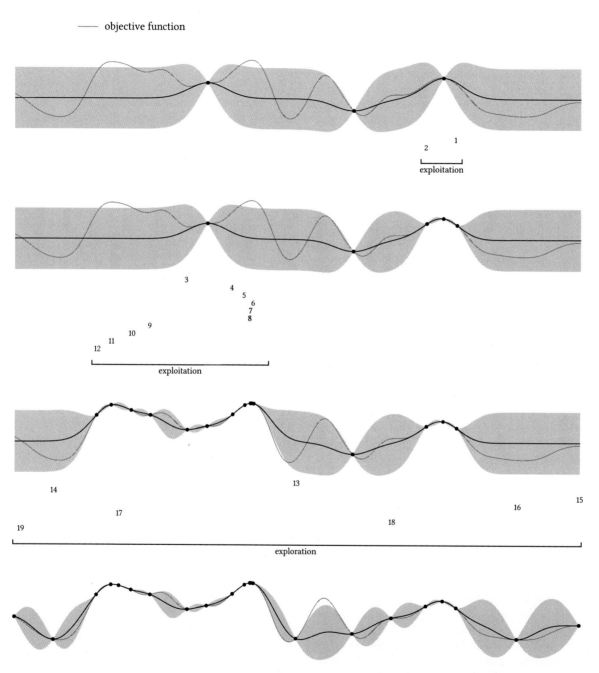

Figure 1.5: The posterior after the indicated number of steps of an example Bayesian optimization policy, starting from the posterior in Figure 1.4. The marks show the points chosen by the policy, progressing from top to bottom. Observations sufficiently close to the optimum are marked in bold; the optimum was located on iteration 7.

emerges *automatically* through the machinery of Gaussian processes and Bayesian decision theory that we will develop over the coming chapters. In this framework, building an optimization policy boils down to:

- choosing a model of the objective function,
- deciding what sort of data we seek to obtain, and
- systematically transforming these beliefs and preferences into an optimization policy.

Over the following chapters, we will develop tools for achieving each of these goals: Gaussian processes (Chapters 2–4) for expressing what we believe about the objective function, utility functions (Chapter 6) for expressing what we value in data, and Bayesian decision theory (Chapter 5) for building optimization policies aware of the uncertainty encoded in the model and guided by the preferences encoded in the utility function. In Chapter 7 we will combine these fundamental components to realize complete Bayesian optimization policies, at which point we will be equipped to replicate this example from first principles.

GAUSSIAN PROCESSES

The central object in optimization is an objective function $f: \mathcal{X} \to \mathbb{R}$, and the primary challenge in algorithm design is inherent *uncertainty* about this function: most importantly, where is the function maximized and what is its maximal value? Prior to optimization, we may very well have no idea. Optimization affords us the opportunity to acquire information about the objective – through observations of our own design – to shed light on these questions. However, this process is itself fraught with uncertainty, as we cannot know the outcomes and implications of these observations at the time of their design. Notably, we face this uncertainty even when we have a closed-form expression for the objective function, a favorable position as many objectives act as "black boxes."

Reflecting on this situation, DIACONIS posed an intriguing question:[1] "what does it mean to 'know' a function?" The answer is unclear when an analytic expression, which might at first glance seem to encapsulate the essence of the function, is insufficient to determine features of interest. However, DIACONIS argued that although we may not know *everything* about a function, we often have *some* prior knowledge that can facilitate a numerical procedure such as optimization. For example, we may expect an objective function to be smooth (or rough), or to assume values in a given range, or to feature a relatively simple underlying trend, or to depend on some hidden low-dimensional representation we hope to uncover.[2] All of this knowledge could be instrumental in accelerating optimization if it could be systematically captured and exploited.

Having identifiable information about an objective function prior to optimization motivates the Bayesian approach we will explore throughout this book. We will address uncertainty in the objective function through the unifying framework of Bayesian inference, treating f – as well as ancillary quantities such as x^* and f^* (1.1) – as random variables to be inferred from observations revealed during optimization.

To pursue this approach, we must first determine how to build useful prior distributions for objective functions and how to compute a posterior belief given observations. If the system under investigation is well understood, we may be able to identify an appropriate parametric form $f(x; \theta)$ and infer the parameters θ directly. This approach is likely the best course of action when possible;[3] however, many objective functions have no obvious parametric form, and most models used in Bayesian optimization are thus nonparametric to avoid undue assumptions.[4]

In this chapter we will introduce *Gaussian processes* (GPS), a convenient class of nonparametric regression models widely used in Bayesian optimization. We will begin by defining Gaussian processes and deriving some basic properties, then demonstrate how to perform inference from observations. In the case of exact observation and additive Gaussian noise, we can perform this inference *exactly*, resulting in an updated posterior Gaussian process. We will continue by considering some theoretical properties of Gaussian processes relevant to optimization and inference with non-Gaussian observation models.

1 P. DIACONIS (1988). Bayesian Numerical Analysis. In: *Statistical Decision Theory and Related Topics IV*.

2 We will explore all of these possibilities in the next chapter, p. 45.

Bayesian inference of the objective function: § 1.2, p. 8

3 V. DALIBARD et al. (2017). BOAT: Building Auto-Tuners with Structured Bayesian Optimization. *WWW 2017*.

4 The term "nonparametric" is something of a misnomer. A nonparametric objective function model has parameters but their dimension is infinite – we effectively parameterize the objective by its value at every point.

The literature on Gaussian processes is vast, and we do not intend this chapter to serve as a standalone introduction but rather as companion to the existing literature. Although our discussion will be comprehensive, our focus on optimization will sometimes bias its scope. For a broad overview, the interested reader may consult RASMUSSEN and WILLIAMS's classic monograph.[5]

5 C. E. RASMUSSEN and C. K. I. WILLIAMS (2006). *Gaussian Processes for Machine Learning*. MIT Press.

2.1 DEFINITION AND BASIC PROPERTIES

multivariate normal distribution: § A.2, p. 296

A *Gaussian process* is an extension of the familiar multivariate normal distribution suitable for modeling functions on infinite domains. Gaussian processes inherit the convenient mathematical properties of the multivariate normal distribution without sacrificing computational tractability. Further, by modifying the structure of a GP, we can model functions with a rich variety of behavior; we will explore this capability in the next chapter. This combination of mathematical elegance and flexibility in modeling has established Gaussian processes as the workhorse of Bayesian approaches to numerical tasks, including optimization.[6,7]

Chapter 3: Modeling with Gaussian Processes, p. 45

6 P. HENNIG et al. (2015). Probabilistic Numerics and Uncertainty in Computations. *Proceedings of the Royal Society A: Mathematical, Physical and Engineering Sciences* 471(2179):20150142.

7 P. HENNIG et al. (2022). *Probabilistic Numerics: Computation as Machine Learning*. Cambridge University Press.

Definition

Consider an objective function $f\colon \mathcal{X} \to \mathbb{R}$ of interest over an arbitrary infinite domain $\mathcal{X}$.[8] We will take a nonparametric approach and reason about the function as an infinite collection of random variables, one corresponding to the function value at every point in the domain. Mutual dependence between these random variables will then determine the statistical properties of the function's shape.

8 If $\mathcal{X}$ is finite, there is no distinction between a Gaussian process and a multivariate normal distribution, so only the infinite case is interesting for this discussion.

It is perhaps not immediately clear how we can specify a useful distribution over infinitely many random variables, a construction known as a *stochastic process*. However, a result known as the *Kolmogorov extension theorem* allows us to construct a stochastic process by defining only the distribution of arbitrary *finite* sets of function values, subject to natural consistency constraints.[9] For a Gaussian process, these finite-dimensional distributions are all multivariate Gaussian, hence its name.

9 B. ØKSENDAL (2013). *Stochastic Differential Equations: An Introduction with Applications*. Springer–Verlag. [§ 2.1]

In this light, we build a Gaussian process by replacing the parameters in the finite-dimensional case – a mean vector and a positive semidefinite covariance matrix – by analogous *functions* over the domain. We specify a Gaussian process on f:[10]

10 Writing the process as if it were a function-valued probability density function is an abuse of notation, but a useful and harmless one.

$$p(f) = \mathcal{GP}(f; \mu, K)$$

mean function, μ
covariance function (kernel), K
value of objective at x, ϕ

by a *mean function* $\mu\colon \mathcal{X} \to \mathbb{R}$ and a positive semidefinite *covariance function* (or *kernel*) $K\colon \mathcal{X} \times \mathcal{X} \to \mathbb{R}$. The mean function determines the expected function value $\phi = f(x)$ at any location x:

$$\mu(x) = \mathbb{E}[\phi \mid x],$$

thus serving as a location parameter representing the function's central tendency. The covariance function determines how deviations from the mean are structured, encoding expected properties of the function's behavior. Defining $\phi' = f(x')$, we have:

value of objective at x', ϕ'

$$K(x, x') = \text{cov}[\phi, \phi' \mid x, x']. \tag{2.1}$$

The mean and covariance functions of the process allow us to compute any finite-dimensional marginal distribution on demand. Let $\mathbf{x} \subset \mathcal{X}$ be finite and let $\boldsymbol{\phi} = f(\mathbf{x})$ be the corresponding function values, a vector-valued random variable. For the Gaussian process (2.1), the distribution of $\boldsymbol{\phi}$ is multivariate normal with parameters determined by the mean and covariance functions:

values of objective at $\mathbf{x}$, $\boldsymbol{\phi} = f(\mathbf{x})$

$$p(\boldsymbol{\phi} \mid \mathbf{x}) = \mathcal{N}(\boldsymbol{\phi}; \boldsymbol{\mu}, \Sigma), \tag{2.2}$$

where

$$\boldsymbol{\mu} = \mathbb{E}[\boldsymbol{\phi} \mid \mathbf{x}] = \mu(\mathbf{x}); \qquad \Sigma = \text{cov}[\boldsymbol{\phi} \mid \mathbf{x}] = K(\mathbf{x}, \mathbf{x}). \tag{2.3}$$

Here $K(\mathbf{x}, \mathbf{x})$ is the matrix formed by evaluating the covariance function for each pair of points: $\Sigma_{ij} = K(x_i, x_j)$, also called the *Gram matrix* of $\mathbf{x}$.

Gram matrix of $\mathbf{x}$, $\Sigma = K(\mathbf{x}, \mathbf{x})$

In many ways, Gaussian processes behave like "really big" Gaussian distributions, and one can intuit many of their properties from this heuristic alone. For example, the Gaussian marginal property in (2.2–2.3) corresponds precisely with the analogous formula in the finite-dimensional case (A.13). Further, this property automatically ensures global consistency in the following sense.[11] If $\mathbf{x}$ is an arbitrary set of points and $\mathbf{x}' \supset \mathbf{x}$ is a superset, then we arrive at the same belief about $\boldsymbol{\phi}$ whether we compute it directly from (2.2–2.3) or indirectly by first computing $p(\boldsymbol{\phi}' \mid \mathbf{x}')$ then marginalizing $\mathbf{x}' \setminus \mathbf{x}$ (A.13).

11 In fact, this is precisely the consistency required by the Kolmogorov extension theorem mentioned on the facing page.

marginalizing multivariate normal distributions, § A.2, p. 299

Example and basic properties

Let us construct and explore an explicit Gaussian process for a function on the interval $\mathcal{X} = [0, 30]$. For the mean function we take the zero function $\mu \equiv 0$, indicating a constant central tendency. For the covariance function, we take the prototypical *squared exponential* covariance:

squared exponential covariance: § 3.3, p. 51

$$K(x, x') = \exp\left(-\tfrac{1}{2}|x - x'|^2\right). \tag{2.4}$$

Let us pause to consider the implications of this choice. First, note that $\text{var}[\phi \mid x] = K(x, x) = 1$ at every point $x \in \mathcal{X}$, and thus the covariance function (2.4) also measures the *correlation* between the function values ϕ and ϕ'. This correlation decreases with the distance between x and x', falling from unity to zero as these points become increasingly separated; see the illustration in the margin. We can loosely interpret this as a statistical consequence of continuity: function values at nearby locations are highly correlated, whereas function values at distant locations are effectively independent. This assumption also implies that observing the function at some point x provides nontrivial information about the function at sufficiently nearby locations (roughly when $|x - x'| < 3$). We will explore this implication further shortly.

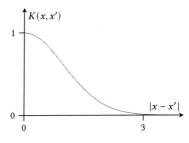

The squared exponential covariance (2.4) as a function of the distance between inputs.

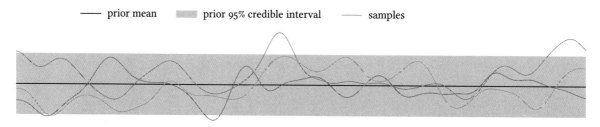

Figure 2.1: Our example Gaussian process on the domain $\mathcal{X} = [0, 30]$. We illustrate the marginal belief at every location with its mean and a 95% credible interval and also show three example functions sampled from the process.

predictive credible intervals

For a Gaussian process, the marginal distribution of any *single* function value is univariate normal (2.2):

$$p(\phi \mid x) = \mathcal{N}(\phi; \mu, \sigma^2); \qquad \mu = \mu(x); \qquad \sigma^2 = K(x, x), \qquad (2.5)$$

where we have abused notation slightly by overloading the symbol μ. This allows us to derive pointwise credible intervals; for example, the familiar $\mu \pm 1.96\sigma$ is a 95% credible interval for ϕ. Examining our example GP, the marginal distribution of every function value is in fact *standard* normal. We provide a rough visual summary of the process via its mean function and pointwise 95% predictive credible intervals in Figure 2.1. There is nothing terribly exciting we can glean from these marginal distributions alone, and no interesting structure in the process is yet apparent.

Sampling

We may gain more insight by inspecting samples drawn from our example process reflecting the *joint* distribution of function values. Although it is impossible to represent an arbitrary function on $\mathcal{X}$ in finite memory, we can approximate the sampling process by taking a dense grid $\mathbf{x} \subset \mathcal{X}$ and sampling the corresponding function values from their joint multivariate normal distribution (2.2). Plotting the sampled vectors against the chosen grid reveals curves approximating draws from the Gaussian process. Figure 2.1 illustrates this procedure for our example using a grid of 1000 equally spaced points. Each sample is smooth and has several local optima distributed throughout the domain – for some applications, this might be a reasonable model for an objective function on $\mathcal{X}$.

sampling from a multivariate normal distribution: § A.2, p. 299

2.2   INFERENCE WITH EXACT AND NOISY OBSERVATIONS

We now turn to our attention to *inference*: given a Gaussian process prior on an objective function, how can we condition this initial belief on observations obtained during optimization?

example and discussion

Let us look at an example to build intuition before diving into the details. Figure 2.2 shows the effect of conditioning our example GP from

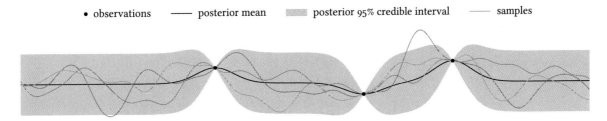

Figure 2.2: The posterior for our example scenario in Figure 2.1 conditioned on three exact observations.

the previous section on three exact measurements of the function. The updated belief reflects both our prior assumptions and the information contained in the data, the hallmark of Bayesian inference. To elaborate, the posterior mean smoothly interpolates through the observed values, agreeing with both the measured values and the smoothness encoded in the prior covariance function. The posterior credible intervals are reduced in the neighborhood of the measured locations – where the prior covariance function encodes nontrivial dependence on at least one observed value – and vanish where the function value has been exactly determined. On the other hand, our marginal belief remains effectively unchanged from the prior in regions sufficiently isolated from the data, where the prior covariance function encodes effectively no correlation.

Conveniently, inference is straightforward for the pervasive observation models of exact measurement and additive Gaussian noise, where the self-conjugacy of the normal distribution yields a *Gaussian process* posterior with updated parameters we can compute in closed form. The reasoning underlying inference for both observation models is identical and is subsumed by a flexible general argument we will present first.

Inference from arbitrary jointly Gaussian observations

We may exactly condition a Gaussian process $p(f) = \mathcal{GP}(f; \mu, K)$ on the observation of *any* vector $\mathbf{y}$ sharing a joint Gaussian distribution with f:

vector of observed values, $\mathbf{y}$

$$p(f, \mathbf{y}) = \mathcal{GP}\left(\begin{bmatrix} f \\ \mathbf{y} \end{bmatrix}; \begin{bmatrix} \mu \\ \mathbf{m} \end{bmatrix}, \begin{bmatrix} K & \kappa^\top \\ \kappa & C \end{bmatrix} \right). \qquad (2.6)$$

This notation, analogous to (A.12), extends the Gaussian process on f to include the entries of $\mathbf{y}$; that is, we assume the distribution of any finite subset of function and/or observed values is multivariate normal. We specify the joint distribution via the marginal distribution of $\mathbf{y}$:[12]

12 We assume C is positive definite; if it were only positive *semi*definite, there would be wasteful linear dependence among observations.

observation mean and covariance, $\mathbf{m}, C$

$$p(\mathbf{y}) = \mathcal{N}(\mathbf{y}; \mathbf{m}, C) \qquad (2.7)$$

and the cross-covariance function between $\mathbf{y}$ and f:

cross-covariance between observations and function values, κ

$$\kappa(x) = \text{cov}[\mathbf{y}, \phi \mid x]. \qquad (2.8)$$

Although it may seem absurd that we could identify and observe a vector satisfying such strong restrictions on its distribution, we can already deduce several examples from first principles, including:

inference from exact observations: § 2.2, p. 22

- any vector of function values (2.2),

affine transformations: § A.2, p. 298

- any affine transformation of function values (A.10), and

derivatives and expectations: § 2.6, p. 30

- limits of such quantities, such as partial derivatives or expectations.

Further, we may condition on any of the above even if corrupted by independent additive Gaussian noise, as we will shortly demonstrate.

conditioning a multivariate normal distribution: § A.2, p. 299

We may condition the joint distribution (2.6) on $\mathbf{y}$ analogously to the finite-dimensional case (A.14), resulting in a Gaussian process posterior on f. Writing $\mathcal{D} = \mathbf{y}$ for the observed data, we have:

$$p(f \mid \mathcal{D}) = \mathcal{GP}(f; \mu_\mathcal{D}, K_\mathcal{D}), \tag{2.9}$$

where

posterior mean and covariance, $\mu_\mathcal{D}$, $K_\mathcal{D}$

$$\mu_\mathcal{D}(x) = \mu(x) + \kappa(x)^\top \mathbf{C}^{-1}(\mathbf{y} - \mathbf{m});$$
$$K_\mathcal{D}(x, x') = K(x, x') - \kappa(x)^\top \mathbf{C}^{-1} \kappa(x'). \tag{2.10}$$

This can be verified by computing the joint distribution of an arbitrary finite set of function values and $\mathbf{y}$ and conditioning on the latter (A.14).[13]

13   This is a useful exercise! The result will be a stochastic process with multivariate normal finite-dimensional distributions, a Gaussian process by definition (2.5).

The above result provides a simple procedure for GP posterior inference from any vector of observations satisfying (2.6):

1. compute the marginal distribution of $\mathbf{y}$ (2.7),
2. derive the cross-covariance function κ (2.8), and
3. find the posterior distribution of f via (2.9–2.10).

We will realize this procedure for several special cases below. However, we will first demonstrate how we may seamlessly handle measurements corrupted by additive Gaussian noise and build intuition for the posterior distribution by dissecting its moments in terms of the statistics of the observations and the correlation structure of the prior.

Corruption by additive Gaussian noise

We pause to make one observation of immense practical importance: any vector satisfying (2.6) would continue to suffice even if corrupted by independent additive Gaussian noise, and thus we can use the above result to condition a Gaussian process on *noisy* observations as well.

noisy observation of y, z
vector of random errors, ε
noise covariance matrix, N

Suppose that rather than observing $\mathbf{y}$ exactly, our measurement mechanism only allowed observing $\mathbf{z} = \mathbf{y} + \varepsilon$ instead, where ε is a vector of random errors independent of $\mathbf{y}$. If the errors are normally distributed with mean zero and known (arbitrary) covariance $\mathbf{N}$:

$$p(\varepsilon \mid \mathbf{N}) = \mathcal{N}(\varepsilon; \mathbf{0}, \mathbf{N}), \tag{2.11}$$

sums of normal vectors: § A.2, p. 300

then we have

$$p(\mathbf{z} \mid \mathbf{N}) = \mathcal{N}(\mathbf{z}; \mathbf{m}, \mathbf{C} + \mathbf{N}); \qquad \text{cov}[\mathbf{z}, \phi \mid x] = \text{cov}[\mathbf{y}, \phi \mid x] = \kappa(x).$$

Thus we can condition on an observation of the corrupted vector $\mathbf{z}$ by simply replacing $\mathbf{C}$ with $\mathbf{C} + \mathbf{N}$ in the prior (2.6) and posterior (2.10).[14] Note that the posterior converges to that from a direct observation of $\mathbf{y}$ if we take the noise covariance $\mathbf{N} \to \mathbf{0}$ in the positive semidefinite cone, a reassuring result.

14 Assuming zero-mean errors is not strictly necessary but is overwhelmingly common in practice. A nonzero mean $\mathbb{E}[\boldsymbol{\varepsilon}] = \mathbf{n}$ is possible by further replacing $(\mathbf{y} - \boldsymbol{\mu})$ with $(\mathbf{y} - [\boldsymbol{\mu} + \mathbf{n}])$ in (2.10), where $\boldsymbol{\mu} + \mathbf{n} = \mathbb{E}[\mathbf{y}]$.

Interpretation of posterior moments

The moments of the posterior Gaussian process (2.10) contain update terms adjusting the prior moments in light of the data. These updates have intuitive interpretations in terms of the nature of the prior process and the observed values, which we may unravel with some care.

We can gain some initial insight by considering the case where we observe a *single* value with y distribution $\mathcal{N}(y; m, s^2)$ and breaking down its impact on our belief. Consider an arbitrary function value ϕ with prior distribution $\mathcal{N}(\phi; \mu, \sigma^2)$ (2.5) and define

z-score of measurement y, z

$$z = \frac{y - m}{s}$$

to be the z-score of the observed value y and

correlation between measurement y and function value ϕ, ρ

$$\rho = \text{corr}[y, \phi \mid x] = \frac{\kappa(x)}{\sigma s}$$

to be the correlation between y and ϕ. Then the posterior mean and standard deviation of ϕ are, respectively:

posterior moments of ϕ from a scalar observation

$$\mu + \sigma\rho z; \qquad \sigma\sqrt{1 - \rho^2}. \tag{2.12}$$

The z-score of the posterior mean, with respect to the prior distribution of ϕ, is ρz. An independent measurement with $\rho = 0$ thus leaves the prior mean unchanged, whereas a perfectly dependent measurement with $|\rho| = 1$ shifts the mean up or down by z standard deviations (depending on the sign of the correlation) to match the magnitude of the measurement's z-score. Measurements with partial dependence result in outcomes between these extremes. Further, *surprising* measurements – that is, those with large $|z|$ – yield larger shifts in the mean, whereas an entirely expected measurement with $y = m$ leaves the mean unchanged.

interpretation of moments

Turning to the posterior standard deviation, the measurement reduces our uncertainty in ϕ by a factor depending on the correlation ρ, but *not* on the value observed. An independent measurement again leaves the prior intact, whereas a perfectly dependent measurement collapses the posterior standard deviation to zero as the value of ϕ would be completely determined. The relative reduction in posterior uncertainty as a function of the absolute correlation is illustrated in the margin.

In the case of vector-valued observations, we can interpret similar structure in the posterior, although dependence between entries of $\mathbf{y}$ must also be accounted for. We may factor the observation covariance matrix as

$$\mathbf{C} = \mathbf{SPS}, \tag{2.13}$$

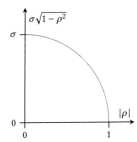

The posterior standard deviation of ϕ as a function of the strength of relationship with y, $|\rho|$.

where S is diagonal with $S_{ii} = \sqrt{C_{ii}} = \text{std}[y_i]$ and $\mathbf{P} = \text{corr}[\mathbf{y}]$ is the observation correlation matrix. We may then rewrite the posterior mean of ϕ as

$$\mu + \sigma \boldsymbol{\rho}^\top \mathbf{P}^{-1} \mathbf{z},$$

where $\mathbf{z}$ and $\boldsymbol{\rho}$ represent the vectors of measurement z-scores and the cross-correlation between ϕ and $\mathbf{y}$, respectively:

$$z_i = \frac{y_i - m_i}{s_i}; \qquad \rho_i = \frac{[\kappa(x)]_i}{\sigma s_i}.$$

The posterior mean is now in the same form as the scalar case (2.12), with the introduction of the observation correlation matrix moderating the z-scores to account for dependence between the observed values.[15]

The posterior standard deviation of ϕ in the vector-valued case is

$$\sigma \sqrt{1 - \boldsymbol{\rho}^\top \mathbf{P}^{-1} \boldsymbol{\rho}},$$

again analogous to (2.12). Noting that the inverse correlation matrix $\mathbf{P}^{-1}$ is positive definite,[16] the posterior covariance again reflects a global reduction in the marginal uncertainty of every function value. In fact, the *joint* distribution of any set of function values has reduced uncertainty in the posterior in terms of the differential entropy (A.16), as[17]

$$|K(\mathbf{x}, \mathbf{x}) - \kappa(\mathbf{x})^\top \mathbf{C}^{-1} \kappa(\mathbf{x})| \leq |K(\mathbf{x}, \mathbf{x})|.$$

The reduction of uncertainty again depends on the strength of dependence between function values and the observed data, with independence ($\boldsymbol{\rho} = \mathbf{0}$) resulting in no change. The reduction also depends on the precision of the measurements: all other things held equal, observations with greater precision in terms of the Löwner order[18] on the precision matrix $\mathbf{C}^{-1}$ provide a globally better informed posterior. In particular, as $(\mathbf{C} + \mathbf{N})^{-1} \prec \mathbf{C}^{-1}$ for any noise covariance $\mathbf{N}$, noisy measurements (2.11) categorically provide *less* information about the function than direct observations, as one should hope.

Inference with exact function evaluations

We will now explicitly demonstrate the general process of Gaussian process inference for important special cases, beginning with the simplest possible observation mechanism: exact observation.

Suppose we have observed f at some set of locations $\mathbf{x}$, revealing the corresponding function values $\phi = f(\mathbf{x})$, and let $\mathcal{D} = (\mathbf{x}, \phi)$ denote this dataset. The observed vector shares a joint Gaussian distribution with any other set of function values by the GP assumption on f (2.2), so we may follow the above procedure to derive the posterior. The marginal distribution of ϕ is Gaussian (2.3):

$$p(\phi \mid \mathbf{x}) = \mathcal{N}(\phi; \mu, \Sigma),$$

15 It can be instructive to contrast the behavior of the posterior when conditioning on two highly correlated values versus two independent ones. In the former case, the posterior does not change much as a result of the second measurement, as dependence reduces the effective number of measurements.

16 P is congruent to C (2.13) and is thus positive definite from Sylvester's law of inertia.

17 For positive semidefinite $\mathbf{A}, \mathbf{B}$, $|\mathbf{A}| \leq |\mathbf{A} + \mathbf{B}|$.

18 The Löwner order is the partial order induced by the convex cone of positive-semidefinite matrices. For symmetric $\mathbf{A}, \mathbf{B}$, we define $\mathbf{A} \prec \mathbf{B}$ if and only if $\mathbf{B} - \mathbf{A}$ is positive definite:

K. LÖWNER (1934). Über monotone Matrixfunktionen. *Mathematische Zeitschrift* 38:177–216.

observed data, $\mathcal{D} = (\mathbf{x}, \phi)$

and the cross-covariance between an arbitrary function value and $\boldsymbol{\phi}$ is by definition given by the covariance function:

$$\kappa(x) = \mathrm{cov}[\boldsymbol{\phi}, \phi \mid \mathbf{x}, x] = K(\mathbf{x}, x).$$

Appealing to (2.9–2.10) we have:

$$p(f \mid \mathcal{D}) = \mathcal{GP}(f; \mu_\mathcal{D}, K_\mathcal{D}),$$

where

$$\mu_\mathcal{D}(x) = \mu(x) + K(x, \mathbf{x})\Sigma^{-1}(\boldsymbol{\phi} - \boldsymbol{\mu});$$
$$K_\mathcal{D}(x, x') = K(x, x') - K(x, \mathbf{x})\Sigma^{-1}K(\mathbf{x}, x'). \tag{2.14}$$

Our previous Figure 2.2 illustrates the posterior resulting from conditioning our GP prior in Figure 2.1 on three exact measurements, with high-level analysis of its behavior in the accompanying text.

example and discussion

Inference with function evaluations corrupted by additive Gaussian noise

With the notable exception of optimizing the output of a deterministic computer program or simulation, observations of an objective function are typically corrupted by noise due to measurement limitations or statistical approximation; we must be able to handle such noisy observations to maximize utility. Fortunately, in the important case of additive Gaussian noise, we may perform exact inference following the general procedure described above. In fact, the derivation below follows directly from our previous discussion on arbitrary additive Gaussian noise, but the case of additive Gaussian noise in function evaluations is important enough to merit its own discussion.

arbitrary additive Gaussian noise: § 2.2, p. 20

Suppose we make observations of f at locations $\mathbf{x}$, revealing corrupted values $\mathbf{y} = \boldsymbol{\phi} + \boldsymbol{\varepsilon}$. Suppose the measurement errors $\boldsymbol{\varepsilon}$ are independent of $\boldsymbol{\phi}$ and normally distributed with mean zero and covariance $\mathbf{N}$, which may optionally depend on $\mathbf{x}$:

[19] Allowing nondiagonal N departs from our typical convention of assuming conditional independence between observations (1.3), but doing so does not complicate inference, so there is no harm in this generality.

$$p(\boldsymbol{\varepsilon} \mid \mathbf{x}, \mathbf{N}) = \mathcal{N}(\boldsymbol{\varepsilon}; \mathbf{0}, \mathbf{N}). \tag{2.15}$$

As before we aggregate the observations into a dataset $\mathcal{D} = (\mathbf{x}, \mathbf{y})$.

The observation noise covariance can in principle be arbitrary;[19] however, the most common models in practice are independent homoskedastic noise with scale σ_n:

special case: independent homoskedastic noise

$$\mathbf{N} = \sigma_n^2 \mathbf{I}, \tag{2.16}$$

and independent heteroskedastic noise with scale depending on location according to a function $\sigma_n \colon \mathcal{X} \to \mathbb{R}_{\geq 0}$:

special case: independent heteroskedastic noise

$$\mathbf{N} = \mathrm{diag}\,\sigma_n^2(\mathbf{x}). \tag{2.17}$$

For a given observation location x, we will simply write σ_n for the associated noise scale, leaving any dependence on x implicit.

observation noise scale, σ_n

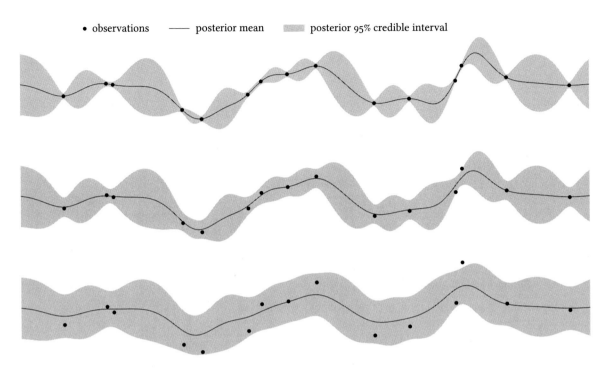

Figure 2.3: Posteriors for our example GP from Figure 2.1 conditioned on 15 noisy observations with independent homoskedastic noise (2.16). The signal-to-noise ratio is 10 for the top example, 3 for the middle example, and 1 for the bottom example.

The prior distribution of the observations is now multivariate normal (2.3, A.15):

$$p(\mathbf{y} \mid \mathbf{x}, \mathbf{N}) = \mathcal{N}(\mathbf{y}; \boldsymbol{\mu}, \Sigma + \mathbf{N}). \tag{2.18}$$

Due to independence of the noise, the cross-covariance remains the same as in the exact observation case:

$$\kappa(x) = \text{cov}[\mathbf{y}, \phi \mid \mathbf{x}, x] = K(\mathbf{x}, x).$$

Conditioning on the observed value now yields a GP posterior with

$$\mu_{\mathcal{D}}(x) = \mu(x) + K(x, \mathbf{x})(\Sigma + \mathbf{N})^{-1}(\mathbf{y} - \boldsymbol{\mu});$$
$$K_{\mathcal{D}}(x, x') = K(x, x') - K(x, \mathbf{x})(\Sigma + \mathbf{N})^{-1}K(\mathbf{x}, x'). \tag{2.19}$$

homoskedastic example and discussion

Figure 2.3 shows a sequence of posterior distributions resulting from conditioning our example GP on data corrupted by increasing levels of homoskedastic noise (2.16). As the noise level increases, the observations have diminishing influence on our belief, with some extreme values eventually being partially explained away as outliers. As measurements are assumed to be inexact, the posterior mean is not compelled to interpolate perfectly through the observations, as in the exact case (Figure

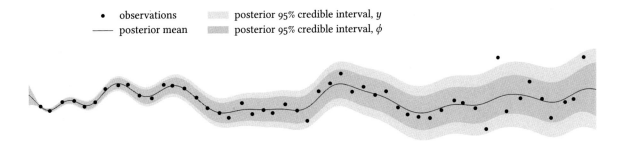

- observations   posterior 95% credible interval, y
- —— posterior mean   posterior 95% credible interval, ϕ

Figure 2.4: The posterior distribution for our example GP from Figure 2.1 conditioned on 50 observations with heteroskedastic observation noise (2.17). We show predictive credible intervals for both the latent objective function and noisy observations; the standard deviation of the observation noise increases linearly from left-to-right.

2.2). Further, with increasing levels of noise, our posterior belief reflects significant residual uncertainty in the function, even in regions with multiple nearby observations.

We illustrate an example of Gaussian process inference with heteroskedastic noise (2.17) in Figure 2.4, where the signal-to-noise ratio decreases smoothly from left-to-right over the domain. Although the observations provide relatively even coverage, our posterior uncertainty is minimal on the left-hand side of the domain – where the measurements provide maximal information – and increases as our observations become more noisy and less informative.

heteroskedastic example and discussion

We will often require the posterior predictive distribution for a noisy measurement y that would result from observing at a given location x. The posterior distribution on f (2.19) provides the posterior predictive distribution for the latent function value $\phi = f(x)$ (2.5):

posterior predictive distribution for noisy observations

$$p(\phi \mid x, \mathcal{D}) = \mathcal{N}(\phi; \mu, \sigma^2); \qquad \mu = \mu_{\mathcal{D}}(x); \qquad \sigma^2 = K_{\mathcal{D}}(x, x),$$

but does not account for the effect of observation noise. In the case of independent additive Gaussian noise (2.16–2.17), deriving the posterior predictive distribution is trivial; we have (A.15):

$$p(y \mid x, \mathcal{D}, \sigma_n) = \mathcal{N}(y; \mu, \sigma^2 + \sigma_n^2). \tag{2.20}$$

This predictive distribution is illustrated in Figure 2.4; the credible intervals for noisy measurements reflect inflation of the credible intervals for the underlying function value commensurate with the scale of the noise.

If the noise contains nondiagonal correlation structure, we must account for dependence between training and test errors in the predictive distribution. The easiest way to proceed is to recognize that the noisy observation process $y = \phi + \varepsilon$, as a function of x, is itself a Gaussian process with mean function μ and covariance function

predictive distribution with correlated noise

covariance function for noisy measurements, C

$$C(x, x') = \mathrm{cov}[y, y' \mid x, x'] = K(x, x') + N(x, x'),$$

covariance function for observation noise, N

where N is the noise covariance: $N(x, x') = \text{cov}[\varepsilon, \varepsilon' \mid x, x']$. The posterior of the observation process is then a GP with

$$
\mathbb{E}[y \mid x, \mathcal{D}] = \mu(x) + C(x, \mathbf{x})(\Sigma + \mathbf{N})^{-1}(\mathbf{y} - \boldsymbol{\mu});
$$
$$
\text{cov}[y, y' \mid x, x', \mathcal{D}] = C(x, x') - C(x, \mathbf{x})(\Sigma + \mathbf{N})^{-1}C(\mathbf{x}, x'),
$$

(2.21)

from which we can derive predictive distributions via (2.2).

2.3 OVERVIEW OF REMAINDER OF CHAPTER

In the remainder of this chapter we will cover some additional, somewhat niche and/or technical aspects of Gaussian processes that see occasional use in Bayesian optimization. Modulo mathematical nuances irrelevant in practical settings, an *intuitive* (but not entirely accurate!) summary follows:[20]

20 In particular the claims regarding continuity and differentiability are slightly more complicated than stated below.

- a *joint Gaussian process* (discussed below) allows us to model *multiple* related functions simultaneously, which is critical for some scenarios such as multifidelity and multiobjective optimization;

- GP sample paths are continuous if the mean function is continuous and the covariance function is continuous along the "diagonal" $x = x'$;

- GP sample paths are differentiable if the mean function is differentiable and the covariance function is differentiable along the "diagonal" $x = x'$;

- a function with a sufficiently smooth GP distribution shares a joint GP distribution with its gradient; among other things, this allows us to condition on (potentially noisy) derivative observations via exact inference;

- GP sample paths attain a maximum when sample paths are continuous and the domain is compact;

- GP sample paths attain a *unique* maximum under the additional condition that no two unique function values are perfectly correlated; and

- several methods are available for approximating the posterior process of a GP conditioned on information incompatible with exact inference.

If satisfied with the above summary, the reader may safely skip this material for now and move on with the next chapter. For those who wish to see the gritty details, dive in below!

2.4 JOINT GAUSSIAN PROCESSES

In some settings, we may wish to reason *jointly* about two-or-more related functions, such as an objective function and its gradient or an expensive objective function and a cheaper surrogate. To this end we can extend Gaussian processes to yield a joint distribution over the values assumed by multiple functions. The key to the construction is to "paste together" a collection of functions into a single function on a larger domain, then construct a standard GP on this combined function.

Definition

To elaborate, consider a set of functions $\{f_i\colon \mathcal{X}_i \to \mathbb{R}\}$ we wish to model.[21] We define the *disjoint union* of these functions $\sqcup f$ – defined on the disjoint union[22] of their domains $\mathcal{X} = \bigsqcup \mathcal{X}_i$ – by insisting its restriction to each domain be compatible with the corresponding function:

$$\sqcup f\colon \mathcal{X} \to \mathbb{R}; \qquad \sqcup f|_{\mathcal{X}_i} \equiv f_i.$$

We now can define a GP on $\sqcup f$ by choosing mean and covariance functions on $\mathcal{X}$ as desired:

$$p(\sqcup f) = \mathcal{GP}(\sqcup f; \mu, K). \tag{2.22}$$

We will call this construction a *joint Gaussian process* on $\{f_i\}$.

It is often convenient to decompose the moments of a joint GP into their restrictions on relevant subspaces. For example, consider a joint GP (2.22) on $f\colon \mathcal{F} \to \mathbb{R}$ and $g\colon \mathcal{G} \to \mathbb{R}$. After defining

$$\mu_f \equiv \mu|_{\mathcal{F}}; \qquad \mu_g \equiv \mu|_{\mathcal{G}};$$
$$K_f \equiv K|_{\mathcal{F}\times\mathcal{F}}; \quad K_g \equiv K|_{\mathcal{G}\times\mathcal{G}}; \quad K_{fg} \equiv K|_{\mathcal{F}\times\mathcal{G}}; \quad K_{gf} \equiv K|_{\mathcal{G}\times\mathcal{F}},$$

we can see that f and g in fact have marginal GP distributions:[23]

$$p(f) = \mathcal{GP}(f; \mu_f, K_f); \qquad p(g) = \mathcal{GP}(g; \mu_g, K_g), \tag{2.23}$$

that are coupled by the *cross-covariance functions* K_{fg} and K_{gf}. Given vectors $\mathbf{x} \subset \mathcal{F}$ and $\mathbf{x}' \subset \mathcal{G}$, these compute the covariance between the corresponding function values $\boldsymbol{\phi} = f(\mathbf{x})$ and $\boldsymbol{\gamma} = g(\mathbf{x}')$:

$$\begin{aligned} K_{fg}(\mathbf{x}, \mathbf{x}') &= \mathrm{cov}[\boldsymbol{\phi}, \boldsymbol{\gamma} \mid \mathbf{x}, \mathbf{x}']; \\ K_{gf}(\mathbf{x}, \mathbf{x}') &= \mathrm{cov}[\boldsymbol{\gamma}, \boldsymbol{\phi} \mid \mathbf{x}, \mathbf{x}'] = K_{fg}(\mathbf{x}, \mathbf{x}')^{\top}. \end{aligned} \tag{2.24}$$

When convenient we will notate a joint GP in terms of these decomposed functions, here writing:[24]

$$p(f, g) = \mathcal{GP}\left(\begin{bmatrix} f \\ g \end{bmatrix}; \begin{bmatrix} \mu_f \\ \mu_g \end{bmatrix}, \begin{bmatrix} K_f & K_{fg} \\ K_{gf} & K_g \end{bmatrix}\right). \tag{2.25}$$

With this notation, the marginal GP property (2.23) is perfectly analogous to the marginal property of the multivariate Gaussian distribution (A.13).

We can also use this construction to define a GP on a *vector*-valued function $\mathbf{f}\colon \mathcal{X} \to \mathbb{R}^d$ by defining a joint Gaussian process on its d coordinate functions $\{f_i\}\colon \mathcal{X} \to \mathbb{R}$. In this case we typically write the resulting model using the standard notation $\mathcal{GP}(\mathbf{f}; \mu, K)$, where the mean and covariance functions are now understood to map to $\mathbb{R}^d$ and $\mathbb{R}^{d\times d}$.

Example

We can demonstrate the behavior of a joint Gaussian process by extending our running example GP on $f\colon [0, 30] \to \mathbb{R}$. Recall the prior on f has

---

Sidenotes:

disjoint union of $\{f_i\}$, $\sqcup f$
disjoint union of $\{\mathcal{X}_i\}$, $\mathcal{X}$

21 The domains need not be equal, but they often are in practice.

22 A disjoint union represents a point $x \in \mathcal{X}_i$ by the pair (x, i), thereby combining the domains while retaining their identities.

joint Gaussian process

23 In fact, *any* restriction of a GP-distributed function has a GP (or multivariate normal) distribution.

24 We also used this notation in (2.6), where the "domain" of the vector $\mathbf{y}$ can be taken to be some finite index set of appropriate size.

extension to vector-valued functions

—— prior mean   ▨ prior 95% credible interval   —— sample

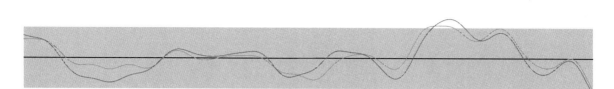

Figure 2.5: A joint Gaussian process over two functions on the shared domain $\mathcal{X} = [0, 30]$. The marginal belief over both functions is the same as our example GP from Figure 2.1, but the cross-covariance (2.26) between the functions strongly couples their behavior. We also show a sample from the joint distribution illustrating the strong correlation induced by the joint prior.

zero mean function $\mu \equiv 0$ and squared exponential covariance function (2.4). We augment our original function with a companion function g, defined on the same domain, that has exactly the same marginal GP distribution. However, we couple the distribution of f and g by defining a nontrivial cross-covariance function K_{fg} (2.24):

$$K_{fg}(x, x') = 0.9K(x, x'), \tag{2.26}$$

where K is the marginal covariance function of f and g. A consequence of this choice is that for any given point $x \in \mathcal{X}$, the correlation of the corresponding function values $\phi = f(x)$ and $\gamma = g(x)$ is quite strong:

$$\text{corr}[\phi, \gamma \mid x] = 0.9. \tag{2.27}$$

We illustrate the resulting joint GP in Figure 2.5. The marginal credible intervals for f (and now g) have not changed from our original example in Figure 2.1. However, drawing a sample of the functions from their joint distribution reveals the strong coupling encoded in the prior (2.26–2.27).

Inference for joint Gaussian processes

The construction in (2.22) allows us to reason about a joint Gaussian process as if it were a single GP. This allows us to condition a joint GP on observations of jointly Gaussian distributed values following the procedure outlined previously. In Figure 2.6, we condition the joint GP prior from Figure 2.5 on ten observations: five exact observations of f on the left-hand side of the domain and five exact observations of g on the right-hand side. Due to the strong correlation between the two functions, an observation of either function strongly informs our belief about the other, even in regions where there are no direct observations.

inference from jointly Gaussian distributed observations: § 2.2, p. 18

2.5   CONTINUITY

In this and the following sections we will establish some important properties of Gaussian processes determined by the properties of their

- • observations (direct)
- • observations (other function)
— posterior mean
posterior 95% credible interval

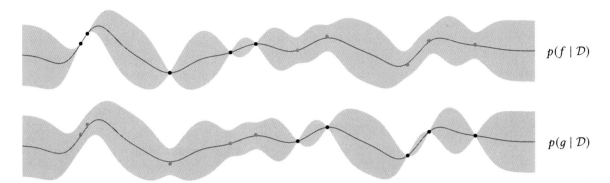

$p(f \mid \mathcal{D})$

$p(g \mid \mathcal{D})$

Figure 2.6: The joint posterior for our example joint GP prior in Figure 2.5 conditioned on five exact observations of each function.

moments. As a GP is completely specified by its mean and covariance functions, it should not be surprising that the nature of these functions has far-reaching implications regarding properties of the function being modeled. A good familiarity with these implications can help guide model design in practice – the focus of the next two chapters.

To begin, a fundamental question regarding Gaussian processes is whether sample paths are almost surely continuous, and if so how many times differentiable they may be. This is obviously an important consideration for modeling and is also critical to ensure that global optimization is a well-posed problem, as we will discuss later in this chapter. Fortunately, continuity of Gaussian processes is a well-understood property that can be guaranteed almost surely under simple conditions on the mean and covariance functions.

existence of global maxima: § 2.7, p. 34

Suppose $f\colon \mathcal{X} \to \mathbb{R}$ has distribution $\mathcal{GP}(f; \mu, K)$. Recall that f is continuous at x if $f(x) - f(x') = \phi - \phi' \to 0$ when $x' \to x$. Continuity is thus a limiting property of differences in function values. But under the Gaussian process assumption, this difference is Gaussian distributed (2.5, A.9)! We have

$$p(\phi - \phi' \mid x, x') = \mathcal{N}(\phi - \phi'; m, s^2),$$

where

$$m = \mu(x) - \mu(x'); \qquad s^2 = K(x, x) - 2K(x, x') + K(x', x').$$

Now if μ is continuous at x and K is continuous at $x = x'$, then both $m \to 0$ and $s^2 \to 0$ as $x \to x'$, and thus $\phi - \phi'$ converges in probability to 0. This intuitive condition of continuous moments is known as *continuity in mean square* at x; if μ and K are both continuous over the entire domain (the latter along the "diagonal" $x = x'$), then we say the entire process is continuous in mean square.

continuity in mean square

sample path continuity

25 R. J. ADLER and J. E. TAYLOR (2007). *Random Fields and Geometry*. Springer–Verlag. [§§ 1.3–1.4]

It turns out that continuity in mean square is not quite sufficient to guarantee that f is simultaneously continuous at every $x \in \mathcal{X}$ with probability one, a property known as *sample path continuity*. However, very slightly stronger conditions on the moments of a GP are sufficient to guarantee sample path continuity.[25] The following result is adequate for most settings arising in practice and may be proven as a corollary to the slightly weaker (and slightly more complicated) conditions assumed in ADLER and TAYLOR's theorem 1.4.1.

Theorem. *Suppose $\mathcal{X} \subset \mathbb{R}^d$ is compact and $f \colon \mathcal{X} \to \mathbb{R}$ has Gaussian process distribution $\mathcal{GP}(f; \mu, K)$, where μ is continuous and K is Hölder continuous.[26] Then f is almost surely continuous on $\mathcal{X}$.*

26 Hölder continuity is a generalization of Lipschitz continuity. Effectively, the covariance function must, in some sense, be "predictably" continuous.

27 W. RUDIN (1976). *Principles of Mathematical Analysis*. McGraw–Hill. [theorem 2.41]

28 Following the discussion in the next section, they in fact are *infinitely* differentiable.

The condition that $\mathcal{X} \subset \mathbb{R}^d$ be compact is equivalent to the domain being closed and bounded, by the Heine–Borel theorem.[27] Applying this result to our example GP in Figure 2.1, we conclude that samples from the process are continuous with probability one as the domain $\mathcal{X} = [0, 30]$ is compact and the squared exponential covariance function (2.4) is Hölder continuous. Indeed, the generated samples are very smooth.[28]

Sample path continuity can also be guaranteed on non-Euclidean domains under similar smoothness conditions.[25]

2.6   DIFFERENTIABILITY

We can approach the question of differentiability by again reasoning about the limiting behavior of linear transformations of function values. Suppose $f \colon \mathcal{X} \to \mathbb{R}$ with $\mathcal{X} \subset \mathbb{R}^d$ has distribution $\mathcal{GP}(f; \mu, K)$, and consider the ith partial derivative of f at $\mathbf{x}$, if it exists:

$$\frac{\partial f}{\partial x_i}(\mathbf{x}) = \lim_{h \to 0} \frac{f(\mathbf{x} + h\mathbf{e}_i) - f(\mathbf{x})}{h},$$

where $\mathbf{e}_i$ is the ith standard basis vector. For $h > 0$, the value in the limit is Gaussian distributed as a linear transformation of Gaussian-distributed random variables (A.9). Assuming the corresponding partial derivative of the mean exists at $\mathbf{x}$ and the corresponding partial derivative with respect to each input of the covariance function exists at $\mathbf{x} = \mathbf{x}'$, then as $h \to 0$ the partial derivative converges in distribution to a Gaussian:

sequences of normal RVs: § A.2, p. 300

$$p\left(\frac{\partial f}{\partial x_i}(\mathbf{x}) \mid \mathbf{x}\right) = \mathcal{N}\left(\frac{\partial f}{\partial x_i}(\mathbf{x}); \frac{\partial \mu}{\partial x_i}(\mathbf{x}), \frac{\partial^2 K}{\partial x_i \, \partial x_i'}(\mathbf{x}, \mathbf{x})\right).$$

If this property holds for each coordinate $1 \leq i \leq d$, then f is said to be *differentiable in mean square* at $\mathbf{x}$.

differentiability in mean square

joint GP between function and gradient

If f is differentiable in mean square everywhere in the domain, the process itself is called differentiable in mean square, and we have the remarkable result that the function and its gradient have a *joint* Gaussian process distribution:

$$p(f, \nabla f) = \mathcal{GP}\left(\begin{bmatrix} f \\ \nabla f \end{bmatrix}; \begin{bmatrix} \mu \\ \nabla \mu \end{bmatrix}, \begin{bmatrix} K & K\nabla^\top \\ \nabla K & \nabla K \nabla^\top \end{bmatrix}\right). \tag{2.28}$$

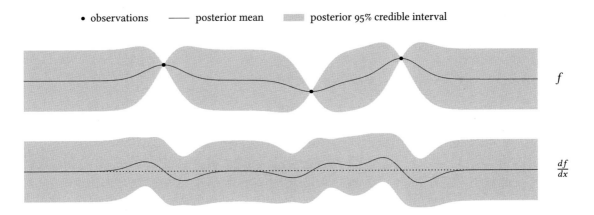

Figure 2.7: The joint posterior of the function and its derivative for our example Gaussian process from Figure 2.2. The dashed line in the lower plot corresponds to a derivative of zero.

Here by writing the gradient operator ∇ on the left-hand side of K we mean the result of taking the gradient with respect to its *first* input, and by writing $\nabla^\top$ on the right-hand side of K we mean taking the gradient with respect to its *second* input and transposing the result. Thus $\nabla K \colon \mathcal{X} \times \mathcal{X} \to \mathbb{R}^d$ maps pairs of points to column vectors:

covariance between $\nabla f(\mathbf{x})$ and $f(\mathbf{x}')$, ∇K

$$\left[\nabla K(\mathbf{x}, \mathbf{x}')\right]_i = \mathrm{cov}\left[\frac{\partial f}{\partial x_i}(\mathbf{x}), f(\mathbf{x}') \mid \mathbf{x}, \mathbf{x}'\right] = \frac{\partial K}{\partial x_i}(\mathbf{x}, \mathbf{x}'),$$

and $K\nabla^\top \colon \mathcal{X} \times \mathcal{X} \to (\mathbb{R}^d)^*$ maps pairs of points to row vectors:

transpose of covariance between $f(\mathbf{x})$ and $\nabla f(\mathbf{x}')$, $K\nabla^\top$

$$K\nabla^\top(\mathbf{x}, \mathbf{x}') = \left[\nabla K(\mathbf{x}', \mathbf{x})\right]^\top.$$

Finally, the function $\nabla K \nabla^\top \colon \mathcal{X} \times \mathcal{X} \to \mathbb{R}^{d \times d}$ represents the result of applying both operations, mapping a pair of points to the covariance matrix between the entries of the corresponding gradients:

covariance between $\nabla f(\mathbf{x})$ and $\nabla f(\mathbf{x}')$, $\nabla K \nabla^\top$

$$\left[\nabla K \nabla^\top(\mathbf{x}, \mathbf{x}')\right]_{ij} = \mathrm{cov}\left[\frac{\partial f}{\partial x_i}(\mathbf{x}), \frac{\partial f}{\partial x'_j}(\mathbf{x}') \mid \mathbf{x}, \mathbf{x}'\right] = \frac{\partial^2 K}{\partial x_i \, \partial x'_j}(\mathbf{x}, \mathbf{x}').$$

As the gradient of f has a Gaussian process marginal distribution (2.28), we can reduce the question of *continuous* differentiability to sample path continuity of the gradient process following the discussion above.

continuous differentiability

Figure 2.7 shows the posterior distribution for the derivative of our example Gaussian process alongside the posterior for the function itself. We can observe a clear correspondence between the two distributions; for example, the posterior mean of the derivative vanishes at critical points of the posterior mean of the function. Notably, we have a great deal of residual uncertainty about the derivative, even at the observed locations. That is because the relatively high spacing between the existing observations limits our ability to accurately estimate the derivative

example and discussion

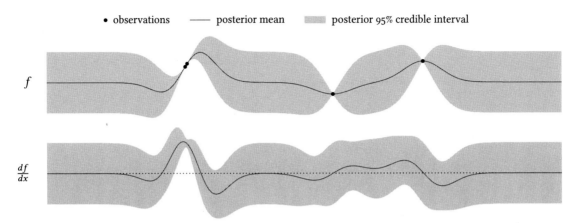

Figure 2.8: The joint posterior of the derivative of our example Gaussian process after adding a new observation nearby another suggesting a large positive slope. The dashed line in the lower plot corresponds to a derivative of zero.

anywhere. Adding an observation immediately next to a previous one significantly reduces the uncertainty in the derivative in that region by effectively providing a finite-difference approximation; see Figure 2.8.

Conditioning on derivative observations

inference from jointly Gaussian distributed observations: § 2.2, p. 18

However, we can be more direct in specifying derivatives than finite differencing. We can instead condition the joint GP (2.28) *directly* on a derivative observation, as described previously. Figure 2.9 shows the joint posterior after conditioning on an exact observation of the derivative at the left-most observation location, where the uncertainty in the derivative now vanishes entirely. This capability allows the seamless incorporation of derivative information into an objective function model. Notably, we can even condition a Gaussian process on *noisy* derivative observations as well, as we might obtain in stochastic gradient descent.

29 For K we again only need to consider the "diagonal" $\mathbf{x} = \mathbf{x}'$.

30 Recall the Hessian is symmetric (assuming the second partial derivatives are continuous) and thus redundant. The *half-vectorization* operator vech $\mathbf{A}$ maps the upper triangular part of a square, symmetric matrix $\mathbf{A}$ to a vector.

We can reason about derivatives past the first recursively. For example, if μ and K are *twice* differentiable,[29] then the (e.g., half-vectorized[30]) Hessian of f will also have a joint GP distribution with f and its gradient. Defining $\mathbf{h}$ to be the operator mapping a function to its half-vectorized Hessian:

$$\mathbf{h}f = \text{vech } \nabla\nabla^{\top}f,$$

for a Gaussian process with suitably differentiable moments, we have

$$p(\mathbf{h}f) = \mathcal{GP}\big(\mathbf{h}f; \mathbf{h}\mu, \mathbf{h}K\mathbf{h}^{\top}\big), \tag{2.29}$$

where we have used the same notational convention for the transpose. Further, f, ∇f, and $\mathbf{h}f$ will have a joint Gaussian process distribution given by augmenting (2.28) with the marginal in (2.29) and the cross-covariance functions

$$\text{cov}[\mathbf{h}f, f] = \mathbf{h}K; \qquad \text{cov}[\mathbf{h}f, \nabla f] = \mathbf{h}K\nabla^{\top}.$$

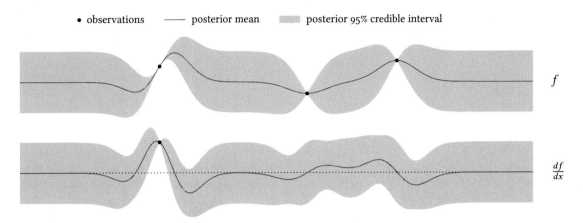

Figure 2.9: The joint posterior of the derivative of our example Gaussian process after adding an exact observation of the derivative at the indicated location. The dashed line in the lower plot corresponds to a derivative of zero.

We can continue further in this vein if needed; however, we rarely reason about derivatives of third-or-higher order in Bayesian optimization.[31]

31 This is true in classical optimization as well!

Other linear transformations

The joint GP distribution between a suitably smooth GP-distributed function and its gradient (2.28) is simply an infinite-dimensional analog of the general result that Gaussian random variables are jointly Gaussian distributed with arbitrary linear transformations (A.10), after noting that differentiation is a linear operator. We can extend this result to reason about other linear transformations of GP-distributed functions. DIACONIS's original motivation for studying Bayesian numerical methods was *quadrature*, the numerical estimation of intractable integrals.[32] It turns out that Gaussian processes are a rather convenient model for this task: if $p(f) = \mathcal{GP}(f; \mu, K)$ and we want to reason about the expectation

$$Z = \int f(x)\, p(x)\, \mathrm{d}x,$$

then (under mild conditions) we again have a joint Gaussian process distribution over f and Z.[33] This enables both inference about Z and conditioning on noisy observations of integrals, such as a Monte Carlo estimate of an expectation. The former is the basis for *Bayesian quadrature*, an analog of Bayesian optimization bringing Bayesian experimental design to bear on numerical integration.[32,34,35]

32 P. DIACONIS (1988). Bayesian Numerical Analysis. In: *Statistical Decision Theory and Related Topics IV*.

33 This can be shown, for example, by considering the limiting distribution of Riemann sums.

34 A. O'HAGAN (1991). Bayes–Hermite Quadrature. *Journal of Statistical Planning and Inference* 29(3):245–260.

35 C. E. RASMUSSEN and Z. GHAHRAMANI (2002). Bayesian Monte Carlo. *NeurIPS 2002*.

2.7   EXISTENCE AND UNIQUENESS OF GLOBAL MAXIMA

The primary use of GPs in Bayesian optimization is to inform optimization decisions, which will be our focus for the majority of this book. Before continuing down this path, we pause to consider whether global optimization of a GP-distributed function is a well-posed problem, in particular, whether the model guarantees the existence of a global maximum at all.

Consider a function $f: \mathcal{X} \to \mathbb{R}$ with distribution $\mathcal{GP}(f; \mu, K)$, and consider the location and value of its global optimum, if one exists:

$$x^* = \arg\max_{x \in \mathcal{X}} f(x); \qquad f^* = \max_{x \in \mathcal{X}} f(x) = f(x^*).$$

mutual information and entropy search: § 7.6, p. 135

As f is unknown, these quantities are random variables. Many Bayesian optimization algorithms operate by reasoning about the distributions of (and uncertainties in) these quantities induced by our belief on f.

There are two technical issues we must address. The first is whether we can be certain that a globally optimal value f^* exists when the objective function is random. If existence is not guaranteed, then its distribution is meaningless. The second issue is one of uniqueness: assuming the objective does attain a maximal value, can we be certain the optimum is unique? In general x^* is a *set*-valued random variable, and thus its distribution might have support over arbitrary subsets of the domain, rendering it complicated to reason about. However, if we could ensure the uniqueness of x^*, its distribution would have support on $\mathcal{X}$ rather than its power set, allowing more straightforward inference.

Both the existence of f^* and uniqueness of x^* are tacitly assumed throughout the Bayesian optimization literature when building algorithms based on distributions of these quantities, but these properties are not guaranteed for arbitrary Gaussian processes. However, we can ensure these properties hold almost surely under mild conditions.

Existence of global maxima

To begin, guaranteeing the existence of an optimal value is straightforward if we suppose the domain $\mathcal{X}$ is compact, a pervasive assumption in optimization. This is no coincidence! In this case, if f is continuous then it achieves a global optimum by the extreme value theorem.[36] Thus sample path continuity of f and compactness of $\mathcal{X}$ is sufficient to ensure that f^* exists almost surely. Both conditions can be readily established: sample path continuity by following our previous discussion, and compactness of the domain by standard arguments (for example, ensuring that $\mathcal{X} \subset \mathbb{R}^d$ be closed and bounded).

36 W. RUDIN (1976). *Principles of Mathematical Analysis*. McGraw–Hill. [theorem 4.16]

sample path continuity: § 2.5, p. 28

Uniqueness of global maxima

We now turn to the question of uniqueness of x^*, which obviously only becomes a meaningful question after presupposing that f^* exists. Again, this condition is easy to ensure almost surely under simple conditions on the covariance function of a Gaussian process.

KIM and POLLARD considered this issue and provided straightforward conditions under which the uniqueness of x^* is guaranteed for a centered Gaussian process.[37],[38] Namely, no two unique points in the domain can

37 A centered Gaussian process has identically zero mean function $\mu \equiv 0$.

38 J. KIM and D. POLLARD (1990). Cube Root Asymptotics. *The Annals of Statistics* 18(1):191–219. [lemma 2.6]

have perfectly correlated function values, a natural condition that can be easily verified.

Theorem (KIM and POLLARD, 1990). *Let $\mathcal{X}$ be a compact metric space.*[39] *Suppose $f \colon \mathcal{X} \to \mathbb{R}$ has distribution $\mathcal{GP}(f; \mu \equiv 0, K)$, and that f is sample path continuous. If for all $x, x' \in \mathcal{X}$ with $x \neq x'$ we have*

$$\mathrm{var}[\phi - \phi' \mid x, x'] = K(x, x) - 2K(x, x') + K(x', x') \neq 0,$$

then f almost surely has a unique maximum on $\mathcal{X}$.

ARCONES provided slightly weaker conditions for uniqueness of the supremum, avoiding the requirement of sample path continuity.[40]

Counterexamples

Although the above conditions for ensuring existence of f^* and uniqueness of x^* are fairly mild, it is easy to construct counterexamples.

Consider a function on the closed unit interval, which we note is compact: $f \colon [0, 1] \to \mathbb{R}$. We endow f with a "white noise"[41] Gaussian process with

$$\mu(x) \equiv 0; \qquad K(x, x') = [x = x'].$$

Now f almost surely does not have a maximum. Roughly, because the value of f at every point in the domain is independent of every other, there will almost always be a point with value exceeding any putative maximum.[42] However, the conditions of sample path continuity were violated as the covariance is discontinuous at $x = x'$.

We may also construct a Gaussian process that almost surely achieves a maximum that is not unique. Consider a random function f defined on the (compact) interval $[0, 4\pi]$ defined by the parametric model

$$f(x) = \alpha \cos x + \beta \sin x,$$

where α and β are independent standard normal random variables. Then f has a Gaussian process distribution with

$$\mu(x) \equiv 0; \qquad K(x, x') = \cos(x - x'). \tag{2.30}$$

Here μ is continuous and K is Hölder continuous, and thus f is sample path continuous and almost surely achieves a global maximum. However, f is also periodic with period 2π with probability one and will thus almost surely achieve its maximum *twice*. Note that the covariance function does not satisfy the conditions outlined in the above theorem, as any input locations separated by 2π have perfectly correlated function values.

2.8 INFERENCE WITH NON-GAUSSIAN OBSERVATIONS AND CONSTRAINTS

Gaussian process inference is tractable when the observed values are jointly Gaussian distributed with the function of interest (2.6). However, this may not always hold for all relevant information we may receive.

---

39 Although unlikely to matter in practice, KIM and POLLARD allow $\mathcal{X}$ to be σ-compact and show that the supremum (rather than the maximum) is unique under the same conditions.

40 M. A. ARCONES (1992). On the arg max of a Gaussian Process. *Statistics & Probability Letters* 15(5):373–374.

41 It turns out this naïve model of white noise has horrible mathematical properties, but it is sufficient for this counterexample.

42 Let $Q = \mathbb{Q} \cap [0, 1] = \{q_i\}$ be the rationals in the domain and let f^* be a putative maximum. Defining $\phi_i = f(q_i)$, we must have $\phi_i \leq f^*$ for every i; call this event A.

Define the event A_k by f^* exceeding the first k elements of Q. From independence,

$$\Pr(A_k) = \prod_{i=1}^{k} \Pr(\phi_i \leq f^*) = \Phi(f^*)^k,$$

so $\Pr(A_k) \to 0$ as $k \to \infty$. But $\{A_k\} \nearrow A$, so $\Pr(A) = 0$, and f^* is almost surely not the maximum.

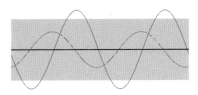

Our counterexample GP without a unique maximum. Every sample achieves its maximum twice.

inference from jointly Gaussian distributed observations: § 2.2, p. 18

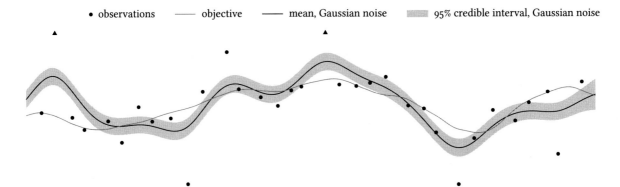

observations   —— objective   —— mean, Gaussian noise   ▨ 95% credible interval, Gaussian noise

Figure 2.10: Regression with observations corrupted with heavy-tailed noise. The triangular marks indicate observations lying beyond the plotted range. Shown is the posterior distribution of an objective function (along with ground truth) modeling the errors as Gaussian. The posterior is heavily affected by the outliers.

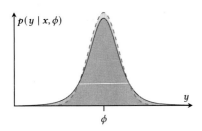

A Student-t error model (solid) with a Gaussian error model (dashed) for reference. The heavier tails of the Student-t model can better explain large outliers.

43 K. L. LANGE et al. (1989). Robust Statistical Modeling Using the t Distribution. *Journal of the American Statistical Association* 84(408):881–896.

differentiability, derivative observations: § 2.6, p. 30

One obvious limitation is an incompatibility with naturally non-Gaussian observations. A scenario particularly relevant to optimization is heavy-tailed noise. Consider the data shown in Figure 2.10, where some observations represent extreme outliers. These errors are poorly modeled as Gaussian, and attempting to infer the underlying objective function with the additive Gaussian noise model leads to overfitting and poor predictive performance. A Student-t error model with $v \approx 4$ degrees of freedom provides a robust alternative:[43]

$$p(y \mid x, \phi) = \mathcal{T}(y; \phi, \sigma_n^2, v). \tag{2.31}$$

The heavier tails of this model can better explain large outliers; unfortunately, the non-Gaussian nature of this model also renders exact inference impossible. We will demonstrate how to overcome this impasse.

Constraints on an objective function, such as bounds on given function values, can also provide valuable information during optimization, but many natural constraints cannot be reduced to observations that can be handled in closed form. Several Bayesian optimization policies impose hypothetical constraints on the objective function when designing each observation, requiring inference from intractable constraints even when the observations themselves pose no difficulties.

To see how constraints might arise in optimization, consider a Gaussian process belief on a one-dimensional objective f, and suppose we wish to condition on f on having a *local* maximum at a given location x. Assuming the function is twice differentiable, we can invoke the second-derivative test to encode this information in two constraints:

$$f'(x) = 0; \qquad f''(x) < 0. \tag{2.32}$$

We can condition a GP on the first of these conditions by following our previous discussion. However, *no* GP is compatible with the second

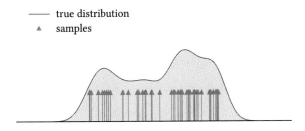

— true distribution

▲ samples

Figure 2.11: The probability density function of an example distribution along with 50 samples drawn independently from the distribution. In Monte Carlo approaches, the distribution is effectively approximated by a mixture of Dirac delta distributions at the sample locations.

condition as $f''(x)$ would necessarily have a Gaussian distribution with unbounded support (2.29). We need some other means to proceed.

Non-Gaussian observations: general case

We can address both non-Gaussian observations and constraints with the following general case, which is flexible enough to handle a large range of information. As in our discussion on exact inference, suppose there is some vector $\mathbf{y}$ sharing a joint Gaussian process distribution with a function of interest f (2.6):

$$p(f, \mathbf{y}) = \mathcal{GP}\left(\begin{bmatrix} f \\ \mathbf{y} \end{bmatrix}; \begin{bmatrix} \mu \\ \mathbf{m} \end{bmatrix}, \begin{bmatrix} K & \kappa^\top \\ \kappa & C \end{bmatrix}\right).$$

Suppose we receive some information about $\mathbf{y}$ in the form of information $\mathcal{D}$ inducing a non-Gaussian posterior on $\mathbf{y}$. Here, it is convenient to adopt the language of factor graphs[44] and write the resulting posterior as proportional to the prior weighted by a function $t(\mathbf{y})$ encoding the available information, which may factorize:

$$p(\mathbf{y} \mid \mathcal{D}) \propto p(\mathbf{y}) \, t(\mathbf{y}) = \mathcal{N}(\mathbf{y}; \mathbf{m}, C) \prod_i t_i(\mathbf{y}). \qquad (2.33)$$

The functions $\{t_i\}$ are called *factors* or *local functions* that may comprise a likelihood augmented by any desired (hard or soft) constraints. The term "local functions" arises because each factor often depends only on a low-dimensional subspace of $\mathbf{y}$, often a single entry.[45]

The posterior on $\mathbf{y}$ (2.33) in turn induces a posterior on f:

$$p(f \mid \mathcal{D}) = \int p(f \mid \mathbf{y}) \, p(\mathbf{y} \mid \mathcal{D}) \, d\mathbf{y}. \qquad (2.34)$$

At first glance, we may hope to resolve this posterior easily as $p(f \mid \mathbf{y})$ is a Gaussian process (2.9–2.10). Unfortunately, the non-Gaussian posterior on $\mathbf{y}$ usually renders the posterior on f intractable.

Monte Carlo sampling

A Monte Carlo approach to approximating the f posterior (2.34) begins by drawing samples from the $\mathbf{y}$ posterior (2.33):

$$\{\mathbf{y}_i\}_{i=1}^s \sim p(\mathbf{y} \mid \mathcal{D}).$$

44 F. R. KSCHISCHANG et al. (2001). Factor Graphs and the Sum–Product Algorithm. *IEEE Transactions on Information Theory* 47(2):498–519.

factors, local functions, $\{t_i\}$

45 For example, when observations are conditionally independent given the corresponding function values, the likelihood factorizes into a product of one-dimensional factors (1.3):

$$p(\mathbf{y} \mid \mathbf{x}, \boldsymbol{\phi}) = \prod_i p(y_i \mid x_i, \phi_i).$$

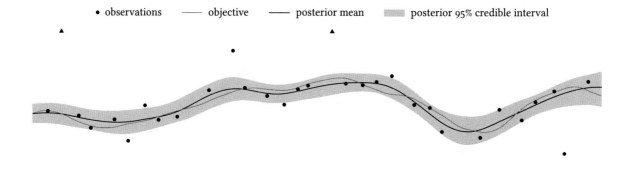

• observations   —— objective   —— posterior mean   ▨ posterior 95% credible interval

Figure 2.12: Regression with observations corrupted with heavy-tailed noise. The triangular marks indicate observations lying beyond the plotted range. Shown is the posterior distribution of an objective function (along with ground truth) modeling the errors as Student-t distributed with $\nu = 4$ degrees of freedom. The posterior was approximated from 100 000 Monte Carlo samples. Comparing with the additive Gaussian noise model from Figure 2.10, this model effectively ignores the outliers and the fit is excellent.

46 *Handbook of Markov Chain Monte Carlo* (2011). Chapman & Hall.

47 I. MURRAY et al. (2010). Elliptical Slice Sampling. *AISTATS 2010*.

We may generate these by appealing to one of numerous Markov chain Monte Carlo (MCMC) routines.[46] One natural choice would be *elliptical slice sampling*,[47] which is specifically tailored for latent Gaussian models of this form. Samples from a one-dimensional toy example distribution are shown in Figure 2.11.

Given posterior samples of **y**, we may then approximate (2.34) via the standard Monte Carlo estimator

$$p(f \mid \mathcal{D}) \approx \frac{1}{s} \sum_{i=1}^{s} p(f \mid \mathbf{y}_i) = \frac{1}{s} \sum_{i=1}^{s} \mathcal{GP}(f; \mu_{\mathcal{D}_i}, K_{\mathcal{D}}). \qquad (2.35)$$

This is a mixture of Gaussian processes, each of the form in (2.9–2.10). The posterior mean functions depend on the corresponding **y** samples, whereas the posterior covariance functions are identical as there is no dependence on the observed values. In this approximation, the marginal belief about any function value is then a mixture of univariate Gaussians:

$$p(\phi \mid x, \mathcal{D}) \approx \frac{1}{s} \sum_{i=1}^{s} \mathcal{N}(\phi; \mu_i, \sigma^2); \quad \mu_i = \mu_{\mathcal{D}_i}(x); \quad \sigma^2 = K_{\mathcal{D}}(x, x). \tag{2.36}$$

Although slightly more complex than the Gaussian marginals of a Gaussian process, this is often convenient enough for most needs.

example: Student-t observation model

A Monte Carlo approximation to the posterior for the heavy-tailed dataset from Figure 2.10 is shown in Figure 2.12. The observations were modeled as corrupted by Student-t errors with $\nu = 4$ degrees of freedom. The posterior was approximated using a truly excessive number of samples (100 000, with a burn-in of 10 000) from the **y** posterior drawn using elliptical slice sampling.[47] The outliers in the data are ignored and the predictive performance is excellent.

Gaussian approximate inference

An alternative to sampling is *approximate inference,* where we make a parametric approximation to the $\mathbf{y}$ posterior that yields a tractable posterior on f. In particular, if the posterior (2.33) were actually *normal,* it would induce a Gaussian process posterior on f. This insight is the basis for most approximation schemes.

In this vein, we proceed by first – somehow – approximating the true posterior over $\mathbf{y}$ with a multivariate Gaussian distribution:

$$p(\mathbf{y} \mid \mathcal{D}) \approx q(\mathbf{y} \mid \mathcal{D}) = \mathcal{N}(\mathbf{y}; \tilde{\mathbf{m}}, \tilde{\mathbf{C}}). \qquad (2.37)$$

We are free to design this approximation as we see fit. There are several general-purpose approaches available, distinguished by how they approach maximizing the fidelity of fitting the true posterior (2.33). These include the Laplace approximation, Gaussian expectation propagation, and variational Bayesian inference. The first two of these methods are covered in Appendix B, and NICKISCH and RASMUSSEN provide an extensive survey of these and other approaches in the context of Gaussian process binary classification.[48]

Regardless of the details of the approximation scheme, the high-level result is the same – the normal approximation (2.37) in turn induces an approximate Gaussian process posterior on f. To demonstrate this, we consider the posterior on f that would arise from a direct observation of $\mathbf{y}$ (2.9–2.10) and integrate against the approximate posterior (2.37):

$$p(f \mid \mathcal{D}) \approx \int p(f \mid \mathbf{y})\, q(\mathbf{y} \mid \mathcal{D})\, \mathrm{d}\mathbf{y} = \mathcal{GP}(f; \mu_{\mathcal{D}}, K_{\mathcal{D}}), \qquad (2.38)$$

where

$$\mu_{\mathcal{D}}(x) = \mu(x) + \kappa(x)^{\top}\mathbf{C}^{-1}(\tilde{\mathbf{m}} - \mathbf{m});$$
$$K_{\mathcal{D}}(x, x') = K(x, x') - \kappa(x)^{\top}\mathbf{C}^{-1}(\mathbf{C} - \tilde{\mathbf{C}})\mathbf{C}^{-1}\kappa(x'). \qquad (2.39)$$

For most approximation schemes, the posterior covariance on f simplifies to a nicer, more familiar form. Most approximations to the $\mathbf{y}$ posterior (2.37) yield an approximate posterior covariance of the form

$$\tilde{\mathbf{C}} = \mathbf{C} - \mathbf{C}(\mathbf{C} + \mathbf{N})^{-1}\mathbf{C}, \qquad (2.40)$$

where $\mathbf{N}$ is positive definite. Although this might appear mysterious, it is actually a natural form: it is the posterior covariance that would result from observing $\mathbf{y}$ corrupted by additive Gaussian noise with covariance $\mathbf{N}$ (2.19), except we are now free to design the noise covariance to maximize the fit. For approximations of this form (2.40), the approximate posterior covariance function on f simplifies to the more familiar

$$K_{\mathcal{D}}(x, x') = K(x, x') - \kappa(x)^{\top}(\mathbf{C} + \mathbf{N})^{-1}\kappa(x'). \qquad (2.41)$$

To demonstrate the power of approximate inference, we return to our motivating scenario of conditioning a one-dimensional process on having a local maximum at an identified point x, which we can achieve by

Laplace approximation: § B.1, p. 301

Gaussian expectation propagation: § B.2 p. 302

48 H. NICKISCH and C. E. RASMUSSEN (2008). Approximations for Binary Gaussian Process Classification. *Journal of Machine Learning Research* 9(Oct):2035–2078.

example: conditioning on a local optimum

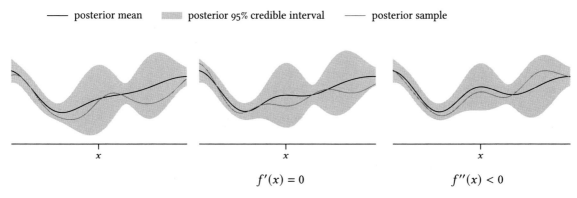

— posterior mean ▨ posterior 95% credible interval — posterior sample

$f'(x) = 0$ $f''(x) < 0$

Figure 2.13: Approximately conditioning a Gaussian process to have a local maximum at the marked point x. We show each stage of the conditioning process with a sample drawn from the corresponding posterior. We begin with the unconstrained process (left), which we condition on the first derivative being zero at x using exact inference (middle). Finally we use Gaussian expectation propagation to approximately condition on the second derivative being negative at x.

derivative observations: § 2.6, p. 32

conditioning the first derivative to be zero and constraining the second derivative to be negative at x (2.32). We illustrate an approximation to the resulting posterior step-by-step in Figure 2.13, beginning with the example Gaussian process in the left-most panel. We first condition the process on the first derivative observation $f'(x) = 0$ using *exact* inference; the result is shown in the middle panel. Both the updated posterior mean and the sample reflect this information; however, the sample displays a local *minimum* at x, as the second-derivative constraint has not yet been addressed.

To incorporate the second-derivative constraint, we begin with this updated GP and consider the second derivative $h = f''(x)$, which is Gaussian distributed prior to the constraint (2.29):

$$p(h) = \mathcal{N}(h; m, s^2).$$

The negativity constraint induces a posterior on h incorporating the factor $[h < 0]$ (2.33); see Figure 2.14:

$$p(h \mid \mathcal{D}) \propto p(h) \, [h < 0].$$

The result is a truncated normal posterior on h. We may use Gaussian expectation propagation, which is especially convenient for handling bound constraints of this form, to produce a Gaussian approximation:

$$p(h \mid \mathcal{D}) \approx q(h \mid \mathcal{D}) = \mathcal{N}(h; \tilde{m}, \tilde{s}^2).$$

Incorporating the updated belief on h into the Gaussian process (2.39) yields the approximate posterior in the right-most panel of Figure 2.13. Although there is still some residual probability that the second derivative is positive at x in the approximate posterior (approximately 8%; see Figure 2.14), the belief reflects the desired information reasonably faithfully.

49 P. MCCULLAGH and J. A. NELDER (1989). *Generalized Linear Models.* Chapman & Hall.

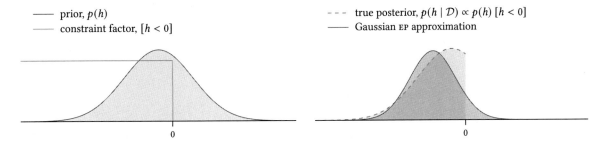

—— prior, $p(h)$
—— constraint factor, $[h < 0]$

--- true posterior, $p(h \mid \mathcal{D}) \propto p(h) \, [h < 0]$
—— Gaussian EP approximation

Figure 2.14: A demonstration of Gaussian expectation propagation. On the left we have a Gaussian belief on the second derivative, $p(h)$. We wish to constrain this value to be negative, introducing a step-function factor encoding the constraint, $[h < 0]$. The resulting distribution is non-Gaussian (right), but we can approximate it with a Gaussian, which induces an updated GP posterior on the function approximately incorporating the constraint.

Going beyond this example, we may use the approach outlined above to realize a general framework for Bayesian nonlinear regression by combining a GP prior on a latent function with an observation model appropriate for the task at hand, then approximating the posterior as desired. The convenience and modeling flexibility offered by Gaussian processes can easily justify any extra effort required for approximating the posterior. This can be seen as a nonlinear extension of the well-known family of *generalized linear models*.[49]

This approach is quite popular and has been realized countless times. Notable examples include binary classification using a logistic or probit observation model,[50] modeling point processes as a nonhomogeneous Poisson process with unknown intensity,[51,52] and robust regression with heavy-tailed additive noise such as Laplace[53] or Student-t[54,55] distributed errors. With regard to the latter and our previous heavy-tailed noise example, a Laplace approximation to the posterior for the data in Figures 2.10–2.12 with the Student-t observation model produces an approximate posterior in excellent agreement with the Monte Carlo approximation in Figure 2.12; see Figure 2.15. The cost of approximate inference in this case was dramatically (several orders of magnitude) cheaper than Monte Carlo sampling.

2.9   SUMMARY OF MAJOR IDEAS

Gaussian processes have been studied – in one form or another – for over 100 years.[56] Although we have covered a lot of ground in this chapter, we have only scratched the surface of an expansive body of literature. A good entry point to that literature is RASMUSSEN and WILLIAMS's monograph, which focuses on machine learning applications of Gaussian processes but also covers their theoretical underpinnings and properties in depth.[57] A good companion to this work is the book of ADLER and TAYLOR, which takes a deep dive into the properties and geometry of sample paths, including statistical properties of their maxima.[58]

50 H. NICKISCH and C. E. RASMUSSEN (2008). Approximations for Binary Gaussian Process Classification. *Journal of Machine Learning Research* 9(Oct):2035–2078.

51 J. MØLLER et al. (1998). Log Gaussian Cox Processes. *Scandinavian Journal of Statistics* 25(3): 451–482.

52 R. P. ADAMS et al. (2009). Tractable Nonparametric Bayesian Inference in Poisson Processes with Gaussian Process Intensities. *ICML 2009*.

53 M. KUSS (2006). Gaussian Process Models for Robust Regression, Classification, and Reinforcement Learning. Ph.D. thesis. Technische Universität Darmstadt. [§ 5.4]

54 R. M. NEAL (1997). *Monte Carlo Implementation of Gaussian Process Models for Bayesian Regression and Classification.* Technical report (9702). Department of Statistics, University of Toronto.

55 P. JYLÄNKI et al. (2011). Robust Gaussian Process Regression with a Student-t Likelihood. *Journal of Machine Learning Research* 12(99): 3227–3257.

56 DIACONIS identified an early application of GPs by POINCARÉ for nonlinear regression:

P. DIACONIS (1988). Bayesian Numerical Analysis. In: *Statistical Decision Theory and Related Topics IV*.

H. POINCARÉ (1912). *Calcul des probabilités.* Gauthier–Villars.

57 C. E. RASMUSSEN and C. K. I. WILLIAMS (2006). *Gaussian Processes for Machine Learning.* MIT Press.

58 R. J. ADLER and J. E. TAYLOR (2007). *Random Fields and Geometry.* Springer–Verlag.

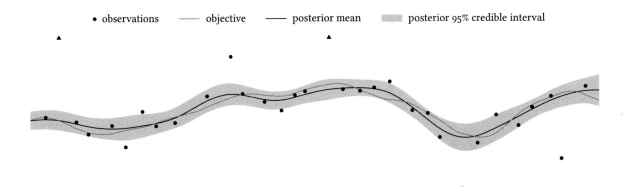

Figure 2.15: A Laplace approximation to the posterior from Figure 2.12.

Fortunately, the basic definitions and properties covered in § 2.1 and exact inference procedure covered in § 2.2 already provide a sufficient foundation for the majority of practical applications of Bayesian optimization. This material also provides sufficient background knowledge for the majority of the remainder of the book. However, we wish to underscore the major results from this chapter at a high level.

- Gaussian processes extend the multivariate normal distribution to model functions on infinite domains. As in the finite-dimensional case, Gaussian processes are specified by their first two moments – a mean function and a positive-definite covariance function – which endow any finite set of function values with a multivariate normal distribution (2.2–2.3).

- Conditioning a Gaussian process on function observations that are either exact or corrupted by additive Gaussian noise yields a Gaussian process posterior with updated moments reflecting the assumptions in the prior and the information in the observations (2.9–2.10).

inference from arbitrary joint Gaussian observations: § 2.2, p. 22

- In fact, we may condition a Gaussian process on the observation of *any* observations sharing a joint Gaussian distribution with the function of interest.

interpretation of posterior moments: § 2.2, p. 21

- In the case of exact inference, the posterior moments of a Gaussian process can be rewritten in terms of correlations among function values and z-scores of the observed values in a manner that may be more intuitive than the standard formulas.

joint Gaussian processes: § 2.4, p. 26

Extensions and Related Settings: Chapter 11, p. 245

- We may extend Gaussian processes to jointly model multiple correlated functions via careful bookkeeping, a construction known as a *joint Gaussian process*. Joint GPs are widely used in optimization settings involving multiple objectives and/or cheaper surrogates for an expensive objective.

continuity: § 2.5, p. 28
differentiability: § 2.6, p. 30

- Continuity and differentiability of Gaussian process sample paths can be guaranteed under mild assumptions on the mean and covariance functions. When these functions are sufficiently differentiable, a GP-distributed function shares a joint GP distribution with its gradient (2.28).

This joint distribution allows us to condition a Gaussian process on (potentially noisy) derivative observations.

derivative observations: § 2.6, p. 32

- The existence and uniqueness of global maxima for Gaussian process sample paths can be guaranteed under mild assumptions on the mean and covariance functions. Establishing these properties ensures that the location x^* and value f^* of the global maximum are well-founded random variables, which will be critical for some optimization methods introduced later in the book.[59]

existence and uniqueness of global maxima: § 2.7, p. 33

59 In particular, policies grounded in information theory under the umbrella of "entropy search." See § 7.6, p. 135 for more.

- Inference from non-Gaussian observations and constraints is possible via Monte Carlo sampling or Gaussian approximate inference.

inference with non-Gaussian observations and constraints: § 2.8, p. 35

Looking forward, the focus of this chapter has been on theoretical rather than practical properties of Gaussian processes. A huge outstanding question is how to actually *design* a Gaussian process to model a given system. This will be our focus for the next two chapters. In the next chapter, we will explore model *construction,* and in the following chapter we will consider model *assessment* in light of available data.

Finally, we have not yet discussed any computational issues inherent to Gaussian process inference, including, most importantly, how the cost of computing the posterior grows with respect to the number of observations. We will discuss implementation details and scaling in a dedicated chapter later in the book.

implementation and scaling of Gaussian process inference: § 9.1, p. 201

MODELING WITH GAUSSIAN PROCESSES

Bayesian optimization relies on a faithful model of the system of interest to make well-informed decisions. In fact, even more so than the details of the optimization policy, the fidelity of the underlying model of the objective function is the most decisive factor determining optimization performance. This has been long acknowledged, with MOCKUS for example commenting in his seminal work that:[1]

> The development of some system of a priori distributions suitable for different classes of the function f is probably the most important problem in the application of [the] Bayesian approach to... global optimization.

The importance of careful modeling has not waned in the intervening years, but our capacity for building sophisticated models has improved.

Recall our approach to modeling observations obtained during optimization combines a prior process for a (perhaps not directly observable) objective function (1.8) and an observation model linking the values of the objective to measured values (1.2). Both distributions must be specified before we can derive a posterior belief about the objective function (1.10) and predictive distribution for proposed observations (1.7), which together serve as the key enablers of Bayesian optimization policies.

In practice, the choice of observation model is often noncontroversial,[2] and our running prototypes of exact observation and additive Gaussian noise suffice for many systems. The bulk of modeling effort is thus spent crafting the prior process. Although specifying a *Gaussian* process is seemingly as simple as choosing a mean and covariance function, it can be difficult to intuit appropriate choices without a great deal of knowledge about the system of interest. As an alternative to prior knowledge, we may appeal to a data-driven approach, where we establish a space of candidate models and search through this space for those offering the best explanation of available data. Almost all Gaussian process models used in practice are designed in this manner, and we will lay the groundwork for this approach in this chapter and the next.

As a Gaussian process is specified by its first two moments, data-driven model design boils down to searching for the prior mean and covariance functions most harmonious with our observations. This can be a daunting task as the space of possibilities is limitless. However, we do not need to begin from scratch: there are mean and covariance functions available off-the-shelf for modeling a range of behavioral archetypes, and by systematically combining these components we may model functions with a rich variety of behavior. We will explore the world of possibilities in this chapter, while addressing details important to optimization.

Once we have established a space of candidate models, we will require some mechanism to differentiate possible choices based on their merits, a process known as *model assessment* that we will explore at length in the next chapter. We will begin the present discussion by revisiting the topic

3

1 J. MOCKUS (1974). On Bayesian Methods for Seeking the Extremum. *Optimization Techniques: IFIP Technical Conference.*

Bayesian inference of the objective function: § 1.2, p. 8

2 However, we may not be certain about some details, such as the scale of observation noise, an issue we will address in the next chapter.

Chapter 4: Model Assessment, Selection, and Averaging, p. 67

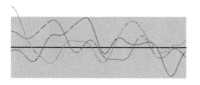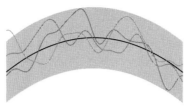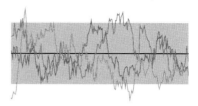

Figure 3.1: The importance of the prior mean function in determining sample path behavior. The models in the first two panels differ in their mean function but share the same covariance function. Sample path behavior is identical up to translation. The model in the third panel features the same mean function as the first panel but a different covariance function. Samples exhibit dramatically different behavior.

of prior mean and covariance functions with an eye toward practical utility.

3.1   THE PRIOR MEAN FUNCTION

Recall the mean function of a Gaussian process specifies the expected value of an arbitrary function value $\phi = f(x)$:

$$\mu(x) = \mathbb{E}[\phi \mid x].$$

Although this is obviously a fundamental concern, the choice of prior mean function has received relatively little consideration in the Bayesian optimization literature.

impact of prior mean on sample paths

There are several reasons for this. To begin, it is actually the *covariance* function rather than the mean function that largely determines the behavior of sample paths. This should not be surprising: the mean function only affects the *marginal* distribution of function values, whereas the covariance function can further modify the *joint* distribution of function values. To elaborate, consider an arbitrary Gaussian process $\mathcal{GP}(f; \mu, K)$. Its sample paths are distributed identically to those from the corresponding centered process $f - \mu$, after shifting pointwise by μ. Therefore the sample paths of *any* Gaussian process with the same covariance function are effectively the same up to translation, and it is the covariance function determining their behavior otherwise; see the demonstration in Figure 3.1.

impact of prior mean on posterior mean

It is also important to understand the role of the prior mean function in the posterior process. Suppose we condition a Gaussian process $\mathcal{GP}(f; \mu, K)$ on the observation of a vector $\mathbf{y}$ with marginal distribution (2.7) and cross-covariance function (2.24)

$$p(\mathbf{y}) = \mathcal{N}(\mathbf{y}; \mathbf{m}, \mathbf{C}); \qquad \kappa(x) = \mathrm{cov}[\mathbf{y}, \phi \mid x].$$

The prior mean influences the posterior process *only* through the posterior mean (2.10):

$$\mu_{\mathcal{D}}(x) = \mu(x) + \kappa(x)^\top \mathbf{C}^{-1}(\mathbf{y} - \mathbf{m}).$$

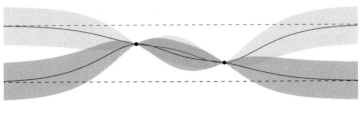

extrapolation   interpolation   extrapolation

Figure 3.2: The influence of the prior mean on the posterior mean. We show two Gaussian process posteriors differing only in their prior mean functions, shown as dashed lines. In the "interpolatory" region between the observations, the posterior means are mostly determined by the data, but devolve to the respective prior means when extrapolating outside this region.

We can roughly understand the behavior of the posterior mean by identifying two regimes determined by the strength of correlation between a given function value and the observations. In "interpolatory" regions, where function values have significant correlation with one-or-more observed value, the posterior mean is mostly determined by the data rather than the prior mean. On the other hand, in "extrapolatory" regions, where $\kappa(x) \approx 0$, the data have little influence and the posterior mean effectively equals the prior mean. Figure 3.2 demonstrates this effect.

behavior in interpolatory and extrapolatory regions

Constant mean function

The primary impact of the prior mean on our predictions – and on an optimization policy informed by these predictions – is in the extrapolatory regime. However, extrapolation without strong prior knowledge can be a dangerous business. As a result, in Bayesian optimization, the prior mean is often taken to be a constant:

$$\mu(x; c) \equiv c, \tag{3.1}$$

in order to avoid any unwanted bias on our decisions caused by spurious structure in the prior process. This simple choice is supported empirically by a study comparing optimization performance across a range of problems as a function of the choice of prior mean.[3]

3 G. DE ATH et al. (2020). What Do You Mean? The Role of the Mean Function in Bayesian Optimization. *GECCO 2020*.

When adopting a constant mean, the value of the constant c is usually treated as a parameter to be estimated or (approximately) marginalized, as we will discuss in the next chapter. However, we can actually do better in some cases. Consider a parametric Gaussian process prior with constant mean (3.1) and arbitrary covariance function:

marginalizing constant prior mean

model selection and averaging: §§ 4.3–4.4, p. 73

$$p(f \mid c) = \mathcal{GP}(f; \mu \equiv c, K),$$

and suppose we place a normal prior on c:

$$p(c) = \mathcal{N}(c; a, b^2). \tag{3.2}$$

Then we can marginalize the unknown constant mean *exactly* to derive the marginal Gaussian process

$$p(f) = \int p(f \mid c) \, p(c) \, dc = \mathcal{GP}(f; \mu \equiv a, K + b^2), \tag{3.3}$$

4 Noting that c and f form a joint Gaussian process, we may perform inference as described in § 2.4, p. 26 to reveal their joint posterior.

5 The basis functions can be arbitrarily complex, such as the output layer of a deep neural network:

J. SNOEK et al. (2015). Scalable Bayesian Optimization Using Deep Neural Networks. *ICML 2015*.

basis functions, $\boldsymbol{\psi}$

weight vector, $\boldsymbol{\beta}$

6 A. O'HAGAN (1978). Curve Fitting and Optimal Design for Prediction. *Journal of the Royal Statistical Society Series B (Methodological)* 40(1): 1–42.

7 C. E. RASMUSSEN and C. K. I. WILLIAMS (2006). *Gaussian Processes for Machine Learning*. MIT Press. [§ 2.7]

8 For an example of such modeling in physics, where the mean function was taken to be the output of a physically informed model, see:

M. A. ZIATDINOV et al. (2021). Physics Makes the Difference: Bayesian Optimization and Active Learning via Augmented Gaussian Process. arXiv: 2108.10280 [physics.comp-ph].

9 This mean function was proposed in the context of Bayesian optimization (with diagonal A) by

J. SNOEK et al. (2015). Scalable Bayesian Optimization Using Deep Neural Networks. *ICML 2015*,

who also proposed appropriate priors for **A** and **b**. The mean was also proposed in the related context of Bayesian quadrature (see § 2.6, p. 33) by

L. ACERBI (2018). Variational Bayesian Monte Carlo. *NeurIPS 2018*.

where the uncertainty in the mean has been absorbed into the prior covariance function. We may now use this prior directly, avoiding any estimation of c. The unknown mean will be automatically marginalized in both the prior and posterior process, and we may additionally derive the posterior belief over c given data if it is of interest.[4]

Linear combination of basis functions

We may extend the above result to marginalize the weights of an *arbitrary* linear combination of basis functions under a normal prior, making this a particularly convenient class of mean functions. Namely, consider a parametric mean function of the form

$$\mu(x; \boldsymbol{\beta}) = \boldsymbol{\beta}^\top \boldsymbol{\psi}(x), \tag{3.4}$$

where the vector-valued function $\boldsymbol{\psi} \colon \mathcal{X} \to \mathbb{R}^n$ defines the basis functions and $\boldsymbol{\beta}$ is a vector of weights.[5]

Now consider a parametric Gaussian process prior with a mean function of this form (3.4) and arbitrary covariance function K. Placing a multivariate normal prior on $\boldsymbol{\beta}$,

$$p(\boldsymbol{\beta}) = \mathcal{N}(\boldsymbol{\beta}; \mathbf{a}, \mathbf{B}), \tag{3.5}$$

and marginalizing yields the marginal prior,[6,7]

$$p(f) = \mathcal{GP}(f; m, C),$$

where

$$m(x) = \mathbf{a}^\top \boldsymbol{\psi}(x); \qquad C(x, x') = K(x, x') + \boldsymbol{\psi}(x)^\top \mathbf{B} \boldsymbol{\psi}(x'). \tag{3.6}$$

We may recover the constant mean case above by taking $\psi(x) \equiv 1$.

Other options

We stress that a constant or linear mean function is by no means necessary, and when a system is understood sufficiently well to suggest a plausible alternative – perhaps the output of a baseline predictive model – it should be strongly considered. However, it is hard to provide general advice, as this modeling will be situation dependent.[8]

One option that might be a reasonable choice in some optimization contexts is a concave quadratic mean:

$$\mu(\mathbf{x}; \mathbf{A}, \mathbf{b}, c) = (\mathbf{x} - \mathbf{b})^\top \mathbf{A}^{-1}(\mathbf{x} - \mathbf{b}) + c, \tag{3.7}$$

where $\mathbf{A} \prec 0$.[9] This mean encodes that values near $\mathbf{b}$ (according to the Mahalanobis distance (A.8)) are expected to be higher than those farther away and could reasonably model an objective function expected to be "bowl-shaped" to a first approximation. The middle panel of Figure 3.1 incorporates a mean of this form; note that the maxima of sample paths are of course not constrained to agree with that of the prior mean.

3.2 THE PRIOR COVARIANCE FUNCTION

The prior covariance function determines the covariance between the function values corresponding to a pair of input locations x and x':

$$K(x, x') = \text{cov}[\phi, \phi' \mid x, x']. \tag{3.8}$$

The covariance function determines fundamental properties of sample path behavior, including continuity, differentiability, and aspects of the global optima, as we have already seen. Perhaps more so than the mean function, careful design of the covariance function is critical to ensure fidelity in modeling. We will devote considerable discussion to this topic, beginning with some important properties and moving on to useful examples and mechanisms for systematically modifying and composing multiple covariance functions together to model complex behavior.

> sample path continuity: § 2.5, p. 28
> sample path differentiability: § 2.6, p. 30
> existence and uniqueness of global maxima: § 2.7, p. 33

After appropriate normalization, a covariance function K may be loosely interpreted as a measure of similarity between points in the domain. Namely, given $x, x' \in \mathcal{X}$, the correlation between the corresponding function values is

> correlation between function values, ρ

$$\rho = \text{corr}[\phi, \phi' \mid x, x'] = \frac{K(x, x')}{\sqrt{K(x, x)\, K(x', x')}}, \tag{3.9}$$

and we may interpret the strength of this dependence as a measure of similarity between the input locations. This intuition can be useful, but some caveats are in order. To begin, note that correlation may be *negative,* which might be interpreted as indicating *dis*-similarity as the function values react to information with opposite sign.

Further, for a proposed covariance function K to be admissible, it must satisfy two global consistency properties ensuring that the collection of random variables comprising f are able to satisfy the purported relationships. First, we can immediately deduce from its definition (3.8) that K must be *symmetric* in its inputs. Second, the covariance function must be *positive semidefinite;* that is, given any finite set of points $\mathbf{x} \subset \mathcal{X}$, the Gram matrix $K(\mathbf{x}, \mathbf{x})$ must have only nonnegative eigenvalues.[10]

> symmetry and positive semidefiniteness

> 10 Symmetry guarantees the eigenvalues are real.

> consequences of positive semidefiniteness

To illustrate how positive semidefiniteness ensures statistical validity, note that a direct consequence is that $K(x, x) = \text{var}[\phi \mid x] \geq 0$, and thus marginal variance is always nonnegative. On a slightly less trivial level, consider a pair of points $\mathbf{x} = (x, x')$ and normalize the corresponding Gram matrix $\Sigma = K(\mathbf{x}, \mathbf{x})$ to yield the correlation matrix:

$$\mathbf{P} = \text{corr}[\boldsymbol{\phi} \mid \mathbf{x}] = \begin{bmatrix} 1 & \rho \\ \rho & 1 \end{bmatrix},$$

where ρ is given by (3.9). For this matrix to be valid, we must have $\rho \in [-1, 1]$. This happens precisely when $\mathbf{P}$ is positive semidefinite, as its eigenvalues are $1 \pm \rho$. Finally, noting that $\mathbf{P}$ is congruent to Σ,[11] we conclude the implied correlations are consistent if and only if Σ is positive semidefinite. With more than two points, the positive semidefiniteness of K ensures similar consistency at higher orders.

> 11 We have $\Sigma = \text{SPS}$, where S is diagonal with $S_{ii} = \sqrt{\Sigma_{ii}}$.

Figure 3.3: Left: a sample from a stationary Gaussian process in two dimensions. The joint distribution of function values is translation- but not rotation-invariant, as the function tends to vary faster in some directions than others. Right: a sample from an isotropic process. The joint distribution of function values is both translation- and rotation-invariant.

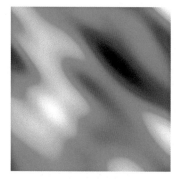 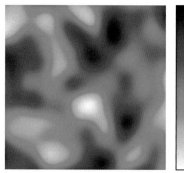

stationary and anisotropic   stationary and isotropic

Stationarity, isotropy, and Bochner's theorem

Some covariance functions exhibit structure giving rise to certain computational benefits. Namely, a covariance function $K(x, x')$ that only depends on the difference $x - x'$ is called *stationary*.[12] When convenient, we will abuse notation and write a stationary covariance function in terms of a single input, writing $K(x - x')$ for $K(x, x') = K(x - x', 0)$. If a GP has a stationary covariance function and *constant* mean function (3.1), then the process itself is also called stationary. A consequence of stationarity is that the distribution of any set of function values is invariant under translation; that is, the function "acts the same" everywhere from a statistical viewpoint. The left panel of Figure 3.3 shows a sample from a $2d$ stationary GP, demonstrating this translation-invariant behavior.

stationary covariance function, $K(x - x')$

Stationarity is a convenient assumption when modeling, as defining the *local* behavior around a single point suffices to specify the *global* behavior of an entire function. Many common covariance functions have this property as a result. However, this may not always be a valid assumption in the context of optimization, as an objective function may for example exhibit markedly different behavior near the optimum than elsewhere. We will shortly see some general approaches for addressing nonstationarity when appropriate.

If $\mathcal{X} \subset \mathbb{R}^n$, a covariance function $K(x, x')$ only depending on the Euclidean distance $d = |x - x'|$ is called *isotropic*. Again, when convenient, we will notate such a covariance with $K(d)$. Isotropy is a more restrictive assumption than stationarity – indeed it trivially implies stationarity – as it implies the covariance is invariant to both translation *and* rotation, and thus the function has identical behavior in every direction from every point. An example sample from a $2d$ isotropic GP is shown in the right panel of Figure 3.3. Many of the standard covariance functions we will define shortly will be isotropic on first definition, but we will again develop generic mechanisms to modify them in order to induce anisotropic behavior when desired.

isotropic covariance function, $K(d)$

BOCHNER's *theorem* is an landmark result characterizing stationary covariance functions in terms of their Fourier transforms:[13,14]

---

12 Of course this definition requires $x - x'$ to be well defined. This is trivial in Euclidean spaces; a fairly general treatment for more exotic spaces would assume an abelian group structure on $\mathcal{X}$ with binary operation $+$ and inverse $-$ and define $x - x' = x + (-x')$.

13 S. BOCHNER (1933). Monotone Funktionen, Stieltjessche Integrale und harmonische Analyse. *Mathematische Annalen* 108:378–410.

14 We do not quote the most general version of the theorem here; the result can be extended to complex-valued covariance functions on arbitrary locally compact abelian groups if necessary. It is remarkably universal.

Theorem (BOCHNER, 1933). *A continuous function $K\colon \mathbb{R}^n \to \mathbb{R}$ is positive semidefinite (that is, represents a stationary covariance function) if and only if we have*

$$K(\mathbf{x}) = \int \exp(2\pi i \mathbf{x}^\top \xi)\, \mathrm{d}\nu,$$

where ν is a finite, positive Borel measure on $\mathbb{R}^n$. Further, this measure is symmetric around the origin; that is, $\nu(A) = \nu(-A)$ for any Borel set $A \subset \mathbb{R}^n$, where $-A$ is the "negation" of A: $-A = \{-a \mid a \in A\}$.

To summarize, BOCHNER's theorem states that the Fourier transform of any stationary covariance function on $\mathbb{R}^n$ is proportional to a probability measure and vice versa; the constant of proportionality is $K(\mathbf{0})$. The measure ν corresponding to K is called the *spectral measure* of K. When a corresponding density function κ exists, it is called the *spectral density* of K and forms a Fourier pair with K:

spectral measure, ν

spectral density, κ

$$K(\mathbf{x}) = \int \exp(2\pi i \mathbf{x}^\top \xi)\, \kappa(\xi)\, \mathrm{d}\xi; \quad \kappa(\xi) = \int \exp(-2\pi i \mathbf{x}^\top \xi)\, K(\mathbf{x})\, \mathrm{d}\mathbf{x}.$$

(3.10)

The symmetry of the spectral measure implies a similar symmetry in the spectral density: $\kappa(\xi) = \kappa(-\xi)$ for all $\xi \in \mathbb{R}^n$.

symmetry of spectral density

BOCHNER's theorem is surprisingly useful in practice, allowing us to approximate an arbitrary stationary covariance function by approximating (e.g., by modeling or sampling from) its spectral density. This is the basis of the *spectral mixture covariance* described in the next section, as well as the *sparse spectrum approximation* scheme, which facilitates the computation of some Bayesian optimization policies.

sparse spectrum approximation: § 8.7, p. 178

3.3 NOTABLE COVARIANCE FUNCTIONS

It can be difficult to define a new covariance function for a given scenario *de novo*, as the positive-semidefinite criterion can be nontrivial to guarantee for what might otherwise be an intuitive notion of similarity. In practice, it is common to instead construct covariance functions by combining and transforming established "building blocks" modeling various atomic behaviors while following rules guaranteeing the result will be valid. We describe several useful examples below.[15]

Our presentation will depart from most in that several of the covariance functions below will initially be defined without parameters that some readers may be expecting. We will shortly demonstrate how coupling these covariance functions with particular transformations of the function domain and output gives rise to common covariance function parameters such as *characteristic length scales* and *output scales*.

15 For a more complete survey, see

C. E. RASMUSSEN and C. K. I. WILLIAMS (2006). *Gaussian Processes for Machine Learning.* MIT Press. [chapter 4]

The Matérn family

If there is one class of covariance functions to be familiar with, it is the *Matérn family*. This is a versatile family of covariance functions for modeling isotropic behavior on Euclidean domains $\mathcal{X} \subset \mathbb{R}^n$ of any

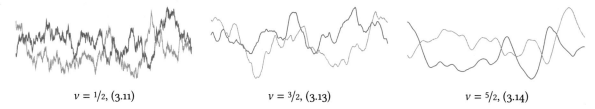

$$\nu = 1/2, \text{(3.11)} \qquad\qquad \nu = 3/2, \text{(3.13)} \qquad\qquad \nu = 5/2, \text{(3.14)}$$

Figure 3.4: Samples from centered Gaussian processes with the Matérn covariance function with different values of the smoothness parameter ν. Sample paths with $\nu = 1/2$ are continuous but not differentiable; incrementing this parameter by one unit increases the number of continuous derivatives by one.

sample path differentiability: § 2.6, p. 30

16 In theoretical contexts, general values for the smoothness parameter $\nu \in R_{>0}$ are considered, but lead to unwieldy expressions (10.12).

exponential covariance function

Ornstein–Uhlenbeck (OU) process

Samples from a centered Gaussian process with squared exponential covariance K_{SE}.

17 M. L. STEIN (1999). *Interpolation of Spatial Data: Some Theory for Kriging.* Springer–Verlag. [§ 1.7]

desired degree of smoothness, in terms of the differentiability of sample paths. The Matérn covariance $K_{M(\nu)}$ depends on a parameter $\nu \in \mathbb{R}_{>0}$ determining this smoothness; sample paths from a centered Gaussian process with this covariance are $\lceil \nu \rceil - 1$ times continuously differentiable. In practice ν is almost always taken to be a half-integer,[16] in which case the expression for the covariance assumes a simple form as a function of the Euclidean distance $d = |x - x'|$.

To begin with the extremes, the case $\nu = 1/2$ yields the so-called *exponential covariance*:

$$K_{M1/2}(x, x') = \exp(-d). \tag{3.11}$$

Sample paths from a centered Gaussian process with exponential covariance are continuous but nowhere differentiable, which is perhaps too rough to be interesting in most optimization contexts. However, this covariance is often encountered in historical literature. In the one-dimensional case $\mathcal{X} \subset \mathbb{R}$, a Gaussian process with this covariance is known as a *Ornstein–Uhlenbeck* (OU) process and satisfies a continuous-time Markov property that renders its posterior moments particularly convenient.

Taking the limit of increasing smoothness $\nu \to \infty$ yields the *squared exponential* covariance from the previous chapter:

$$K_{SE}(x, x') = \exp\left(-\tfrac{1}{2}d^2\right). \tag{3.12}$$

We will refer to the Matérn and the limiting case of the squared exponential covariance functions together as the *Matérn family*. The squared exponential covariance is without a doubt the most prevalent covariance function in the statistical and machine learning literature. However, it may not always be a good choice in practice. Sample paths from a centered Gaussian process with squared exponential covariance are *infinitely* differentiable, which has been ridiculed as an absurd assumption for most physical processes.[17] STEIN does not mince words on this, starting off a three-sentence "summary of practical suggestions" with "use the Matérn model" and devoting significant effort to discouraging the use of the squared exponential in the context of geostatistics.

Between these extremes are the cases $v = 3/2$ and $v = 5/2$, which respectively model once- and twice-differentiable functions:

$$K_{\mathrm{M}3/2}(x, x') = \left(1 + \sqrt{3}d\right) \exp\left(-\sqrt{3}d\right); \tag{3.13}$$

$$K_{\mathrm{M}5/2}(x, x') = \left(1 + \sqrt{5}d + \tfrac{5}{3}d^2\right) \exp\left(-\sqrt{5}d\right). \tag{3.14}$$

Figure 3.4 illustrates samples from centered Gaussian processes with different values of the smoothness parameters v. The $v = 5/2$ case in particular has been singled out as a prudent off-the-shelf choice for Bayesian optimization when no better alternative is obvious.[18]

18 J. SNOEK et al. (2012). Practical Bayesian Optimization of Machine Learning Algorithms. *NeurIPS 2012.*

The spectral mixture covariance

Covariance functions in the Matérn family express fairly simple correlation structure, with the covariance dropping monotonically to zero as the distance $d = |x - x'|$ increases. All differences in sample path behavior such as differentiability, etc. are expressed entirely through nuances in the tail behavior of the covariance functions; see the figure in the margin.

The Fourier transforms of these covariances are also broadly comparable: all are proportional to unimodal distributions centered on the origin. However, BOCHNER's theorem indicates that there is a vast world of stationary covariance functions indexed by the *entire* space of symmetric spectral measures, which may have considerably more complex structure. Several authors have sought to exploit this characterization to build stationary covariance functions with virtually unlimited flexibility.

A notable contribution in this direction is the *spectral mixture covariance* function proposed by WILSON and ADAMS.[19] The idea is simple but powerful: we parameterize a space of stationary covariance functions by some suitable family of mixture distributions in the Fourier domain representing their spectral density. The parameters of this spectral mixture distribution specify a covariance function via the correspondence in (3.10), and we can make the resulting family as rich as desired by adjusting the number of components in the mixture. WILSON and ADAMS proposed Gaussian mixtures for the spectral density, which are universal approximators and have a convenient Fourier transform. We define a Gaussian mixture spectral density κ as

$$k(\xi) = \sum_i w_i \mathcal{N}(\xi; \mu_i, \Sigma_i); \qquad \kappa(\xi) = \tfrac{1}{2}\left[k(\xi) + k(-\xi)\right],$$

where the indirect construction via k ensures the required symmetry. Note that the weights $\{w_i\}$ must be positive but need not sum to unity. Taking the inverse Fourier transform (3.10), the corresponding covariance function is

$$K_{\mathrm{SM}}\left(\mathbf{x}, \mathbf{x}'; \{w_i\}, \{\mu_i\}, \{\Sigma_i\}\right) =$$
$$\sum_i w_i \exp\left(-2\pi^2 (\mathbf{x} - \mathbf{x}')^\top \Sigma_i (\mathbf{x} - \mathbf{x}')\right) \cos\left(2\pi (\mathbf{x} - \mathbf{x}')^\top \mu_i\right). \tag{3.15}$$

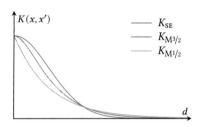

Some members of the Matérn family and the squared exponential covariance as a function of the distance between inputs. All decay to zero correlation as distance increases.

19 A. G. WILSON and R. P. ADAMS (2013). Gaussian Process Kernels for Pattern Discovery and Extrapolation. *ICML 2013.*

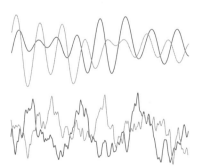

Samples from centered Gaussian processes with two realizations of a Gaussian spectral mixture covariance function, offering a glimpse into the flexibility of this class.

Inspecting this expression, we can see that every covariance function induced by a Gaussian mixture spectral density is infinitely differentiable, and one might object to this choice on the grounds of overly smooth sample paths. This can be mitigated by using enough mixture components to induce sufficiently complex structure in the covariance (on the order of ~5 is common). Another option would be to use a different family of spectral distributions; for example, a mixture of Cauchy distributions would induce a family of continuous but nondifferentiable covariance functions analogous to the exponential covariance (3.11), but this idea has not been explored.

Linear covariance function

Another useful covariance function arises from a Bayesian realization of linear regression. Let the domain be Euclidean, $\mathcal{X} \subset \mathbb{R}^n$, and consider the model

$$f(\mathbf{x}) = \beta + \boldsymbol{\beta}^\top \mathbf{x},$$

where we have abused notation slightly to distinguish the constant term from the remaining coefficients. Following our discussion on linear basis functions, if we take independent[20] normal priors on β and $\boldsymbol{\beta}$:

$$p(\beta) = \mathcal{N}(\beta; a, b^2); \qquad p(\boldsymbol{\beta}) = \mathcal{N}(\boldsymbol{\beta}; \mathbf{a}, \mathbf{B}),$$

we arrive at the so-called *linear covariance*:

$$K_{\text{LIN}}(\mathbf{x}, \mathbf{x}'; b, \mathbf{B}) = b^2 + \mathbf{x}^\top \mathbf{B} \mathbf{x}. \tag{3.16}$$

Although this covariance is unlikely to be of any direct use in Bayesian optimization (linear programming is much simpler!), it can be a useful component of more complex composite covariance structures.

3.4   MODIFYING AND COMBINING COVARIANCE FUNCTIONS

With the notable exception of the spectral mixture covariance, which can approximate any stationary covariance function, several of the covariances introduced in the last section are still too rigid to be useful.

In particular, consider any of the Matérn family (3.11–3.14). Each of these covariances encodes several explicit and possibly dubious assumptions about the function of interest. To begin, each prescribes unit variance for every function value:

$$\text{var}[\phi \mid x] = K(x, x) = 1, \tag{3.17}$$

which is an arbitrary, possibly inappropriate choice of scale. Further, each of these covariance functions fixes an isotropic *characteristic length scale* of correlation of approximately one unit:[21] at a separation of $|x - x'| = 1$, the correlation between the corresponding function values drops to roughly

$$\text{corr}[\phi, \phi' \mid x, x'] \approx 0.5, \tag{3.18}$$

Samples from a centered Gaussian process with linear covariance K_{LIN}.

---

[20] Independence is usual but not necessary; an arbitrary joint prior would add a term of $2\mathbf{b}^\top \mathbf{x}$ to (3.16), where $\mathbf{b} = \text{cov}[\boldsymbol{\beta}, \beta]$.

linear basis functions: § 3.1, p. 48

[21] Although an important concept, there is no clear-cut definition of characteristic length scale. It is simply a convenient separation distance for which correlation remains appreciable, but beyond which correlation begins to noticeably decay.

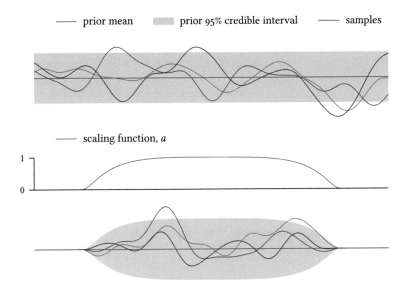

Figure 3.5: Scaling a stationary covariance by a nonconstant function (here, a smooth bump function of compact support) to yield a nonstationary covariance.

and this correlation continues to drop effectively to zero at a separation of approximately five units. Again, this choice of scale is arbitrary, and the assumption of isotropy is particularly restrictive.

In general, a Gaussian process encodes strong assumptions regarding the joint distribution of function values (2.5), which may not be compatible with a given function "out of the box." However, we can often improve model fit by appropriate transformations of the objective. In fact, *linear* transformations of function inputs and outputs are almost universally considered, although only implicitly by introducing parameters conveying the effects of these transformations. We will show how both linear and nonlinear transformations of function input and output lead to more expressive models and give rise to common model parameters.

Scaling function outputs

We first address the issue of scale in function output (3.17) by considering the statistical effects of arbitrary scaling. Consider a random function $f: \mathcal{X} \to \mathbb{R}$ with covariance function K and let $a: \mathcal{X} \to \mathbb{R}$ be a known scaling function.[22] Then the pointwise product $af: x \mapsto a(x)f(x)$ has covariance function

22 For this result f need not have a GP distribution.

$$\mathrm{cov}[af \mid a] = a(x)K(x,x')a(x'), \tag{3.19}$$

by the bilinearity of covariance. If the scaling function is *constant*, $a \equiv \lambda$, then we have

$$\mathrm{cov}[\lambda f \mid \lambda] = \lambda^2 K. \tag{3.20}$$

This simple result allows us to extend a "base" covariance K with fixed scale, as in (3.17), to a parametric family with arbitrary scale:

$$K'(x,x';\lambda) = \lambda^2 K(x,x').$$

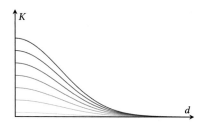

The squared exponential covariance K_{SE} scaled by a range of output scales λ (3.20).

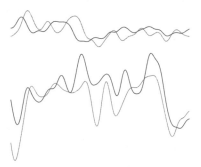

Sample paths from centered GPs with smaller (top) and larger (bottom) output scales.

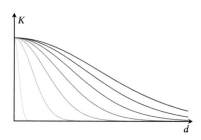

The squared exponential covariance K_{SE} dilated by a range of length scales ℓ (3.22).

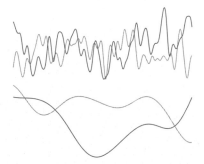

Sample paths from centered GPs with shorter (top) and longer (bottom) characteristic length scales.

In this context the parameter λ is known as an *output scale,* or when the base covariance is stationary with $K(x, x) = 1$, the *signal variance,* as it determines the variance of any function value: $\mathrm{var}[\phi \mid x, \lambda] = \lambda^2$. The illustration in the margin shows the effect of scaling the squared exponential covariance function by a series of increasing output scales.

We can also of course consider *nonlinear* transformations of the function output as well. This can be useful for modeling constraints – such as nonegativity or boundedness – that are not compatible with the Gaussian assumption. However, a nonlinear transformation of a Gaussian process is no longer Gaussian, so it is often more convenient to model the transformed function after "removing the constraint."

We may use the general form of this scaling result (3.19) to transform a stationary covariance into a nonstationary one, as any nonconstant scaling is sufficient to break translation invariance. We show an example of such a transformation in Figure 3.5, where we have scaled a stationary covariance by a bump function to create a prior on smooth functions with compact support.

Transforming the domain and length scale parameters

We now address the issue of the scaling of correlation as a function of distance (3.18) by introducing a powerful tool: transforming the domain of the function of interest into a more convenient space for modeling.

Namely, suppose we wish to reason about a function $f: \mathcal{X} \to \mathbb{R}$, and let $g: \mathcal{X} \to \mathcal{Z}$ be a map from the domain to some arbitrary space $\mathcal{Z}$, which might also be $\mathcal{X}$. If $K_{\mathcal{Z}}$ is a covariance function on $\mathcal{Z}$, then the composition

$$K_{\mathcal{X}}(x, x') = K_{\mathcal{Z}}\big(g(x), g(x')\big) \tag{3.21}$$

is trivially a covariance function on $\mathcal{X}$. This allows us to define a covariance for f indirectly by jointly designing a map g to another space and a corresponding covariance $K_{\mathcal{Z}}$ (and mean $\mu_{\mathcal{Z}}$) on that space. This approach offers a lot of flexibility, as we are free to design these components as we see fit to impose any desired structure.

We will spend some time exploring this idea, beginning with the relatively simple but immensely useful case of combining a *linear* transformation on a Euclidean domain $\mathcal{X} \subset \mathbb{R}^n$ with an *isotropic* covariance on the output. Perhaps the simplest example is the dilation $\mathbf{x} \mapsto \mathbf{x}/\ell$, which simply scales distance by ℓ^{-1}. Incorporating this transformation into an isotropic base covariance $K(d)$ on $\mathcal{X}$ yields a parametric family of dilated versions:

$$K'(x, x'; \ell) = K(d/\ell). \tag{3.22}$$

If the base covariance has a characteristic length scale of one unit, the length scale of the dilated version will be ℓ; for this reason, this parameter is simply called *the* characteristic length scale of the parameterized covariance (3.22). Adjusting the length scale allows us to model functions with a range of "wiggliness," where shorter length scale implies more wiggly behavior; see the margin for examples.

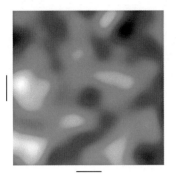 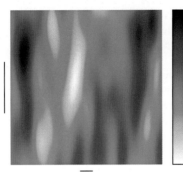

Figure 3.6: Left: a sample from a centered Gaussian process in two dimensions with isotropic squared exponential covariance. Right: a sample from a centered Gaussian process with an ARD squared exponential covariance. The length of the lines on each axis are proportional to the length scale along that axis.

Taking this one step further, we may consider dilating each axis by a separate factor:

$$x_i \mapsto x_i/\ell_i; \qquad \mathbf{x} \mapsto [\operatorname{diag} \boldsymbol{\ell}]^{-1}\mathbf{x}, \tag{3.23}$$

which induces the weighted Euclidean distance

$$d_{\boldsymbol{\ell}} = \sqrt{\sum_i \frac{(x_i - x_i')^2}{\ell_i}}. \tag{3.24}$$

Geometrically, the effect of this map is to transform surfaces of equal distance around each point – which represent curves of constant covariance for an isotropic covariance – from spheres into axis-aligned ellipsoids; see the figure in the margin. Incorporating into an isotropic base covariance $K(d)$ produces a parametric family of *anisotropic* covariances with different characteristic length scales along each axis, corresponding to the parameters $\boldsymbol{\ell}$:

$$K'(x, x'; \boldsymbol{\ell}) = K(d_{\boldsymbol{\ell}}). \tag{3.25}$$

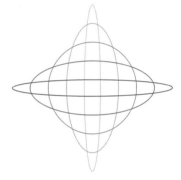

Possible surfaces of equal covariance with the center when combining separate dilation of each axis with an isotropic covariance.

When the length scale parameters are inferred from data, this construction is known as *automatic relevance determination* (ARD). The motivation for the name is that if the function has only weak dependence on some mostly irrelevant dimension of the input, we could hope to infer a very long length scale for that dimension. The contribution to the weighted distance (3.24) for that dimension would then be effectively nullified, and the resulting covariance would effectively "ignore" that dimension.

automatic relevance determination, ARD

Figure 3.6 shows samples from $2d$ centered Gaussian processes, comparing behavior with an isotropic covariance and an ARD modified version that contracts the horizontal and expands the vertical axis (see curves of constant covariance in the margin). The result is anisotropic behavior with a longer characteristic length scale in the vertical direction than in the horizontal direction, but with the behavior of local features remaining aligned with the axes overall.

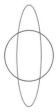

Finally, we may also consider an arbitrary linear transformation $g \colon \mathbf{x} \mapsto \mathbf{A}\mathbf{x}$, which induces the Mahalanobis distance (A.8)

$$d_{\mathbf{A}} = |\mathbf{A}\mathbf{x} - \mathbf{A}\mathbf{x}'|.$$

Surfaces of equal covariance with the center for the examples in Figure 3.6: the isotropic covariance in the left panel (the smaller circle), and the ARD covariance in the right panel (the elongated ellipse).

Possible surfaces of equal covariance with the center when combining an arbitrary linear transformation with an isotropic covariance.

high-dimensional domains: § 3.5, p. 61

23 We did see a periodic GP in the previous chapter (2.30); however, that model only had support on *perfectly* sinusoidal functions.

24 D. J. C. MACKAY (1998). Introduction to Gaussian Processes. In: *Neural Networks and Machine Learning.* [§ 5.2]

25 The covariance on the circle is usually inherited from a covariance on $\mathbb{R}^2$. The result of composing with the squared exponential covariance in particular is often called "the" periodic covariance, but we stress that any other covariance on $\mathbb{R}^2$ could be used instead.

A sample path of a centered GP with Matérn covariance with $\nu = 5/2$ (3.14) after applying the periodic warping function (3.27).

26 J. SNOEK et al. (2014). Input Warping for Bayesian Optimization of Non-Stationary Functions. *ICML 2014.*

As before, we may incorporate this map into an isotropic base covariance K to realize a family of anisotropic covariance functions:

$$K'(x, x'; \mathbf{A}) = K(d_\mathbf{A}). \tag{3.26}$$

Geometrically, an arbitrary linear map can transform surfaces of constant covariance from spheres into arbitrary ellipsoids; see the figure in the margin. The sample from the left-hand side of Figure 3.3 was generated by composing an isotropic covariance with a map inducing both anisotropic scaling and rotation. The effect of the underlying transformation can be seen in the shapes of local features, which are not aligned with the axes.

Due to the inherent number of parameters required to specify a general transformation, this construction is perhaps most useful when the map is to a much lower-dimensional space: $\mathbb{R}^n \to \mathbb{R}^k$, $k \ll n$. This has been promoted as one strategy for modeling functions on high-dimensional domains suspected of having hidden low-dimensional structure – if this low-dimensional structure is along a linear subspace of the domain, we could capture it by an appropriately designed projection $\mathbf{A}$. We will discuss this idea further in the next section.

Nonlinear warping

When using a covariance function with an inherent length scale, such as a Matérn or squared exponential covariance, *some* linear transformation of the domain is almost always considered, whether it be simple dilation (3.22), anisotropic scaling (3.25), or a general transformation (3.26). However, *nonlinear* transformations can also be useful for imposing structure on the domain, a process commonly referred to as *warping*.

To provide an example that may not often be useful in optimization but is illustrative nonetheless, suppose we wish to model a function $f \colon \mathbb{R} \to \mathbb{R}$ that we believe to be smooth and *periodic* with period p. None of the covariance functions introduced thus far would be able to induce the periodic correlations that this assumption would entail.[23] A construction due to MACKAY is to compose a map onto a circle of radius $r = p/(2\pi)$:[24]

$$x \mapsto \begin{bmatrix} r \cos x \\ r \sin x \end{bmatrix} \tag{3.27}$$

with a covariance function on that space reflecting any desired properties of f.[25] As this map identifies points separated by any multiple of the period, the corresponding function values are perfectly correlated, as desired. A sample from a Gaussian process employing this construction with a Matérn covariance after warping is shown in the margin.

A compelling use of warping is to build nonstationary models by composing a nonlinear map with a stationary covariance, an idea SNOEK et al. explored in the context of Bayesian optimization.[26] Many objective functions exhibit different behavior depending on the proximity to the optimum, suggesting that nonstationary models may sometimes be worth exploring. SNOEK et al. proposed a flexible family of warping functions for optimization problems with box-bounded constraints, where

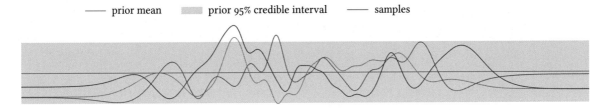

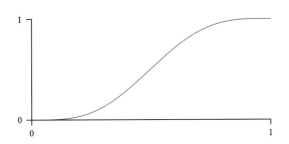

Figure 3.7: An example of the beta warping method proposed by SNOEK et al. We show three samples of the stationary Gaussian process prior from Figure 2.1 (above) after applying a nonlinear warping through a beta CDF (3.28) with $(\alpha, \beta) = (4, 4)$ (right). The length scale is compressed in the center of the domain and expanded near the boundary.

we may take the domain to be the unit cube by scaling and translating as necessary: $\mathcal{X} = [0, 1]^n$ The idea is to warp each coordinate of the input via the cumulative distribution function of a beta distribution:

$$x_i \mapsto I(x_i; \alpha_i, \beta_i), \tag{3.28}$$

where (α_i, β_i) are shape parameters and I is the regularized beta function. This represents a monotonic bijection on the unit interval that can assume several shapes; see the marginal figure for examples. The map may contract portions of the domain and expand others, effectively decreasing and increasing the length scale in those regions. Finally, taking $\alpha = \beta = 1$ recovers the identity map, allowing us to degrade gracefully to the unwarped case if desired.

In Figure 3.7 we combine a beta warping on a one-dimensional domain with a stationary covariance on the output. The chosen warping shortens the length scale near the center of the domain and extends it near the boundary, which might be reasonable for an objective expected to exhibit the most "interesting" behavior on the interior of its domain.

A recent innovation is to use sophisticated artificial neural networks as warping maps for modeling functions of high-dimensional data with complex structure. Notable examples of this approach include the families of *manifold Gaussian processes* introduced by CALANDRA et al.[27] and *deep kernels* introduced contemporaneously by WILSON et al.[28] Here the warping function was taken to be an arbitrary neural network, the output layer of which was fed into a suitable stationary covariance function. This gives a highly parameterized covariance function where the parameters of the base covariance *and* the neural map become parameters of the resulting model. In the context of Bayesian optimization, this can be especially useful when there is sufficient data to learn a useful representation of the domain via unsupervised methods.

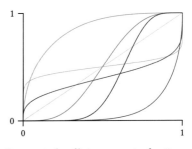

Some examples of beta CDF warping functions (3.28).

[27] R. CALANDRA et al. (2016). Manifold Gaussian Processes for Regression. *IJCNN 2016*.

[28] A. G. WILSON et al. (2016). Deep Kernel Learning. *AISTATS 2016*.

neural representation learning: § 8.11, p. 198

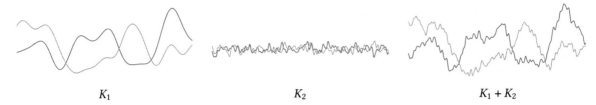

$$K_1 \qquad\qquad K_2 \qquad\qquad K_1 + K_2$$

Figure 3.8: Samples from centered Gaussian processes with different covariance functions: (left) a squared exponential covariance, (middle) a squared exponential covariance with smaller output scale and shorter length scale, and (right) the sum of the two. Samples from the process with the sum covariance show smooth variation on two different scales.

Combining covariance functions

In addition to modifying covariance functions via scaling the output and/or transforming the domain, we may also combine multiple covariance functions together to model functions influenced by multiple random processes.

Let $f, g\colon \mathcal{X} \to \mathbb{R}$ be two centered, independent (not necessarily Gaussian) random functions with covariance functions K_f and K_g, respectively. By the properties of covariance, the sum and pointwise product of these functions have covariance functions with the same structure:

$$\operatorname{cov}[f + g] = K_f + K_g; \qquad \operatorname{cov}[fg] = K_f K_g, \tag{3.29}$$

29 The assumption of the processes being centered is needed for the product result only; otherwise, there would be additional terms involving scaled versions of each individual covariance as in (3.19). The sum result does not depend on any assumptions regarding the mean functions.

and thus covariance functions are closed under addition and pointwise multiplication.[29] Combining this result with (3.20), we have that *any* polynomial of covariance functions with nonnegative coefficients forms a valid covariance. This enables us to construct infinite families of increasingly complex covariance functions from simple components.

We may use a sum of covariance functions to model a function with independent additive contributions, such as random behavior on several length scales. Precisely such a construction is illustrated in Figure 3.8. If the covariance functions are nonnegative and have roughly the same scale, the effect of addition is roughly one of logical disjunction: the sum will assume nontrivial values whenever any one of its constituents does.

Meanwhile, a product of covariance functions can loosely be interpreted in terms of logical conjunction, with function values having appreciable covariance only when every individual covariance function does. A prototypical example of this effect is a covariance function modeling functions that are "almost periodic," formed by the product of a bump-shaped isotropic covariance function such as a squared exponential (3.12) with a warped version modeling perfectly periodic functions (3.27). The former moderates the influence of the latter by driving the correlation between function values to zero for inputs that are sufficiently separated, regardless of their positions in the periodic cycle. We show a sample from such a covariance in the margin, where the length scale of the modulation term is three times the period.

A sample from a centered Gaussian process with an "almost periodic" covariance function.

3.5 MODELING FUNCTIONS ON HIGH-DIMENSIONAL DOMAINS

Optimization on a high-dimensional domain can be challenging, as we can succumb to the *curse of dimensionality* if we are not careful. As an example, consider optimizing an objective function on the unit cube $[0, 1]^n$. Suppose we model this function with an isotropic covariance from the Matérn family, taking the length scale to be $\ell = 1/10$ so that ten length scales span the domain along each axis.[30] This choice implies that function values on the corners of the domain would be effectively independent, as $\exp(-10) < 10^{-4}$ (3.11) and $\exp(-50)$ is smaller still (3.12). If we were to demand even a modicum of confidence in these regions at termination, say by having a measurement within one length scale of every corner, we would need 2^n observations! This exponential growth in the number of observations required to cover the domain is the tyrannical curse of dimensionality.

However, compelling objectives do not tend to have so many degrees of freedom; if they did, we should perhaps give up on the idea of global optimization altogether. Rather, many authors have noted a tendency toward low *intrinsic dimensionality* in real-world problems: that is, most of the variation in the objective is confined to a low-dimensional subspace of the domain. This phenomenon has been noted for example in hyperparameter optimization[31] and optimizing the parameters of neural networks.[32] LEVINA and BICKEL suggested that "hidden" low-dimensional structure is actually a *universal* requirement for success on any task:[33]

> There is a consensus in the high-dimensional data analysis community that the only reason any methods work in very high dimensions is that, in fact, the data are not truly high dimensional.

The global optimization community shares a similar consensus: typical high-dimensional objectives are not "truly" high dimensional. This intuition presents us with an opportunity: if we could only identify inherent low-dimensional structure during optimization, we could sidestep the curse of dimensionality by restricting our search accordingly.

Several strategies are available for capturing low intrinsic dimension with Gaussian process models. The general approach closely follows our discussion from the previous section: we identify some appropriate mapping from the high-dimensional domain to a lower-dimensional space, then model the objective function after composing with this embedding (3.21). This is one realization of the general class of manifold Gaussian processes,[34] where the sought-after manifold is low dimensional. Adopting this approach then raises the issue of identifying *useful* families of mappings that can suitably reduce dimension while preserving enough structure of the objective to keep optimization feasible.

Neural embeddings

Given the success of deep learning in designing feature representations for complex, high-dimensional objects, *neural* embeddings – as used in

curse of dimensionality

30 This is far from excessive: the domain for the marginal sampling examples in this chapter spans 15 length scales and there's just enough room for interesting behavior to emerge.

31 J. BERGSTRA and Y. BENGIO (2012). Random Search for Hyper-Parameter Optimization. *Journal of Machine Learning Research* 13:281–305.

32 C. LI et al. (2018a). Measuring the Intrinsic Dimension of Objective Landscapes. *ICLR 2018.* arXiv: 1804.08838 [cs.LG].

33 E. LEVINA and P.J. BICKEL (2004). Maximum Likelihood Estimation of Intrinsic Dimension. *NeurIPS 2004.*

34 R. CALANDRA et al. (2016). Manifold Gaussian Processes for Regression. *IJCNN 2016.*

Figure 3.9: An objective function on a two-dimensional domain (left) with intrinsic dimension 1. The entire variation of the objective is determined on the one-dimensional linear subspace $\mathcal{Z}$ corresponding to the diagonal black line, which we can model in its inherent dimension (right).

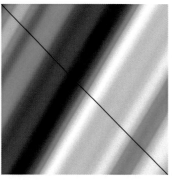

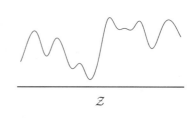

35 A. G. WILSON et al. (2016). Deep Kernel Learning. *AISTATS 2016*.

neural representation learning: § 8.11, p. 198

36 J. SNOEK et al. (2015). Scalable Bayesian Optimization Using Deep Neural Networks. *ICML 2015*.

cost of Gaussian process inference: § 9.1, p. 201

37 J. BERGSTRA and Y. BENGIO (2012). Random Search for Hyper-Parameter Optimization. *Journal of Machine Learning Research* 13:281–305.

38 F. VIVARELLI and C. K. I. WILLIAMS (1998). Discovering Hidden Features with Gaussian Process Regression. *NeurIPS 1998*.

39 Z. WANG et al. (2016b). Bayesian Optimization in a Billion Dimensions via Random Embeddings. *Journal of Artificial Intelligence Research* 55:361–387.

the family of deep kernels[35] – present a tantalizing option. Neural embeddings have shown some success in Bayesian optimization, where they can facilitate optimization over complex structured objects by providing a nice continuous latent space to work in.

SNOEK et al. demonstrated excellent performance on hyperparameter tuning tasks by interpreting the output layer of a deep neural network as a set of custom nonlinear basis functions for Bayesian linear regression, as in (3.6).[36] An advantage of this particular construction is that Gaussian process inference and prediction is accelerated dramatically by adopting the linear covariance (3.6) – the cost of inference scales linearly with the number of observations, rather than cubically as in the general case.

Linear embeddings

Another line of attack is to search for a low-dimensional *linear* subspace of the domain encompassing the relevant variation in inputs and model the function after projection onto that space. For an objective f on a high-dimensional domain $\mathcal{X} \subset \mathbb{R}^n$, we consider models of the form

$$f(\mathbf{x}) = g(\mathbf{A}\mathbf{x}); \qquad \mathbf{A} \in \mathbb{R}^{k \times n} \tag{3.30}$$

where $g \colon \mathbb{R}^k \to \mathbb{R}$ is a $(k \ll n)$-dimensional surrogate for f.

The simplest such approach is automatic relevance determination (3.25), where we learn separate length scales along each dimension.[37] Although the corresponding linear transformation (3.23) does not reduce dimension, axes with sufficiently long length scales are *effectively* eliminated, as they do not have strong influence on the covariance. This can be effective when some dimensions are likely to be irrelevant, but limits us to axis-aligned subspaces only.

A more flexible option is to consider *arbitrary* linear transformations in the model (3.26, 3.30), an idea that has seen significant attention for Gaussian process modeling in general[38] and for Bayesian optimization in particular.[39] Figure 3.9 illustrates a simple example where a one-dimensional objective function is embedded in two dimensions in a non-axis-aligned manner. Both axes would appear important for explaining the function when using ARD, but a one-dimensional subspace suffices

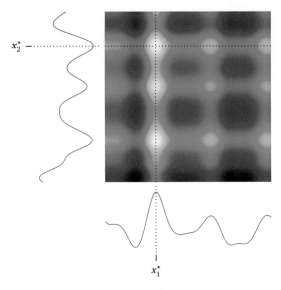

Figure 3.10: A sample from a GP in two dimensions with the decomposition $f(\mathbf{x}) = g_1(x_1) + g_2(x_2)$. Here a nominally two-dimensional function is actually the sum of two one-dimensional components defined along each axis with no interaction. The maximum of the function is achieved at the point corresponding to the maxima of the individual components.

if chosen carefully. This approach offers considerably more modeling flexibility than ARD at the expense of a k-fold increase in the number of parameters that must be specified. However, several algorithms have been proposed for efficiently identifying a suitable map $\mathbf{A}$,[40,41] and WANG et al. demonstrated success in optimizing objectives in extremely high dimension by simply searching along a *random* low-dimensional subspace. The authors also provided theoretical guarantees regarding the recoverability of the global optimum with this approach, assuming the hypothesis of low intrinsic dimensionality holds.

40 J. DJOLONGA et al. (2013). High-Dimensional Gaussian Process Bandits. *NeurIPS 2013*.

41 R. GARNETT et al. (2014). Active Learning of Linear Embeddings for Gaussian Processes. *UAI 2014*.

If more flexibility is desired, we may represent an objective function as a sum of contributions on multiple relevant linear subspaces:

$$f(\mathbf{x}) = \sum_i g_i(\mathbf{A}_i \mathbf{x}). \tag{3.31}$$

This decomposition is similar in spirit to the classical family of *generalized additive models*,[42] where the linear maps can be arbitrary and of variable dimension. If we assume the additive components in (3.31) are independent, each with Gaussian process prior $\mathcal{GP}(g_i; \mu_i, K_i)$, then the resulting model for f is a Gaussian process with additive moments (3.29):

$$\mu(\mathbf{x}) = \sum_i \mu_i(\mathbf{A}_i \mathbf{x}); \qquad K(\mathbf{x}, \mathbf{x}') = \sum_i K_i(\mathbf{A}_i \mathbf{x}, \mathbf{A}_i \mathbf{x}').$$

42 T. HASTIE and R. TIBSHIRANI (1986). Generalized Additive Models. *Statistical Science* 1(3): 297–318.

Several specific schemes have been proposed for building such decompositions. One convenient approach is to partition the coordinates of the input into disjoint groups and add a contribution defined on each subset.[43,44] Figure 3.10 shows an example, where a two-dimensional objective is the sum of independent axis-aligned components. We might use such a model when every feature of the input is likely to be relevant but only through interaction with a limited number of additional variables.

43 K. KANDASAMY et al. (2015). High Dimensional Bayesian Optimisation and Bandits via Additive Models. *ICML 2015*.

44 J. R. GARDNER et al. (2017). Discovering and Exploiting Additive Structure for Bayesian Optimization. *AISTATS 2017*.

45 P. ROLLAND et al. (2018). High-Dimensional Bayesian Optimization via Additive Models with Overlapping Groups. *AISTATS 2018*.

46 M. MUTNÝ and A. KRAUSE (2018). Efficient High Dimensional Bayesian Optimization with Additivity and Quadrature Fourier Features. *NeurIPS 2018*.

47 T. N. HOANG et al. (2018). Decentralized High-Dimensional Bayesian Optimization with Factor Graphs. *AAAI 2018*.

48 E. GILBOA et al. (2013). Scaling Multidimensional Gaussian Processes Using Projected Additive Approximations. *ICML 2013*.

49 C.-L. LI et al. (2016). High Dimensional Bayesian Optimization via Restricted Projection Pursuit Models. *AISTATS 2016*.

prior mean function: § 3.1, p. 46

impact on sample path behavior: Figure 3.1, p. 46 and surrounding discussion

impact on extrapolation: Figure 3.2, p. 47 and surrounding discussion

prior covariance function: § 3.2, p. 49

An advantage of a disjoint partition is that we may reduce optimization of the high-dimensional objective to separate optimization of each of its lower-dimensional components (3.31). Several other additive schemes have been proposed as well, including partitions with (perhaps sparsely) overlapping groups[45,46,47] and decompositions of the general form (3.31) with arbitrary projection matrices.[48,49]

3.6   SUMMARY OF MAJOR IDEAS

Specifying a Gaussian process entails choosing a mean and covariance function for the function of interest. As we saw in the previous chapter, the structure of these functions has important implications regarding sample path behavior, and as we will see in the next chapter, important implications regarding its ability to explain a given set of data.

In practice, the design of a Gaussian process model is usually data-driven: we establish some space of candidate models to consider, then search this space for the models providing the best explanation of available data. In this chapter we offered some guidance for the construction of models – or parametric spaces of models – as possible explanations of a given system. We will continue the discussion in the next chapter by taking up the question of assessing model quality in light of data. Below we summarize the important ideas arising in the present discussion.

- The mean function of a Gaussian process determines the expected value of function values. Although an important concern, the mean function can only affect sample path behavior through pointwise translation, and most interesting properties of sample paths are determined by the covariance function instead.

- Nonetheless, the mean function has important implications for prediction, namely, in *extrapolation*. When making predictions in locations poorly explained by available data – that is, locations where function value are not strongly correlated with any observation – the prior mean function effectively determines the posterior predictive mean.

- There are no restrictions on the mean function of a Gaussian process, and we are free to use any sensible choice in a given scenario. In practice, unless a better option is apparent, the mean function is usually taken to have some relatively simple parametric form, such as a constant (3.1) or a low-order polynomial (3.7). Such choices are both simple and unlikely to cause grossly undesirable extrapolatory behavior.

- When the mean function includes a *linear* combination of basis functions, we may exactly marginalize the coefficients under a multivariate normal prior (3.5). The result is a marginal Gaussian process where uncertainty in the linear terms of the mean is absorbed into the covariance function (3.6). As an important special case, we may marginalize the value of a constant mean (3.3) under a normal prior (3.2).

- The covariance function of a Gaussian process is critical to determining the behavior of its sample paths. To be valid, a covariance function must be symmetric and positive semidefinite. The latter condition can be difficult to guarantee for arbitrary "similarity measures," but covariance functions are closed under several natural operations, allowing us to build complex covariance functions from simple building blocks.

- In particular, sums and pointwise products of covariance functions are valid covariance functions, and by extension any polynomial expression of covariance functions with positive coefficients.

sums and products of covariance functions: § 3.4, p. 55

- Many common covariance functions are invariant to translation of their inputs, a property known as *stationarity*. An important result known as BOCHNER's *theorem* provides a useful representation for the space of stationary covariance functions: their Fourier transforms are symmetric, finite measures, and vice versa. This result has important implications for modeling and computation, as the Fourier representation can be much easier to work with than the covariance function itself.

stationarity: § 3.2, p. 50

BOCHNER's theorem: § 3.2, p. 51

- Numerous useful covariance functions are available "off-the-shelf." The family of *Matérn covariances* – and its limiting case the *squared exponential covariance* – can model functions with any desired degree of smoothness (3.11–3.14). A notable special case is the Matérn covariance with $v = 5/2$ (3.14), which has been promoted as a reasonable default.

the Matérn family and squared exponential covariance: § 3.3, p. 51

- The *spectral mixture covariance* (3.15) appeals to BOCHNER's theorem to provide a parametric family of covariance functions able to approximate *any* stationary covariance.

spectral mixture covariance: § 3.3, p. 53

- Covariance functions can be modified by arbitrary scaling of function outputs (3.19) and/or arbitrary transformation of function inputs (3.21). This ability allows us to create *parametric* families of covariance functions with tunable behavior.

scaling function outputs: § 3.4, p. 55
transforming function inputs: § 3.4, p. 56

- Considering arbitrary *constant* scaling of function outputs gives rise to parameters known as *output scales* (3.20).

- Considering arbitrary *dilations* of function inputs gives rise to parameters known as *characteristic length scales* (3.22). Taking the dilation to be anisotropic introduces a characteristic length scale for each input dimension, a construction known as *automatic relevance determination* (ARD). With an ARD covariance, setting a given dimension's length scale very high effectively "turns off" its influence on the model.

- *Nonlinear* warping of function inputs is also possible. This enables us to easily build custom *nonstationary* covariance functions by combining a nonlinear warping with a stationary base covariance.

nonlinear warping: Figure 3.7, p. 59 and surrounding discussion

- Optimization can be especially challenging in high dimensions due to the curse of dimensionality. However, if an objective function has intrinsic low-dimensional structure, we can avoid some of the challenges by finding a structure-preserving mapping to a lower-dimensional space and modeling the function on the "smaller" space. This idea has repeatedly proven successful, and several general-purpose constructions are available.

modeling functions on high-dimensional domains: § 3.5, p. 61

MODEL ASSESSMENT, SELECTION, AND AVERAGING

4

The previous chapter offered a glimpse into the flexibility of Gaussian processes, which can evidently model functions with a wide range of behavior. However, a critical question remains: how can we identify *which* models are most appropriate in a given situation?

The difficulty of this question is compounded by several factors. To begin, the number of possible choices is staggering. *Any* function can serve as a mean function for a Gaussian process, and we may construct arbitrary complex covariance functions through a variety of mechanisms. Even if we fix the general form of the moment functions, introducing natural parameters such as output and length scales yields an infinite spectrum of possible models.

prior mean function: § 3.1, p. 46
prior covariance function: § 3.2, p. 49

output and length scales: § 3.4, p. 54

Further, many systems of interest act as "black boxes," about which we may have little prior knowledge. Before optimization, we may have only a vague notion of which models might be reasonable for a given objective function or how any parameters of these models should be set. We might even be uncertain about aspects of the observation process, such as the nature or precise scale of observation noise. Therefore, we may find ourselves in the unfavorable position of having infinitely many possible models to choose from and no idea how to choose!

Acquiring *data*, however, provides a way out of this conundrum. After obtaining some observations of the system, we may determine which models are the most compatible with the data and thereby establish preferences over possible choices, a process known as *model assessment.* Model assessment is a surprisingly complex and nuanced subject – even if we limit the scope to Bayesian methods – and no method can rightfully be called "the" Bayesian approach.[1] In this chapter we will present one convenient framework for model assessment via Bayesian inference over models, which are evaluated based on their ability to explain observed data and our prior beliefs.

1 The interested reader can find an overview of this rich subject in:

A. VEHTARI and J. OJANEN (2012). A Survey of Bayesian Predictive Methods for Model Assessment, Selection and Comparison. *Statistics Surveys* 6:142–228.

models and model structures: § 4.1, p. 68

We will begin our presentation by carefully defining the models we will be assessing and discussing how we may build useful spaces of models for consideration. With Gaussian processes, these spaces will most often be built from what we will call *model structures,* comprising a parametric mean function, covariance function, and observation model; in the context of model assessment, the parameters of these model components are known as *hyperparameters.* We will then show how to perform Bayesian inference over the hyperparameters of a model structure from observations, resulting in a *model posterior* enabling model assessment and other tasks. We will later extend this process to multiple model structures and show how we can even *automatically* search for better model structures.

Bayesian inference over parametric model spaces: § 4.2, p. 70

multiple model structures: § 4.5, p. 78
automating model structure search: § 4.6, p. 81

Central to this approach is a fundamental measure of model fit known as the *marginal likelihood* of the data or *model evidence.* Gaussian process models are routinely selected by maximizing this score, which can produce excellent results when sufficient data are available to unambiguously determine the best-fitting model. However, model construction

marginal likelihood, model evidence: § 4.2, p. 71

model selection via MAP inference: § 4.3, p. 73

in the context of Bayesian optimization is unusual as the expense of gathering observations relegates us to the realm of *small data*. Effective modeling with small datasets requires careful consideration of model uncertainty: models explaining the data equally well may disagree drastically in their predictions, and committing to a single model may yield biased predictions with poorly calibrated uncertainty – and disappointing optimization performance as a result. *Model averaging* is one solution that has proven effective in Bayesian optimization, where the predictions of multiple models are combined in the interest of robustness.

model averaging: § 4.4, p. 74

4.1   MODELS AND MODEL STRUCTURES

In *model assessment,* we seek to evaluate a space of models according to their ability to explain a set of observations $\mathcal{D} = (\mathbf{x}, \mathbf{y})$. Before taking up this problem in earnest, let us establish exactly what we mean by "model" in this context, which is a model for the given *observations,* rather than of a latent function alone as was our focus in the previous chapter.

model, $p(\mathbf{y} \mid \mathbf{x})$

For this discussion we will define a *model* to be a prior probability distribution over the measured values $\mathbf{y}$ that would result from observing at a set of locations $\mathbf{x}$: $p(\mathbf{y} \mid \mathbf{x})$. In the overarching approach we have adopted for this book, a model is specified *indirectly* via a prior process on a latent function f and an observation model linking this function to the observed values:

$$\big[p(f), p(y \mid x, \phi) \big]. \tag{4.1}$$

model induced by prior process and observation model

Given explicit choices for these components, we may form the desired distribution by marginalizing the latent function values $\phi = f(\mathbf{x})$ through the observation model:

$$p(\mathbf{y} \mid \mathbf{x}) = \int p(\mathbf{y} \mid \mathbf{x}, \phi) \, p(\phi \mid \mathbf{x}) \, \mathrm{d}\phi. \tag{4.2}$$

All models we consider below will be of this composite form (4.1), but the assessment framework we describe will accommodate arbitrary models.

Spaces of candidate models

2 Although defining a space of candidate models may seem natural and innocuous, this is actually a major point of contention between different approaches to Bayesian model assessment. If we subscribe to the maxim "all models are wrong," we might conclude that the *true* model will *never* be contained in any space we define, no matter how expansive. However, some are likely "more wrong" than others, and we can still reasonably establish preferences over the given space.

To proceed, we must establish some space of candidate models we wish to consider as possible explanations of the observed data.[2] Although this space can in principle be arbitrary, with Gaussian process models it is convenient to consider *parametric* collections of models defined by parametric forms for the observation model and the prior mean and covariance functions of the latent function. We invested significant effort in the last chapter laying the groundwork to enable this approach: a running theme was the introduction of flexible parametric mean and covariance functions that can assume a wide range of different shapes – perfect building blocks for expressive model spaces.

model structure

We will call a particular combination of observation model, prior mean function μ, and prior covariance function K a *model structure.*

Corresponding to each model structure is a natural model space formed by exhaustively traversing the joint parameter space:

model space, $\mathcal{M}$

$$\mathcal{M} = \left\{ \left[p(f \mid \boldsymbol{\theta}), p(y \mid x, \phi, \boldsymbol{\theta}) \right] \mid \boldsymbol{\theta} \in \Theta \right\}, \qquad (4.3)$$

where

$$p(f \mid \boldsymbol{\theta}) = \mathcal{GP}\big(f; \mu(x; \boldsymbol{\theta}), K(x, x'; \boldsymbol{\theta})\big).$$

We have indexed the space by a vector $\boldsymbol{\theta}$, the entries of which jointly specify any necessary parameters from their joint range Θ. The entries of $\boldsymbol{\theta}$ are known as *hyperparameters* of the model structure, as they parameterize the prior distribution for the observations, $p(y \mid x, \boldsymbol{\theta})$ (4.2).

vector of hyperparameters, $\boldsymbol{\theta}$

range of hyperparameter values, Θ

In many cases we may be happy with a single suitably flexible model structure for the data, in which case we can proceed with the corresponding space (4.3) as the set of candidate models. We may also consider multiple model structures for the data by taking a discrete union of such spaces, an idea we will return to later in this chapter.

multiple model structures: § 4.5, p. 78

Example

Let us momentarily take a step back from abstraction and create an explicit model space for optimization on the interval $\mathcal{X} = [a, b]$.[3] Suppose our initial beliefs are that the objective will exhibit stationary behavior with a constant trend near zero, and that our observations will be corrupted by additive noise with unknown signal-to-noise ratio.

3 The interval can be arbitrary; our discussion will be purely qualitative.

For the observation model, we take homoskedastic additive Gaussian noise, a reasonable choice when there is no obvious alternative:

observation model: additive Gaussian noise with unknown scale

$$p(y \mid \phi, \sigma_n) = \mathcal{N}(y; \phi, \sigma_n^2), \qquad (4.4)$$

and leave the scale of the observation noise σ_n as a hyperparameter. Turning to the prior process, we assume a constant mean function (3.1) with a zero-mean normal prior on the unknown constant:

prior mean function: constant mean with unknown value

$$\mu(x; c) \equiv c; \qquad p(c) = \mathcal{N}(c; 0, b^2),$$

and select the Matérn covariance function with $\nu = 5/2$ (3.14) with unknown output scale λ (3.20) and unknown length scale ℓ (3.22):

prior covariance function: Matérn $\nu = 5/2$ with unknown output and length scales

$$K(x, x'; \lambda, \ell) = \lambda^2 K_{\text{M5/2}}(d/\ell).$$

Following our discussion in the last chapter, we may eliminate one of the parameters above by marginalizing the unknown constant mean under its assumed prior,[4] leaving us with the identically zero mean function and an additive contribution to the covariance function (3.3):

eliminating mean parameter via marginalization: § 3.1, p. 47

4 We would ideally marginalize the other parameters as well, but it would not result in a Gaussian process, as we will discuss shortly.

$$\mu(x) \equiv 0; \qquad K(x, x'; \lambda, \ell) = b^2 + \lambda^2 K_{\text{M5/2}}(d/\ell). \qquad (4.5)$$

This, combined with (4.4), completes the specification of a model structure with three hyperparameters: $\boldsymbol{\theta} = [\sigma_n, \lambda, \ell]^\top$. Figure 4.1 illustrates

Figure 4.1: Samples from our example model space for a range of the hyperparameters: σ_n, the observation noise scale, and ℓ, the characteristic length scale. The output scale λ is fixed for each example. Each example demonstrates a sample of the latent function and observations resulting from measurements at a fixed set of 15 locations $\mathbf{x}$. Elements of the model space can model functions with short- or long-scale correlations that are observed with a range of fidelity from virtually exact observation to extreme noise.

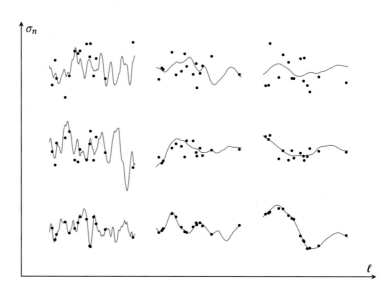

samples from the joint prior over the objective function and the observed values $\mathbf{y}$ that would result from measurements at 15 locations $\mathbf{x}$ (4.2) for a range of these hyperparameters. Even this simple model space is quite flexible, offering degrees of freedom for the variation in the objective function and the precision of our measurements.

4.2   BAYESIAN INFERENCE OVER PARAMETRIC MODEL SPACES

Given a space of candidate models, we now turn to the question of assessing the quality of these models in light of data. There are multiple paths forward,[5] but Bayesian inference offers one effective solution. By accepting that we can never be absolutely certain regarding which model is the most faithful representation of a given system, we can – as with anything unknown in the Bayesian approach – treat that "best model" as a random variable to be inferred from data and prior beliefs.

We will limit this initial discussion to parametric model spaces built from a single model structure (4.1), which will simplify notation and allow us to conflate models and their corresponding hyperparameters $\boldsymbol{\theta}$ as convenient. We will consider more complex spaces comprising multiple alternative model structures presently.

Model prior

We first endow the model space with a prior encoding which models are more plausible a priori, $p(\boldsymbol{\theta})$.[6] For convenience, it is common to design the model hyperparameters such that the uninformative (and possibly improper) "uniform prior"

$$p(\boldsymbol{\theta}) \propto 1 \qquad (4.6)$$

5   A. VEHTARI and J. OJANEN (2012). A Survey of Bayesian Predictive Methods for Model Assessment, Selection and Comparison. *Statistics Surveys* 6:142–228.

6   As it is most likely that *no* model among the candidates actually *generated* the data, some authors have suggested that any choice of prior is dubious. If this bothers the reader, it can help to frame the inference as being over the model "closest to the truth" rather than over the "true model" itself.

model prior, $p(\boldsymbol{\theta})$

Figure 4.2: The dataset for our model assessment example, generated using a hidden model from the space on the facing page.

may be used, in which case the model prior may not be explicitly acknowledged at all. However, it can be helpful to express at least weakly informative prior beliefs – especially when working with small datasets – as it can offer gentle regularization away from patently absurd choices. This should be possible for most hyperparameters in practice. For example, when modeling a physical system, it would be unlikely that interaction length scales of say one nanometer and one kilometer would be equally plausible a priori; we might capture this intuition with a wide prior on the logarithm of the length scale.

Model posterior

Given a set of observations $\mathcal{D} = (\mathbf{x}, \mathbf{y})$, we may appeal to Bayes' theorem to derive the posterior distribution over the candidate models:

$$p(\boldsymbol{\theta} \mid \mathcal{D}) \propto p(\boldsymbol{\theta}) \, p(\mathbf{y} \mid \mathbf{x}, \boldsymbol{\theta}). \tag{4.7}$$

model posterior, $p(\boldsymbol{\theta} \mid \mathcal{D})$

The model posterior provides support to the models most consistent with our prior beliefs and the observed data. Consistency with the data is encapsulated by the $p(\mathbf{y} \mid \mathbf{x}, \boldsymbol{\theta})$ term, the prior PDF over observations evaluated on the actual data.[7] This value is known as the *model evidence* or the *marginal likelihood* of the data, as it serves as a likelihood in Bayes' theorem (4.7) and, in our class of latent function models, is computed by marginalizing the latent function values at the observed locations (4.2).

7 Recall that this distribution is precisely what a model defines: § 4.1, p. 68.

model evidence, marginal likelihood, $p(\mathbf{y} \mid \mathbf{x}, \boldsymbol{\theta})$

Marginal likelihood and Bayesian Occam's razor

Model assessment becomes trivial in light of the model posterior if we simply establish preferences over models according to their posterior probability. When using the uniform model prior (4.6) (perhaps implicitly), the model posterior is proportional to the marginal likelihood alone, which can be then used directly for model assessment.

It is commonly argued that the model evidence encodes automatic penalization for model complexity, a phenomenon known as *Bayesian Occam's razor*.[8] MACKAY outlines a simple argument for this effect by noting that a model $p(\mathbf{y} \mid \mathbf{x})$ must integrate to unity over all possible measurements $\mathbf{y}$. Thus if a "simpler" model wishes to become more "complex" by putting support over a wider range of possible observations, it can only do so by reducing the support for the datasets that are already well explained; see the illustration in the margin.

The marginal likelihood of a given dataset can be conveniently computed in closed form for Gaussian process models with additive Gaussian

8 D. J. C. MACKAY (2003). *Information Theory, Inference, and Learning Algorithms*. Cambridge University Press. [chapter 28]

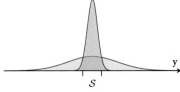

A cartoon of the Bayesian Occam's razor effect due to MACKAY. Interpreting models as PDFs over measurements $\mathbf{y}$, a "simple" model that explains datasets in $\mathcal{S}$ well, but not elsewhere. The "complex" alternative model explains datasets outside $\mathcal{S}$ better, but in $\mathcal{S}$ worse; the probability density must be lower there to explain a broader range of data.

Figure 4.3: The posterior distribution over the model space from Figure 4.1 (the range of the axes are compatible with that figure) conditioned on the dataset in Figure 4.2. The output scale is fixed (to its true value) for the purposes of illustration. Significant uncertainty remains in the exact values of the hyperparameters, but the model posterior favors models featuring either short length scales with low noise or long length scales with high noise. The points marked 1–3 are referenced in Figure 4.4; the point marked $*$ is the MAP (Figure 4.5).

noise or exact observation. In this case, we have (2.18):

$$p(\mathbf{y} \mid \mathbf{x}, \boldsymbol{\theta}) = \mathcal{N}(\mathbf{y}; \boldsymbol{\mu}, \Sigma + \mathbf{N}),$$

where $\boldsymbol{\mu}$ and Σ are the prior mean and covariance of the latent objective function values $\boldsymbol{\phi}$ (2.3), and $\mathbf{N}$ is the observation noise covariance matrix (the zero matrix for exact observation) – all of which may depend on $\boldsymbol{\theta}$. As this value can be exceptionally small and have high dynamic range, the logarithm of the marginal likelihood is usually preferred for computational purposes (A.6–A.7):

marginal likelihood for Gaussian process models with additive Gaussian noise

$$\log p(\mathbf{y} \mid \mathbf{x}, \boldsymbol{\theta}) = \\ -\tfrac{1}{2}\big[(\mathbf{y} - \boldsymbol{\mu})^{\top}(\Sigma + \mathbf{N})^{-1}(\mathbf{y} - \boldsymbol{\mu}) + \log|\Sigma + \mathbf{N}| + n\log 2\pi\big]. \quad (4.8)$$

interpretation of terms

The first term of this expression is the sum of the squared Mahalanobis norms (A.8) of the observations under the prior and represents a measure of data fit. The second term serves as a complexity penalty: the volume of any confidence ellipsoid under the prior is proportional to $|\Sigma + \mathbf{N}|$, and thus this term scales according to the volume of the model's support in observation space. The third term simply ensures normalization.

Return to example

Let us return to our example scenario and model space. We invite the reader to consider the hypothetical set of 15 observations in Figure 4.2 from our example system of interest and contemplate which models from our space of candidates in Figure 4.1 might be the most compatible with these observations.[9]

We illustrate the model posterior given this data in Figure 4.3, where, in the interest of visualization, we have fixed the covariance output

9 The dataset was realized using a moderate length scale (30 length scales spanning the domain) and a small amount of additive noise, shown below. But this is *impossible* to know from inspection of the data alone, and many alternative explanations are just as plausible according to the model posterior!

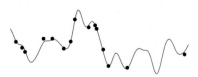

—— posterior mean

▨ posterior 95% credible interval, y ▨ posterior 95% credible interval, ϕ

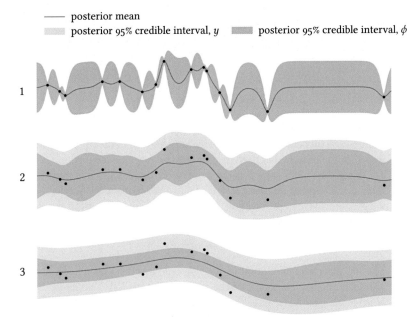

Figure 4.4: Posterior distributions given the observed data corresponding to the three settings of the model hyperparameters marked in Figure 4.3. Although remarkably different in their interpretations, each model represents an equally plausible explanation in the model posterior. Model 1 favors near-exact observations with a short length scale, and models 2–3 favor large observation noise with a range of length scales.

scale to its true value and set the range of the axes to be compatible with the samples from Figure 4.1. The model prior was designed to be weakly informative regarding the expected order of magnitude of the hyperparameters by taking independent, wide Gaussian priors on the logarithm of the observation noise and covariance length scale.[10]

The first observation we can make regarding the model posterior is that it is remarkably *broad,* with many settings of the model hyperparameters remaining plausible after observing the data. However, the model posterior does express a preference for models with either low noise and short length scale or high noise combined with a range of compatible length scales. Figure 4.4 provides examples of objective function and observation posteriors corresponding to the hyperparameters indicated in Figure 4.3. Although each is equally plausible in the posterior,[11] their explanations of the data are diverse.

10 Both parameters are nonnegative, so the prior has support on the entire parameter range.

11 The posterior probability density of these points is approximately 10% of the maximum.

4.3 MODEL SELECTION VIA POSTERIOR MAXIMIZATION

Winnowing down a space of candidate models to a *single* model for use in inference and prediction is known as *model selection.* Model selection becomes straightforward if we agree to rank candidates according to the model posterior, as we may then select the maximum a posteriori (MAP) (4.7) model:[12]

$$\hat{\theta} = \arg\max_{\theta} p(\theta)\, p(\mathbf{y} \mid \mathbf{x}, \theta). \tag{4.9}$$

When the model prior is flat (4.6), the MAP model corresponds to the maximum likelihood estimate (MLE) of the model hyperparameters. Fig-

12 If we only wish to find the maximum, there is no benefit to normalizing the posterior.

Figure 4.5: The predictions of the maximum a posteriori (MAP) model from the example data in Figure 4.2.

ure 4.5 shows the predictions made by the MAP model for our running example; in this case, the MAP hyperparameters are in fact a reasonable match to the parameters used to generate the example dataset.

acceleration via gradient-based optimization

When the model space is defined over a continuous space of hyperparameters, computation of the MAP model can be significantly accelerated via gradient-based optimization. Here it is advisable to work in the log domain, where the objective becomes the unnormalized log posterior:

$$\log p(\boldsymbol{\theta}) + \log p(\mathbf{y} \mid \mathbf{x}, \boldsymbol{\theta}). \tag{4.10}$$

gradient of log marginal likelihood with respect to $\boldsymbol{\theta}$: § c.1, p. 307

The log marginal likelihood is given in (4.8), noting that $\boldsymbol{\mu}$, Σ, and $\mathbf{N}$ are all implicitly functions of the hyperparameters $\boldsymbol{\theta}$. This objective (4.10) is differentiable with respect to $\boldsymbol{\theta}$ assuming the Gaussian process prior moments, the noise covariance, and the model prior are as well, in which case we may appeal to off-the-shelf gradient methods for solving (4.9). However, a word of warning is in order: the model posterior is not guaranteed to be concave and may have multiple local maxima, so multistart optimization is prudent.

4.4 MODEL AVERAGING

Reliance on a single model is questionable when the model posterior is not well determined by the data. For example, in our running example, a diverse range of models is consistent with the data (Figures 4.3–4.4). Committing to a single model in this case may systematically bias our predictions and underestimate predictive uncertainty – note how the diversity in predictions from Figure 4.4 is lost in the MAP model (4.5).

model-marginal objective posterior, $p(f \mid \mathcal{D})$
model-marginal predictive distribution, $p(y \mid x, \mathcal{D})$

An alternative is to *marginalize* the model with respect to the model posterior, a process known as *model averaging*:

$$p(f \mid \mathcal{D}) = \int p(f \mid \mathcal{D}, \boldsymbol{\theta}) \, p(\boldsymbol{\theta} \mid \mathcal{D}) \, \mathrm{d}\boldsymbol{\theta}; \tag{4.11}$$

$$p(y \mid x, \mathcal{D}) = \iint p(y \mid x, \phi, \boldsymbol{\theta}) \, p(\phi \mid x, \mathcal{D}, \boldsymbol{\theta}) \, p(\boldsymbol{\theta} \mid \mathcal{D}) \, \mathrm{d}\phi \, \mathrm{d}\boldsymbol{\theta}, \tag{4.12}$$

where we have marginalized the hyperparameters of both the objective and observation models. Model averaging is more consistent with the ideal Bayesian convention of marginalizing nuisance parameters when possible[13] and promises robustness to model misspecification, at least over the chosen model space.

13 Although it may be unusual to consider the choice of model a "nuisance!"

Unfortunately, neither of these model-marginal distributions (4.11–4.12) can be computed exactly for Gaussian process models except in

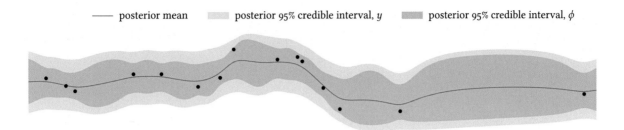

—— posterior mean   ▮ posterior 95% credible interval, y ▮ posterior 95% credible interval, ϕ

Figure 4.6: A Monte Carlo estimate to the model-marginal predictive distribution (4.11) for our example sceneario using 100 samples drawn from the model posterior in Figure 4.3 (4.14–4.15); see illustration in margin. Samples from the objective function posterior display a variety of behavior due to being associated with different hyperparameters.

some special cases,[14] so we must resort to approximation if we wish to pursue this approach. In fact, maximum a posteriori estimation can be interpreted as one rather crude approximation scheme where the model posterior is replaced by a Dirac delta distribution at the MAP hyperparameters:

$$p(\boldsymbol{\theta} \mid \mathcal{D}) \approx \delta(\boldsymbol{\theta} - \hat{\boldsymbol{\theta}}).$$

This can be defensible when the dataset is large compared to the number of hyperparameters, in which case the model posterior is often unimodal with little residual uncertainty. However, large datasets are the exception rather than the rule in Bayesian optimization, and more sophisticated approximations can pay off when model uncertainty is significant.

Monte Carlo approximation

Monte Carlo approximation is one straightforward path forward. Drawing a set of hyperparameter samples from the model posterior,

$$\{\boldsymbol{\theta}_i\}_{i=1}^{s} \sim p(\boldsymbol{\theta} \mid \mathcal{D}), \tag{4.13}$$

yields the following simple Monte Carlo estimates:

$$p(f \mid \mathcal{D}) \approx \frac{1}{s} \sum_{i=1}^{s} \mathcal{GP}\big(f; \mu_{\mathcal{D}}(\boldsymbol{\theta}_i), K_{\mathcal{D}}(\boldsymbol{\theta}_i)\big); \tag{4.14}$$

$$p(y \mid x, \mathcal{D}) \approx \frac{1}{s} \sum_{i=1}^{s} \int p(y \mid x, \phi, \boldsymbol{\theta}_i)\, p(\phi \mid x, \mathcal{D}, \boldsymbol{\theta}_i)\, \mathrm{d}\phi. \tag{4.15}$$

The objective function posterior is approximated by a *mixture* of Gaussian processes corresponding to the sampled hyperparameters, and the posterior predictive distribution for observations is then derived by integrating a Gaussian mixture (2.36) against the observation model.

Any Markov chain Monte Carlo procedure could be used to generate the hyperparameter samples (4.13); a variation on Hamiltonian Monte

14 A notable example is marginalizing the coefficients of a linear prior mean against a Gaussian prior: § 3.1, p. 47.

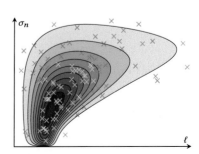

The 100 hyperparameter samples used to produce Figure 4.6.

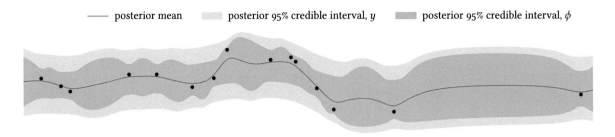

—— posterior mean   ▨ posterior 95% credible interval, y ▨ posterior 95% credible interval, ϕ

Figure 4.7: An approximation to the model-marginal posterior (4.11) using the central composite design approach proposed by RUE et al. A total of nine hyperparameter samples are used for the approximation, illustrated in the margin below.

15 M. D. HOFFMAN and A. GELMAN (2014). The No-U-turn Sampler: Adaptively Setting Path Lengths in Hamiltonian Monte Carlo. *Journal of Machine Learning Research* 15(4):1593–1623.

Carlo (HMC) such as the no u-turn sampler (NUTS) would be a reasonable choice when the gradient of the log posterior (4.10) is available, as it can exploit this information to accelerate mixing.[15]

Figure 4.6 demonstrates a Monte Carlo approximation to the model-marginal posterior (4.11–4.12) for our running example. Comparing with the MAP approximation in Figure 4.5, the predictive uncertainty of both objective function values and observations has increased considerably due to accounting for model uncertainty in the predictive distributions.

Deterministic approximation schemes

The downside of Monte Carlo approximation is relatively inefficient use of the hyperparameter samples – the price of random sampling rather than careful design. This inefficiency in turn leads to an increased computational burden for inference and prediction from having to derive a GP posterior for each sample. Several more efficient (but less accurate) alternative approximations for hyperparameter marginalization have also been proposed. A common simplifying tactic taken by these cheaper procedures is to approximate the hyperparameter posterior with a multivariate normal via a Laplace approximation:

Laplace approximation: § B.1, p. 301

$$p(\boldsymbol{\theta} \mid \mathcal{D}) \approx \mathcal{N}(\boldsymbol{\theta}; \hat{\boldsymbol{\theta}}, \mathbf{C}), \qquad (4.16)$$

where $\hat{\boldsymbol{\theta}}$ is the MAP (4.9). Integrating this approximation into (4.11) gives

$$p(f \mid \mathcal{D}) \approx \int \mathcal{GP}\big(f; \mu_{\mathcal{D}}(\boldsymbol{\theta}), K_{\mathcal{D}}(\boldsymbol{\theta})\big)\, \mathcal{N}(\boldsymbol{\theta}; \hat{\boldsymbol{\theta}}, \mathbf{C})\, \mathrm{d}\boldsymbol{\theta}. \qquad (4.17)$$

16 H. RUE et al. (2009). Approximate Bayesian Inference for Latent Gaussian Models by Using Integrated Nested Laplace Approximations. *Journal of the Royal Statistical Society Series B (Methodological)* 71(2):319–392.

17 G. E. P. BOX and K. B. WILSON (1951). On the Experimental Attainment of Optimum Conditions. *Journal of the Royal Statistical Society Series B (Methodological)* 13(1):1–45.

Unfortunately this integral remains intractable due to the nonlinear dependence of the posterior moments on the hyperparameters, but reducing to this common form allows us to derive *deterministic* approximations against a single assumed posterior.

RUE et al. introduced several approximation schemes representing different tradeoffs between efficiency and fidelity.[16] Notable among these is a simple, sample-efficient procedure grounded in classical experimental design. Here a central composite design[17] in hyperparameter

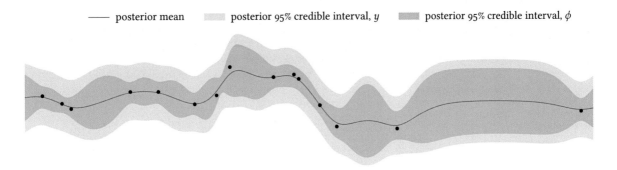

— posterior mean   ▨ posterior 95% credible interval, y ▨ posterior 95% credible interval, ϕ

Figure 4.8: The approximation to the model-marginal posterior (4.11) for our running example using the approach proposed by OSBORNE et al.

space is transformed to agree with the moments of (4.16), then used as nodes in a numerical quadrature approximation to (4.17). The resulting approximation again takes the form of a (now weighted) mixture of Gaussian processes (4.14): the MAP model augmented by a small number of additional models designed to reflect the important variation in the hyperparameter posterior. The number of hyperparamater samples required by this scheme grows relatively slowly with the dimension of the hyperparameter space: less than 100 for $|\theta| \leq 8$ and less than 1000 for $|\theta| \leq 21$.[18] The nine samples required for our running example are shown in the marginal figure. Figure 4.7 shows the resulting approximate posterior; comparing with the gold-standard Monte Carlo approximation from Figure 4.6, the agreement is excellent.

An even more lightweight approximation was proposed by OSBORNE et al., which despite its crudeness is arguably still preferable to MAP estimation and can be used as a drop-in replacement.[19] This approach again relies on a Laplace approximation to the hyperparameter posterior (4.16–4.17). The key observation is that under the admittedly strong assumption that the posterior mean were in fact *linear* in θ and the posterior covariance *independent* of θ, we could resolve (4.17) in closed form. We proceed by taking the best linear approximation to the posterior mean around the MAP:[20]

$$\mu_{\mathcal{D}}(x;\theta) \approx \mu_{\mathcal{D}}(x;\hat{\theta}) + \mathbf{g}(x)^\top(\theta - \hat{\theta}); \qquad \mathbf{g}(x) = \frac{\partial \mu_{\mathcal{D}}(x;\theta)}{\partial \theta}(\hat{\theta}),$$

and assuming the MAP posterior covariance is universal: $K_{\mathcal{D}}(\theta) \approx K_{\mathcal{D}}(\hat{\theta})$. The result is a *single* Gaussian process approximation to the posterior:

$$p(f \mid \mathcal{D}) \approx \mathcal{GP}(f; \hat{\mu}_{\mathcal{D}}, \hat{K}_{\mathcal{D}}), \qquad (4.18)$$

where

$$\hat{\mu}_{\mathcal{D}}(x) = \mu_{\mathcal{D}}(x;\hat{\theta}); \qquad \hat{K}_{\mathcal{D}}(x,x') = K_{\mathcal{D}}(x,x';\hat{\theta}) + \mathbf{g}(x)^\top \mathbf{C} \mathbf{g}(x').$$

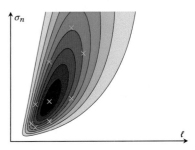

A Laplace approximation to the model posterior (performed in the log domain) and hyperparameter settings corresponding to the central composite design proposed by RUE et al. The samples do a good job covering the support of the true posterior.

18 S. M. SANCHEZ and P. J. SANCHEZ (2005). Very Large Fractional Factorial and Central Composite Designs. ACM *Transactions on Modeling and Computer Simulation* 15(4):362–377.

19 M. A. OSBORNE et al. (2012). Active Learning of Model Evidence Using Bayesian Quadrature. *NeurIPS 2012.*

20 This is analogous to the linearization step in the extended Kalman filter, whereas the central composite design approach is closer to the unscented Kalman filter in pushing samples through the nonlinear transformation.

This is the MAP model with covariance inflated by a term determined by the dependence of the posterior mean on the hyperparameters, g, and the uncertainty in the hyperparameters, C.[21]

OSBORNE et al. did not address how to account for uncertainty in observation model parameters when approximating $p(y \mid x, \mathcal{D})$, but we can derive a natural approach for independent additive Gaussian noise with unknown scale σ_n. Given x, let $p(\phi \mid x, \mathcal{D}) \approx \mathcal{N}(\phi; \mu, \sigma^2)$ as in (4.18). We must approximate[22]

$$p(y \mid x, \mathcal{D}) \approx \int \mathcal{N}(y; \mu, \sigma^2 + \sigma_n^2) \, p(\sigma_n \mid x, \mathcal{D}) \, d\sigma_n.$$

A moment-matched approximation $p(y \mid x, \mathcal{D}) \approx \mathcal{N}(y; m, s^2)$ is possible by appealing to the law of total variance:

$$m = \mathbb{E}[y \mid x, \mathcal{D}] \approx \mu; \qquad s^2 = \text{var}[y \mid x, \mathcal{D}] \approx \sigma^2 + \mathbb{E}[\sigma_n^2 \mid x, \mathcal{D}].$$

If the noise scale is parameterized by its logarithm, then the Laplace approximation (4.16) in particular yields

$$p(\log \sigma_n \mid x, \mathcal{D}) \approx \mathcal{N}(\log \sigma_n; \log \hat{\sigma}_n, s^2); \qquad \mathbb{E}[\sigma_n^2 \mid x, \mathcal{D}] \approx \hat{\sigma}_n^2 \exp(2s^2).$$

Thus we predict with the MAP estimate $\hat{\sigma}_n$ inflated by a factor commensurate with the residual uncertainty in the noise contribution.

Figure 4.8 shows the resulting approximation for our running example. Although not perfect, the predictive uncertainty in the observations is more faithful than the MAP model from Figure 4.5, which severely underestimates the scale of observation noise in the posterior.

4.5   MULTIPLE MODEL STRUCTURES

We have now covered model inference, selection, and averaging with a *single* parametric model space (4.1). With a bit of extra bookkeeping, we may extend this framework to handle multiple model structures comprising different combinations of parametric prior moments and observation models.

To begin, we may build a space of candidate models by taking a discrete union of parametric spaces as in (4.1), with one built from each desired model structure: $\{\mathcal{M}_i\}$. It is natural to index this space by $(\theta, \mathcal{M})$, where θ is understood to be a vector of hyperparameters associated with the specified model structure; the size and interpretation of this vector may differ across structures. All that remains is to derive our previous results while managing this compound structure–hyperparameter index.

We may define a model prior over this compound space by combining a prior over the chosen model structures with priors over the hyperparameters of each:

$$p(\theta, \mathcal{M}) = \Pr(\mathcal{M}) \, p(\theta \mid \mathcal{M}). \tag{4.19}$$

Given data, the model posterior has a similar form as before (4.7):

$$p(\theta, \mathcal{M} \mid \mathcal{D}) = \Pr(\mathcal{M} \mid \mathcal{D}) \, p(\theta \mid \mathcal{D}, \mathcal{M}). \tag{4.20}$$

---

uncertainty in additive noise scale σ_n

21 This term vanishes if the hyperparameters are completely determined by the data, in which case the approximation regresses gracefully to the MAP estimate.

22 In general we have

$$p(y \mid x, \mathcal{D}) =$$
$$\iint p(y \mid x, \phi, \sigma_n) \, p(\phi, \sigma_n \mid x, \mathcal{D}) \, d\phi \, d\sigma_n,$$

and we have resolved the integral on ϕ using the single-GP approximation.

model structure index, $\mathcal{M}$

model structure prior, $\Pr(\mathcal{M})$

Figure 4.9: The objective and dataset for our multiple-model example.

The structure-conditional hyperparameter posterior $p(\boldsymbol{\theta} \mid \mathcal{D}, \mathcal{M})$ is as in (4.7) and may be reasoned about following our previous discussion. The model structure posterior is then given by

model structure posterior, $\Pr(\mathcal{M} \mid \mathcal{D})$

$$\Pr(\mathcal{M} \mid \mathcal{D}) \propto \Pr(\mathcal{M})\,p(\mathbf{y} \mid \mathbf{x}, \mathcal{M}); \quad (4.21)$$

$$p(\mathbf{y} \mid \mathbf{x}, \mathcal{M}) = \int p(\mathbf{y} \mid \mathbf{x}, \boldsymbol{\theta}, \mathcal{M})\,p(\boldsymbol{\theta} \mid \mathcal{M})\,\mathrm{d}\boldsymbol{\theta}. \quad (4.22)$$

The expression in (4.22) is the normalizing constant of the structure-conditional hyperparameter posterior (4.7), which we could ignore when there was only a single model structure. This integral is in general intractable, but several approximations are feasible. One effective choice is the Laplace approximation (4.16), which provides an approximation to the integral as a side effect (B.2). The classical *Bayesian information criterion* (BIC) may be seen as an approximation to this approximation.[23]

Laplace approximation: § B.1, p. 301

23 S. KONISHI and G. KITAGAWA (2008). *Information Criteria and Statistical Modeling.* Springer-Verlag. [chapter 9]

Model selection may now be pursued by maximizing the model posterior over the model space as before, although we may no longer appeal to gradient methods as the model space is not continuous with multiple model structures. A simple approach would be to find the MAP hyperparameters for each of the model structures separately, then use these MAP points to approximate (4.22) for each structure via the Laplace approximation or BIC. This would be sufficient to estimate (4.20–4.21) and maximize over the MAP models.

model selection

Turning to model averaging, the model-marginal posterior to the objective function is:

model averaging

$$p(f \mid \mathcal{D}) = \sum_i \Pr(\mathcal{M}_i \mid \mathcal{D})\,p(f \mid \mathcal{D}, \mathcal{M}_i). \quad (4.23)$$

The structure-conditional, hyperparameter-marginal distribution on each space $p(f \mid \mathcal{D}, \mathcal{M})$ is as before (4.11) and may be approximated following our previous discussion. These are now combined in a mixture distribution weighted by the model structure posterior (4.21).

Multiple structure example

We now present an example of model inference, selection, and averaging over multiple model structures using the dataset in Figure 4.9.[24] The data were sampled from a Gaussian process with linear prior mean (a linear trend with positive slope is evident) and Matérn $\nu = \frac{3}{2}$ prior covariance (3.13), with a small amount of additive Gaussian noise. We also show a sample from the objective function posterior corresponding to the true model generating the data for reference.

24 The data are used as a demo in the code released with:

C. E. RASMUSSEN and C. K. I. WILLIAMS (2006). *Gaussian Processes for Machine Learning.* MIT Press.

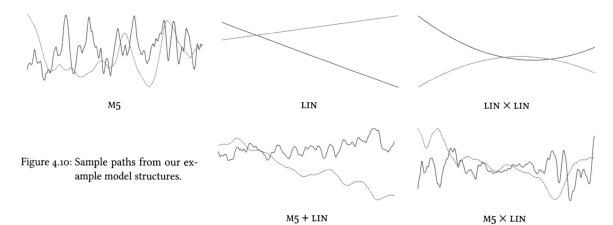

M5   LIN   LIN × LIN

Figure 4.10: Sample paths from our example model structures.

M5 + LIN   M5 × LIN

initial model structure: p. 69

We build a model space comprising several model structures by augmenting our previous space with structures incorporating additional
covariance functions. The treatment of the prior mean (unknown constant marginalized against a Gaussian prior) and observation model
(additive Gaussian noise with unknown scale) will remain the same
for all. The model structures reflect a variety of hypotheses positing
potential linear or quadratic behavior:

M5: the Matérn $\nu = 5/2$ covariance (3.14) from our previous example;

LIN: the linear covariance (3.16), where the the prior on the slope is vague
and centered at zero and the prior on the intercept agrees with the M5
model;

LIN × LIN: the product of two linear covariances designed as above, modeling a
latent quadratic function with unknown coefficients;

M5 + LIN: the sum of a Matérn $\nu = 5/2$ and linear covariance designed as in the
corresponding individual model structures; and

M5 × LIN: the product of a Matérn $\nu = 5/2$ and linear covariance designed as in the
corresponding individual model structures.

Objective function samples from models in each of these structures are
shown in Figure 4.10. Among these, the model structure closest to the
truth is arguably M5 + LIN.

approximation to model structure posterior

Following the above discussion, we find the MAP hyperparameters
for each of these model structures separately and use a Laplace approximation (4.16) to approximate the hyperparameter posterior on each
space, along with the normalizing constant (4.22). Normalizing over the
structures provides an approximate model structure posterior:

$$\Pr(\text{M5} \mid \mathcal{D}) \approx 10.8\%;$$
$$\Pr(\text{M5} + \text{LIN} \mid \mathcal{D}) \approx 71.8\%;$$
$$\Pr(\text{M5} \times \text{LIN} \mid \mathcal{D}) \approx 17.0\%,$$

with the remaining model structures (LIN and LIN × LIN) sharing the re-

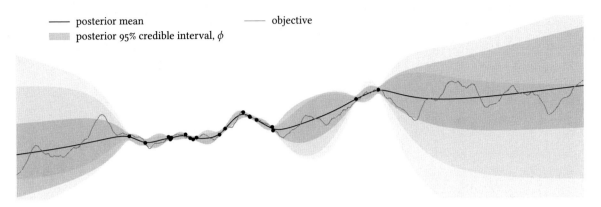

— posterior mean   — objective
▨ posterior 95% credible interval, ϕ

Figure 4.11: An approximation to the model-marginal posterior (4.23) for our multiple-model example. The posterior on each model structure is approximated separately as a mixture of Gaussian processes following RUE et al. (see Figure 4.7); these are then combined by weighting by an approximation of the model structure posterior (4.21). We show the result with three superimposed, transparent credible intervals, which are shaded with respect to their weight in contributing to the final approximation.

maining 0.4%. The M5 + LIN model structure is the clear winner, and there is strong evidence that the purely polynomial models are insufficient for explaining the data alone.

Figure 4.11 illustrates an approximation to the model-marginal posterior (4.23), approximated by applying RUE et al.'s central composite design approach to each of the model structures, then combining these into a Gaussian process mixture by weighting by the approximate model structure posterior. The highly asymmetric credible intervals reflect the diversity in explanations for the data offered by the chosen model structures, and the combined model makes reasonable predictions of our example objective function sampled from the true model.

For this example, averaging over the model structure has important implications regarding the behavior of the resulting optimization policy. Figure 4.12 illustrates a common acquisition function[25] built from the off-the-shelf M5 model, as well as from the structure-marginal model. The former chooses to exploit near what it believes is a local optimum, but the latter has a strong belief in an underlying linear trend and chooses to explore the right-hand side of the domain instead. For our example objective function sample, this would in fact reveal the global optimum with the next observation.

approximation to marginal predictive distribution

averaging over a space of Gaussian processes in policy computation: § 8.10, p. 192

25 to be specific, expected improvement: § 7.3, p. 127

4.6 AUTOMATING MODEL STRUCTURE SEARCH

We now have a comprehensive framework for reasoning about model uncertainty, including methods for model assessment, selection, and averaging across one or multiple model structures. However, it is still not clear how we should determine which model structures to consider for a given system. This is critical as our model inference procedure requires

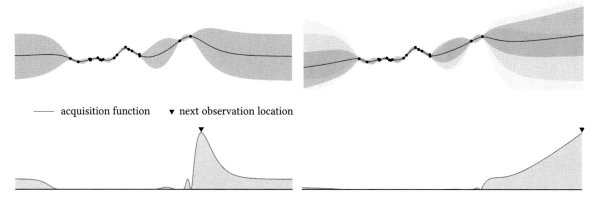

Figure 4.12: Optimization policies built from the MAP M5 model (left) and the structure-marginal posterior (right). The M5 model chooses to exploit near the local optimum, but the structure-marginal model is aware of the underlying linear trend and chooses to explore the right-hand side as a result.

the space of candidate models to be predefined; equivalently, the model prior (4.19) is implicitly set to zero for every model outside this space. Ideally, we would simply enumerate every possible model structure and average over all of them, but even a naïve approximation of this ideal would entail overwhelming computational effort.

However, the set of model structures we consider for a given dataset can be *adaptively* tailored as we gather data. One powerful idea is to appeal to metaheuristics such as local search: by establishing a suitable space of candidate model structures, we can dynamically explore this space for the best explanations of available data.

Spaces of candidate model structures

26 D. DUVENAUD et al. (2013). Structure Discovery in Nonparametric Regression through Compositional Kernel Search. *ICML 2013*.

addition and multiplication of covariance functions: § 3.4, p. 60

base kernels, B

To enable this approach, we must first establish a sufficiently rich space of candidate model structures. DUVENAUD et al. proposed one convenient mechanism for defining such a space via a simple productive grammar.[26] The idea is to appeal to the closure of covariance functions under addition and pointwise multiplication to systematically build up families of increasingly complex models from simple components. We begin by choosing a set of so-called *base kernels*, B, modeling relatively simple behavior, then extend this set to an infinite family of compositions via the following context-free grammar:

$$K \rightarrow B$$
$$K \rightarrow K + K$$
$$K \rightarrow KK$$
$$K \rightarrow (K).$$

The symbol B in the first rule represents any desired base kernel. The five model structures considered in our multiple-structure example above in fact represent five members of the language generated by this grammar with the base kernels $\mathcal{B} = \{K_{M5/2}, K_{LIN}\}$ or simply $\mathcal{B} = \{M5, LIN\}$. The grammar however also generates arbitrarily more complicated expressions such as

$$(M5 + (M5 + LIN)M5)(M5 + M5) + LIN. \qquad (4.24)$$

We are free to design the base kernels to capture any potential atomic behavior in the objective function. For example, if the domain is high dimensional and we suspect that the objective may depend only on sparse interactions of mostly independent variables, we might design the base kernels to model variations in single variables at a time, then rely on the grammar to generate an array of possible interaction structures.

Other spaces of model structures have also been proposed for automated structure search. With an eye toward high-dimensional domains, GARDNER et al. for example considered spaces of additive model structures indexed by every possible partition of the input variables.[27] This is an expressive class of model structures, but the number of partitions grows so rapidly that exhaustive search is not feasible.

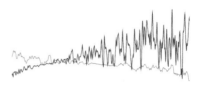

Samples from objective function models incorporating the example covariance structure (4.24).

additive decompositions, §3.5, p. 61

27 J. R. GARDNER et al. (2017). Discovering and Exploiting Additive Structure for Bayesian Optimization. *AISTATS 2017*.

Searching over model structures

Once a space of candidate model structures has been established, we may develop a search procedure seeking the most promising structures to explain a given dataset. Several approaches have been proposed for this search with a range of complexity, all of which frame the problem in terms of optimizing some figure of merit over the space. Although any score could be used in this context, a natural choice is an approximation to the (unnormalized) model structure posterior (4.21) such as the Laplace approximation or the Bayesian information criterion, and every method described below uses one of these two scores.

DUVENAUD et al. suggested traversing their kernel grammar via greedy search – here, we first evaluate the base kernels, then subject the productive rules to the best among them to generate similar structures to search next.[26] We continue in this manner as desired, alternating between evaluating the newly proposed structures, then using the grammar to expand around the best-seen structure to generate new proposals. This simple procedure is easy to implement and offers a strong baseline.

MALKOMES et al. refined this approach by replacing greedy search with *Bayesian optimization* over the space of model structures.[28] As in the DUVENAUD et al. procedure, the authors pose the problem in terms of maximizing a score over model structures: a Laplace approximation of the (log) unnormalized structure posterior (4.21). This objective function was then modeled using a Gaussian process, which informed a sequential Bayesian optimization procedure seeking to effectively manage the exploration–exploitation tradeoff in the space of candidate structures. The Gaussian process in model space requires a covariance function over model structures, and the authors proposed an exotic "kernel kernel" evaluating the similarity of proposed structures in terms of the overlap

28 G. MALKOMES et al. (2016). Bayesian Optimization for Automated Model Selection. *NeurIPS 2016*.

between their hyperparameter-marginal priors for the given dataset. The resulting optimization procedure was found to rapidly locate promising models across a range of regression tasks.

End-to-end automation

Follow-on work demonstrated a *completely automated* Bayesian optimization system built on this structure search procedure avoiding any manual modeling at all.[29] The key idea was to dynamically maintain a set of plausible model structures throughout optimization. Predictions are made via model averaging over this set, offering robustness to model misspecification when computing the outer optimization policy. Every time a new observation is obtained, the set of model structures is then updated via a continual Bayesian optimization in model space given the new data. This interleaving of Bayesian optimization in data space and model space offered promising performance.

Finally, GARDNER et al. offered an alternative to *optimization* over model structures by constructing a Markov chain Monte Carlo routine to *sample* model structures from their posterior (4.21).[30] The proposed sampler was a realization of the Metropolis–Hastings algorithm with a custom proposal distribution making minor modifications to the incumbent structure. In the case of the additive decompositions considered in that work, this step consisted of applying random atomic operations such as merging or splitting components of the existing decomposition. Despite the absolutely enormous number of possible additive decompositions, this MCMC routine was able to quickly locate promising structures, and averaging over the sampled structures for prediction resulted in superior optimization performance as well.

29 G. MALKOMES and R. GARNETT (2018). Automating Bayesian Optimization with Bayesian Optimization. *NeurIPS 2018*.

30 J. R. GARDNER et al. (2017). Discovering and Exploiting Additive Structure for Bayesian Optimization. *AISTATS 2017*.

4.7 SUMMARY OF MAJOR IDEAS

We have presented a convenient framework for model assessment, selection, and averaging grounded in Bayesian inference; this is the predominant approach with Gaussian process models. In the context of Bayesian optimization, perhaps the most important development was the notion of *model averaging,* which has proven beneficial to empirical performance[31] and has become standard practice.

31 J. SNOEK et al. (2012). Practical Bayesian Optimization of Machine Learning Algorithms. *NeurIPS 2012*.

- Model assessment entails deriving preferences over a space of candidate models of a given system in light of available data.

models and model structures: § 4.1, p. 68

- In its purest form, a *model* in this context is a prior distribution over observed values $\mathbf{y}$ arising from observations at a given set of locations $\mathbf{x}$, $p(\mathbf{y} \mid \mathbf{x})$. A convenient mechanism for specifying a model is via a prior process for a latent function, $p(f)$, and an observation model conditioned on this function, $p(y \mid x, \phi)$ (4.1–4.2).

- With Gaussian process models, it is convenient to work with combinations of *parametric* forms for the prior mean function, prior covariance function, and observation model, a construct we call a *model structure*. A model structure defines a space of corresponding models by traversing its parameter space (4.3), allowing us to build expressive model spaces.

- Once we delineate a space of candidate models, model assessment becomes straightforward if we make the – perhaps dubious but nonetheless practical – assumption that the mechanism generating our data is contained within this space. This allows us to treat that true model as a random variable and proceed via Bayesian inference over the chosen model space.

Bayesian inference over (parametric) model spaces: § 4.2, p. 70

- This inference proceeds as usual. We first define a *model prior* capturing any initial beliefs over the model space. Then, given a set of observations $\mathcal{D} = (\mathbf{x}, \mathbf{y})$, the model posterior is proportional to the model prior and a measure of model fit known as the *marginal likelihood* or *model evidence*, the probability (density) of the observed data under the model.

- In addition to quantifying fit, the model evidence encodes an automatic penalty for model complexity, an effect known as *Bayesian Occam's razor*.

Bayesian Occam's razor, § 4.2, p. 71

- Model evidence can be computed in closed form for Gaussian process models with additive Gaussian observation noise (4.8).

- Model inference is especially convenient when the model space is a single model structure, but can be extended to spaces built from multiple model structures with a bit of extra bookkeeping.

multiple model structures: § 4.5, p. 78

- The model posterior provides a simple means of model assessment by establishing preferences according to posterior probability. If we must commit to a *single* model to explain the data – a task known as *model selection* – we then select the maximum a posteriori (MAP) model.

model selection via MAP inference: § 4.3, p. 73

- Model selection may not be prudent when the model posterior is very flat, which is common when observations are scarce. In this case many models may be compatible with the data but incompatible in their predictions, which should be accounted for in the interest of robustness. *Model averaging* is a natural solution, where we marginalize the unknown model when making predictions according to the model posterior.

model averaging: § 4.4, p. 74

- Model averaging cannot in general be performed in closed form for Gaussian process models; however, we may proceed via MCMC sampling (4.14–4.15) or by appealing to more lightweight approximation schemes.

approximations to model-marginal posterior: Figures 4.6–4.8 and surrounding text

- Appealing to metaheuristics allows us to *automatically* search a space of candidate model *structures* to explain a given dataset. Once sufficiently mature, such schemes may some day enable fully automated Bayesian optimization pipelines that sidestep explicit modeling altogether.

automating model structure search: § 4.6, p. 81

The next chapter marks a major departure from our discussion thus far, which has focused on modeling and making predictions from data. We will now shift our attention from inference to decision making, with the goal of building effective optimization policies informed by the models we have now fully developed. This endeavor will consume the bulk of the remainder of the book.

The first step will be to develop a framework for optimal decision making under uncertainty. Our work to this point will serve an essential component of this framework, as every such decision will be made with reference to a posterior belief about what might happen as a result. In the context of optimization, this belief will take the form of a posterior predictive distribution for proposed observations given data, and our investment in building faithful models will pay off in spades.

DECISION THEORY FOR OPTIMIZATION

5

Optimization entails a series of decisions. Most obviously, we must repeatedly decide where to make each observation guided by the available data. Some settings also demand we decide when to terminate optimization, weighing the potential benefit from continuing optimization against any costs that may be incurred. It is not obvious how we should make these decisions, especially in the face of incomplete and constantly evolving knowledge about the objective function that is only refined via the outcomes of our own actions.

In the previous four chapters, we established Bayesian inference as a framework for reasoning about uncertainty that offers partial guidance. The primary obstacle to decision making during optimization is uncertainty about the objective function, and, by extension, the outcomes of proposed observations. Bayesian inference allows us to reason about an unknown objective function with a probability distribution over plausible functions that we may seamlessly update as we gather new information. This belief over the objective function in turn enables prediction of proposed observations via the posterior predictive distribution.

How can we use these beliefs to guide our decisions? Bayesian inference offers no direct answer, but in this chapter we will bridge this gap. We will develop *Bayesian decision theory* as a principled means of decision making under uncertainty and apply this approach in the context of optimization, demonstrating how to use a probabilistic belief about an objective function to inform intelligent optimization policies.

Bayesian decision theory

Recall our model of sequential optimization outlined in Algorithm 1.1, repeated for convenience on the following page. We begin with an arbitrary set of data, which we build upon through a sequence of observations of our own design. The core of the procedure is an *optimization policy*, which examines any already gathered data and makes the fundamental decision of where to make the next observation. With a policy in hand, optimization proceeds by repeating a straightforward pattern: the policy selects the next observation location, then we acquire the requested measurement and update our data accordingly. We repeat this process until satisfied, at which point we return the collected data.

formalization of optimization, § 1.1, p. 2

optimization policy

Barring the question of termination, the behavior of this procedure is entirely determined by the policy, and constructing optimization policies will be our primary concern in this and the following chapters. We will begin with sheer audacity: we will derive the *optimal* policy – in terms of maximizing the expected quality of the returned data – in a generic setting. The reader may wonder why this book is so long if the optimal policy is apparently so simple. As it turns out, this theoretically optimal procedure is usually impossible to compute and rarely of practical value. However, our careful derivation will shed light on how we might derive effective approximations. This is a common theme in Bayesian optimization and will be our focus in Chapters 7 and 8.

optimal optimization policies: § 5.2, p. 91

running time and approximation: § 5.3, p. 99

Chapter 7: Common Bayesian Optimization Policies, p. 123

Chapter 8: Computing Policies with Gaussian Processes, p. 157

The question of when to terminate optimization also represents a decision that can be of critical importance in some applications. A

Algorithm 1.1: Sequential optimization.

> **input**: initial dataset $\mathcal{D}$ ▸ can be empty
> **repeat**
> $x \leftarrow \textsc{policy}(\mathcal{D})$ ▸ select the next observation location
> $y \leftarrow \textsc{observe}(x)$ ▸ observe at the chosen location
> $\mathcal{D} \leftarrow \mathcal{D} \cup \{(x, y)\}$ ▸ update dataset
> **until** termination condition reached   ▸ e.g., budget exhausted
> **return** $\mathcal{D}$

stopping rule

1 A predominant example is a preallocated budget on the number of allowed observations, in which case we are compelled to stop after exhausting the budget regardless of progress.

optimal stopping rules: § 5.4, p. 103

practical stopping rules: § 9.3, p. 210

Chapter 6: Utility Functions for Optimization, p. 109

acquisition function, infill function, figure of merit

acquisition function, $\alpha(x; \mathcal{D})$

procedure for inspecting an observed dataset and deciding whether to stop or continue optimization is called a *stopping rule*. In optimization, the stopping rule is often fixed and known before we begin, in which case we do not need to worry over its design.[1] However, in some scenarios, we may wish instead to consider our evolving understanding of the objective function and the expected cost of further observations to dynamically decide when to stop, requiring more subtle adaptive stopping rules. We will also address termination decisions in this chapter and will again begin by deriving the *optimal* – but intractable – stopping procedure, which will inspire efficient and effective approximations.

Practical optimization routines will return datasets that reflect significant progress on our global optimization problem (1.1) in some way. For example, we may wish to return datasets containing near-optimal values of the objective function. Alternatively, we may be satisfied returning datasets that indirectly reveal likely locations of the global optimum or achieve some other related goal. We will formalize this notion of a returned dataset's *utility* shortly and use it to guide optimization. First, we pause to introduce a useful and pervasive technique for implicitly defining an optimization policy by maximizing a score function over the domain.

Defining optimization policies via acquisition functions

A convenient mechanism for defining an optimization policy is by first specifying an intermediate so-called *acquisition function* (also called an *infill function* or *figure of merit*) that provides a score to each potential observation location commensurate with its propensity for aiding the optimization task. We may then define a policy by observing at a point judged most promising by the acquisition function. Nearly all Bayesian optimization policies are defined in this manner, and this relationship is so intimate that the phrase "acquisition function" is often used interchangeably with "policy" in the literature and conversation, with *maximization* of the acquisition function understood.

Specifically, an acquisition function $\alpha \colon \mathcal{X} \to \mathbb{R}$ assigns a score to each point in the domain reflecting our preferences over locations for the next observation. Of course, these preferences will presumably depend on the data we have already observed. To make this dependence explicit, we adopt the notation $\alpha(x; \mathcal{D})$ for a general acquisition function, where available data serve as parameters shaping our preferences. In the Bayesian approach, acquisition functions are invariably defined by deriving the posterior belief of the objective function given the data, $p(f \mid \mathcal{D})$, then defining preferences with respect to this belief.

An acquisition function α encodes preferences over potential observation locations by inducing a total order over the domain: given data $\mathcal{D}$, observing at a point x is preferred over another point x' whenever $\alpha(x; \mathcal{D}) > \alpha(x'; \mathcal{D})$. Thus a rational action in light of these preferences is (any) one maximizing the acquisition function:[2]

encoding preferences with an acquisition function

2 Ties may be broken arbitrarily.

$$x \in \arg\max_{x' \in \mathcal{X}} \alpha(x'; \mathcal{D}). \tag{5.1}$$

Solving (5.1) maps a set of observed data $\mathcal{D}$ to a point $x \in \mathcal{X}$ to observe next, exactly the role of an optimization policy.

At first this idea may sound absurd: we have proposed solving a global optimization problem (1.1) by repeatedly solving global optimization problems (5.1)! To resolve this apparent paradox, we note that acquisition functions in common use have properties rendering their optimization considerably more tractable than the problem we ultimately wish to solve. Typical acquisition functions are both cheap to evaluate and analytically differentiable, allowing the use of off-the-shelf optimizers when computing the policy (5.1). The objective function, on the other hand, is assumed to be expensive to evaluate, and its gradient is often unavailable. Therefore we can reduce a difficult, expensive problem to a series of simpler, inexpensive problems – a reasonable pursuit!

the paradox of Bayesian optimization: global optimization via…global optimization?

Numerous acquisition functions have been proposed for Bayesian optimization, and we will describe many popular choices in detail in Chapter 7. The most prominent means to constructing acquisition functions is *Bayesian decision theory,* an approach to optimal decision making we will discuss over the remainder of the chapter.

Chapter 7: Common Bayesian Optimization Policies, p. 123

5.1 INTRODUCTION TO BAYESIAN DECISION THEORY

Bayesian decision theory is a framework for decision making under uncertainty that is flexible enough to handle effectively any scenario. Instead of presenting the entire theory in complete abstraction, we will introduce the essential concepts with an eye to the context of optimization. For a more in-depth and theoretical treatment, the interested reader may refer to numerous comprehensive reviews of the subject.[3] A good familiarity with this material can demystify some key ideas that are often glossed over in the Bayesian optimization literature, as it serves as the "hidden origin" of many common acquisition functions.

3 The following would be excellent companion texts:

M. H. DEGROOT (1970). *Optimal Statistical Decisions.* McGraw–Hill.

J. O. BERGER (1985). *Statistical Decision Theory and Bayesian Analysis.* Springer–Verlag.

In this section we will introduce the Bayesian approach to decision making and demonstrate how to make optimal decisions in the case of a single isolated decision. Ultimately, we will require a theory for making a *sequence* of decisions to reason over an entire optimization session. In the next section, we will extend the line of reasoning presented below to address sequential decision making and the construction of optimization policies.

Isolated decisions

action space, $\mathcal{A}$

A decision problem under uncertainty has two defining characteristics. The first is the *action space* $\mathcal{A}$, the set of all available decisions. Our task is to select an action from this space. For example, in sequential optimization, an optimization policy decision must select a point in the domain $\mathcal{X}$ for observation, and so we have $\mathcal{A} = \mathcal{X}$.

unknown variables affecting decision outcome, ψ

relevant observed data, $\mathcal{D}$
posterior belief about ψ, $p(\psi \mid \mathcal{D})$

The second critical feature is the presence of *uncertain* elements of the world influencing the outcomes of our actions, complicating our decision. Let ψ represent a random variable encompassing any relevant uncertain elements when making and evaluating a decision. Although we may lack perfect knowledge, Bayesian inference allows us to reason about ψ in light of data via the posterior distribution $p(\psi \mid \mathcal{D})$, and we will use this belief to inform our decision.

utility function, $u(a, \psi, \mathcal{D})$

Suppose now we must select a decision from an action space $\mathcal{A}$ under uncertainty in ψ, informed by a set of observed data $\mathcal{D}$. To guide our choice, we select a real-valued *utility function* $u(a, \psi, \mathcal{D})$. This function measures the quality of selecting the action a if the true state of the world were revealed to be ψ, with higher utilities indicating more favorable outcomes. The arguments to a utility function comprise everything required to judge the quality of a decision in hindsight: the proposed action a, what we know (the data $\mathcal{D}$), and what we don't know (the uncertain elements ψ).[4]

4 Typical presentations of Bayesian decision theory omit the data from the utility function, but including it offers more generality, and this allowance will be important when we turn our attention to optimization policies.

We cannot know the exact utility that would result from selecting any given action a priori, due to our incomplete knowledge of ψ. We can, however, compute the *expected* utility that would result from selecting an action a, according to our posterior belief:

expected utility

$$\mathbb{E}\big[u(a, \psi, \mathcal{D}) \mid a, \mathcal{D}\big] = \int u(a, \psi, \mathcal{D}) \, p(\psi \mid \mathcal{D}) \, \mathrm{d}\psi. \tag{5.2}$$

This expected utility maps each available action to a real value, inducing a total order and providing a straightforward mechanism for making our decision. We pick an action maximizing the expected utility:

$$a \in \arg\max_{a' \in \mathcal{A}} \mathbb{E}\big[u(a', \psi, \mathcal{D}) \mid a', \mathcal{D}\big]. \tag{5.3}$$

5 One may question whether this framework is complete in some sense: is it possible to make rational decisions in some other manner? The *von Neumann–Morgenstern theorem* shows that the answer is, surprisingly, no. Assuming a certain set of rationality axioms, *any* rational preferences over uncertain outcomes can be captured by the expectation of some utility function. Thus every rational decision maximizes an expected utility:

J. VON NEUMANN and O. MORGENSTERN (1944). *Theory of Games and Economic Behavior.* Princeton University Press. [appendix A]

This decision is optimal in the sense that no other action results in greater expected utility. (By definition!) This procedure for acting optimally under uncertainty – computing expected utility with respect to relevant unknown variables and maximizing to select an action – is the central tenant of Bayesian decision making.[5]

Example: recommending a point for use after optimization

With this abstract decision-making framework established, let us analyze an example decision that might be faced in the context of optimization. Consider a scenario where the purpose of optimization is to identify a single point $x \in \mathcal{X}$ for perpetual use in a production system, preferring locations achieving higher values of the objective function. If we run an optimizer and it returns some dataset $\mathcal{D}$, which point should we select for our final recommendation?

We may model this choice as a decision problem with action space $\mathcal{A} = \mathcal{X}$, where we must reason under uncertainty about the objective function f. We first select a utility function quantifying the quality of a given recommendation x in hindsight. One natural choice would be

$$u(x, f) = f(x) = \phi,$$

which rewards points for achieving high values of the objective function. Now if our optimization procedure returned a dataset $\mathcal{D}$, the expected utility from recommending a point x is simply the posterior mean of the corresponding function value:

$$\mathbb{E}[u(x, f) \mid x, \mathcal{D}] = \mathbb{E}[\phi \mid x, \mathcal{D}] = \mu_{\mathcal{D}}(x). \tag{5.4}$$

Therefore, an optimal recommendation maximizes the posterior mean:

$$x \in \arg\max_{x' \in \mathcal{X}} \mu_{\mathcal{D}}(x').$$

Of course, other considerations in a given scenario such as risk aversion might suggest some other utility function or action space would be more appropriate, in which case we are free to select any alternative as we see fit. We will discuss terminal recommendations at length in the next chapter, including alternative utility functions and action spaces.

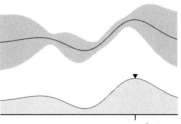

recommendation

Optimal terminal recommendation. Above: posterior belief about an objective function given the data returned by an optimizer, $p(f \mid \mathcal{D})$. Below: the expected utility for our example, the posterior mean $\mu_{\mathcal{D}}(x)$. The optimal recommendation maximizes the expected utility.

terminal recommendations: § 6.1, p. 109

5.2 SEQUENTIAL DECISIONS WITH A FIXED BUDGET

We have now introduced Bayesian decision theory as a framework for computing optimal decisions informed by data. The key idea is to measure the post hoc quality of a decision with an appropriately designed utility function, then choose actions maximizing expected utility according to our beliefs. We will now apply this idea to the construction of optimization policies. This setting is considerably more complicated because each decision we make over the course of optimization will shape the context of all future decisions.

Modeling policy decisions

To define an optimization routine, we must design a policy to adaptively design a sequence of observations seeking the optimum. Following our discussion in the previous section, we will model each of these choices as a decision problem under uncertainty. Some aspects of this modeling will be straightforward and others will take some care. To begin, the action space of each decision is the domain $\mathcal{X}$, and we must act under uncertainty about the objective function f, which induces uncertainty about the outcomes of proposed observations. Fortunately, we may make each decision guided by any data obtained from previous decisions.

Bayesian inference of the objective function:
§ 1.2, p. 8

To reason about uncertainty in the objective function, we follow the path laid out in the preceding chapters and maintain a probabilistic belief throughout optimization, $p(f \mid \mathcal{D})$. We make no assumptions regarding the nature of this distribution, and in particular it need not be a Gaussian process. Equipped with this belief, we may reason about the result of making an observation at some point x via the posterior predictive distribution $p(y \mid x, \mathcal{D})$ (1.7), which will play a key role below.

optimization utility function, $u(\mathcal{D})$

The ultimate purpose of optimization is to collect and return a dataset $\mathcal{D}$. Before we can reason about what data we should acquire, we must first clarify what data we *would like* to acquire. Following the previous section, we will accomplish this by defining a utility function $u(\mathcal{D})$ to evaluate the quality of data returned by an optimizer. This utility function will serve to establish preferences over optimization outcomes: all other things being equal, we would prefer to return a dataset with higher utility than any dataset with lower utility. As before, we will use this utility to guide the design of policies, by making observations that, in expectation, promise the biggest improvement in utility. We will define and motivate several utility functions used for optimization in the next chapter, and some readers may wish to jump ahead to that discussion for explicit examples before continuing. In the following, we will develop the general theory in terms of an arbitrary utility function.

Chapter 6: Utility Functions for Optimization, p. 109

Uncertainty faced during optimization

Suppose $\mathcal{D}$ is a dataset of previous observations and that we must select the next observation location x. This is the core decision defining an optimization policy, and we will make all such decisions in the same manner: by maximizing the expected utility of the data we will return.

Although this sounds straightforward, let us consider the uncertainty faced when contemplating this decision in more detail. When evaluating a potential action x, uncertainty in the objective function induces uncertainty in the corresponding value y we will observe. Bayesian inference allows us to reason about this uncertain outcome via the posterior predictive distribution (1.7), and we may hope to be able to address this uncertainty without much trouble. However, we must also consider that evaluating at x would add the unknown observation (x, y) to our dataset, and that the contents of this updated dataset would be consulted for all future decisions. Thus we must reason not only about the outcome of the present observation but also its impact on the *entire remainder of optimization*. This requires special attention and distinguishes sequential decisions from the isolated decisions discussed in the last section.

Intuitively, we might suspect that decisions made closer to termination should be easier, as fewer future decisions depend on their outcomes. This is indeed the case, and it will be prudent to define optimization policies *in reverse*.[6] We will first reason about the *final* decision – when we are freed from the burden of having to ponder any future observations – and proceed backwards to the choice of the first observation location, working out optimal behavior every step along the way.

6 In fact, we have already begun by analyzing a decision *after* optimization has completed!

In this section we will consider the construction of optimization policies assuming that we have a fixed and known budget on the number of observations we will make. This scenario is both common in practice and convenient for analysis, as we can for now ignore the question of when to terminate optimization. Note that this assumption effectively implies that every observation has a constant acquisition cost, which may not always be reasonable. We will address variable observation costs and the question of when to stop optimization later in this chapter.

Assuming a fixed observation budget allows us to reason about optimization policies in terms of the number of observations remaining to termination, which will always be known. The problem we will consider in this section then becomes the following: provided an arbitrary set of data, how should we design our next evaluation location when exactly τ observations remain before termination? In sequential decision making, this value is known as the decision *horizon,* as it indicates how far we must look ahead into the future when reasoning about the present.

To facilitate our discussion, we pause to define notation for future data that will be encountered during optimization relative to the present. When considering an observation at some point x, we will call the value resulting from an observation there y. We will then call the dataset available at the next stage of optimization $\mathcal{D}_1 = \mathcal{D} \cup \{(x, y)\}$, where the subscript indicates the number of future observations incorporated into the current data. We will write (x_2, y_2) for the following observation, which when acquired will form $\mathcal{D}_2$, etc. Our final observation τ steps in the future will then be (x_τ, y_τ), and the dataset returned by our optimization procedure will be $\mathcal{D}_\tau$, with utility $u(\mathcal{D}_\tau)$.

This utility of the data we return is our ultimate concern and will serve as the utility function used to design every observation. Note we may write this utility in the same form we introduced in our general discussion:

$$u(\mathcal{D}_\tau) = u(\underbrace{\mathcal{D},}_{\text{known}}\ \underbrace{x,}_{\text{action}}\ \underbrace{y, x_2, y_2, \ldots, x_\tau, y_\tau}_{\text{unknown}}),$$

which expresses the terminal utility in terms of a proposed current action x, the known data $\mathcal{D}$, and the unknown future data to be obtained: the not-yet observed value y, and the locations $\{x_2, \ldots, x_\tau\}$ and values $\{y_2, \ldots, y_\tau\}$ of any following observations.

Following our treatment of isolated decisions, we evaluate a potential observation location x via the expected utility at termination ultimately obtained if we observe at that point next:

$$\mathbb{E}\big[u(\mathcal{D}_\tau) \mid x, \mathcal{D}\big], \tag{5.5}$$

and define an optimization policy via maximization:

$$x \in \arg\max_{x' \in \mathcal{X}} \mathbb{E}\big[u(\mathcal{D}_\tau) \mid x', \mathcal{D}\big]. \tag{5.6}$$

On its surface, this proposal is relatively simple. However, we must now consider how to actually *compute* the expected terminal utility (5.5).

fixed, known budget

cost-aware optimization: § 5.4, p. 103

number of remaining observations (horizon), τ

putative next observation and dataset: (x, y), $\mathcal{D}_1$

putative following observation and dataset: (x_2, y_2), $\mathcal{D}_2$

putative final observation and dataset: (x_τ, y_τ), $\mathcal{D}_\tau$

expected terminal utility, $\mathbb{E}\big[u(\mathcal{D}_\tau) \mid x, \mathcal{D}\big]$

Explicitly writing out the expectation over the future data in (5.5) yields the following expression:

$$\int \cdots \int u(\mathcal{D}_\tau)\, p(y \mid x, \mathcal{D}) \prod_{i=2}^{\tau} p(x_i, y_i \mid \mathcal{D}_{i-1})\, \mathrm{d}y\, \mathrm{d}\{(x_i, y_i)\}. \qquad (5.7)$$

This integral certainly appears unwieldy! In particular, it is unclear how to reason about uncertainty in our future actions, as we should hope that these actions are made to maximize our welfare rather than generated by a random process. We will show how to compute this expression under the bold but rational assumption that we *make all future decisions optimally*,[7] and this analysis will reveal the optimal optimization policy.

We will proceed via induction on the number of evaluations remaining before termination, τ. We will first determine optimal behavior when only one observation remains and then inductively consider increasingly long horizons.[8] For this analysis it will be useful to introduce notation for the expected *increase* in utility achieved when beginning from an arbitrary dataset $\mathcal{D}$, making an observation at x, and then continuing optimally until termination τ steps in the future. We will write

$$\alpha_\tau(x; \mathcal{D}) = \mathbb{E}\big[u(\mathcal{D}_\tau) \mid x, \mathcal{D}\big] - u(\mathcal{D})$$

for this quantity, which is simply the expected terminal utility (5.5) shifted by the utility of our existing data, $u(\mathcal{D})$. It is no coincidence this notation echoes our notation for acquisition functions! We will characterize the optimal optimization policy by a family of acquisition functions defined in this manner.

defining a policy by maximizing an acquisition function: § 5, p. 88

Fixed budget: one observation remaining

We first consider the case where only one observation remains before termination; that is, the horizon is $\tau = 1$. In this case the terminal dataset will be the current dataset augmented with a single additional observation. As there are no following decisions to consider, we may analyze the decision using the framework we have already developed for isolated decisions. The marginal gain in utility from a final evaluation at x is an expectation over the corresponding value y with respect to the posterior predictive distribution:

isolated decisions: § 5.1, p. 89

$$\alpha_1(x; \mathcal{D}) = \int u(\mathcal{D}_1)\, p(y \mid x, \mathcal{D})\, \mathrm{d}y - u(\mathcal{D}). \qquad (5.8)$$

The optimal observation maximizes the expected marginal gain:

$$x \in \arg\max_{x' \in \mathcal{X}} \alpha_1(x'; \mathcal{D}), \qquad (5.9)$$

and leads to our returning a dataset with expected utility

$$u(\mathcal{D}) + \alpha_1^*(\mathcal{D}); \qquad \alpha_1^*(\mathcal{D}) = \max_{x' \in \mathcal{X}} \alpha_1(x'; \mathcal{D}). \qquad (5.10)$$

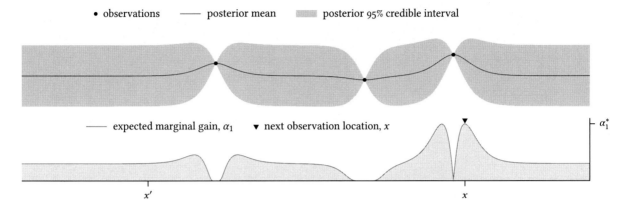

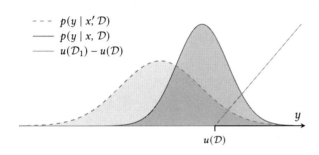

Figure 5.1: Illustration of the optimal optimization policy with a horizon of one. Above: we compute the expected marginal gain α_1 over the domain and design our next observation x by maximizing this score. Left: the computation of the expected marginal gain for the optimal point x and a suboptimal point x' indicated above. In this example the marginal gain is a simple piecewise linear function of the observed value (5.11), and the optimal point maximizes its expectation.

Here we have defined the symbol $\alpha_\tau^*(\mathcal{D})$ to represent the expected increase in utility when starting with $\mathcal{D}$ and continuing *optimally* for τ additional observations. This is called the *value* of the dataset with a horizon of τ and will serve a central role below. We have now shown how to compute the value of any dataset with a horizon of $\tau = 1$ (5.10) and how to identify a corresponding optimal action (5.9). This completes the base case of our argument.

We illustrate the optimal optimization policy with one observation remaining in Figure 5.1. In this scenario the belief over the objective function $p(f \mid \mathcal{D})$ is a Gaussian process, and for simplicity we assume our observations reveal exact values of the objective. We consider an intuitive utility function: the maximal objective value contained in the data, $u(\mathcal{D}) = \max f(\mathbf{x})$.[9] The marginal gain in utility offered by a putative final observation (x, y) is then a piecewise linear function of the observed value:

$$u(\mathcal{D}_1) - u(\mathcal{D}) = \max\{y - u(\mathcal{D}), 0\}; \qquad (5.11)$$

that is, the utility increases linearly if we exceed the previously best-seen value and otherwise remains constant. To design the optimal final observation, we compute the expectation of this quantity over the domain and choose the point maximizing it, as shown in the top panels. We also illustrate the computation of this expectation for the optimal choice and

value of $\mathcal{D}$ with horizon τ, $\alpha_\tau^*(\mathcal{D})$

illustration of one-step optimal optimization policy

9 This is a special case of the *simple reward* utility function, which we discuss further in the next chapter (§ 6.1, p. 109). The corresponding expected marginal gain is the well-known *expected improvement* acquisition function (§ 7.3, p. 127).

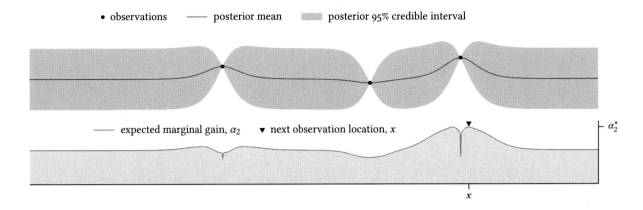

Figure 5.2: Illustration of the optimal optimization policy with a horizon of two. Above: the expected two-step marginal gain α_2. Right: computation of α_2 for the optimal point x. The marginal gain is decomposed into two components (5.13): the immediate gain $u(\mathcal{D}_1) - u(\mathcal{D})$ and the expected future gain $\mathbb{E}[u(\mathcal{D}_2) - u(\mathcal{D}_1)]$. The chosen point offers a high expected future reward even if the immediate reward is zero; see the facing page for the scenarios resulting from the marked values.

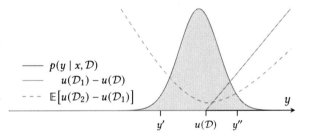

a suboptimal alternative in the bottom panel. We expect an observation at the chosen location to improve utility by a greater amount than any alternative.

Fixed budget: two observations remaining

Rather than proceeding immediately to the inductive case, let us consider the specific case of two observations remaining: $\tau = 2$. Suppose we have obtained an arbitrary dataset $\mathcal{D}$ and must decide where to make the *penultimate* observation x. The reasoning for this special case presents the inductive argument most clearly.

We again consider the expected increase in utility by termination, now after two observations:

$$\alpha_2(x; \mathcal{D}) = \mathbb{E}[u(\mathcal{D}_2) \mid x, \mathcal{D}] - u(\mathcal{D}). \tag{5.12}$$

Nominally this expectation requires marginalizing the observation y, as well as the final observation location x_2 and its value y_2 (5.7). However, *if we assume optimal future behavior*, we can simplify our treatment of the final decision x_2. First, we rewrite the two-step expected gain α_2 in terms of the one-step expected gain α_1, a function for which we have already established a good understanding. We write the two-step difference in

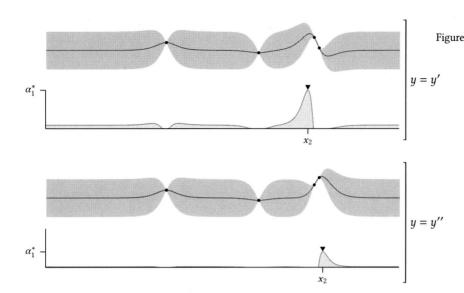

Figure 5.3: The posterior of the objective function given two possible observations resulting from the optimal two-step observation x illustrated on the facing page. The relatively low value y' offers no immediate reward, but reveals a new local optimum and the expected future reward from the optimal final decision x_2 is high. The relatively high value y'' offers a large immediate reward and respectable prospects from the optimal final decision as well.

utility as a telescoping sum:

$$u(\mathcal{D}_2) - u(\mathcal{D}) = \big[u(\mathcal{D}_1) - u(\mathcal{D})\big] + \big[u(\mathcal{D}_2) - u(\mathcal{D}_1)\big],$$

which yields

$$\alpha_2(x; \mathcal{D}) = \alpha_1(x; \mathcal{D}) + \mathbb{E}\big[\alpha_1(x_2; \mathcal{D}_1) \mid x, \mathcal{D}\big].$$

That is, the expected increase in utility after two observations can be decomposed as the expected increase after our first observation x – the expected *immediate* gain – plus the expected additional increase from the final observation x_2 – the expected *future* gain.

decomposition of expected marginal gain

It is still not clear how to address the second term in this expression. However, from our analysis of the base case, we can reason as follows. Given y (and thus knowledge of $\mathcal{D}_1$), the *optimal* final decision x_2 (5.9) results in an expected marginal gain of $\alpha_1^*(\mathcal{D}_1)$, a quantity we know how to compute (5.10). Therefore, assuming optimal future behavior, we have:

$$\alpha_2(x; \mathcal{D}) = \alpha_1(x; \mathcal{D}) + \mathbb{E}\big[\alpha_1^*(\mathcal{D}_1) \mid x, \mathcal{D}\big], \tag{5.13}$$

which expresses the desired quantity as an expectation with respect to the current observation y only – the future value α_1^* (5.10) does not depend on either x_2 (due to maximization) or y_2 (due to expectation). The optimal penultimate observation location maximizes the expected gain as usual:

$$x \in \arg\max_{x' \in \mathcal{X}} \alpha_2(x'; \mathcal{D}), \tag{5.14}$$

and provides an expected terminal utility of

$$u(\mathcal{D}) + \alpha_2^*(\mathcal{D}); \qquad \alpha_2^*(\mathcal{D}) = \max_{x' \in \mathcal{X}} \alpha_2(x'; \mathcal{D}).$$

This demonstrates we can achieve optimal behavior for a horizon of $\tau = 2$ and compute the value of any dataset with this horizon.

The optimal policy with two observations remaining is illustrated in Figures 5.2 and 5.3. The former shows the expected two-step marginal gain α_2 and the optimal action. This quantity depends both on the immediate gain from the next observation and the expected future gain from the optimal final action. The chosen observation appears quite promising: even if the result offers no immediate gain, it will likely provide information that can be exploited with the optimal final decision x_2. We show the situation that would be faced in the final stage of optimization for two potential values in Figure 5.3. The relatively low value y' offers no immediate gain but sets up an encouraging final decision, whereas the relatively high value y'' offers a significant immediate gain with some chance of further improvement.

Fixed budget: inductive case

We now present the general inductive argument, which closely follows the $\tau = 2$ analysis above. Let τ be an arbitrary decision horizon, and for the sake of induction assume we can compute the value of any dataset with a horizon of $\tau - 1$. Suppose we have an arbitrary dataset $\mathcal{D}$ and must decide where to make the next observation. We will show how to do so optimally and how to compute its value with a horizon of τ.

Consider the τ-step expected gain in utility from observing at some point x:

$$\alpha_\tau(x; \mathcal{D}) = \mathbb{E}\big[u(\mathcal{D}_\tau) \mid x, \mathcal{D}\big] - u(\mathcal{D}),$$

which we seek to maximize. We decompose this expression in terms of shorter-horizon quantities through a telescoping sum:[10]

$$\alpha_\tau(x; \mathcal{D}) = \alpha_1(x; \mathcal{D}) + \mathbb{E}\big[\alpha_{\tau-1}(x_2; \mathcal{D}_1) \mid x, \mathcal{D}\big].$$

Now if we knew y (and thus $\mathcal{D}_1$), optimal continued behavior would provide an expected further gain of $\alpha^*_{\tau-1}(\mathcal{D}_1)$, a quantity we can compute via the inductive hypothesis. Therefore, assuming optimal behavior for all remaining decisions, we have:

$$\alpha_\tau(x; \mathcal{D}) = \alpha_1(x; \mathcal{D}) + \mathbb{E}\big[\alpha^*_{\tau-1}(\mathcal{D}_1) \mid x, \mathcal{D}\big], \tag{5.15}$$

which is an expectation with respect to y of a function we can compute. To find the optimal decision and the τ-step value of the data, we maximize:

$$x \in \arg\max_{x' \in \mathcal{X}} \alpha_\tau(x'; \mathcal{D}); \tag{5.16}$$

$$\alpha^*_\tau(\mathcal{D}) = \max_{x' \in \mathcal{X}} \alpha_\tau(x'; \mathcal{D}). \tag{5.17}$$

This demonstrates we can achieve optimal behavior for a horizon of τ given an arbitrary dataset and compute its corresponding value, establishing the inductive case and completing our analysis.

illustration of two-step optimal optimization policy

10 Namely:

$$u(\mathcal{D}_\tau) - u(\mathcal{D}) =$$
$$\big[u(\mathcal{D}_1) - u(\mathcal{D})\big] + \big[u(\mathcal{D}_\tau) - u(\mathcal{D}_1)\big].$$

We pause to note that the value of any dataset with null horizon is $\alpha_0^*(\mathcal{D}) = 0$, and thus the expressions in (5.15–5.17) are valid for any horizon and compactly express the proposed policy. Further, we have actually shown that this policy is *optimal* in the sense of maximizing expected terminal utility over the space of all policies, at least with respect to our model of the objective function and observations. This follows from our induction: the base case is established in (5.9), and the inductive case by the sequential maximization in (5.16).[11]

Bellman optimality and the Bellman equation

Substituting (5.15) into (5.17), we may derive the following recursive definition of the value in terms of the value of future data:

$$\alpha_\tau^*(\mathcal{D}) = \max_{x' \in \mathcal{X}} \left\{ \alpha_1(x'; \mathcal{D}) + \mathbb{E}\left[\alpha_{\tau-1}^*(\mathcal{D}_1) \mid x', \mathcal{D} \right] \right\}. \qquad (5.18)$$

This is known as the *Bellman equation* and is a central result in the theory of optimal sequential decisions.[12] The treatment of future decisions in this equation – recursively assuming that we will always act to maximize expected terminal utility given the available data – reflects BELLMAN's *principle of optimality*, which characterizes optimal sequential decision policies in terms of the optimality of subpolicies:[13]

> An optimal policy has the property that whatever the initial state and initial decision are, the remaining decisions must constitute an optimal policy with regard to the state resulting from the first decision.

That is, to make a sequence of optimal decisions, we make the first decision optimally, then make all following decisions optimally given the outcome!

5.3 COST AND APPROXIMATION OF THE OPTIMAL POLICY

Although the framework presented in the previous section is conceptually simple and theoretically attractive, the optimal policy is unfortunately prohibitive to compute except for very short decision horizons.

To demonstrate the key computational barrier, consider the selection of the penultimate observation location. The expected two-step marginal gain to be maximized is (5.13):

$$\alpha_2(x; \mathcal{D}) = \alpha_1(x; \mathcal{D}) + \mathbb{E}\left[\alpha_1^*(\mathcal{D}_1) \mid x, \mathcal{D} \right].$$

The second term appears to be a straightforward expectation over the one-dimensional random variable y. However, evaluating the integrand in this expectation requires solving a nontrivial global optimization problem (5.10)! Even with only two evaluations remaining, we must solve a doubly nested global optimization problem, an onerous task.

Close inspection of the recursively defined optimal policy (5.15–5.16) reveals that when faced with a horizon of τ, we must solve τ nested

optimal policy: compact notation

optimality

11 Since ties in (5.16) may be broken arbitrarily, this argument does not rule out the possibility of there being multiple, equally good optimal policies.

12 R. BELLMAN (1952). On the Theory of Dynamic Programming. *Proceedings of the National Academy of Sciences* 38(8):716–719.

Bellman equation

BELLMAN's principle of optimality

13 R. BELLMAN (1957). *Dynamic Programming.* Princeton University Press.

"unrolling" the optimal sequential policy

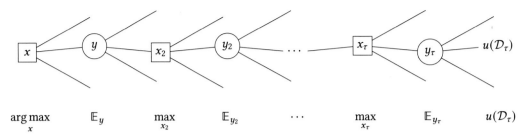

Figure 5.4: The optimal optimization policy as a decision tree. Squares indicate decisions (the choice of each observation), and circles represent expectations with respect to random variables (the outcomes of observations). Only one possible optimization path is shown; dangling edges lead to different futures, and all possibilities are always considered. We maximize the expected terminal utility $u(\mathcal{D}_\tau)$, recursively assuming optimal future behavior.

optimization problems to find the optimal decision. Temporarily adopting compact notation, we may "unroll" the optimal policy as follows:

$$x \in \arg\max \alpha_\tau;$$

$$\begin{aligned}
\alpha_\tau &= \alpha_1 + \mathbb{E}[\alpha_{\tau-1}^*] \\
&= \alpha_1 + \mathbb{E}[\max \alpha_{\tau-1}] \\
&= \alpha_1 + \mathbb{E}[\max\{\alpha_1 + \mathbb{E}[\alpha_{\tau-2}^*]\}] \\
&= \alpha_1 + \mathbb{E}[\max\{\alpha_1 + \mathbb{E}[\max\{\alpha_1 + \mathbb{E}[\max\{\alpha_1 + \cdots\}]\}]\}].
\end{aligned}$$

The design of each optimal decision requires repeated maximization over the domain and expectation over unknown observations until the horizon is reached. This computation is visualized as a decision tree in Figure 5.4, where it is clear that each unknown quantity contributes a significant branching factor. Computing the expected utility at x exactly requires a complete traversal of this tree.

running time of optimal policy

The cost of computing the optimal policy clearly grows with the horizon. Let us perform a careful running time analysis for a naïve implementation via exhaustive traversal of the decision tree in Figure 5.4 with off-the-shelf procedures. Suppose we use an optimization routine for each maximization and a numerical quadrature routine for each expectation encountered in this computation. If we allow n evaluations of the objective for each call to the optimizer and q observations of the integrand for each call to the quadrature routine, then each decision along the horizon will contribute a multiplicative factor of $\mathcal{O}(nq)$ to the total running time. Computing the optimal decision with a horizon of τ thus requires $\mathcal{O}(n^\tau q^\tau)$ work, an exponential growth in running time with respect to the horizon.

evaluation budget for optimization, n
evaluation budget for quadrature, q

Evidently, the computational effort required for realizing the optimal policy quickly becomes intractable, and we must find some alternative mechanism for designing effective optimization policies. General approximation schemes for the optimal policy have been studied in depth under the name *approximate dynamic programming*,[14] and usually operate as

14 Detailed references are provided by:

W. B. POWELL (2011). *Approximate Dynamic Programming: Solving the Curses of Dimensionality*. John Wiley & Sons.

D. P. BERTSEKAS (2017). *Dynamic Programming and Optimal Control*. Vol. 1. Athena Scientific.

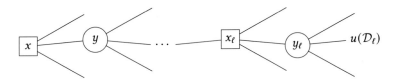

Figure 5.5: A lookahead approximation to the optimal optimization policy. We choose the optimal decision for a limited horizon $\ell \ll \tau$ decisions, ignoring any observations that would follow.

follows. We begin with the intractable optimal expected marginal gain (5.15):

$$\alpha_\tau(x; \mathcal{D}) = \alpha_1(x; \mathcal{D}) + \mathbb{E}\big[\alpha^*_{\tau-1}(\mathcal{D}_1) \mid x, \mathcal{D}\big],$$

and substitute a tractable approximation for the "hard" part of the expression: the recursively defined future value α^* (5.18). The result is an acquisition function inducing a suboptimal – but rationally guided – approximate policy. Two particular approximations schemes have proven useful in Bayesian optimization: *limited lookahead* and *rollout*.

Limited lookahead

One widespread and surprisingly effective approximation is to simply limit how many future observations we consider in each decision. This is practical as decisions closer to termination require substantially less computation than earlier decisions.

   With this in mind, we can construct a natural family of approximations to the optimal policy defined by artificially limiting the horizon used throughout optimization to some computationally feasible maximum ℓ. When faced with an infeasible decision horizon τ, we make the crude approximation

$$\alpha_\tau(x; \mathcal{D}) \approx \alpha_\ell(x; \mathcal{D}),$$

and by maximizing this score, we act optimally under the incorrect but convenient assumption that only ℓ observations remain. This effectively assumes $u(\mathcal{D}_\tau) \approx u(\mathcal{D}_\ell)$.[15] This may be reasonable if we expect decreasing marginal gains, implying a significant fraction of potential gains can be attained within the truncated horizon. This scheme is often described (sometimes disparagingly) as *myopic*, as we limit our sight to only the next few observations rather than looking ahead to the full horizon.

   A policy that designs each observation to maximize the limited-horizon acquisition function $\alpha_{\min\{\ell,\tau\}}$ is called an *ℓ-step lookahead* policy.[16] This is also called a *rolling horizon* strategy, as the fixed horizon "rolls along" with us as we go. By limiting the horizon, we bound the computational effort required for each decision to at-most $\mathcal{O}(n^\ell q^\ell)$ time with the implementation described above. This can be a considerable speedup when the observation budget is much greater than the selected lookahead. A lookahead policy is illustrated as a decision tree in Figure 5.5. Comparing to the optimal policy in Figure 5.4, we simply "cut off" and ignore any portion of the tree lying deeper than ℓ steps in the future.

15 Equivalently, we approximate the true future value $\alpha^*_{\tau-1}$ with $\alpha^*_{\ell-1}$.

myopic approximations

ℓ-step lookahead
rolling horizon

16 We take the minimum to ensure we don't look *beyond* the true horizon, which would be nonsense.

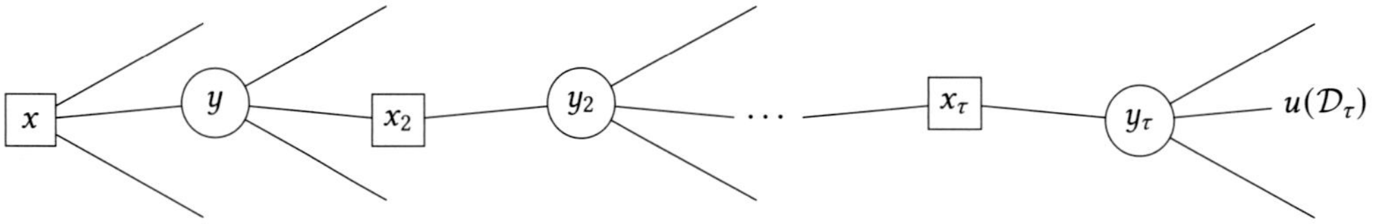

Figure 5.6: A decision tree representing a rollout policy. Comparing to the optimal policy in Figure 5.4, we simulate future decisions starting with x_2 using an efficient but *suboptimal* heuristic policy, rather than the intractable optimal policy. We maximize the expected terminal utility $u(\mathcal{D}_\tau)$, assuming potentially suboptimal future behavior.

one-step lookahead

Particularly important in Bayesian optimization is the special case of *one-step lookahead,* which successively maximizes the expected marginal gain after acquiring a single additional observation, α_1. One-step lookahead is the most efficient lookahead approximation (barring the absurdity that would be "zero-step" lookahead), and it is often possible to derive closed-form, analytically differentiable expressions for α_1, enabling efficient implementation. Many well-known acquisition functions represent one-step lookahead approximations for some implicit choice of utility function, as we will see in Chapter 7.

Chapter 7: Common Bayesian Optimization Policies, p. 123

Rollout

The optimal policy evaluates a potential observation location by simulating the entire remainder of optimization following that choice, recursively assuming we will use the *optimal* policy for every future decision. Although sensible, this is clearly intractable. *Rollout* is an approach to approximate policy design that emulates the structure of the optimal policy, but using a tractable *suboptimal* policy to simulate future decisions.

A rollout policy is illustrated as a decision tree in Figure 5.6. Given a putative next observation (x, y), we use an inexpensive so-called *base* or *heuristic* policy to simulate a plausible – but perhaps suboptimal – realization of the following decision x_2. Note there is no branching in the tree corresponding to this decision, as it does not depend on the exhaustively enumerated subtree required by the optimal policy. We then take an expectation with respect to the unknown value y_2 as usual. Given a putative value of y_2, we use the base policy to select x_3 and continue in this manner until reaching the decision horizon. We use the terminal utilities in the resulting pruned tree to estimate the expected marginal gain α_τ, which we maximize as a function of x.

base policy, heuristic policy

choice of base policy

There are no constraints on the design of the base policy used in rollout; however, for this approximation to be sensible, we must choose something relatively efficient. One common and often effective choice is to simulate future decisions with one-step lookahead. If we again use off-the-shelf optimization and quadrature routines to traverse the rollout decision tree in Figure 5.6 with this particular choice, the running time of the policy with a horizon of τ is $\mathcal{O}(n^2 q^\tau)$, significantly faster

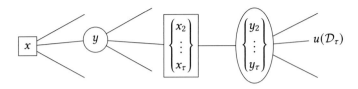

Figure 5.7: A batch rollout policy as a decision tree. Given a putative value for the next evaluation (x, y), we design all remaining decisions simultaneously using a batch base policy and take the expectation of the terminal utility with respect to their values.

than the optimal policy. Although there is still exponential growth with respect to q, we typically have $q \ll n$,[17] so we can usually entertain farther horizons with rollout than with limited lookahead with the same amount of computational effort.

Due to the flexibility in the design of the base policy, rollout is a remarkably flexible approximation scheme. For example, we can combine rollout with the idea of limiting the decision horizon to yield approximate policies with tunable running time. In fact, we can interpret ℓ-step lookahead as a special case of rollout, where the base policy designs the next $\ell - 1$ decisions optimally assuming a myopic horizon and then simply *terminates early*, discarding any remaining budget.

We may also adopt a base policy that designs all remaining observations *simultaneously*. Ignoring the dependence between these decisions can provide a computational advantage while retaining awareness of the evolving decision horizon, and such *batch rollout* schemes have proven useful in Bayesian optimization. A batch rollout policy is illustrated as a decision tree in Figure 5.7. Although we account for the entire horizon, the tree depth is reduced dramatically compared to the optimal policy.

17 For estimating a one-dimensional expectation we might take q on the order of roughly 10, but for optimizing a nonconvex acquisition function over the domain we might take n on the order of thousands or more.

limited lookahead as rollout

batch rollout

5.4 COST-AWARE OPTIMIZATION AND TERMINATION AS A DECISION

Thus far we have only considered the construction of optimization policies under a known budget on the total number of observations. Although this scenario is pervasive, it is not universal. In some situations, we might wish instead to use our evolving beliefs about the objective function to decide *dynamically* when termination is the best course of action.

Dynamic termination can be especially prudent when we want to reason explicitly about the cost of data acquisition during optimization. For example, if this cost were to *vary* across the domain, it would not be sensible to define a budget in terms of function evaluations. However, by accounting for observation costs in the utility function, we can reason about cost–benefit tradeoffs during optimization and seek to terminate whenever the expected cost of further observation outweighs any expected benefit it might provide.

Modeling termination decisions and the optimal policy

We consider a modification to the sequential decision problem we analyzed in the known-budget case, wherein we now allow ourselves to

action space, $\mathcal{A}$

termination option, $\varnothing$

bound on total number of observations, τ_{max}

18 It is possible to consider unbounded sequential decision problems, but this is probably not of practical interest in Bayesian optimization:

M. H. DEGROOT (1970). *Optimal Statistical Decisions*. McGraw–Hill. [§ 12.7]

19 This can be proven through various "information never hurts" (in expectation) results.

terminate optimization at any time of our choosing. Suppose we are at an arbitrary point of optimization and have already obtained data $\mathcal{D}$. We face the following decision: should we terminate optimization immediately and return $\mathcal{D}$? If not, where should we make our next observation?

We model this scenario as a decision problem under uncertainty with an action space equal to the domain $\mathcal{X}$, representing potential observation locations if we decide to continue, augmented with a special additional action $\varnothing$ representing immediate termination:

$$\mathcal{A} = \mathcal{X} \cup \{\varnothing\}. \qquad (5.19)$$

For the sake of analysis, after the termination action has been selected, it is convenient to model the decision process as not actually terminating, but rather continuing with the collapsed action space $\mathcal{A} = \{\varnothing\}$ – once you terminate, there's no going back.

As before, we may derive the optimal optimization policy in the adaptive termination case via induction on the decision horizon τ. However, we must address one technical issue: the base case of the induction, which analyzes the "final" decision, breaks down if we allow the possibility of a nonterminating sequence of decisions. To sidestep this issue, we assume there is a fixed and known upper bound τ_{max} on the total number of observations we may make, at which point optimization is compelled to terminate regardless of any other concern. This is not an overly restrictive assumption in the context of Bayesian optimization. Because observations are assumed to be expensive, we can adopt some suitably absurd upper bound without issue; for example, $\tau_{max} = 1\,000\,000$ would suffice for an overwhelming majority of plausible scenarios.[18]

After assuming the decision process is bounded, our previous inductive argument carries through after we demonstrate how to compute the value of the termination action. Fortunately, this is straightforward: termination does not augment our data, and once this action is taken, no other action will ever again be allowed. Therefore the expected marginal gain from termination is always zero:

$$\alpha_\tau(\varnothing; \mathcal{D}) = 0. \qquad (5.20)$$

With this, substituting $\mathcal{A}$ for $\mathcal{X}$ in (5.15–5.17) now gives the optimal policy.

Intuitively, the result in (5.20) implies that termination is only the optimal decision if there is no observation offering positive expected gain in utility. For the utility functions described in the next chapter – all of which are agnostic to costs and measure optimization progress alone – reaching this state is actually *impossible*.[19] However, explicitly accounting for observation costs in addition to optimization progress in the utility function resolves this issue, as we will demonstrate.

Example: cost-aware optimization

To illustrate the behavior of a policy allowing early termination, we return to our motivating scenario of accounting for observation costs.

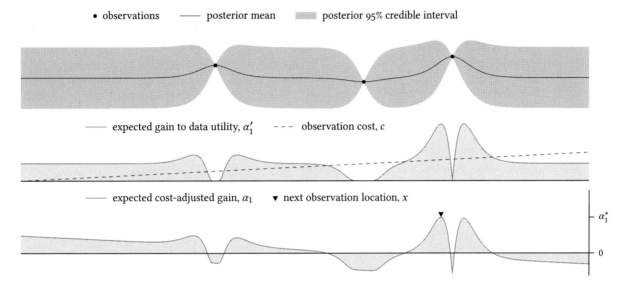

Figure 5.8: Illustration of one-step lookahead with the option to terminate. With a linear utility and additive costs, the expected marginal gain α_1 is the expected marginal gain to the data utility α_1' adjusted for the cost of acquisition c. For some points, the cost-adjusted expected gain is negative, in which case we would prefer immediate termination to observing there. However, continuing with the chosen point is expected to increase the utility of the current data.

Consider the objective function belief in the top panel of Figure 5.8 (which is identical to that from our running example from Figures 5.1–5.3) and suppose that the cost of observation now depends on location according to a known cost function $c(x)$,[20] illustrated in the middle panel.

If we wish to reason about observation costs in the optimization policy, we must account for them somehow, and the most natural place to do so is in the utility function. Depending on the situation, there are many ways we could proceed;[21] however, one natural approach is to first select a utility function measuring the quality of a returned dataset alone, ignoring any costs incurred to acquire it. We call this quantity the *data utility* and notate it with $u'(\mathcal{D})$. The data utility is akin to the cost-agnostic utility from the known-budget case, and any one of the options described in the next chapter could reasonably fill this role.

We now adjust the data utility to account for the cost of data acquisition. In many applications, these costs are additive, so that the total cost of gathering a dataset $\mathcal{D}$ is simply

$$c(\mathcal{D}) = \sum_{x \in \mathcal{D}} c(x). \tag{5.21}$$

If the acquisition cost can be expressed in the same units as the data utility – for example, if both can be expressed in monetary terms[22] – then we might reasonably evaluate a dataset $\mathcal{D}$ by the cost-adjusted utility:

$$u(\mathcal{D}) = u'(\mathcal{D}) - c(\mathcal{D}). \tag{5.22}$$

20 We will consider unknown and stochastic costs in § 11.1, p. 245.

observation cost function, $c(x)$

21 We wish to stress this point – there is considerable flexibility beyond the scheme we describe.

data utility, $u'(\mathcal{D})$

Chapter 6: Utility Functions for Optimization, p. 109

observation costs, $c(\mathcal{D})$

22 Some additional discussion on this natural approach can be found in:

H. RAIFFA and R. SCHLAIFER (1961). *Applied Statistical Decision Theory*. Division of Research, Graduate School of Business Administration, Harvard University. [chapter 4]

Demonstration: one-step lookahead with cost-aware utility

Returning to the scenario in Figure 5.8, let us adopt a cost-aware utility function of the above form (5.22) and consider the behavior of a one-step lookahead approximation to the optimal optimization policy.

For these choices, if we were to continue optimization by evaluating at a point x, the resulting one-step marginal gain in utility would be:

$$u(\mathcal{D}_1) - u(\mathcal{D}) = \left[u'(\mathcal{D}_1) - u'(\mathcal{D})\right] - c(x),$$

the cost-adjusted marginal gain in the data utility alone. Therefore the expected marginal gain in utility is:

$$\alpha_1(x; \mathcal{D}) = \alpha'_1(x; \mathcal{D}) - c(x),$$

where α'_1 is the one-step expected gain in the data utility (5.8). That is, we simply adjust what would have been the acquisition function in the cost-agnostic setting by subtracting the cost of data acquisition. To prefer evaluating at x to immediate termination, this quantity must have positive expected value (5.20).

The resulting policy is illustrated in Figure 5.8. The middle panel shows the cost-agnostic acquisition function α'_1 (from Figure 5.1), which is then adjusted for observation cost in the bottom panel. This renders the expected marginal gain negative in some locations, where observations are not expected to be worth their cost. However, in this case there are still regions where observation is favored to termination, and optimization continues at the selected location. Comparing with the cost-agnostic setting in Figure 5.1, the optimal observation has shifted from the right-hand side to the left-hand side of the previously best-seen point, as an observation there is more cost-effective.

example and discussion

5.5   SUMMARY OF MAJOR IDEAS

defining optimization policies via acquisition functions: p. 88

- Optimization policies can be conveniently defined via an *acquisition function* assigning a score to each potential observation location. We then design observations by maximizing the acquisition function (5.1).

- *Bayesian decision theory* is a general framework for optimal decision making under uncertainty, through which we can derive optimal optimization policies and stopping rules.

introduction to Bayesian decision theory: §5.1, p. 89

- The key elements of a decision problem under uncertainty are:

  - an *action space* $\mathcal{A}$, from which we must choose an action a,
  - uncertainty in elements ψ relevant to the decision, represented by a posterior belief $p(\psi \mid \mathcal{D})$, and
  - a *utility function* $u(a, \psi, \mathcal{D})$ quantifying the quality of the action a assuming a given realization of the uncertain elements ψ.

  Given these, an optimal decision maximizes the expected utility (5.2–5.3).

modeling policy decisions: §5.2, p. 91

- Optimization policy decisions may be cast in this framework by defining a utility function for the data returned by an optimizer, then designing each observation location to maximize the expected utility with respect to all future data yet to be obtained (5.5–5.6).

- To ensure the optimality of a *sequence* of decisions, we must recursively assume the optimality of all future decisions. This is known as BELLMAN's *principle of optimality*. Under this assumption, the optimal policy can be derived inductively and assumes a simple recursive form (5.15–5.17).

BELLMAN's principle of optimality: § 5.2, p. 99

- The cost of computing the optimal policy grows exponentially with the decision horizon, but several techniques under the umbrella *approximate dynamic programming* provide tractable approximations. Two notable examples are *limited lookahead,* where the decision horizon is artificially limited, and *rollout,* where future decisions are simulated suboptimally.

computational burden and approximation of the optimal policy: § 5.3, p. 99

- Through careful accounting, we may explicitly account for the (possibly nonuniform) cost of data acquisition in the utility function. Offering a termination option and computing the resulting optimal policy then allows us to adaptively terminate optimization when continuing optimization becomes a losing battle of cost versus expected gain.

termination as a decision: § 5.4, p. 103

In the next chapter we will discuss several prominent utility functions for measuring the quality of a dataset returned by an optimization procedure. In the following chapter, we will demonstrate how many common acquisition functions for Bayesian optimization may be realized by performing one-step lookahead with these utility functions.

Chapter 7: Common Bayesian Optimization Policies, p. 123

UTILITY FUNCTIONS FOR OPTIMIZATION

In the last chapter we introduced Bayesian decision theory, a framework for decision making under uncertainty through which we can derive theoretically optimal optimization policies. Central to this approach is the notion of a *utility function* evaluating the quality of a dataset returned from an optimization routine. Given a model of the objective function – conveying our *beliefs* in the face of uncertainty – and a utility function – expressing our *preferences* over outcomes – computing the optimal policy is purely mechanical: we design every observation to maximize the expected utility of the returned dataset (5.15–5.17). Setting aside computational issues, adopting this approach entails only two major hurdles: building an objective function model consistent with our beliefs and designing a utility function consistent with our preferences.

Neither of these tasks is trivial! Beliefs and preferences are so innate to the human experience that distilling them down to mathematical symbols can be challenging. Fortunately, expressive and mathematically convenient options for both are readily available. We devoted significant attention to model building in the first part of this book, and we will address the construction of utility functions in this chapter. We will introduce a number of common utility functions designed for optimization, each carrying a different perspective on how optimization performance should be quantified. We hope that the underlying motivation for these utility functions may inspire the design of novel alternatives when called for. In the next chapter, we will demonstrate how approximating the optimal optimization policy corresponding to the utility functions described here yields many widespread Bayesian optimization algorithms.

Chapter 7: Common Bayesian Optimization Policies, p. 123

Although we will be using Gaussian process models in our illustrations throughout the chapter, we will not assume the objective function model is a Gaussian process in our discussion. As in the previous chapters, we will use the notation $\mu_\mathcal{D}(x) = \mathbb{E}[\phi \mid x, \mathcal{D}]$ for the posterior mean of the objective function; this should not be interpreted as implying any particular model structure beyond admitting a posterior mean.

posterior mean function, $\mu_\mathcal{D}$

6.1 EXPECTED UTILITY OF TERMINAL RECOMMENDATION

The purpose of optimization is often to explore a space of possibilities in search of the single best alternative, and after investing in optimization, we commit to using some chosen point in a subsequent procedure. In this context, the only purpose of the data collected during optimization is to help select this final point. For example, in hyperparameter tuning, we may evaluate numerous hyperparameters during model development, only to use the apparently best settings found in a production system.

selecting a point for permanent use

Selecting a point for permanent use represents a *decision,* which we may analyze using Bayesian decision theory. If the sole purpose of optimization is to inform a final decision, it is natural to design the policy to maximize the expected utility of the terminal decision directly, and several popular policies are defined in this manner.

Chapter 5: Decision Theory for Optimization, p. 87

1 Dependence on ϕ alone is not strictly necessary. For example, in the interest of robustness
we might wish to ensure that function values
are high in the *neighborhood* of our recommendation as well. This would be possible in
the same framework by redefining the utility
function as desired.

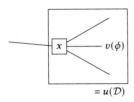

$$= u(\mathcal{D})$$

We may also interpret this class of utility functions as augmenting the decision tree in Figure
5.4 with a final layer corresponding to the terminal decision. The utility of the data is then
the expected utility of this subtree, assuming
optimal behavior.

bound on uncertainty

2   M. A. OSBORNE et al. (2009). Gaussian Processes
for Global Optimization. *LION 3*.

Formalization of terminal recommendation decision

Suppose we have run an optimization routine, which returned a dataset
$\mathcal{D} = (\mathbf{x}, \mathbf{y})$, and suppose we now wish to recommend a point $x \in \mathcal{X}$
for use in some task, with performance determined by the underlying
objective function value $\phi = f(x)$.[1] This represents a decision under
uncertainty about ϕ, informed by the predictive distribution, $p(\phi \mid x, \mathcal{D})$.

To completely specify the decision problem, we must identify an
action space $\mathcal{A} \subset \mathcal{X}$ for our recommendation and a utility function $v(\phi)$
evaluating a recommendation in hindsight according to its objective
value ϕ. Given these, a rational recommendation maximizes the expected
utility:

$$x \in \arg\max_{x' \in \mathcal{A}} \mathbb{E}\big[v(\phi') \mid x', \mathcal{D}\big].$$

The expected utility of the optimal recommendation only depends on
the data returned by the optimizer; it does not depend on the optimal
recommendation x (due to maximization) nor its objective value ϕ (due
to expectation). This suggests a natural utility for use in optimization:
the expected quality of an optimal terminal recommendation given the
data,

$$u(\mathcal{D}) = \max_{x' \in \mathcal{A}} \mathbb{E}\big[v(\phi') \mid x', \mathcal{D}\big]. \tag{6.1}$$

In the context of the sequential decision tree from Figure 5.4, this utility
function effectively "collapses" the expected utility of a final decision
into a utility for the returned data; see the illustration in the margin.
We are free to select the action space and utility function for the final
recommendation as we see fit; we provide some advice below.

Choosing an action space

We begin with the action space $\mathcal{A} \subset \mathcal{X}$. One extreme option is to restrict
our choice to only the visited points $\mathbf{x}$. This ensures at least some knowledge of the objective function at the recommended point, which may be
prudent when the objective function model may be misspecified. The
other extreme is the maximally permissive alternative: the entire domain
$\mathcal{X}$, allowing us to recommend any point, including those arbitrarily far
from our observations. The wisdom of recommending an unvisited point
for perpetual use is ultimately a question of faith in the model's beliefs.

Compromises between these extremes have also been occasionally
suggested in the literature. OSBORNE et al. for example proposed restricting the choice of final recommendation to only those points where the
objective function is known with acceptable tolerance.[2] Such a scheme
can limit unwanted surprise from recommending points where the objective function value is not known with sufficient certainty. One might
accomplish this in several ways; OSBORNE et al. adopted a parametric,
data-dependent action space of the form

$$\mathcal{A}(\varepsilon; \mathcal{D}) = \big\{x \mid \mathrm{std}[\phi \mid x, \mathcal{D}] \leq \varepsilon\big\},$$

where ε is a threshold specifying the largest acceptable uncertainty.

Choosing a utility function and risk tolerance

In addition to selecting an action space, we must also select a utility function $v(\phi)$ evaluating a recommendation at x in light of the corresponding function value ϕ. As our focus is on maximization (1.1), it is clear that the utility should be monotonically increasing in ϕ, but it is not necessarily clear what shape this function should assume. The answer depends on our *risk tolerance,* a concept demonstrated in the margin. When making our final recommendation, we may wish to consider not only the *expected* function value of a given point but also our *uncertainty* in this value, as points with greater uncertainty may result in more surprising and potentially disappointing results.

By controlling the shape of the utility function $v(\phi)$, we may induce different behavior with respect to risk. The simplest and most common option encountered in Bayesian optimization is a linear utility:

$$v(\phi) = \phi. \tag{6.2}$$

In this case, the expected utility from recommending x is simply the posterior mean of ϕ, as we have already seen (5.4):

$$\mathbb{E}[v(\phi) \mid x, \mathcal{D}] = \mu_{\mathcal{D}}(x),$$

and an optimal recommendation maximizes the posterior mean over the action space:

$$x = \arg\max_{x' \in \mathcal{A}} \mu_{\mathcal{D}}(x').$$

Uncertainty in the objective function is not considered in this decision at all! Rather, we are indifferent between points with equal expected value, regardless of their uncertainty – that is, we are *risk neutral.*

Risk neutrality is computationally convenient due to the simple form of the expected utility, but may not always reflect our true preferences. In the margin we show beliefs over the objective values for two potential recommendations with equal expected value but significantly different risk. In many scenarios we would have a clear preference between the two alternatives, but a risk-neutral utility induces complete indifference.

A useful concept when reasoning about risk preferences is the so-called *certainty equivalent.* Consider a risky potential recommendation x, that is, a point for which we do not know the objective value exactly. The certainty equivalent for x is the value of a hypothetical *risk-free* alternative for which our preferences would be indifferent. That is, the certainty equivalent for x corresponds to an objective function value ϕ' such that

$$v(\phi') = \mathbb{E}[v(\phi) \mid x, \mathcal{D}].$$

Under a risk-neutral utility function, the certainty equivalent of a point x is simply its expected value: $\phi' = \mu_{\mathcal{D}}(x)$. Thus we would abandon a potential recommendation for another only if it had greater expected value, independent of risk. However, we may encode risk-aware preferences with appropriately designed *nonlinear* utility functions.

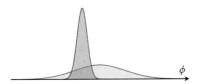

Consider the illustrated beliefs about the objective function value corresponding to two possible recommendations. One option has a higher expected value, but also greater uncertainty, and proposing it entails some risk. The alternative has a lower expected value but is perhaps a safer option. A risk-averse agent might prefer the latter option, whereas a risk-tolerant agent might prefer the former.

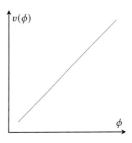

A risk-neutral (linear) utility function.

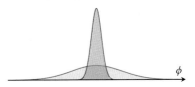

Beliefs over two recommendations with equal expected value. A risk-neutral agent would be indifferent between these alternatives, a risk-averse agent would prefer the more certain option, and a risk-seeking agent would prefer the more uncertain option.

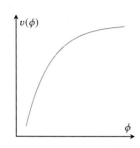

A risk-averse (concave) utility function.

A risk-averse agent may be indifferent between a risky recommendation (the wide distribution) and its risk-free certainty equivalent with lower expected value (the Dirac delta).

3 One flexible family is the *hyperbolic absolute risk aversion* (HARA) class, which includes many popular choices as special cases:

J. E. INGERSOLL JR. (1987). *Theory of Financial Decision Making.* Rowman & Littlefield. [chapter 1]

4 Under Gaussian beliefs on function values, one can find a family of concave (or convex) utility functions inducing equivalent recommendations. See § 8.26, p. 171 for related discussion.

5 Note that expected reward (μ) and risk (σ) have compatible units in this formulation, so this weighted combination is sensible.

6 This name contrasts with the *cumulative reward*: § 6.2, p. 114.

7 One technical caveat is in order: when the dataset is empty, the maximum degererates and we have $u(\varnothing) = -\infty$.

If our preferences indicate *risk aversion,* we might be willing to recommend a point with lower expected value if it also entailed less risk. We may induce risk-averse preferences by adopting a utility function that is a concave function of the objective value. In this case, by Jensen's inequality we have

$$v(\phi') = \mathbb{E}\big[v(\phi) \mid x, \mathcal{D}\big] \leq v\big(\mathbb{E}[\phi \mid x, \mathcal{D}]\big) = v\big(\mu_{\mathcal{D}}(x)\big),$$

and thus the certainty equivalent of a risky recommendation is *less* than its expected value; see the example in the margin. Similarly, we may induce *risk-seeking* preferences with a convex utility function, in which case the certainty equivalent of a risky recommendation is *greater* than its expected value – our preferences encode an inclination toward gambling. Risk-averse and risk-seeking utilities are rarely encountered in the Bayesian optimization literature; however, they may be preferable in some practical settings, as risk neutrality is often questionable.

Numerous risk-averse utility functions have been proposed in the economics and decision theory literature,[3] and a full discussion is beyond the scope of this book. However, one natural approach is to quantify the risk associated with recommending an uncertain value ϕ by its standard deviation:

$$\sigma = \text{std}[\phi \mid x, \mathcal{D}].$$

Now we may establish preferences over potential recommendations consistent with[4] a weighted combination of a point x's expected reward, $\mu = \mu_{\mathcal{D}}(x)$, and its risk, σ:[5]

$$\mu + \beta\sigma.$$

Here β serves as a tunable risk-tolerance parameter: values $\beta < 0$ penalize risk and induce risk-averse behavior, values $\beta > 0$ reward risk and induce risk-seeking behavior, and $\beta = 0$ induces risk neutrality (6.2).

Two particular utility functions from this general framework are widely encountered in Bayesian optimization, both representing the expected utility of a risk-neutral optimal terminal recommendation.

Simple reward

Suppose an optimization routine returned data $\mathcal{D} = (\mathbf{x}, \mathbf{y})$ to inform a terminal recommendation, and that we will make this decision using the risk-neutral utility function $v(\phi) = \phi$ (6.2). If we limit the action space of this recommendation to only the locations evaluated during optimization $\mathbf{x}$, the expected utility of the optimal recommendation is the so-called *simple reward*:[6,7]

$$u(\mathcal{D}) = \max \mu_{\mathcal{D}}(\mathbf{x}). \tag{6.3}$$

In the special case of exact observations, where $\mathbf{y} = f(\mathbf{x}) = \boldsymbol{\phi}$, the simple reward reduces to the maximal function value encountered during optimization:

$$u(\mathcal{D}) = \max \boldsymbol{\phi}. \tag{6.4}$$

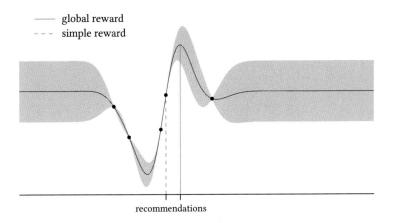

—— global reward
- - - simple reward

recommendations

Figure 6.1: The terminal recommendations corresponding to the simple reward and global reward for an example dataset comprising five observations. The prior distribution for the objective for this demonstration is illustrated in Figure 6.3.

One-step lookahead with the simple reward utility function produces a widely used acquisition function known as *expected improvement*, which we will discuss in detail in the next two chapters.

expected improvement: § 7.3 p. 127

Global reward

Another prominent utility is the *global reward*.[8] Here we again consider a risk-neutral terminal recommendation, but now expand the action space for this recommendation to the entire domain $\mathcal{X}$. The expected utility of this recommendation is the global maximum of the posterior mean:

8 "Global *simple* reward" would be a more accurate (but annoyingly bulky) name.

$$u(\mathcal{D}) = \max_{x \in \mathcal{X}} \mu_{\mathcal{D}}(x). \qquad (6.5)$$

An example dataset exhibiting a large discrepancy between the simple reward (6.3) and global reward (6.5) utilities is illustrated in Figure 6.1. The larger action space underlying global reward leads to a markedly different and somewhat riskier recommendation.

One-step lookahead with global reward (6.5) yields the *knowledge gradient* acquisition function, which we will also consider at length in the following chapters.

knowledge gradient: § 7.4, p. 129

A tempting, but nonsensical alternative

There is an alternative utility deceptively similar to the simple reward that is sometimes encountered in the Bayesian optimization literature, namely, the maximum *noisy* observed value contained in the dataset:[9]

9 The "questionable equality" symbol $\overset{?}{=}$ is reserved for this single dubious equation.

$$u(\mathcal{D}) \overset{?}{=} \max \mathbf{y}. \qquad (6.6)$$

In the case of *exact* observations of the objective function, this value coincides with the simple reward (6.4), which has a natural interpretation as the expected utility of a particular optimal terminal recommendation. However, this correspondence does *not* hold in the case of inexact or noisy observations, and the proposed utility is rendered absurd.

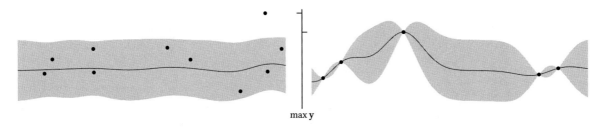

max **y**

Figure 6.2: The utility $u(\mathcal{D})$ = max **y** would prefer the excessively noisy dataset on the left to the less-noisy dataset on the right with smaller maximum value. The data on the left reveal little information about the objective function, and the maximum observed value is very likely to be an outlier, whereas the data on the right indicate reasonable progress.

large-but-noisy observations are not necessarily preferable

This is simple to demonstrate by contemplating the preferences over outcomes encoded in the utility, which may not align with intuition. This disparity is especially notable in situations with excessively noisy observations, where the maximum value observed will likely reflect spurious noise rather than actual optimization progress.

example and discussion

Figure 6.2 shows an extreme but illustrative example. We consider two optimization outcomes over the same domain, one with excessively noisy observations and the other with exact measurements. The noisy dataset contains a large observation on the right-hand side of the domain, but this is almost certainly the result of noise, as indicated by the objective function posterior. Although the other dataset has a lower maximal value, the observations are more trustworthy and represent a plainly better outcome. But the proposed utility (6.6) prefers the noisier dataset! On the other hand, both the simple and global reward utilities prefer the noiseless dataset, as the data produce a larger effect on the posterior mean – and thus yield more promising recommendations.

approximation to the simple reward

Of course, errors in noisy measurements are not always as extreme as in this example. When the signal-to-noise ratio is relatively high, the utility (6.6) can serve as a reasonable *approximation* to the simple reward. We will discuss this approximation scheme further in the context of expected improvement.

expected improvement: § 7.3, p. 127

6.2   CUMULATIVE REWARD

Simple and global reward are motivated by supposing that the goal of optimization is to discover the best *single* point from a space of alternatives. To this end, we evaluate data according to the highest function value revealed and assume that the values of any suboptimal points encountered are irrelevant.

In other settings, the value of *every* individual observation might be significant, for example, if the optimization procedure is controlling a critical external system. If the consequences of these decisions are nontrivial, we might wish to discourage observing where we might encounter unexpectedly low objective function values.

Cumulative reward encourages obtaining observations with large *average* value. For a dataset $\mathcal{D} = (\mathbf{x}, \mathbf{y})$, its cumulative reward is simply the sum of the observed values:

$$u(\mathcal{D}) = \sum_i y_i. \qquad (6.7)$$

One notable use of cumulative reward is in *active search,* a simple mathematical model of scientific discovery. Here, we successively select points for investigation seeking novel members of a rare, valuable class $\mathcal{V} \subset \mathcal{X}$. Observing at a point $x \in \mathcal{X}$ yields a *binary* observation indicating membership in the desired class: $y = [x \in \mathcal{V}]$. Most studies of active search seek to maximize the cumulative reward (6.7) of the gathered data, hoping to discover as many valuable items as possible.

active search: § 11.11, p. 282

6.3 INFORMATION GAIN

Simple, global, and cumulative reward judge optimization performance based solely on having found high objective function values, a natural and pragmatic concern. *Information theory*[10] provides an alternative approach to measuring utility that is often used in Bayesian optimization. An information-theoretic approach to sequential experimental design (including optimization) identifies some random variable that we wish to learn about through our observations. We then evaluate performance by quantifying the amount of information about this random variable revealed by data, favoring datasets containing more information. This line of reasoning gives rise to the notion of *information gain.*

Let ω be a random variable of interest that we wish to determine through the observation of data. The choice of ω is open-ended and should be guided by the application at hand. Natural choices aligned with optimization include the location of the global optimum, x^*, and the maximal value of the objective, f^* (1.1), each of which has been considered in depth in this context.

We may quantify our initial uncertainty about ω via the (differential) *entropy* of its prior distribution, $p(\omega)$:

$$H[\omega] = -\int p(\omega) \log p(\omega) \, d\omega.$$

The *information gain* offered by a dataset $\mathcal{D}$ is then the reduction in entropy when moving from the prior to the posterior distribution:

$$u(\mathcal{D}) = H[\omega] - H[\omega \mid \mathcal{D}], \qquad (6.8)$$

where $H[\omega \mid \mathcal{D}]$ is the differential entropy of the posterior:[11]

$$H[\omega \mid \mathcal{D}] = -\int p(\omega \mid \mathcal{D}) \log p(\omega \mid \mathcal{D}) \, d\omega.$$

Somewhat confusingly, some authors use an alternative definition of information gain – the *Kullback–Leibler (KL) divergence* between the

entropy

[10] A broad introduction to information theory is provided by the classical text:

T. M. COVER and J. A. THOMAS (2006). *Elements of Information Theory.* John Wiley & Sons,

and a treatment focusing on the connections to Bayesian inference can be found in:

D. J. C. MACKAY (2003). *Information Theory, Inference, and Learning Algorithms.* Cambridge University Press.

[11] A caveat is in order regarding this notation, which is not standard. In information theory $H[\omega \mid \mathcal{D}]$ denotes the *conditional entropy* of ω given $\mathcal{D}$, which is the expectation of the given quantity over the observed values $\mathbf{y}$. For our purposes it will be more useful for this to signify the differential entropy of the notationally parallel posterior $p(\omega \mid \mathcal{D})$. When needed, we will write conditional entropy with an explicit expectation: $\mathbb{E}[H[\omega \mid \mathcal{D}] \mid \mathbf{x}]$.

Kullback–Leibler (KL) divergence

12 A simple example: suppose $\omega \in (0, 1)$ is the unknown bias of a coin, with prior

12 A simple example: suppose $\omega \in (0, 1)$ is the unknown bias of a coin, with prior

$$p(\omega) = \text{Beta}(\omega; 2, 1); \quad H \approx -0.193.$$

After flipping and observing "tails," the posterior becomes

$$p(\omega \mid \mathcal{D}) = \text{Beta}(\omega; 2, 2); \quad H \approx -0.125.$$

The information "gained" was

$$H[\omega] - H[\omega \mid \mathcal{D}] \approx -0.068 < 0.$$

Of course, the most likely outcome of the flip a priori was "heads," so the outcome was surprising. Indeed the *expected* information gain before the experiment was

$$H[\omega] - \mathbb{E}[H[\omega \mid \mathcal{D}]] \approx 0.137 > 0.$$

13 See p. 138 for a proof.

mutual information, entropy search: § 7.6, p. 135

information-theoretic policies as the scientific method: § 7.6, p. 136

posterior distribution and the prior distribution:

$$u(\mathcal{D}) = D_{\text{KL}}\big[p(\omega \mid \mathcal{D}) \parallel p(\omega)\big] = \int p(\omega \mid \mathcal{D}) \log \frac{p(\omega \mid \mathcal{D})}{p(\omega)} \, \mathrm{d}\omega. \quad (6.9)$$

That is, we quantify the information contained in data by how much our belief in the ω changes as a result of collecting it. This definition has some convenient properties compared to the previous one (6.8); namely, the expression in (6.9) is invariant to reparameterization of ω and always nonnegative, whereas "surprising" observations may cause the information gain in (6.8) to become negative.[12] However, the previous definition as the direct reduction in entropy may be more intuitive.

Fortunately (and perhaps surprisingly!), there is a strong connection between these two "information gains" (6.8–6.9) in the context of sequential decision making. Namely, their expected values with respect to observed values are equal, and thus maximizing expected utility with either leads to identical decisions.[13] For this reason, the reader may simply choose whichever definition they find more intuitive.

One-step lookahead with (either) information gain yields an acquisition function known as *mutual information*. This is the basis for a family of related Bayesian optimization procedures sharing the moniker *entropy search*, which we will discuss further in the following chapters.

Unlike the other utility functions discussed thus far, information gain is not intimately linked to optimization, and may be adapted to a wide variety of tasks by selecting the random variable ω appropriately. Rather, this scheme of refining knowledge through experiment is effectively a mathematical formulation of scientific inquiry.

6.4 DEPENDENCE ON MODEL OF OBJECTIVE FUNCTION

One striking feature of most of the utility functions defined in this chapter is implicit dependence on an underlying model of the objective function. Both the simple and global reward are defined in terms of the posterior mean function $\mu_\mathcal{D}$, and information gain about the location or value of the optimum is defined in terms of the posterior belief about these values, $p(x^*, f^* \mid \mathcal{D})$; both of these quantities are byproducts of the objective function posterior.

model averaging: §§ 4.4–4.5, p. 74
model-agnostic alternatives

14 The effect on simple and global reward is to maximize a model-marginal posterior mean, and the effect on information gain is to evaluate changes in model-marginal beliefs about ω.

One way to mitigate model dependence in the computation of utility is via model averaging (4.11, 4.23).[14] We may also attempt to define purely model-agnostic utility functions in terms of the data alone, without reference to a model; however, the possibilities are somewhat limited if we wish the resulting utility to be sensible. Cumulative reward (6.7) is one example, as it depends only on the observed values $\mathbf{y}$. The maximum function value observed is another possibility (6.6), but, as we have shown, it is dubious when observations are corrupted by noise. Other similarly defined alternatives may suffer the same fate – for additive noise with zero mean, the expected contribution from noise to the cumulative reward is zero; however, noise will bias many other natural measures such as order statistics (including the maximum) of the observations.

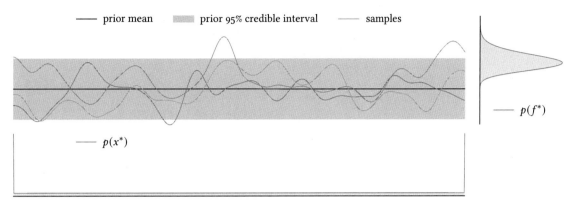

Figure 6.3: The objective function prior used throughout our utility function comparison. Marginal beliefs of function values are shown, as well as the induced beliefs over the location of the global optimum, $p(x^*)$, and the value of the global optimum, $p(f^*)$. Note that there is a significant probability that the global optimum is achieved on the boundary of the domain, reflected by large point masses.

6.5   COMPARISON OF UTILITY FUNCTIONS

We have now presented several utility functions for evaluating a dataset returned by an optimization routine. Each utility quantifies progress on our model optimization problem (1.1) in some way, but it may be difficult at this point to appreciate their, sometimes subtle, differences in approach. Here we will present and discuss example datasets for which different utility functions diverge in their opinion of quality.

We particularly wish to contrast the behavior of the simple reward (6.3) with other utility functions. Simple reward is probably the most prevalent utility in the Bayesian optimization literature (especially in applications), as it corresponds to the widespread expected improvement acquisition function. A distinguishing feature of simple reward is that it evaluates data based only on *local* properties of the objective function posterior. This locality is both computationally convenient and pragmatic. Simple reward is derived from the premise that we will be recommending one of the points observed during the course of optimization for permanent use, and thus it is sensible to judge performance based on the objective function values at the observed locations alone.

Several alternatives instead measure *global* properties of the objective function posterior. The global reward (6.5), for example, considers the entire posterior mean function, reflecting a willingless to recommend an unevaluated point after termination. Information gain (6.8) about the location or value of the optimum considers the posterior entropy of these quantities, again a global property. The consequences of reasoning about local or global properties of the posterior can sometimes lead to significant disagreement between the simple reward and other utilities.

In the following examples, we consider optimization on an interval with exact measurements. We model the objective function with a Gaussian process with constant mean (3.1) and squared exponential

local vs. global properties of posterior

expected improvement: § 7.3, p. 127

model of objective function

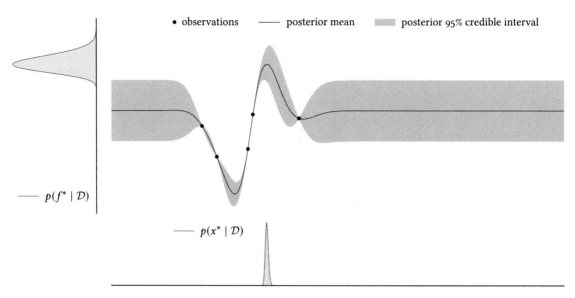

Figure 6.4: An example dataset of five observations and the resulting posterior belief of the objective function. This dataset exhibits relatively low simple reward (6.3) but relatively high global reward (6.5) and information gain (6.8) about the location x^* and value f^* of the optimum.

covariance (3.12). This prior is illustrated in Figure 6.3, along with the induced beliefs about the location x^* and value f^* of the global optimum. Both distributions reflect considerable uncertainty.[15] We will examine two datasets that might be returned by an optimizer using this model and discuss how different utility functions would evaluate these outcomes.

Good global outcome but poor local outcome

Consider the dataset in Figure 6.4 and the resulting posterior belief about the objective and its optimum. In this example, the simple reward is relatively low as the posterior mean at our observations is unremarkable. In fact, every observation was lower than the prior mean, a seemingly unlucky outcome. However, the global reward is relatively high: the data imply a steep derivative in one location, inducing high values of the posterior mean away from our data. This is a significant accomplishment from the point of view of the global reward, as the model expects a terminal recommendation in that region to be especially valuable.

Figure 6.1 shows the optimal final recommendations associated with these two utility functions. The simple reward recommendation prioritizes safety over reward, whereas the global reward recommendation reflects more risk tolerance. Neither is inherently better: although the global reward recommendation has a larger expected value, this expectation is computed using a model that might be mistaken. Further, comparing the posterior distribution in Figure 6.4 with the prior in Figure

low simple reward

high global reward

final recommendations

high information gain

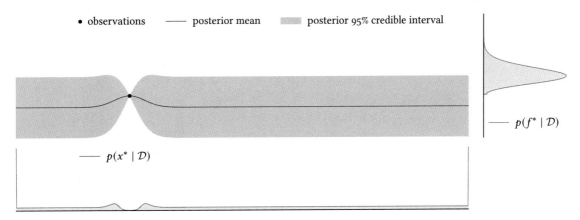

Figure 6.5: An example dataset containing a single observation and the resulting posterior belief of the objective function. This dataset exhibits relatively high simple reward (6.3) but relatively low global reward (6.5) and information gain (6.8) about the location x^* and value f^* of the optimum.

6.3, we see this example dataset also induces a significant reduction in our uncertainty about both the location and value of the global optimum, despite not containing any particularly notable values itself. Therefore, despite a somewhat low simple reward, observing this dataset results in relatively high information gain about these quantities.

Good local outcome but poor global outcome

We illustrate a different example dataset in Figure 6.5. The dataset contains a single observation with value somewhat higher than the prior mean. Although this dataset may not appear particularly impressive, its simple reward is higher than the previous dataset, as this observation exceeds every value seen in that scenario.

high simple reward

However, this dataset has lower value than the previous dataset when evaluated by other utility functions. Its global reward is lower than in the first scenario, as the global maximum of the posterior mean is lower. This can be verified by visual inspection of Figures 6.4 and 6.5, whose vertical axes are compatible. Further, the single observation in this scenario provides nearly no information regarding the location nor the value of the global maximum. The observation of a moderately high value provides only weak evidence that the global optimum may be located nearby, barely influencing our posterior belief about x^*. The observation does truncate our belief of the value of the global optimum f^* but only rules out a relatively small portion of its lower tail.

low global reward

low information gain

6.6 SUMMARY OF MAJOR IDEAS

In Bayesian decision theory, preferences over outcomes are encoded by a *utility function,* which in the context of optimization policy design,

16 Just like human taste, there is no right or wrong when it comes to preferences, at least not over *certain* outcomes. The von Neumann–Morgenstern theorem mentioned on p. 90 entails rationality axioms, but these only apply to preferences over *uncertain* outcomes.

expected utility of terminal recommendation: § 6.1, p. 109

risk tolerance: § 6.1, p. 111

simple reward: § 6.1, p. 112
global reward: § 6.1, p. 113

cumulative reward: § 6.2, p. 114

information gain: § 6.3, p. 115

comparison of utility functions: § 6.5, p. 117

assesses the quality of data returned by an optimization routine, $u(\mathcal{D})$. The optimization policy then seeks to design observations to maximize the *expected* utility of the returned data. The general theory presented in the last chapter makes no assumptions regarding the utility function.[16] However, in the context of optimization, some utility functions are particularly easy to motivate.

- In many cases there is a decision following optimization in which we must recommend a single point in the domain for perpetual use. In this case, it is sensible to define an optimization utility function in terms of the expected utility of the optimal terminal recommendation informed by the returned data. This requires fully specifying that terminal recommendation, including its action space and utility function, after which we may "pass through" the optimal expected utility (6.1).

- When designing a terminal recommendation – especially when we may recommend points with residual uncertainty in their underlying objective value – it may be prudent to consider our *risk tolerance*. Careful design of the terminal utility allows for us to tune our appetite for risk, in terms of trading off a point's expected value against its uncertainty. Most utilities encountered in Bayesian optimization are *risk neutral*, but this need not necessarily be the case.

- Two notable realizations of this scheme are *simple reward* (6.3) and *global reward* (6.5), both of which represent the expected utility of an optimal terminal recommendation with a risk-neutral utility. The action space for simple reward is the points visited during optimization, and the action space for global reward is the entire domain.

- The simple reward simplifies when observations are exact (6.4).

- An alternative to the simple reward is the *cumulative reward* (6.7), which evaluates a dataset based on the *average*, rather than maximum, value observed. This does not see too much direct use in policy design, but is an important concept for the analysis of algorithms.

- *Information gain* provides an information-theoretic approach to quantifying the value of data in terms of the information provided by the data regarding some quantity of interest. This can be quantified by either measuring the reduction in differential entropy moving from the prior to the posterior (6.8) or by the KL divergence between the posterior and prior (6.9) – either induces the same one-step lookahead policy.

- In the context of optimization, information gain regarding either the location x^* or value f^* of the global optimum (1.1) are judicious realizations of this general approach to utility design.

- An important feature distinguishing simple reward from most other utility functions is its dependence on the posterior belief at the observed locations *alone*, rather than the posterior belief over the entire objective function. Even in relatively simple examples, this may lead to disagreement between simple reward and other utility functions in judging the quality of a given dataset.

The utility functions presented in this chapter form the backbone of the most popular Bayesian optimization algorithms. In particular, many common policies are realized by maximizing the one-step expected marginal gain to one of these utilities, as we will show in the next chapter.

one-step lookahead: § 5.3, p. 101

COMMON BAYESIAN OPTIMIZATION POLICIES

7

The heart of an optimization routine is its policy, which sequentially designs each observation in light of available data.[1] In the Bayesian approach to optimization, policies are designed with reference to a probabilistic belief about the objective function, with this belief guiding the policy in making decisions likely to yield beneficial outcomes. Numerous Bayesian optimization policies have been proposed in the literature, many of which enjoy widespread use. In this chapter we will present an overview of popular Bayesian optimization policies and emphasize common themes in their construction. In the next chapter we will provide explicit computational details for implementing these policies with Gaussian process models of the objective function.

Nearly all Bayesian optimization algorithms result from one of two primary approaches to policy design. The most popular is *Bayesian decision theory*, the focus of the previous two chapters. In Chapter 5 we introduced Bayesian decision theory as a general framework for deriving optimal, but computationally prohibitive, optimization policies. In this chapter, we will apply the ideas underlying these optimal procedures to realize computationally tractable and practically useful policies. We will see that a majority of popular Bayesian optimization algorithms can be interpreted in a uniform manner as performing one-step lookahead for some underlying utility function.

Another avenue for policy design is to adopt algorithms for *multi-armed bandits* to the optimization setting. A multi-armed bandit is a finite-dimensional model of sequential optimization with noisy observations. We consider an agent faced with a finite set of alternatives ("arms"), who is compelled to select a sequence of items from this set. Choosing a given item yields a stochastic reward drawn from an unknown distribution associated with that arm. We seek a sequential policy for selecting arms maximizing the expected cumulative reward (6.7).[2]

Multi-armed bandits have seen decades of sustained study, and some policies have strong theoretical guarantees on their performance, suggesting these policies may also be useful for optimization. To this end, we may model optimization as an *infinite-armed bandit*, where each point in the domain $x \in \mathcal{X}$ represents an arm with uncertain reward depending on the objective function value $\phi = f(x)$. Our belief about the objective function then provides a mechanism to reason about these rewards and derive a policy. This analogy has inspired several Bayesian optimization policies, many of which enjoy strong performance guarantees.

A central concern in bandit problems is the *exploration–exploitation dilemma*: we must repeatedly decide whether to allocate resources to an arm already known to yield high reward ("exploitation") or to an arm with uncertain reward to learn about its reward distribution ("exploration"). Exploitation may yield a high instantaneous reward, but exploration may provide valuable information for improving future rewards. This tradeoff between instant payoff and learning for the future has been called "a conflict evident in all human action."[3] A similar choice is faced

1 The reader may wish to recall our model optimization procedure: Algorithm 1.1, p. 3.

Chapter 8: Computing Policies with Gaussian Processes, p. 157

Chapter 5: Decision Theory for Optimization, p. 87

one-step lookahead: § 5.3, p. 101
Chapter 6: Utility Functions for Optimization: p. 109

multi-armed bandits

2 The name references a gambler contemplating how to allocate their bankroll among a wall of slot machines. Slot machines are known as "one-armed bandits" in American vernacular, as they eventually steal all your money.

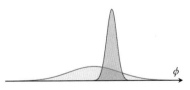

Exploration vs. exploitation. We show reward distributions for two possible options. The more certain option returns higher expected reward, but the alternative reflects more uncertainty and may actually be superior. Which should we prefer?

3 P. WHITTLE (1982). *Optimization over Time: Dynamic Programming and Stochastic Control.* Vol. 1. John Wiley & Sons.

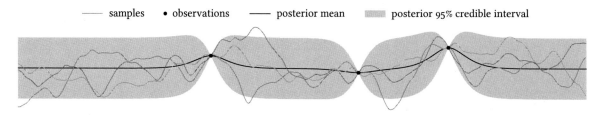

Figure 7.1: The scenario we will consider for illustrating optimization policies. The objective function prior is a Gaussian process with constant mean and Mátern covariance with $\nu = 5/2$ (3.14). We show the marginal predictive distributions and three samples from the posterior conditioned on the indicated observations.

throughout optimization, as we must continually decide whether to focus on a suspected local maximum (exploitation) or to explore unknown regions of the domain seeking new maxima (exploration). We will see that typical Bayesian optimization policies reflect consideration of this dilemma in some way, whether by explicit design on or as a consequence of decision-theoretic reasoning.

Before diving into policy design, we pause to introduce a running example we will carry through the chapter and notation to facilitate our discussion. We will then derive a series of policies stemming from Bayesian decision theory, and finally consider bandit-inspired algorithms.

7.1 EXAMPLE OPTIMIZATION SCENARIO

Throughout this chapter we will demonstrate the behavior of optimization policies on an example scenario illustrated in Figure 7.1.[4] We consider a one-dimensional objective function observed without noise and adopt a Gaussian process prior belief about this function. The prior mean function is constant (3.1), and the prior covariance function is a Mátern covariance with $\nu = 5/2$ (3.14). The parameters are fixed so that the domain spans exactly 30 length scales. We condition this prior on three observations, inducing two local maxima in the posterior mean and a range of marginal predictive uncertainty.

We will illustrate the behavior of policies by simulating optimization to design a sequence of additional observations for this running example. The ground truth objective function we will use for these simulations is shown in Figure 7.2 and was drawn from the corresponding model. The objective features numerous undiscovered local maxima and exhibits an unusually high global maximum on the left-hand side of the domain.

7.2 DECISION-THEORETIC POLICIES

Central to decision-theoretic optimization is a utility function $u(\mathcal{D})$ measuring the quality of a dataset returned by an optimizer. After selecting a utility function and a model of the objective function and our observations, we may design each observation to maximize the expected utility

4 Take note of the legend; it will not be repeated.

Chapter 2: Gaussian Processes, p. 15

objective function for simulation

Chapter 6: Utility Functions for Optimization: p. 109

optimal policies: § 5.2, p. 91

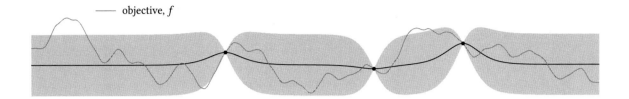

Figure 7.2: The true objective function used for simulating optimization policies.

of the returned data (5.16). This policy is optimal in the average case: it maximizes the expected utility of the returned dataset over the space of all possible policies.[5] Unfortunately, optimality comes at a great cost. Computing the optimal policy requires recursive simulation of the entire remainder of optimization, a random process due to uncertainty in the outcomes of our observations. In general, the cost of computing the optimal policy grows exponentially with the horizon, the number of observations remaining before termination.

However, the structure of the optimal policy suggests a natural family of *lookahead* approximations based on fixing a computationally tractable maximum horizon throughout optimization. This line of reasoning has led to many of the practical policies available for Bayesian optimization. In fact, most popular algorithms represent *one*-step lookahead, where in each iteration we greedily maximize the expected utility after obtaining only a single additional observation. Although these policies are maximally myopic, they are also maximally efficient among lookahead approximations and have delivered impressive empirical performance in a wide range of settings.

It may seem surprising that such dramatically myopic policies have any use at all. There is a huge difference between the scale of reasoning in one-step lookahead compared with the optimal procedure, which may consider hundreds of future decisions or more when designing an observation. However, the situation is somewhat more nuanced than it might appear. In a seminal paper, KUSHNER argued that myopic policies may in fact show *better* empirical performance than a theoretically optimal policy, and his argument remains convincing:[6]

Since a mathematical model of [f] is available, it is theoretically possible, once a criterion of optimality is given, to determine the mathematically optimal sampling policy. However...determination of the optimum sampling policies is extremely difficult. Because of this, the development of our sampling laws has been guided primarily by heuristic considerations.[7] There are some advantages to the approximate approach...[and] its use may yield better results than would a procedure that is optimum for the model. Although the model selected for [f] is the best we have found for our purposes, it is sometimes too general...

5 To be precise, optimality is defined with respect to a model for the objective function $p(f)$, an observation model $p(y \mid x, \phi)$, a utility function $u(\mathcal{D})$, and an upper bound on the number of observations allowed τ. Bayesian decision theory provides a policy achieving the maximal expected utility at termination with respect to these choices.

running time of optimal policy and efficient approximations: § 5.3, p. 99

limited lookahead: § 5.3, p. 101

6 H. J. KUSHNER (1964). A New Method of Locating the Maximum Point of an Arbitrary Multi-peak Curve in the Presence of Noise. *Journal of Basic Engineering* 86(1):97–106.

7 Specifically, maximizing probability of improvement: § 7.5, p. 131.

What could possibly cause such a seemingly contradictory finding? As KUSHNER suggests, one possible reason could be model misspecification. The optimal policy is only defined with respect to a chosen model of the objective function and our observations, which is bound to be imperfect. By relying *less* on the model's belief, we may gain some robustness alongside considerable computational savings.

The intimate relationship between many Bayesian optimization methods and one-step lookahead is often glossed over, with a policy often introduced *ex nihilo* and the implied choice of utility function left unstated. This disconnect can sometimes lead to policies that are nonsensical from a decision-theoretic perspective or that incorporate implicit approximations that may not always be appropriate. We intend to clarify these connections here. We hope that our presentation can help guide practitioners in navigating the increasingly crowded space of available policies when presented with a novel scenario.

One-step lookahead

notation for one-step lookahead policies

Let us review the generic procedure for developing a one-step lookahead policy and adopt standard notation to facilitate their description. Suppose we have selected an arbitrary utility function $u(\mathcal{D})$ to evaluate a returned dataset. Suppose further that we have already gathered an arbitrary dataset $\mathcal{D} = (\mathbf{x}, \mathbf{y})$ and wish to select the next evaluation location. This is the fundamental role of an optimization policy.

proposed next point x with putative value y
updated dataset $\mathcal{D}' = \mathcal{D} \cup (x, y)$

If we were to choose some point x, we would observe a corresponding value y and update our dataset, forming $\mathcal{D}' = (\mathbf{x}', \mathbf{y}') = \mathcal{D} \cup \{(x, y)\}$. Note that in our discussion on decision theory in Chapter 5, we noted this updated dataset with the symbol $\mathcal{D}_1$, as we needed to be able to distinguish between datasets after the incorporation of a variable number of additional observations. As our focus in this chapter will be on one-step lookahead, we can simplify notation by dropping subscripts indicating time. Instead, we will systematically use the prime symbol to indicate future quantities after the acquisition of the next observation.

expected marginal gain

In one-step lookahead, we evaluate a proposed point x via the expected marginal gain in utility after incorporating an observation there (5.8):

$$\alpha(x; \mathcal{D}) = \mathbb{E}\big[u(\mathcal{D}') \mid x, \mathcal{D}\big] - u(\mathcal{D}),$$

acquisition functions: § 5, p. 88

which serves as an acquisition function inducing preferences over possible observation locations. We design each observation by maximizing this score:

$$x \in \underset{x' \in \mathcal{X}}{\arg\max}\, \alpha(x'; \mathcal{D}). \tag{7.1}$$

value of sample information

When the utility function $u(\mathcal{D})$ represents the expected utility of a decision informed by the data, such as a terminal recommendation following optimization, the expected marginal gain is also known as the *value of sample information* from observing at x. This term originates from the study of decision making in an economic context. Consider

utility function, $u(\mathcal{D})$	expected one-step marginal gain
simple reward, (6.3)	expected improvement, §7.3
global reward, (6.5)	knowledge gradient, §7.4
improvement to simple reward	probability of improvement, §7.5
information gain, (6.8) or (6.9)	mutual information, §7.6
cumulative reward, (6.7)	posterior mean, §7.10

Table 7.1: Summary of one-step lookahead optimization policies.

an agent who must make a decision under uncertainty, and suppose they have access to a third party who is willing to provide potentially insightful advice in exchange for a fee. By reasoning about the potential impact of this advice on the ultimate decision, we may quantify the expected value of the information,[8,9] and determine whether the offered advice is worth the investment.

8 J. MARSCHAK and R. RADNER (1972). *Economic Theory of Teams.* Yale University Press. [§2.12]

9 H. RAIFFA and R. SCHLAIFER (1961). *Applied Statistical Decision Theory.* Division of Research, Graduate School of Business Administration, Harvard University. [§4.5]

Due to its simplicity and inherent computational efficiency, one-step lookahead is a pervasive approximation scheme in Bayesian optimization. Table 7.1 provides a list of common acquisition functions, each representing the expected one-step marginal gain to a corresponding utility function. We will discuss each in detail below.

7.3 EXPECTED IMPROVEMENT

Adopting the simple reward utility function (6.3) and performing one-step lookahead defines the *expected improvement* acquisition function. Sequential maximization of expected improvement is perhaps the most widespread policy in all of Bayesian optimization.

simple reward: §6.1, p. 109

Suppose that we wish to locate a single location in the domain with the highest possible objective value and ultimately wish to recommend one of the points investigated during optimization for permanent use. The simple reward utility function evaluates a dataset $\mathcal{D}$ precisely by the expected value of an optimal final recommendation informed by the data, assuming risk neutrality:

risk neutrality: §6.1, p. 109

$$u(\mathcal{D}) = \max \mu_{\mathcal{D}}(\mathbf{x}).$$

Suppose we have already gathered observations $\mathcal{D} = (\mathbf{x}, \mathbf{y})$ and wish to choose the next evaluation location. Expected improvement is derived by measuring the expected marginal gain in utility, or the instantaneous *improvement*, $u(\mathcal{D}') - u(\mathcal{D})$,[10] offered by making the next observation at a proposed location x:[11]

$$\alpha_{\text{EI}}(x; \mathcal{D}) = \int \left[\max \mu_{\mathcal{D}'}(\mathbf{x}')\right] p(y \mid x, \mathcal{D}) \, \mathrm{d}y - \max \mu_{\mathcal{D}}(\mathbf{x}). \quad (7.2)$$

Expected improvement reduces to a particularly nice expression in the case of exact observations of the objective, where the utility takes a simpler form (6.4). Suppose that, when we elect to make an observation at a location x, we observe the exact objective value $\phi = f(x)$. Consider

10 This reasoning is the same for *all* one-step lookahead policies, which could all be described as maximizing "expected improvement." But this name has been claimed for the simple reward utility alone.

11 As mentioned in the last chapter, simple reward degenerates with an empty dataset; expected improvement does as well. In that case we can simply ignore the second term and compute the first, which for zero-mean additive noise becomes the mean function of the prior process.

expected improvement without noise

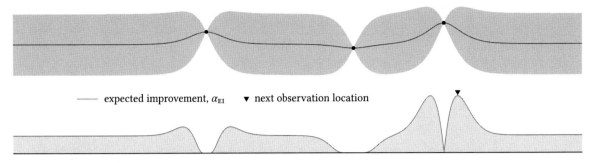

—— expected improvement, α_{EI} ▼ next observation location

Figure 7.3: The expected improvement acquisition function (7.2) corresponding to our running example.

maximal value observed, incumbent ϕ^*

12 The value ϕ^* is incumbent as it is currently "holding office" as our standing recommendation until it is deposed by a better candidate.

a dataset $\mathcal{D} = (\mathbf{x}, \boldsymbol{\phi})$, and define $\phi^* = \max \boldsymbol{\phi}$ to be the so-called *incumbent*: the maximal objective value yet seen.[12] As a consequence of exact observation, we have

$$u(\mathcal{D}) = \phi^*; \qquad u(\mathcal{D}') = \max(\phi^*, \phi);$$

and thus

$$u(\mathcal{D}') - u(\mathcal{D}) = \max(\phi - \phi^*, 0).$$

Substituting into (7.2), in the noiseless case we have

$$\alpha_{\text{EI}}(x; \mathcal{D}) = \int \max(\phi - \phi^*, 0)\, p(\phi \mid x, \mathcal{D})\, d\phi. \qquad (7.3)$$

example and interpretation

Expected improvement is illustrated for our running example in Figure 7.3. In this case, maximizing expected improvement will select a point near the previous best point found, an example of exploitation. Notice that the expected improvement vanishes near regions where we have existing observations. Although these locations may be likely to yield values higher than ϕ^* due to relatively high expected value, the relatively narrow credible intervals suggest that the magnitude of any improvement is likely to be small. Expected improvement is thus considering the exploration–exploitation dilemma in the selection of the next observation location, and the tradeoff between these two concerns is considered automatically.

simulated optimization and interpretation

Figure 7.4 shows the posterior belief of the objective after sequentially maximizing expected improvement to gather 20 additional observations of our example objective function. The global optimum was efficiently located. The distribution of the sample locations, with more evaluations in the most promising regions, reflects consideration of the exploration–exploitation dilemma. However, there seems to have been a focus on exploitation throughout the entire process; the first ten observations for example never strayed from the initially known local optimum. This behavior is a reflection of the simple reward utility function underlying the policy, which only rewards the discovery of high objective function values at *observed* locations. As a result, one-step lookahead may

exploitative behavior resulting from myopia

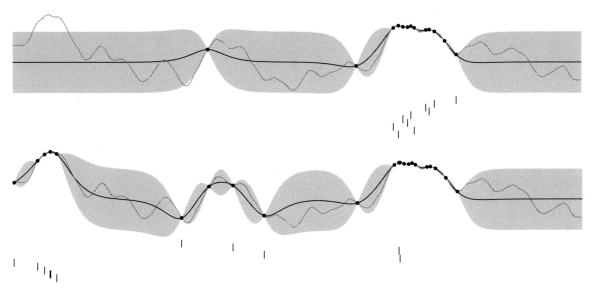

Figure 7.4: The posterior after 10 (top) and 20 (bottom) steps of the optimization policy induced by the expected improvement acquisition function (7.2) on our running example. The tick marks show the points chosen by the policy, progressing from top to bottom, during iterations 1–10 (top) and 11–20 (bottom). Observations within 0.2 length scales of the optimum have thicker marks; the optimum was located on iteration 19.

rationally choose to make marginal improvements to the value of the best-seen point, even if the underlying function value is known with a fair amount of confidence.

7.4 KNOWLEDGE GRADIENT

Adopting the global reward utility (6.5) and performing one-step-lookahead yields an acquisition function known as the *knowledge gradient*.

global reward: § 6.1, p. 109

Assume that, just as in the situation leading to the derivation of expected improvement, we again wish to identify a single point in the domain maximizing the objective function. However, imagine that at termination we are willing to commit to a location possibly never evaluated during optimization. To this end, we adopt the global reward utility function to measure our progress:

$$u(\mathcal{D}) = \max_{x \in \mathcal{X}} \mu_{\mathcal{D}}(x),$$

which rewards data for increasing the posterior mean, irrespective of location. Computing the one-step marginal gain to this utility results in the knowledge gradient acquisition function:

$$\alpha_{\text{KG}}(x; \mathcal{D}) = \int \left[\max_{x' \in \mathcal{X}} \mu_{\mathcal{D}'}(x') \right] p(y \mid x, \mathcal{D}) \, \mathrm{d}y - \max_{x' \in \mathcal{X}} \mu_{\mathcal{D}}(x'). \quad (7.4)$$

The knowledge gradient moniker was coined by FRAZIER and POW-ELL,[13] who interpreted the global reward as the amount of "knowledge"

13 P. FRAZIER and W. POWELL (2007). The Knowledge Gradient Policy for Offline Learning with Independent Normal Rewards. *ADPRL 2007*.

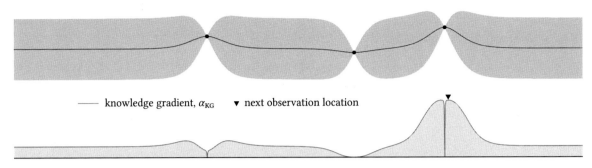

Figure 7.5: The knowledge gradient acquisition function (7.4) corresponding to our running example.

Figure 7.6: Samples of the updated posterior mean when evaluating at the location chosen by the knowledge gradient, illustrated in Figure 7.5. Only the right-hand section of the domain is shown.

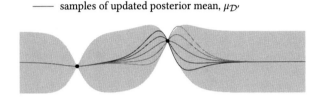

about the global maximum offered by a dataset $\mathcal{D}$. The knowledge gradient $\alpha_{KG}(x; \mathcal{D})$ can then be interpreted as the expected change in knowledge (that is, a discrete-time gradient) offered by a measurement at x.

example and interpretation

The knowledge gradient is illustrated for our running example in Figure 7.5. Perhaps surprisingly, the chosen observation location is remarkably close to the previously best-seen point. At first glance, this may seem wasteful, as we are already fairly confident about the value we might observe.

reason for selected observation

However, the knowledge gradient seeks to maximize the *global* maximum of the posterior mean, regardless of its location. With this in mind, we may reason as follows. There must be a local maximum of the objective function in the neighborhood of the best-seen point, but our current knowledge is insufficient to pinpoint its location. Further, as the relevant local maximum is probably not located precisely at this point, the objective function is either increasing or decreasing as it passes through. If we were to learn the *derivative* of the objective at this point, we would adjust our posterior belief to reflect that knowledge. Regardless of the sign or exact value of the derivative, our updated belief would reflect the discovery of a new, higher local maximum of the posterior mean in the indicated direction. By evaluating at the location selected by the knowledge gradient, we can effectively estimate the derivative of the objective; this is the principle behind finite differencing.

In Figure 7.6, we show samples of the updated posterior mean function $\mu_{\mathcal{D}'}(x)$ derived from sampling from the predictive distribution at the chosen evaluation location and conditioning. Indeed, these samples exhibit newly located global maxima on either side of the selected point, depending on the sign of the implied derivative. Note that the locations

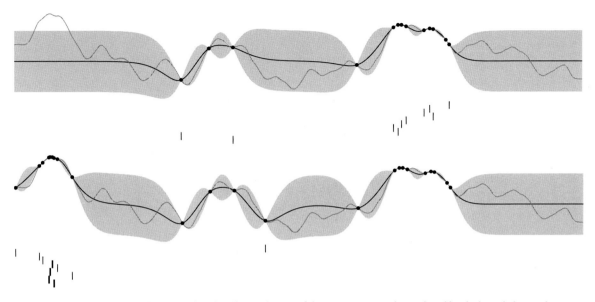

Figure 7.7: The posterior after 10 (top) and 20 (bottom) steps of the optimization policy induced by the knowledge gradient acquisition function (7.4) on our running example. The tick marks show the points chosen by the policy, progressing from top to bottom, during iterations 1–10 (top) and 11–20 (bottom). Observations within 0.2 length scales of the optimum have thicker marks; the optimum was located on iteration 15.

of these new maxima coincide with local maxima of the expected improvement acquisition function; see Figure 7.3 for comparison. This is not a coincidence! One way to interpret this relation is that, due to rewarding large values of the posterior mean at observed locations only, expected improvement must essentially guess on which side the hidden local optimum of the objective lies and hope to be correct. The knowledge gradient, on the other hand, considers identifying this maximum on either side a success, and guessing is not necessary.

Figure 7.7 illustrates the behavior of the knowledge gradient policy on our example optimization scenario. The global optimum was located efficiently. Comparing the decisions made by the knowledge gradient to those made by expected improvement (see Figure 7.4), we can observe a somewhat more even exploration of the domain, including in local maxima. The knowledge gradient policy does not necessarily need to expend observations to verify a suspected maximum, instead putting more trust into the model to have correct beliefs in these regions.

simulated optimization and interpretation

more exploration than expected improvement from more-relaxed utility

7.5 PROBABILITY OF IMPROVEMENT

As its name suggests, the *probability of improvement* acquisition function computes the probability of an observed value to improve upon some chosen threshold, regardless of the magnitude of this improvement.

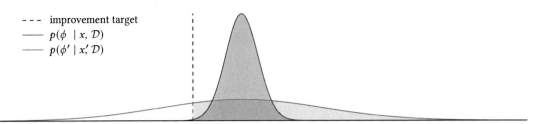

- - - improvement target
—— $p(\phi \mid x, \mathcal{D})$
—— $p(\phi' \mid x', \mathcal{D})$

Figure 7.8: An illustrative example comparing the behavior of probability of improvement with expected improvement computed with respect to the dashed target. The predictive distributions for two points x and x' are shown. The distributions have equal mean but the distribution at x' has larger predictive standard deviation. The shaded regions represent the region of improvement. The relatively safe x is preferred by probability of improvement, whereas the more-risky x' is preferred by expected improvement.

simple reward: § 6.1, p. 109

Consider the simple reward of an already gathered dataset $\mathcal{D} = (\mathbf{x}, \mathbf{y})$:

$$u(\mathcal{D}) = \max \mu_{\mathcal{D}}(\mathbf{x}).$$

The probability of improvement acquisition function scores a proposed observation location x according to the probability that an observation there will improve this utility by at least some margin ε. Let us denote the desired utility threshold with $\tau = u(\mathcal{D}) + \varepsilon$; we will use both the absolute threshold τ and the marginal threshold ε in the following discussion as convenient. The probability of improvement is then the probability that the updated utility $u(\mathcal{D}')$ exceeds the chosen threshold:

desired margin of improvement, ε
desired improvement threshold, τ

$$\alpha_{\text{PI}}(x; \mathcal{D}, \tau) = \Pr\big(u(\mathcal{D}') > \tau \mid x, \mathcal{D}\big). \tag{7.5}$$

utility formulation

We may interpret probability of improvement in the Bayesian decision-theoretic framework as computing the expected one-step marginal gain in a peculiar choice of utility function: a utility offering unit reward for each observation increasing the simple reward by the desired amount.

noiseless case

In the case of exact observation, we have

$$u(\mathcal{D}) = \max f(\mathbf{x}) = \phi^*; \qquad u(\mathcal{D}') = \max(\phi^*, \phi),$$

and we may write the probability of improvement in the somewhat simpler form

$$\alpha_{\text{PI}}(x; \mathcal{D}, \tau) = \Pr(\phi > \tau \mid x, \mathcal{D}). \tag{7.6}$$

In this case, the probability of improvement is simply the complementary cumulative distribution function of the predictive distribution evaluated at the improvement threshold τ. This form of probability of improvement is sometimes encountered in the literature, but our modification in terms of the simple reward allows for inexact observations as well.

comparison with expected improvement

It can be illustrative to compare the preferences over observation locations implied by the probability of improvement and expected improvement acquisition functions. In general, probability of improvement is somewhat more risk-averse than expected improvement, because probability of improvement would prefer a certain improvement of modest

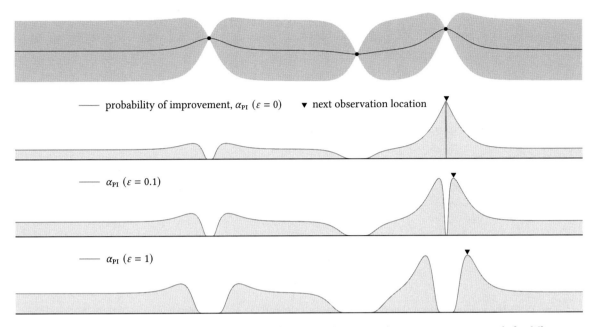

Figure 7.9: The probability of improvement acquisition function (7.5) corresponding to our running example for different values of the target improvement ε. The target is expressed as a fraction of the range of the posterior mean over the space. Increasing the target improvement leads to increasingly exploratory behavior.

magnitude to an uncertain improvement of potentially large magnitude. Figure 7.8 illustrates this phenomenon. Shown are the predictive distributions for the objective function values at two points x and x'. Both points have equal predictive means; however, x' has a significantly larger predictive standard deviation. We consider improvement with respect to the illustrated target. The shaded regions represent the regions of improvement; the probability mass of these regions equal the probabilities of improvement. Improvement is near certain at x ($\alpha_{\text{PI}} = 99.9\%$), whereas it is somewhat smaller at x' ($\alpha_{\text{PI}} = 72.6\%$), and thus probability of improvement would prefer to observe at x. The *expected* improvement at x, however, is small compared to x' with its longer tail:

$$\frac{\alpha_{\text{EI}}(x'; \mathcal{D})}{\alpha_{\text{EI}}(x; \mathcal{D})} = 1.28.$$

The expected improvement at x' is 28% larger than at x, indicating a preference for a less-certain but potentially larger payout.

The role of the improvement target

The magnitude of the required improvement plays a crucial role in shaping the behavior of probability of improvement policies. By adjusting this parameter, we may encourage exploration (with large ε) or exploitation (with small ε). Figure 7.9 shows the probability of improvement for

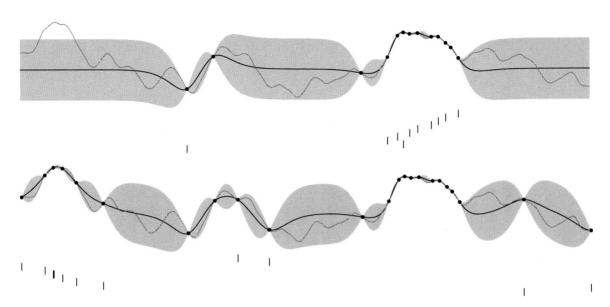

Figure 7.10: The posterior after 10 (top) and 20 (bottom) steps of the optimization policy induced by probability of improvement with $\varepsilon = 0.1\left[\max \mu_{\mathcal{D}}(x) - \min \mu_{\mathcal{D}}(x)\right]$ (7.5) on our running example. The tick marks show the points chosen by the policy, progressing from top to bottom, during iterations 1–10 (top) and 11–20 (bottom). Observations within 0.2 length scales of the optimum have thicker marks; the optimum was located on iteration 15.

our example scenario with thresholds corresponding to infinitesimal improvement, a modest improvement, and a significant improvement. The shift toward exploratory behavior for larger improvement thresholds can be clearly seen.

In Figure 7.10, we see 20 evaluations chosen by maximizing probability of improvement with the target dynamically set to 10% of the range of the posterior mean function. The global optimum was located, and the domain appears sufficiently explored. Although performance was quite reasonable here, the improvement threshold was set somewhat arbitrarily, and it is not always clear how one should set this parameter.

the $\varepsilon = 0$ case

On one extreme, some authors define a parameter-free (and probably too literal) version of probability of improvement by fixing the improvement target to $\varepsilon = 0$, rewarding even infinitesimal improvement to the current data. Intuitively, this low bar can induce overly exploitative behavior. Examining the probability of improvement with $\varepsilon = 0$ for our running example in Figure 7.9, we see that the acquisition function is maximized directly next to the previously best-found point. This decision represents extreme exploitation and potentially undesirable behavior. The situation after applying probability of improvement with $\varepsilon = 0$ to select 20 additional observation locations, shown in Figure 7.11, clearly demonstrates a drastic focus on exploitation. Notably, the global optimum was not identified.

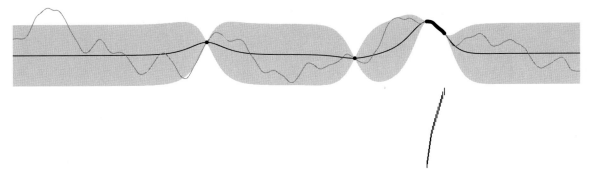

Figure 7.11: The posterior after 20 steps of the optimization policy induced by probability of improvement with $\varepsilon = 0$ (7.5) on our running example. The tick marks show the points chosen by the policy, progressing from top to bottom.

Evidently we must carefully select the desired improvement threshold to achieve ideal behavior. JONES provided some simple, data-driven advice for choosing improvement thresholds that remains sound.[14] Define

$$\mu^* = \max_{x \in \mathcal{X}} \mu_{\mathcal{D}}(x); \qquad r = \max \mu_{\mathcal{D}}(\mathbf{x}) - \min \mu_{\mathcal{D}}(\mathbf{x});$$

to represent the global maximum of the posterior mean and the range of the posterior mean at the observed locations. JONES suggests considering targets of the form

$$\mu^* + \alpha r,$$

where $\alpha \geq 0$ controls the amount of desired improvement in terms of the range of observed data. He provides a table of 27 suggested values for α in the range $[0, 3]$ and remarks that the points optimizing the set of induced acquisition functions typically cluster together in a small number of locations, each representing a different tradeoff between exploration and exploitation.[15] JONES continued to recommend selecting one point from each of these clusters to evaluate in parallel, defining a batch optimization policy. Although this may not always be possible, the recommended parameterization of the desired improvement is natural and would be appropriate for general use.

This proposal is illustrated for our running example in Figure 7.12. We begin with the posterior after selecting 10 points in our previous demo (see Figure 7.10), and indicate the points maximizing the probability of improvement for JONES's proposed improvement targets. The points cluster together in four regions reflecting varying exploration–exploitation tradeoffs.

14 D. R. JONES (2001). A Taxonomy of Global Optimization Methods Based on Response Surfaces. *Journal of Global Optimization* 21(4):345–383.

15 The proposed values for α given by JONES are compiled below.

	α	
0	0.07	0.25
0.0001	0.08	0.3
0.001	0.09	0.4
0.01	0.1	0.5
0.02	0.11	0.75
0.03	0.12	1
0.04	0.13	1.5
0.05	0.15	2
0.06	0.2	3

7.6 MUTUAL INFORMATION AND ENTROPY SEARCH

A family of information-theoretic optimization policies have been proposed in recent years, most with variations on the name *entropy search*.

Figure 7.12: The points maximizing probability of improvement using the 27 improvement thresholds proposed by JONES, beginning with the posterior from Figure 7.10 after 10 total observations have been obtained. The tick marks show the chosen points and cluster together in four regions representing different tradeoffs between exploration and exploitation.

16 T. M. COVER and J. A. THOMAS (2006). *Elements of Information Theory.* John Wiley & Sons.

17 D. J. C. MACKAY (2003). *Information Theory, Inference, and Learning Algorithms.* Cambridge University Press.

information-theoretic decision making as a model of the scientific method

information gain: § 6.3, p. 115

18 D. V. LINDLEY (1956). On a Measure of the Information Provided by an Experiment. *The Annals of Mathematical Statistics* 27(4):986–1005.

19 B. SETTLES (2012). *Active Learning.* Morgan & Claypool.

The acquisition function in these methods is *mutual information*, a measure of dependence between random variables that is a central concept in information theory.[16,17]

The reasoning underlying entropy search policies is somewhat different from and more general than the other acquisition functions we have considered thus far, all of which ultimately focus on maximizing the posterior mean function. Although this is a pragmatic concern, it is intimately linked to optimization. Information-theoretic experimental design is instead motivated by an abstract pursuit of *knowledge*, and may be interpreted as a mathematical formulation of the scientific method.

We begin by identifying some unknown feature of the world that we wish to learn about; in the context of Bayesian inference, this will be some random variable ω. We then view each observation we make as an opportunity to learn about this random variable, and seek to gather data that will, in aggregate, provide considerable information about ω. This process is analogous to a scientist designing a sequence of experiments to understand some natural phenomenon, where each experiment may be chosen to challenge or confirm constantly evolving beliefs.

The framework of information theory allows us to formalize this process. We may quantify the amount of information provided about a random variable ω by a dataset $\mathcal{D}$ via the *information gain*, a concept for which we provided two definitions in the last chapter. Adopting either definition as a utility function and performing one-step lookahead yields mutual information as an acquisition function.

Information-theoretic optimization policies select ω such that its determination gives insight into our optimization problem (1.1). However, by selecting different choices for ω, we can generate radically different policies, each attempting to learn about a different aspect of the system of interest. Maximizing mutual information has long been promoted as a general framework for optimal experimental design,[18] and this framework has been applied in numerous *active learning* settings.[19]

Before showing how mutual information arises in a decision-theoretic context, we pause to define the concept and derive some important properties.

Mutual information

Let ω and ψ be random variables with probability density functions $p(\omega)$ and $p(\psi)$. The mutual information between ω and ψ is

$$I(\omega; \psi) = \iint p(\omega, \psi) \log \frac{p(\omega, \psi)}{p(\omega)\, p(\psi)} \, \mathrm{d}\omega \, \mathrm{d}\psi. \qquad (7.7)$$

definition

This expression may be recognized as the Kullback–Leibler divergence between the joint distribution of the random variables and the product of their marginal distributions:

$$I(\omega; \psi) = D_{\mathrm{KL}}\big[p(\omega, \psi) \,\|\, p(\omega)\, p(\psi) \big].$$

We may extend this definition to conditional probability distributions as well. Given an arbitrary set of observed data $\mathcal{D}$, we define the conditional mutual information between ω and ψ by:[20]

conditional mutual information, $I(\omega; \psi \mid \mathcal{D})$

$$I(\omega; \psi \mid \mathcal{D}) = \iint p(\omega, \psi \mid \mathcal{D}) \log \frac{p(\omega, \psi \mid \mathcal{D})}{p(\omega \mid \mathcal{D})\, p(\psi \mid \mathcal{D})} \, \mathrm{d}\omega \, \mathrm{d}\psi.$$

20 Some authors use the notation $I(\omega; \psi \mid \mathcal{D})$ to represent the *expectation* of the given quantity with respect to the dataset $\mathcal{D}$. In optimization, we will always have an explicit dataset in hand, in which case the provided definition is more useful.

Here we have simply conditioned all distributions on the data and applied the definition in (7.7) to the posterior beliefs.

Several properties of mutual information are immediately evident from its definition. First, mutual information is symmetric in its arguments:

symmetry

$$I(\omega; \psi) = I(\psi; \omega). \qquad (7.8)$$

We also have that if ω and ψ are independent, then $p(\omega, \psi) = p(\omega)\, p(\psi)$ and the mutual information is zero:

$$I(\omega; \psi) = \iint p(\omega, \psi) \log \frac{p(\omega)\, p(\psi)}{p(\omega)\, p(\psi)} \, \mathrm{d}\omega \, \mathrm{d}\psi = 0.$$

Further, recognition of mutual information as a Kullback–Leibler divergence implies several additional inherited properties, including nonnegativity. Thus mutual information attains its minimal value when ω and ψ are independent.

nonnegativity

We may also manipulate (7.7) by twice applying the identity

$$p(\omega, \psi) = p(\psi)\, p(\omega \mid \psi)$$

expected reduction in entropy

to derive an equivalent expression for the mutual information:

$$\begin{aligned} I(\omega; \psi) &= \iint p(\omega, \psi) \log \frac{p(\omega, \psi)}{p(\omega)\, p(\psi)} \, \mathrm{d}\omega \, \mathrm{d}\psi \\ &= \iint p(\omega, \psi) \log p(\omega \mid \psi) \, \mathrm{d}\omega \, \mathrm{d}\psi - \int p(\omega) \log p(\omega) \, \mathrm{d}\omega \\ &= \int p(\psi) \left[\int p(\omega \mid \psi) \log p(\omega \mid \psi) \, \mathrm{d}\omega \right] \mathrm{d}\psi + H[\omega] \\ &= H[\omega] - \mathbb{E}\big[H[\omega \mid \psi] \big]. \qquad (7.9) \end{aligned}$$

It is important to note that this is true only in expectation. Consider two random variables x and y with the following joint distribution. x takes value 0 or 1 with probability $1/2$ each. If x is 0, y takes value 0 or 1 with probability $1/2$ each. If x is 1, y takes value 0 or -1 with probability $1/2$ each. The entropy of x is 1 bit and the entropy of y is 1.5 bits. Observing x always yields 0.5 bits about y. However, observing y produces either *no information* about x (0 bits), with probability $1/2$, or *complete information* about x (1 bit), with probability $1/2$. So the information gain about x from y and about y from x is actually *never* equal. However, the *expected* information gain *is* equal, $I(x; y) = 0.5$ bits.

22 Setting $u(\mathcal{D}) = D_{\mathrm{KL}}\big[p(\omega \mid \mathcal{D}) \parallel p(\omega)\big]$, we have:

$$\mathbb{E}\big[u(\mathcal{D}') \mid x, \mathcal{D}\big]$$
$$= \mathbb{E}\Bigg[\int p(\omega \mid \mathcal{D}') \log p(\omega \mid \mathcal{D}')\, d\omega \mid x, \mathcal{D}\Bigg]$$
$$\quad - \int p(\omega \mid \mathcal{D}) \log p(\omega)\, d\omega$$
$$= -\mathbb{E}\big[H[\omega \mid x, \mathcal{D}'] \mid \mathcal{D}\big]$$
$$\quad - \int p(\omega \mid \mathcal{D}) \log p(\omega)\, d\omega.$$

Here the second term is known as the *cross entropy* between $p(\omega)$ and $p(\omega \mid \mathcal{D})$. We can also rewrite the utility in similar terms:

$$u(\mathcal{D}) = \int p(\omega \mid \mathcal{D}) \frac{\log p(\omega \mid \mathcal{D})}{\log p(\omega)}\, d\omega$$
$$= \int p(\omega \mid \mathcal{D}) \log p(\omega \mid \mathcal{D})\, d\omega$$
$$\quad - \int p(\omega \mid \mathcal{D}) \log p(\omega)\, d\omega$$
$$= -H[\omega \mid \mathcal{D}]$$
$$\quad - \int p(\omega \mid \mathcal{D}) \log p(\omega)\, d\omega.$$

If we subtract, the cross-entropy terms cancel and we obtain mutual information:

$$\mathbb{E}\big[u(\mathcal{D}') \mid x, \mathcal{D}\big] - u(\mathcal{D}) = $$
$$H[\omega \mid \mathcal{D}] - \mathbb{E}\big[H[\omega \mid \mathcal{D}'] \mid \mathcal{D}\big].$$

Thus the mutual information between ω and ψ is the expected decrease in the differential entropy of ω if we were to observe ψ. Due to symmetry (7.8), we may swap the roles of ω and ψ to derive an equivalent expression in the other direction:

$$I(\omega; \psi) = H[\omega] - \mathbb{E}_\psi\big[H[\omega \mid \psi]\big] = H[\psi] - \mathbb{E}_\omega\big[H[\psi \mid \omega]\big]. \quad (7.10)$$

Observing either ω or ψ will, in expectation, provide the same amount of information about the other: the mutual information $I(\omega; \psi)$.[21]

Maximizing mutual information as an optimization policy

Mutual information arises naturally in Bayesian sequential experimental design as the one-step expected information gain resulting from an observation. In the previous chapter, we introduced two different methods for quantifying this information gain. The first was the reduction in the differential entropy of ω from the prior to the posterior:

$$u(\mathcal{D}) = H[\omega] - H[\omega \mid \mathcal{D}] \quad (7.11)$$
$$= \int p(\omega \mid \mathcal{D}) \log p(\omega \mid \mathcal{D})\, d\omega - \int p(\omega) \log p(\omega)\, d\omega.$$

The second was the Kullback–Leibler divergence between the posterior and the prior:

$$u(\mathcal{D}) = D_{\mathrm{KL}}\big[p(\omega \mid \mathcal{D}) \parallel p(\omega)\big] = \int p(\omega \mid \mathcal{D}) \log \frac{p(\omega \mid \mathcal{D})}{p(\omega)}\, d\omega. \quad (7.12)$$

Remarkably, performing one-step lookahead with either choice yields mutual information as an acquisition function.

Let us first compute the expected marginal gain in (7.11). In this case the marginal information gain is:

$$H[\omega \mid \mathcal{D}] - H[\omega \mid \mathcal{D}'],$$

and the expected marginal information gain is then:

$$\alpha_{\mathrm{MI}}(x; \mathcal{D}) = H[\omega \mid \mathcal{D}] - \mathbb{E}\big[H[\omega \mid \mathcal{D}'] \mid x, \mathcal{D}\big] \quad (7.13)$$
$$= I(y; \omega \mid x, \mathcal{D}),$$

where we have recognized the expected reduction in entropy in (7.13) as the mutual information between y and ω given the putative location x and the available data $\mathcal{D}$ (7.9). It is simple to verify that the expected marginal improvement to the alternative information gain definition (7.12) gives the same expression; several terms cancel when computing the expectation, and those that remain are identical to those in (7.13).[22]

Due to the symmetry of mutual information, we have several equivalent forms for this acquisition function (7.10):

$$\alpha_{\mathrm{MI}}(x; \mathcal{D}) = I(y; \omega \mid x, \mathcal{D})$$
$$= H[\omega \mid \mathcal{D}] - \mathbb{E}_y\big[H[\omega \mid \mathcal{D}'] \mid x, \mathcal{D}\big] \quad (7.14)$$
$$= H[y \mid x, \mathcal{D}] - \mathbb{E}_\omega\big[H[y \mid \omega, x, \mathcal{D}] \mid x, \mathcal{D}\big]. \quad (7.15)$$

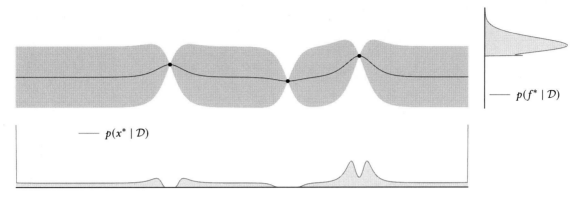

Figure 7.13: The posterior belief about the location of the global optimum, $p(x^* \mid \mathcal{D})$, and about the value of the global optimum, $p(f^* \mid \mathcal{D})$, for our running example. Note the significant probability mass associated with the optimum lying on the boundary.

Depending on the application, one of these two forms may be preferable, and maximizing either results in the same policy.

Adopting mutual information as an acquisition function for optimization requires that ω be selected to support the optimization task. Two natural options present themselves: the location of the global optimum, x^*, and the maximum value attained, $f^* = f(x^*)$ (1.1). Both have received extensive consideration, and we will discuss each in turn.

Mutual information with x^*

Several authors have proposed mutual information with the location of the global optimum x^* as an acquisition function:[23]

$$\alpha_{x^*}(x; \mathcal{D}) = I(y; x^* \mid x, \mathcal{D}). \tag{7.16}$$

The distribution of x^* is illustrated for our running example in Figure 7.13. Even for this simple example, the distribution of the global optimum is nontrivial and multimodal. In fact, in this case, there is a significant probability that the global maximum occurs on the *boundary* of the domain, which has Lebesgue measure zero, so x^* does not even have a proper probability density function.[24] We will nonetheless use the notation $p(x^* \mid \mathcal{D})$ in our discussion below.

The middle panel of Figure 7.14 shows the mutual information with x^* (7.16) for our running example. The next evaluation location will be chosen to investigate the neighborhood of the best-seen point. It is interesting to compare the behavior of the mutual information with other acquisition functions near the boundary of the domain. Although there is a significant probability that the maximum is achieved on the boundary, mutual information indicates that we cannot expect to reveal much information regarding x^* by measuring there. More information tends to be revealed by evaluating away from the boundary, as we can reduce our

23 We tacitly assume the location of the global optimum is unique to simplify discussion. Technically x^* is a set-valued random variable. For Gaussian process models, the uniqueness of x^* can be guaranteed under mild assumptions (§ 2.7, p. 34).

24 A proper treatment would separate the probability density on the interior of $\mathcal{X}$ from the distribution restricted to the boundary, but in practice we will only ever be sampling from this distribution, as it is simply too complicated to work with directly.

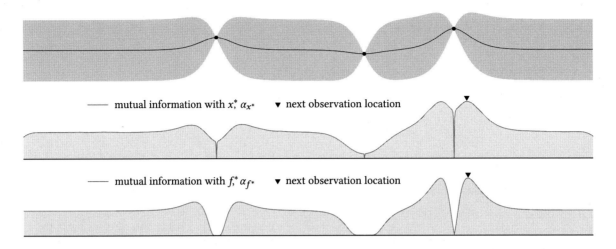

—— mutual information with x^*, α_{x^*} ▼ next observation location

—— mutual information with f^*, α_{f^*} ▼ next observation location

Figure 7.14: The mutual information between the observed value and the location of the global optimum, α_{x^*} (middle panel), and between the observed value and the value of the global optimum, α_{f^*} (bottom panel), for our running example.

uncertainty about the objective function over a larger volume. Expected improvement (Figure 7.3) and probability of improvement (Figure 7.9), on the other hand, are computed only from inspection of the marginal predictive distribution $p(y \mid x, \mathcal{D})$. As a result, they cannot differentiate observation locations based on their global impact on our belief.

In Figure 7.15, we demonstrate optimization by maximizing the mutual information with x^* (7.16) for our scenario. We also show the posterior belief about the maximum location at termination, $p(x^* \mid \mathcal{D})$. The global optimum was discovered efficiently and with remarkable confidence. Further, the posterior mode matches the true optimal location.

Mutual information with f^*

Mutual information with the value of the global optimum f^* has also been investigated as an acquisition function:[25]

$$\alpha_{f^*}(x; \mathcal{D}) = I(y; f^* \mid x, \mathcal{D}). \tag{7.17}$$

25 Again we assume in this discussion that a global optimum f^* exists almost surely. This assumption can be guaranteed for Gaussian process models under mild assumptions (§ 2.7, p. 34).

The distribution of this quantity is illustrated for our running example in Figure 7.13. There is a sharp mode in the distribution corresponding to the best-seen value in fact being near-optimal, and there is no mass *below* the best-seen value, as it serves as a lower bound on the maximum due to the assumption of exact observation.

example and discussion

The bottom panel of Figure 7.14 shows the mutual information with f^* (7.17) for our running example. The next evaluation location will be chosen to investigate the neighborhood of the best-seen point. It is interesting to contrast this surface with that of the mutual information with x^* in Figure 7.16. Mutual information with f^* is heavily penalized near

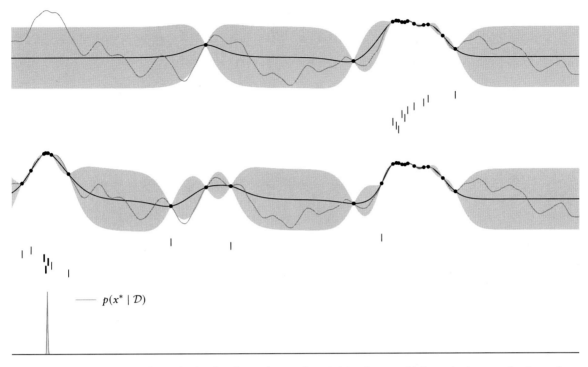

Figure 7.15: The posterior after 10 (top) and 20 (bottom) steps of maximizing the mutual information between the observed value y and the location of the global maximum x^* (7.16) on our running example. The tick marks show the points chosen by the policy, progressing from top to bottom. Observations within 0.2 length scales of the optimum have thicker marks; the optimum was located on iteration 16.

existing observations, even those with relatively high values. Observing at these points would contribute relatively little information about the value of the optimum, as their predictive distributions already reflect a narrow range of possibilities and contribute little to the distribution of f^*. Further, points on the boundary were less favored when seeking to learn about x^*. However, these points are expected to provide just as much information about f^* as neighboring points.

Figure 7.16 illustrates 25 evaluations chosen by sequentially maximizing the mutual information with f^* (7.17) for our scenario, along with the posterior belief about the value of the maximum given these observations, $p(f^* \mid \mathcal{D})$. The global optimum was discovered after 23 iterations, somewhat slower than the alternatives described above. The value of the optimum is known with almost complete confidence at termination.

7.7 MULTI-ARMED BANDITS AND OPTIMIZATION

Several Bayesian optimization algorithms have been inspired by policies for *multi-armed bandits,* a model system for sequential decision making

multi-armed bandits

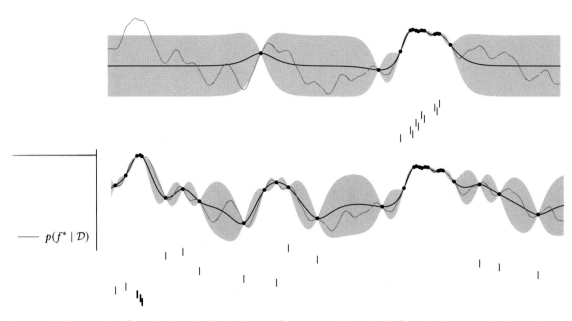

Figure 7.16: The posterior after 10 (top) and 25 (bottom) steps of maximizing the mutual information between the observed value y and the location of the global maximum f^* (7.17) on our running example. The tick marks show the points chosen by the policy, progressing from top to bottom. Observations within 0.2 length scales of the optimum have thicker marks; the optimum was located on iteration 23.

—— $p(f^* \mid \mathcal{D})$

under uncertainty. A multi-armed bandit problem can be interpreted as a particular finite-dimensional analog of sequential optimization, and effective algorithm design in both settings requires addressing many shared concerns.

set of arms, $\mathcal{X}$

The classical multi-armed bandit problem considers a finite set of "arms" $\mathcal{X}$ and an agent who must select a sequence of items from this set. Selecting an arm x results in a stochastic reward y drawn from an unknown distribution $p(y \mid x)$ associated with that arm; these rewards are assumed to be independent of time and conditionally independent given the chosen arm. The goal of the agent is to select a sequence of arms $\{x_i\}$ to maximize the cumulative reward (6.7) received, $\sum y_i$.

cumulative reward: § 6.2, p. 114

Multi-armed bandits have been studied as a model of many sequential decision processes arising in practice. For example, consider a doctor caring for a series of patients with the same condition, who must determine which of two possible treatments is the best course of action. We could model the sequence of treatment decisions as a two-armed bandit, with patient outcomes determining the rewards. The Hippocratic oath compels the doctor to discover the optimal arm (the best treatment) as efficiently and confidently as possible to minimize patient harm, creating a dilemma of effective assignment. In fact, this scenario of sequential clinical trials was precisely the original motivation for studying multi-armed bandits.[26]

26 W. R. THOMPSON (1933). On the Likelihood That One Unknown Probability Exceeds Another in View of the Evidence of Two Samples. *Biometrika* 25(3–4):285–294.

To facilitate the following discussion, for each arm $x \in \mathcal{X}$, we define $\phi = \mathbb{E}[y \mid x]$ to be its expected reward and will aggregate these into a vector $\mathbf{f}$ when convenient. We also define

$$x^* \in \arg\max_{x \in \mathcal{X}} \mathbb{E}[y \mid x] = \arg\max \mathbf{f}; \qquad f^* = \max_{x \in \mathcal{X}} \mathbb{E}[y \mid x] = \max \mathbf{f}$$

optimal policy with known rewards

to be the index of an arm with maximal expected reward and the value of that optimal reward, respectively.[27] If the reward distributions associated with each arm were known a priori, the optimal policy would be trivial: we would always select the arm with the highest expected reward. This policy generates expected reward f^* in each iteration, and it is clear from linearity of expectation that this is optimal. Unfortunately, the reward distributions are *unknown* to the agent and must be learned from observations instead. This complicates policy design considerably.

The only way we can learn about the reward distributions is to allocate resources to each arm and observe the outcomes. If the reward distributions have considerable spread and/or overlap with each other, a large number of observations may be necessary before the agent can confidently conclude which arm is optimal. The agent thus faces an exploration–exploitation dilemma, constantly forced to decide whether to select an arm believed to have high expected reward (exploitation) or whether to sample an uncertain arm to better understand its reward distribution (exploration). Ideally, the agent would have a policy that *efficiently* explores the arms, so that in the limit of many decisions the agent would eventually allocate an overwhelming majority of resources to the best possible alternative.

challenges in policy design

Dozens of policies for the multi-armed bandit problem have been proposed and studied from both the Bayesian and frequentist perspectives, and many strong convergence results are known.[28] Numerous variations on the basic formulation outlined above have also received consideration in the literature, and the interested reader may refer to one of several available exhaustive surveys for more information.[29,30,31]

The Bayesian optimal policy

A multi-armed bandit is fundamentally a sequential decision problem under uncertainty, and we may derive an optimal expected-case policy following our discussion in Chapter 5. The selection of each arm is a decision with action space $\mathcal{X}$, and we must act under uncertainty about the expected reward vector $\mathbf{f}$. Over the course of τ decisions, we will gather a dataset $\mathcal{D}_\tau = (\mathbf{x}_\tau, \mathbf{y}_\tau)$, seeking to maximize the cumulative reward (6.7): $u(\mathcal{D}_\tau) = \sum y_i$.

The key to the Bayesian approach is maintaining a belief about the expected reward of each arm. We begin by choosing a prior over the expected rewards, $p(\mathbf{f})$, and an observation model for the observed rewards given the index of an arm and its expected reward, $p(y \mid x, \phi)$.[32] Now given an arbitrary set of previous observations $\mathcal{D}$, we may derive a posterior belief about the expected rewards, $p(\mathbf{f} \mid \mathcal{D})$.

belief about expected rewards

27 All of the notation throughout this section is chosen to align with that for optimization. In a multi-armed bandit, an arm x is associated with expected reward $\phi = \mathbb{E}[y \mid x]$. In optimization with zero-mean additive noise, a point x is associated with expected observed value $\phi = f(x) = \mathbb{E}[y \mid x]$.

28 We will explore these connections in our discussion on theoretical convergence results for Bayesian optimization algorithms in Chapter 10, p. 213.

29 D. A. BERRY and B. FRISTEDT (1985). *Bandit Problems: Sequential Allocation of Experiments.* Chapman & Hall.

30 S. BUBECK and N. CESA-BIANCHI (2012). Regret Analysis of Stochastic and Nonstochastic Multi-Armed Bandit Problems. *Foundations and Trends in Machine Learning* 5(1):1–122.

31 T. LATTIMORE and C. SZEPESVÁRI (2020). *Bandit Algorithms.* Cambridge University Press.

32 This model is often conditionally independent of the arm given the expected reward, allowing the definition of a single observation model $p(y \mid \phi)$.

optimal policy: § 5.2, p. 91

The optimal policy may now be derived following our previous analysis. We make each decision by maximizing the expected reward by termination, recursively assuming optimal future behavior (5.15–5.17). Notably, the optimal decision for the *last* round is the arm maximizing the posterior mean reward, reflecting pure exploitation:[33]

$$x_\tau \in \arg\max \mathbb{E}[\mathbf{f} \mid \mathcal{D}_{\tau-1}].$$

More exploratory behavior begins with the penultimate decision and increases with the decision horizon.

running time of optimal policy: § 5.3, p. 99

Unfortunately, the cost of computing the optimal policy increases exponentially with the horizon. We must therefore find some mechanism to design computationally efficient but empirically effective policies for use in practice. This is precisely the same situation we face in optimization!

Optimization as an infinite-armed bandit

We may model continuous optimization as an *infinite-armed* bandit problem,[34] and this analogy has proven fruitful. Suppose we seek to optimize an objective function $f: \mathcal{X} \to \mathbb{R}$, where the domain $\mathcal{X}$ is now infinite. We assume as usual that we can observe this function at any point x of our choosing, revealing an observation y with distribution $p(y \mid x, \phi); \phi = f(x)$. For the bandit analogy to be maximally appropriate, we will further assume that the expected value of this observation is ϕ: $\mathbb{E}[y \mid \phi] = \phi$; this is not unduly restrictive and is satisfied for example by zero-mean additive noise.

Assuming an evaluation budget of τ observations, we may formulate this scenario to a multi-armed bandit. We interpret each point $x \in \mathcal{X}$ as one of infinitely many arms, with each arm returning an expected reward determined by the underlying objective function value ϕ. With some care, we may now adapt a multi-armed bandit policy to this setting.

correlation of rewards

In the traditional multi-armed bandit problem, we assume that rewards are conditionally independent given the chosen arm index. As a consequence, the reward from any selected arm provides no information about the rewards of other arms. However, this independence would render an infinite-armed bandit hopeless, as we would never be able to determine the best arm with a finite budget. Instead, we must assume that the rewards are *correlated* over the domain, so that each observation can potentially inform us about the rewards of every other arm.[35]

This assumption is natural in optimization; the objective function must reflect some nontrivial structure, or optimization would also be hopeless. In the Bayesian framework, we formalize our assumptions regarding the structure of correlations between function values by choosing an appropriate prior distribution, which we may condition on available data to form the posterior belief, $p(f \mid \mathcal{D})$. In our bandit analogy, this distribution encapsulates beliefs about the expected rewards of each arm that can be used to derive effective policies.

cumulative vs. simple reward

Why should we reduce optimization to the multi-armed bandit at all? Notably, in optimization we are usually concerned with identifying

33 See § 7.10 for an analogous result in optimization.

34 R. AGRAWAL (1995). The Continuum-Armed Bandit Problem. *SIAM Journal on Control and Optimization* 33(6):1926–1951.

35 In the multi-armed bandit literature, bandits with correlated rewards are known as *restless bandits*, as our belief about arms may change even when they are not selected (left alone):

P. WHITTLE (1988). Restless Bandits: Activity Allocation in a Changing World. *Journal of Applied Probability* 25(A):287–298.

a *single* point in the domain maximizing the function, and variations on the simple reward directly measure progress toward this end. It may seem odd to focus on maximizing the *cumulative* reward, which judges a dataset based on the *average* value observed rather than the maximum.

These aims are not necessarily incompatible. In the limit of many observations, we hope to guarantee the best arm will be eventually identified so that we can guarantee convergence to optimal behavior. Bandit algorithms are typically analyzed in terms of their *cumulative regret,* the difference between the cumulative reward received and that expected from the optimal policy. If this quantity decreases sufficiently quickly, we may conclude that the optimal arm is eventually identified and selected. In our infinite-armed case, this implies the global optimum of the objective will eventually be located,[36] suggesting the multi-armed bandit reduction is indeed reasonable.

cumulative regret and convergence: § 10.1, p. 214

[36] In the infinite-armed case, establishing the no-regret property (§ 10.1, p. 214) is not sufficient to guarantee the global optimum will ever be evaluated exactly; however, we can conclude that we evaluate points achieving objective values within any desired tolerance of the maximum.

7.8 MAXIMIZING A STATISTICAL UPPER BOUND

Effective strategies for both bandits and optimization require careful consideration of the exploration–exploitation dilemma for success. Numerous bandit algorithms have been built on the unifying principle of *optimism in the face of uncertainty,*[37] which has proven to be an effective heuristic for balancing these concerns. The key idea is to use any available data to both estimate the expected reward of each arm and to quantify the uncertainty in these estimates. When faced with a decision, we then always select the arm that would be optimal when allowing "the benefit of the doubt": the arm with the highest *plausible* expected reward given the currently available information. Arms with highly uncertain reward will have a correspondingly wide range of plausible values, and this mechanism thus provides underexplored arms a so-called *exploration bonus*[38] commensurate with their uncertainty, encouraging exploration of plausible optimal locations.

To be more precise, assume we have gathered an arbitrary dataset $\mathcal{D}$, and consider an arbitrary point x. Consider the *quantile function* associated with the predictive distribution $p(\phi \mid x, \mathcal{D})$:[39]

$$q(\pi; x, \mathcal{D}) = \inf \left\{ \phi' \mid \Pr(\phi \leq \phi' \mid x, \mathcal{D}) \geq \pi \right\}.$$

We can interpret this function as a statistical *upper confidence bound* on ϕ: the value will exceed the bound only with tunable probability $1 - \pi$.

As a function of x, we can interpret $q(\pi; x, \mathcal{D})$ as an optimistic estimate of the entire objective function. The principle of optimism in the face of uncertainty then suggests observing where this upper confidence bound is maximized, yielding the acquisition function

$$\alpha_{\text{UCB}}(x; \mathcal{D}, \pi) = q(\pi; x, \mathcal{D}). \tag{7.18}$$

Figure 7.17 shows upper confidence bounds for our example scenario corresponding to three values of the confidence parameter π. Unlike the acquisition functions considered previously in this chapter, an upper

optimism in the face of uncertainty

[37] A. W. MOORE and C. G. ATKESON (1993). Memory-Based Reinforcement Learning: Efficient Computation with Prioritized Sweeping. *NeurIPS 1992.*

[38] R. S. SUTTON (1990). Integrated Architectures for Learning, Planning, and Reacting Based on Approximating Dynamic Programming. *ICML 1990.*

[39] The quantile function satisfies the relation that $\phi \leq q(\pi; x, \mathcal{D})$ with probability π.

upper confidence bound

example and discussion

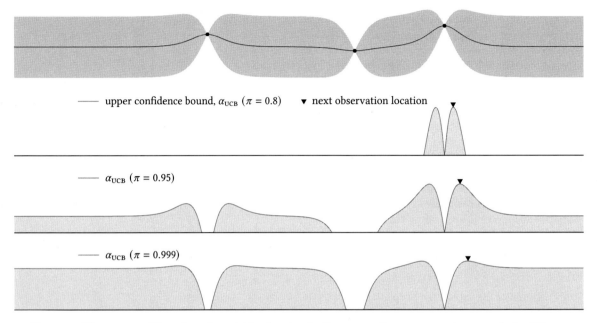

Figure 7.17: The upper confidence bound acquisition function (7.18) corresponding to our running example for different values of the confidence parameter π. The vertical axis for each acquisition function is shifted to the largest observed function value. Increasing the confidence parameter leads to increasingly exploratory behavior.

correspondence between certainty parameter and exploration proclivity

confidence bound need not be nonnegative, so we shift the acquisition function in these plots so that the best-seen function value intersects the horizontal axis. We can see that relatively low confidence values ($\pi = 0.8$) give little credit to locations with high uncertainty, and exploitation is heavily favored. By increasing this parameter, our actions reflect more exploratory behavior.

In Figure 7.18, we sequentially maximize the upper confidence bound on our example function to select 20 observation locations using confidence parameter $\pi = 0.999$, corresponding to the bottom and most exploratory example in Figure 7.17. The global maximum was located efficiently. Notably, the observation locations chosen in the early stages of the search reflect more exploration than all the other methods we have discussed thus far.

adjusting the exploration parameter

Using an upper confidence bound policy in practice requires specifying the exploration parameter π, and it may not always be clear how best to do so. We face a similar challenge when choosing the improvement target parameter for probability of improvement, and in fact this analogy is sometimes remarkably intimate. For some models of the objective function, including Gaussian processes, a point maximizing the probability of improvement over a given threshold τ also maximizes an upper confidence bound for some confidence parameter π, and vice versa.[40] Therefore the sets of points obtained by maximizing these acquisition

40 D. R. JONES (2001). A Taxonomy of Global Optimization Methods Based on Response Surfaces. *Journal of Global Optimization* 21(4):345–383.

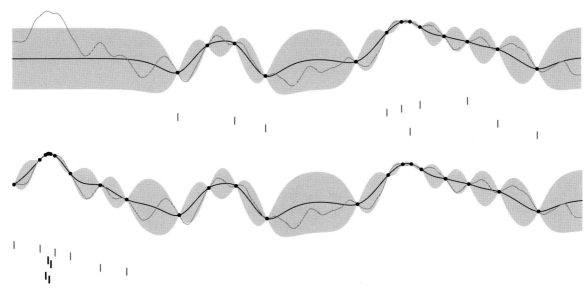

Figure 7.18: The posterior after 10 (top) and 20 (bottom) steps of the optimization policy induced by the upper confidence bound acquisition function (7.2) on our running example. The confidence parameter was set to $\pi = 0.999$. The tick marks show the points chosen by the policy, progressing from top to bottom, during iterations 1–10 (top) and 11–20 (bottom). Observations within 0.2 length scales of the optimum have thicker marks; the optimum was located on iteration 15.

functions over the range of their respective parameters are identical. We will establish this relationship for Gaussian process models in the next chapter.

equivalence of α_{PI} and α_{UCB} for GPS: § 8.4, p. 170

Little concrete advice is available for selecting the confidence parameter, as concerns such as model selection and calibration may have effects on the upper confidence bound that are hard to foresee and account for. Most authors select relatively large values in the approximate range $\pi \in (0.98, 1)$, with values of $\pi \approx 0.999$ being perhaps the most common. In line with his advice regarding probability of improvement parameter selection, JONES suggests considering a wide range of confidence values,[41] reflecting different exploration–exploitation tradeoffs. Figure 7.12 illustrates this concept by maximizing the probability of improvement for a range of improvement thresholds; by the correspondence between these policies for Gaussian process models, this is also illustrative for maximizing upper confidence bounds.

selecting improvement threshold: § 7.5, p. 134

41 D. R. JONES (2001). A Taxonomy of Global Optimization Methods Based on Response Surfaces. *Journal of Global Optimization* 21(4):345–383.

Chapter 10: Theoretical Analysis, p. 213

The policy realized by sequentially maximizing upper confidence bounds enjoys strong theoretical guarantees. For Gaussian process models, SRINIVAS et al. proved this policy is guaranteed to effectively maximize the objective at a nontrivial rate under reasonable assumptions.[42] One of these assumptions is that the confidence parameter must increase asymptotically to 1 at a particular rate. Intuitively, the reason for this growth is that our uncertainty in the objective function will typically

42 N. SRINIVAS et al. (2010). Gaussian Process Optimization in the Bandit Setting: No Regret and Experimental Design. *ICML 2010*.

These results will be discussed at length in Chapter 10, p. 213.

decrease as we continue to gather more data. As a result, we must simultaneously increase the confidence parameter to maintain a sufficient rate of exploration. This idea of slowly increasing the confidence parameter throughout optimization may be useful as a practical heuristic as well as a theoretical device.

7.9   THOMPSON SAMPLING

In the early 20th century, THOMPSON proposed a simple and effective *stochastic* policy for the multi-armed bandit problem that has come to be known as *Thompson sampling*.[43] Faced with a set of alternatives, the basic idea is to maintain a belief about which of these options is optimal in light of available information. We then design each evaluation by sampling from this distribution, yielding an adaptive stochastic policy. This procedure elegantly addresses the exploration–exploitation dilemma: sampling observations proportional to their probability of optimality automatically encourages exploitation, while the inherent randomness of the policy guarantees constant exploration. Thompson sampling can be adopted from finite-armed bandits to continuous optimization, and has enjoyed some interest in the Bayesian optimization literature.

43 W. R. THOMPSON (1933). On the Likelihood That One Unknown Probability Exceeds Another in View of the Evidence of Two Samples. *Biometrika* 25(3–4):285–294.

definition

Suppose we are at an arbitrary stage of optimization with data $\mathcal{D}$. The key object in Thompson sampling is the posterior distribution of the location of the global maximum x^*, $p(x^* \mid \mathcal{D})$, a distribution we have already encountered in our discussion on mutual information. Whereas maximizing mutual information carefully maximizes the information we expect to receive, Thompson sampling employs a considerably simpler mechanism. We choose the next observation location by sampling from this belief, yielding a nondeterministic optimization policy:

mutual information with x^*: § 7.6, p. 139

$$x \sim p(x^* \mid \mathcal{D}). \tag{7.19}$$

alternative interpretation: optimizing a random acquisition function

At first glance, Thompson sampling appears fundamentally different from the previous policies we have discussed, which were all defined in terms of maximizing an acquisition function. However, we may resolve this discrepancy while gaining some insight: Thompson sampling in fact designs each observation by maximizing a *random* acquisition function.

The location of the global maximum x^* is completely determined by the objective function f, and we may exploit this relationship to yield a simple two-stage implementation of Thompson sampling. We first sample a random realization of the objective function from its posterior:[44]

44 We give the sample a suggestive name!

$$\alpha_{\text{TS}}(x; \mathcal{D}) \sim p(f \mid \mathcal{D}). \tag{7.20}$$

We then optimize this function to yield the desired sample from $p(x^* \mid \mathcal{D})$, our next observation location:

$$x \in \arg\max_{x' \in \mathcal{X}} \alpha_{\text{TS}}(x'; \mathcal{D}).$$

From this point of view, we can interpret the sampled objective function α_{TS} as an ordinary acquisition function that is maximized as usual.

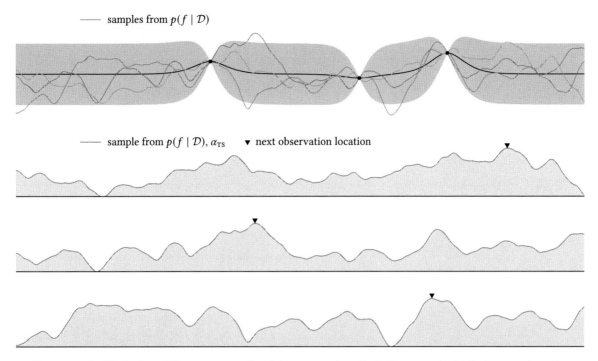

Figure 7.19: An illustration of Thompson sampling for our example optimization scenario. At the top, we show the objective function posterior $p(f \mid \mathcal{D})$ and three samples from this belief. Thompson sampling selects the next observation location by maximizing one of these samples. In the bottom three panels we show three possible outcomes of this process, corresponding to each of the sampled objective functions illustrated in the top panel.

Rather than representing an expected utility or a statistical upper bound, the acquisition function used in each round of Thompson sampling is a hallucinated objective function that is plausible under our belief. Whereas a Bayesian decision-theoretic policy chooses the optimal action in expectation while *averaging* over the uncertain objective function, Thompson sampling chooses the optimal action for a *randomly sampled* objective function. This interpretation of Thompson sampling is illustrated for our example scenario in Figure 7.19, showing three possible outcomes for Thompson sampling. In this case, two samples would exploit the region surrounding the best-seen point, and one would explore the region around the left-most observation.

Figure 7.20 shows the posterior belief of the objective after 15 rounds of Thompson sampling for our example scenario. The global maximum was located remarkably quickly. Of course, as a stochastic policy, it is not guaranteed that the behavior of Thompson sampling will resemble this outcome. In fact, this was a remarkably lucky run! The most likely locations of the optimum were ignored in the first rounds, quickly leading to the discovery of the optimum on the left. Figure 7.21 shows another

optimal decision for random sample

example and discussion

example of slow convergence

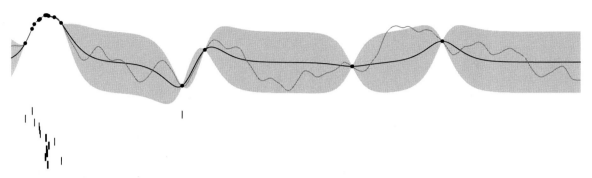

Figure 7.20: The posterior after 15 steps of Thompson sampling (7.19) on our running example. The tick marks show the points chosen by the policy, progressing from top to bottom. Observations within 0.2 length scales of the optimum have thicker marks; the optimum was located on iteration 8.

run of Thompson sampling on the same scenario. The global optimum was not found nearly as quickly; however, it was eventually located after approximately 80 iterations. In 100 repetitions of the policy varying the random seed, the median iteration for discovering the optimum on this example was 38, with only 12 seeds resulting in discovery in the first 20 iterations. Despite this sometimes slow convergence, the distribution of the chosen evaluation locations nonetheless demonstrates continual management of the exploration–exploitation tradeoff.

7.10   OTHER IDEAS IN POLICY CONSTRUCTION

We have now discussed the two most pervasive approaches to policy construction in Bayesian optimization: one-step lookahead and adapting policies for multi-armed bandits. We have also introduced the most popular Bayesian optimization policies encountered in the literature, all of which stem from one of these two methods. However, there are some additional ideas worthy of discussion.

Approximate dynamic programming beyond one-step lookahead

One-step lookahead offers tremendous computational benefits, but the cost of these savings is extreme myopia in decision making. As we are oblivious to anything that might happen beyond the present observation, one-step lookahead can focus too much on exploitation. However, some less myopic alternatives have been proposed based on more complex (and more costly!) approximations to the optimal policy.

approximate dynamic programming: § 5.3, p. 101

The simplest idea in this direction is to extend the lookahead horizon, and the most tractable option is of course two-step lookahead. Given an arbitrary one-step lookahead acquisition function $\alpha(x; \mathcal{D})$, the two-step analog is (5.12):

two-step lookahead

$$\alpha_2(x; \mathcal{D}) = \alpha(x; \mathcal{D}) + \mathbb{E}\left[\max_{x' \in \mathcal{X}} \alpha(x'; \mathcal{D}') \mid x, \mathcal{D}\right].$$

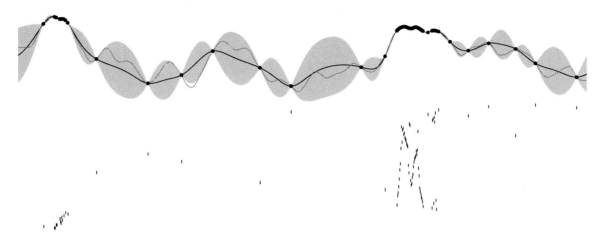

Figure 7.21: The posterior after 80 steps of Thompson sampling (7.19) on our running example, using a random seed different from Figure 7.20. The global optimum was located on iteration 78.

Although this door is open for any of the decision-theoretic policies considered in this chapter, two-step expected improvement has received the most attention. OSBORNE et al. derived two-step expected improvement and demonstrated good empirical performance on some test functions compared with the one-step alternative.[45] However, it is telling that they restricted their investigation to a limited number of functions due to the inherent computational expense. GINSBOURGER and LE RICHE completed a contemporaneous exploration of two-step expected improvement and provided an explicit example showing superior behavior from the less myopic policy.[46] Recently, several authors have revisited (2+)-step lookahead and developed sophisticated implementation schemes rendering longer horizons more feasible.[47,48]

We provided an in-depth illustration and deconstruction of two-step expected improvement for our example scenario in Figures 5.2–5.3. Note that the two-step expected improvement is appreciable even for the (useless!) options of evaluating at the previously observed locations, as we can still make conscientious use of the following observation.

Figure 7.22 illustrates the progress of 20 evaluations designed by maximizing two-step expected improvement for our example scenario. Comparing with the one-step alternative in Figure 7.4, the less myopic policy exhibits somewhat more exploratory behavior and discovered the optimum more efficiently – after 15 rather than 19 evaluations.

Rollout has also been considered as an approach to building nonmyopic optimization policies. Again the focus of these investigations has been on expected improvement (or the related knowledge gradient), but the underlying principles could be extended to other policies.

LAM et al. combined expected improvement with several steps of rollout, again maximizing expected improvement as the base policy.[49] The authors also proposed optionally adjusting the utility function through

45 M. A. OSBORNE et al. (2009). Gaussian Processes for Global Optimization. *LION 3*.

46 D. GINSBOURGER and R. LE RICHE (2010). Towards Gaussian Process-Based Optimization with Finite Time Horizon. *MODA 9*.

47 J. WU and P. I. FRAZIER (2019). Practical Two-Step Look-Ahead Bayesian Optimization. *NeurIPS 2019*.

48 S. JIANG et al. (2020b). Efficient Nonmyopic Bayesian Optimization via One-Shot Multi-Step Trees. *NeurIPS 2020*.

rollout: § 5.3, p. 102

49 R. R. LAM et al. (2016). Bayesian Optimization with a Finite Budget: An Approximate Dynamic Programming Approach. *NeurIPS 2016*.

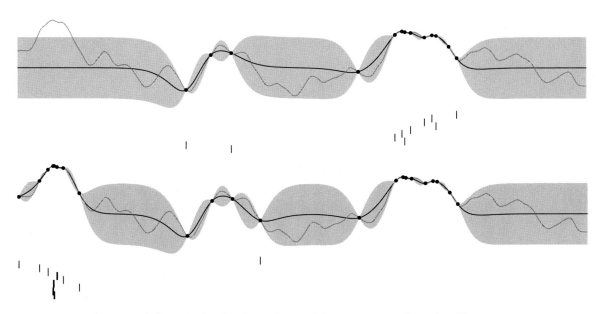

Figure 7.22: The posterior after 10 (top) and 20 (bottom) steps of the optimization policy induced by maximizing two-step expected improvement on our running example. The tick marks show the points chosen by the policy, progressing from top to bottom, during iterations 1–10 (top) and 11–20 (bottom). Observations within 0.2 length scales of the optimum have thicker marks; the optimum was located on iteration 15.

50 Such a discount factor is common in infinite-horizon decision problems:

D. P. BERTSEKAS (2017). *Dynamic Programming and Optimal Control.* Vol. 1. Athena Scientific.

51 X. YUE and R. AL KONTAR (2020). Why Non-Myopic Bayesian Optimization Is Promising and How Far Should We Look-ahead? A Study via Rollout. *AISTATS 2020.*

52 See p. 125.

batch rollout: § 5.3, p. 103

53 J. GONZÁLEZ et al. (2016b). GLASSES: Relieving the Myopia of Bayesian Optimisation. *AISTATS 2016.*

54 The policy used in GLASSES is described in

J. GONZÁLEZ et al. (2016a). Batch Bayesian Optimization via Local Penalization. *AISTATS 2016,*

as well as in § 11.3, p. 257; however, any desired alternative could also be used.

multiplicative discounting to encourage earlier rather than later progress during the rollout steps.[50] For some combinations of the rollout horizon and the discount factor, the resulting policies outperformed common one-step lookahead policies on a suite of synthetic test functions. YUE and AL KONTAR described a mechanism for dynamically choosing the rollout horizon based on the potential impact of a misspecified model,[51] exactly the issue that gave KUSHNER pause.[52]

The additional computational burden of rollout limited LAM et al. to a relatively short rollout horizon on the order of 4–5. Although considerably less myopic than one-step lookahead, the true decision horizon can be much greater, especially during the early stages of optimization. GONZÁLEZ et al. proposed an alternative approach based on batch rollout that can effectively look farther ahead at the expense of ignoring dependence among future decisions.[53] The algorithm – dubbed GLASSES by the authors as it counteracts myopia – augments expected improvement with a single rollout step that designs a batch of additional observation locations of size equal to the remaining evaluation budget.[54] These points serve as a rough simulation of the decisions that might follow after making a proposed observation. A potential observation location is then evaluated by the expected improvement gained by simultaneously evaluating at that point as well as the constructed batch, realizing an efficient and budget-aware nonmyopic policy. GLASSES outperformed myopic and nonmyopic baselines on synthetic test functions, and the

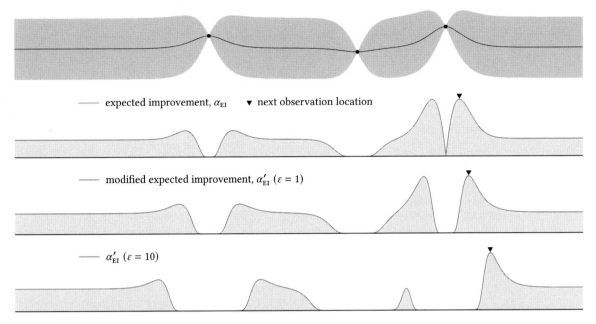

Figure 7.23: The modified expected improvement acquisition function (7.21) for our running example for different values of the target improvement ε. The target is expressed as a fraction of the range of the posterior mean over the space. Increasing the target improvement leads to increasingly exploratory behavior.

authors also demonstrated that dynamically setting the batch size to the remaining budget outperformed an arbitrary fixed size, suggesting that budget adaptation was important for success.

JIANG et al. continued this thread with an even more dramatic approximation dubbed BINOCULARS, potentially initiating an arms race toward increasingly nonmyopic acronyms.[55] The idea is to construct a *single* batch observation in each iteration, then select a point from this batch for evaluation. This represents an extreme computational savings over GLASSES, which must construct a batch anew for every proposed observation location. However, the method retains the same fundamental motivation: well-designed batch policies automatically induce *diversity* among batch members, encouraging exploration in the resulting sequential policy (see Figure 11.3). The strong connection between the optimal batch and sequential policies (11.9–11.10) provides further motivation for this approach. JIANG et al. also conducted a study of optimization performance versus the cost of computing the policy: one-step lookahead, BINOCULARS, GLASSES, and rollout comprised the Pareto frontier, with each method increasing computational effort by an order of magnitude.

Artificially encouraging exploration

Another more indirect approach to nonmyopic policy design is to modify a one-step lookahead acquisition function to artificially encourage more

55 S. JIANG et al. (2020a). BINOCULARS for Efficient, Nonmyopic Sequential Experimental Design. *ICML 2020.*

batch observations: § 11.3, p. 252

Pareto frontier: § 11.7, p. 269

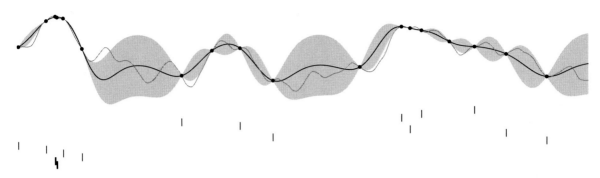

Figure 7.24: The posterior after 15 steps of the STRELTSOV and VAKILI optimization policy on our running example. The tick marks show the points chosen by the policy, progressing from top to bottom. Observations within 0.2 length scales of the optimum have thicker marks; the optimum was located on iteration 14.

exploratory behavior when the remaining budget is significant. This can be motivated by the nature of the optimal policy, which maximizes a combination of immediate reward (exploitation) with expected future reward (exploration) (5.18). As the decision horizon increases, the exploration term may become increasingly dominant in this score, suggesting that optimal behavior entails early exploration of the domain followed by later exploitation and refinement.

Both the probability of improvement (7.5) and upper confidence bound acquisition functions already feature a parameter controlling the exploration–exploitation tradeoff, which can be dynamically maintained throughout optimization. This idea is quite old, reaching back to the earliest papers on Bayesian optimization. KUSHNER for example provided detailed advice on adjusting the threshold in probability of improvement to transition from early exploration to increasing levels of exploitation when appropriate.[56]

56 H. J. KUSHNER (1964). A New Method of Locating the Maximum Point of an Arbitrary Multipeak Curve in the Presence of Noise. *Journal of Basic Engineering* 86(1):97–106.

In the case of exact observation, it is also possible to modify expected improvement (7.3) to incorporate a similar parameter. Rather than measuring improvement with respect to the utility of the current data $u(\mathcal{D}) = \phi^*$, we measure with respect to an inflated value $\phi^* + \varepsilon$, with no credit given for improvements less than this amount. The result is a modified expected improvement acquisition function:

$$\alpha'_{\text{EI}}(x; \mathcal{D}, \varepsilon) = \mathbb{E}\big[\max\{\phi - [\phi^* + \varepsilon], 0\} \mid x, \mathcal{D}\big]. \qquad (7.21)$$

As with probability of improvement, larger improvement thresholds encourage increasing exploration, as illustrated in Figure 7.23. For extreme values, the modified expected improvement drops to effectively zero except in regions with significant uncertainty. It is not obvious how this idea can be extended to handle noisy observations, as the simple reward of the updated dataset may in fact *decrease,* raising the question of how to correctly define "sufficient improvement."

MOCKUS proposed a scheme to set the threshold for Gaussian process models with constant mean and stationary covariance where the threshold was set dynamically based on the remaining budget, using the asymptotic behavior of the maximum of iid Gaussian random variables.[57] This can be interpreted as an approximate batch rollout policy where remaining decisions are simulated by fictitious uncorrelated observations; for some models this serves as an efficient simulation of random rollout.

57 J. MOCKUS (1989). *Bayesian Approach to Global Optimization: Theory and Applications.* Kluwer Academic Publishers. [§ 2.5]

The modified expected improvement (7.21) was also the basis for an unusual policy proposed by STRELTSOV and VAKILI.[58] Let $c \colon \mathcal{X} \to \mathbb{R}^{>0}$ quantify the cost of making an observation at any proposed location; in the simplest case we could take the cost to be constant. To evaluate the promise of making an observation at x, we solve the equation

$$\alpha'_{\mathrm{EI}}(x; \mathcal{D}, \alpha_{\mathrm{SV}}) = c(x)$$

58 S. STRELTSOV and P. VAKILI (1999). A Non-Myopic Utility Function for Statistical Global Optimization Algorithms. *Journal of Global Optimization* 14(3):283–298.

for α_{SV}, which will serve as the acquisition function value at x.[59] That is, we solve for the improvement threshold that would render an observation at x cost-prohibitive in expectation, and design each observation to coincide with the last point to be ruled out when considering increasingly demanding thresholds. The resulting policy shows interesting behavior, at least on our running example; see Figure 7.24. After effective initial exploration, the global optimum was located on iteration 14. The behavior is similar to the upper confidence bound approach in Figure 7.18, and indeed STRELTSOV and VAKILI showed that the proposed method can be understood as a variation on this method with a location-dependent upper confidence quantile depending on observation cost and uncertainty.

59 As α'_{EI} is monotonically decreasing with respect to α_{SV} and approaches zero as $\alpha_{\mathrm{SV}} \to \infty$, the unique solution can be found efficiently via bisection.

An even simpler mechanism for injecting exploration into an existing policy is to occasionally make decisions *randomly* or via some other policy encouraging pure exploration. DE ATH et al. for example considered a family of ε-greedy policies where a one-step lookahead policy is interrupted, with probability ε in each iteration, by evaluating at a location chosen uniformly at random from the domain.[60] These policies delivered impressive empirical performance, even when the one-step lookahead policy was as simple as maximizing the posterior mean (see below).

60 G. DE ATH et al. (2021). Greed Is Good: Exploration and Exploitation Trade-offs in Bayesian Optimisation. *ACM Transactions on Evolutionary Learning and Optimization* 1(1):1–22.

Lookahead for cumulative reward?

Notably missing from our discussion on one-step lookahead policies was the cumulative reward utility function. Unfortunately, in this case one-step lookahead does not produce a particularly useful optimization policy. Suppose we adopt the cumulative reward utility function (6.7), $u(\mathcal{D}) = \sum y_i$. Then marginal gain in utility from a measurement at x is simply the observed value y. Therefore the expected one-step marginal gain is the posterior predictive mean:

cumulative reward: § 6.2, p. 114

$$\alpha(x; \mathcal{D}) = \mathbb{E}[y \mid x, \mathcal{D}],$$

which for zero-mean additive noise reduces to the posterior mean of f:

posterior mean acquisition function

$$\alpha(x; \mathcal{D}) = \mu_{\mathcal{D}}(x).$$

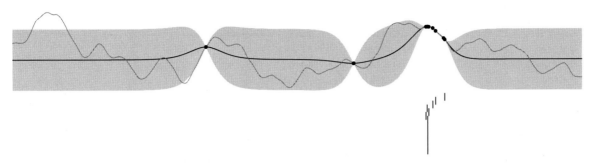

Figure 7.25: The posterior after 15 steps of two-step lookahead for cumulative reward (7.22) on our running example. The tick marks show the points chosen by the policy, progressing from top to bottom. The policy becomes stuck on iteration 7.

becoming "stuck"

two-step lookahead for cumulative reward

From cursory inspection of our example scenario in Figure 7.1, we can see that maximizing this acquisition function can cause the policy to become "stuck" with no chance of recovery. In our example, the posterior mean is maximized at the previously best-seen point, so the policy will select this point forevermore.

It is also interesting to consider two-step lookahead, where the acquisition function becomes (5.12):

$$\alpha_2(x; \mathcal{D}) = \mu_{\mathcal{D}}(x) + \mathbb{E}\left[\max_{x' \in \mathcal{X}} \mu_{\mathcal{D}'}(x') \mid x, \mathcal{D}\right].$$

After subtracting a constant (the global reward of the current data), we have

$$\alpha_2(x; \mathcal{D}) = \mu_{\mathcal{D}}(x) + \alpha_{\text{KG}}(x; \mathcal{D}), \tag{7.22}$$

the sum of the posterior mean and the knowledge gradient (7.4), reflecting both exploitation and exploration. Unfortunately even this less myopic option can become stuck due to overexploitation, as illustrated in Figure 7.25.

7.11   SUMMARY OF MAJOR IDEAS

one-step lookahead: § 7.2, p. 124
multi-armed bandits: § 7.7, p. 141

Although we have covered a lot of ground in this chapter, there were really only two big ideas in policy construction: one-step lookahead and adopting successful policies from multi-armed bandits. However, there remains significant opportunity for novelty in this space.

COMPUTING POLICIES WITH GAUSSIAN PROCESSES

8

In the last chapter we introduced several notable Bayesian optimization policies in a model-agnostic setting, concentrating on their motivation and behavior while ignoring computational details. In this chapter we will provide further information for effectively implementing these policies. We will focus on Gaussian process models of the objective function, combined with either an exact or additive Gaussian noise observation model; this family accounts for the vast majority of models encountered in practice. However, we will discuss computation for alternative model classes such as Bayesian neural networks at the end of the chapter.

Chapter 2: Gaussian Processes, p. 15

observation models: § 1.1, p. 4

alternative models: § 8.11, p. 196

Implementing each policy in the previous chapter ultimately requires optimizing some acquisition function over the domain:[1]

$$x \in \underset{x' \in \mathcal{X}}{\arg\max}\, \alpha(x'; \mathcal{D}).$$

1 Even the nondeterministic Thompson sampling policy, which may be realized by optimizing a random acquisition function: § 7.9, p. 148.

We will demonstrate how to compute (or approximate) each of these acquisition functions with respect to Gaussian process models. Some will admit exact analytical expressions; when this is not possible, we will describe effective approximation schemes. In Euclidean domains, we will also show how to compute the gradient of these acquisition functions with respect to the proposed observation location, allowing efficient optimization via gradient methods. These gradient computations will sometimes be somewhat involved (but not difficult), and we will defer some details to an appendix for the sake of brevity.

gradients of common acquisition functions: § C.3, p. 308

The order of our presentation will differ from that in the previous chapter. Here we will begin with the acquisition functions for which exact computation is possible, then develop approximation techniques for those that remain. First, we pause to establish notation for important reoccurring quantities.

8.1 NOTATION FOR OBJECTIVE FUNCTION MODEL

As usual, let us consider an objective function $f: \mathcal{X} \to \mathbb{R}$, with a Gaussian process belief conditioned on arbitrary observations $\mathcal{D} = (\mathbf{x}, \mathbf{y})$:

$$p(f \mid \mathcal{D}) = \mathcal{GP}(f; \mu_{\mathcal{D}}, K_{\mathcal{D}}). \tag{8.1}$$

Gaussian process on f, $\mathcal{GP}(f; \mu_{\mathcal{D}}, K_{\mathcal{D}})$

Our main task in this chapter will be to compute a given acquisition function at an arbitrary location $x \in \mathcal{X}$ with respect to this belief. Given a proposed location x, we will write the predictive distribution for $\phi = f(x)$ as:

$$p(\phi \mid x, \mathcal{D}) = \mathcal{N}(\phi; \mu, \sigma^2), \tag{8.2}$$

predictive distribution for ϕ, $\mathcal{N}(\phi; \mu, \sigma^2)$

where the predictive mean and variance

$$\mu = \mu_{\mathcal{D}}(x); \qquad \sigma^2 = K_{\mathcal{D}}(x, x) \tag{8.3}$$

predictive mean and variance for ϕ: μ, σ^2

depend implicitly on x. We will always treat x as given and fixed, so this convention will not lead to ambiguity.

We will also require the predictive distribution for the observed value y resulting from a measurement at x. In addition to the straightforward case of exact measurements, where $y = \phi$ and the predictive distribution is given above (8.2), we will also consider corruption by independent, zero-mean additive Gaussian noise:

$$p(y \mid \phi, \sigma_n) = \mathcal{N}(y; \phi, \sigma_n^2). \tag{8.4}$$

observation noise scale, σ_n
predictive distribution for y, $\mathcal{N}(y; \mu, s^2)$

Again we allow the noise scale σ_n to depend on x if desired. We will notate the resulting predictive distribution for y with:

$$p(y \mid x, \mathcal{D}, \sigma_n) = \mathcal{N}(y; \mu, \sigma^2 + \sigma_n^2) = \mathcal{N}(y; \mu, s^2), \tag{8.5}$$

predictive variance for y, s^2

where μ and σ^2 are the predictive moments of ϕ (8.3) and $s^2 = \sigma^2 + \sigma_n^2$ is the predictive variance for y, which again depends implicitly on x. When no distinction between exact and noisy observations is necessary, we will use the above general notation (8.5). With exact observations, the observation noise scale is identically zero, and we have $s^2 = \sigma^2$.

prime notation for post-observation quantities

We will retain our convention from the last chapter of indicating quantities available after acquiring a proposed observation with a prime symbol. For example $\mathbf{x}' = \mathbf{x} \cup \{x\}$ represents the updated set of observation locations after adding an observation at x, and $\mathcal{D}' = (\mathbf{x}', \mathbf{y}')$ represents the current data augmented with the observation (x, y) – a random variable.

general form of gradient and dependence on parameter gradients

The value of an acquisition function α at a point x will naturally depend on the distribution of the corresponding observation y, and its gradient must reflect this dependence. Applying the chain rule, the general form of the gradient will be written in terms of the gradient of the predictive parameters:

$$\frac{\partial \alpha}{\partial x} = \frac{\partial \alpha}{\partial \mu} \frac{\partial \mu}{\partial x} + \frac{\partial \alpha}{\partial s} \frac{\partial s}{\partial x}. \tag{8.6}$$

gradients of GP predictive distribution: § C.2, p. 308

The gradients of the predictive mean and standard deviation for a Gaussian process are easily computable assuming the prior mean and covariance functions and the observation noise scale are differentiable, and general expressions are provided in an appendix.

8.2   EXPECTED IMPROVEMENT

expected improvement: § 7.3, p. 127
simple reward: § 6.1, p. 112

We first consider the expected improvement acquisition function (7.2), the expected marginal gain in simple reward (6.3):

$$\alpha_{\text{EI}}(x; \mathcal{D}) = \mathbb{E}\big[\max \mu_{\mathcal{D}'}(\mathbf{x}') \mid x, \mathcal{D}\big] - \max \mu_{\mathcal{D}}(\mathbf{x}). \tag{8.7}$$

Remarkably, this expectation can be computed analytically for Gaussian processes with both exact and noisy observations. We will consider each case separately, as the former is considerably simpler and the latter involves minor controversy.

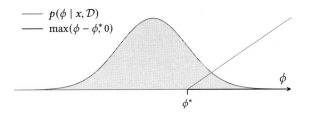

— $p(\phi \mid x, \mathcal{D})$
— $\max(\phi - \phi^*, 0)$

Figure 8.1: The expectation required to compute noiseless expected improvement: linear improvement for values exceeding the incumbent ϕ^*, integrated against a Gaussian distribution (8.2).

Expected improvement without noise

Expected improvement assumes a convenient form when measurements are exact (7.3):

$$\alpha_{\text{EI}}(x; \mathcal{D}) = \int \max(\phi - \phi^*, 0)\, \mathcal{N}(\phi; \mu, \sigma^2)\, d\phi. \tag{8.8}$$

Here ϕ^* is the previously best-seen, *incumbent* objective function value, and $\max(\phi - \phi^*, 0)$ measures the improvement offered by observing a value of ϕ. Figure 8.1 illustrates this integral.

incumbent function value, ϕ^*

To proceed, we resolve the max operator to yield two integrals:

$$\alpha_{\text{EI}}(x; \mathcal{D}) = \int_{\phi^*}^{\infty} \phi\, \mathcal{N}(\phi; \mu, \sigma^2)\, d\phi - \phi^* \int_{\phi^*}^{\infty} \mathcal{N}(\phi; \mu, \sigma^2)\, d\phi,$$

both of which can be computed easily assuming $\sigma > 0$.[2] The first term is proportional to the expected value of a normal distribution truncated at ϕ^*, and the second term is the complementary normal CDF scaled by ϕ^*. The resulting acquisition function can be written conveniently in terms of the standard normal PDF and CDF:

2 In the degenerate case $\sigma = 0$, we simply have $\alpha_{\text{EI}}(x; \mathcal{D}) = \max(\mu - \phi^*, 0)$.

$$\alpha_{\text{EI}}(x; \mathcal{D}) = (\mu - \phi^*)\, \Phi\!\left(\frac{\mu - \phi^*}{\sigma}\right) + \sigma\phi\!\left(\frac{\mu - \phi^*}{\sigma}\right). \tag{8.9}$$

Examining this expression, it is tempting to interpret its two terms as respectively encouraging exploitation (favoring points with high expected value μ) and exploration (favoring points with high uncertainty σ). Indeed, taking partial derivatives with respect to μ and σ, we have:

exploitation and exploration

partial derivatives with respect to predictive distribution parameters

$$\frac{\partial \alpha_{\text{EI}}}{\partial \mu} = \Phi\!\left(\frac{\mu - \phi^*}{\sigma}\right) > 0; \qquad \frac{\partial \alpha_{\text{EI}}}{\partial \sigma} = \phi\!\left(\frac{\mu - \phi^*}{\sigma}\right) > 0.$$

Expected improvement is thus monotonically increasing in both μ and σ. Increasing a point's expected value naturally makes the point more favorable for exploitation, and increasing its uncertainty makes it more favorable for exploration. Either action would increase the expected improvement. The tradeoff between these two concerns is considered automatically and is reflected in the magnitude of the derivatives above.

Maximization of expected improvement in Euclidean domains may be guided by its gradient with respect to the proposed evaluation location x. Using the results above and applying the chain rule, we have (8.6):

gradient of expected improvement without noise

$$\frac{\partial \alpha_{\text{EI}}}{\partial x} = \Phi\!\left(\frac{\mu - \phi^*}{\sigma}\right)\frac{\partial \mu}{\partial x} + \phi\!\left(\frac{\mu - \phi^*}{\sigma}\right)\frac{\partial \sigma}{\partial x},$$

which expresses the gradient in terms of the implicit exploration–exploitation tradeoff parameter and the change in the predictive distribution.

Expected improvement with noise

Computing expected improvement with noisy observations is somewhat more complicated than in the noiseless case. In fact, there is not even universal agreement regarding what the definition of noisy expected improvement should be! The situation is so nuanced that JONES et al. sidestepped the issue entirely in their landmark paper:[3]

3 D. R. JONES et al. (1998). Efficient Global Optimization of Expensive Black-Box Functions. *Journal of Global Optimization* 13(4):455–492.

> Unfortunately it is not immediately clear how to extend our *optimization algorithm* to the case of noisy functions. With noisy data, we really want to find the point where the *signal* is optimized. Similarly, our expected improvement criterion should be defined in terms of the signal component. [emphasis added by JONES et al.]

This summarizes the main challenge to optimization with noisy observations: how can we determine whether a particularly high observed value reflects a true underlying effect or is merely an artifact of noise? Several alternative definitions and heuristics have been proposed to address this question, which we will discuss further shortly.

We will first argue that seeking to maximize the simple reward utility (6.3) is *precisely* aligned with the goal outlined by JONES et al. With appropriate modeling of observation noise, the objective function posterior exactly represents our belief about the "signal component": the latent objective f. Simple reward evaluates progress directly with respect to this belief, only ascribing merit to observations that improve the maximum of the posterior mean and thus the expected outcome of an optimal terminal recommendation. Notably, an excessively noisy observation has weak correlation with the underlying objective function value and thus yields little change in the posterior mean (2.12). Therefore even an extremely high outcome would produce only a minor improvement to the simple reward. As a result, the expected improvement of such a point would be relatively small, exactly the desired behavior.

behavior of posterior moments: § 2.2, p. 21

any point may maximize the posterior mean

Unfortunately, observation noise renders expected improvement somewhat more complicated than the exact case, due to the nature of the updated simple reward. After an exact observation, the simple reward can only be achieved at one of two locations: either the observed point or the incumbent. However, with noisy observations, inherent uncertainty in the objective function implies that the updated simple reward could be achieved *anywhere,* including a point that previously appeared suboptimal. We must account for this possibility in the computation, increasing its complexity. Fortunately, exact computation is still possible for Gaussian processes and additive Gaussian noise by adopting a procedure originally described by FRAZIER et al. for computing the knowledge gradient on a discrete domain;[4] we will return to this method in our discussion on knowledge gradient in the next section.

4 P. FRAZIER et al. (2009). The Knowledge-Gradient Policy for Correlated Normal Beliefs. *INFORMS Journal on Computing* 21(4):599–613.

If we define $\mu^* = \max \mu_{\mathcal{D}}(\mathbf{x})$ to represent the simple reward of the current data, then we must compute:

$$\alpha_{\text{EI}}(x; \mathcal{D}) = \int \left[\max \mu_{\mathcal{D}'}(\mathbf{x}') - \mu^* \right] \mathcal{N}(y; \mu, s^2) \, dy.$$

We first reduce this computation to an expectation of the general form

$$g(\mathbf{a}, \mathbf{b}) = \int \max(\mathbf{a} + \mathbf{b}z) \, \phi(z) \, dz, \qquad (8.10)$$

where $\mathbf{a}, \mathbf{b} \in \mathbb{R}^n$ are arbitrary vectors and z is a standard normal random variable.[5] Note that given the observation y, the updated posterior mean at $\mathbf{x}'$ is a vector we may compute in closed form (2.19):

$$\mu_{\mathcal{D}'}(\mathbf{x}') = \mu_{\mathcal{D}}(\mathbf{x}') + \frac{K_{\mathcal{D}}(\mathbf{x}', x)}{s} \frac{y - \mu}{s}.$$

This update is linear in y. Applying the transformation $y = \mu + sz$ yields

$$\mu_{\mathcal{D}'}(\mathbf{x}') = \mathbf{a} + \mathbf{b}z, \qquad (8.11)$$

where

$$\mathbf{a} = \mu_{\mathcal{D}}(\mathbf{x}'); \qquad \mathbf{b} = \frac{K_{\mathcal{D}}(\mathbf{x}', x)}{s}, \qquad (8.12)$$

and we may express expected improvement in the desired form:

$$\alpha_{\text{EI}}(x; \mathcal{D}) = g(\mathbf{a}, \mathbf{b}) - \mu^*. \qquad (8.13)$$

As a function of z, $\mathbf{a} + \mathbf{b}z$ is a set of lines with intercepts and slopes given by the entries of the $\mathbf{a}$ and $\mathbf{b}$ vectors, respectively. In the context of expected improvement, these lines represent the updated posterior mean values for each point of interest $\mathbf{x}'$ as a function of the z-score of the noisy observation y. See Figure 8.2 for an illustration. Note that the points with the highest correlation with the proposed point have the greatest slope (8.12), as our belief at these locations will be strongly affected by the outcome.

Now $\max(\mathbf{a} + \mathbf{b}z)$ is the upper envelope of these lines, a convex piecewise linear function shown in Figure 8.3. The interpretation of this envelope is the simple reward of the updated dataset given the z-score of y, which will be achieved at some point in $\mathbf{x}'$. For this example, the updated posterior mean could be maximized at one of four locations: either at one of the points on the far right given a relatively high observation, or at a backup point farther left given a relatively low observation. Note that in the latter case the simple reward will decrease.[6]

With this geometric intuition in mind, we can deduce that g is invariant to transformations that do not alter the upper envelope. In particular, g is invariant both to reordering the lines by applying an identical permutation to $\mathbf{a}$ and $\mathbf{b}$ and also to the deletion of lines that never dominate. In the interest of notational simplicity, we will take advantage of these invariances and only consider evaluating g when every given line achieves

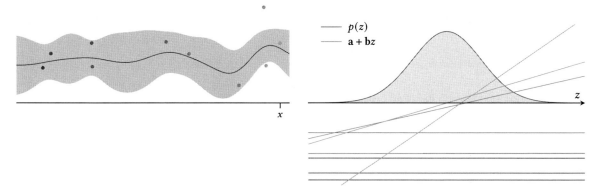

Figure 8.2: The geometric intuition of the $g(\mathbf{a}, \mathbf{b})$ function. Left: if we make a measurement at x, the z-score of the observed value completely determines the updated posterior mean at that point and all previously observed points. Right: as a function of z, the updated posterior mean at each of these points is linear; here the lightness of each line corresponds to the matching point on the left. The slope and intercept of each line can be determined from the posterior (8.12). Not all lines are visible.

maximal value on some interval and the lines appear in strictly increasing order of slope:

$$b_1 < b_2 < \cdots < b_n.$$

7 Briefly, we sort the lines in ascending order of slope, then add each line in turn to a set of dominating lines, checking whether any previously added lines need to be removed and updating the intervals of dominance.

FRAZIER et al. give a simple and efficient algorithm to process a set of n lines to eliminate any always-dominated lines, reorder the remainder in increasing slope, and identify their intervals of dominance in $\mathcal{O}(n \log n)$ time.[7] The output of this procedure is a permutation matrix $\mathbf{P}$, possibly with some rows deleted, such that

$$g(\mathbf{a}, \mathbf{b}) = g(\mathbf{Pa}, \mathbf{Pb}) = g(\boldsymbol{\alpha}, \boldsymbol{\beta}), \tag{8.14}$$

and the new inputs $(\boldsymbol{\alpha}, \boldsymbol{\beta})$ satisfy the desired properties. We will assume below that the inputs have been preprocessed in such a manner.

Given a set of lines in the desired form, we may partition the real line into a collection of n intervals

$$(-\infty = c_1, c_2) \cup (c_2, c_3) \cup \cdots \cup (c_n, c_{n+1} = +\infty), \tag{8.15}$$

8 Reordering the lines in order of increasing slope guarantees this correspondence: the line with minimal slope is always the "leftmost" in the upper envelope, etc.

such that the ith line $a_i + b_i z$ dominates on the corresponding interval (c_i, c_{i+1}).[8] This allows us to decompose the desired expectation (8.10) into a sum of contributions on each interval:

$$g(\mathbf{a}, \mathbf{b}) = \sum_i \int_{c_i}^{c_{i+1}} (a_i + b_i z)\, \phi(z)\, \mathrm{d}z.$$

Finally, we may compute each integral in the sum in closed form:

$$g(\mathbf{a}, \mathbf{b}) = \sum_i a_i \big[\Phi(c_{i+1}) - \Phi(c_i)\big] + b_i \big[\phi(c_i) - \phi(c_{i+1})\big], \tag{8.16}$$

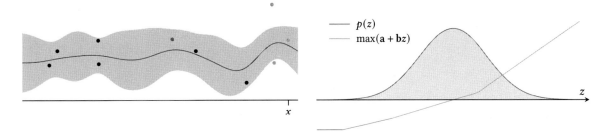

Figure 8.3: After a measurement at x, the updated simple reward can be achieved at one of four points (left), whose corresponding lines comprise the upper envelope $\max(\mathbf{a} + \mathbf{b}z)$ (right). The lightness of the line segments on the right correspond to the possible updated maximum locations on the left. The lightest point on the left serves as a "backup option" if the observed value is low.

allowing efficient and exact computation of expected improvement in the noisy case. The main bottleneck is the modest $\mathcal{O}(n \log n)$ preprocessing step required.

This expression reverts to that for exact measurements (8.9) in the absence of noise. In that case, we have $\mathbf{b} = [0, s]^{\top}$ and the upper envelope only contains lines corresponding to the incumbent and newly observed point, which intersect at the incumbent value $c_1 = \phi^{*}$. Geometrically, the situation collapses to that in Figure 8.1, and it is easy to confirm (8.9) and (8.16) coincide.

compatibility with noiseless case

Although tedious, we may compute the gradient of g and thus the gradient of expected improvement (8.13); the details are in an appendix.

gradient of noisy expected improvement: § C.3, p. 308

Alternative formulations of noisy expected improvement

Although thematically consistent and mathematically straightforward, our approach of computing expected improvement as the expected marginal gain in simple reward is not common and may be unfamiliar to some readers.

Over the years, numerous authors have grappled with the best definition of noisy expected improvement. A typical approach is to begin with the convenient formula (8.9) in the noiseless regime, then work "backwards" by identifying potential issues with its application to noisy data and suggesting a heuristic correction. This strategy of "fixing" exact expected improvement is in opposition to our ground-up approach of first defining a well-grounded utility function and only then working out the expected marginal gain. PICHENY et al. provided a survey of such approximations – representing a total of 11 different acquisition strategies – accompanied by a thorough empirical investigation.[9] Notably, the authors were familiar with the exact computation we outlined in the previous section and recommended it for use in practice.

One popular idea in this direction is to take the formula from the exact case (8.9) and substitute a plug-in estimate for the now unknown

9 V. PICHENY et al. (2013b). A Benchmark of Kriging-Based Infill Criteria for Noisy Optimization. Structural and Multidisciplinary Optimization 48(3):607–626.

expected improvement with plug-in estimator of ϕ^{*}

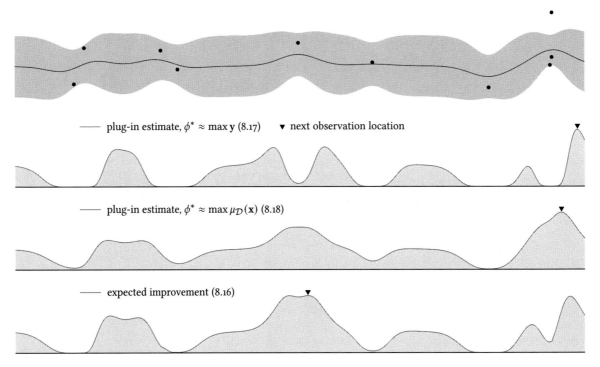

Figure 8.4: Expected improvement using different plug-in estimators (8.17–8.18) compared with the noisy expected improvement as the expected marginal gain in simple reward (8.7).

incumbent value ϕ^*. Several possibilities for this estimate have been put forward. One option is to plug in the maximum noisy observation:

$$\phi^* \approx \max \mathbf{y}. \tag{8.17}$$

maximum noisy value "utility" function: § 6.1, p. 113

inflating expected improvement threshold: § 7.10, p. 154

However, this may not always behave as expected for the same reason the maximum observed value does not serve as a sensible utility function (6.6). With very noisy data, the maximum observed value is most likely spurious rather than a meaningful goalpost. Further, as we are likely to overestimate our progress due to bias in this estimate, the resulting behavior may become excessively exploratory. The approximation will eventually devolve to expected improvement against an inflated threshold (7.21), which may overly encourage exploration; see Figure 7.23. An especially spurious observation can bias the estimate in (8.17) (and our behavior) for a considerable time.

Opinions on the proposed approximation using this simple plug-in estimate (8.17) vary dramatically. PICHENY et al. discarded the idea out of hand as "naïve" and lacking robustness.[10] The authors also found it empirically inferior in their investigation and described the same over-exploratory effect and explanation given above. On the other hand, NGUYEN et al. described the estimator as "standard" and concluded it was empirically preferable![11]

10 V. PICHENY et al. (2013b). A Benchmark of Kriging-Based Infill Criteria for Noisy Optimization. *Structural and Multidisciplinary Optimization* 48(3):607–626.

11 V. NGUYEN et al. (2017). Regret for Expected Improvement over the Best-Observed Value and Stopping Condition. *ACML 2017*.

An alternative estimator is the simple reward of the data (6.3):[12,13]

$$\phi^* \approx \max \mu_{\mathcal{D}}(\mathbf{x}), \tag{8.18}$$

which is less biased and may be preferable. A simple extension is to maximize other predictive quantiles,[10,14] and HUANG et al. recommend using a relatively low quantile, specifically $\Phi(-1) \approx 0.16$, in the interest of risk aversion.

In Figure 8.4 we compare noisy expected improvement with two plug-in approximations. The plug-in estimators agree that sampling on the right-hand side of the domain is the most promising course of action, but our formulation of noisy expected improvement prefers a less explored region. This decision is motivated by the interesting behavior of the posterior, which shows considerable disagreement regarding the updated posterior mean; see Figure 8.6. This nuance is only revealed as our formulation reasons about the *joint* predictive distribution of $\mathbf{y}'$, whereas the plug-in estimators only inspect the marginals.

Another proposed approximation scheme for noisy expected improvement is reinterpolation. We fit a *noiseless* Gaussian process to imputed values of the objective function at the observed locations $\boldsymbol{\phi} = f(\mathbf{x})$, then compute the exact expected improvement for this surrogate. A natural choice considered by FORRESTER et al. is to impute using the posterior mean:[15]

$$\boldsymbol{\phi} \approx \mu_{\mathcal{D}}(\mathbf{x}),$$

resulting in the approximation (computed with respect to the surrogate):

$$\alpha_{\mathrm{EI}}(x; \mathcal{D}) \approx \alpha_{\mathrm{EI}}(x; \mathbf{x}, \boldsymbol{\phi}). \tag{8.19}$$

This procedure is illustrated in Figure 8.5. The resulting decision is very similar to that made by noisy expected improvement.

LETHAM et al. also promoted this basic approach, but proposed marginalizing rather than imputing the latent objective function values:[16]

$$\alpha_{\mathrm{EI}}(x; \mathcal{D}) \approx \int \alpha_{\mathrm{EI}}(x; \mathbf{x}, \boldsymbol{\phi}) \, p(\boldsymbol{\phi} \mid \mathbf{x}, \mathcal{D}) \, \mathrm{d}\boldsymbol{\phi}. \tag{8.20}$$

The approximate acquisition function is the expectation of the exact expected improvement if we had access to exact observations. Although this integral cannot be computed exactly, the authors described a straightforward and effective quasi-Monte Carlo approximation. LETHAM et al.'s approximation is illustrated in Figure 8.6. There is good agreement with the expected improvement acquisition function from Figure 8.4, *except* near the observation location chosen by that policy.

This stark disagreement is a consequence of reinterpolation: the acquisition function vanishes at previously observed locations – just as the exact expected improvement does – regardless of the observed values. Thus repeated measurements at the same location are barred, strongly encouraging exploration. HUANG et al. cite this property as undesirable,[17] as repeated measurements can reinforce our understanding

12 E. VAZQUEZ et al. (2008). Global Optimization Based on Noisy Evaluations: An Empirical Study of Two Statistical Approaches. *ICIPE 2008*.

13 Z. WANG and N. DE FREITAS (2014). Theoretical Analysis of Bayesian Optimization with Unknown Gaussian Process Hyper-Parameters. arXiv: 1406.7758 [stat.ML].

14 D. HUANG et al. (2006b). Global Optimization of Stochastic Black-Box Systems via Sequential Kriging Meta-Models. *Journal of Global Optimization* 34(3):441–466.

approximating through reinterpolation

15 A. I. J. FORRESTER et al. (2006). Design and Analysis of "Noisy" Computer Experiments. *AIAA Journal* 44(10):2331–2339.

16 B. LETHAM et al. (2019). Constrained Bayesian Optimization with Noisy Experiments. *Bayesian Analysis* 14(2):495–519.

reduction to zero at observed locations

17 D. HUANG et al. (2006b). Global Optimization of Stochastic Black-Box Systems via Sequential Kriging Meta-Models. *Journal of Global Optimization* 34(3):441–466.

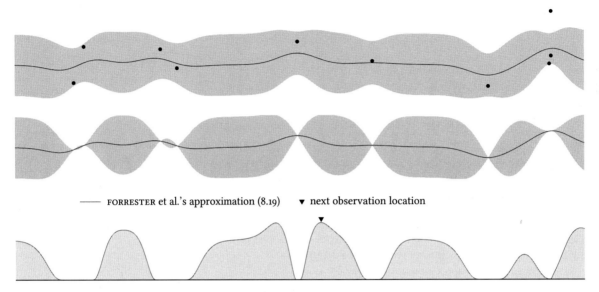

—— FORRESTER et al.'s approximation (8.19)   ▼ next observation location

Figure 8.5: FORRESTER et al.'s approximation to noisy expected improvement (8.19). Given a Gaussian process fit to noisy data, we compute the exact expected improvement (8.9) for a noiseless Gaussian process fit to the posterior mean.

adjusting for observation noise

18 D. HUANG et al. (2006b). Global Optimization of Stochastic Black-Box Systems via Sequential Kriging Meta-Models. *Journal of Global Optimization* 34(3):441–466.

19 This is only sensible when the signal-to-noise ratio is at least one.

of the optimum by reducing uncertainty. LETHAM et al. on the other hand suggest the exploration boost is beneficial for optimization and point out we may reduce uncertainty through measurements in neighboring locations if desired.

A weakness shared by all these approximations is that the underlying noiseless expected improvement incorrectly assumes that our observation will reveal the *exact* objective value. In fact, observation noise is ignored entirely, as all these acquisition functions are expectations with respect to the *unobservable* quantity ϕ rather than the observed quantity y. This represents a disconnect between the reasoning of the optimization policy and the true nature of the observation process. HUANG et al. acknowledged this issue and proposed an *augmented expected improvement* measure accounting for observation noise[18] by multiplying by the factor $1 - \sigma_n/s$,[19] penalizing locations with low signal-to-noise ratios.

Ignoring the distribution of the observed value can be especially problematic with heteroskedastic noise, as shown in Figure 8.7. Both the augmented[18] and noisy expected improvement acquisition functions are biased toward the left-hand side of the domain, where observations reveal more information. Plug-in approximations, on the other hand, are oblivious to this distinction and elect to explore the noisy region on the right; see Figure 8.4.

Our opinion is that all approximation schemes based on reducing to exact expected improvement should be avoided with significant noise levels, but can be a reasonable choice otherwise. With low noise, observed

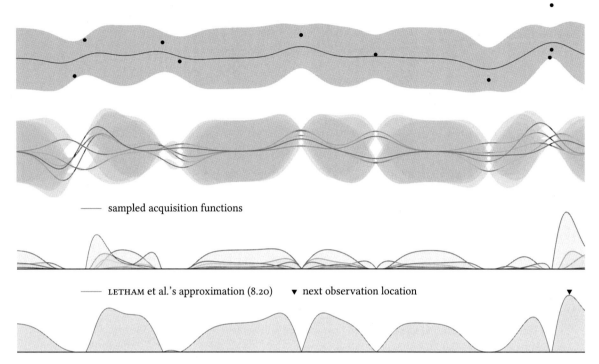

Figure 8.6: LETHAM et al.'s approximation to noisy expected improvement (8.20). We take the expectation of the exact expected improvement (8.9) for a noiseless Gaussian process fit to exact observations at the observed locations. The middle panels show realizations of the reinterpolated process and the resulting expected improvement.

values cannot stray too far from the true underlying objective function value. Thus we have $y \approx \phi$; $s \approx \sigma$, and any inaccuracy in (8.17), (8.18), or (8.20) will be minor. However, this heuristic argument breaks down in high-noise regimes.

8.3 PROBABILITY OF IMPROVEMENT

Probability of improvement (7.5) represents the probability that the simple reward of our data (6.3) will exceed a threshold τ after obtaining an observation at x:

probability of improvement: § 7.5, p. 131

$$\alpha_{\text{PI}}(x; \mathcal{D}) = \Pr(u(\mathcal{D}') > \tau \mid x, \mathcal{D}).$$

Like expected improvement, this quantity can be computed exactly for our chosen model class.

Probability of improvement without noise

The probability of improvement after an exact observation at x is simply the probability that the observed value will exceed τ (7.6). For a Gaussian

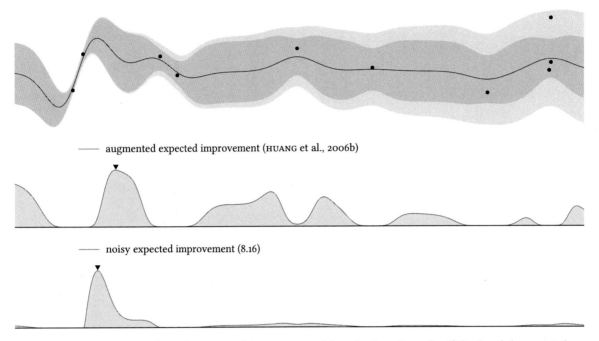

—— augmented expected improvement (HUANG et al., 2006b)

—— noisy expected improvement (8.16)

Figure 8.7: A comparison of noiseless expected improvement with a plug-in estimate for ϕ^* (8.17) and the expected one-step marginal gain in simple reward (7.2). Here the noise variance increases linearly from zero on the left-hand side of the domain to a signal-to-noise ratio of 1 on the right-hand side. The larger enveloping area shows 95% credible intervals for the noisy observation y, whereas the smaller area provides the same credible intervals for the objective function.

process, this probability is given by the complementary Gaussian CDF:

$$\alpha_{\text{PI}}(x; \mathcal{D}, \tau) = \Phi\left(\frac{\mu - \tau}{\sigma}\right). \tag{8.21}$$

equivalent acquisition function, α'_{PI}

As our policy will ultimately be determined by maximizing the probability of improvement, it is prudent to transform this expression into the simpler and better-behaved acquisition function

$$\alpha'_{\text{PI}}(x; \mathcal{D}, \tau) = \frac{\mu - \tau}{\sigma}, \tag{8.22}$$

which shares the same maxima but is slightly cheaper to compute and does not suffer from a vanishing gradient for extreme values of τ.

partial derivatives with respect to predictive distribution parameters

We may gain some insight into the behavior of probability of improvement by computing the gradient of this alternative expression (8.22) with respect to the parameters of the predictive distribution:

$$\frac{\partial \alpha'_{\text{PI}}}{\partial \mu} = \frac{1}{\sigma}; \qquad \frac{\partial \alpha'_{\text{PI}}}{\partial \sigma} = \frac{\tau - \mu}{\sigma^2}.$$

We observe that probability of improvement is monotonically increasing with μ, universally encouraging exploitation. Probability of improvement

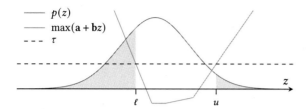

Figure 8.8: Probability of improvement with noise. The piecewise linear curve represents the updated simple reward given the z-score of the observed value. The probability of improvement is the probability this value exceeds a threshold τ, the area of the shaded region.

is also increasing with σ when the target value is greater than the predictive mean, or equivalently when the probability of improvement is less than $1/2$. Therefore probability of improvement also tends to encourage exploration in this typical case. However, when the predictive mean is greater than the improvement threshold, probability of improvement is, perhaps surprisingly, *decreasing* with σ, discouraging exploration in this favorable regime. Probability of improvement favors a relatively safe option returning a certain but modest improvement over a more-risky alternative offering a potentially larger but less-certain improvement, as demonstrated in Figure 7.8.

risk aversion of probability of improvement: § 7.5, p. 132

With the partial derivatives computed above, we may readily compute the gradient of (8.22) with respect to the proposed evaluation location x in the noiseless case (8.6):

gradient of probability of improvement without noise

$$\frac{\partial \alpha'_{\text{PI}}}{\partial x} = \frac{1}{\sigma}\left[\frac{\partial \mu}{\partial x} - \alpha'_{\text{PI}}\frac{\partial \sigma}{\partial x}\right].$$

Probability of improvement with noise

As with expected improvement, computing probability of improvement with noisy observations is slightly more complicated than with exact observations, and for the same reason. A noisy observation can affect the posterior mean at every previously observed location, and thus improvement to the simple reward can occur at any point. However, we can compute probability of improvement exactly by adapting the techniques we used to compute noisy expected improvement (8.16).

As before, the key observation is that the updated posterior mean is linear in the observed value y (8.11), allowing us to express the updated simple reward as

$$u(\mathcal{D}') = \max(\mathbf{a} + \mathbf{b}z),$$

where $\mathbf{a}$ and $\mathbf{b}$ are defined in (8.12) and z is the z-score of the observation. Now we can write the probability of improvement as the expectation of an indicator against a standard normal random variable; see Figure 8.8:

$$\alpha_{\text{PI}}(x;\mathcal{D}) = \int \left[\max(\mathbf{a} + \mathbf{b}z) > \tau\right]\phi(z)\,dz.$$

Due to the convexity of the updated simple reward, improvement occurs on at-most two intervals:[20]

20 In the case that improvement is impossible or occurs at a single point, the probability of improvement is zero.

$$(-\infty, \ell) \cup (u, \infty).$$

The endpoints of these intervals may be computed directly by inspecting the intersections of the lines $\mathbf{a} + \mathbf{b}z$ with the threshold:

$$\ell = \max_i \left\{ (\tau - a_i)/b_i \mid b_i < 0 \right\}; \qquad u = \min_i \left\{ (\tau - a_i)/b_i \mid b_i > 0 \right\}.$$

Note that one of these endpoints may not exist, for example if every slope in the $\mathbf{b}$ vector were positive; see Figure 8.3 for an example. In this case we may take $\ell = -\infty$ or $u = \infty$ as appropriate. Now given the endpoints (ℓ, u), the probability of improvement may be computed in terms of the standard normal CDF:

$$\alpha_{\text{PI}}(x; \mathcal{D}) = \Phi(\ell) + \Phi(-u). \tag{8.23}$$

gradient of noisy probability of improvement: § C.3, p. 309

We may compute the gradient of this noisy formulation of probability of improvement; details are given in the appendix.

8.4 UPPER CONFIDENCE BOUND

upper confidence bound: § 7.8, p. 145

Computing an upper confidence bound (7.18) for a Gaussian process is trivial. Given a confidence parameter $\pi \in (0, 1)$, we must compute a pointwise upper bound for the objective function with that confidence:

$$\alpha_{\text{UCB}}(x; \mathcal{D}, \pi) = q(\pi; x, \mathcal{D}), \tag{8.24}$$

where q is the quantile function of the predictive distribution. For a Gaussian process, this quantile takes the simple form

$$\alpha_{\text{UCB}}(x; \mathcal{D}, \pi) = \mu + \beta\sigma, \tag{8.25}$$

exploration parameter, β

21 A word of warning: the exploration parameter is sometimes denoted $\sqrt{\beta}$, so that β is a weight on the variance σ^2 instead.

gradient of upper confidence bound

where $\beta = \Phi^{-1}(\pi)$ depends on the confidence level and can be computed from the inverse Gaussian CDF. This acquisition function is normally parameterized directly in terms of β rather than the confidence level π. In this case β can be interpreted as an "exploration parameter," as higher values clearly reward uncertainty more than smaller values.[21] No special care is required in computing (8.25), and its gradient with respect to the proposed observation location x can also be computed easily:

$$\frac{\partial \alpha_{\text{UCB}}}{\partial x} = \frac{\partial \mu}{\partial x} + \beta \frac{\partial \sigma}{\partial x}.$$

Correspondence with probability of improvement

22 D. R. JONES (2001). A Taxonomy of Global Optimization Methods Based on Response Surfaces. *Journal of Global Optimization* 21(4):345–383. [§ 6]

23 Z. WANG et al. (2016a). Optimization as Estimation with Gaussian Processes in Bandit Settings. *AISTATS 2016*. [lemma 3.1]

For Gaussian processes, we can derive an intimate correspondence between the (noiseless) probability of improvement and upper confidence bound acquisition functions. Namely, a point maximizing probability of improvement for a given target also maximizes some statistical upper bound of the objective and vice versa, a fact that has been noted by several authors, including JONES[22] and, independently, WANG et al.[23]

To establish this result, let an arbitrary exploration parameter β be given. Consider a point optimizing the upper confidence bound:

$$x \in \argmax_{x' \in \mathcal{X}} \mu + \beta\sigma,$$

and define

equivalent improvement target, $\tau(\beta)$

$$\tau(\beta) = \max_{x' \in \mathcal{X}} \mu + \beta\sigma$$

to be its optimal value. Then the following equalities are satisfied at x:

$$\tau(\beta) = \mu + \beta\sigma; \qquad \beta = \frac{\tau(\beta) - \mu}{\sigma}.$$

Now it is easy to show that x also minimizes the score

$$x \in \arg\min_{x' \in \mathcal{X}} \frac{\tau(\beta) - \mu}{\sigma}, \tag{8.26}$$

because if there were some other point x' with

$$\frac{\tau(\beta) - \mu'}{\sigma'} < \beta,$$

then we would have

$$\mu' + \beta\sigma' > \tau(\beta),$$

contradicting the optimality of x. Therefore x also maximizes probability of improvement with target $\tau(\beta)$ (8.22).

It is important to note that the value of this target $\tau(\beta)$ is data- and model-dependent and may change from iteration to iteration. Therefore sequentially maximizing an upper confidence bound with a fixed exploration parameter is not equivalent to maximizing probability of improvement with a fixed improvement target.

data-dependence of relationship

8.5 APPROXIMATE COMPUTATION FOR ONE-STEP LOOKAHEAD

Unfortunately we have exhausted the acquisition functions for which exact computation is possible with Gaussian process models. However, we can still proceed effectively with appropriate approximations. We will begin by discussing the implementation of arbitrary one-step lookahead policies when exact computation is not possible.

Recall that one-step lookahead entails maximizing the expected marginal gain to a utility function $u(\mathcal{D})$ after making an observation at a proposed location x:

one-step lookahead: § 5.3, p. 101

$$\alpha(x; \mathcal{D}) = \int \left[u(\mathcal{D}') - u(\mathcal{D}) \right] \mathcal{N}(y; \mu, s^2) \, dy.$$

If this integral is intractable, we must resort to analytic approximation or numerical integration to evaluate and optimize the acquisition function. Fortunately in the case of sequential optimization, this is a one-dimensional integral that can be approximated using standard tools.

It will be convenient below to introduce simple notation for the marginal gain in utility resulting from a putative observation (x, y). We will write

marginal gain from observation (x, y), $\Delta(x, y)$

$$\Delta(x, y) = u(\mathcal{D}') - u(\mathcal{D})$$

for this quantity, leaving the dependence on $\mathcal{D}$ implicit. Now we seek to approximate

$$\alpha(x; \mathcal{D}) = \int \Delta(x, y)\, \mathcal{N}(y; \mu, s^2)\, dy. \qquad (8.27)$$

Gauss–Hermite quadrature

We recommend using off-the-shelf quadrature methods to estimate the expected marginal gain (8.27).[24] The most natural approach is *Gauss–Hermite quadrature*, a classical approach for approximating integrals of the form

$$I = \int h(z) \exp(-z^2)\, dz. \qquad (8.28)$$

24 P. J. DAVIS and P. RABINOWITZ (1984). *Methods of Numerical Integration*. Academic Press.

integration nodes, $\{z_i\}$

Like all numerical integration methods, Gauss–Hermite quadrature entails measuring the integrand h at a set of n points, called *nodes*, $\{z_i\}$, then approximating the integral by a weighted sum of the measured values:

$$I \approx \sum_{i=1}^{n} w_i h(z_i).$$

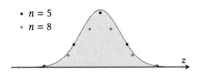

- $n = 5$
- $n = 8$

Gauss–Hermite nodes/weights for $n \in \{5, 8\}$.

Remarkably, this estimator is *exact* when the integrand is a polynomial of degree less than $2n - 1$. This guarantee provides some guidance for selecting the order of the quadrature rule depending on how well the marginal gain Δ may be approximated by a polynomial over the range of plausible observations. Tables of integration nodes and quadrature weights for n up to 64 are readily available, although such a high order should rarely be needed.[25]

25 T. S. SHAO et al. (1964). Tables of Zeros and Gaussian Weights of Certain Associated Laguerre Polynomials and the Related Generalized Hermite Polynomials. *Mathematics of Computation* 18(88):598–616.

Through a simple transformation,[26] we can rewrite the arbitrary Gaussian expectation (8.27) in the Gauss–Hermite form (8.28):

$$\int \Delta(x, y)\, \mathcal{N}(y; \mu, s^2)\, dy = \frac{1}{\sqrt{\pi}} \int \Delta(x, \mu + \sqrt{2}sz) \exp(-z^2)\, dz.$$

26 We take

$$y = \mu + \sqrt{2}sz \quad \Leftrightarrow \quad z = \frac{y - \mu}{\sqrt{2}s}.$$

Note we must account for the normalization factor $(\sqrt{2\pi}s)^{-1}$ of the Gaussian distribution, hence the constant that appears.

If we define appropriately renormalized weights

$$\bar{w}_i = w_i / \sqrt{\pi},$$

then we arrive at the following approximation to the acquisition function:

$$\alpha(x; \mathcal{D}) \approx \sum_{i=1}^{n} \bar{w}_i \Delta(x, y_i); \qquad y_i = \mu + \sqrt{2}z_i s. \qquad (8.29)$$

approximating gradient via Gauss–Hermite quadrature: § c.3, p. 309

We may also extend this scheme to approximate the gradient of the acquisition function using the same nodes and weights; details are provided in the accompanying appendix.

8.6 KNOWLEDGE GRADIENT

knowledge gradient: § 7.4, p. 129

The knowledge gradient is the expected one-step gain in the global reward (6.5). If we define

$$\mu^* = \max_{x \in \mathcal{X}} \mu_{\mathcal{D}}(x)$$

to be the utility of the current dataset, then we must compute:

$$\alpha_{\text{KG}}(x; \mathcal{D}) = \int \left[\max_{x' \in \mathcal{X}} \mu_{\mathcal{D}'}(x') - \mu^* \right] p(y \mid x, \mathcal{D}) \, dy. \qquad (8.30)$$

The global optimization in the expectation renders the knowledge gradient nontrivial to compute in most cases, so we must resort to quadrature or other approximation.

Exact computation in discrete domains

FRAZIER et al. first proposed the knowledge gradient for optimization on a *discrete* domain $\mathcal{X} = \{1, 2, \ldots, n\}$.[27] In this case, the objective is simply a vector $\mathbf{f} \in \mathbb{R}^n$ and a Gaussian process belief about the objective is simply a multivariate normal distribution:

$$p(\mathbf{f} \mid \mathcal{D}) = \mathcal{N}(\mathbf{f}; \boldsymbol{\mu}, \Sigma).$$

27 P. FRAZIER et al. (2009). The Knowledge-Gradient Policy for Correlated Normal Beliefs. *INFORMS Journal on Computing* 21(4):599–613.

The knowledge gradient now reduces to the expected marginal gain in the maximum of the posterior mean vector:

$$\alpha_{\text{KG}}(x; \mathcal{D}) = \int \left[\max \boldsymbol{\mu}' - \mu^* \right] p(y \mid x, \mathcal{D}) \, dy.$$

We may compute this expectation in closed form following our analysis of noisy expected improvement, which was merely a slight adaptation of FRAZIER et al.'s approach.

computation of noisy expected improvement: § 8.2, p. 160

The updated posterior mean vector $\boldsymbol{\mu}'$ after observing an observation (x, y) is linear in the observed value y:

$$\boldsymbol{\mu}' = \boldsymbol{\mu} + \frac{\Sigma_x}{s} \frac{y - \mu_x}{s},$$

where μ_x is the entry of $\boldsymbol{\mu}$ corresponding to the index x, and Σ_x is similarly the corresponding column of Σ. If we define

$$\mathbf{a} = \boldsymbol{\mu}; \qquad \mathbf{b} = \frac{\Sigma_x}{s},$$

then we may rewrite the knowledge gradient in terms of the g function introduced in the context of noisy expected improvement (8.10):

computation in terms of $g(\mathbf{a}, \mathbf{b})$

$$\alpha_{\text{KG}}(x; \mathcal{D}) = g(\mathbf{a}, \mathbf{b}) - \mu^*$$

We may evaluate this expression exactly in $\mathcal{O}(n \log n)$ time following our previous discussion. Thus we may compute the knowledge gradient policy with a discrete domain in $\mathcal{O}(n^2 \log n)$ time per iteration by exhaustive computation of the acquisition function.

computation of g: § 8.2, p. 161

Approximation via numerical quadrature

Although the knowledge gradient acquisition function can be computed exactly over discrete domains, the situation becomes significantly more

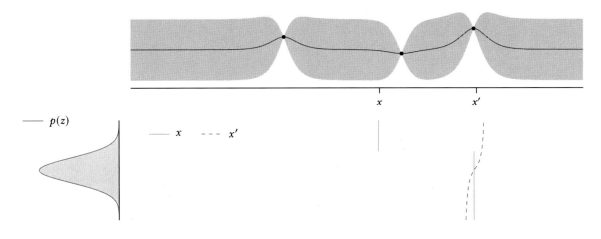

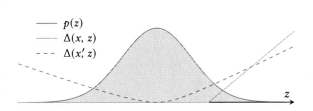

Figure 8.9: The complex behavior of the updated global reward. Above: the location of the posterior mean maximum given the z-score of an observation at two points, x and x'. An observation at x' always results in shoring up the existing maximum, whereas an observation at x reveals a new maximum given a sufficiently high observation. Below: the marginal gain in the global reward as a function of the z-score of an observation at these locations.

exact computation for special cases

28 H. J. KUSHNER (1964). A New Method of Locating the Maximum Point of an Arbitrary Multipeak Curve in the Presence of Noise. *Journal of Basic Engineering* 86(1):97–106.

29 J. MOCKUS (1972). Bayesian Methods of Search for an Extremum. *Avtomatika i Vychislitel'naya Tekhnika (Automatic Control and Computer Sciences)* 6(3):53–62.

complicated in continuous domains. The culprit is the nonconvex global optimization in (8.30), which makes the knowledge gradient intractable except in a few special cases.

Some Gaussian processes give rise to convenient structure in the posterior distribution facilitating computation of the knowledge gradient. For example, in one dimension the Wiener or Ohrstein–Uhlenbeck processes satisfy a Markov property guaranteeing the posterior mean is always maximized at an observed location. As a result the simple reward and global reward are always equal, and the knowledge gradient reduces to expected improvement. This structure was often exploited in the early literature on Bayesian optimization.[28,29]

Figure 8.9 give some insight into the complexity of the knowledge gradient integral (8.30). We illustrate the possible results from adding an observation at two locations as a function of the z-score of the observed value. For the point on the left, the behavior is similar to expected improvement: a sufficiently high value moves the maximum of the posterior mean to that point; otherwise, we retain the incumbent. The marginal gain in utility is a piecewise linear function corresponding to these two outcomes, as in expected improvement. The point on the right displays entirely different behavior – the marginal gain in utility is smooth, and nearly any outcome would be beneficial.

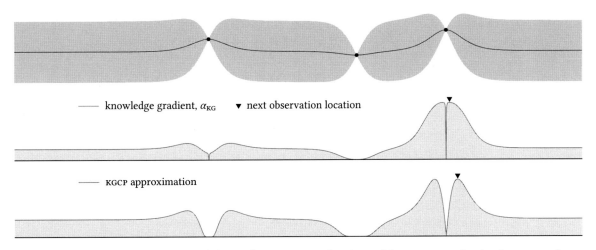

Figure 8.10: A comparison of the knowledge gradient acquisition function and the KGCP approximation for an example scenario. In this case the KGCP approximation reverts to expected improvement.

When exact computation is not possible, we must resort to numerical integration or an analytic approximation when adopting the knowledge gradient policy. The former path was explored in depth by WU et al.[30] To compute the acquisition function at a given point, we can compute a high-accuracy approximation following the numerical techniques outlined in the previous section. Order-n Gauss–Hermite quadrature for example, would approximate with (8.29):

30 J. WU et al. (2017). Bayesian Optimization with Gradients. *NeurIPS 2017*.

$$\alpha_{\text{KG}}(x; \mathcal{D}) \approx \frac{1}{\sqrt{\pi}} \sum_{i=1}^{n} w_i \Delta(x, y_i); \qquad \Delta(x, y_i) = \max_{x' \in \mathcal{X}} \mu_{\mathcal{D}'}(x') - \mu^*.$$

With some care, we can also approximate the gradient of the knowledge gradient in this scheme; details are given in an appendix.

approximating gradient of knowledge gradient: § C.3, p. 310

Knowledge gradient for continuous parameters approximation

SCOTT et al. suggested an alternative and lightweight approximation scheme for the knowledge gradient the authors called the *knowledge gradient for continuous parameters* (KGCP).[31] The KGCP approximation entails replacing the domain of the maximization in the definition of the global reward utility, normally the entire domain $\mathcal{X}$, with a conveniently chosen discrete set: the already observed locations $\mathbf{x}$ and the proposed new observation location x. Let $\mathbf{x}'$ represent this set. We approximate the current and future utility with

31 W. SCOTT et al. (2011). The Correlated Knowledge Gradient for Simulation Optimization of Continuous Parameters Using Gaussian Process Regression. *SIAM Journal on Optimization* 21(3):996–1026.

$$u(\mathcal{D}) \approx \max \mu_{\mathcal{D}}(\mathbf{x}'); \qquad u(\mathcal{D}') \approx \max \mu_{\mathcal{D}'}(\mathbf{x}'),$$

yielding the approximation

$$\alpha_{\text{KG}}(x; \mathcal{D}) \approx \mathbb{E}\big[\max \mu_{\mathcal{D}'}(\mathbf{x}') \mid x, \mathcal{D}\big] - \max \mu_{\mathcal{D}}(\mathbf{x}'). \qquad (8.31)$$

comparison with expected improvement

This expression is almost identical to expected improvement (8.7)! In fact, if we define

$$\mu^* = \max \mu_{\mathcal{D}}(\mathbf{x}),$$

then a simple manipulation gives:

$$\alpha_{\text{KG}}(x; \mathcal{D}) \approx \alpha_{\text{EI}}(x; \mathcal{D}) - \max(\mu - \mu^*, 0).$$

Effectively, the KGCP approximation is a simple adjustment to expected improvement where we punish points for already having large expected value. From the point of view of the global reward, these points already represent success and their large expected values are already reflected in the current utility. Therefore, we should not necessarily waste precious evaluations confirming what we already believe.

gradient of KGCP approximation

The gradient of the KGCP approximation may also be computed in terms of the gradient of expected improvement and the posterior mean:

$$\frac{\partial \alpha_{\text{KG}}}{\partial x} \approx \frac{\partial \alpha_{\text{EI}}}{\partial x} - [\mu > \mu^*] \frac{\partial \mu}{\partial x}.$$

example and discussion

In the case of our example scenario, the posterior mean never exceeds the highest observed point. Therefore, the KGCP approximation to the knowledge gradient globally reduces to the expected improvement; see Figure 8.10 and compare with the expected improvement in Figure 7.3. Comparing with true knowledge gradient, we can see that this approximation cannot necessarily be trusted to be unconditionally faithful. However, the KGCP approximation has the advantage of efficient computation and may be used as a drop-in replacement for expected improvement that may offer a slight boost in performance when the global reward utility is preferred to simple reward.

8.7 THOMPSON SAMPLING

Thompson sampling: § 7.9, p. 148

Thompson sampling designs each observation by sampling a point proportional to its probability of maximizing the objective (7.19):

$$x \sim p(x^* \mid \mathcal{D}).$$

A major barrier to Thompson sampling with Gaussian processes is the complex nature of this distribution. Except in a small number of special cases,[32] this distribution cannot be computed analytically. Figure 8.11 illustrates the complicated nature of this distribution for our running example, which was only revealed via brute-force sampling. However, a straightforward implementation strategy is to maximize a draw from the objective function posterior, which assumes the role of an acquisition function:

$$\alpha_{\text{TS}}(x; \mathcal{D}) \sim p(f \mid \mathcal{D}).$$

The global optimum of α_{TS} is then a sample from the desired distribution.

This procedure in fact yields a sample from the *joint* distribution of the location and value of the optimum, $p(x^*, f^* \mid \mathcal{D})$, as the value of

32 One notable example is the Wiener process, where x^* famously has an arcsine distribution:

P. LÉVY (1948). *Processus stochastiques et mouvement brownien.* Gauthier–Villars.

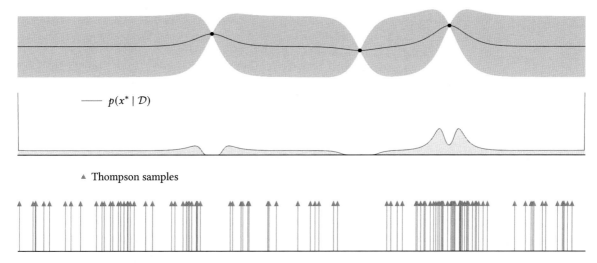

$$p(x^* \mid \mathcal{D})$$

▲ Thompson samples

Figure 8.11: The distribution of the location of the global maximum, $p(x^* \mid \mathcal{D})$, for an example scenario, and 100 samples drawn from this distribution.

the sampled objective function α_{TS} at its maximum provides a sample from $p(f^* \mid x^*, \mathcal{D})$; see the margin. We discuss Thompson sampling now because the ability to sample from these distributions will be critical for computing mutual information, our focus in the following sections.

Exhaustive sampling

In "small" domains, we can realize Thompson sampling via brute force. If the domain can be exhaustively covered by a sufficiently small set of points ξ (for example, with a dense grid or a low-discrepancy sequence) then we can simply sample the associated objective function values $\boldsymbol{\phi} = f(\boldsymbol{\xi})$ and maximize:[33]

$$x = \arg\max \boldsymbol{\phi}; \qquad \boldsymbol{\phi} \sim p(\boldsymbol{\phi} \mid \boldsymbol{\xi}, \mathcal{D}).$$

The distribution of $\boldsymbol{\phi}$ is multivariate normal, making sampling easy:

$$p(\boldsymbol{\phi} \mid \boldsymbol{\xi}, \mathcal{D}) = \mathcal{N}(\boldsymbol{\phi}; \boldsymbol{\mu}, \boldsymbol{\Sigma}); \qquad \boldsymbol{\mu} = \mu_{\mathcal{D}}(\boldsymbol{\xi}); \qquad \boldsymbol{\Sigma} = K_{\mathcal{D}}(\boldsymbol{\xi}, \boldsymbol{\xi}).$$

The running time of this procedure grows quickly with the size of ξ, although sophisticated numerical methods enable scaling to roughly 50 000 points.[34]

Figure 8.11 shows 100 Thompson samples for our example scenario generated via exhaustive sampling, taking ξ to be a grid of 1000 points.

On-demand sampling

An alternative to exhaustive sampling is to use off-the-shelf optimization routines to maximize a draw from the objective function posterior we

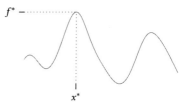

Maximizing a draw from a Gaussian process naturally samples from $p(x^*, f^* \mid \mathcal{D})$

33 We are taking a slight liberty with notation here as we have previously used $\boldsymbol{\phi}$ for $f(\mathbf{x})$, the latent objective function values at the observed locations. However, for the remainder of this discussion we will be assuming the general, potentially noisy case where our data will be written $\mathcal{D} = (\mathbf{x}, \mathbf{y})$ and we will have no need to refer to $f(\mathbf{x})$.

34 G. PLEISS et al. (2020). Fast Matrix Square Roots with Applications to Gaussian Processes and Bayesian Optimization. *NeurIPS 2020*.

Algorithm 8.1: On-demand sampling.

$\mathcal{D}_{\text{TS}} \leftarrow \mathcal{D}$ ▸ initialize fictitious dataset with current data
repeat
    given request for observation at x:
      $\phi \;\;\leftarrow p(\phi \mid x, \mathcal{D}_{\text{TS}})$ ▸ sample value at x
      $\mathcal{D}_{\text{TS}} \leftarrow \mathcal{D}_{\text{TS}} \cup (x, \phi)$ ▸ update fictitious dataset
    yield ϕ
until external optimizer terminates

build progressively on demand. Namely, when an optimization routine requests an evaluation of α_{TS} at a point x, we sample an objective function value at that location:

$$\phi \sim p(\phi \mid x, \mathcal{D}),$$

then augment our dataset with the simulated observation (x, ϕ). We proceed in this manner until the optimizer terminates. This procedure avoids simulating the entire objective function while guaranteeing the joint distribution of the provided evaluations is correct via the chain rule of probability. Pseudocode is provided in Algorithm 8.1 in the form of a generator function; the "yield" statement returns a value while maintaining state. Using rank-one updates to update the posterior, the computational cost of generating each evaluation scales quadratically with the size of the fictitious dataset $\mathcal{D}_{\text{TS}}$.

If desired, we may use gradient methods to optimize the generated sample by sampling from the joint posterior of the function value and its gradient at each requested location:

$$p(\phi, \nabla\phi \mid x, \mathcal{D}_{\text{TS}}).$$

However, in high dimensions, the additional cost required to condition on these gradient observations may become excessive. In d dimensions, returning gradients effectively reduces the number of function evaluations we can allow for the optimizer by a factor of $(d + 1)$ if we wish to maintain the same total computational effort.

Sparse spectrum approximation for stationary covariance functions

If the prior covariance function K of the Gaussian process is stationary, we may use a *sparse spectrum approximation*[35] to the posterior Gaussian process to dramatically accelerate Thompson sampling.[36]

Consider a stationary covariance function K on $\mathbb{R}^d$ with spectral density κ. The key idea in sparse spectrum approximation is to interpret the characterization in (3.10) as an expectation with respect to the spectral density:[37]

$$K(\mathbf{x} - \mathbf{x}') = K(0)\,\mathbb{E}_\xi\big[\exp\big(2\pi i(\mathbf{x} - \mathbf{x}')^\top \xi\big)\big], \tag{8.32}$$

and approximate via Monte Carlo integration. We first sample a set of m frequencies, called *spectral points,* from the spectral density: $\{\xi_i\} \sim \kappa(\xi)$.

Margin notes:

low-rank updates: § 9.1, p. 202
running time

using gradient methods

35 M. LÁZARO-GREDILLA et al. (2010). Sparse Spectrum Gaussian Process Regression. *Journal of Machine Learning Research* 11(Jun):1865–1881.

36 J. M. HERNÁNDEZ-LOBATO et al. (2014). Predictive Entropy Search for Efficient Global Optimization of Black-Box Functions. *NeurIPS 2014.*

stationarity: § 3.2, p. 50

37 Recall the convention of writing a stationary covariance with respect to a single input, $K(\mathbf{x}, \mathbf{x}') = K(\mathbf{x} - \mathbf{x}')$.

spectral points, $\{\xi_i\}$

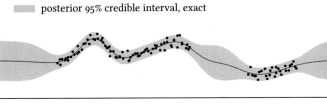

—— posterior mean, exact
▨ posterior 95% credible interval, exact

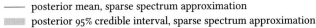

—— posterior mean, sparse spectrum approximation
▨ posterior 95% credible interval, sparse spectrum approximation

Figure 8.12: Sparse spectrum approximation. Top: the exact posterior belief (about noisy observations rather than the latent function) for a Gaussian process conditioned on 200 observations. Bottom: a sparse spectrum approximation using 100 spectral points sampled from the spectral density.

To enforce the symmetry around the origin inherent to the spectral density (theorem 3.2), we augment each sample ξ_i with its negation, $-\xi_i$.

Using these samples for a Monte Carlo approximation to (8.32) has the effect of approximating a Gaussian process $\mathcal{GP}(f; \mu, K)$ with a *finite-dimensional* Gaussian process:

$$f(\mathbf{x}) \approx \mu(\mathbf{x}) + \boldsymbol{\beta}^\top \boldsymbol{\psi}(\mathbf{x}). \tag{8.33}$$

Here $\boldsymbol{\beta}$ is a vector of normally distributed weights and $\boldsymbol{\psi} \colon \mathbb{R}^d \to \mathbb{R}^{2m}$ is a feature representation determined by the spectral points:

weight vector, $\boldsymbol{\beta}$
feature representation, $\boldsymbol{\psi}$

$$\psi_{2i-1}(\mathbf{x}) = \cos(2\pi \boldsymbol{\xi}_i^\top \mathbf{x}); \qquad \psi_{2i}(\mathbf{x}) = \sin(2\pi \boldsymbol{\xi}_i^\top \mathbf{x}).$$

For the additive Gaussian noise model, if $\mathbf{N}$ is the covariance of the noise contributions to the observed values $\mathbf{y}$, the posterior moments of the weight vector in this approximation are:

noise covariance matrix, $\mathbf{N}$

$$\mathbb{E}[\boldsymbol{\beta} \mid \mathcal{D}] = \boldsymbol{\Psi}^\top (\boldsymbol{\Psi}\boldsymbol{\Psi}^\top + a^{-2}\mathbf{N})^{-1}(\mathbf{y} - \boldsymbol{\mu});$$
$$\mathrm{cov}[\boldsymbol{\beta} \mid \mathcal{D}] = a^2 \big[\mathbf{I} - \boldsymbol{\Psi}^\top (\boldsymbol{\Psi}\boldsymbol{\Psi}^\top + a^{-2}\mathbf{N})^{-1}\boldsymbol{\Psi}\big],$$

where $a^2 = K(\mathbf{0})/m$, $\boldsymbol{\mu}$ is the prior mean of $\mathbf{y}$, and $\boldsymbol{\Psi}$ is a matrix whose rows comprise the feature representations of the observed locations.

training features, $\boldsymbol{\Psi}$

The sparse spectrum approximation allows us to generate a posterior sample of the objective function in time $\mathcal{O}(nm^2)$ by drawing a sample from the weight posterior and appealing to the representation in (8.33). The resulting sample is nontrivial to maximize due to the nonlinear nature of the representation, but with the sampled weights in hand, we can generate requested function and gradient evaluations in constant time, enabling exhaustive optimization via gradient methods.

sampling from a multivariate normal distribution: § A.2, p. 299

A sparse spectrum approximation is illustrated in Figure 8.12, using a total of 100 spectral points. The approximation is quite reasonable near data and acceptable in extrapolatory regions as well.

8.8 MUTUAL INFORMATION WITH x^*

mutual information: § 7.6, p. 135

Mutual information measures the expected information gain (6.3) provided by an observation at x about some random variable of interest ω, which can be expressed in two equivalent forms (7.14–7.15):

$$\alpha_{\text{MI}}(x; \mathcal{D}) = H[\omega \mid \mathcal{D}] - \mathbb{E}_y\big[H[\omega \mid \mathcal{D}'] \mid x, \mathcal{D}\big] \tag{8.34}$$

$$= H[y \mid x, \mathcal{D}] - \mathbb{E}_\omega\big[H[y \mid \omega, x, \mathcal{D}] \mid x, \mathcal{D}\big]. \tag{8.35}$$

In the context of Bayesian optimization, the most natural choices for ω are the location x^* and value f^* of the global optimum, both of which were discussed in the previous chapter. Unfortunately, a Gaussian process belief on the objective function in general induces complex distributions for these quantities, which makes even *approximating* mutual information somewhat involved. However, several effective approximation schemes are available for both options. We will consider each in turn, beginning with x^*.

Direct form of mutual information

Of the two equivalent formulations of mutual information above, the former (8.34) is perhaps the most natural, as it reasons directly about changes in the entropy of the variable of interest. Initial work on mutual information with x^* considered approximations to this direct expression[38] – including the work coining the now-common moniker *entropy search* for information-theoretic optimization policies[39] – but this approach has fallen out of favor in preference for the latter formulation (8.35), discussed below.

The main computational difficulty in approximating (8.34) is the unwieldy (and potentially high-dimensional) distribution $p(x^* \mid \mathcal{D})$; see even the simple example in Figure 8.11. There is no general method for computing the entropy of this distribution in closed form, and overcoming this barrier requires approximation. The usual approach is to make a discrete approximation to this distribution via a set of carefully maintained so-called *representer points,* then reason about changes in the entropy of this surrogate distribution via further layers of approximation.

Predictive form of mutual information

HERNÁNDEZ-LOBATO et al. proposed a faithful approximation to the mutual information with x^* based on the formulation in (8.35):[40]

$$\alpha_{x^*}(x; \mathcal{D}) = H[y \mid x, \mathcal{D}] - \mathbb{E}\big[H[y \mid x, x^*, \mathcal{D}] \mid x, \mathcal{D}\big]. \tag{8.36}$$

Compared to the direct form (8.34), this formulation is attractive as all entropy computations are restricted to the one-dimensional predictive distribution $p(y \mid x, \mathcal{D})$; however, considerable approximation is still required to realize an effective policy, as we will see.[41] The authors named their approach *predictive entropy search* to highlight this focus.

38 J. VILLEMONTEIX et al. (2009). An Informational Approach to the Global Optimization of Expensive-to-evaluate Functions. *Journal of Global Optimization* 44(4):509–534.

39 P. HENNIG and C. J. SCHULER (2012). Entropy Search for Information-Efficient Global Optimization. *Journal of Machine Learning Research* 13(Jun):1809–1837.

40 J. M. HERNÁNDEZ-LOBATO et al. (2014). Predictive Entropy Search for Efficient Global Optimization of Black-Box Functions. *NeurIPS 2014.*

41 With careful implementation, the two schemes are comparable in terms of computational cost. We focus on the predictive formulation because it is now more commonly encountered and serves as the foundation for several extensions described in Chapter 11.

predictive entropy search

computing first term

Let us consider the evaluation of (8.36) for a Gaussian process model with additive Gaussian noise. To begin, the first term is simply the differential entropy of a one-dimensional Gaussian distribution (8.5) and may be computed in closed form (A.17):

$$H[y \mid x, \mathcal{D}] = \tfrac{1}{2} \log(2\pi e s^2).$$

Unfortunately, the second term is significantly more complicated to work with, and we can identify two primary challenges.

Approximating expectation with respect to x^*

First, we must compute an expectation with respect to the location of the global optimum x^*. The complexity of its distribution limits our options, but Monte Carlo integration remains a viable option. We use Thompson sampling to generate samples of the optimal location $\{x_i^*\}_{i=1}^n \sim p(x^* \mid \mathcal{D})$ and estimate the expected updated entropy with:

Thompson sampling for GPs: § 8.7, p. 176

$$\mathbb{E}\big[H[y \mid x, x^*, \mathcal{D}] \mid x, \mathcal{D}\big] \approx \frac{1}{n} \sum_{i=1}^n H[y \mid x, x_i^*, \mathcal{D}].$$

When the prior covariance function is stationary, HERNÁNDEZ-LOBATO et al. further propose to exploit the efficient approximate Thompson sampling scheme via sparse spectrum approximation described in the last section. When feasible, this reduces the cost of drawing the samples, but it is not necessary for correctness.

sparse spectrum approximation for Thompson sampling: § 8.7, p. 178

Gaussian approximation to conditional predictive distribution

Now we must address the predictive distribution conditioned on the location of the global optimum, $p(y \mid x, x^*, \mathcal{D})$, which we may express as the result of marginalizing the latent objective value ϕ:

$$p(y \mid x, x^*, \mathcal{D}) = \int p(y \mid x, \phi) \, p(\phi \mid x, x^*, \mathcal{D}) \, d\phi. \tag{8.37}$$

It is unclear how we can condition our belief on the objective function given knowledge of the optimum, and – as the resulting posterior on ϕ will be non-Gaussian – how we can resolve the resulting integral (8.37). A key insight is that if the predictive distribution $p(\phi \mid x, x^*, \mathcal{D})$ *were* Gaussian, we could compute (8.37) in closed form,[42] suggesting a promising path forward. In particular, consider an arbitrary Gaussian approximation:

$$p(\phi \mid x, x^*, \mathcal{D}) \approx \mathcal{N}(\phi; \mu_*, \sigma_*^2), \tag{8.38}$$

whose parameters depend x^* as their subscripts indicate. Plugging into (8.37), we may estimate the predictive variance of y given x^* with (A.15):

42 In this case, the integral in (8.37) becomes the convolution of two Gaussians, which may be interpreted as the distribution of the sum of independent Gaussian random variables – see § A.2, p. 300.

approximate variance of y given x^*, s_*^2

$$\mathrm{var}[y \mid x, x^*, \mathcal{D}] \approx \sigma_*^2 + \sigma_n^2 = s_*^2, \tag{8.39}$$

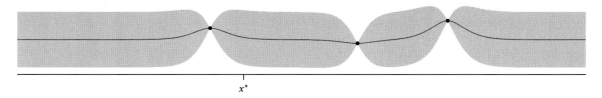

Figure 8.13: The example scenario we will consider for illustrating the predictive entropy search approximation to $p(f \mid x, x_*^*, \mathcal{D})$, using the marked location for x_*^*.

and thus its differential entropy with (A.17):

$$H[y \mid x, x_*^*, \mathcal{D}] \approx \tfrac{1}{2} \log(2\pi e s_*^2). \tag{8.40}$$

After simplification, the resulting approximation to (8.36) becomes:

$$\alpha_{x^*}(x; \mathcal{D}) \approx \alpha_{\text{PES}}(x; \mathcal{D}) = \log s - \frac{1}{n} \sum_{i=1}^{n} \log s_{*_i}. \tag{8.41}$$

Approximation via Gaussian expectation propagation

To realize a complete algorithm, we need some way of finding a suitable Gaussian approximation to $p(\phi \mid x, x_*^*, \mathcal{D})$, and HERNÁNDEZ-LOBATO et al. describe one effective approach. The high-level idea is to begin with the objective function posterior $p(f \mid \mathcal{D})$, impose a series of constraints implied by knowledge of x_*^*, then approximate the desired posterior via approximate inference. We will describe the procedure for an arbitrary putative optimum x_*^*, illustrating each step of the approximation for the example scenario and assumed optimum location shown in Figure 8.13. For the moment, we will proceed with complete disregard for computational efficiency, and return to the question of implementation shortly.

Ensuring x^* is a local optimum

We first condition our belief on x^* being a *local* optimum by insisting that the point satisfies the second partial derivative test. Let ∇^* and $\mathbf{H}^*$ respectively represent the gradient and Hessian of the objective function at x_*^*. Local optimality implies that the gradient is zero and the Hessian is negative definite:[43]

$$\nabla^* = \mathbf{0}; \tag{8.42}$$

$$\mathbf{H}^* < \mathbf{0}. \tag{8.43}$$

Enforcing the gradient constraint (8.42) is straightforward, as we can directly condition on a gradient observation. We show the result for our example scenario in the top panel of Figure 8.14.

The Hessian constraint (8.43) however is nonlinear and we must resort to approximate inference. HERNÁNDEZ-LOBATO et al. approximate

gradient, Hessian at x^*: ∇^*, $\mathbf{H}^*$

43 We discussed a simpler, one-dimensional analog of this task in § 2.8, p. 39.

gradient constraint: $\nabla^* = 0$

first Hessian constraint: diagonal entries are negative

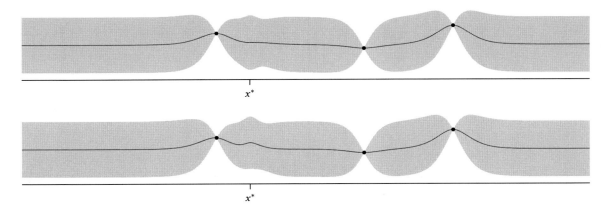

Figure 8.14: Top: the posterior for our example after conditioning on the derivative being zero at x^* (8.42). Bottom: the approximate posterior after conditioning on the second derivative being negative at x^* (8.44).

this condition by breaking it into two complementary components. First, we compel every diagonal entry of the Hessian to be negative. Letting $\mathbf{h}^* = \operatorname{diag} \mathbf{H}^*$; we assume:

diagonal of Hessian at x^*, $\mathbf{h}^*$

$$\forall i: h_i^* < 0. \tag{8.44}$$

We then *fix* the off-diagonal entries of the Hessian to values of our choosing. One simple option is to set all off-diagonal entries to zero:

second Hessian constraint: off-diagonal entries are fixed

$$\operatorname{upper} \mathbf{H}^* = \mathbf{0}, \tag{8.45}$$

which combined with the diagonal constraint guarantees negative definiteness.[44] The combination of these conditions (8.44–8.45) is stricter than mere negative definiteness, as we eliminate all degrees of freedom for the off-diagonal entries. However, an advantage of this approach is that we can enforce the off-diagonal constraint via exact conditioning.

[44] HERNÁNDEZ-LOBATO et al. point out this may not be faithful to the model and suggest the alternative of matching the off-diagonal entries of the Hessian of the objective function sample that generated x^*. However, this does not guarantee negative definiteness without tweaking (8.44).

To proceed we dispense with the constraints we can condition on exactly. Let $\mathcal{D}'$ represent our dataset augmented with the gradient (8.42) and off-diagonal Hessian (8.45) observations. The joint distribution of the latent objective value ϕ, the purportedly optimal value $\phi^* = f(x^*)$, and the diagonal of the Hessian $\mathbf{h}^*$ given this additional information is multivariate normal:

$$p(\phi, \phi^*, \mathbf{h}^* \mid x^*, \mathcal{D}') = \mathcal{N}(\phi, \phi^*, \mathbf{h}^*; \boldsymbol{\mu}^*, \Sigma^*). \tag{8.46}$$

We will now subject this initial belief to a series of factors corresponding to desired nonlinear constraints. These factors will be compatible with Gaussian expectation propagation, which we will use to finally derive the desired Gaussian approximation to the posterior (8.38). To begin, the Hessian diagonal constraint (8.44) contributes one factor for each entry:

Gaussian EP: § B.2, p. 302

truncating a variable with EP: § B.2, p. 305

$$\prod_i [h_i^* < 0]. \tag{8.47}$$

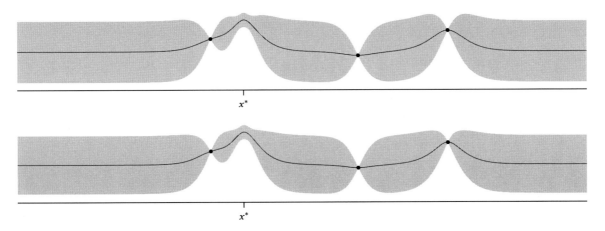

Figure 8.15: Top: the approximate posterior after conditioning on ϕ^* exceeding the function values at previously measured locations (8.49). Bottom: the approximate posterior after conditioning on ϕ^* dominating elsewhere (8.50).

45 For this and the following demonstrations, we show the expectation propagation approximation to the entire objective function posterior; this is not required to approximate the marginal predictive distribution and is only for illustration.

Our approximate posterior after incorporating (8.47) and performing expectation propagation is shown in the bottom panel of Figure 8.14.[45]

Ensuring x^* is a global optimum

Our belief now reflects our desire that x^* be a *local* maximum; however, we wish for x^* to be the *global* maximum. Global optimality is not easy to enforce, as it entails infinitely many constraints bounding the objective at every point in the domain. HERNÁNDEZ-LOBATO et al. instead approximate this condition with optimality at the most relevant locations: the already-observed points $\mathbf{x}$ and the proposed point x.

ensuring $\phi^* > \max \boldsymbol{\phi}$

To enforce that ϕ^* exceed the objective function values at the observed points, we could theoretically add $\boldsymbol{\phi} = f(\mathbf{x})$ to our prior (8.46), then add one factor for each observation: $\prod_j [\phi_j < \phi^*]$. However, this approach requires an increasing number of factors as we gather more data, rendering expectation propagation (and thus the acquisition function) increasingly expensive. Further, factors corresponding to obviously suboptimal observations are uninformative and simply represent extra work for no benefit.

truncating with respect to an unknown threshold with EP: § B.2, p. 306

Instead, we enforce this constraint through a single factor truncating with respect to the maximal value of $\boldsymbol{\phi}$: $[\phi^* < \max \boldsymbol{\phi}]$. In general, this threshold will be a random variable unless our observations are noiseless. Fortunately, expectation propagation enables tractable approximate truncation at an *unknown*, Gaussian-distributed threshold. Define

$$\mu_{\max} = \mathbb{E}[\max \boldsymbol{\phi} \mid \mathcal{D}]; \qquad \sigma_{\max}^2 = \mathrm{var}[\max \boldsymbol{\phi} \mid \mathcal{D}]; \qquad (8.48)$$

46 C. E. CLARK (1961). The Greatest of a Finite Set of Random Variables. *Operations Research* 9(2): 145–162.

these moments can be approximated via either sampling or an assumed density filtering approach described by CLARK.[46] Taking a moment-matched Gaussian approximation to $\max \boldsymbol{\phi}$ and integrating yields the

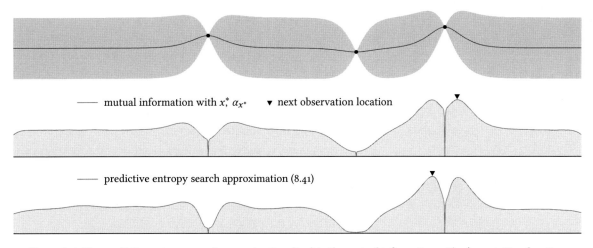

Figure 8.16: The predictive entropy search approximation (8.41) to the mutual information with x^* acquisition function (8.36) using the 100 Thompson samples from Figure 8.11.

factor (B.13):[47]

$$\Phi\left(\frac{\phi^* - \mu_{\max}}{\sigma_{\max}}\right). \tag{8.49}$$

We show the approximate posterior for our running example after incorporating this factor in the top panel of Figure 8.15. The probability mass at x^* has shifted up dramatically.

Finally, to constrain ϕ^* to dominate the objective function value at a point of interest x, we add one additional factor:

$$[\phi < \phi^*]. \tag{8.50}$$

We obtain the final approximation to $p(\phi \mid x, x^*, \mathcal{D})$ by combining the prior in (8.46) with the factors (8.47, 8.49–8.50):

$$\mathcal{N}(\phi, \phi^*, \mathbf{h}^*; \boldsymbol{\mu}^*, \Sigma^*)\, [\phi < \phi^*]\, \Phi\left(\frac{\phi^* - \mu_{\max}}{\sigma_{\max}}\right) \prod_i [h_i^* < 0],$$

approximating with Gaussian expectation propagation, and deriving the marginal belief about ϕ. The resulting final approximate posterior for our example scenario is shown in the bottom panel of Figure 8.15. Our predictive uncertainty has been moderated in response to the final constraint (8.50).

With the ability to approximate the latent predictive posterior, we can now compute the predictive entropy search acquisition function (8.41) via Thompson sampling and following the above procedure for each sample. Figure 8.16 shows the approximation computed with 1000 Thompson samples. The approximation is excellent and induces a near-optimal decision. Any deviation from the truth mostly reflects bias in the Thompson sample distribution.

[47] With high noise, this approximation could be improved slightly by computing moments of max $\boldsymbol{\phi}$ given $\mathcal{D}'$, at additional expense.

ensuring $\phi^* > \phi$
enforcing order with EP: § B.2, p. 306

Efficient implementation

A practical realization of predictive entropy search can benefit from careful precomputation and reuse of partial results. We will outline an efficient implementation strategy, beginning with three steps of one-time initial work.

1. Estimate the moments of $\max \boldsymbol{\phi}$ (8.48).

2. Generate a set of Thompson samples $\{x_i^*\}$.

3. For each sample x_i^* derive the joint distribution of the function value, gradient, and Hessian at x^*. Let $\mathbf{z}^* = (\phi_*^*, \mathbf{h}_*^*, \text{upper } \mathbf{H}_*^*, \nabla^*)$ represent a vector comprising these random variables, with those that will be subjected to expectation propagation first. We compute:

$$p(\mathbf{z}^* \mid x_*^*, \mathcal{D}) = \mathcal{N}(\mathbf{z}^*; \boldsymbol{\mu}_*^*, \Sigma^*).$$

Find the marginal belief over $(\phi_*^*, \mathbf{h}^*)$ and use Gaussian expectation propagation to approximate the posterior after incorporating the factors (8.47, 8.49). Let vectors $\tilde{\boldsymbol{\mu}}$ and $\tilde{\boldsymbol{\sigma}}^2$ denote the site parameters at termination. Finally, precompute[48]

$$\mathbf{V}_*^{-1} = \left[\Sigma^* + \begin{bmatrix} \tilde{\Sigma} & 0 \\ 0 & 0 \end{bmatrix}\right]^{-1}; \qquad \boldsymbol{\alpha}^* = \mathbf{V}_*^{-1}\left[\begin{bmatrix} \tilde{\boldsymbol{\mu}} \\ 0 \end{bmatrix} - \boldsymbol{\mu}^*\right],$$

where $\tilde{\Sigma} = \text{diag } \tilde{\boldsymbol{\sigma}}^2$. These quantities do not depend on x and will be repeatedly reused during prediction.

After completing the preparations above, suppose a proposed observation location x is given. For each sample x_*^* we compute the joint distribution of ϕ and ϕ^*:

$$p(\phi, \phi^* \mid x, x_*^*, \mathcal{D}) = \mathcal{N}(\phi, \phi^*; \boldsymbol{\mu}, \Sigma),$$

and derive the approximate posterior given the exact gradient (8.42) and off-diagonal Hessian (8.45) observations and the factors (8.47, 8.49). Defining

$$\mathbf{K} = \begin{bmatrix} \mathbf{k}^\top \\ \mathbf{k}_*^\top \end{bmatrix} = \text{cov}\big([\phi, \phi^*]_*^\top, \mathbf{z}^*\big),$$

the desired distribution is $\mathcal{N}(\phi, \phi^*; \mathbf{m}, \mathbf{S})$, where:[49]

$$\mathbf{m} = \begin{bmatrix} m \\ m^* \end{bmatrix} = \boldsymbol{\mu} + \mathbf{K}\boldsymbol{\alpha}^* \qquad \mathbf{S} = \begin{bmatrix} \varsigma^2 & \rho \\ \rho & \varsigma_*^2 \end{bmatrix} = \Sigma - \mathbf{K}\mathbf{V}_*^{-1}\mathbf{K}^\top \qquad (8.51)$$

We now apply the prediction constraint (8.50) with one final step of expectation propagation. Define (B.7, B.11–B.12):

$$\bar{\mu} = m - m^*; \qquad \bar{\sigma}^2 = \varsigma^2 - 2\rho + \varsigma_*^2;$$

$$z = -\frac{\bar{\mu}}{\bar{\sigma}}; \qquad \alpha = -\frac{\phi(z)}{\Phi(z)\bar{\sigma}}; \qquad \gamma = -\frac{\bar{\sigma}}{\alpha}\left(\frac{\phi(z)}{\Phi(z)} + z\right)^{-1}.$$

48 In the interest of numerical stability, the inverse of $\mathbf{V}_*$ should not be stored directly; for relevant practical advice see:

C. E. RASMUSSEN and C. K. I. WILLIAMS (2006). *Gaussian Processes for Machine Learning*. MIT Press.

J. P. CUNNINGHAM et al. (2011). Gaussian Probabilities and Expectation Propagation. arXiv: 1111.6832 [stat.ML].

49 This can be derived by marginalizing $\mathbf{z}^*$ according to its approximate posterior from step 3 above:

$$\int p(\phi, \phi^* \mid \mathbf{z}^*)\, p(\mathbf{z}^*)\, d\mathbf{z}_*^*$$

The final approximation to the predictive variance of ϕ given x^* is

$$\sigma_*^2 = \varsigma^2 - (\varsigma^2 - \rho)^2 / \gamma, \qquad (8.52)$$

from which we can compute the contribution to the acquisition function from this sample with (8.39–8.40).

Although it may seem unimaginable at this point, in Euclidean domains we may compute the gradient of the predictive entropy search acquisition function; see the accompanying appendix for details.

gradient of predictive entropy search acquisition function: § c.3, p. 311

8.9 MUTUAL INFORMATION WITH f^*

Finally, we consider the computation of the mutual information between the observed value y and the value of the global maximum f^* (8.53). Several authors have considered this acquisition function in its predictive form (8.35), which is the most convenient choice for Gaussian process models:

mutual information with f^*: § 7.6, p. 140

$$\alpha_{f^*}(x; \mathcal{D}) = H[y \mid x, \mathcal{D}] - \mathbb{E}\big[H[y \mid x, f^*, \mathcal{D}] \mid x, \mathcal{D}\big]. \qquad (8.53)$$

Unfortunately, this expression cannot be computed exactly due to the complexity of the distribution $p(f^* \mid \mathcal{D})$; see Figure 8.17 for an example. However, several effective approximations have been proposed, including *max-value entropy search* (MES)[50] and *output-space predictive entropy search* (OPES).[51]

The issues we face in estimating (8.53), and the strategies we use to overcome them, largely mirror those in predictive entropy search. To begin, the first term is the differential entropy of a Gaussian and may be computed exactly:

50 z. wang and s. jegelka (2017). Max-value Entropy Search for Efficient Bayesian Optimization. *ICML 2017*.

51 m. w. hoffman and z. ghahramani (2015). Output-Space Predictive Entropy Search for Flexible Global Optimization. *Bayesian Optimization Workshop, NeurIPS 2015*.

$$H[y \mid x, \mathcal{D}] = \tfrac{1}{2} \log(2\pi e s^2). \qquad (8.54)$$

The second term, however, presents some challenges, and the available approximations to (8.53) diverge in their estimation approach. We will discuss the MES and OPES approximations in parallel, as they share the same basic strategy and only differ in some details along the way.

Approximating expectation with respect to f^*

The first complication in evaluating the second term of (8.53) is that we must compute an expectation with respect to f^*. Although Thompson sampling and simple Monte Carlo approximation is one way forward, we can exploit the fact that f^* is one dimensional to pursue more sophisticated approximations. One convenient and rapidly converging strategy is to design n samples $\{f_i^*\}_{i=1}^n$ to be equally spaced quantiles of f^*, then use the familiar estimator

$$\mathbb{E}\big[H[y \mid x, f^*, \mathcal{D}] \mid x, \mathcal{D}\big] \approx \frac{1}{n} \sum_{i=1}^n H[y \mid x, f_i^*, \mathcal{D}]. \qquad (8.55)$$

52 R. E. CAFLISCH (1998). Monte Carlo and Quasi-Monte Carlo Methods. *Acta Numerica* 7:1–49.

53 The chosen samples are the first *n* points from a base-*n* van de Corput sequence:

J. G. VAN DE CORPUT (1935). Verteilungsfunktionen: Erste Mitteilung. *Proceedings of the Koninklijke Nederlandse Akademie van Wetenschappen* 38:813–821

mapped to the desired distribution via the inverse CDF. These points have the minimum possible discrepancy for a set of size *n*.

54 C. E. CLARK (1961). The Greatest of a Finite Set of Random Variables. *Operations Research* 9(2): 145–162.

55 A. M. ROSS (2010). Computing Bounds on the Expected Maximum of Correlated Normal Variables. *Methodology and Computing in Applied Probability* 12(1):111–138.

56 R. P. BRENT (1973). *Algorithms for Minimization without Derivatives.* Prentice–Hall. [chapter 4]

57 D. SLEPIAN (1962). The One-Sided Barrier Problem for Gaussian Noise. *The Bell System Technical Journal* 41(2):463–501.

58 This result requires the posterior covariance function to be positive everywhere, which is not guaranteed even if true for the prior covariance function. However, it is "usually true" for typical models in high-dimensional spaces.

This represents a *quasi*-Monte Carlo[52] approximation that converges considerably faster than simple Monte Carlo integration.[53] Further, this scheme only requires the ability to estimate quantiles of f^*.

Approximating quantiles of f^*

WANG and JEGELKA proposed estimating the quantiles of f^* via a convenient analytic approximation. To build this approximation, they proposed selecting a set of *representer points* ξ and approximating the distribution of f^* with that of the maximum function value restricted to these locations. Let $\boldsymbol{\phi} = f(\boldsymbol{\xi})$ and define the random variable $\phi^* = \max \boldsymbol{\phi}$. We estimate:

$$p(f^* \mid \mathcal{D}) \approx p(\phi^* \mid \xi, \mathcal{D}).$$

Unfortunately, the distribution of the maximum of dependent Gaussian random variables is intractable in general, even if the dimension is finite,[54,55] so we must resort to further approximation.

We could proceed in several ways, but WANG and JEGELKA propose using an exhaustive, dense set of representer points (for example, covering the domain with a low-discrepancy sequence) and then making the simplifying assumption that the associated function values are *independent*. If the marginal belief at each representer point is

$$p(\phi_i \mid \xi_i, \mathcal{D}) = \mathcal{N}(\phi_i; \mu_i, \sigma_i^2),$$

then we may approximate the cumulative distribution function of ϕ^* with a product of normal CDFs:

$$\Pr(\phi^* < z \mid \xi, \mathcal{D}) \approx \prod_i \Phi\left(\frac{z - \mu_i}{\sigma_i}\right). \tag{8.56}$$

We can now estimate the quantiles of f^* via numerical inversion of (8.56); Brent's[56] method applied to the log CDF would offer rapid convergence. The resulting approximation for our example scenario is shown in Figure 8.17 using 100 equally spaced representer points covering the domain. In general, the independence assumption tends to overestimate the maximal value, a finding WANG and JEGELKA explained heuristically by appealing to SLEPIAN's lemma.[57,58]

A diametrically opposing alternative to using dense representer points with a crude approximation (8.56) would be using a few, carefully chosen representer points with a better approximation to the distribution of ϕ^*. For example, we could generate a set of Thompson samples, $\xi_i \sim p(x^* \mid \mathcal{D})$, then approximate the quantiles of ϕ^* by repeatedly sampling their corresponding function values $\boldsymbol{\phi}$. Figure 8.17 shows such an approximation for our example scenario using 100 Thompson samples. The agreement with the true distribution is excellent, but the computational cost was significant compared to the independent approximation. However, in high-dimensional spaces where dense coverage of the domain is not possible, such a direct approach may become appealing.

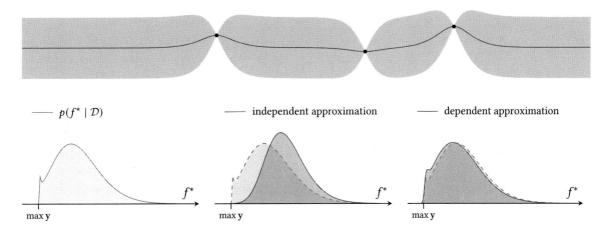

$$\text{—— } p(f^* \mid \mathcal{D}) \qquad\qquad \text{—— independent approximation} \qquad\qquad \text{—— dependent approximation}$$

Figure 8.17: Left: the true distribution $p(f^* \mid \mathcal{D})$ for our running scenario, estimated using exhaustive sampling. Middle: WANG and JEGELKA's approximation to $p(f^* \mid \mathcal{D})$ (8.56) using a grid of 100 equally spaced representer points. Right: an approximation to $p(f^* \mid \mathcal{D})$ from sampling the function values at the 100 Thompson samples from Figure 8.11.

Predictive entropy with exact observations

Regardless of the exact estimator we use to approximate the second term of the acquisition function, we will need to compute the entropy of the predictive distribution for y given the optimal value f^*:

$$p(y \mid x, f^*, \mathcal{D}) = \int p(y \mid x, \phi)\, p(\phi \mid x, f^*, \mathcal{D})\, d\phi. \tag{8.57}$$

The latent predictive distribution of ϕ given f^* can be reasonably approximated as a normal distribution with upper tail truncated at f^*:[59]

$$p(\phi \mid x, f^*, \mathcal{D}) \approx \mathcal{TN}\big(\phi; \mu, \sigma^2, (-\infty, f^*)\big). \tag{8.58}$$

Remarkably, this approximation is sufficient to provide a closed-form *upper bound* on the differential entropy of the true marginal:[60]

$$H[\phi \mid x, f^*, \mathcal{D}] \le \frac{1}{2}\left[\log\big(2\pi e \sigma^2 \Phi(z)^2\big) - z\frac{\phi(z)}{\Phi(z)}\right]; \quad z = \frac{f^* - \mu}{\sigma}. \tag{8.59}$$

In the absence of observation noise, this result is sufficient to realize a complete algorithm by combining (8.59) with (8.53–8.55). After simplification, this yields the final MES approximation, which ignores the effect of observation noise in the predictive distribution:

$$\alpha_{\text{MES}}(x; \mathcal{D}) \approx \frac{1}{2n} \sum_{i=1}^{n} \left[z_i \frac{\phi(z_i)}{\Phi(z_i)} - \log \Phi(z_i)^2 \right]; \quad z_i = \frac{f_i^* - \mu}{\sigma}. \tag{8.60}$$

Figure 8.18 illustrates this approximation for our running example using the independent approximation to $p(f^* \mid \mathcal{D})$ (8.56). The approximation is faithful and induces a near-optimal decision.

[59] It is possible, but expensive, to compute better approximations by "correcting" this truncated normal to account for correlations between ϕ and the rest of f, which must satisfy the constraint globally:

J. CARTINHOUR (1989). One-Dimensional Marginal Density Functions of a Truncated Multivariate Normal Density Function. *Communications in Statistics – Theory and Methods* 19(1):197–203.

[60] This is a consequence of the fact that "information never hurts." We are conditioning ϕ to be less than f_i^*, but every other function value is similarly bounded – a fact we ignore.

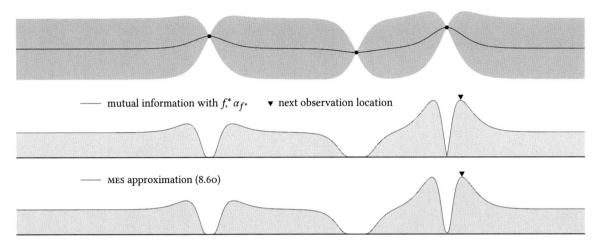

Figure 8.18: An approximation to the mutual information between the observed value y and the value of the global optimum $\alpha_{f^*} = I(y; f^* \mid x, \mathcal{D})$ for our running example using the independent approximation to $p(f^* \mid \mathcal{D})$ (8.56) and numerical integration.

Approximating predictive entropy with noisy observations

direct computation of predictive entropy

In the case of additive Gaussian noise, however, the predictive distribution of y (8.57) is better approximated as the convolution of a centered normal distribution and a truncated normal distribution; see Figure 8.19 for an illustration of a particularly noisy scenario. TURBAN provides a closed form for the resulting probability density function:[61,62]

61 S. TURBAN (2010). *Convolution of a Truncated Normal and a Centered Normal Variable.* Technical report. Columbia University.

62 Thus equality is only approximate due to the approximation in (8.58); the convolution of the truncated normal and normal distribution is exact.

$$p(y \mid x, f^*, \mathcal{D}) \approx \gamma \Phi\!\left(\frac{\alpha(y) - y + f^*}{\beta}\right) \exp\!\left(-\frac{(y-\mu)^2}{2s^2}\right),$$

where

$$\alpha(y) = \frac{\sigma_n^2(y-\mu)}{s^2}; \qquad \beta = \frac{\sigma_n \sigma}{s}; \qquad \gamma = \frac{1}{\sqrt{2\pi}s\,\Phi(z)},$$

and z is defined in (8.59). Unfortunately this distribution does not admit a closed-form expression for its entropy, although we can approximate the entropy effectively via numerical quadrature.

analytic approximation to predictive entropy

Alternatively, we can appeal to analytic approximation to estimate the predictive entropy, and both WANG and JEGELKA and HOFFMAN and GHAHRAMANI take this approach.[63] The MES approximation simply *ignores* the observation noise in the acquisition function (8.60) and instead computes the mutual information between the latent function value ϕ and f^*. This approach overestimates the true mutual information by assuming exact observations, but serves as a reasonable approximation when the signal-to-noise ratio is high. This approximation is illustrated in Figure 8.20 for a scenario with relatively high noise; although the approximation is not perfect, the chosen point is close to optimal.

63 However, the closed form for the predictive distribution above was not discussed by either and perhaps deserves further consideration.

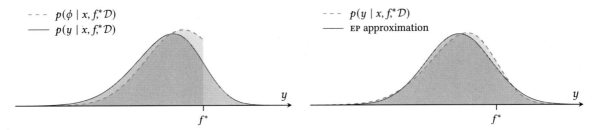

Figure 8.19: Left: an example of the latent predictive distribution $p(\phi \mid x, f^*\mathcal{D})$, which takes the form of a truncated normal distribution (8.58), and the resulting predictive distribution $p(y \mid x, f^*\mathcal{D})$, which is a convolution with a centered normal distribution accounting for Gaussian observation noise. Right: a Gaussian expectation propagation approximation to the predictive distribution (8.62).

HOFFMAN and GHAHRAMANI instead approximate the latent predictive distribution (8.58) using Gaussian expectation propagation:

truncating a variable with EP: § B.2, p. 305

$$p(\phi \mid x, f^*\mathcal{D}) \approx \mathcal{N}(\phi; \mu_*, \sigma_*^2),$$

where

$$\sigma_*^2 = \sigma^2 \left[1 - z\frac{\phi(z)}{\Phi(z)} - \frac{\phi(z)^2}{\Phi(z)^2} \right] \tag{8.61}$$

is the variance of the truncated normal latent predictive distribution (8.58) and z is defined in (8.59). We may now approximate the differential entropy of y with

$$\begin{aligned} \mathrm{var}[y \mid x, f^*\mathcal{D}] &\approx \sigma_*^2 + \sigma_n^2 = s_*^2; \\ H[y \mid x, f^*\mathcal{D}] &\approx \tfrac{1}{2}\log(2\pi e s_*^2). \end{aligned} \tag{8.62}$$

This is similar to the strategy used in predictive entropy search, although computing the approximate latent posterior is considerably easier in this case, only requiring the single factor $[\phi < f^*]$. Figure 8.19 shows the resulting Gaussian approximation to the predictive distribution for an example point; the approximation is excellent. Estimating the expectation over f^* with (8.55) and simplifying, the final OPES approximation to (8.53) is

$$\alpha_{\mathrm{OPES}}(x; \mathcal{D}) = \log s - \frac{1}{n}\sum_{i=1}^{n} \log s_{*_i}, \tag{8.63}$$

where s_{*_i} is the approximate predictive standard deviation corresponding to the sample f_i^*. This takes the same form as the predictive entropy search approximation to the mutual information with x^* (8.41), although the approximations to the predictive distribution are of course different. The OPES approximation (8.63) is shown for a high-noise scenario in Figure 8.20; the approximation is almost perfect and in this case yields the optimal decision.

Both the MES and OPES approximations to the mutual information can be differentiated with respect to the proposed observation location.

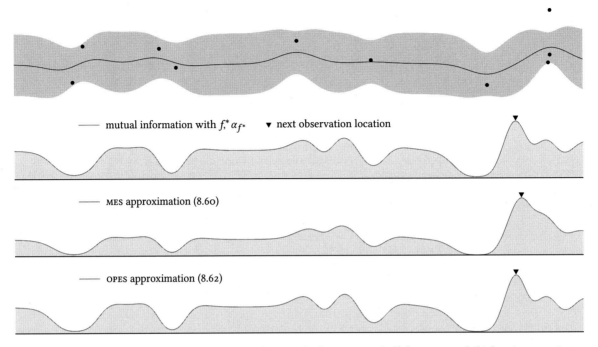

Figure 8.20: The MES and OPES approximations to the mutual information with f^* for an example high-noise scenario with unit signal-to-noise ratio. Both use the independent representer point approximation to $p(f^* \mid \mathcal{D})$ (8.56).

For the former, we simply differentiate (8.60):

$$\frac{\partial \alpha_{\text{MES}}}{\partial x} = \frac{1}{2n\sigma} \sum_{i=1}^{n} \frac{\phi(z_i)}{\Phi(z_i)} \left[\frac{\partial \mu}{\partial x} + z_i \frac{\partial \sigma}{\partial x} \right] \left[1 + z_i \frac{\phi(z_i)}{\Phi(z_i)} + z_i^2 \right];$$

note the $\{f_i^*\}$ samples will in general not depend on x, so we do not need to worry about any dependence of their distribution on the observation location. The details for the OPES approximation are provided in the appendix.

gradient of OPES acquisition function: § C.3, p. 311

8.10 AVERAGING OVER A SPACE OF GAUSSIAN PROCESSES

Throughout this chapter we have assumed our belief regarding the objective function is given by a single Gaussian process. However, especially when our dataset is relatively small, we may seek robustness to model misspecification by averaging over multiple plausible models. Here we will provide some guidance for policy computation when performing Bayesian model averaging over a space of Gaussian processes. Although this may seem straightforward, there is some nuance involved.

model averaging: § 4.4, p. 74

Below we will consider a space of Gaussian processes indexed by a vector of hyperparameters θ, which determines both the moments of the objective function prior and any relevant parameters of the observation noise process. Bayesian model averaging over this space yields marginal posterior and predictive distributions:

$$p(f \mid \mathcal{D}) = \int p(f \mid \mathcal{D}, \boldsymbol{\theta}) \, p(\boldsymbol{\theta} \mid \mathcal{D}) \, \mathrm{d}\boldsymbol{\theta}; \qquad (8.64)$$

$$p(y \mid x, \mathcal{D}) = \int p(y \mid x, \mathcal{D}, \boldsymbol{\theta}) \, p(\boldsymbol{\theta} \mid \mathcal{D}) \, \mathrm{d}\boldsymbol{\theta}, \qquad (8.65)$$

which are integrated against the model posterior $p(\boldsymbol{\theta} \mid \mathcal{D})$ (4.7). Both of these distributions are in general intractable, but we developed several viable approximations in Chapter 3, all of which approximate the objective function posterior (8.64) with a mixture of Gaussian processes and the posterior predictive distribution (8.65) with a mixture of Gaussians.

model posterior, $p(\boldsymbol{\theta} \mid \mathcal{D})$

Noiseless expected improvement and probability of improvement

When observations are exact, the marginal gain in utility underlying both expected improvement and probability of improvement depends *only* on the objective function value ϕ and the value of the incumbent ϕ^*:

$$\Delta_{\mathrm{EI}}(x, \phi) = \max(\phi - \phi^*, 0); \qquad \Delta_{\mathrm{PI}}(x, \phi) = [\phi > \phi^*].$$

As a result, the formulas we derived for these acquisition functions given a GP belief on the objective (8.9, 8.21) depend only on the moments of the (Gaussian) predictive distribution $p(\phi \mid x, \mathcal{D})$.[64] With a Gaussian *mixture* approximation to the predictive distribution, the expected marginal gain,

64 In fact, a Gaussian process belief is not required at all, only Gaussian predictive distributions. This will be important in the next section.

$$\alpha(x; \mathcal{D}) = \int \Delta(x, \phi) \, p(\phi \mid x, \mathcal{D}) \, \mathrm{d}\phi,$$

is simply a weighted combination of these results by linearity of expectation.

Model-dependent utility functions

For the remaining decision-theoretic acquisition functions, noisy expected improvement and probability of improvement, knowledge gradient, and mutual information with any relevant random variable ω, the situation is somewhat more complicated, because the underlying utility functions *depend on the model of the objective function.* The first three depend on the posterior mean function, and the last depends on the posterior belief $p(\omega \mid \mathcal{D})$, both of which are induced by our belief regarding the objective function. To make this dependence explicit, for a model $\boldsymbol{\theta}$ in our space of interest, let us respectively notate the utility, marginal gain in utility, and expected marginal gain in utility with:

dependence on objective function model

$$u(\mathcal{D}; \boldsymbol{\theta}); \qquad \Delta(x, y; \boldsymbol{\theta}); \qquad \alpha(x; \mathcal{D}, \boldsymbol{\theta}).$$

There are two natural ways we might address this dependence when averaging over models. One is to seek to maximize the *expected* utility

average model-conditional utility, $\mathbb{E}u$

of the data, averaged over the choice of model:

$$\mathbb{E}u(\mathcal{D}) = \int u(\mathcal{D};\boldsymbol{\theta})\, p(\boldsymbol{\theta} \mid \mathcal{D})\, \mathrm{d}\boldsymbol{\theta}. \tag{8.66}$$

marginal gain in $\mathbb{E}u$, $\mathbb{E}\Delta$
expected marginal gain in $\mathbb{E}u$, $\mathbb{E}\alpha$

Writing the marginal gain in expected utility as $\mathbb{E}\Delta$, we may derive an acquisition function via one-step lookahead:

$$\begin{aligned}
\mathbb{E}\alpha(x;\mathcal{D}) &= \int \mathbb{E}\Delta(x,y)\, p(y \mid x, \mathcal{D})\, \mathrm{d}y \\
&= \int \left[\int \Delta(x,y;\boldsymbol{\theta})\, p(y \mid x, \mathcal{D}, \boldsymbol{\theta})\, \mathrm{d}y \right] p(\boldsymbol{\theta} \mid \mathcal{D})\, \mathrm{d}\boldsymbol{\theta} \\
&= \int \alpha(x;\mathcal{D},\boldsymbol{\theta})\, p(\boldsymbol{\theta} \mid \mathcal{D})\, \mathrm{d}\boldsymbol{\theta}. \tag{8.67}
\end{aligned}$$

As hinted by its notation, this is simply the expectation of the conditional acquisition functions, which we can approximate via standard methods.

Although this approach is certainly convenient, it may overestimate optimization progress as utility *is only measured under the assumption of a perfectly identified model* – the utility function is "blind" to model uncertainty. An arguably more appealing alternative is to evaluate utility with respect to the marginal objective function model (8.64) from the start, defining simple and global reward with respect to the marginal posterior mean:

marginal posterior mean

$$\int \mu_{\mathcal{D}}(x;\boldsymbol{\theta})\, p(\boldsymbol{\theta} \mid \mathcal{D})\, \mathrm{d}\boldsymbol{\theta}, \tag{8.68}$$

marginal belief about ω

and information gain about ω with respect to its marginal belief:

$$\int p(\omega \mid \mathcal{D}, \boldsymbol{\theta})\, p(\boldsymbol{\theta} \mid \mathcal{D})\, \mathrm{d}\boldsymbol{\theta}. \tag{8.69}$$

utility of marginal model, $u\mathbb{E}$
(expected) marginal gain in utility of marginal model: $\Delta\mathbb{E}$, $\alpha\mathbb{E}$

Let us notate a utility function defined in this manner with $u\mathbb{E}(\mathcal{D})$, contrasting with its post hoc averaging equivalent, $\mathbb{E}u(\mathcal{D})$ (8.66). Similarly, let us notate its marginal gain with $\Delta\mathbb{E}$ and its expected marginal gain with:

$$\alpha\mathbb{E}(x;\mathcal{D}) = \int \Delta\mathbb{E}(x,y)\, p(y \mid x, \mathcal{D})\, \mathrm{d}y. \tag{8.70}$$

Example and discussion

We may shed some light on the differences between these approaches with a barebones example. Let us work with the knowledge gradient, and consider a pair of simple models for an objective function on the interval $\mathcal{X} = [-1, 1]$: either $f = x$ or $f = -x$, with equal probability.[65]

The model-conditional global reward in either case is 1, and thus the expected utility (8.66) *does not depend on the data*: $\mathbb{E}u(\mathcal{D}) \equiv 1$. What a strange set of affairs – although we know the maximal *value* of the objective a priori, we need data to tell us where it is! For this particular model space, an optimal recommendation for either model is maximally *suboptimal* if that model is incorrect.

65 These models may be interpreted as degenerate Gaussian processes with covariance $K \equiv 0$.

In contrast, the global reward of the marginal model *does* depend on the data via the model posterior. The global reward is monotonic in the probability of the model most favored by the data, π:

$$u\mathbb{E}(\mathcal{D}) = 2\pi - 1.$$

A priori, the utility is $u\mathbb{E}(\varnothing) = 0$ – the marginal mean function is $\mu \equiv 0$, and no compelling recommendation is possible until we determine the correct model.

As the expected utility $\mathbb{E}u$ (8.66) is independent of the data, it does not lead to an especially insightful policy. In contrast, the marginal gain in $u\mathbb{E}$ (8.70) can differentiate potential observation locations via their expected impact on the model posterior. We illustrate this acquisition function in the margin given an empty dataset and assuming moderate additive Gaussian noise. As one might hope, it prefers evaluating on the boundary of the domain, where observations are expected to provide more information regarding the model and thus greater improvement in model-marginal utility.

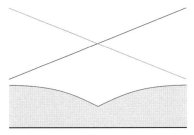

Above: the two possible objectives for our comparison of the $\mathbb{E}u$ and $u\mathbb{E}$. Below: the expected marginal gain in $u\mathbb{E}$, which prefers sampling on the boundary to reveal more information regarding the model. The expected marginal gain in $\mathbb{E}u$ is constant.

Computing expected gain in marginal utility

Unfortunately, the expected gain in utility for the marginal model (8.70) does not simplify as before (8.66), as we must account for the effect of the observed data on the model posterior in the utility function. However, we may sketch a Monte Carlo approximation using samples from the model posterior, $\{\theta_i\} \sim p(\theta \mid \mathcal{D})$.

For utility functions based on the marginal posterior mean (8.68), the resulting approximation to the expected marginal gain (8.70) is a weighted sum of Gaussian expectations of $\Delta\mathbb{E}$, each of which we may approximate via Gauss–Hermite quadrature. To approximate $\Delta\mathbb{E}$ for a putative observation (x, y), a simple sequential Monte Carlo approximation to the updated model posterior would reweight each sample θ_i by $p(y \mid x, \mathcal{D}, \theta_i)$, then approximate the updated marginal posterior mean by a weighted sum.

To approximate the predictive form of mutual information with x^* or f^* (8.36, 8.53):

$$H[y \mid x, \mathcal{D}] - \mathbb{E}_\omega\big[H[y \mid x, \omega, \mathcal{D}] \mid x, \mathcal{D}\big],$$

we first note that the first term is the entropy of a Gaussian mixture, which we can approximate via quadrature. We may approximate the expectation in the second term via Thompson sampling (see below); for each of these samples, we may approximate the updated predictive distribution as before, reweighting the mixture by $p(\omega \mid \mathcal{D}, \theta)$.[66]

Gauss–Hermite quadrature: § 8.5, p. 171

66 This requires one final layer of approximation, which is produced as a byproduct of expectation propagation in the case of x^* (B.6), and may be dealt with without much trouble in the case of the univariate random variable f^*.

Upper confidence bound and Thompson sampling

We may compute any desired upper confidence bound of a Gaussian process mixture at x by bisecting the cumulative distribution function of ϕ, which is a weighted sum of Gaussian CDFs.

Thompson sampling for GPs: § 8.7, p. 176

Finally, to perform Thompson sampling from the marginal posterior, we first sample from the model posterior, $\theta \sim p(\theta \mid \mathcal{D})$; the conditional posterior $p(f \mid \mathcal{D}, \theta)$ is then a GP, and we may proceed via the previous discussion.

8.11 ALTERNATIVE MODELS: BAYESIAN NEURAL NETWORKS, ETC.

Although Gaussian processes are without question the most prominent objective function model used in Bayesian optimization, we are of course free to use any other model when prudent. Below we briefly outline some notable alternative model classes that have received some attention in the context of Bayesian optimization and comment on any issues arising in computing common policies with these surrogates.

Random forests

67   L. BREIMAN (2001). Random Forests. *Machine Learning* 45(1):5–32.

Random forests[67] are a popular model class renown for their excellent off-the-shelf performance,[68] offering good generalization, strong resistance to overfitting, and efficient training and prediction. Of particular relevance for optimization, random forests are adept at handling high-dimensional data and categorical and conditional features, and may be a better choice than Gaussian processes for objectives featuring any of these characteristics.

68   M. FERNÁNDEZ-DELGADO et al. (2014). Do We Need Hundreds of Classifiers to Solve Real World Classification Problems? *Journal of Machine Learning Research* 15(90):3133–3181.

Algorithm configuration is one setting where these capabilities are critical: complex algorithms such as compilers or SAT solvers often have complex configuration schemata with many mutually dependent parameters, and it can be difficult to build nontrivial covariance functions for such inputs. Random forests require no special treatment in this setting and have delivered impressive performance in predicting algorithmic performance measures such as runtime.[69] They are thus a natural choice for Bayesian optimization of these same measures.[70]

69   F. HUTTER et al. (2014). Algorithm Runtime Prediction: Methods & Evaluation. *Artificial Intelligence* 206:79–111.

70   F. HUTTER et al. (2011). Sequential Model-Based Optimization for General Algorithm Configuration. *LION 5*.

Classical random forests are not particularly adept at quantifying uncertainty in predictions off-the-shelf. Seeking more nuanced uncertainty quantification, HUTTER et al. proposed a modification of the vanilla model wherein leaves store both the mean (as usual) and the standard deviation of the training data terminating there.[69] We then estimate the predictive distribution with a mixture of Gaussians with moments corresponding to the predictions of the member trees.[71,72] Figure 8.21 compares the predictions of a Gaussian process and a random forest model on a toy dataset. Although they differ in their extrapolatory behavior, the models make very similar predictions otherwise.

71   HUTTER et al. then fit a single Gaussian distribution to this mixture via moment matching, although this is not strictly necessary.

72   A similar approach can also be used to estimate arbitrary predictive quantiles:

N. MEINSHAUSEN (2006). Quantile Regression Forests. *Journal of Machine Learning Research* 7(35):983–999.

To realize an optimization policy with a random forest, HUTTER et al. suggested approximating acquisition functions depending only on marginal predictions – such as (noiseless) expected improvement or probability of improvement – by simply plugging this Gaussian approximation into the expressions derived in this chapter (8.9, 8.22). Either can be computed easily from a Gaussian mixture predictive distribution as well due to linearity of expectation.

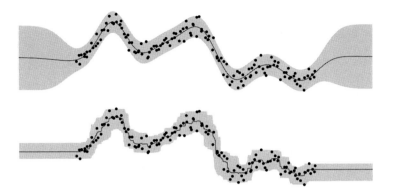

Figure 8.21: The predictions of a Gaussian process model (above) and a random forest model comprising 100 regression trees (below) for an example dataset; the credible intervals of the latter are not symmetric as the predictive distribution is estimated with a Gaussian mixture.

Density ratio estimation

BERGSTRA et al. described a lightweight Bayesian optimization algorithm that operates by maximizing probability of improvement (7.3) via a reduction to density ratio estimation.[73,74]

We begin each iteration of this algorithm by choosing some reference value y^* that we wish to exceed with our next observation; we will then select the next observation location to maximize the probability of improvement over this threshold:[75]

$$\alpha_{\text{PI}}(x; \mathcal{D}, y^*) = \Pr(y > y^* \mid x, \mathcal{D}). \qquad (8.71)$$

We will discuss the selection of the improvement target y^* shortly.

We now consider two conditional probability density functions depending on this threshold:

$$\begin{aligned} g(x) &= p(x \mid y > y^*, \mathcal{D}); \\ \ell(x) &= p(x \mid y \le y^*, \mathcal{D}); \end{aligned} \qquad (8.72)$$

that is, g is the probability density of observation locations exceeding the threshold, and ℓ of locations failing to. Note that both densities are proportional to quantities related to the probability of improvement:

$$\begin{aligned} g(x) &\propto \Pr(y > y^* \mid x, \mathcal{D})\, p(x) = \quad \alpha_{\text{PI}}\ p(x); \\ \ell(x) &\propto \Pr(y \le y^* \mid x, \mathcal{D})\, p(x) = (1 - \alpha_{\text{PI}})\, p(x), \end{aligned} \qquad (8.73)$$

where $p(x)$ is an arbitrary prior density that we will dispose of shortly.

BERGSTRA et al. now define an acquisition function as the ratio of these densities:

$$\alpha(x; \mathcal{D}) = \frac{g(x)}{\ell(x)} \propto \frac{\alpha_{\text{PI}}}{1 - \alpha_{\text{PI}}}, \qquad (8.74)$$

where the prior density $p(x)$ appearing in (8.73) cancels.[76] As this ratio is monotonically increasing with the probability of improvement (8.71), maximizing the density ratio yields the same policy.

To proceed, we require some mechanism for estimating this density ratio (8.74). BERGSTRA et al. appealed to density estimation, constructing

73 J. BERGSTRA et al. (2011). Algorithms for Hyper-Parameter Optimization. *NeurIPS 2011.*

74 Although the source material claims that *expected* improvement is maximized, this was the result of a minor mathematical error.

75 Although we have spent considerable effort arguing *against* maximizing "improvement" over a noisy observation – at least in the presence of high noise – we will see that this choice provides considerable computational benefit.

76 There is, however, a tacit assumption that the prior density has support over the whole domain to enable this cancellation.

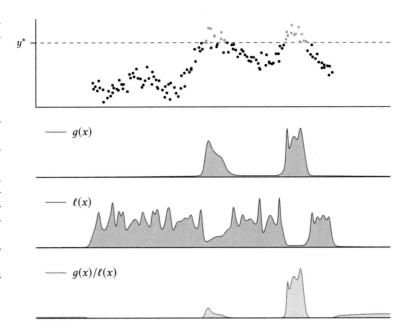

Figure 8.22: BERGSTRA et al.'s Parzen estimation optimization policy. The top panel shows an example dataset along with a threshold y^* set to be the 85th percentile of the observed values. The next two panels illustrate the central kernel density estimates (8.72) for the density of observation locations above and below this threshold. The "wiggliness" of these estimates stems from the kernel bandwidth scheme proposed by BERGSTRA et al. The bottom panel shows the ratio of these densities, which is monotonic in the probability of improvement over y^* (8.74).

77 B. W. SILVERMAN (1986). *Density Estimation for Statistics and Data Analysis.* Chapman & Hall.

78 The details of BERGSTRA et al.'s scheme are somewhat complicated due to the particular optimization problems they were considering. Their focus was on hyperparameter tuning, where conditional dependence among variables can lead to complex structure in the domain. To address this dependence, BERGSTRA et al. considered domains with *tree* structure, where each node represents a variable that can be assigned provided the assignments of its parents. They then built separate conditional density estimates for each variable appearing in the tree.

79 L. C. TIAO et al. (2021). BORE: Bayesian Optimization by Density-Ratio Estimation. *ICML 2021.*

role of improvement threshold in probability of improvement: § 7.5, p. 133

kernel (Parzen) density estimates[77] of g and ℓ and directly maximizing their ratio (8.74) to realize a policy.[78] One advantage of this scheme is that the cost of computing the policy only scales linearly with respect to the number of observations. Figure 8.22 illustrates the key components of this algorithm for a toy problem in one dimension.

An alternative to density estimation is to approximate the density ratio in (8.74) directly, an option promoted by TIAO et al.[79] Here we effectively reduce the problem to binary classification, building a probabilistic classifier to predict the binary label $[y > y^*]$, then interpreting the predictions of this classifier in terms of the probability of improvement. Any probabilistic classifier could be used to this end, so the scheme offers a great deal of latitude in modeling beyond Gaussian processes or related models; in fact we do not need to model the objective function at all!

For either of these approaches to be feasible, we must have enough observations to either accurately estimate the required densities (8.72) or to accurately train a classifier predicting $[y > y^*]$. BERGSTRA et al. addressed this issue by taking y^* to be a relatively (but not exceedingly) high quantile of the observed data, using the 85th percentile in their experiments. TIAO et al. provided some discussion on the role of y^* in balancing exploration and exploitation, but ultimately used the 66th percentile of the observed data in their experiments for simplicity.

Bayesian neural networks

Neural networks represent the state-of-the-art in numerous learning tasks due to their flexibility in modeling and impressive predictive performance. For this reason, it is tempting to use (Bayesian) neural networks for modeling in Bayesian optimization. However, there are two obstacles that must be addressed in order to build a successful system. First, the typically considerable cost of obtaining new data in Bayesian optimization limits the amount of data that might be used to train a neural network, imposing a ceiling on model complexity and perhaps ruling out deep architectures. Second, in order to guide an optimization policy, a neural network must yield useful estimates of uncertainty.

SNOEK et al. took an early step in this direction and reported success with a relatively simple construction.[80] The authors first trained a typical (non-Bayesian) neural network using empirical loss minimization, then replaced the final layer with Bayesian linear regression. The weights in all but the final layer were fixed for the remainder of the procedure; the resulting model can thus be interpreted as Bayesian linear regression using neural basis functions. As this is in fact a Gaussian process,[81] we may appeal to the computational details outlined earlier in this chapter to compute any policy we desire.

A somewhat more involved (and, arguably, "more Bayesian") approach was proposed by SPRINGENBERG et al.,[82] who combined a parametric objective function model $f(x; \mathbf{w})$ – the output of a neural network with input x and weights $\mathbf{w}$ – with an additive Gaussian noise observation model:

$$p(y \mid x, \mathbf{w}, \sigma) = \mathcal{N}(y; f(x; \mathbf{w}), \sigma^2).$$

Bayesian inference proceeds by selecting a prior $p(\mathbf{w}, \sigma)$ and computing the posterior from the observed data. The posterior is intractable, but SPRINGENBERG et al. described a Hamiltonian Monte Carlo scheme for drawing samples $\{\mathbf{w}_i, \sigma_i\}_{i=1}^{s}$ from the posterior, from which we may form a Gaussian mixture approximation to the predictive distribution.[83] This is sufficient to compute policies such as (noiseless) expected improvement and probability of improvement (8.9, 8.22).

Several other neural and/or deep models have also been explored in the context of Bayesian optimization, including deep Gaussian processes[84] and (probabilistic) transformers.[85]

The impressive performance of modern deep neural networks is largely due to their ability to learn sophisticated feature representations of complex data, a process that requires enormous amounts of data and may be out of reach in most Bayesian optimization settings. However, when the domain consists of structured objects with sufficiently many *unlabeled* examples available, one path forward is to train a generative latent variable model – such as a variational autoencoder or generalized adversarial network – using unsupervised (or semi-supervised) methods. We can then perform optimization in the resulting latent space, for example by simply constructing a Gaussian process over the learned neural representation.[86] This approach has notably proven useful in the design of molecules[87] and biological sequences.[88] In both of these settings, enormous databases (on the order of hundreds of millions of examples) are available for learning a representation prior to optimization.[89,90]

80 J. SNOEK et al. (2015). Scalable Bayesian Optimization Using Deep Neural Networks. *ICML 2015*.

81 See the result in (3.6), setting $K \equiv 0$ as there is no nonlinear component in the model. One beneficial side effect of this model is that the cost of inference for Bayesian linear regression is only linear with the number of observations.

82 J. T. SPRINGENBERG et al. (2016). Bayesian Optimization with Robust Bayesian Neural Networks. *NeurIPS 2016*.

83 Namely, we approximate with:

$$p(y \mid x, \mathcal{D}) \approx \frac{1}{s} \sum_{i=1}^{s} \mathcal{N}(y; f(x; \mathbf{w}_i), \sigma_i^2).$$

Following HUTTER et al.'s approach to optimization with random forests, SPRINGENBERG et al. fit a single Gaussian distribution to this mixture via moment matching, but this is optional.

84 Z. DAI et al. (2016). Variational Auto-encoded Deep Gaussian Processes. *ICLR 2016*. arXiv: 1511.06455 [cs.LG].

85 A. MARAVAL et al. (2022). Sample-Efficient Optimisation with Probabilistic Transformer Surrogates. arXiv: 2205.13902 [cs.LG].

86 This construction represents a realization of a manifold Gaussian process/deep kernel; see § 3.4, p. 59.

87 R. GÓMEZ-BOMBARELLI et al. (2018). Automatic Chemical Design Using a Data-Driven Continuous Representation of Molecules. *ACS Central Science* 4(2):268–276.

88 Numerous example systems are outlined in:

B. L. HIE and K. K. YANG (2021). Adaptive Machine Learning for Protein Engineering. arXiv: 2106.05466 [q-bio.QM]. [table 1]

89 J. J. IRWIN et al. (2020). ZINC20 – A Free Ultralarge-Scale Chemical Database for Ligand Discovery. *Journal of Chemical Information and Modeling* 60(12):6065–6073.

90 THE UNIPROT CONSORTIUM (2021). UniProt: The Universal Protein Knowledgebase in 2021. *Nucleic Acids Research* 49(D1):D480–D489.

91 D. ZHOU et al. (2020). Neural Contextual Bandits with UCB-Based Exploration. *ICML 2020*.

92 W. ZHANG et al. (2021). Neural Thompson Sampling. *ICLR 2021*. arXiv: 2010.00827 [cs.LG].

93 C. RIQUELME et al. (2018). Deep Bayesian Bandits Showdown. *ICLR 2018*. arXiv: 1802.09127 [cs.LG].

Finally, neural networks have also received some attention in the bandit literature as models for contextual bandits, which has led to theoretical regret bounds.[91,92] RIQUELME et al. conducted an empirical "showdown" of various neural models in this setting.[93] Although there was no clear "winner," the authors concluded that "decoupled" models – where uncertainty quantification is handled post hoc by feeding the output layer of a neural network into a simple model such as Bayesian linear regression – tended to perform better than end-to-end training.

8.12 SUMMARY OF MAJOR IDEAS

In this chapter we considered the computation of the popular optimization policies described in the last chapter for Gaussian process models of an objective function with an exact or additive Gaussian noise observation model. The acquisition functions for most of these policies represent the one-step expected marginal gain to some underlying utility function:

$$\alpha(x; \mathcal{D}) = \int \Delta(x, y) \, \mathcal{N}(y; \mu, s^2) \, dy,$$

where $\Delta(x, y)$ is the gain in utility resulting from the observation (x, y) (8.27). When Δ is a piecewise linear function of y, this integral can be resolved analytically in terms of the standard normal CDF. This is the case for the expected improvement and probability of improvement acquisition functions, both with and without observation noise.

However, when Δ is a more complicated function of the putative observation, we must in general rely on approximate computation to resolve this integral. When the predictive distribution is normal – as in the model class considered in this chapter – *Gauss–Hermite quadrature* provides a useful and sample-efficient approximation via a weighted average of carefully chosen integration nodes. This allows us to address some more complex acquisition functions such as the knowledge gradient.

The computation of mutual information with x^* or f^* entails an expectation with respect to these random variables, which cannot be approximated using simple quadrature schemes. Instead, we must rely on schemes such as Thompson sampling – a notable policy in its own right – to generate samples and proceed via (simple or quasi-) Monte Carlo integration, and in some cases, further approximations to the conditional predictive distributions resulting from these samples.

Finally, Bayesian optimization is of course not limited to a single Gaussian process belief on the objective function, which may be objectionable even when Gaussian processes are the preferred model class due to uncertainty in hyperparameters or model structure. Averaging over a space of Gaussian processes is possible – with some care – by adopting a Gaussian process mixture approximation to the marginal objective function posterior and relying on results from the single GP case. If desired, we may also abandon the model class entirely and compute policies with respect to an alternative such as random forests or Bayesian neural networks.

IMPLEMENTATION

There is a rich and mature software ecosystem available for Gaussian process modeling and Bayesian optimization, and it is relatively easy to build sophisticated optimization routines using off-the-shelf libraries. However, successful implementation of the underlying algorithms requires attending to some nitty-gritty details to ensure optimal performance, and what may appear to be simple equations on the page can be challenging to realize in a limited-precision environment. In this chapter we will provide a brief overview of the computational details that practitioners should be aware of when designing Bayesian optimization algorithms, even when availing themselves of existing software libraries.

9.1 GAUSSIAN PROCESS INFERENCE, SCALING, AND APPROXIMATION

As is typical with nonparametric models, the computational cost of Gaussian process inference grows (considerably!) with the number of observations, and it is important to understand the nature of this growth and be aware of methods for scaling to large-scale data when necessary.

The primary computational bottleneck in Gaussian process inference is solving systems of linear equations that scale with the number of observed values. Consider the general case of exact inference where we condition a Gaussian process $\mathcal{GP}(f; \mu, K)$ on the observation of a length-n vector of values $\mathbf{y}$ with marginal distribution and cross-covariance function (2.6):

solving linear systems with respect to the observation covariance $\mathbf{C}$

number of observed values, $n = |\mathbf{y}|$

$$p(\mathbf{y}) = \mathcal{N}(\mathbf{y}; \mathbf{m}, \mathbf{C}); \qquad \kappa(x) = \text{cov}[\mathbf{y}, \phi \mid x]. \qquad (9.1)$$

The posterior is a Gaussian process with moments (2.10):

$$\mu_{\mathcal{D}}(x) = \mu(x) + \kappa(x)^\top \mathbf{C}^{-1}(\mathbf{y} - \mathbf{m});$$
$$K_{\mathcal{D}}(x, x') = K(x, x') - \kappa(x)^\top \mathbf{C}^{-1} \kappa(x'). \qquad (9.2)$$

Evaluating either the posterior mean or the posterior covariance requires solving a linear system with respect to the observation covariance $\mathbf{C}$. Inference with non-Gaussian observations using Monte Carlo sampling or Gaussian approximate inference also entails solving linear systems with respect to this matrix (2.35, 2.39–2.41).

Direct computation via Cholesky decomposition

NEAL outlined a straightforward implementation based on direct numerical methods that suffices for the small-to-moderate datasets typical in Bayesian optimization.[1] We take advantage of the fact that $\mathbf{C}$ is symmetric and positive definite and precompute and store its Cholesky factorization:[2]

$$\mathbf{L} = \text{chol}\, \mathbf{C}; \qquad \mathbf{L}\mathbf{L}^\top = \mathbf{C}.$$

This computation requires one-time $\mathcal{O}(n^3)$ work and represents the bulk of effort spent in this implementation. Note that despite having the same

1 R. M. NEAL (1998). Regression and Classification Using Gaussian Process Priors. In: *Bayesian Statistics 6.*

2 G. H. GOLUB and C. F. VAN LOAN (2013). *Matrix Computations.* Johns Hopkins University Press. [§ 4.2]

asymptotic running time as the general-purpose LU decomposition, the Cholesky factorization exploits symmetry to run twice as fast.

With the Cholesky factor in hand, we may solve an arbitrary linear system $\mathbf{Cx} = \mathbf{b}$ in time $\mathcal{O}(n^2)$ via forward–backward substitution by rewriting as $\mathbf{LL}^\top \mathbf{x} = \mathbf{b}$ and twice applying a triangular solver. We exploit this fact to additionally precompute the vector

$$\boldsymbol{\alpha} = \mathbf{C}^{-1}(\mathbf{y} - \mathbf{m})$$

appearing in the posterior mean. After this initial precomputation of $\mathbf{L}$ and $\boldsymbol{\alpha}$, we may compute the posterior mean

$$\mu_{\mathcal{D}}(x) = \mu(x) + \kappa(x)^\top \boldsymbol{\alpha}$$

on demand in linear time and the posterior covariance

$$K_{\mathcal{D}}(x, x') = K(x, x') - \left[\mathbf{L}^{-1}\kappa(x)\right]^\top \left[\mathbf{L}^{-1}\kappa(x')\right]$$

in quadratic time. We may also efficiently compute the log marginal likelihood (4.8) of the data in linear time:[3]

$$\log p(\mathbf{y} \mid \mathbf{x}) = -\tfrac{1}{2}\left[(\mathbf{y} - \mathbf{m})^\top \boldsymbol{\alpha} + 2\sum_i \log L_{ii} + n \log 2\pi\right].$$

3 The $2\sum_i \log L_{ii}$ term is the log determinant of C, where we have exploited the Cholesky factorization and the fact that L is triangular.

Low-rank updates to the Cholesky factorization for sequential inference

Optimization is an inherently sequential procedure, where our dataset grows incrementally as we gather new observations. In this setting, we can accelerate sequential inference with a *fixed* Gaussian process[4] by replacing direct computation of the Cholesky decomposition in favor of fast incremental updates to previously computed Cholesky factors.

4 That is, a Gaussian process whose hyperparameters are fixed, rather than dependent on the data.

For the sake of argument, suppose we have computed the Cholesky factor $\mathbf{L} = \text{chol}\,\mathbf{C}$ for a set of n observations $\mathbf{y}$ with covariance $\mathbf{C}$. Suppose we then receive k additional observations $\boldsymbol{v}$, resulting in the augmented observation vector

$$\mathbf{y}' = \begin{bmatrix} \mathbf{y} \\ \boldsymbol{v} \end{bmatrix}.$$

The covariance matrix of $\mathbf{y}'$ is formed by appending the previous covariance $\mathbf{C}$ with new rows/columns:

$$\text{cov}[\mathbf{y}'] = \mathbf{C}' = \begin{bmatrix} \mathbf{C} & \mathbf{X}_1^\top \\ \mathbf{X}_1 & \mathbf{X}_2 \end{bmatrix}.$$

The Cholesky factor of the updated covariance matrix has the form

$$\text{chol}\,\mathbf{C}' = \begin{bmatrix} \mathbf{L} & \mathbf{0} \\ \boldsymbol{\Lambda}_1 & \boldsymbol{\Lambda}_2 \end{bmatrix}.$$

Note that the upper-left block is simply the previously computed Cholesky factor, which we can reuse. The new blocks may be computed as

$$\boldsymbol{\Lambda}_1 = \mathbf{X}_1 \mathbf{L}^{-\top}; \qquad \boldsymbol{\Lambda}_2 = \text{chol}\left[\mathbf{X}_2 - \boldsymbol{\Lambda}_1 \boldsymbol{\Lambda}_1^\top\right].$$

The first of these blocks can be computed efficiently using a triangular solver with the previous Cholesky factor, and the second block only requires factoring a $(k \times k)$ matrix.

This low-rank update requires $\mathcal{O}(kn^2)$ work to compute, compared to the $\mathcal{O}(n^3 + kn^2)$ work required to compute the Cholesky decomposition of $\mathbf{C}'$ from scratch; asymptotically, the low-rank update is $\mathcal{O}(n/k)$ times faster. In particular, if we begin with an empty dataset and sequentially apply this update for a total of n observations (in any order and with any number of observations at a time) the *total* cost of inference would be $\mathcal{O}(n^3)$. This is equivalent to the cost of one-time inference with the full dataset, so the update scheme is as efficient as one could hope for.

amortized analysis

Ill-conditioned covariance matrices

When an optimization policy elects to make an observation in the pursuit of "exploitation," the value observed is (by design!) highly correlated with at least one existing observation. Although these decisions may be well grounded, the resulting highly correlated observations can wreak havoc on numerical linear algebra routines.

To sketch the problems that may arise, consider the following scenario. Suppose the covariance function is stationary, that observations are corrupted by additive Gaussian noise with scale σ_n^2, and that the signal-to-noise ratio is large. Now, if two locations in the dataset correspond to highly correlated values, the corresponding rows/columns in the observation covariance matrix $\mathbf{C}$ will be nearly equal, and $\mathbf{C}$ will thus be nearly singular – one-or-more eigenvalues will be near zero, and in extreme cases, some may even become (numerically) negative. This poor conditioning[5] can cause loss of precision when solving a linear system via the Cholesky decomposition, and a negative eigenvalue will cause the Cholesky routine to fail altogether.

When necessary, we may sidestep these issues with a number of "tricks." One simple solution is to add a small (in terms of σ_n^2) multiple of the identity to the observation covariance, replacing $\mathbf{C}$ by $\mathbf{C} + \varepsilon \mathbf{I}$. Numerically, this shifts the singular values of $\mathbf{C}$ by ε, improving conditioning; practically, this caps the signal-to-noise ratio by increasing the noise floor. When high correlation is a result of small spatial separation, OSBORNE et al. suggested replacing problematic observations of the objective function with (noisy) observations of directional derivatives,[6] which are only weakly correlated with the corresponding function values.[7] Another option is to appeal to iterative numerical methods, discussed below, which actually *benefit* from having numerous eigenvalues clustered around zero.

Iterative numerical methods

Direct methods can handle datasets of perhaps a few tens of thousands of observations before the cubic scaling becomes too much to bear. In most settings where Bayesian optimization would be considered, the

5 Numerical conditioning of $\mathbf{C}$ is usually evaluated by its *condition number*, defined in terms of its singular values $\sigma = \{\sigma_i\}$:

$$\kappa = \frac{\max \sigma}{\min \sigma}.$$

Given infinite precision, the singular values are equal to the (nonnegative) eigenvalues of $\mathbf{C}$, but very poor conditioning can cause negative (numerical) eigenvalues.

6 That is, we replace observations of $f(x)$ and $f(x')$ with one of $f(x)$ and one of the directional derivative in the direction of $x - x'$, evaluated at the midpoint $(x + x')/2$.

7 M. A. OSBORNE et al. (2009). Gaussian Processes for Global Optimization. *LION 3*.

8 M. R. HESTENES and E. STIEFEL (1952). Methods of Conjugate Gradients for Solving Linear Systems. *Journal of Research of the National Bureau of Standards* 49(6):409–436.

9 If $\mathbf{C}\mathbf{x} = \mathbf{b}$, then $|\mathbf{C}\mathbf{x} - \mathbf{b}| = 0$. As this norm is nonnegative and only vanishes at $\mathbf{x}$, squaring gives

$$\mathbf{x} = \arg\min_{\mathbf{y}} \mathbf{y}^\top \mathbf{C}\mathbf{y} - 2\mathbf{b}^\top\mathbf{y}.$$

Thus $\mathbf{x}$ is also the solution of an unconstrained quadratic optimization problem, which is convex as $\mathbf{C}$ is symmetric positive definite.

10 G. H. GOLUB and C. F. VAN LOAN (2013). *Matrix Computations.* Johns Hopkins University Press. [§ 11.5]

11 K. CUTAJAR et al. (2016). Preconditioning Kernel Matrices. *ICML 2016.*

12 M. N. GIBBS (1997). Bayesian Gaussian Processes for Regression and Classification. Ph.D. thesis. University of Cambridge.

13 J. R. GARDNER et al. (2018). GPyTorch: Blackbox Matrix–Matrix Gaussian Process Inference with GPU Acceleration. *NeurIPS 2018.*

Gaussian approximate inference: § 2.8, p. 39

cost of observation will preclude obtaining a dataset anywhere near this size, in which case we need not consider the issue further. However, when necessary, we may appeal to more complex approximate inference schemes to scale to larger datasets.

One line of work in this direction is to solve the linear systems arising in the posterior with iterative rather than direct numerical methods. The method of *conjugate gradients* is especially well suited as it is designed for symmetric positive-definite systems such as appear in the GP posterior.[8] The main idea behind the conjugate gradient method is to reinterpret the solution of the linear system $\mathbf{C}\mathbf{x} = \mathbf{b}$ as the solution of a related and particularly well-behaved convex optimization problem.[9] With this insight, we may derive a simple procedure to construct a sequence of vectors $\{\mathbf{x}_i\}$ guaranteed to converge in finite time to the desired solution. For a system of size n, each iteration of this procedure requires only $\mathcal{O}(n^2)$ work; the most expensive operation is a single matrix–vector multiplication with $\mathbf{C}$.

The method of conjugate gradients is guaranteed to converge (up to round-off error) after n iterations, but this does not offer any speedup over direct methods. However, when $\mathbf{C}$ has a well-behaved spectrum – that is, it is well conditioned and/or has clustered eigenvalues – the sequence converges rapidly. In many cases we may terminate after only $k \ll n$ iterations with an accurate estimate of the solution, for an effectively quadratic running time of $\mathcal{O}(kn^2)$. Although many covariance matrices arising in practice are not necessarily well conditioned, we may use a technique known as *preconditioning* to transform a poorly conditioned matrix to speed up convergence, with only minor overhead.[10,11]

The use of conjugate gradients for GP inference can be traced back to the doctoral work of GIBBS.[12] Numerous authors have provided enhancements in the intervening years, and there is a now a substantial body of related work. A good starting point is the work of GARDNER et al., who provide a review of the literature and the key ideas from numerical linear algebra required for large-scale GP inference.[13] The authors refine these tools to exploit modern massively parallel hardware and build an accompanying software package scaling inference to hundreds of thousands of observations.

Sparse approximations

An alternative approach for scaling to large datasets is *sparse approximation.* Here rather than approximating the linear algebra arising in the exact posterior, we approximate the posterior distribution itself with a Gaussian process admitting tractable computation with direct numerical methods. A large family of sparse approximations have been proposed, which differ in their details but share the same general approach.

As we have seen, specifying an *arbitrary* Gaussian distribution for a set of values jointly Gaussian distributed with a function of interest induces a GP posterior consistent with that belief (2.39). This is a powerful tool, used in approximate inference to optimize the fit of the induced

Gaussian process to a true, intractable posterior. Sparse approximation methods make use of this property as well, but to achieve computational rather than mathematical tractability. The idea is to craft a Gaussian belief for a sufficiently small set of values such that the induced posterior is a faithful, but tractable approximation to the true posterior.

For this discussion it is important that we explicitly account for any observation noise that may be present in the values we wish to condition on, as only *independent* noise – that is, with diagonal error covariance – is suitable for sparse approximation. Consider conditioning a Gaussian process on a vector of n values $\mathbf{z}$, for large n. We will assume the observation model $\mathbf{z} = \mathbf{y} + \boldsymbol{\varepsilon}$, where $\mathbf{y}$ is a vector of jointly Gaussian distributed values as in (9.1), and $\boldsymbol{\varepsilon}$ is a vector of independent, zero-mean Gaussian measurement noise with diagonal covariance matrix $\mathbf{N}$.

observed values, $\mathbf{z}$; $|\mathbf{z}| = n$

diagonal noise covariance, $\mathbf{N}$

The first step of sparse approximation is to identify a set of $m \ll n$ values $\boldsymbol{v}$, called *inducing values*, whose distribution can in some sense capture most of the information in the full dataset. We will discuss the selection of inducing values shortly; for the moment we assume an arbitrary set has been chosen. The joint prior distribution of the observed and inducing values is Gaussian:

inducing values, $\boldsymbol{v}$; $|\boldsymbol{v}| = m \ll n$

$$p(\boldsymbol{v}, \mathbf{z}) = \mathcal{N}\left(\begin{bmatrix} \boldsymbol{v} \\ \mathbf{z} \end{bmatrix}; \begin{bmatrix} \boldsymbol{\mu} \\ \mathbf{m} \end{bmatrix}, \begin{bmatrix} \boldsymbol{\Sigma} & \mathbf{K}^{\top} \\ \mathbf{K} & \mathbf{C} + \mathbf{N} \end{bmatrix}\right), \quad (9.3)$$

and we will write the cross-covariance function for $\boldsymbol{v}$ as

$$k(x) = \text{cov}[\boldsymbol{v}, \phi \mid x].$$

Conditioning (9.3) on $\mathbf{z}$ would yield the true Gaussian posterior on the inducing values, but computing this posterior would be intractable. In a sparse approximation, we instead *prescribe* a computationally tractable posterior for $\boldsymbol{v}$ informed by the available observations:

$$p(\boldsymbol{v} \mid \mathbf{z}) \approx q(\boldsymbol{v} \mid \mathbf{z}) = \mathcal{N}(\boldsymbol{v}; \tilde{\boldsymbol{\mu}}, \tilde{\boldsymbol{\Sigma}}).$$

This assumed distribution then induces (hence the moniker inducing values) a Gaussian process posterior on f:

$$p(f \mid \mathbf{z}) \approx \int p(f \mid \boldsymbol{v}) \, q(\boldsymbol{v} \mid \mathbf{z}) \, d\boldsymbol{v} = \mathcal{GP}(f; \mu_{\mathcal{D}}, K_{\mathcal{D}}),$$

which represents the sparse approximation. After transliteration of notation, the posterior moments take the same form as (2.38), and the cost of computation now scales according to the number of inducing values.

To complete this approximation scheme, we must specify a procedure for identifying a set of inducing values $\boldsymbol{v}$ as well as the approximate posterior $q(\boldsymbol{v} \mid \mathbf{z})$, and it is in these details that the various available methods differ. The inducing values are usually taken to be function values at a set of locations $\boldsymbol{\xi}$ called *pseudo-* or *inducing points*, taking $\boldsymbol{v} = f(\boldsymbol{\xi})$.[14] These inducing points are fictitious and do not need to coincide with any actual observations. Once a suitable parameterization

14 This is not strictly necessary. We could consider using other values such as derivatives as inducing values for added flexibility.

pseudopoints, inducing points

Figure 9.1: Sparse approximation. Top: the exact posterior belief (about noisy observations rather than the latent function) for a Gaussian process conditioned on 200 observations. Bottom: a sparse approximation (9.5–9.7) using ten inducing values corresponding to the indicated inducing points, designed to minimize the KL divergence between the induced and true posterior distributions (9.4).

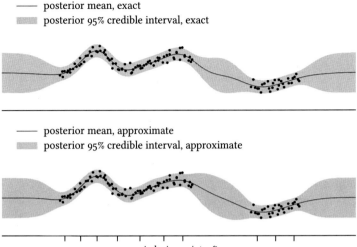

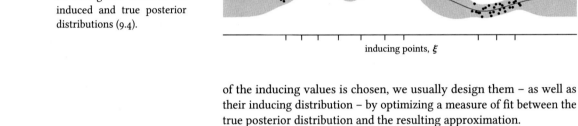

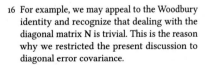

inducing points, ξ

of the inducing values is chosen, we usually design them – as well as their inducing distribution – by optimizing a measure of fit between the true posterior distribution and the resulting approximation.

TITSIAS introduced a variational approach that has gained prominence.[15] The idea is to minimize the Kullback–Leibler divergence between the true and induced posteriors on $\mathbf{y}$ and the inducing values $\boldsymbol{v}$:

$$D_{\text{KL}}\big[q(\mathbf{y},\boldsymbol{v} \mid \mathbf{z}) \parallel p(\mathbf{y},\boldsymbol{v} \mid \mathbf{z})\big], \qquad (9.4)$$

where

$$q(\mathbf{y},\boldsymbol{v} \mid \mathbf{z}) = p(\mathbf{y} \mid \boldsymbol{v})\, q(\boldsymbol{v} \mid \mathbf{z})$$

is the implied joint distribution in the approximate posterior. Once optimal inducing values are determined, the optimal inducing distribution is as well, and examining the resulting approximate posterior gives insight into the typical behavior of sparse approximations. The approximate posterior mean is

$$\mu_{\mathcal{D}}(x) = \mu(x) + \big[\mathbf{K}\Sigma^{-1}k(x)\big]^{\top}(\mathbf{K}\Sigma^{-1}\mathbf{K}^{\top} + \mathbf{N})^{-1}(\mathbf{z} - \mathbf{m}). \qquad (9.5)$$

Although this expression nominally entails solving a linear system of size n, the low-rank-plus-diagonal structure of the matrix $\mathbf{K}\Sigma^{-1}\mathbf{K}^{\top} + \mathbf{N}$ allows the system to be solved in time $\mathcal{O}(nm^2)$, merely linear in the size of the dataset.[16] With this favorable cost, sparse approximation can scale Gaussian process inference to millions of observations without issue.

Comparing this expression (9.5) with the true posterior mean:

$$\mu_{\mathcal{D}}(x) = \mu(x) + \kappa(x)^{\top}(\mathbf{C} + \mathbf{N})^{-1}(\mathbf{z} - \mathbf{m}),$$

we can identify a key approximation to the covariance structure of the GP prior. Namely, we approximate the covariance function with:

$$K(x, x') \approx k(x)^{\top}\Sigma^{-1}k(x') = \text{cov}[x, \boldsymbol{v}]\, \text{cov}[\boldsymbol{v}, \boldsymbol{v}]^{-1}\, \text{cov}[\boldsymbol{v}, x'], \qquad (9.6)$$

15 M. TITSIAS (2009). Variational Learning of Inducing Variables in Sparse Gaussian Processes. *AISTATS 2009.*

16 For example, we may appeal to the Woodbury identity and recognize that dealing with the diagonal matrix $\mathbf{N}$ is trivial. This is the reason why we restricted the present discussion to diagonal error covariance.

—— posterior mean, exact
▨ posterior 95% credible interval, exact

—— posterior mean, approximate
▨ posterior 95% credible interval, approximate

that is, we assume that all covariance between function values is moderated through the inducing values. This is a popular approximation scheme known as the *Nyström method*.[17] Importantly, however, we note that the posterior mean does still reflect the information contained in the entire dataset through the true residuals $(z - m)$ and noise N. The approximate posterior covariance also reflects this approximation:

$$K(x, x') - \left[K\Sigma^{-1}k(x)\right]^\top (K\Sigma^{-1}K^\top + N)^{-1} \left[K\Sigma^{-1}k(x')\right] \quad (9.7)$$
$$\approx K(x, x') - \quad \kappa(x)^\top \quad (C + N)^{-1} \quad \kappa(x').$$

17 C. K. I. WILLIAMS and M. SEEGER (2000). Using the Nyström Method to Speed up Kernel Machines. *NeurIPS 2000.*

Figure 9.1 illustrates a sparse approximation for a toy example following this approach. Here the inducing values were taken to be the function[17] values at ten inducing points, and both the inducing points and their distribution were designed to minimize the KL divergence between the true and induced posterior distributions (9.4). The approximation is faithful: the posterior mean is nearly identical to the true mean and the posterior credible intervals only display some minor differences from the truth. Increasing the number of inducing values would naturally improve the approximation.

Sparse approximation for Gaussian processes has a long history, beginning in earnest with investigation into the Nyström approximation (9.6).[18,19] In addition to the variational approach mentioned above, an approximation known as the *fully independent training conditional* (FITC) approximation has also received significant attention[20] and gives rise to a similar approximate posterior. HENSMAN et al. provided a variational sparse approximation for non-Gaussian observation models, allowing for scaling general GP latent models to large datasets.[21]

19 A. J. SMOLA and B. SCHÖLKOPF (2000). Sparse Greedy Matrix Approximation for Machine Learning. *ICML 2000.*

20 E. SNELSON and Z. GHAHRAMANI (2005). Sparse Gaussian Processes Using Pseudo-inputs. *NeurIPS 2005.*

21 J. HENSMAN et al. (2015). MCMC for Variationally Sparse Gaussian Processes. *NeurIPS 2015.*

9.2 OPTIMIZING ACQUISITION FUNCTIONS

In our discussion on computing optimization policies with Gaussian processes, we considered the *pointwise* evaluation of common acquisition functions and their gradient with respect to the proposed observation location. However, we realize an optimization policy via the global *optimization* of an acquisition function:

Chapter 8: Computing Policies with Gaussian Processes, p. 157

$$x \in \arg\max_{x' \in \mathcal{X}} \alpha(x'; \mathcal{D}). \quad (9.8)$$

Every common Bayesian acquisition function is nonconvex in general, so we must resort to some generic global optimization routine for this inner optimization. Some care is required to guarantee success in this optimization, as the behavior of a typical acquisition function can make it a somewhat unusual objective function. In particular, consider a prototypical Gaussian process model combining:

- a constant mean function (3.1),
- a stationary covariance function decaying to zero as $|x - x'| \to \infty$, and
- independent, homoskedastic observation noise (2.16).

stationarity: § 3.2, p. 50

For such a model, the prior predictive distribution $p(y \mid x)$ is identical regardless of location. However, the *posterior* predictive distribution $p(y \mid x, \mathcal{D})$ also degenerates to the prior for locations sufficiently far from observed locations, due to the decay of the covariance function. In these regions, the gradients of the posterior predictive parameters effectively vanish:

$$\frac{\partial \mu}{\partial x} \approx 0; \qquad \frac{\partial s}{\partial x} \approx 0.$$

curse of dimensionality: § 3.5, p. 61

As a result, the gradient of the acquisition function (8.6) vanishes as well! This vanishing gradient is especially problematic in high-dimensional spaces, where the acquisition function will be flat on an overwhelming fraction of the domain unless the prior encodes absurdly long-scale correlations, a consequence of the unshakable *curse of dimensionality*. Thus, the acquisition function will only exhibit interesting behavior in the neighborhood of previous observations – where the posterior predictive distribution is nontrivial – and it is here we should spend most of our effort during optimization.

Optimization approaches

There are two common lines of attack for optimizing acquisition functions in Bayesian optimization. One approach is to use an off-the-shelf derivative-free global optimization method such as the "dividing rectangles" (DIRECT) algorithm of JONES et al.[22] or a member of the covariance matrix adaptation evolution strategy (CMA–ES) family of algorithms.[23] Although a popular choice in the literature, we argue that neither is a particularly good choice in situations where the acquisition function may devolve into effective flatness as described above. However, an algorithm of this class may be reasonable in modest dimension where optimization can be somewhat exhaustive.

In general, a better alternative is multistart *local* optimization, making use of the gradients computed in the previous chapter for rapid convergence. KIM and CHOI provided an extensive comparison of the theoretical and empirical performance of global and local optimization routines for acquisition function optimization, and ultimately recommended multistart local optimization as best practice.[24] This is also the approach used in (at least some) sophisticated modern software packages for Bayesian optimization.[25]

To ensure success, we must carefully select starting points to ensure that the relevant regions of the domain are searched. JONES (the same JONES of the DIRECT algorithm) recognized the problem of vanishing gradients described above and suggested a simple heuristic for selecting local optimization starting points by enumerating and pruning the midpoints between all pairs of observed points.[26] A more brute-force approach is to measure the acquisition function on an exhaustive covering of the domain – generated for example by a low-discrepancy sequence – then begin local searches from the highest values seen. This can be effective if the initial set of points is dense enough to probe the neigh-

22 D. R. JONES et al. (1993). Lipschitzian Optimization without the Lipschitz Constant. *Journal of Optimization Theory and Application* 79(1): 157–181.

23 N. HANSEN (2016). The CMA Evolution Strategy: A Tutorial. arXiv: 1604.00772 [cs.LG].

24 J. KIM and S. CHOI (2020). On Local Optimizers of Acquisition Functions in Bayesian Optimization. 12458:675–690.

25 M. BALANDAT et al. (2020). BoTorch: A Framework for Efficient Monte-Carlo Bayesian Optimization. *NeurIPS 2020*.

26 D. R. JONES (2001). A Taxonomy of Global Optimization Methods Based on Response Surfaces. *Journal of Global Optimization* 21(4):345–383.

borhoods of previous observations; otherwise, it would be prudent to augment with a locally motivated approach such as JONES's.

Multistart local optimization has the advantage of being embarrassingly parallel. Further, both global and multistart local optimization of the acquisition function can be treated as *anytime* algorithms that constantly improve their proposed observations until we are ready to act.[27]

27 E. BROCHU et al. (2010). A Tutorial on Bayesian Optimization of Expensive Cost Functions, with Application to Active User Modeling and Hierarchical Reinforcement Learning. arXiv: 1012.2599 [cs.LG].

Optimization in latent spaces

A common approach for modeling on high-dimensional domains is to apply some mapping from the domain to some lower-dimensional representation space, then construct a Gaussian process on that space. With such a model, it is tempting to optimize an acquisition function on the latent space rather than on the original domain so as to at least partially sidestep the curse of dimensionality. This can be an effective approach when we can faithfully "decode" from the latent space back into the original domain for evaluation, a process that can require careful thought even when the latent embedding is *linear* (3.30) due to the nonbijective nature of the map.[28]

modeling functions on high-dimensional domains: § 3.5, p. 61

28 Detailed advice for this setting is provided by:

Z. WANG et al. (2016b). Bayesian Optimization in a Billion Dimensions via Random Embeddings. *Journal of Artificial Intelligence Research* 55:361–387.

linear embeddings: § 3.5, p. 62
neural embeddings: § 3.5, p. 61, § 8.11, p. 199

Fortunately, modern neural embedding techniques such as (variational) autoencoders provide a decoding mechanism as a natural side effect of their construction. When we are fortunate enough to have sufficient unlabeled data to learn a useful unsupervised representation prior to optimization, we may simply optimize in the latent space and feed each chosen observation location through the decoder. GÓMEZ-BOMBARELLI et al. for example applied Bayesian optimization to *de novo* molecular design.[29] Their model combined a pretrained variational autoencoder for molecular structures with a Gaussian process on the latent embedding space; the autoencoder was trained on a large precompiled database of known molecules.[30] A welcome side effect of this construction was that, by optimizing the acquisition function over the continuous embedding space, the decoding process had the freedom to generate novel structures not seen in the autoencoder's training data.

de novo molecular design: Appendix D, p. 314

29 R. GÓMEZ-BOMBARELLI et al. (2018). Automatic Chemical Design Using a Data-Driven Continuous Representation of Molecules. *ACS Central Science* 4(2):268–276.

30 J.J. IRWIN et al. (2020). ZINC20 – A Free Ultralarge-Scale Chemical Database for Ligand Discovery. *Journal of Chemical Information and Modeling* 60(12):6065–6073.

We may also pursue this approach even when we begin optimization without any data at all. For example, MORICONI et al. demonstrated success jointly learning a nonlinear low-dimensional representation as well as a corresponding decoding stage throughout optimization on the fly.[31]

31 R. MORICONI et al. (2020). High-Dimensional Bayesian Optimization Using Low-Dimensional Feature Spaces. *Machine Learning* 109(9–10):1925–1943.

Optimization on combinatorial domains

Combinatorial domains present a challenge for Bayesian optimization as the optimization policy (9.8) requires combinatorial optimization of the acquisition function. It is difficult to provide concrete advice for such a situation, as the details of the domain may in some cases suggest a natural path forward. One potential solution is outlined above: when the domain is a space of discrete structured objects such as graphs (say,

gene and protein design: Appendix D, p. 319

32 B. L. HIE and K. K. YANG (2021). Adaptive Machine Learning for Protein Engineering. arXiv: 2106.05466 [q-bio.QM].

33 H. B. MOSS et al. (2020). BOSS: Bayesian Optimization over String Spaces. *NeurIPS 2020*.

34 As evaluated by the covariance function.

35 R. GARNETT et al. (2010). Bayesian Optimization for Sensor Set Selection. *IPSN 2010*.

36 R. BAPTISTA and M. POLOCZEK (2018). Bayesian Optimization of Combinatorial Structures. *ICML 2018*.

37 C. OH et al. (2019). Combinatorial Bayesian Optimization Using the Graph Cartesian Product. *NeurIPS 2019*.

38 J. KIM et al. (2021). Bayesian Optimization with Approximate Set Kernels. *Machine Learning* 110(5):857–879.

molecules), we might find a useful *continuous* embedding of the domain and simply work there instead.[29]

Applications such as gene or protein design entail combinatorial optimization over *strings,* whose nature presents problems both in modeling and optimizing acquisition functions, although optimizing a neural encoding remains a viable option.[32] MOSS et al. described a more direct approach for Bayesian optimization over strings when this is not possible.[33] The objective function was modeled by a Gaussian process with a special-purpose *string kernel,* and the induced acquisition function was then optimized using genetic algorithms, which are well suited for string optimization. The authors also showed how to incorporate a context-free grammar into the optimization policy to impose desired constraints on the structure of the strings investigated.

In the general case, we note that our previous sketch of how a "typical" acquisition function behaves with a "typical" model – with its most interesting behavior near observed data – carries over to combinatorial domains and may lead to useful heuristics. For example, rather than enumerating the domain (presumably impossible) or sampling from the domain (presumably yielding poor coverage), we might instead curate a small list of candidate points offering options for both exploitation and exploration. We could perhaps generate a list of points similar to[34] the thus-far best-seen points, encouraging exploitation, and augment with a small set of points constructed to cover the domain, encouraging exploration. This approach was used for example by GARNETT et al. for Bayesian set function optimization.[35]

Other approaches are also possible. For example, several authors have constructed GP models for particular combinatorial spaces whose structure simplifies the (usually approximate but near-optimal) optimization of particular acquisition functions induced from the model.[36,37,38]

The benefit of imperfect optimization?

We conclude this discussion with one paradoxical remark. In some cases it may actually be advantageous to optimize an acquisition function *imperfectly.* As many common policies are based on extremely myopic (one-step) reasoning, imperfect optimization may yield a useful exploration benefit as a side effect. This phenomenon, and the effect it may have on empirical performance, deserves thoughtful consideration.

9.3   STARTING AND STOPPING OPTIMIZATION

Finally, we briefly consider the part of optimization that happens *outside* the application of an optimization policy: initialization and termination.

Initialization

Theoretically, one can begin a Bayesian optimization routine with a completely empty dataset $\mathcal{D} = \emptyset$ and then use an optimization policy to design every observation, and indeed this has been our working model of Bayesian optimization since sketching the basic idea in Algorithm 1.1. However, Bayesian optimization policies are informed by an underlying belief about the objective function, which can be significantly misinformed when too little data are available, especially when relying on point estimation for model selection rather than accounting for (significant!) uncertainty in model hyperparameters and/or model structures.

Due to the sequential nature of optimization and the dependence of each decision on the data observed in previous iterations, it can be wise to use a model-*independent* procedure to design a small number of initial observations before beginning optimization in earnest. This procedure can be as simple as random sampling[39] or a space-filling design such as a low-discrepancy sequence or Latin hypercube design.[40] When repeatedly solving related optimization problems, we may even be able to *learn* how to initialize Bayesian optimization routines from experience. Some authors have proposed sophisticated "warm start" initialization procedures for hyperparameter tuning using so-called *metafeatures* characterizing the datasets under consideration.[41]

Termination

In many applications of Bayesian optimization, we assume a preallocated budget on the number of observations we will make and simply terminate optimization when that budget is expended. However, we may also treat termination as a *decision* and adaptively determine when to stop based on collected data. Of course, in practice we are free to design a stopping rule however we see fit, but we can outline some possible options.

Especially when using a policy grounded in decision theory, it is natural to terminate optimization when the maximum of our chosen acquisition function drops below some threshold c, which may depend on x:

$$\left[\max_{x \in \mathcal{X}} \left[\alpha(x; \mathcal{D}) - c(x) \right] < 0 \right]. \tag{9.9}$$

For acquisition functions derived from decision theory, such a stopping rule may be justified theoretically: we stop when the expected gain from the optimal observation is no longer worth the cost of acquisition.[42] A majority of the stopping rules described in the literature assume this form, with the threshold c often being determined dynamically based on the scale of observed data.[43] DAI et al. combined a stopping rule of this form with an otherwise non-decision-theoretic policy (GP-UCB) and showed that its asymptotic performance in terms of expected regret was not adversely affected despite the mismatch in motivation between the policy and stopping rule.[44]

It may also be prudent to consider purely data-dependent stopping rules in order to avoid undue expense arising from miscalibrated models fruitlessly continuing optimization based on incorrect beliefs. For example, ACERBI and MA proposed augmenting a bound on the total number of

model averaging: § 4.4, p. 74

39 These approaches are discussed and evaluated in:

M. W. HOFFMAN and B. SHAHRIARI (2014). Modular Mechanisms for Bayesian Optimization. *Bayesian Optimization Workshop, NeurIPS 2014.*

40 D. R. JONES et al. (1998). Efficient Global Optimization of Expensive Black-Box Functions. *Journal of Global Optimization* 13(4):455–492.

41 M. FEURER et al. (2015). Initializing Bayesian Hyperparameter Optimization via Meta-Learning. *AAAI 2015.*

optimal stopping rules: § 5.4, p. 103

42 See in particular our discussion of the one-step optimal stopping rule, p. 104.

43 Some early (but surely not the earliest!) examples:

D. D. COX and S. JOHN (1992). A Statistical Method for Global Optimization. *SMC 1992.*

D. R. JONES et al. (1998). Efficient Global Optimization of Expensive Black-Box Functions. *Journal of Global Optimization* 13(4):455–492.

44 Z. DAI et al. (2019). Bayesian Optimization Meets Bayesian Optimal Stopping. *ICML 2019.*

45 L. ACERBI and W. J. MA (2017). Practical Bayesian Optimization for Model Fitting with Bayesian Adaptive Direct Search. *NeurIPS 2017.*

observations with an early stopping option if no optimization progress is made over a given number of observations.[45]

9.4   SUMMARY OF MAJOR IDEAS

- Gaussian process inference requires solving a system of linear equations whose size grows with the number of observed values (9.2).

direct computation via Cholesky decomposition: § 9.1, p. 201

- A direct implementation via the Cholesky decomposition is a straightforward option, but scales cubically with the number of observed values.

iterative numerical methods: § 9.1, p. 203

sparse approximation: § 9.1, p. 204

- Scaling to larger datasets is possible by appealing to iterative numerical methods such as the method of *conjugate gradients,* or to *sparse approximation,* where we approximate an intractable posterior Gaussian process with a Gaussian process conditioned on carefully designed, fictitious observations at locations called *inducing points.* These methods can scale inference to hundreds of thousands of observations or more.

the potential for vanishing gradients: § 9.2, p. 207

- When optimizing acquisition functions, it is important to be aware of the potential for vanishing gradients in extrapolatory regions of the domain and plan accordingly.

initialization: § 9.3, p. 210

- It is usually a good idea to begin optimization with a small set of observations designed in a model-agnostic fashion in order to begin with a somewhat informed model of the objective function.

termination: § 9.3, p. 211

- When dynamic termination is desired, simple schemes based on thresholding the acquisition function can be effective.

THEORETICAL ANALYSIS

10

The Bayesian optimization procedures we have developed throughout this book have demonstrated remarkable empirical performance in a huge swath of practical settings, many of which are outlined in Appendix D. However, good empirical performance may not be enough to satisfy those who value rigor over results. Fortunately, many Bayesian optimization algorithms are also backed by strong theoretical guarantees on their performance. The literature on this topic is now quite vast, and convergence has been studied by different authors in different ways, sometimes involving slight nuances in approach and interpretation. We will take an in-depth look at this topic in this chapter, covering the most common lines of attack and outlining the state-of-the-art in results.

Appendix D, p. 313: Annotated Bibliography of Applications

A running theme throughout this chapter will be understanding how various measures of optimization error decrease asymptotically as an optimization policy is repeatedly executed. To facilitate this discussion, we will universally use τ in this chapter to indicate dataset size, or equivalently to indicate the number of steps an optimization procedure is assumed to have run. As we will primarily be interested in asymptotic results as $\tau \to \infty$, this convention does not rule out the possibility of starting optimization with some arbitrary dataset of fixed size. We will use subscripts to indicate dataset size when necessary, notating the dataset comprising the first τ observations with:

size of dataset, τ

dataset after τ observations, $\mathcal{D}_\tau$

$$\mathcal{D}_\tau = (\mathbf{x}_\tau, \mathbf{y}_\tau) = \big\{(x_i, y_i)\big\}_{i=1}^{\tau}.$$

When studying the convergence of a global optimization algorithm, we must be careful to define exactly what we *mean* by "convergence." In general, a convergence argument entails:

what does it mean to converge?

- choosing some measure of optimization error,
- choosing some space of possible objective functions, and
- establishing some guarantee for the chosen error on the chosen function space, such as an asymptotic bound on the worst- or average-case error in the large-sample limit $\tau \to \infty$.

There is a great deal of freedom in the last of these steps, and we will discuss several important results and proof strategies later in this chapter. However, there are well-established conventions for the first two of these steps, which we will introduce in the following two sections. We begin with the notion of *regret*, which provides a natural measure of optimization error.

regret: below
useful spaces of objective functions: § 10.2, p. 215

10.1 REGRET

Regret is a core concept in the analysis of optimization algorithms, Bayesian or otherwise. The role of regret is to quantify optimization progress in a manner suitable for establishing convergence to the global optimum and studying the rate of this convergence. There are several definitions

5 Occasionally a slightly different definition of simple regret is used, analogous to the global reward (6.5), where we measure regret with respect to the maximum of the posterior mean:

$$r_\tau = f^* - \max_{x \in \mathcal{X}} \mu_{\mathcal{D}_\tau}(x).$$

convergence goal: show $r_\tau \to 0$

instantaneous regret, ρ

cumulative regret of $\mathcal{D}_\tau$, R_τ

of regret used in different contexts, all based on the same idea: comparing the objective function values visited during optimization to the globally optimal value, f^*. The larger this gap, the more "regret" we incur in retrospect for having invested in observations at suboptimal locations.[1]

Regret is an unavoidable consequence of decision making under uncertainty. Without foreknowledge of the global optimum, we must of course spend some time searching for it, and even what may be *optimal* actions in the face of uncertainty may seem disappointing in retrospect.[2] However, such actions are necessary in order to learn about the environment and inform future decisions. This reasoning gives rise to the classic tension between exploration and exploitation in policy design: although exploration may not yield immediate progress, it enables future success, and if we are careful, reduces future regret. Of course, exploration alone is not sufficient to realize a compelling optimization strategy,[3] as we must also exploit what we have learned and adapt our behavior accordingly. An ideal algorithm thus explores *efficiently* enough that its regret can at least be limited in the long run.

Most analysis is performed in terms of one of two closely related notions of regret: *simple* or *cumulative regret,* defined below.

Simple regret

Let $\mathcal{D}_\tau$ represent some set of (potentially noisy) observations gathered during optimization,[4] and let $\boldsymbol{\phi}_\tau = f(\mathbf{x}_\tau)$ represent the objective function values at the observed locations. The *simple regret* associated with this data is the difference between the global maximum of the objective and the maximum restricted to the observed locations:[5]

$$r_\tau = f^* - \max \boldsymbol{\phi}_\tau. \tag{10.1}$$

It is immediate from its definition that simple regret is nonnegative and vanishes only if the data contain a global optimum. With this in mind, a common goal is to show that the simple regret of data obtained by some policy approaches zero, implying the policy will eventually (and perhaps efficiently) identify the global optimum, up to vanishing error.

Cumulative regret

To define cumulative regret, we first introduce the *instantaneous regret* ρ corresponding to an observation at some point x, which is the difference between the global maximum of the objective and the function value ϕ:

$$\rho = f^* - \phi. \tag{10.2}$$

The *cumulative regret* for a dataset $\mathcal{D}_\tau$ is then the total instantaneous regret incurred:

$$R_\tau = \sum_i \rho_i = \tau f^* - \sum_i \phi_i. \tag{10.3}$$

Relationship between simple and cumulative regret

Simple and cumulative regret are analogous to the simple (6.3) and cumulative (6.7) reward utility functions, and any intuition regarding these utilities transfers to their regret counterparts.[6]

However, these two definitions of regret are not directly comparable, even on the same data – for starters, simple regret is nonincreasing as more data are collected, whereas cumulative regret is nondecreasing. However, suitable normalization allows some useful comparison.[7] Namely, consider the *average,* rather than cumulative, regret:

$$\frac{R_\tau}{\tau} = f^* - \frac{1}{\tau} \sum_i \phi_i.$$

As the mean of a vector is a lower bound on its maximum, we may derive an upper bound on simple regret in terms of cumulative regret:

$$r_\tau \le \frac{R_\tau}{\tau}. \tag{10.4}$$

In this light, a common goal is to show that an optimization algorithm has the so-called *no-regret property,* which means that its average regret vanishes with increasing data:

$$\lim_{\tau \to \infty} \frac{R_\tau}{\tau} = 0. \tag{10.5}$$

Equivalently, a policy achieves no regret if its cumulative regret grows sublinearly with the dataset size τ. This is sufficient to prove convergence in terms of simple regret as well by appealing to the squeeze theorem:

$$0 \le r_\tau \le \frac{R_\tau}{\tau} \to 0.$$

Although no regret guarantees convergence in simple regret, the reverse is not necessarily the case. It is easy to find counterexamples – consider, for example, modifying a no-regret policy to select a *fixed* suboptimal point every other observation. The simple regret would still vanish (half as fast), but constant instantaneous regret on alternating iterations would prevent sublinear cumulative regret. Thus the no-regret property is somewhat stronger than convergence in simple regret alone. From another perspective, simple regret is more tolerant of exploration: we only need to visit the global optimum *once* to converge in terms of simple regret, whereas effectively *all* observations must eventually become effectively optimal to achieve the no-regret property.

10.2 USEFUL FUNCTION SPACES FOR STUDYING CONVERGENCE

Identifying the "right" function space to consider when studying convergence is a subtle decision, as we must strike a balance between generality and practicality. One obvious choice would be the space of *all* continuous

6 Note that neither notion of regret represents a valid utility function itself, as in general both f^* and ϕ would be random variables in that context.

7 For a deeper discussion on the connections between simple and cumulative regret, see:

S. BUBECK et al. (2009). Pure Exploration in Multi-Armed Bandits Problems. *ALT 2009.*

convergence goal: show $R_\tau / \tau \to 0$

no-regret property implies convergence in simple regret

convergence in simple regret does not imply the no-regret property

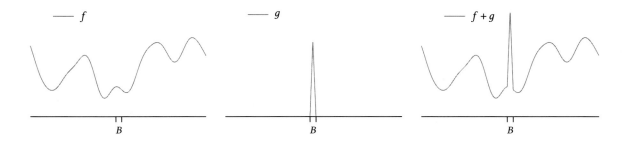

Figure 10.1: Modifying a continuous function f (left) to feature a "needle" on some ball (here an interval) B. We construct a continuous function g vanishing on the complement of B (middle), then add this "correction" to f (right).

functions. However, it turns out this space is far too large to be of much theoretical interest, as it contains functions that are arbitrarily hard to optimize. Nonetheless, it is easy to characterize convergence (in terms of simple regret) on this space, and some convergence guarantees of this type are known for select Bayesian optimization algorithms. We will begin our discussion here.

We may gain some traction by considering a family of more plausible, "nice" functions whose complexity can be controlled enough to guarantee rapid convergence. In particular, choosing a Gaussian process prior for the objective function implies strong correlation structure, and this insight leads to natural function spaces to study. This has become the standard approach in modern analysis, and we will consider it shortly.

convergence on "nice" continuous functions:
p. 218

Convergence on all continuous functions

The largest reasonable space we might want to consider is the space of all continuous functions. However, continuous functions can be poorly behaved from the point of view of optimization, and we cannot hope for strong convergence guarantees as a result. There is simply too much freedom for functions to "hide" their optima in inconvenient places.

To begin, we establish a simple characterization of convergence on all continuous functions in terms of eventual density of observation.

Theorem. *Let $\mathcal{X}$ be a compact metric space. An optimization policy converges in terms of simple regret on all continuous functions $f\colon \mathcal{X} \to \mathbb{R}$ if and only if the set of eventually observed points $\bigcup_{i=1}^{\infty}\{x_i\}$ is always dense.*

The proof is instructive as it shows what can go wrong with general continuous functions. First, if the set of eventually observed points is dense in $\mathcal{X}$, we may construct a sequence of observations converging to a global maximum x^*.[8] The associated function values $\{\phi_i\}$ then converge to f^* by continuity, and thus $r_\tau \to 0$.

If density *fails*[9] for some continuous function f – and thus there is some ball $B \subset \mathcal{X}$ that will never contain an observation – then we may foil the policy with a "needle in a haystack." We construct a continuous

8 For example by taking x_i within a ball of radius $1/i$ around x^*.

9 Some care would be required to make the following argument rigorous for stochastic observations and/or policies, but the spirit would remain intact.

function g vanishing on the complement of B and achieving arbitrarily high values on B.[10] Adding the needle to f creates a continuous function $f + g$ with arbitrary – and, once the needle is sufficiently tall, never observed – maximum; see Figure 10.1. As f and $f + g$ agree outside B, the policy cannot distinguish between these functions, and thus the policy can have arbitrarily high simple regret.

We can use this strategy of building adversarial "needles in haystacks" to further show that, even if we can guarantee convergence on all continuous functions, we cannot hope to demonstrate *rapid* convergence in simple regret, at least not in the worst case. Unless the domain is finite, running any policy for any finite number of iterations will leave unobserved "holes" that we can fill in with arbitrarily tall "needles," and thus the worst-case regret will be unbounded at every stage of the algorithm.

Convergence results for all continuous functions on the unit interval

Establishing the density criterion above has proven difficult for Bayesian optimization algorithms in general spaces with arbitrary models. However, restricting the domain to the unit interval $\mathcal{X} = [0, 1]$ and limiting the objective function and observation models to certain well-behaved combinations has yielded universal convergence guarantees for some Bayesian procedures.

For example, KUSHNER sketched a proof of convergence in simple regret when maximizing probability of improvement on the unit interval, when the objective function model is the Wiener process and observations are exact or corrupted by additive Gaussian noise.[11] ŽILINSKAS later provided a proof in the noiseless case.[12] This particular model exhibits a Markov property that enables relatively straightforward analysis by characterizing its behavior on each of the subintervals subdivided by the data. This structure enables a simple proof strategy by assuming some subinterval is never subdivided and arriving at a contradiction.

Convergence guarantees for this policy (under the name the "P-algorithm") on the unit interval have also been established for smoother models of the objective function – that is, with differentiable rather than merely continuous sample paths[13] – including the once-integrated Wiener process.[14] Convergence rates for these algorithms for general continuous functions have also been derived.[13,14,15] In light of the above discussion, these convergence rates are not in terms of simple regret but rather in terms of shrinkage in the size of the subinterval containing the global optimum, and thus the distance from the closest observed location to the global optimum. The proofs of these results all relied on exact observation of the objective function.

Convergence on all continuous functions on the unit interval has also been established for maximizing expected improvement, in the special case of exact observation and a Wiener process model on the objective.[16] The proof strategy again relied on the special structure of the posterior to show that the observed locations will always subdivide the domain such that no "hole" is left behind.

10 For example, we may scale the distance to the complement of B.

worst-case simple regret unbounded

11 H. J. KUSHNER (1964). A New Method of Locating the Maximum Point of an Arbitrary Multipeak Curve in the Presence of Noise. *Journal of Basic Engineering* 86(1):97–106.

12 A. G. ŽILINSKAS (1975). Single-Step Bayesian Search Method for an Extremum of Functions of a Single Variable. *Kibernetika (Cybernetics)* 11(1):160–166.

13 J. CALVIN and A. ŽILINSKAS (1999). On the Convergence of the P-Algorithm for One-Dimensional Global Optimization of Smooth Functions. *Journal of Optimization Theory and Applications* 102(3):479–495.

14 J. M. CALVIN and A. ŽILINSKAS (2001). On Convergence of a P-Algorithm Based on a Statistical Model of Continuously Differentiable Functions. *Journal of Global Optimization* 19(3):229–245.

15 J. M. CALVIN (2000). Convergence Rate of the P-Algorithm for Optimization of Continuous Functions. In: *Approximation and Complexity in Numerical Optimization: Continuous and Discrete Problems*.

16 M. LOCATELLI (1997). Bayesian Algorithms for One-Dimensional Global Optimization. *Journal of Global Optimization* 10(1):57–76.

Convergence on "nice" continuous functions

In the pursuit of stronger convergence results, we may abandon the space of all continuous functions and focus on some space of suitably well-behaved objectives. By limiting the complexity of the functions we consider, we can avoid complications arising from adversarial examples like "needles in haystacks." This can be motivated from the basic assumption that optimization is to be feasible at all, which is not the case when facing an adversary creating arbitrarily difficult problems. Instead, we may seek strong performance guarantees when optimizing "plausible" objective functions. Conveniently, a Gaussian process model on the objective $\mathcal{GP}(f; \mu, K)$ gives rise to several paths forward.[17]

Sample paths of a Gaussian process

In a Bayesian analysis, it is natural to assume that the objective function is a sample path from the Gaussian process used to model it. Assuming sample path continuity, sample paths of a Gaussian process are much better behaved than general continuous functions. The covariance function provides regularization on the behavior of sample paths via the induced correlations among function values; see the figure in the margin. As a result, we can ensure that functions with exceptionally bad behavior (such as hidden "needles") are also exceptionally rare.

The sample path assumption provides a known distribution for the function values at observed locations (2.2–2.3), allowing us to derive average-case results. An important concept here is the *Bayesian* (or simply *Bayes*) *regret* of a policy, which is the expected value of the (simple or cumulative) regret incurred when following the policy, say for τ steps:

$$\mathbb{E}[r_\tau]; \quad \mathbb{E}[R_\tau]. \tag{10.6}$$

This expectation is taken with respect to uncertainty in the objective function f, the observation locations $\mathbf{x}$, and the observed values $\mathbf{y}$.[18]

The worst-case alternative

The GP sample path assumption is not always desirable, for example in the context of a frequentist (that is, worst-case) analysis of a Bayesian optimization algorithm. This is not as contradictory as it may seem, as Bayesian analyses can lack robustness to model misspecification – a certainty in practice. An alternative is to assume that the objective function lies in some explicit space of "nice" functions $\mathcal{H}$, then find worst-case convergence guarantees for the Bayesian algorithm on inputs satisfying this regularity assumption. For example, we might seek to bound the worst-case expected (simple or cumulative) regret for a function in this space after τ decisions:

$$\bar{r}_\tau[\mathcal{H}] = \sup_{f \in \mathcal{H}} \mathbb{E}[r_\tau]; \qquad \bar{R}_\tau[\mathcal{H}] = \sup_{f \in \mathcal{H}} \mathbb{E}[R_\tau]. \tag{10.7}$$

17 All of the algorithms we will study for the remainder of the chapter will use a Gaussian process belief on the objective function, where the theory is mature.

sample path continuity: § 2.5, p. 28

Sample paths of a stationary Gaussian process with Matérn $\nu = 5/2$ covariance (3.14) show more regularity than arbitrary continuous functions.

Bayesian (Bayes) regret

18 In some analyses, we may also seek bounds on the regret that hold with high probability with respect to these random variables rather than bounds on the expected regret.

worst-case regret on $\mathcal{H}$ after τ steps: $\bar{r}(\tau, \mathcal{H})$, $\bar{R}(\tau, \mathcal{H})$

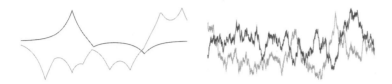

Figure 10.2: Left: functions in the RKHS corresponding to the Matérn $v = 1/2$ covariance function (3.11). Right: sample paths from a GP with the same covariance.

Here the expectation is over with respect to the observed locations $\mathbf{x}$ and the observed values $\mathbf{y}$,[19] but uncertainty in the objective function – presumably the most troubling factor in a Bayesian analysis – is replaced by a pessimistic bound on the functions in $\mathcal{H}$. Note that the algorithms we will analyze still *use* a Gaussian process belief on f in making decisions, but the objective function is not generated according to that model.

[19] In the special case of exact observation and a deterministic policy, such a bound would entail no probabilistic elements.

Reproducing kernel Hilbert spaces

Corresponding to every covariance function K is a natural companion function space, its *reproducing kernel Hilbert space* (RKHS) $\mathcal{H}_K$. There is a strong connection between this space and a centered Gaussian process with the same covariance function, $\mathcal{GP}(f; \mu \equiv 0, K)$. Namely, consider the set of functions of the form

$$x \mapsto \sum_{i=1}^{n} \alpha_i K(x_i, x), \qquad (10.8)$$

reproducing kernel Hilbert space corresponding to K, $\mathcal{H}_K$

where $\{x_i\} \subset \mathcal{X}$ is an arbitrary finite set of input locations with corresponding real-valued weights $\{\alpha_i\}$.[20] Note this is *precisely* the set of all possible posterior mean functions for the Gaussian process arising from exact inference![21] The RKHS $\mathcal{H}_K$ is then the completion of this space endowed with the inner product

[20] Equivalently, this is the span of the set of covariance functions with one input held fixed: $\text{span}\{x \mapsto K(x, x') \mid x' \in \mathcal{X}\}$.

[21] Inspection of the general posterior mean functions in (2.14, 2.19) reveals they can always be (and can *only* be) written in this form.

$$\left\langle \sum_{i=1}^{n} \alpha_i K(x_i, x), \sum_{j=1}^{m} \beta_j K(x'_j, x) \right\rangle = \sum_{i=1}^{n} \sum_{j=1}^{m} \alpha_i \beta_j K(x_i, x'_j). \qquad (10.9)$$

That is, the RKHS is roughly the set of functions "as smooth as" a posterior mean function of the corresponding GP, according to a notion of "explainability" by the covariance function.

It turns out that belonging to the RKHS $\mathcal{H}_K$ is a stronger regularity assumption than being a sample path of the corresponding GP. In fact, unless the RKHS is finite-dimensional (which is not normally the case), sample paths from a Gaussian process almost surely do *not* lie in the corresponding RKHS:[22,23] $\Pr(f \in \mathcal{H}_K) = 0$. However, the posterior mean function of the same process *always* lies in the RKHS by the above construction. Figure 10.2 illustrates a striking example of this phenomenon: sample paths from a stationary GP with Matérn covariance function with $v = 1/2$ (3.11) are *nowhere* differentiable, whereas members of the corresponding RKHS are *almost everywhere* differentiable. Effectively, the process of averaging over sample paths "smooths out" their erratic behavior in the posterior mean, and elements of the RKHS exhibit similar smoothness.

[22] M. N. LUKIĆ and J. H. BEDER (2001). Stochastic Processes with Sample Paths in Reproducing Kernel Hilbert Spaces. *Transactions of the American Mathematical Society* 353(10):3945–3969.

[23] However, for the Matérn family, sample paths *do* lie in a "larger" RKHS we can determine from the covariance function. Namely, sample paths of processes with a Matérn covariance with finite v are (almost everywhere) one-time less differentiable than the functions in the corresponding RKHS; see Figure 10.2 for an illustration of this phenomenon with $v = 1/2$. Sample paths for the squared exponential covariance, meanwhile, lie "just barely" outside the corresponding RHKS. For more details, see:

M. KANAGAWA et al. (2018). Gaussian Processes and Kernel Methods: A Review on Connections and Equivalences. arXiv: 1807.02582 [stat.ML]. [theorem 4.12]

Reproducing kernel Hilbert space norm

RKHS norm, $\|f\|_{\mathcal{H}_K}$

Associated with an RKHS $\mathcal{H}_K$ is a norm $\|f\|_{\mathcal{H}_K}$ that can be interpreted as a measure of function complexity with respect to the covariance function K. The RKHS norm derives from the pre-completion inner product (10.9), and we can build intuition for the norm by drawing a connection between that inner product and familiar concepts from Gaussian process regression. The key is the characterization of the pre-completion function space (10.8) as the space of all possible posterior mean functions for the corresponding centered Gaussian process $\mathcal{GP}(f; \mu \equiv 0, K)$.

RKHS norm of posterior mean function

To be more explicit, consider the posterior mean after observing a dataset of *exact* observations $\mathcal{D} = (\mathbf{x}, \mathbf{y})$, inducing the posterior mean (2.14):

$$\mu_{\mathcal{D}}(x) = K(x, \mathbf{x})\Sigma^{-1}\mathbf{y},$$

24 For this example we have $\boldsymbol{\alpha} = \Sigma^{-1}\mathbf{y}$ in (10.8).

where $\Sigma = K(\mathbf{x}, \mathbf{x})$. Then the (squared) RKHS norm of the posterior mean is:[24]

$$\|\mu_{\mathcal{D}}\|^2_{\mathcal{H}_K} = \langle \mu_{\mathcal{D}}, \mu_{\mathcal{D}} \rangle = \mathbf{y}^\top \Sigma^{-1} \mathbf{y}. \tag{10.10}$$

That is, the RKHS norm of the posterior mean is the Mahalanobis norm of the observed data $\mathbf{y}$ under their Gaussian prior distribution (2.2–2.3).

connection between RKHS norm and GP marginal likelihood

25 The remaining terms are independent of data.

We have actually seen this score before: it appears in the log marginal likelihood of the data under the Gaussian process (4.8), where we interpreted it as a score of data fit.[25] This reveals a deep connection between the RKHS norm and the associated Gaussian process: posterior mean functions arising from "more unusual" observations from the point of view of the GP have higher complexity from the point of view of the RKHS. Whereas the Gaussian process judges the *data* $\mathbf{y}$ to be complex via the marginal likelihood, the RKHS judges the resulting *posterior mean* $\mu_{\mathcal{D}}$ to be complex via the RKHS norm – but these are simply two ways of interpreting the same scenario.[26]

26 The "needles in a haystack" constructed earlier would have extraordinarily large RKHS norm, if they lie in a given RKHS at all.

The role of the RKHS norm in quantifying function complexity suggests a natural space of objective functions to work with when seeking worst-case results (10.7). We take the *RKHS ball* of radius B, the space of functions with complexity bounded by B in the RKHS:

RKHS ball of radius B, $\mathcal{H}_K[B]$

$$\mathcal{H}_K[B] = \left\{ f \mid \|f\|_{\mathcal{H}_K} \leq B \right\}. \tag{10.11}$$

The radius B is left as a parameter that is absorbed into derived bounds.

10.3 RELEVANT PROPERTIES OF COVARIANCE FUNCTIONS

A sizable majority of the results discussed in the remainder of this chapter concern optimization performance on one of the function spaces discussed in the previous section: sample paths of a centered Gaussian process with covariance function K or functions in the corresponding RKHS $\mathcal{H}_K$. Given the fundamental role the covariance function plays in determining sample path behavior, it should not be surprising that the nature of the covariance function also has profound influence on optimization performance.

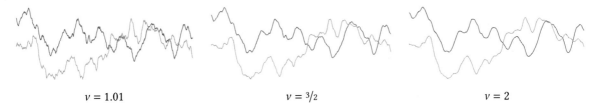

$$\nu = 1.01 \qquad\qquad \nu = 3/2 \qquad\qquad \nu = 2$$

Figure 10.3: Sample paths from a centered GP with Matérn covariance with smoothness parameter ν ranging from just over 1 (left) to 2 (right). The random seed is shared so that corresponding paths are comparable across the panels. All samples are once differentiable, but some are smoother than others.

One might intuitively expect that optimizing smoother functions should be easier than optimizing rougher functions, as a rougher function gives the optimum more places to "hide"; see the figure in the margin. This intuition turns out to be correct. The key insight is that rougher functions require more *information* to describe than smoother ones. As each observation we make is limited in how much information it can reveal regarding the objective function, rougher objectives require more observations to learn with a similar level of confidence, and to optimize with a similar level of success. We can make this intuition precise through the concept of *information capacity*, which bounds the rate at which we can learn about the objective through noisy observations and serves as a fundamental measure of function complexity appearing in numerous analyses.

Smoothness of sample paths

The connection between sample path smoothness and the inherent difficulty of learning is best understood for the Matérn covariance family and the limiting case of the squared exponential covariance. Combined, these covariance functions allow us to model functions with a *continuum* of smoothness. To this end, there is a general form of the Matérn covariance function modeling functions of any finite smoothness, controlled by a parameter $\nu > 0$:[27]

$$K_{\text{M}}(d; \nu) = \frac{2^{1-\nu}}{\Gamma(\nu)} \left(\sqrt{2\nu}d\right)^{\nu} K_{\nu}\left(\sqrt{2\nu}d\right), \qquad (10.12)$$

where $d = |x - x'|$ and K_{ν} is the modified Bessel function of the second kind. Sample paths from a centered Gaussian process with this covariance are $\lceil \nu \rceil - 1$ times continuously differentiable, but the smoothness of sample paths is not as granular as a simple count of derivatives. Rather, the parameter ν allows us to fine-tune sample path smoothness as desired.[28] Figure 10.3 illustrates sample paths generated from a Matérn covariance with a range of smoothness from $\nu = 1.01$ to $\nu = 2$. All of these samples are exactly once differentiable, but we might say that the $\nu = 1.01$ samples are "just barely" so, and that the $\nu = 2$ samples are "very nearly" twice differentiable.

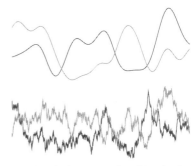

Sample paths from a smooth GP (above) and a rough one (below). The rough samples have more degrees of freedom – and far more local maxima – and we might conclude they are harder to optimize as a result.

Matérn and squared exponential covariance functions: § 3.3, p. 51

27 The given expression has unit length and output scale; if desired, we can introduce parameters for these following § 3.4.

smoothness parameter, ν

28 This can be made precise through the coefficient of Hölder continuity in the "final" derivative of K_{M}, which controls the smoothness of the final derivative of sample paths. Except when ν is an integer, the Matérn covariance with parameter ν belongs to the Hölder space

$$\mathcal{C}^{\alpha,\beta}; \quad \alpha = \lfloor 2\nu \rfloor; \quad \beta = 2\nu - \lfloor 2\nu \rfloor,$$

and we can expect the final derivative of sample paths to be $(\nu - \lfloor \nu \rfloor)$-Hölder continuous.

Matérn family

Taking the limit $v \to \infty$ recovers the squared exponential covariance K_{SE}. This serves as the extreme end of the continuum, modeling functions with infinitely many continuous derivatives. Together, the Matérn and squared exponential covariances allow us to model functions with any smoothness $v \in (0, \infty]$; we will call this collection the *Matérn family*.

Information capacity

We now require some way to relate the complexity of sample path behavior to our ability to learn about an unknown function. Information theory provides an answer through the concept of *information capacity*, the maximum rate of information transfer through a noisy observation mechanism.

In the analysis of Bayesian optimization algorithms, the central concern is how efficiently we can learn about a GP-distributed objective function $\mathcal{GP}(f; \mu, K)$ through a set of τ noisy observations $\mathcal{D}_\tau$. The information capacity of this observation process, as a function of the number of observations τ, provides a fundamental bound on our ability to learn about f. For this discussion, let us adopt the common observation model of independent and homoskedastic additive Gaussian noise with scale $\sigma_n > 0$ (2.16). In this case, information capacity is a function of:

- the covariance K, which determines the information content of f, and
- the noise scale σ_n, which limits the amount of information obtainable through a single observation.

29 We have $H[\mathbf{y} \mid f] = H[\mathbf{y} \mid \boldsymbol{\phi}]$ by conditional independence (1.3).

The information regarding f contained in an arbitrary set of observations $\mathcal{D} = (\mathbf{x}, \mathbf{y})$ can be quantified by the *mutual information* (A.16):[29]

$$I(\mathbf{y}; f) = H[\mathbf{y}] - H[\mathbf{y} \mid \boldsymbol{\phi}] = \tfrac{1}{2} \log |\mathbf{I} + \sigma_n^{-2} \Sigma|, \qquad (10.13)$$

30 For more on information gain, see § 6.3, p. 115. Thus far we have primarily concerned ourselves with information gain regarding x^* or f^*; here we are reasoning about the function f itself.

information capacity, γ_τ

where $\Sigma = K(\mathbf{x}, \mathbf{x})$. Note that the entropy of $\mathbf{y}$ given $\boldsymbol{\phi}$ does not depend on the actual value of $\boldsymbol{\phi}$, and thus the mutual information $I(\mathbf{y}; f)$ is also the *information gain* about f provided by the data.[30] The *information capacity* (also known as the *maximum information gain*) of this observation process is now the maximum amount of information about f obtainable through any set of τ observations:

$$\gamma_\tau = \sup_{|\mathbf{x}|=\tau} I(\mathbf{y}; f). \qquad (10.14)$$

Known bounds on information capacity

The information capacity of a GP observation process (10.14) is commonly invoked in theoretical analyses of algorithms making use of this model class. Unfortunately, working with information capacity is somewhat unwieldy for two reasons. First, as mentioned above, information capacity is a function of the covariance function K, which can be verified through the explicit formula in (10.13). Thus performance guarantees in terms of information capacity require further analysis to derive explicit results for a particular choice of model. Second, information capacity of any given model is in general NP-hard to compute due to the difficulty of the set function maximization in (10.14).[31]

For these reasons, the typical strategy is to derive *agnostic* convergence results in terms of the information capacity of an arbitrary observation process, then seek to derive bounds on the information capacity for notable covariance functions such as those in the Matérn family. A common proof strategy for bounding the information gain is to relate the information capacity to the spectrum of the covariance function, with faster spectral decay yielding stronger bounds on information capacity. The first explicit bounds on information capacity for the Matérn and squared exponential covariances were provided by SRINIVAS et al.,[32] and the bounds for the Matérn covariance have since been sharpened using similar techniques.[33,34]

For a compact domain $\mathcal{X} \subset \mathbb{R}^d$ and fixed noise scale σ_n, we have the following asymptotic bounds on the information capacity. For the Matérn covariance function with smoothness v, we have:[34]

$$\gamma_\tau = \mathcal{O}\big(\tau^\alpha (\log \tau)^{1-\alpha}\big), \quad \alpha = \frac{d}{2v + d}; \tag{10.15}$$

and for the squared exponential covariance, we have:[32]

$$\gamma_\tau = \mathcal{O}\big((\log \tau)^{d+1}\big). \tag{10.16}$$

These results embody our stated goal of characterizing smoother sample paths (as measured by v) as being inherently less complex than rougher sample paths. The information capacity decreases steadily as $v \to \infty$, eventually dropping to only logarithmic growth in τ for the squared exponential covariance. The correct interpretation of this result is that the smoother sample paths require *less* information to describe, and thus the maximum amount of information one *could* learn is limited compared to rougher sample paths.

Bounding the sum of predictive variances

A key result linking information capacity to an optimization policy is the following.[32] Suppose some optimization policy selected an arbitrary sequence of τ observation locations $\{x_i\}$, and let $\{\sigma_i\}$ be the corresponding predictive standard deviations at the time of selection. By applying the chain rule for mutual information, we can rewrite the information gain (10.13) from observing **y** in terms of the marginal predictive variances:

predictive standard deviation of ϕ_i, σ_i

$$I(\mathbf{y}; f) = \frac{1}{2} \sum_{i=1}^{\tau} \log\Big(1 + \frac{\sigma_i^2}{\sigma_n^2}\Big). \tag{10.17}$$

Now assume that the prior covariance function is bounded: $K(x, x) \le M$. Noting that $z^2 / \log(1 + z^2)$ is increasing for $z > 0$ and that $\sigma_i^2 \le M$, the following inequality holds for every observation:

bound on prior variance $K(x, x)$, M

posterior variance is nonincreasing: § 2.2, p. 22

$$\sigma_i^2 \le \frac{M}{\log(1 + \sigma_n^{-2} M)} \log\Big(1 + \frac{\sigma_i^2}{\sigma_n^2}\Big).$$

31 C.-W. KO et al. (1995). An Exact Algorithm for Maximum Entropy Sampling. *Operations Research* 43(4):684–691.

32 N. SRINIVAS et al. (2010). Gaussian Process Optimization in the Bandit Setting: No Regret and Experimental Design. *ICML 2010*.

33 D. JANZ et al. (2020). Bandit Optimisation of Functions in the Matérn Kernel RKHS. *AISTATS 2020*.

34 S. VAKILI et al. (2021b). On Information Gain and Regret Bounds in Gaussian Process Bandits. *AISTATS 2021*.

If an explicit leading constant is desired, we have $\sum_i \sigma_i^2 \le c\gamma_\tau$ with

$$c = \frac{2M}{\log(1 + \sigma_n^{-2}M)}.$$

We can now bound the sum of the predictive variances in terms of the information capacity:[35]

$$\sum_{i=1}^{\tau} \sigma_i^2 = \mathcal{O}(\gamma_\tau). \tag{10.18}$$

This bound will repeatedly prove useful below.

10.4 BAYESIAN REGRET WITH OBSERVATION NOISE

We have now covered the background required to understand – or at least to meaningfully interpret – most of the theoretical convergence results appearing in the literature. In the remainder of the chapter we will summarize some notable results built upon these ideas. The literature is expansive, and navigation can be challenging. Broadly, we can categorize these results according to certain dichotomies in their approach and focus, listed below.

analysis: frequentist or Bayesian?

- The first is whether the result is regarding the average-case (Bayesian) or worst-case (frequentist) regret. In the former case, we assume the objective function is a sample path from a Gaussian process $\mathcal{GP}(f; \mu, K)$ and seek to bound the expected regret (10.6). In the latter case, we assume the objective function lies in some RKHS $\mathcal{H}_K$ with bounded norm (10.11) and seek to bound the worst-case regret on this space (10.7).

observations: noisy or exact?

- The second is the assumption and treatment of observation noise. Stronger guarantees can often be derived in the noiseless setting, as we can learn much faster about the objective function. Observation noise is also modeled somewhat differently in the Bayesian and frequentist settings.

In this and the following sections, we will provide an overview of convergence results for all combinations of these choices: frequentist and Bayesian guarantees, with and without noise. For each of these cases, we will discuss both upper bounds on regret, which provide guarantees for the performance of specific Bayesian optimization algorithms, and also lower bounds on regret, which provide algorithm-agnostic bounds on the best possible performance. Here we will begin with results for Bayesian regret in the noisy setting.

To facilitate the discussion, we will adopt the notation $\mathcal{O}^*$ (sometimes written $\tilde{\mathcal{O}}$ in other texts) to describe asymptotic bounds in which *dimension-independent* logarithmic factors of τ are suppressed:

asymptotic behavior with logarithmic factors suppressed, $\mathcal{O}^*$

$$f(\tau) = \mathcal{O}\big(g(\tau)(\log \tau)^k\big); \implies f(\tau) = \mathcal{O}^*\big(g(\tau)\big).$$

Common assumptions

assumption: f is a sample path from $\mathcal{GP}(f; \mu \equiv 0, K)$

assumption: observations are corrupted by iid Gaussian noise with scale σ_n

In this section, we will assume that the objective function $f \colon \mathcal{X} \to \mathbb{R}$ is a sample path from a centered Gaussian process $\mathcal{GP}(f; \mu \equiv 0, K)$, and that observation noise is independent, homoskedastic Gaussian noise with scale $\sigma_n > 0$ (2.16). The domain $\mathcal{X}$ will at various times be either a *finite* set (as a stepping stone toward the continuous case) or a compact and convex subset of a d-dimensional cube: $\mathcal{X} \subset [0, m]^d$ We will also be assuming that the covariance function is continuous and bounded on $\mathcal{X}$: $K(x, x) \leq 1$. Since the covariance function is guaranteed to be bounded anyway (as $\mathcal{X}$ is compact) this simply fixes the scale without loss of generality.

assumption: $K(x, x) \leq 1$ is bounded

Upper confidence bound

In a landmark paper, SRINIVAS et al. derived sublinear cumulative regret bounds for the Gaussian process upper confidence bound (GP-UCB) policy in the Bayesian setting with noise.[36] The authors considered policies of the form (8.25):

upper confidence bound: § 7.8, p. 145, § 8.4, p. 170

$$x_i = \arg\max_{x \in \mathcal{X}} \mu + \beta_i \sigma, \tag{10.19}$$

where x_i is the point chosen in the ith iteration of the policy, μ and σ are shorthand for the posterior mean and standard deviation of $\phi = f(x)$ given the data available at time i, $\mathcal{D}_{i-1}$, and β_i is a time-dependent exploration parameter. The authors were able to demonstrate that if this exploration parameter is carefully tuned over the course of optimization, then the cumulative regret of the policy can be asymptotically bounded, with high probability, in terms of the information capacity.

We will discuss this result and its derivation in some detail below, as it demonstrates important proof strategies that will be repeated throughout this section and the next.

[36] N. SRINIVAS et al. (2010). Gaussian Process Optimization in the Bandit Setting: No Regret and Experimental Design. *ICML 2010*.

information capacity: § 10.3, p. 222

Regret bound on finite domains

To proceed, we first assume the domain $\mathcal{X}$ is finite; we will lift this to the continuous case shortly via a secondary argument.[37]

The construction of the UCB policy suggests the following *confidence interval* condition is likely to hold for any point $x \in \mathcal{X}$ at any time i:

$$\phi \in [\mu - \beta_i \sigma, \mu + \beta_i \sigma] = \mathcal{B}_i(x). \tag{10.20}$$

In fact, we can show that for appropriately chosen confidence parameters $\{\beta_i\}$, *every* such confidence interval is *always* valid, with high probability.

This may seem like a strong claim, but it is simply a consequence of the exponentially decreasing tails of the Gaussian distribution. At time i, we can use tail bounds on the Gaussian CDF to bound the probability of a given confidence interval failing in terms of β_i,[38] then use the union bound to bound the probability of (10.20) failing anywhere at time i.[39] Finally, we show that by increasing the confidence parameter β_i over time – so that the probability of failure decreases suitably quickly – the probability of failure anywhere and at any time is small. SRINIVAS et al. showed in particular that for any $\delta \in (0, 1)$, taking[40]

$$\beta_i^2 = 2\log\left(\frac{i^2 \pi^2 |\mathcal{X}|}{6\delta}\right) \tag{10.21}$$

[37] The general strategy for this case was established in the linear bandit setting in:

V. DANI et al. (2008). Stochastic Linear Optimization under Bandit Feedback. *COLT 2008*.

[38] SRINIVAS et al. use

$$\Pr(\phi \notin \mathcal{B}_i(x)) \leq \exp(-\beta_i^2/2).$$

[39] Using the above bound, the probability of failure anywhere at time i is at most

$$|\mathcal{X}| \exp(-\beta_i^2/2).$$

[40] The mysterious appearance of $\pi^2/6$ comes from

$$\sum_{i=1}^{\infty} \frac{1}{i^2} = \frac{\pi^2}{6}.$$

step 1: show confidence intervals (10.20) are universally valid with high probability

step 2: bound instantaneous regret by width of chosen confidence interval

guarantees that the confidence intervals (10.20) are universally valid with probability at least $1 - \delta$.

With this, we are actually almost finished. The next key insight is that if the confidence intervals in (10.20) *are* universally valid, then we can bound the instantaneous regret of the policy in every iteration by noting that the confidence interval of the chosen point always contains the global optimum:

$$f^* \in \mathcal{B}_i(x_i). \tag{10.22}$$

the lower bound of every point holds for f^*

the upper bound of the chosen point holds for every function value

To show this, we first note that the lower bound of every confidence interval applies to f^*_i, as all intervals are valid and f^* is the global maximum. Further, the upper bound of the chosen confidence interval is valid for f^*_i as it is the maximal upper bound by definition (and thus is valid for *every* function value) (10.19).

This result allows us to bound, with high probability, the instantaneous regret (10.2) in every iteration by the width of the confidence interval of the chosen point:

$$\rho_i \leq 2\beta_i \sigma_i. \tag{10.23}$$

41 D. RUSSO and B. VAN ROY (2014). Learning to Optimize via Posterior Sampling. *Mathematics of Operations Research* 39(4):1221–1243.

step 3: bound cumulative regret via bound on instantaneous regret

RUSSO and VAN ROY interpret this bound on the instantaneous regret as guaranteeing that regret can only be high when we also *learn* a great deal about the objective function to compensate (10.17).[41]

Finally, we bound the cumulative regret. Assuming the confidence intervals (10.20) are universally valid, we may bound the sum of the squared instantaneous regret up to time τ by

$$\sum_{i=1}^{\tau} \rho_i^2 \leq 4 \sum_{i=1}^{\tau} \beta_i^2 \sigma_i^2 \leq 4\beta_\tau^2 \sum_{i=1}^{\tau} \sigma_i^2 = \mathcal{O}(\beta_\tau^2 \gamma_\tau). \tag{10.24}$$

42 We have $M = 1$ as a bound on $K(x, x)$ according to our common assumptions (p. 224).

From left-to-right, we plug in (10.23), note that $\{\beta_i\}$ is nondecreasing (10.21), and appeal to the information capacity bound on the sum of predictive variances (10.18).[42] Plugging in β_τ and appealing to the Cauchy–Schwartz inequality gives

$$R_\tau = \mathcal{O}^*(\sqrt{\tau \gamma_\tau \log |\mathcal{X}|}) \tag{10.25}$$

with probability at least $1 - \delta$.

Extending to continuous domains

The above analysis can be extended to continuous domains via a discretization argument. The proof is technical, but the technique is often useful in other settings, so we provide a sketch of a general argument:

assumption: $\mathcal{X}$ is convex and compact

- We assume that the domain $\mathcal{X} \subset [0, m]^d$ is convex and compact.

assumption: f is Lipschitz continuous

- We assume that the objective function is continuously differentiable. As $\mathcal{X}$ is compact, this implies the objective is in fact *Lipschitz* continuous with some Lipschitz constant L.

- Purely for the sake of analysis, in each iteration i, we discretize the domain with a grid $\mathcal{X}_i \subset \mathcal{X}$; these grids become finer over time and eventually dense. The exact details vary, but it is typical to take a regular grid in $[0, m]^d$ with spacing on the order of $\mathcal{O}(1/i^c)$ (for some constant c not depending on d) and take the intersection with $\mathcal{X}$. The resulting discretizations have size $\log |\mathcal{X}_i| = \mathcal{O}(d \log i)$.

- We note that Lipschitz continuity of f allows us to extend valid confidence intervals for the function values at $\mathcal{X}_i$ to all of $\mathcal{X}$ with only slight inflation. Namely, for any $x \in \mathcal{X}$, let $[x]_i$ denote the closest point to x in $\mathcal{X}_i$. By Lipschitz continuity, a valid confidence interval at $[x]_i$ can be extended to one at x with inflation on the order of $\mathcal{O}(L/i^c)$ due to the discretizations becoming finer over time.

- With this intuition, we design a confidence parameter sequence $\{\beta_i\}$ guaranteeing that the function values on both the grids $\{\mathcal{X}_i\}$ and at the points chosen by the algorithm $\{x_i\}$ always lie in their respective confidence intervals with high probability. As everything is discrete, we can generally start from a guarantee such as (10.21), replace $|\mathcal{X}|$ with $|\mathcal{X}_i|$, and fiddle with constants as necessary.

- Finally, we proceed as in the finite case. We bound the instantaneous regret in each iteration in terms of the width of the confidence intervals of the selected points, noting that any extra regret due to discretization shrinks rapidly as $\mathcal{O}(L/i^c)$ and, if we are careful, does not affect the asymptotic regret. Generally the resulting bound simply replaces any factors of $\log |\mathcal{X}|$ with factors of $\log |\mathcal{X}_i| = \mathcal{O}(d \log i)$.

For the particular case of bounding the Bayesian regret of GP-UCB, we can effectively follow the above argument but must deal with some nuance regarding the Lipschitz constant of the objective function. First, note that if the covariance function of our Gaussian process is smooth enough, its sample paths will be continuously differentiable[43] and Lipschitz continuous – but with *random* Lipschitz constant. SRINIVAS et al. proceed by assuming that the covariance function is sufficiently smooth to ensure that the Lipschitz constant has an exponential tail bound of the following form:

$$\forall \lambda > 0: \ \Pr(L > \lambda) \leq da \exp(-\lambda^2/b^2), \quad (10.26)$$

where $a, b > 0$; this allows us to derive a high-probability upper bound on L. We will say more about this assumption shortly.

SRINIVAS et al. showed that, under this assumption, a slight modification of the confidence parameter sequence from the finite case[44] (10.21) is sufficient to ensure

$$R_\tau = \mathcal{O}^*(\sqrt{d\tau\gamma_\tau}) \quad (10.27)$$

with high probability. Thus, assuming the Gaussian process sample paths are smooth enough, the cumulative regret of GP-UCB on continuous domains grows at rate comparable to the discrete case.

Plugging in the information capacity bounds in (10.15–10.16) and dropping the $\sqrt{d}$ factor, we have the following high-probability regret

---

step 1: discretize the domain with a sequence of increasingly fine grids $\{X_i\}$

size of discretizations: $\log |\mathcal{X}_i| = \mathcal{O}(d \log i)$

step 2: valid confidence intervals on $\mathcal{X}_i$ can be extended to all of $\mathcal{X}$ with slight inflation

inflation in iteration i: $\mathcal{O}(L/i^c)$

step 3: find a confidence parameter sequence $\{\beta_i\}$ guaranteeing validity on $\{x_i\}$ and $\{\mathcal{X}_i\}$

step 4: proceed as in the discrete case

sample path differentiability: § 2.6, p. 30

43 Hölder continuity of the derivative process covariance is sufficient; this holds for the Matérn family with $\nu > 1$.

44 Specifically, SRINIVAS et al. took:

$$\beta_i^2 = 2\log\left(\frac{2i^2\pi^2}{3\delta}\right) + 2d\log\left(i^2 dbm\sqrt{\log(4da/\delta)}\right).$$

The resulting bound holds with probability at least $1 - \delta$.

bounds for specific covariance functions. For the Matérn covariance, we have

$$R_\tau = \mathcal{O}^*\big(\tau^\alpha (\log \tau)^\beta\big), \quad \alpha = \frac{v+d}{2v+d}, \quad \beta = \frac{2v}{2v+d}, \qquad (10.28)$$

and for the squared exponential we have

$$R_\tau = \mathcal{O}^*\big(\sqrt{\tau(\log \tau)^d}\big). \qquad (10.29)$$

The growth is sublinear for all values of the smoothness parameter v, so GP-UCB achieves no regret with high probability for the Matérn family.

The Lipschitz tail bound condition

Finally, we address the exponential tail bound assumption on the Lipschitz constant (10.26). Despite its seeming strength in controlling the behavior of sample paths, it is actually a fairly weak assumption on the Gaussian process. In fact, all that is needed is that sample paths be continuously differentiable. In this case, each coordinate of the gradient, $f_i = \partial f / \partial x_i$, is a sample path continuous Gaussian process. By compactness, each f_i is then almost surely bounded on $\mathcal{X}$. Now the Borell–TIS inequality ensures that for any $\lambda > 0$ we have:[45]

$$\Pr\big(\max |f_i| > \lambda\big) \le 4\exp(-\lambda^2/b_i^2), \quad b_i = 2\sqrt{2}\,\mathbb{E}\big[\max |f_i|\big]. \quad (10.30)$$

45 A. W. VAN DER VAART and J. A. WELLNER (1996). *Weak Convergence and Empirical Processes with Applications to Statistics.* Springer–Verlag. [proposition A.2.1]

Taking a union bound then establishes a bound of the desired form (10.26). In particular, this argument applies to the Matérn covariance with $v > 1$, which has continuously differentiable sample paths. Thus GP-UCB can achieve sublinear cumulative regret for all but the roughest of sample paths.

However, the bound in (10.30) does not immediately lead to an algorithm we can realize in practice, as the expected extremum $\mathbb{E}[\max |f_i|]$ is difficult to compute (or even bound). Things simplify considerably if sample paths are *twice* differentiable, in which case GHOSAL and ROY showed how to derive bounds of the above form (10.30) for each of the coordinates of the gradient process with *explicitly* computable constants,[46] yielding a practical algorithm for the Matérn covariance with $v > 2$.

46 S. GHOSAL and A. ROY (2006). Posterior Consistency of Gaussian Process Prior for Nonparametric Binary Regression. *The Annals of Statistics* 34(5):2413–2429. [lemma 5]

Fortunately, intricate arguments regarding the objective function's Lipschitz constant are only necessary due to its randomness in the Bayesian setting. In the frequentist setting, where f is in some RKHS ball $\mathcal{H}_K[B]$, we can immediately derive a *hard* upper bound L in terms of K and B.[47]

47 N. DE FREITAS et al. (2012a). Regret Bounds for Deterministic Gaussian Process Bandits. arXiv: 1203.2177 [cs.LG]. [lemma 1]

Bounding the expected regret

Without too much effort, we may augment the high-probability bound presented above with a corresponding bound on the expected regret (10.6). However, note that the high-probability regret bound is stronger in the sense that we can guarantee good performance not only on average but also in extremely "unlucky" scenarios as well.

For simplicity, let us begin again with a finite domain $\mathcal{X}$. Consider a run of the GP-UCB algorithm in (10.19) for some confidence parameter sequence $\{\beta_i\}$ to be determined shortly. Let $\{x_i\}$ be the sequence of selected points and let x^* be a global optimum of f. Define

$$u_i = \mu_i + \beta_i \sigma_i; \qquad u_i^* = \mu_i^* + \beta_i \sigma_i^*$$

to be, respectively, the upper confidence bound associated with x_i at the time of its selection and the upper confidence bound associated with x^* at the same time. Since the algorithm always maximizes the upper confidence bound in each iteration, we always have $u_i \leq u_i^*$. This allows us to bound the expected regret as follows:

$$\mathbb{E}[R_\tau] = \sum_{i=1}^{\tau} \mathbb{E}[f^* - \phi_i] \leq \sum_{i=1}^{\tau} \mathbb{E}[f^* - u_i^*] + \sum_{i=1}^{\tau} \mathbb{E}[u_i - \phi_i], \quad (10.31)$$

where we have added $u_i - u_i^* \geq 0$ to each term and rearranged.

In their analysis of the Gaussian process Thompson sampling algorithm (discussed below), RUSSO and VAN ROY showed how to bound each of the terms on the right-hand side. First, they show that the confidence parameter sequence (compare with the analogous and spiritually equivalent sequence used above (10.21))

$$\beta_i^2 = 2\log\left(\frac{(i^2+1)|\mathcal{X}|}{\sqrt{2\pi}}\right)$$

is sufficient to bound the first term by a constant: $\sum_i \mathbb{E}[f^* - u_i^*] \leq 1$.[48] The second term can then be bounded in terms of the information capacity following our previous discussion (10.18, 10.24):[49]

$$\sum_{i=1}^{\tau} \mathbb{E}[u_i - \phi_i] = \sum_{i=1}^{\tau} \beta_i \sigma_i \leq \beta_\tau \sum_{i=1}^{\tau} \sigma_i = \mathcal{O}^*(\sqrt{\tau \gamma_\tau \log|\mathcal{X}|}). \quad (10.32)$$

As before, we may extend this result to the continuous case via a discretization argument to prove $\mathbb{E}[R_\tau] = \mathcal{O}^*(\sqrt{d\tau\gamma_\tau})$, matching the high-probability bound (10.27).[50]

Thompson sampling

RUSSO and VAN ROY developed a general approach for transforming Bayesian regret bounds for a wide class of UCB-style algorithms into regret bounds for analogous Thompson sampling algorithms.[51]

Namely, consider a UCB policy selecting a sequence of points $\{x_i\}$ for observation by maximizing a sequence of "upper confidence bounds," which here can be *any* deterministic functions of the observed data, regardless of their statistical validity. Let $\{u_i\}$ be the sequence of upper confidence bounds associated with the selected points at the time of their selection, and let $\{u_i^*\}$ be the sequence of upper confidence bounds associated with a given global optimum, x^*.

48 This is again a consequence of the rapidly decaying tails of the Gaussian distribution; note that $f^* - u_i^*$ has distribution

$$\mathcal{N}(-\beta_i \sigma_i^*, (\sigma_i^*)^2).$$

As β_i increases without bound, this term will eventually be *negative* with overwhelming probability.

49 $u_i - \phi_i$ has distribution $\mathcal{N}(\beta_i \sigma_i, \sigma_i^2)$.

50 Although used for Thompson sampling, the discretization argument used in the below reference suffices here as well:

K. KANDASAMY et al. (2018). Parallelised Bayesian Optimisation via Thompson Sampling. *AISTATS 2018.* [appendix, theorem 11]

Thompson sampling: § 7.9, p. 148, § 8.7, p. 176

51 D. RUSSO and B. VAN ROY (2014). Learning to Optimize via Posterior Sampling. *Mathematics of Operations Research* 39(4):1221–1243.

Now consider a corresponding Thompson sampling policy selecting $x_i \sim p(x^* \mid \mathcal{D}_{i-1})$. Note that, given the observed data, x_i and x^* are identically distributed by design; because the upper confidence bounds are deterministic functions of the observed data, u_i and u_i^* are thus identically distributed as well. This allows us to express the expected cumulative regret of the Thompson sampling policy entirely in terms of the upper confidence bounds:

$$\mathbb{E}[R_\tau] = \sum_{i=1}^{\tau} \mathbb{E}[f^* - u_i^*] + \sum_{i=1}^{\tau} \mathbb{E}[u_i - \phi_i]. \tag{10.33}$$

This is of the exactly same form as the bound derived above for GP–UCB (10.31), leading immediately to a regret bound for GP-TS matching that for GP-UCB (10.32):

$$\mathbb{E}[R_\tau] = \mathcal{O}^*(\sqrt{\tau \gamma_\tau \log|\mathcal{X}|}); \tag{10.34}$$

once again, we may extend this result to the continuous case to derive a bound matching that for GP-UCB (10.27).[52]

52 K. KANDASAMY et al. (2018). Parallelised Bayesian Optimisation via Thompson Sampling. *AISTATS 2018*.

Upper bounds on simple regret

We may use the bound on simple regret in terms of the average regret in (10.4) to derive bounds on the simple regret of GP-UCB and GP-TS policies. Dropping dependence on the domain size,[53] we have

$$r_\tau \leq \frac{R_\tau}{\tau}$$

53 There is an additional multiplicative factor of $\sqrt{\log|\mathcal{X}|}$ in the finite case and $\sqrt{d}$ in the continuous case.

$$r_\tau = \mathcal{O}^*\left(\sqrt{\gamma_\tau / \tau}\right)$$

for both algorithms, where this is to be understood as either a high-probability (GP-UCB) or expected-case (GP-UCB, GP-TS) result.

Plugging in the information capacity bounds (10.15–10.16), we have the following bounds for the simple regret for specific covariance functions. For the Matérn covariance in dimension d, we have

$$r_\tau = \mathcal{O}^*\left(\tau^\alpha (\log \tau)^\beta\right), \quad \alpha = -\frac{\nu}{2\nu + d}, \quad \beta = \frac{2\nu}{2\nu + d},$$

and for the squared exponential we have

$$r_\tau = \mathcal{O}^*\left(\sqrt{(\log \tau)^d / \tau}\right).$$

Lower bounds and tightness of existing algorithms

We have now derived upper bounds on the regret of particular Bayesian optimization algorithms in the Bayesian setting with noise. A natural question is whether we can derive corresponding algorithm-agnostic *lower* regret bounds establishing the fundamental difficulty of optimization in this setting, which might hint at how much room for improvement there may be.

Lower bounds on Bayesian regret are not easy to come by. As we will see, the frequentist setting offers considerable flexibility in deriving

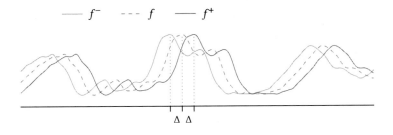

$$— f^- \quad --- f \quad — f^+$$

$$\Delta \quad \Delta$$

Figure 10.4: A sketch of SCARLETT's proof strategy. Given access to a reference function f, which of its translations by Δ, f^- or f^+ is the objective function?

lower bounds, as we can construct explicit *objective functions* in a given RKHS, then prove that they are difficult to optimize. In the Bayesian setting, the objective function is random, so we must instead seek explicit *distributions* over objective functions with enough structure that we can bound the expected regret, a much more challenging task.

That said, nontrivial lower bounds have been derived in this setting, most notably on the unit interval $\mathcal{X} = [0, 1]$. Under the assumption of a stationary Gaussian process with twice differentiable sample paths, SCARLETT demonstrated the following high-probability lower bound on the expected cumulative regret of any optimization algorithm:[54]

$$\mathbb{E}[R_\tau] = \Omega(\sqrt{\tau}). \tag{10.35}$$

This result is as about as good as we could hope for, as it matches the lower bound for optimizing *convex* functions.[55]

The key idea behind this result is to identify multiple plausible objective functions with identical distributions such that an optimization algorithm is prone to "prefer the wrong function," and in doing so, incur high regret. To illustrate the construction, we imagine an objective function on the unit interval is generated *indirectly* by the following process. We first realize an initial sample path f on the larger domain $[-\Delta, 1+\Delta]$, for some $\Delta > 0$.[56] We then take the objective function to be one of the following translations of f with equal probability:

$$f^+ : x \mapsto f(x+\Delta); \qquad f^- : x \mapsto f(x-\Delta). \tag{10.36}$$

As the prior process is assumed to be stationary, this procedure does not change the distribution of the objective function.

To proceed, we consider optimization of the generated objective *given access to the initial reference function f.*[57] We now frame optimization in terms of using a sequence of noisy observations to determine which of the two possible translations (10.36) represents the objective function; see Figure 10.4. *Fano's inequality,*[58] an information-theoretic lower bound on error probability in adaptive hypothesis testing, then allows us to show that there is a significant probability that the data collected by *any* algorithm have better cumulative regret for the *wrong* translation. Finally, we may use assumed statistical properties of the objective function to show that when this happens, the cumulative regret is significant.[59]

On the rougher side of the spectrum, WANG et al. used the same proof strategy to bound the expected regret – both simple and cumulative – of

54 J. SCARLETT (2018). Tight Regret Bounds for Bayesian Optimization in One Dimension. *ICML 2018.*

55 O. SHAMIR (2013). On the Complexity of Bandit and Derivative-Free Stochastic Convex Optimization. *COLT 2013.*

56 This introduces the additional minor requirement that the covariance function be defined on this larger domain.

57 This is a so-called *genie argument:* as the extra information (provided by a "genie") can be ignored, it cannot possibly impede optimization.

58 J. SCARLETT and V. CEVHAR (2021). An Introductory Guide to Fano's Inequality with Applications in Statistical Estimation. In: *Information-Theoretic Methods in Data Science.*

59 Specifically, we need that the global maximum of the reference function is unlikely to be "pushed off the edge" of the domain during translation, and that sample paths are likely to have locally quadratic behavior in a neighborhood of the global optimum. The lower bound on regret then holds with probability depending on these events. For more discussion, see:

N. DE FREITAS et al. (2012b). Exponential Regret Bounds for Gaussian Process Bandits with Deterministic Observations. *ICML 2012.*

60 Z. WANG et al. (2020b). Tight Regret Bounds for Noisy Optimization of a Brownian Motion. arXiv: 2001.09327 [cs.LG].

any algorithm maximizing a (nondifferentiable) sample path of Brownian motion (from the Wiener process) on the unit interval:[60]

$$\mathbb{E}[r_\tau] = \Omega(1/\sqrt{\tau \log \tau}); \qquad \mathbb{E}[R_\tau] = \Omega(\sqrt{\tau/\log \tau}). \qquad (10.37)$$

Both WANG et al. and SCARLETT also described straightforward, but not necessarily practical, optimization algorithms to provide corresponding upper bounds on the unit interval. The algorithms are based on a simple branch-and-bound scheme whereby the domain is adaptively partitioned based on confidence bounds computed from available data. For relatively smooth sample paths,[61] SCARLETT's algorithm achieves cumulative regret

61 Again $\nu > 2$ is sufficient for the Matérn family.

$$\mathbb{E}[R_\tau] = \mathcal{O}(\sqrt{\tau \log \tau})$$

with high probability. This is within a factor of $\sqrt{\log \tau}$ of the corresponding lower bound (10.35), so there is not too much room for improvement on the unit interval. Note that both GP-UCB and GP-TS with the squared exponential covariance match this rate up to logarithmic factors (10.29), but SCARLETT's algorithm is better for the Matérn covariance for $\nu > 2$ (10.28) (as assumed in the analysis). For Brownian motion sample paths, WANG et al. established the following upper bounds:

$$\mathbb{E}[r_\tau] = \mathcal{O}(\log \tau/\sqrt{\tau}); \qquad \mathbb{E}[R_\tau] = \mathcal{O}(\sqrt{\tau} \log \tau), \qquad (10.38)$$

which are within a factor of $(\log \tau)^{3/2}$ of the corresponding lower bounds (10.37), again fairly tight.

10.5   WORST-CASE REGRET WITH OBSERVATION NOISE

We now turn our attention to worst-case (frequentist) results analogous to the expected-case (Bayesian) results discussed in the previous section. Here we no longer reason about the objective function as a sample path from a Gaussian process, but rather as a fixed, but unknown function lying in some reproducing kernel Hilbert space $\mathcal{H}_K$ with norm bounded by some constant B (10.11). We also replace the assumption of independent Gaussian observation errors with somewhat more flexible and agnostic conditions. The goal is then to bound the worst-case (simple or cumulative) regret (10.7) of a given algorithm when applied to such a function, which we will notate with $\bar{r}_\tau[B]$ and $\bar{R}_\tau[B]$, respectively.

worst-case regret on $\mathcal{H}_K[B]$: $\bar{r}_\tau[B]$, $\bar{R}_\tau[B]$

62 Recall that sample paths of a centered Gaussian process with covariance K do *not* lie inside $\mathcal{H}_K$; see p. 219.

Compared with the analysis of Bayesian regret, the analysis of worst-case regret is complicated by model misspecification, as the model assumptions underlying the Bayesian optimization algorithms are no longer valid.[62] We must therefore seek other methods of analysis.

Common assumptions

assumption: $f \in \mathcal{H}_K[B]$
assumption: $\mathcal{X}$ is compact

In this section, we will assume that the objective function $f: \mathcal{X} \to \mathbb{R}$, where $\mathcal{X}$ is compact, lies in a reproducing kernel Hilbert space corresponding to covariance function K and has bounded norm: $f \in \mathcal{H}_K[B]$

(10.11). As in the previous section, we will also assume that the covariance function is continuous and bounded on $\mathcal{X}$: $K(x, x) \leq 1$.

To model observations, we will assume that a sequence of observations $\{y_i\}$ at $\{x_i\}$ are corrupted by additive noise, $y_i = \phi_i + \varepsilon_i$, and that the distribution of the errors satisfies mild regularity conditions. First, we will assume each ε_i has mean zero conditioned on its history:

$$\mathbb{E}[\varepsilon_i \mid \boldsymbol{\varepsilon}_{<i}] = 0,$$

where $\boldsymbol{\varepsilon}_{<i}$ is the vector of errors occurring before time i. We will also make assumptions regarding the scale of the errors. The most typical assumption is that the distribution of each ε_i is σ_n-sub-Gaussian conditioned on its history, that is, the tail of the conditional distribution shrinks at least as quickly as a Gaussian distribution with variance σ_n^2:

$$\forall c > 0\colon\ \Pr\big(|\varepsilon_i| > c \mid \boldsymbol{\varepsilon}_{<i}\big) \leq 2\exp\big(-\tfrac{1}{2}c^2/\sigma_n^2\big).$$

This condition is satisfied, for example, by a distribution bounded on the interval $[-\sigma_n, \sigma_n]$ and by any Gaussian distribution with standard deviation of at most σ_n.

Complementary with the above assumptions, the Bayesian optimization algorithms that we will analyze model the function with the centered Gaussian process $\mathcal{GP}(f; \mu \equiv 0, K)$ and assume independent Gaussian observation noise with scale σ_n.

Upper confidence bound and Thompson sampling

Sublinear bounds on cumulative regret have been established for both the Gaussian process upper confidence bound (GP-UCB) and Thompson sampling (GP-TS) algorithms in this setting, albeit with somewhat slower convergence rates that in the Bayesian setting. However, more complex algorithms built on similar ideas are able to close this gap, as we will discuss shortly.

The primary proof strategy in this setting is to bound the deviation of the Gaussian process posterior mean used in the algorithm from the objective function in the assumed RKHS. A prototypical result is to show that for some sequence of confidence parameters $\{\beta_i\}$, the confidence interval assumption (10.20) is universally valid with high probability:

$$\phi \in [\mu - \beta_i\sigma, \mu + \beta_i\sigma]. \tag{10.39}$$

This would then allow us to bound the cumulative regret in terms of the information capacity following our previous analysis.

The strongest known result of this form was derived by ABBASI-YADKORI in the context of regression[63] and later applied in the context of optimization by CHOWDHURY and GOPALAN.[64] Namely, under our common assumptions for this section and the assumption of σ_n-sub-Gaussian errors, the following confidence parameter sequence yields universally valid confidence intervals with probability at least $1 - \delta$:

$$\beta_i = B + \sigma_n\sqrt{2\gamma_{i-1} + 2\log(1/\delta)}. \tag{10.40}$$

Margin notes

assumption: $K(x, x) \leq 1$ is bounded

assumption: errors have zero mean conditioned on their history

assumption: scale of errors is limited

sub-Gaussian distribution

finite-domain Bayesian analysis of GP-UCB: p. 225

63 Y. ABBASI-YADKORI (2012). *Online Learning for Linearly Parameterized Control Problems.* Ph.D. thesis. University of Alberta. [theorem 3.11, remark 3.13]

64 S. R. CHOWDHURY and A. GOPALAN (2017). On Kernelized Multi-Armed Bandits. *ICML 2017.* [theorem 2]

65 If we wish to retain explicit dependence on the RKHS norm B, we have

$$\bar{R}_\tau[B] = \mathcal{O}^*\left(\sqrt{\tau \gamma_\tau}(B + \sqrt{\gamma_\tau})\right).$$

extending to continuous domains with a discretization argument: p. 226

66 S. R. CHOWDHURY and A. GOPALAN (2017). On Kernelized Multi-Armed Bandits. *ICML 2017*.

67 S. VAKILI et al. (2021c). Open Problem: Tight Online Confidence Intervals for RKHS Elements. *COLT 2021*.

68 A wider family of light-tailed noise distributions was also considered.

69 S. VAKILI et al. (2021a). Optimal Order Simple Regret for Gaussian Process Bandits. *NeurIPS 2021*. [theorem 1]

70 If $\mathcal{X}$ is finite, we can ensure universally valid confidence intervals at all times with probability $1 - \delta$ as in (10.21):

$$\beta_i = B + \sigma_n \sqrt{2 \log(i^2 \pi^2 |\mathcal{X}|/6\delta)}.$$

For continuous domains, we can again rely on discretization arguments. For a convex and compact domain $\mathcal{X} \subset R^d$ coupled with a covariance function in the Matérn family with $\nu > 1$, we may take:

$$\beta_i = B + \sigma_n \sqrt{d \log(i/\delta)}.$$

Unfortunately, these confidence parameters are *much* larger than needed in the Bayesian setting (see (10.21) and footnote 44), and the resulting regret bounds suffer as a result. Following the same argument leading up to (10.24), we may show that, with high probability, the worst-case cumulative regret of GP-UCB is[65]

$$\bar{R}_\tau[B] = \mathcal{O}^*(\sqrt{\tau}\gamma_\tau); \tag{10.41}$$

the same bound holds for GP-TS with an additional factor of $\sqrt{d}$ stemming from a discretization argument.[66]

There is a gap on the order of $\sqrt{\gamma_\tau}$ between these bounds and the analogous bounds in the Bayesian setting (10.27), and for the Matérn family, the best known bounds on the information capacity (10.15–10.16) only guarantee sublinear cumulative regret when $d < 2\nu$. It is unclear whether this gap stems from inherent weakness of the GP-UCB and GP-TS algorithms in this setting or merely from weakness in their analysis to date, and there may be room for improvement by proving that a tighter confidence parameter sequence than above (10.40) would suffice for universally valid confidence intervals.[67]

Simple regret bounds in the nonadaptive setting

Although the best (yet) known worst-case regret bounds for the vanilla GP-UCB and GP-TS algorithms do not grow favorably compared with their Bayesian regret counterparts, several authors have been able to construct spiritually related algorithms that close this gap.

A common idea in the development of these algorithms is to carefully sever some of the dependence between the sequence of points observed throughout optimization $\{x_i\}$ and the corresponding observed values $\{y_i\}$. This may seem counterintuitive, as the power of Bayesian optimization algorithms surely stems from their adaptivity! However, injecting some independence allows us to appeal to significantly more powerful concentration results in their analysis.

The following result illustrates the power of nonadaptivity in this setting. Consider conditioning on a an arbitrary sequence of observation locations $\{x_i\}$ chosen *independently* of the corresponding values $\{y_i\}$. Under our common assumptions for this section and the assumption of σ_n-sub-Gaussian errors,[68] VAKILI et al. showed that for any $x \in \mathcal{X}$, the following confidence interval condition holds with probability at least $1 - \delta$:[69]

$$\phi \in [\mu - \beta\sigma, \mu + \beta\sigma]; \qquad \beta = B + \sigma_n \sqrt{2 \log(1/\delta)}. \tag{10.42}$$

Although this bound only holds for a fixed point at a fixed time, we may extend this result to hold at all points and at all times with only logarithmic inflation of the confidence parameter.[70] Comparing to CHOWDHURY and GOPALAN's corresponding result in the adaptive setting (10.40), the confidence parameter sequence here does *not* depend on the information capacity. Thus we can ensure dramatically tighter confidence intervals when observations are designed nonadaptively.

This result has enabled several strong convergence guarantees in the worst-case setting with noise. VAKILI et al., for example, were able to show that the simple policy of *uncertainty sampling* (also known as *maximum variance reduction*) achieves near-optimal *simple* regret in the worst case.[71] Uncertainty sampling designs each observation by maximizing the posterior predictive variance, which for a Gaussian process does not depend on the observed values (2.19). One insightful interpretation of uncertainty sampling is that, from the perspective of the Gaussian process used in the algorithm, it acts to greedily maximize the information about the objective function revealed by the observations (10.17) – such a policy is sometimes described as performing "pure exploration."

For typical (stationary) processes on typical (convex and compact) domains, uncertainty sampling designs observations seeking to, in a rough sense, cover the domain as evenly as possible; an example run is shown in the marginal figure. In light of the concentration result above, we might expect this space-filling behavior to guarantee that the maximum of the posterior mean cannot stray too far from the maximum of the objective function. VAKILI et al. showed that this is indeed the case for the Matérn family. Namely, under our shared assumptions for this section and the minor additional assumption that $\mathcal{X}$ is convex, the simple regret of uncertainty sampling is, with high probability, bounded by[72]

$$\bar{r}_\tau[B] = \mathcal{O}^*(\sqrt{d\gamma_\tau/\tau}).$$

This rate is within logarithmic factors of the best-known lower bounds for convergence in simple regret, as discussed later in this section.

Closing the cumulative regret bound gap

Although uncertainty sampling achieves near-optimal simple regret in the worst case, we cannot expect to meaningfully bound its *cumulative* regret due to its nonadaptive nature. However, the results discussed above have proven useful for building algorithms that do achieve near-optimal cumulative regret in the worst case. To make the best use of results such as VAKILI et al.'s toward this end, algorithm development becomes a careful balancing act of including enough adaptivity to ensure low cumulative regret while including enough independence to ensure that we can *prove* low cumulative regret.

LI and SCARLETT proposed and analyzed one relatively simple algorithm in this direction.[73] Given an observation budget of τ, we proceed by constructing a sequence of batch observations in a nonadaptive fashion. After each batch observation is resolved, we pause to derive the resulting confidence intervals from the observed data and eliminate any points from consideration whose upper confidence bound is dominated by the maximum *lower* confidence bound among the points remaining under consideration; see the marginal figure. This occasional elimination step is the only time the algorithm exhibits adaptive behavior – in fact, after every elimination step, the GP used in the algorithm is "reset" to the prior

71 This result uses the alternative definition of simple regret mentioned in footnote 5: the difference between the global maximum and the maximum of the posterior mean.

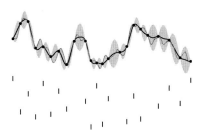

A sequence of 20 observations designed via a nonadaptive uncertainty sampling policy for the running example from Chapter 7.

72 S. VAKILI et al. (2021a). Optimal Order Simple Regret for Gaussian Process Bandits. *NeurIPS 2021*. [theorem 3, remark 2]

73 Z. LI and J. SCARLETT (2021). Gaussian Process Bandit Optimization with Few Batches. arXiv: 2110.07788 [stat.ML].

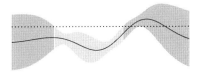

The lighter region of this Gaussian process has upper confidence bounds dominated by the maximum lower confidence bound (dashed line). Assuming the confidence bounds are valid with high probability, points in this region are unlikely to be optimal.

74   X. CAI et al. (2021). Lenient Regret and Good-Action Identification in Gaussian Process Bandits. *ICML 2021*. [§B.4]

75   The pruning scheme ensures that (if the last batch concluded after i steps) the global optimum is very likely among the remaining candidates, and thus the instantaneous regret incurred in each stage of the next batch will be bounded by $\mathcal{O}(\beta_i\sqrt{\gamma_i/i})$ with high probability.

76   M. VALKO et al. (2013). Finite-Time Analysis of Kernelised Contextual Bandits. *UAI 2013*.

77   S. SALGIA et al. (2020). A Computationally Efficient Approach to Black-Box Optimization Using Gaussian Process Models. arXiv: 2010. 13997 [stat.ML].

78   R. CAMILLERI et al. (2021). High-Dimensional Experimental Design and Kernel Bandits. *ICML 2021*.

needles in haystacks: see p. 216

79   J. SCARLETT et al. (2017). Lower Bounds on Regret for Noisy Gaussian Process Bandit Optimization. *COLT 2017*.

The bump function used in SCARLETT et al.'s lower bound analysis, the Fourier transform of a smooth function with compact support as in Figure 10.5.

80   This particular bump function is the prototypical smooth function with compact support:

$$x \mapsto \begin{cases} \exp\!\left(-\frac{1}{1-|x|^2}\right) & |x| < 1; \\ 0 & \text{otherwise.} \end{cases}$$

(on a smaller domain) by discarding all observed data. This ensures that every observation is always gathered nonadaptively.

The intervening batches are constructed by uncertainty sampling. The motivation behind this strategy is that we can bound the width of confidence intervals after i rounds of uncertainty sampling in terms of the information capacity; in particular, we can bound the maximum posterior standard deviation after i rounds of uncertainty sampling with:[74]

$$\max_{x \in \mathcal{X}} \sigma = \mathcal{O}(\sqrt{\gamma_i/i}). \qquad (10.43)$$

By combining this result with the concentration inequality in (10.42), and by periodically eliminating regions that are very likely to be suboptimal throughout optimization,[75] the authors were able to show that the resulting algorithm has worst-case regret

$$\bar{R}_\tau[B] = \mathcal{O}^*(\sqrt{d\tau\gamma_\tau}) \qquad (10.44)$$

with high probability, matching the regret bounds for GP-UCB and GP-TS in the Bayesian setting (10.27).

This is not the only result of this type; several other authors have been able to construct algorithms achieving similar worst-case regret bounds through other means.[76,77,78]

Lower bounds and tightness of existing algorithms

Lower bounds on regret are easier to come by in the frequentist setting than in the Bayesian setting, as we have considerable freedom to construct *explicit* objective functions that are provably difficult to optimize.

A common strategy to this end is to take inspiration from the "needle in a haystack" trick discussed earlier. We construct a large set of suitably well-behaved "needles" that have little overlap, then argue that there will always be some needle "missed" by an algorithm with insufficient budget to distinguish all the functions. Figure 10.5 shows a motivating example with four translations of a smooth bump function with height ε and mutually disjoint support. Given any set of three observations – regardless of how they were chosen – the cumulative regret for at least one of these functions would be 3ε.

This construction embodies the spirit of most of the lower bound arguments appearing in the literature. To yield a full proof, we must show how to construct a large number of suitable needles with bounded RKHS norm. For a *stationary* process, this can usually be accomplished by scaling and translating a suitable bump-shaped function to cover the domain. We also need to bound the regret of an algorithm given an input chosen from this set; here, we can keep the set of potential objectives larger than the optimization budget and appeal to pigeonhole arguments.

In the frequentist setting with noise, the strongest known lower bounds are due to SCARLETT et al.[79] The function class considered in the analysis was scaled and translated versions of a function similar to (in fact,

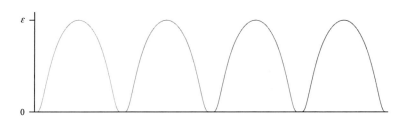

Figure 10.5: Four smooth objective functions with disjoint support.

precisely the Fourier transform of) the bump function in Figure 10.5;[80] this function has the advantage of having "nearly compact" support while having finite RKHS norm in the entire Matérn family. For optimization on the unit cube $\mathcal{X} = [0,1]^d$ with the Matérn covariance function, the authors were able to establish a lower bound on the cumulative regret of any algorithm of

$$\bar{R}_\tau[B] = \Omega(\tau^\alpha); \quad \alpha = \frac{v+d}{2v+d},$$

and for the squared exponential covariance, a lower bound of

$$\bar{R}_\tau[B] = \Omega\left(\sqrt{\tau(\log \tau)^d}\right).$$

These bounds are fairly tight – they are within logarithmic factors of the best-known upper bounds in the worst-case setting (10.15–10.16, 10.44); see also the corresponding Bayesian bounds (10.28–10.29).

SCARLETT et al. also provided lower bounds on the worst-case *simple* regret $\bar{r}_\tau[B]$, in terms of the expected time required to reach a given level of regret. Inverting these bounds in terms of the simple regret at a given time yields rates that are as expected in light of the relation in (10.4).

$r_\tau \leq \frac{R_\tau}{\tau}$

10.6   THE EXACT OBSERVATION CASE

The arguments outlined in the previous sections all ultimately depend on the information capacity of noisy observations of a Gaussian process. An upper bound on this quantity allows us to control the width of posterior confidence intervals through a pivotal result (10.18). After noting that the instantaneous regret of an upper confidence bound algorithm is in turn bounded by the width of these confidence intervals (10.23), we may piece together a bound on its cumulative regret (10.24).

Unfortunately, this line of attack breaks down with exact observations, as the information capacity of the now *deterministic* observation process diverges to infinity.[81] However, all is not lost – we can appeal to different techniques to find much *stronger* bounds on the width of confidence intervals induced by exact observations, and thereby establish much faster rates of convergence than in the noisy case.

Throughout this section, as in the previous two sections, we will assume that the domain $\mathcal{X} \subset \mathbb{R}^d$ is compact and that the covariance function is bounded by unity: $K(x,x) \leq 1$.

81 This can be seen by taking $\sigma_n \to 0$ in (10.17).

assumptions: $\mathcal{X}$ is compact, $K(x,x) \leq 1$ is bounded

maximum posterior standard deviation given exact observations at x, $\bar{\sigma}_{\mathbf{x}}$

82 We previously derived a bound of this form for uncertainty sampling in the noisy regime (10.43).

83 The literature on this topic is substantial, but the following references provide good entry points:

M. KANAGAWA et al. (2018). Gaussian Processes and Kernel Methods: A Review on Connections and Equivalences. arXiv: 1807.02582 [stat.ML]. [§ 5.2]

H. WENDLAND (2004). Scattered Data Approximation. Cambridge University Press. [chapter 11]

fill distance of observation locations x, $\delta_{\mathbf{x}}$

84 Carefully taking this limit yields the following bound for the squared exponential covariance. For sufficiently small $\delta_{\mathbf{x}}$, we have

$$\bar{\sigma}_{\mathbf{x}} \leq \delta_{\mathbf{x}}^{c/\delta_{\mathbf{x}}}$$

for some c not depending on x. Thus the rate of convergence increases as $\delta_{\mathbf{x}} \to 0$:

H. WENDLAND (2004). Scattered Data Approximation. Cambridge University Press. [theorem 11.22]

85 For an excellent survey on both maximin (sphere packing) and minimax (fill distance) optimal designs, see:

L. PRONZATO (2017). Minimax and Maximin Space-Filling Designs: Some Properties and Methods for Construction. Journal de la Société Française de Statistique 158(1):7–36.

86 We successively exhaust all combinations of dyadic rationals $\{i/2^n\}$ with increasing height $n = 0, 1, \ldots$

Bounding the posterior standard deviation

As in the noisy setting, a key idea in deriving regret bounds with exact observations is bounding the width of posterior confidence intervals (10.39) resulting from observations. In this light, let us consider the behavior of a Gaussian process $\mathcal{GP}(f; \mu, K)$ on an objective $f \colon \mathcal{X} \to \mathbb{R}$ as it is conditioned on a set of exact observations. Given some set of observation locations $\mathbf{x} \subset \mathcal{X}$, we seek to bound the *maximum* posterior standard deviation of the process:

$$\bar{\sigma}_{\mathbf{x}} = \max_{x \in \mathcal{X}} \sigma,$$

in terms of properties of x.[82] This would serve as a universal bound on the width of *all* credible intervals, allowing us to bound the cumulative regret of a UCB-style algorithm via previous arguments.

Thankfully, bounds of this type have enjoyed a great deal of attention, and strong results are available.[83] Most of these results bound the posterior standard deviation of a Gaussian process in terms of the *fill distance,* a measure of how densely a given set of observations fills the domain. For a set of observation locations $\mathbf{x} \subset \mathcal{X}$, its fill distance is defined to be

$$\delta_{\mathbf{x}} = \max_{x \in \mathcal{X}} \min_{x_i \in \mathbf{x}} |x - x_i|, \tag{10.45}$$

the largest distance from a point in the domain to the closest observation.

Intuitively, we should expect the maximum posterior standard deviation induced by a set of observations to shrink with its fill distance. This is indeed the case, and particularly nice results for the rate of this shrinkage are available for the Matérn family. Namely, for finite v, once the fill distance is sufficiently small (below a constant depending on the covariance but not x), we have

$$\bar{\sigma}_{\mathbf{x}} \leq c\delta_{\mathbf{x}}^{v}, \tag{10.46}$$

where the constant c does not depend on x. That is, once the observations achieve some critical density, the posterior standard deviation of the process shrinks rapidly with the fill distance, especially as sample paths become increasingly smooth in the limit $v \to \infty$.[84] This result will be instrumental in several results discussed below.

Optimizing fill distance

The question of *optimizing* the fill distance of a given number of points in compact subsets of $\mathbb{R}^d$ – so as to maximally strengthen the bound on prediction error above – is a major open question in geometry. Unfortunately, this problem is exceptionally difficult due to its close connection to the notoriously difficult problem of *sphere packing*.[85]

In the unit cube $\mathcal{X} = [0, 1]^d$, a simple grid strategy[86] achieves asymptotic fill distance $\mathcal{O}(\tau^{-1/d})$, and thus for a Matérn covariance, we can guarantee (10.46):

$$\bar{\sigma}_{\mathbf{x}} = \mathcal{O}(\tau^{-v/d}). \tag{10.47}$$

This will suffice for the arguments to follow.[87] However, this strategy may not be the best choice in practical settings, as the fill distance decreases sporadically by large jumps each time the grid is refined. An alternative with superior "anytime" performance would be a low-discrepancy sequence such as a Sobol or Halton sequence, which would achieve slightly larger (by a factor of $\log \tau$), but more smoothly decreasing, asymptotic fill distance.

Several sophisticated algorithms are also available for (approximately) optimizing the fill distance from a given *fixed* number of points.[85,88]

Worst-case regret with deterministic observations

We now turn our attention to specific results, beginning with bounds on the worst-case regret, where the analysis is somewhat simpler. As in the noisy setting, we assume that the objective function lies in the RKHS ball of radius B corresponding to the covariance function K used to model the objective function during optimization, $\mathcal{H}_K[B]$.

In this setting, we have the remarkable result that posterior confidence intervals with fixed confidence parameter B are *always* valid:[89]

$$\forall x \in \mathcal{X} : \phi \in [\mu - B\sigma, \mu + B\sigma]. \tag{10.48}$$

Combining this with the bound on standard deviation in (10.47) immediately shows that a simple grid strategy achieves worst-case simple regret[90]

$$\bar{r}_\tau[B] = \mathcal{O}(\tau^{-\nu/d})$$

for the Matérn covariance with smoothness ν. BULL provided a corresponding lower bound establishing that this rate is actually *optimal*: $\bar{r}_\tau[B] = \Theta(\tau^{-\nu/d})$.[91] As with previous results, the lower bound derives from an adversarial "needle in haystack" construction as in Figure 10.5.

This result is perhaps not as exciting as it could be, as it demonstrates that no adaptive algorithm can perform (asymptotically) better than grid search in the worst case. However, we may reasonably seek similar guarantees for algorithms that are also effective in practice. BULL was able to show that maximizing expected improvement yields worst-case simple regret

$$\bar{r}_\tau[B] = \mathcal{O}^*(\tau^{-\min(\nu,1)/d}),$$

which is near optimal for $\nu \leq 1$. BULL also showed that augmenting expected improvement with occasional random exploration akin to an ε-greedy policy improves its performance to near optimal for any finite smoothness:

$$\bar{r}_\tau[B] = \mathcal{O}^*(\tau^{-\nu/d}).$$

The added randomness effectively guarantees the fill distance of observations shrinks quickly enough that we can still rely on posterior contraction arguments, and this strategy could be useful for analyzing other policies.

87 We can extend this argument to any arbitrary compact domain $\mathcal{X} \subset \mathbb{R}^d$ by enclosing it in a cube.

88 Y. LYU et al. (2019). Efficient Batch Black-Box Optimization with Deterministic Regret Bounds. arXiv: 1905.10041 [cs.LG].

worst-case regret with noise: p. 232

89 M. KANAGAWA et al. (2018). Gaussian Processes and Kernel Methods: A Review on Connections and Equivalences. arXiv: 1807.02582 [stat.ML]. [corollary 3.11]

90 Here we use the alternative definition in footnote 5. As the confidence intervals (10.48) are always valid, f^* must always be in the (rapidly shrinking) confidence interval of whatever point maximizes the posterior mean.

91 A. D. BULL (2011). Convergence Rates of Efficient Global Optimization Algorithms. *Journal of Machine Learning Research* 12(88):2879–2904.

convergence rates for expected improvement

92 S. GRÜNEWÄLDER et al. (2010). Regret Bounds for Gaussian Process Bandit Problems. *AISTATS 2010*.

93 The upper bound is within a factor of $\sqrt{\log \tau}$ of WANG et al.'s upper bound for the *noisy* optimization of Brownian motion sample paths, where $\alpha = d = 1$ (10.38). The lower bound is identical to that case (10.37).

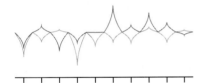

Samples from an example Gaussian process used in deriving GRÜNEWÄLDER et al.'s lower bound. Here 10 ($\frac{1}{2}$)-Hölder continuous "needles" are scaled and translated to cover the unit interval, with one centered on each tick mark. Each needle is then scaled by an independent normal random variable and summed, yielding a Gaussian process with the desired properties.

94 P. MASSART (2007). *Concentration Inequalities and Model Selection: Ecole d'Eté de Probabilités de Saint-Flour XXXIII – 2003*. Vol. 1896. Springer–Verlag.

uniqueness of global maxima: § 2.7, p. 34

95 N. DE FREITAS et al. (2012b). Exponential Regret Bounds for Gaussian Process Bandits with Deterministic Observations. *ICML 2012*.

Bayesian regret with deterministic observations

GRÜNEWÄLDER et al. proved bounds on the Bayesian regret in the exact observation case, although their results are only relevant for particularly rough objectives.[92] The authors considered sample paths of a Gaussian process on the unit cube $[0, 1]^d$ with Lipschitz continuous mean function and α-Hölder continuous covariance function. The latter is an exceptionally weak smoothness assumption: the Matérn covariance with parameter ν is Hölder continuous with $\alpha = \min(2\nu, 1)$, and any distinction in smoothness is lost beyond $\nu > 1/2$, where sample paths are not yet even differentiable. Under these assumptions, GRÜNEWÄLDER et al. proved the following bounds on the Bayesian simple regret, where the lower bound is not universal but rather achieved by a specific construction satisfying the assumptions:[93]

$$\mathbb{E}[r_\tau] = \Omega\big(\tau^{-c}/\sqrt{\log \tau}\big); \quad \mathbb{E}[r_\tau] = \mathcal{O}\big(\tau^{-c}\sqrt{\log \tau}\big); \quad c = -\frac{\alpha}{2d}.$$

The lower bound is achieved by an explicit Gaussian process with Hölder continuous covariance function whose "needle in a haystack" nature makes it difficult to optimize by any strategy. Specifically, the authors show how to cover the unit cube with 2τ disjoint and α-Hölder continuous "needles" of compact support. We may then create a Gaussian process by scaling each of these needles by an independent normal random variable and summing. This construction is perhaps most clearly demonstrated visually, and the marginal figure shows an example on the unit interval with $\tau = 5$ and $\alpha = 1/2$. As the needles are disjoint with independent heights, no policy with a budget of τ can determine more than half of the weights, and we must therefore pay a penalty in terms of expected simple regret.

The upper bound derives from analyzing the performance of a simple grid strategy via classical concentration inequalities.[94] It is remarkable that a nonadaptive strategy would yield such a small gap in regret compared to the corresponding lower bound, but this result is probably best understood as illustrating the inherent difficulty of optimizing rough functions rather than any inherent aptitude of grid search.

To underscore this remark, we may turn to a result of DE FREITAS et al., who showed that we may optimize sample paths of sufficiently smooth Gaussian processes with *exponentially* decreasing expected simple regret in the deterministic setting.[95] This result relies on a few technical properties of the Gaussian process in question, in particular that it has a unique global optimum and that it exhibit "nice" behavior in the neighborhood of the global optimum. A centered Gaussian process with covariance function in the Matérn family satisfies the required assumptions if $\nu > 2$.

The algorithm analyzed by the authors was a simple branch-and-bound policy based on GP-UCB, wherein the domain is recursively subdivided into finer and finer divisions. After each division, we identify the regions that could still contain the global optimum based on the current confidence intervals, then evaluate on these regions such that the fill distance (10.45) is sufficiently small before the next round of subdivision.

In this step, DE FREITAS et al. relied on the bound in (10.46) (with $\nu = 2$) to ensure that the confidence intervals induced by observed data shrink rapidly throughout this procedure.

At some point in this procedure, we will (with high probability) find ourselves having rejected all but the local neighborhood of the global optimum, at which point the assumed "nice" behavior of the sample path guarantees rapid convergence thereafter. Specifically, the authors demonstrate that at some point the *instantaneous* regret of this algorithm will converge exponentially:

$$\mathbb{E}[\rho_\tau] = \mathcal{O}\left(\exp\left(-\frac{c\tau}{(\log \tau)^{d/4}}\right)\right),$$

for some constant $c > 0$ depending on the process but not on τ. This condition implies rapid convergence in terms of simple regret as well (as we obviously have $r_\tau \leq \rho_\tau$) and *bounded* cumulative regret after we have entered the converged regime.[96]

Evidently optimization is *much* easier with deterministic observations than noisy ones, at least in terms of Bayesian regret. Intuitively, the reason for this discrepancy is that noisy observations may compel us to make repeated measurements in the same region in order to shore up our understanding of the objective function, whereas this is never necessary with exact observations.

10.7 THE EFFECT OF UNKNOWN HYPERPARAMETERS

We have now outlined a plethora of convergence results: upper bounds on the regret of specific algorithms and algorithm-agnostic lower bounds, in the expected and worst case, with and without observation noise. However, all of these results assumed *intimate* knowledge about the objective function being optimized: in Bayesian analysis, we assumed the objective is sampled from the prior used to model it, and for worst-case analysis, we assumed the objective lay in the corresponding RKHS. Of course, neither of these assumptions (especially the former!) may hold in practice. Further, in practice the model used to reason about the objective is typically inferred from observed data and constantly updated throughout optimization, but the analysis discussed thus far has assumed the model is not only perfectly informed, but also fixed.

It turns out that violations to these (rather implausible!) assumptions can be disastrous for convergence. For example, consider this prototypical Bayesian optimization algorithm: we model the objective function with an automatic relevance determination (ARD) version of a Matérn covariance function, learn its output (3.20) and length scales (3.25) via maximum likelihood estimation, and design observation locations by maximizing expected improvement. Although this setup has proven remarkably effective in practice,[97] BULL proved that it can actually fail miserably in the frequentist setting: we may construct functions in the RKHS of any such covariance function (that is, with any desired param-

96 This is not inconsistent with GRÜNEWÄLDER et al.'s lower bound: here we assume smoothness consistent with $\nu > 2$ in the Matérn family, whereas the adversarial Gaussian process constructed in the lower bound is only as smooth as $\nu = 1/2$.

Chapter 3: Modeling with Gaussian Processes, p. 45

automatic relevance determination: § 3.4, p. 56
ML estimation of hyperparameters: § 4.3, p. 73

97 J. SNOEK et al. (2012). Practical Bayesian Optimization of Machine Learning Algorithms. *NeurIPS 2012*.

Figure 10.6: The problem with estimating hyperparameters. Above: a function in the RKHS for the $\nu = 5/2$ Matérn covariance with unit norm. Below: a sample path from a Gaussian process with the same covariance. Unless we're lucky, we may never find the "hump" in the former function and thus may never build a reasonable belief regarding the objective.

98 A. D. BULL (2011). Convergence Rates of Efficient Global Optimization Algorithms. *Journal of Machine Learning Research* 12(88):2879–2904. [theorem 3]

99 M. LOCATELLI (1997). Bayesian Algorithms for One-Dimensional Global Optimization. *Journal of Global Optimization* 10(1):57–76.

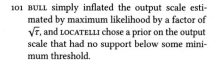

A function given by LOCATELLI for which expected improvement combined with a Wiener process prior will not converge if its output scale is marginalized. The first three observations are at the indicated locations; after iteration 3, the left-hand side of the domain is forever ignored.

100 Recall that sample paths almost surely do not lie in $\mathcal{H}_K$, assuming it is infinite dimensional, and see Figure 10.2 and the surrounding text.

101 BULL simply inflated the output scale estimated by maximum likelihood by a factor of $\sqrt{\tau}$, and LOCATELLI chose a prior on the output scale that had no support below some minimum threshold.

eters) that will "fool" this algorithm into having high regret with high probability.[98]

Estimation of hyperparameters can also cause problems with convergence in the Bayesian setting. For example, LOCATELLI considered optimization on the unit interval $\mathcal{X} = [0, 1]$ from exact observations using a Wiener process prior and maximizing expected improvement. In this relatively straightforward model, the only hyperparameter under consideration was an output scale (3.20). LOCATELLI showed that for a fixed output scale, this procedure converges for *all* continuous functions.[99] However, when the output scale is learned from data – even in a fully Bayesian manner where it is endowed with a prior distribution and marginalized in the predictive distribution – there are extremely simple (piecewise linear!) functions for which this algorithm does *not* recover the optimum. An example is shown in the margin.

In both of these examples, the roadblock to convergence when estimating hyperparameters is a mismatch between the objective function model used by the Bayesian optimization algorithm and the true objective. In the frequentist setting, there is an inherent tension as functions lying in the RKHS $\mathcal{H}_K$ are *not* representative of sample paths from the Gaussian process $\mathcal{GP}(f; \mu, K)$.[100]

Functions in the RKHS are much smoother than sample paths and may feature relatively "flat" regions of little variation, which may in turn lead to poorly fit models. See Figure 10.6 for a striking example. LOCATELLI's piecewise linear counterexample also reflects extreme model misspecification – the function is far too smooth to resemble Brownian motion in any statistical sense, and we should not be surprised that maximum likelihood estimation leads to an inconsistent algorithm.

A line of continuing work has been to derive *robust* algorithms that do not require perfect prior knowledge regarding the objective function in order to provide strong convergence guarantees. There are several ideas in this direction, all of which employ some mechanism to ensure that the space of objective functions considered by the algorithm does not ever become too "small." For example, both BULL and LOCATELLI addressed their counterexamples with schemes wherein the output scale used during optimization is never allowed to shrink so rapidly that true objective function is left behind.[101]

In the frequentist setting, one common strategy is to replace the assumption that the objective function lay in some particular RKHS with the assumption that it lay in some parametric family of RKHSes indexed by a set of hyperparameters. We then slowly expand the space of functions considered in the algorithm over the course of the algorithm such that the objective function is guaranteed to eventually – and forever thereafter – be well explained. In particular, consider augmenting an isotropic covariance function from the Matérn family K with an output scale (3.20) λ and a vector of length scales ℓ (3.25). We have the remarkable property that if a function f is in the RKHS ball of radius B (10.11) for some setting of these hyperparameters:

$$f \in \mathcal{H}_K[B; \lambda, \ell],$$

then the same function is *also* in the RKHS ball for any larger output scale and for any vector of shorter (as in the lexicographic order) length scales:

$$f \in \mathcal{H}_K[B; \lambda', \ell']; \quad \lambda' \geq \lambda; \quad \ell' \leq \ell.$$

With this in mind, a natural idea for deriving theoretical convergence results (but not necessarily for realizing a practical algorithm!) is to ignore any data-dependent scheme for setting hyperparameters and instead simply slowly increase the output scale and slowly decrease the length scales over the course of optimization, so that at some point any function lying in any such RKHS will eventually be captured. This scheme has been used to provide convergence guarantees for both expected improvement[102] and GP-UCB[103] with unknown hyperparameters.

102 Z. WANG and N. DE FREITAS (2014). Theoretical Analysis of Bayesian Optimization with Unknown Gaussian Process Hyper-Parameters. arXiv: 1406.7758 [stat.ML].

103 F. BERKENKAMP et al. (2019). No-Regret Bayesian Optimization with Unknown Hyperparameters. *Journal of Machine Learning Research* 20(50):1–24.

10.8 SUMMARY OF MAJOR IDEAS

- Convergence analysis for Bayesian optimization algorithms entails selecting a measure of optimization performance, a space of objective functions to consider, and deriving bounds on the asymptotic growth of the chosen performance measure on the chosen function space.

- Optimization performance is almost always assessed via one of two related notations of *regret*, both of which depend on the difference between the function value at measured locations and the global optimum.

simple and cumulative regret: § 10.1, p. 213

- Although tempting, the space of all continuous functions is too large to be of much interest in analysis: we may construct "needles in haystacks" to foil any algorithm by any amount. Instead, we may study spaces of objective functions with more plausible behavior. A Gaussian process model suggests two natural possibilities: sample paths from the process and the reproducing kernel Hilbert space (RKHS) associated with the process, the closure of the space of all possible posterior mean functions.

useful function spaces for studying convergence: § 10.2, p. 215

- Putting these pieces together, a Bayesian analysis of regret assumes the objective is a sample path from a Gaussian process and seeks asymptotic bounds on the expected regret (10.6). A frequentist analysis, on the other hand, assumes the objective function is a fixed, but unknown function

upper bounds:
Bayesian regret with noise: § 10.4, p. 224
worst-case regret with noise: § 10.5, p. 232
Bayesian regret without noise: § 10.6, p. 240

worst-case regret without noise: § 10.6, p. 239

this argument is carefully laid out for
Bayesian regret with noise in § 10.4, p. 225

information capacity: § 10.3, p. 222

bounding the posterior standard deviation
with exact observations: § 10.6, p. 238

lower bounds:
Bayesian regret with noise: § 10.4, p. 230
worst-case regret with noise, § 10.5, p. 236
Bayesian regret without noise: § 10.6, p. 240
worst-case regret without noise: § 10.6, p. 239

in a given RKHS and seeks asymptotic bounds on the worst-case regret (10.6).

- Most upper bounds on cumulative regret derive from a proof strategy where we identify some suitable set of predictive credible intervals that are universally valid with high probability. We may then argue that the cumulative regret is bounded in terms of the total width of these intervals. This strategy lends itself most naturally to analyzing the Gaussian process upper confidence bound (GP-UCB) policy, but also yields bounds for Gaussian process Thompson sampling (GP-TS) due to strong theoretical connections between these algorithms (10.33).

- In the presence of noise, a key quantity is the *information capacity,* the maximum information about the objective that can be revealed by a set of noisy observations. Bounds on this quantity yield bounds on the sum of predictive variances (10.18) and thus cumulative regret. With exact observations, we may derive bounds on credible intervals by relating the *fill distance* (10.45) of the observations to the maximum standard deviation of the process, as in (10.46).

- To derive lower bounds on Bayesian regret, we seek arguments limiting the rate at which Gaussian process sample paths can be optimized. For worst-case regret, we may construct explicit objective functions in a given RKHS and prove that they are difficult to optimize; here the "needles in haystacks" idea again proves useful.

EXTENSIONS AND RELATED SETTINGS

11

Thus far we have focused exclusively on a simple model problem (Algorithm 1.1): sequential optimization of a single objective with either a fixed evaluation budget or known observation costs. These assumptions are convenient for study and often reasonable in practice, but not all optimization scenarios fit neatly into this mold. Numerous extensions of this setup have received serious attention in the literature, and we will provide an overview of the most important of these in this chapter.

A running theme throughout this discussion will be adapting the decision-theoretic framework developed in Chapter 5 to derive policies for each of these new settings. In that chapter, we derived optimal optimization policies for our model problem, but we want to stress that the overarching approach to decision making can be extended to effectively any scenario.

Chapter 5: Decision Theory for Optimization, p. 87

Namely, we may derive an optimal policy for *any* sequential experimental design problem by following a simple recipe, an abstraction of our previous presentation:

general procedure for optimal policies

1. Identify the action space $\mathcal{A}$ of each decision.
2. Define preferences over outcomes with a utility function $u(\mathcal{D})$.
3. Identify the uncertain elements ψ relevant for each decision and determine how to compute the posterior belief given data, $p(\psi \mid \mathcal{D})$.
4. Compute the one-step marginal gain α_1 (5.8) for every action.[1]
5. Derive the optimal policy by induction on the horizon (5.15–5.16).

[1] Conveniently, this step also yields the one-step lookahead approximate policy as a side effect.

We will sketch how this scheme can be realized for notable optimization settings not yet addressed. Each will involve additional complexity in building effective policies due to additional complexity in the problem formulation, but we will demonstrate how we can adapt our existing tools by addressing the appropriate steps of the above general procedure. We will also provide a survey of proposed approaches to each of the optimization extensions we will consider, regardless of whether they are grounded in decision theory.

11.1 UNKNOWN OBSERVATION COSTS

In our discussion on cost-aware optimization, we assumed that observation costs were prescribed by a *known* cost function c, which enabled a simple mechanism for dynamic termination through careful accounting. However, in some scenarios the cost of an observation may not be known a priori, but rather only determined through the course of acquisition. These unknown costs reflect additional uncertainty that must be accounted for in policy design, as the utility of the returned data depends critically on their values. The natural solution is to perform inference about observation costs throughout optimization and use the resulting beliefs to guide our decisions, just as we do with an unknown

cost-aware optimization: § 5.4, p. 103
cost function, c

objective function. To adapt the cost-aware policies from Chapter 5 to this setting, we must revisit steps 3–4 of the above procedure.

Inference for unknown cost function

At a high level, reasoning about an unknown cost function given observations is no different from reasoning about an unknown objective function, and we can apply any suitable regression model for this task. The details of this inference will obviously depend on the situation, but we can outline one rather general approach.

First, let us define some notation for cost observations mirroring our notation for the objective function. Suppose that evaluation costs are determined, perhaps stochastically, by an underlying cost function $c\colon \mathcal{X} \to \mathbb{R}$ we wish to infer. Suppose further that an evaluation at a point x now returns both a measured value y, whose distribution depends on the corresponding objective function value $\phi = f(x)$, and an observation cost z, whose distribution depends on the corresponding cost function value $\kappa = c(x)$. We will accumulate these values throughout optimization in an augmented dataset of observations and their costs, $\mathcal{D} = (\mathbf{x}, \mathbf{y}, \mathbf{z})$.

If we can safely model cost observations as conditionally independent of objective observations given the chosen location, then we may follow our modeling strategy for the objective function and assume that each observed cost is generated by an observation model $p(z \mid x, \kappa)$. This allows for modeling a wide range of different scenarios, including nondeterministic costs.[2] Now we can proceed with inference about the cost function as usual. We choose a suitable (possibly parametric) prior process $p(c)$, which we condition on observed costs to form the posterior $p(c \mid \mathcal{D})$. Finally, we can form the predictive distribution for the cost of making an observation at an arbitrary point x by marginalizing the latent cost function:

$$p(z \mid x, \mathcal{D}) = \int p(z \mid x, \kappa)\, p(\kappa \mid x, \mathcal{D})\, \mathrm{d}\kappa.$$

In some applications, observation costs may be nontrivially correlated with the objective function. As an extreme example, consider a common problem in *algorithm configuration*,[3] where the goal is to design the parameters of an algorithm so as to minimize its expected running time. Here the cost of evaluating a proposed configuration might be reasonably defined to be proportional to its running time. Up to scaling, the observation cost is precisely equal to the objective! To model such correlations, we could define a joint prior $p(f, c)$ over the cost and objective functions, as well as a joint observation model $p(y, z \mid x, \phi, \kappa)$. We could then continue as normal, computing expected utilities with respect to the joint predictive distribution

$$p(y, z \mid x, \mathcal{D}) = \iint p(y, z \mid x, \phi, \kappa)\, p(\phi, \kappa \mid x, \mathcal{D})\, \mathrm{d}\phi\, \mathrm{d}\kappa,$$

a setup offering considerable flexibility in modeling.

Margin notes:

notation for observation costs

cost function, c

observed cost at x, z
value of cost function at x, $\kappa = c(x)$

cost observation model, $p(z \mid x, \kappa)$

cost function prior, $p(c)$
cost function posterior, $p(c \mid \mathcal{D})$

predictive distribution for cost, $p(z \mid x, \mathcal{D})$

---

2 As an example use case, suppose evaluating the objective requires train a machine learning model on cloud hardware with variable (e.g., spot) pricing.

3 The related literature is substantial, but a Bayesian optimization perspective can be found in:

F. HUTTER et al. (2011). Sequential Model-Based Optimization for General Algorithm Configuration. *LION 5*.

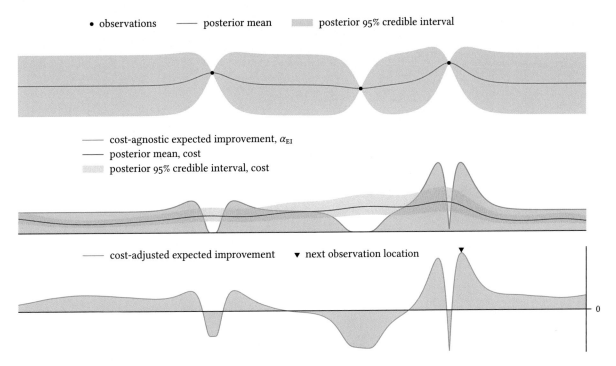

• observations   ——— posterior mean   ▨ posterior 95% credible interval

——— cost-agnostic expected improvement, α_{EI}
——— posterior mean, cost
▨ posterior 95% credible interval, cost

——— cost-adjusted expected improvement   ▼ next observation location

0

Figure 11.1: Decision making with uncertain costs. The middle panel shows the cost-agnostic expected improvement acquisition function along with a belief about an uncertain cost function, here assumed to be independent of the objective. The bottom panel shows the cost-adjusted expected improvement, marginalizing uncertainty in the objective and cost function (11.1).

Decision making with unknown costs

The approach outlined above suffices to maintain a belief about the potential cost of observations proposed throughout optimization, but we still must account for this uncertainty in the optimization policy. Thankfully, this is relatively straightforward in our decision-theoretic framework: we simply compute expected utility accounting for all relevant uncertainty as usual, here to include cost. Given an arbitrary dataset $\mathcal{D}$, now augmented with observation costs, consider the one-step expected marginal gain in utility:

$$\alpha_1(x; \mathcal{D}) = \mathbb{E}\big[u(\mathcal{D}_1) \mid x, \mathcal{D}\big] - u(\mathcal{D}).$$

Computing this expectation now requires integrating over both the unknown measurement y and the unknown observation cost z:

$$\mathbb{E}\big[u(\mathcal{D}_1) \mid x, \mathcal{D}\big] = \iint u\big(\mathcal{D} \cup \{x, y, z\}\big)\, p(y, z \mid x, \mathcal{D})\, dy\, dz. \qquad (11.1)$$

Although there is some slight added complexity in this computation, the optimal policy otherwise remains exactly as derived in (5.15–5.17).[4]

4 Of course, all nested expectations must also be taken with respect to unknown observation costs!

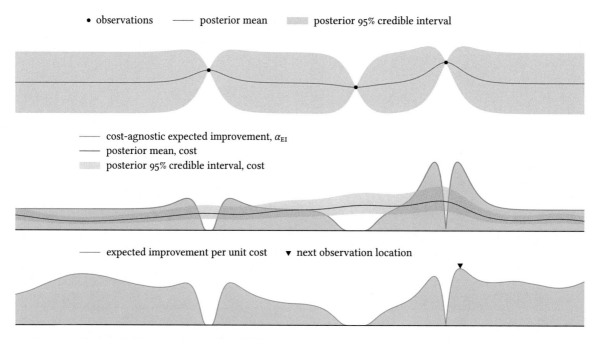

observations —— posterior mean ▦ posterior 95% credible interval

—— cost-agnostic expected improvement, α_{EI}
—— posterior mean, cost
▦ posterior 95% credible interval, cost

—— expected improvement per unit cost ▼ next observation location

Figure 11.2: Expected gain per unit cost. The middle panel shows the cost-agnostic expected improvement acquisition function along with a belief about an uncertain cost function, here assumed to be independent of the objective. The bottom panel shows the expected improvement per unit cost (11.1).

Figure 11.1 illustrates this policy, combining expected improvement with an independent uncertain cost function.

Expected gain per unit cost

Other approaches to dealing with unknown costs are also of course possible. SNOEK et al. proposed one notable option that has gained some popularity based on a heuristic common in *anytime algorithms*[5] – that is, algorithms that seek to maximize the instantaneous *rate* of improvement under the premise that the procedure may be terminated at any time.[6] The idea is simple: we can approximate the expected immediate marginal gain in utility *per unit cost* from an observation at x by

$$\mathbb{E}\left[\frac{u(\mathcal{D}_1) - u(\mathcal{D})}{\kappa} \mid x, \mathcal{D}\right] \approx \frac{\alpha_1(x; \mathcal{D})}{\mathbb{E}[\kappa \mid x, \mathcal{D}]}, \tag{11.2}$$

where α_1 is the expected gain in data utility. This is a first-order approximation to the expected gain-per-cost (which is not the ratio of their respective expectations, even in the independent case) that could be further refined if desired,[7] but works well in practice. The motivating example for SNOEK et al. was hyperparameter tuning of machine learning algorithms with unknown training costs, and the simple heuristic of maximizing "expected improvement per (expected) second" delivered

5 S. ZILBERSTEIN (1996). Using Anytime Algorithms in Intelligent Systems. *AI Magazine* 17(3):73–83.

6 J. SNOEK et al. (2012). Practical Bayesian Optimization of Machine Learning Algorithms. *NeurIPS 2012.*

7 Assuming independence between the objective and cost, a second-order expansion is just as easy to compute:

$$\frac{\alpha_1(x; \mathcal{D})}{\mathbb{E}[\kappa \mid x, \mathcal{D}]} + \frac{\alpha_1(x; \mathcal{D}) \operatorname{var}[\kappa \mid x, \mathcal{D}]}{\mathbb{E}[\kappa \mid x, \mathcal{D}]^3}.$$

promising results in their experiments. This heuristic has since appeared in other contexts.[8]

Figure 11.2 illustrates this policy with the sample example in Figure 11.2. The chosen decision closely matches the decision reached in Figure 11.1. It is interesting to compare the behavior of the two acquisition functions on both sides of the domain: whereas these regions are not especially exciting in the additive cost approach, they are appealing from the anytime view – although they are expected to give only modest improvement, they are also relatively inexpensive.

8 G. MALKOMES et al. (2016). Bayesian Optimization for Automated Model Selection. *NeurIPS 2016*.

11.2 CONSTRAINED OPTIMIZATION AND UNKNOWN CONSTRAINTS

Many optimization problems feature *constraints* restricting allowable solutions in a potentially complex, even uncertain manner. To this end we may extend our running optimization problem (1.1) to incorporate arbitrary constraints; a common formulation is:

$$x^* \in \arg\max_{x \in \mathcal{X}} f(x) \quad \text{subject to} \quad \forall i: g_i(x) \leq 0,$$

where the functions $\{g_i\}: \mathcal{X} \to \mathbb{R}$ comprise a set of inequality constraints. The subset of the domain where all constraints are satisfied is known as the *feasible region*:

inequality constraints, $\{g_i\}$

feasible region, $\mathcal{F}$

$$\mathcal{F} = \big\{ x \in \mathcal{X} \mid \forall i: g_i(x) \leq 0 \big\}.$$

In some situations, the value of some or all of the constraint functions may in fact be *unknown* a priori and only revealed through experimentation, complicating policy design considerably. As an example, consider a business optimizing the parameters of a service to maximize revenue, subject to constraints on customer response. If customer response is measured experimentally – for example via a focus group – we cannot know the feasibility of a proposed solution until after the objective has been measured, and even then only with limited confidence.

uncertain constraints

Further, even if the constraint functions can be computed exactly on demand, constrained optimization of an uncertain objective function is not entirely straightforward. In particular, an observation of the objective at an *infeasible* point may yield useful information regarding behavior on the feasible region, and could represent an optimal decision if that information were compelling enough. Thus simply restricting the action space to the feasible region may not be the best approach to policy design.[9] Instead, to derive effective policies for constrained optimization, we must reconsider steps 2–4 of our general approach.

9 R. B. GRAMACY and H. K. H. LEE (2011). Optimization under Unknown Constraints. In: *Bayesian Statistics 9*.

Modeling constraint functions

To allow for uncertain constraint functions, we begin by modeling the joint observation process of the objective and constraint functions. As with an uncertain cost function, we will assume that each observation of the objective is accompanied by some information regarding constraint satisfaction at the chosen location. Modeling this process is trivial when the constraint functions are known a priori, but otherwise may require some care.

It is difficult to provide concrete advice as information about constraint satisfaction may assume different forms, ranging from exact observation of the constraint functions to mere *binary* indicators of constraint satisfaction. In some situations, we may even face stochastic constraint processes where the feasibility of a given location is only achieved with some unknown probability. Fortunately, our discussion in the previous section regarding modeling an uncertain cost function is general enough to handle any of these situations by choosing an appropriate joint prior processes and observation model for the objective and constraint functions.

Defining a utility function

Next we must define a utility function appropriate for constrained optimization. Most of the utility functions in Chapter 6 can be suitably modified to this end.

simple reward: § 6.1, p. 112

We can realize a constrained version of simple reward by considering the expected utility of a risk-neutral terminal recommendation following optimization. As before, the resulting utility will depend on the action space used for the terminal decision. Perhaps the simplest option would be to limit the recommendation to the *feasible* observed locations (if known!):

$$u(\mathcal{D}) = \max_{x \in \mathbf{x} \cap \mathcal{F}} \mu_{\mathcal{D}}(x), \tag{11.3}$$

resulting in a natural adaptation of the simple reward (6.3). If the entire feasible region is known, we might instead allow recommending any feasible point, giving rise to an adaptation of the global simple reward (6.5):

$$u(\mathcal{D}) = \max_{x \in \mathcal{F}} \mu_{\mathcal{D}}(x). \tag{11.4}$$

Finally, in the case of uncertain constraints, we might limit our recommendation to those points believed to be feasible with sufficient confidence:[10]

10 M. A. GELBART et al. (2014). Bayesian Optimization with Unknown Constraints. *UAI 2014*.

$$u(\mathcal{D}) = \max_{x \in \mathcal{F}(\delta)} \mu_{\mathcal{D}}(x); \quad \mathcal{F}(\delta) = \big\{x \mid \Pr(x \in \mathcal{F} \mid \mathcal{D}) \geq 1 - \delta\big\}. \tag{11.5}$$

With some care, we could also modify other utility functions to be aware of a (possibly uncertain) feasible region, although the variations on simple reward above have received the most attention.

Deriving a policy

After selecting a model for the constraint functions and a utility function for our observations, we can derive a policy for constrained optimization following the standard procedure of induction on the decision horizon.

A policy that has received particular attention is the result of one-step lookahead with (11.3).[10,11,12] If we assume that the constraint functions are conditionally independent of the objective function given the observation location, then the one-step expected marginal gain in utility becomes

$$\alpha(x; \mathcal{D}) = \alpha'_{\text{EI}}(x; \mathcal{D}, \mu^*) \Pr(x \in \mathcal{F} \mid x, \mathcal{D}). \tag{11.6}$$

This is simply the expected improvement, measured with respect to the *feasible incumbent* value $\mu^* = u(\mathcal{D})$ (7.21, 11.3), weighted by the probability of feasibility, a natural policy we might arrive at via purely heuristic arguments. GELBART et al. point out this acquisition function has a slight pathology (also present with unconstrained expected improvement): the utility degenerates when no feasible observations are available, and (11.6) becomes ill-defined. In this case, the authors propose simply maximizing the probability of feasibility:

$$\alpha(x; \mathcal{D}) = \Pr(x \in \mathcal{F} \mid x, \mathcal{D}).$$

The expected feasible improvement (11.6) encodes a strong preference for evaluating on the feasible region only, and in the case where the constraint functions are all known, the resulting policy will *never* evaluate outside the feasible region.[13] This is a natural consequence of the one-step nature of the acquisition function: an infeasible observation cannot yield any immediate improvement to the utility (11.3) and thus cannot be one-step optimal. However, this behavior might be seen as undesirable given our previous comment that infeasible observations may yield valuable information about the objective on the feasible region.

If we wish to realize a policy more open to observing outside the feasible region, there are several paths forward. A less-myopic policy built on the same utility (11.3) is one option; even two-step lookahead could elect to obtain an infeasible measurement. Another possibility is one-step lookahead with a more broadly defined utility such as (11.4–11.5), which can see the merit of infeasible observations through more global evaluation of success.

To encourage infeasible observations when prudent, GRAMACY and LEE proposed a score they called the *integrated expected conditional improvement*:[14]

$$\iint \left[\alpha_{\text{EI}}(x'; \mathcal{D}) - \alpha_{\text{EI}}(x'; \mathcal{D}') \right] \Pr(x' \in \mathcal{F} \mid x', \mathcal{D}) \, p(y \mid x, \mathcal{D}) \, dx' dy,$$

where $\mathcal{D}'$ is the putative updated dataset and the location x' is integrated over the domain. This is a measure of the expected impact of a measurement on the entire acquisition surface over the feasible region, which can effectively capture the potential impact of an infeasible observation when it is useful. A similar approach was taken by PICHENY, who integrated the change in probability of improvement against the feasibility probability.[15] Although these approaches can be heuristically motivated, the required integrals over the acquisition surfaces are intractable, and no obvious approximations are available beyond standard methods.

11 M. SCHONLAU et al. (1998). Global versus Local Search in Constrained Optimization of Computer Models. In: *New Developments and Applications in Experimental Design.*

12 J. R. GARDNER et al. (2014). Bayesian Optimization with Inequality Constraints. *ICML 2014.*

observations in the infeasible region

13 In this case the policy would be equivalent to redefining the domain to encompass only the feasible region $\mathcal{F}$ and maximizing the unmodified expected improvement (7.2).

14 R. B. GRAMACY and H. K. H. LEE (2011). Optimization under Unknown Constraints. In: *Bayesian Statistics 9.*

15 V. PICHENY (2014). A Stepwise Uncertainty Reduction Approach to Constrained Global Optimization. *AISTATS 2014.*

decoupled observations

16 M. A. GELBART et al. (2014). Bayesian Optimization with Unknown Constraints. *UAI 2014*.

17 J. M. HERNÁNDEZ-LOBATO et al. (2016b). A General Framework for Constrained Bayesian Optimization Using Information-Based Search. *Journal of Machine Learning Research* 17:1–53.

predictive entropy search: § 8.8, p. 180

GELBART et al. considered a variation on the constrained optimization problem discussed above wherein observations of the objective and constraints can be "decoupled" – that is, when we can elect to measure any of these functions independent of the others, expanding the action space of the decision problem.[16] The authors noted the expected feasible improvement (11.6) displayed undesirable behavior in this scenario and proposed an alternative policy based on mutual information, which was later refined and expanded into a fully fledged information-theoretic policy for constrained optimization (with or without decoupled observations) based on predictive entropy search.[17]

11.3 SYNCHRONOUS BATCH OBSERVATIONS

Many optimization settings allow for the possibility of making multiple observations in parallel. In fact, some settings such as high-throughput screening for scientific discovery practically *demand* parallel experiments due to the growing capacity of sophisticated automated instruments. Numerous batch policies have been proposed for Bayesian optimization to harness this capability, including variants of virtually every popular sequential policy.

synchronous vs. asynchronous batch construction

Here we can distinguish two settings: *synchronous* and *asynchronous* batch construction. In both cases, multiple experiments must be designed to run in parallel. The distinguishing factor is that in the synchronous case, the results from each entire batch of experiments are obtained before designing the next, whereas in the asynchronous case, each time an experiment completes, we may immediately design a new one in light of those still pending. Bayesian decision theory naturally offers one possible approach to both of these scenarios. We will focus on the synchronous case in this section and will discuss the asynchronous case in the next section.

asynchronous batch observations: § 11.4, p. 262

Decision-theoretic batch construction

Consider an optimization scenario where in each iteration we may design a batch of b points $\mathbf{x} = \{x_1, x_2, \ldots x_b\}$ for simultaneous evaluation, resulting in a corresponding vector of measured values $\mathbf{y}$ obtained before our next action. The design of each batch represents a decision with action space $\mathcal{A} = \mathcal{X}^b$, a modification to step 3 of our general procedure.

batch of observation locations, $\mathbf{x}$
corresponding observed values, $\mathbf{y}$

action space for batch observations, $\mathcal{A} = \mathcal{X}^b$

We proceed by computing the one-step expected gain in utility from a proposed batch measurement $\mathbf{x}$. We will call the corresponding batch acquisition function β_1 to distinguish it from its sequential analog α_1:

expected one-step marginal gain from batch observation, β_1

$$\beta_1(\mathbf{x}; \mathcal{D}) = \mathbb{E}\big[u(\mathcal{D}_1) \mid \mathbf{x}, \mathcal{D}\big] - u(\mathcal{D}).$$

Here $\mathcal{D}_1$ represents the data available after the batch observation is resolved: $\mathcal{D}_1 = \mathcal{D} \cup \big\{(\mathbf{x}, \mathbf{y})\big\}$. Computing this expected marginal gain is an expectation with respect to the unknown values $\mathbf{y}$:

$$\beta_1(\mathbf{x}; \mathcal{D}) + u(\mathcal{D}) = \int u(\mathcal{D}_1)\, p(\mathbf{y} \mid \mathbf{x}, \mathcal{D})\, \mathrm{d}\mathbf{y}, \tag{11.7}$$

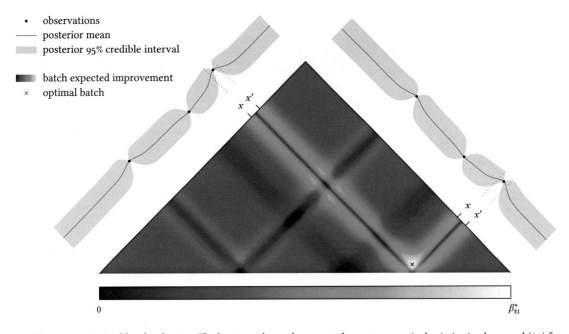

- observations
—— posterior mean
▨ posterior 95% credible interval

▰ batch expected improvement
× optimal batch

Figure 11.3: Optimal batch selection. The heatmap shows the expected one-step marginal gain in simple reward (6.1) from adding a batch of two points – corresponding in location to the belief about the objective plotted along the margins – to the current dataset. Note that the expected marginal gain is symmetric. The optimal batch will observe on both sides of the previously best-seen point. In this example, incorporating either one of the selected points alone would also yield relatively high expected marginal gain.

and an optimal batch with decision horizon $\tau = 1$ maximizes this score:

$$\mathbf{x} \in \underset{\mathbf{x}' \in \mathcal{X}^b}{\arg\max} \, \beta_1(\mathbf{x}'; \mathcal{D}). \qquad (11.8)$$

Finally, we can derive the optimal batch policy for a fixed evaluation budget by induction on the horizon, accounting for the expanded action space for each future decision:

optimal batch policy with fixed evaluation budget

$$\mathbf{x} \in \underset{\mathbf{x}' \in \mathcal{X}^b}{\arg\max} \underbrace{\beta_1(\mathbf{x}'; \mathcal{D}) + \mathbb{E}\big[\beta_{\tau-1}^*(\mathcal{D}_1) \mid \mathbf{x}', \mathcal{D}\big]}_{=\beta_\tau(\mathbf{x}'; \mathcal{D})};$$

$$\beta_\tau^*(\mathcal{D}) = \underset{\mathbf{x}' \in \mathcal{X}^b}{\max} \, \beta_\tau(\mathbf{x}'; \mathcal{D}).$$

If desired, we could also allow for variable-cost observations and the option of dynamic termination by accounting for costs and including a termination option in the action space. Another compelling possibility would be to consider *dynamic* batch sizes by expanding the action space further and assigning an appropriate size-dependent cost function for proposed batch observations.

variable costs and termination option

dynamic batch sizes

Optimal batch selection is illustrated in Figure 11.3 for designing a batch of two points with horizon $\tau = 1$. We compute the expected

example of optimal batch policy

one-step gain in utility (11.7) – here the simple reward (6.1), analogous to expected improvement α_{EI} (7.2) – for every possible batch and observe where the score is maximized. The optimal batch evaluates on either side of the previously best-seen point, achieving distributed exploitation. The expected marginal gain surface has notably complex structure, for example expressing a strong preference for batches containing at least one of the chosen locations over any purely exploratory alternative, as well as severely punishing batches containing an observation too close to an existing one.

connection to b-step lookahead

We may gain some insight into the optimal batch policy by decomposing the expected batch marginal gain in terms of corresponding quantities from the optimal sequential policy. Let us first consider the expected marginal gain from selecting a batch of two points, $\mathbf{x} = \{x, x'\}$, resulting in observed values $\mathbf{y} = \{y, y'\}$. Let $\mathcal{D}'$ represent the current data augmented with the *single* observation (x, y). We may rewrite the marginal gain from the batch observation $(\mathbf{x}, \mathbf{y})$ as a telescoping sum with terms corresponding to the impact of each individual observation:

$$u(\mathcal{D}_1) - u(\mathcal{D}) = \big[u(\mathcal{D}_1) - u(\mathcal{D}')\big] + \big[u(\mathcal{D}') - u(\mathcal{D})\big],$$

which allows us to rewrite the one-step expected batch marginal gain as:

$$\beta_1(\mathbf{x}; \mathcal{D}) = \alpha_1(x; \mathcal{D}) + \mathbb{E}\big[\alpha_1(x'; \mathcal{D}') \mid \mathbf{x}, \mathcal{D}\big].$$

This expression is remarkably similar to the optimal two-step expected sequential marginal gain (5.12):

$$\alpha_2(x; \mathcal{D}) = \alpha_1(x; \mathcal{D}) + \mathbb{E}\Big[\max_{x' \in \mathcal{X}} \alpha_1(x'; \mathcal{D}') \mid x, \mathcal{D}\Big].$$

The main difference is that in the batch setting, we must commit to both observation locations a priori, whereas in the sequential setting, we can design our second observation optimally given the outcome of the first.

"unrolling" the optimal policy: § 5.3, p. 99

We can extend this relationship to the general case. Temporarily adopting compact notation, a horizon-b optimal sequential decision satisfies:

$$x \in \arg\max\Big\{\alpha_1 + \mathbb{E}\big[\max\{\alpha_1 + \mathbb{E}[\max\{\alpha_1 + \cdots]\big]\Big\}, \tag{11.9}$$

and the optimal one-step batch of size b satisfies:

$$\mathbf{x} \in \arg\max\Big\{\alpha_1 + \mathbb{E}\big[\quad \alpha_1 + \mathbb{E}[\quad \alpha_1 + \cdots]\big]\Big\}. \tag{11.10}$$

18 J. VONDRÁK (2005). Probabilistic Methods in Combinatorial and Stochastic Optimization. Ph.D. thesis. Massachusetts Institute of Technology.

Clearly the expected utility gained from making b optimal sequential decisions surpasses the expected utility from a single optimal batch the same size: the sequential policy benefits from designing each successive observation location adaptively, whereas the batch policy must make all decisions simultaneously and cannot benefit from replanning. This unavoidable difference in performance is called the *adaptivity gap* in the analysis of algorithms.[18]

adaptivity gap

---

input: dataset $\mathcal{D}$, batch size b, acquisition function α

$\mathcal{D}' \leftarrow \mathcal{D}$ ▸ initialize fictitious dataset

for $i = 1 \ldots b$ **do**

     $x_i \leftarrow \arg\max_{x \in \mathcal{X}} \alpha(x; \mathcal{D}')$ ▸ select the next batch member

     $\hat{y}_i \leftarrow \textsc{simulate-observation}(x_i, \mathcal{D}')$

     $\mathcal{D}' \leftarrow \mathcal{D}' \cup \{(x_i, \hat{y}_i)\}$ ▸ update fictitious dataset

end for

return x

Algorithm 11.1: Sequential simulation.

Unfortunately, working with the larger action space inherent to batch optimization requires significant computational effort. First, computing the expected marginal gain (11.7) is more expensive than in the sequential setting (5.8), as we must now integrate with respect to the *joint* distribution over outcomes $p(\mathbf{y} \mid \mathbf{x}, \mathcal{D})$. Thus even evaluating the acquisition function at a single point entails more work. Additionally, finding the optimal decision (11.8) requires optimizing this score over a significantly larger domain than in the sequential analog, a nontrivial task due to its potentially complex and multimodal nature – see Figure 11.3.

Despite these computational difficulties, synchronous batch Bayesian optimization has enjoyed significant attention from the research community. We can identify two recurring research thrusts: deriving general strategies for extending arbitrary sequential policies to batch policies and deriving batch extensions of specific sequential policies. We provide a brief survey below.

Batch construction via sequential simulation

Sequential simulation is an efficient strategy for creating batch policies by simulating multiple steps of an existing sequential policy. Pseudocode for this procedure is listed in Algorithm 11.1. Given a sequential acquisition function α, we choose the first batch member by maximization:

first batch member, x_1

$$x_1 \in \arg\max_{x \in \mathcal{X}} \alpha(x; \mathcal{D}),$$

and commit to this choice. We now augment our dataset with the chosen point and a *fictitious* observed value $\hat{y}_1$, forming $\mathcal{D}_1 = \mathcal{D} \cup \{(x_1, \hat{y}_1)\}$, then maximize the acquisition function again to choose the second point:

fictitious observation at x_1, $\hat{y}_1$

second batch member, x_2

$$x_2 \in \arg\max_{x \in \mathcal{X}} \alpha(x; \mathcal{D}_1).$$

We proceed in this manner until the desired batch size has been reached. Sequential simulation entails b optimization problems on $\mathcal{X}$ rather than a single problem on $\mathcal{X}^b$, which can be a significant speed improvement.

When the sequential policy represents one-step lookahead, sequential simulation can be regarded as a natural greedy approximation to the one-step batch policy via the decomposition in (11.10): whereas the optimal batch policy must maximize this score *jointly*, sequential simulation maximizes the score *pointwise*, fixing each point once chosen.

greedy approximation of one-step lookahead

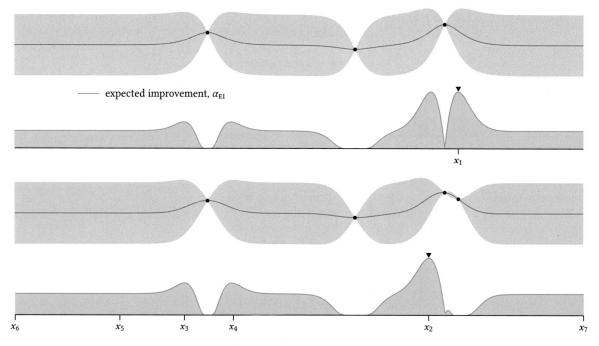

Figure 11.4: Sequential simulation using the expected improvement (7.2) policy and the kriging believer (11.11) imputation strategy. The first point is selected by maximizing expected improvement, and we condition the model on an observation equal to the posterior mean (top panel). We then maximize the updated expected improvement, condition, and repeat as desired. The bottom panel indicates the locations of several further points selected in this manner.

This procedure requires some mechanism for generating fictitious observations as we build the batch. GINSBOURGER et al. described two simple heuristics that have been widely adopted.[19] Perhaps the most natural option is to impute the expected value of each observation, a heuristic GINSBOURGER et al. dubbed the *kriging believer* strategy:

$$\hat{y} = \mathbb{E}[y \mid x, \mathcal{D}]. \qquad (11.11)$$

19 D. GINSBOURGER et al. (2010). Kriging is Well-Suited to Parallelize Optimization. In: *Computational Intelligence in Expensive Optimization Problems*.

kriging believer heuristic

This has the effect of fixing the posterior mean of the objective function throughout simulation. An even simpler option is to impute a constant value independent of the chosen point, which the authors called the *constant liar* strategy:

constant liar heuristic

$$\hat{y} = c. \qquad (11.12)$$

Although this might seem silly, this has the advantage of being model independent and has demonstrated surprisingly good performance in practice. Three natural options for the constant, ranging from the most optimistic to most pessimistic, are to impute the maximum, mean, or minimum of the known observed values y.

example and discussion

Seven steps of sequential simulation with the expected improvement acquisition function (7.2) and the kriging believer strategy (11.11) are

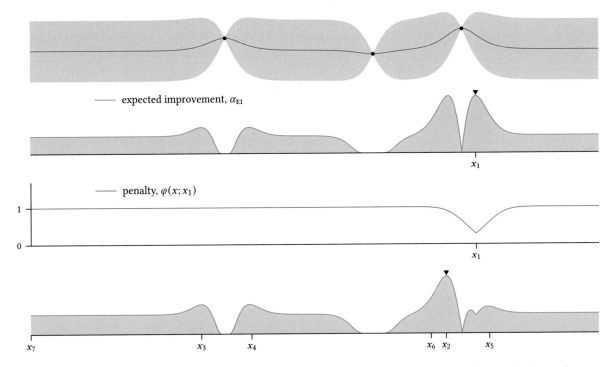

Figure 11.5: Batch construction via local penalization of the expected improvement acquisition function (7.2). We select the first point by maximizing the expected improvement, after which the acquisition function is multiplied by a penalty factor discouraging future batch members in that area. We then maximize the updated acquisition function, penalize, and repeat as desired. The bottom panel indicates the locations of several further points selected in this manner.

demonstrated in Figure 11.4. The selected points appear reasonable: the first two exploit the best-seen observation (and are near optimal for a batch size of two; see Figure 11.3), the next two exploit another local optimum, and the remainder explore the domain.

Batch construction via local penalization

GONZÁLEZ et al. proposed another general mechanism for extending a given sequential policy (defined by the acquisition function α) to the batch setting.[20] Like sequential simulation, we select the first point by maximizing the acquisition function:

$$x_1 \in \arg\max_{x \in \mathcal{X}} \alpha(x; \mathcal{D}).$$

We then incorporate a multiplicative penalty $\varphi(x; x_1)$ into the acquisition function discouraging future batch members from being in a neighborhood of the initial point. This penalty is designed to avoid redundancy between batch members without disrupting the differentiability of the original acquisition function. GONZÁLEZ et al. describe one simple and

20 J. GONZÁLEZ et al. (2016a). Batch Bayesian Optimization via Local Penalization. *AISTATS 2016*.

penalty from selecting x_1, $\varphi(x; x_1)$

effective penalty function from an estimate of the global maximum and Lipschitz constant of the objective function.[21] We now select the second batch member by maximizing the penalized acquisition function

$$x_2 \in \arg\max_{x \in \mathcal{X}} \alpha(x; \mathcal{D})\, \varphi(x; x_1),$$

after which we apply another penalty and continue in this manner as desired. This process is illustrated in Figure 11.5. Comparing with sequential simulation, the first batch members are very similar; however, there is some divergence in the final stages, with local penalization preferring to revisit the local optimum on the right.

Like sequential simulation, local penalization also entails b optimization problems on $\mathcal{X}$ and is in fact even faster than sequential simulation, as the objective function model does not need to be updated along the way.

Approximation via Monte Carlo integration

approximate computation for sequential one-step lookahead: § 8.5, p. 171

If we wish to proceed via joint optimization of (11.7) rather than one of the above heuristics, we will often face the complication that the expectation with respect to the observed values $\mathbf{y}$ is intractable. We can offer some advice for approximating this quantity and its gradient for a Gaussian process model coupled with an exact or additive Gaussian noise observation model. This abbreviated discussion will closely follow the approach for the sequential case.[22]

22 For more discussion on this method, see

J. T. WILSON et al. (2018). Maximizing Acquisition Functions for Bayesian Optimization. *NeurIPS 2018*.

First, we write the one-step marginal gain (11.7) as an expectation of the marginal gain in utility $\Delta(\mathbf{x}, \mathbf{y}) = u(\mathcal{D}') - u(\mathcal{D})$ with respect to a multivariate normal belief on the observations (2.20):

$$\beta(\mathbf{x}; \mathcal{D}) = \int \Delta(\mathbf{x}, \mathbf{y})\, \mathcal{N}(\mathbf{y}; \boldsymbol{\mu}, \mathbf{S})\, d\mathbf{y}. \tag{11.13}$$

23 Gauss–Hermite quadrature, as we recommended in the one-dimensional case, does not scale well with dimension.

We may approximate this expectation via Monte Carlo integration[23] by sampling from this belief. It is convenient to do so by sampling n vectors $\{\mathbf{z}_i\}$ from a *standard* normal distribution, then transforming these via

$$\mathbf{z}_i \mapsto \boldsymbol{\mu} + \Lambda \mathbf{z}_i = \mathbf{y}_i, \tag{11.14}$$

where Λ is the Cholesky factor of $\mathbf{S}$: $\Lambda\Lambda^\top = \mathbf{S}$. Monte Carlo estimation now gives

$$\beta(\mathbf{x}; \mathcal{D}) \approx \frac{1}{n} \sum_{i=1}^{n} \Delta(\mathbf{x}, \mathbf{y}_i). \tag{11.15}$$

Monte Carlo approximation of gradient

As in the sequential case, we may reuse these samples to approximate the gradient of the acquisition function with respect to the proposed observation locations, under mild assumptions (c.4–c.5):

$$\frac{\partial \beta}{\partial \mathbf{x}} \approx \frac{1}{n} \sum_{i=1}^{n} \frac{\partial \Delta}{\partial \mathbf{x}}(\mathbf{x}, \mathbf{y}_i); \quad \frac{\partial \Delta}{\partial x_j}(\mathbf{x}, \mathbf{y}_i) = \left[\frac{\partial \Delta}{\partial x_j} \right]_{\mathbf{y}} + \frac{\partial \Delta}{\partial \mathbf{y}} \left[\frac{\partial \boldsymbol{\mu}}{\partial x_j} + \frac{\partial \Lambda}{\partial x_j} \mathbf{z}_i \right],$$
$$\tag{11.16}$$

where, in the second expression, we account for the dependence of the y samples on x through the transformation (11.14). The gradient of the Cholesky factor Λ can be computed efficiently via automatic differentiation.[24]

We will spend the remainder of this section discussing the details of explicit batch extensions of popular sequential policies.

Expected improvement and knowledge gradient

Both the expected improvement and knowledge gradient policies have been extended to the batch case, closely following the decision-theoretic approach outlined above.

Unlike its sequential counterpart, computation of batch expected improvement for Gaussian process models is rather involved, even in the case of exact observation. The primary challenge is evaluating the expectation of a multivariate truncated normal distribution, a computation whose difficulty increases rapidly with the batch size. There are exact formulas to compute batch expected improvement[25] and its gradient[26] based on the moment-generating function for the truncated multivariate normal derived by TALLIS;[27] however, these formulas require b evaluations of the b-dimensional and b^2 evaluations of the $(b - 1)$-dimensional multivariate normal CDF, itself a notoriously difficult computation that can only effectively be approximated via Monte Carlo methods in dimension greater than four. This limits the utility of the direct approach to relatively small batch sizes, perhaps $b \leq 10$.

For larger batch sizes, GINSBOURGER et al. proposed sequential simulation, and found the constant liar strategy (11.12) using the "optimistic" estimate $\hat{y} = \max y$ to deliver good empirical performance in simulation.[28] WANG et al. proposed an efficient alternative: joint optimization of batch expected improvement via multistart stochastic gradient ascent using the Monte Carlo estimators in (11.15–11.16).[29] The authors demonstrated this procedure scaling up to batch sizes of $b = 128$ with impressive performance and runtime compared with exact computation and sequential simulation.

A similar approach for approximating the batch knowledge gradient policy was described by WU and FRAZIER.[30] The overall approach is effectively the same: multistart stochastic gradient ascent relying on (11.15–11.16). An additional complication in estimating the batch knowledge gradient is the global optimization inherent to the global reward (6.5). WU and FRAZIER suggest a discretization approach where the global reward is estimated on a dynamically managed discrete set of points drawn via Thompson sampling from the objective function posterior.

The batch expected improvement acquisition function is illustrated for an example scenario in Figure 11.3, and batch knowledge gradient for the same scenario in Figure 11.6. In both cases, the optimal batch measures on either side of the previously best-seen point; however, knowledge gradient is more tolerant of batches containing only one observation in this region.

24 I. MURRAY (2016). Differentiation of the Cholesky decomposition. arXiv: 1602.07527 [stat.CO].

expected improvement: § 7.3 p. 127
knowledge gradient: § 7.4 p. 129

25 C. CHEVALIER and D. GINSBOURGER (2013). Fast Computation of the Multi-Points Expected Improvement with Applications in Batch Selection. *LION 7*.

26 S. MARMIN et al. (2015). Differentiating the Multipoint Expected Improvement for Optimal Batch Design. *MOD 2015*.

27 G. M. TALLIS (1961). The Moment Generating Function of the Truncated Multi-Normal Distribution. *Journal of the Royal Statistical Society Series B (Methodological)* 23(1):223–229.

28 D. GINSBOURGER et al. (2010). Kriging is Well-Suited to Parallelize Optimization. In: *Computational Intelligence in Expensive Optimization Problems*.

29 J. WANG et al. (2020a). Parallel Bayesian Global Optimization of Expensive Functions. *Operations Research* 68(6):1850–1865.

30 J. WU and P. I. FRAZIER (2016). The Parallel Knowledge Gradient Method for Batch Bayesian Optimization. *NeurIPS 2016*.

Thompson sampling: 7.9, p. 148

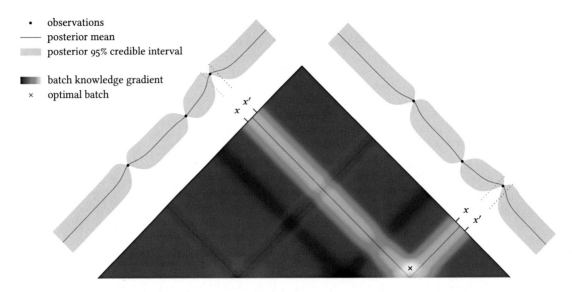

- observations
- —— posterior mean
- posterior 95% credible interval

- batch knowledge gradient
- × optimal batch

Figure 11.6: The batch knowledge gradient acquisition function for an example scenario. The optimal batch exploits the local optimum, but any batch containing at least one point in that neighborhood is near-optimal.

Mutual information with x^*

mutual information with x^*: § 7.6, p. 139

predictive entropy search: § 8.8, p. 180

31 A. SHAH and Z. GHAHRAMANI (2015). Parallel Predictive Entropy Search for Batch Global Optimization of Expensive Objective Functions. *NeurIPS 2015.*

Compared with the difficulty faced in computing (or even approximating) batch analogs of the expected improvement and knowledge gradient acquisition functions, extending the predictive entropy search acquisition function to the batch setting is relatively straightforward.[31] The mutual information between the observed values y and the location of the global maximum x^* is (compare with (8.36)):

$$\beta_{x^*}(\mathbf{x}; \mathcal{D}) = H[\mathbf{y} \mid \mathbf{x}, \mathcal{D}] - \mathbb{E}\big[H[\mathbf{y} \mid \mathbf{x}, x^*, \mathcal{D}] \mid \mathbf{x}, \mathcal{D}\big]. \tag{11.17}$$

The first term is the differential entropy of a multivariate normal and may be computed in closed form (A.16). The second term is somewhat difficult to approximate, but no innovation is required in the batch setting beyond the machinery already developed for the sequential case. We may approximate the expectation with respect to x^* via Thompson sampling and may approximate $p(\mathbf{y} \mid \mathbf{x}, x^*, \mathcal{D})$ as a multivariate normal following the expectation propagation approach described previously.

Thompson sampling: 7.9, p. 148

Probability of improvement

probability of improvement: § 7.5, p. 131

32 See § 7.5, p. 134.

33 D. R. JONES (2001). A Taxonomy of Global Optimization Methods Based on Response Surfaces. *Journal of Global Optimization* 21(4):345–383.

Batch probability of improvement has received relatively little attention, but JONES proposed one simple option in the context of threshold selection.[32,33] The idea is to find the optimal sequential decisions using a range of improvement thresholds, representing a spectrum of exploration–exploitation tradeoffs. JONES then recommends a simple clustering procedure to remove redundant points, resulting in a batch (of variable size) reflecting diversity in location and behavior. A compelling aspect of this procedure is that it is naturally *nonmyopic,* as each batch is explicitly constructed to address both immediate and long-term gain.

This approach is illustrated in Figure 7.12;[34] depending on the aggressiveness of the pruning procedure, the constructed batch would contain 2–4 points chosen from the visible clusters.

34 See p. 136.

Upper confidence bound

Due to the equivalence between the probability of improvement and upper confidence bound policies for Gaussian processes (8.22, 8.26), the procedure proposed by JONES described above may also be used to realize a simple batch upper confidence bound policy for that model class. In this case, we would design each batch by maximizing the upper confidence bound for a range of confidence parameters, clustering, and pruning.

maximizing an upper confidence bound: § 7.8, p. 145

Several more direct batch upper confidence bound policies have been developed, all variations on a theme. DESAUTELS et al. proposed a strategy – dubbed simply *batch upper confidence bound* (BUCB) – based on sequential simulation with the kriging believer strategy (11.11).[35] Batch diversity is automatically encouraged: each point added to the batch globally reduces the upper confidence bound, most dramatically at the locations with the most strongly correlated function values.

35 T. DESAUTELS et al. (2014). Parallelizing Exploration–Exploitation Tradeoffs in Gaussian Process Bandit Optimization. *Journal of Machine Learning Research* 15(119):4053–4103.

The BUCB algorithm was later refined by several authors to encourage more exploration, which can improve both empirical and theoretical performance. Like BUCB, we seed each batch with the maximum of the upper confidence bound (8.25). We now identify the so-called "relevant region" of the domain, defined to be the set of locations whose upper confidence bound exceeds the global maximum of the *lower* confidence bound.[36] The intuition behind this region is that the objective value at any point in its complement is – with high probability – lower than at the point maximizing the lower confidence bound and can thus be discarded with some confidence; see the illustration in the margin.

36 N. DE FREITAS et al. (2012b). Exponential Regret Bounds for Gaussian Process Bandits with Deterministic Observations. *ICML 2012.*

The (disconnected) relevant region (the darker portions of the uncertainty envelope) for an example Gaussian process. Points outside the region (the lighter portion in between) are unlikely to maximize the objective function.

With the relevant region in hand, we design the remaining batch members to promote maximal information gain about the objective on this region. For a Gaussian process, this is intimately related to a diversity-encouraging distribution known as a *k-determinantal point process* (*k*-DPP) built from the posterior covariance function.[37] We may proceed by either a simple greedy procedure[38] or via more nuanced maximization or sampling using methods developed for *k*-DPPs.[39]

37 A. KULESZA and B. TASKAR (2012). Determinantal Point Processes for Machine Learning. *Foundations and Trends in Machine Learning* 5(2–3):123–286.

38 E. CONTAL et al. (2013). Parallel Gaussian Process Optimization with Upper Confidence Bound and Pure Exploration. *ECML PKDD 2013.*

39 T. KATHURIA et al. (2016). Batched Gaussian Process Bandit Optimization via Determinantal Point Processes. *NeurIPS 2016.*

These schemes are all backed by strong theoretical analysis, including sublinear cumulative regret (10.3) bounds under suitable conditions.

Thompson sampling

The stochastic nature of Thompson sampling enables trivial batch construction by drawing b independent samples of the location of the global maximum (7.19):

$$\{x_i\} \sim p(x^* \mid \mathcal{D}).$$

40 J. M. HERNÁNDEZ-LOBATO et al. (2017). Parallel and Distributed Thompson Sampling for Large-Scale Accelerated Exploration of Chemical Space. *ICML 2017*.

41 K. KANDASAMY et al. (2018). Parallelised Bayesian Optimisation via Thompson Sampling. *AISTATS 2018*.

A remarkable advantage of this policy is that the samples may be generated entirely in parallel, which allows linear scaling to arbitrarily large batch sizes. Batch Thompson sampling has delivered impressive performance in a real-world setting with batch sizes up to $b = 500$,[40] and is backed by theoretical guarantees on the asymptotic reduction of the simple regret (10.1).[41]

11.4 ASYNCHRONOUS OBSERVATION WITH PENDING EXPERIMENTS

Some situations allow parallel observation with *asynchronous* execution. For example, when optimizing the result of a computational simulation, access to more than one CPU core (or even better, a cluster of machines) could enable many simulations to be run in parallel. To maximize throughput, we could immediately start a new simulation upon the termination of a previous job, without waiting for the other running processes to finish. An effective optimization policy for this setting must account for the pending experiments when designing each observation.

We may consider a general case where we wish to design a batch of experiments $\mathbf{x} \in \mathcal{X}^b$ when another batch of experiments $\mathbf{x}' \in \mathcal{X}^{b'}$ is under current evaluation, where the number of running and pending experiments may be arbitrary.[42] Here the action space for the current decision is $\mathcal{A} \in \mathcal{X}^b_?$ and we must make the decision under uncertainty both in the observations resulting from the chosen batch, $\mathbf{y}$, and the observations resulting from the pending experiments, $\mathbf{y}'$.

The one-step expected gain in utility from a set of proposed experiments and the pending experiments is

$$\beta_1(\mathbf{x}; \mathbf{x}', \mathcal{D}) = \mathbb{E}\big[u(\mathcal{D}_1) \mid \mathbf{x}, \mathbf{x}', \mathcal{D}\big] - u(\mathcal{D}),$$

where $\mathcal{D}_1 = \mathcal{D} \cup \big\{(\mathbf{x}, \mathbf{y}, \mathbf{x}', \mathbf{y}')\big\}$. This entails an expectation with respect to the unknown values $\mathbf{y}$ and $\mathbf{y}'$:

$$\beta_1(\mathbf{x}; \mathcal{D}) + u(\mathcal{D}) = \iint u(\mathcal{D}_1)\, p(\mathbf{y}, \mathbf{y}' \mid \mathbf{x}, \mathbf{x}', \mathcal{D})\, \mathrm{d}\mathbf{y}\, \mathrm{d}\mathbf{y}'.$$

reduction to synchronous case

This is simply the one-step marginal gain for the combined batch $\mathbf{x} \cup \mathbf{x}'$ from the synchronous case (11.7)! The only difference with respect to one-step lookahead is that we can only maximize this score with respect to $\mathbf{x}$ as we are already committed to the pending experiments. Thus a one-step lookahead policy for the asynchronous case can be reduced to maximizing the corresponding score from the synchronous case with some batch members fixed. This reduction has been pointed out by numerous authors, and effectively every batch policy discussed above may be modified with little effort to work in the asynchronous case.

Moving beyond one-step lookahead may be extremely challenging, however, due to the implications of uncertainty in the order of termination for pending experiments. A full treatment would require a model for the time of termination and accounting for how the decision tree may branch after the present decision. Exact computation of even two-step

42 Perhaps the most prevalent case in practice will be $b = 1$ assuming job termination is governed by a simple random process.

lookahead is likely intractable in most practical situations, but rollout might offer one path forward.

rollout: § 5.3, p. 102

11.5 MULTIFIDELITY OPTIMIZATION

In Bayesian optimization, we typically assume that observations of the objective function are expensive and should be made as sparingly as possible. However, some scenarios offer a potential shortcut: *indirect* inspection of the system of interest via a cheaper surrogate, such as the output of a computer simulation. In some cases, we may even have access to multiple surrogates of varying cost and fidelity. It is tempting to try to accelerate optimization using these surrogates to guide the search. This is the inspiration for *multifidelity optimization,* a cost-aware extension of optimization that has received significant attention.

As a motivating example, consider a problem from materials science where we wish to optimize the properties of a material as a function of its composition, process parameters, etc. Materials scientists have several mechanisms available[43] to investigate a proposed material, ranging from relatively inexpensive computer simulations (molecular dynamics, density functional theory, etc.) to extremely expensive synthesis and characterization in a laboratory. State-of-the-art materials discovery pipelines rely on these computational surrogates to winnow the search space for experimental campaigns.

Automated machine learning provides another motivating example. Suppose we wish to tune the hyperparameters of a model by minimizing validation error after training on a large training set. Although training on the full dataset may be costly, we can estimate performance by training on only a subset of the data[44] or by terminating the training procedure early.[45] We may reasonably hope to accelerate hyperparameter tuning by exploiting these noisy, but cost-effective surrogates.

We will outline a decision-theoretic approach to multifidelity optimization below. The complexity of this setting will require readdressing every step of the procedure outlined at the top of this chapter. We will focus on the first three steps, as deriving the optimal policy is mechanical once the model and decision problem are completely specified.

Formalization of problem and action space

Suppose that in addition to the objective function f, we have access to one-or-more surrogate functions $\{f_i\}\colon \mathcal{X} \to \mathbb{R}$, indexed by a parameter $i \in \mathcal{I}$. Most often we take the surrogate functions to form a discrete set, but in some cases we may wish to consider multidimensional and/or continuous surrogate spaces.[46] We denote the objective function itself with the special index $* \in \mathcal{I}$, writing $f = f_*$. We consider an optimization scenario where we may design each observation to be either of the objective or a surrogate as we see fit, by selecting a location $x \in \mathcal{X}$ for our next observation and an index $i \in \mathcal{I}$ specifying the desired surrogate. The action space for each such decision is $\mathcal{A} = \mathcal{X} \times \mathcal{I}$.

In multifidelity optimization, we wish to optimize an expensive objective function (the darker curve) aided by access to cheaper – but still informative – surrogates (the lighter curves).

materials science applications: Appendix D, p. 313

43 "Relatively" should be stressed; these simulations can be quite expensive in absolute terms, but still much cheaper than synthesis.

44 A. KLEIN et al. (2015). Towards Efficient Bayesian Optimization for Big Data. *Bayesian Optimization Workshop, NeurIPS 2015.*

45 K. SWERSKY et al. (2014). Freeze–Thaw Bayesian Optimization. arXiv: 1406 . 3896 [stat.ML].

surrogate functions, $\{f_i\}$
surrogate index set, $\mathcal{I}$

objective function, f_*

46 K. KANDASAMY et al. (2017). Multi-Fidelity Bayesian Optimisation with Continuous Approximations. *ICML 2017.*

action space, $\mathcal{A} = \mathcal{X} \times \mathcal{I}$

Modeling surrogate functions and observations

If surrogate observations are to be useful, they must provide information about the objective function, and the relationship between the objective and its surrogates is captured by a joint model over their values. We first design a joint prior process $p(\{f_i\})$ specifying the expected structure of each individual function and the nature of correlations between the functions. Next we must create an observation model linking the value y observed at a point $[x, i]$ to the underlying function value $\phi = f_i(x)$: $p(y \mid x, i, \phi)$. Now, given a set of observed data $\mathcal{D}$, we may derive the posterior belief over the functions, $p(\{f_i\} \mid \mathcal{D})$, and the posterior predictive distribution, $p(y \mid x, i, \mathcal{D})$, with which we can reason about proposed observations.

joint prior process, $p(\{f_i\})$

observation model, $p(y \mid x, i, \phi)$
posterior distribution, $p(\{f_i\} \mid \mathcal{D})$
posterior predictive distribution,
$p(y \mid x, i, \mathcal{D})$
joint Gaussian processes: § 2.4, p. 26

In practice, the joint prior process is usually a joint *Gaussian* process over the objective and its surrogates. The primary challenge in crafting a joint Gaussian process is in defining cross-covariance functions

$$K_{ij} = \mathrm{cov}[f_i, f_j]$$

that adequately encode the correlations between the functions of interest, which can take some care to ensure the resulting joint covariance function over the collection $\{f_i\}$ is positive definite.

Fortunately, a great deal of effort has been invested in developing this model class into a flexible and expressive family.[47,48] One simple construction offering some intuition is the *separable* covariance

47 M. A. ÁLVAREZ et al. (2012). Kernels for Vector-Valued Functions: A Review. *Foundations and Trends in Machine Learning* 4(3):195–266.

48 K. ULRICH et al. (2015). GP Kernels for Cross-Spectrum Analysis. *NeurIPS 2015*.

$$K([x, i], [x', i']) = K_\mathcal{X}(x, x') K_\mathcal{I}(i, i'), \tag{11.18}$$

which decomposes the joint covariance into a covariance function on the domain $K_\mathcal{X}$ shared by each individual function and a covariance function between the functions, $K_\mathcal{I}$ (which would be a covariance *matrix* if $\mathcal{I}$ is finite). In this construction, the marginal covariance and cross-covariance functions are all scaled versions of $K_\mathcal{X}$, with the $K_\mathcal{I}$ covariance scaling each marginal belief and encoding (constant) cross-correlations across functions as well. Figures 2.5 and 2.6[49] illustrate the behavior of this model for two highly correlated functions on a shared one-dimensional domain.

shared domain covariance, $K_\mathcal{X}$
cross-function covariance, $K_\mathcal{I}$

49 See pp. 28–29.

Defining a utility function

We have now addressed steps 2 and 3 of our general procedure for multifidelity optimization, by identifying the expanded action space implied by the problem and determining how to reason about the potential outcomes of these actions. Before we can proceed with deriving a policy, however, we must establish preferences over outcomes with a utility function $u(\mathcal{D})$. It is difficult to provide specific guidance for this choice, as these preferences are inherently bound to a given situation. One natural approach would be to choose a cost-aware utility function measuring optimization progress limited to the objective function alone, adjusted

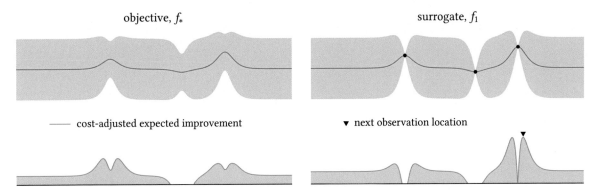

Figure 11.7: Cost-adjusted multifidelity expected improvement for a toy scenario. The objective (left) and its surrogate (right) are modeled as a joint Gaussian process with marginals equivalent to the example from Figure 7.1 and constant cross-correlation 0.8. The cost of observation was assumed to be ten times greater for the objective than its surrogate. Maximizing the cost-adjusted multifidelity expected improvement elects to continue evaluating the surrogate.

for the variable costs of each observation obtained. For example we might quantify the cost of observing the objective function or each of the surrogate functions with values $\{c_i\}$, and adjust a data utility $u'(\mathcal{D})$ appropriately, by defining

observation costs, $\{c_i\}$

$$u(\mathcal{D}) = u'(\mathcal{D}) - \sum_{(x,i)\in\mathcal{D}} c_i.$$

With an appropriate utility function in hand, we can then proceed to derive the optimal policy as usual.

As an example, we can realize an analog of expected improvement (7.2) through a suitable redefinition of the simple reward (6.3). Suppose that at termination we wish to recommend a location visited during optimization, with *any* fidelity, using a risk-neutral utility. Given a multifidelity dataset $\mathcal{D} = \big([\mathbf{x}, \mathbf{i}], \mathbf{y}\big)$, the expected utility of this recommendation would be

multifidelity expected improvement

$$u'(\mathcal{D}) = \max_{x'\in\mathbf{x}} \mu_{\mathcal{D}}\big([x', *]\big),$$

the maximum of the posterior mean for the objective function at the observed locations.

Figure 11.7 illustrates one-step lookahead policy with this utility function for a one-dimensional objective function f_* (left) and a surrogate f_1 (right). The marginal belief about each function is a Gaussian process identical to our running example from Chapter 7; see Figure 7.1. These are coupled together via the separable covariance (11.18) with $K_{\mathcal{I}}(*, *) = K_{\mathcal{I}}(1, 1) = 1$ and cross-correlation $K_{\mathcal{I}}(1, *) = 0.8$. We begin with three surrogate observations and compute the cost-adjusted expected improvement as described above, where the cost of observing the objective was set to ten times that of the surrogate. In this case, the one-step optimal decision is to continue evaluating the surrogate around the best-seen surrogate observation.

example and discussion

—— objective, f_*

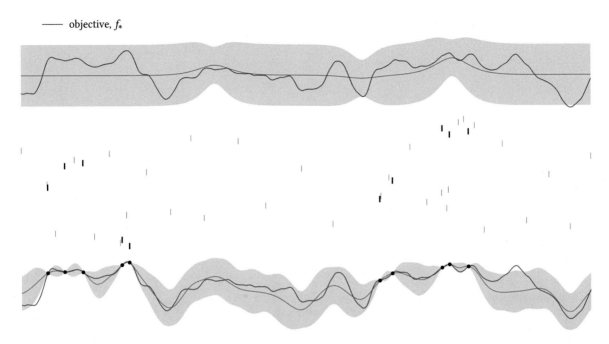

Figure 11.8: A simulation of optimization with the cost-adjusted multifidelity expected improvement starting from the scenario in Figure 11.7. We simulate sequential observations of either the objective or the surrogate, illustrated using the running tick marks. The lighter marks correspond to surrogate observations and the heavier marks correspond to objective observations. The optimum was found after 10 objective observations and 32 surrogate observations. The prior (top) and posterior (bottom) of the objective function conditioned on all observations are also shown.

50 D. HUANG et al. (2006a). Sequential Kriging Optimization Using Multiple-Fidelity Evaluations. *Structural and Multidisciplinary Optimization* 32(5):369–382.

51 V. PICHENY et al. (2013a). Quantile-Based Optimization of Noisy Computer Experiments with Tunable Precision. *Technometrics* 55(1): 2–13.

52 J. WU et al. (2019). Practical Multi-Fidelity Bayesian Optimization for Hyperparameter Tuning. *UAI 2019*.

53 K. KANDASAMY et al. (2016). Gaussian Process Bandit Optimisation with Multi-Fidelity Evaluations. *NeurIPS 2016*.

54 K. KANDASAMY et al. (2017). Multi-Fidelity Bayesian Optimisation with Continuous Approximations. *ICML 2017*.

55 K. SWERSKY et al. (2013). Multi-Task Bayesian Optimization. *NeurIPS 2013*.

Figure 11.8 simulates sequential multifidelity optimization using this policy; here the optimum was discovered after only 10 evaluations of the objective, guided by 32 observations of the cheaper surrogate. A remarkable feature we can see in the posterior is that *all* evaluations made of the objective function are above the prior mean, nearly all with z-scores of approximately $z = 1$ or greater. This can be ascribed not to extreme luck, but rather to efficient use of the surrogate to rule out regions unlikely to contain the optimum.

Multifidelity Bayesian optimization has enjoyed sustained interest from the research community, and numerous policies have been available. These include adaptations of the expected improvement,[50,51] knowledge gradient,[52] upper confidence bound,[53,54] and mutual information with x^*[55,56] and f^*[57] acquisition functions, as well as novel approaches.[58]

11.6 MULTITASK OPTIMIZATION

Multitask optimization addresses the sequential or simultaneous optimization of multiple objectives $\{f_i\}\colon \mathcal{X} \to \mathbb{R}$ representing performance on related tasks. Like multifidelity optimization, the underlying idea in multitask optimization is that if performance on the various tasks is *correlated* as a function of the input, we may accelerate optimization by transferring information between tasks.

As a motivating example of sequential multitask optimization, consider a web service wishing to retune the parameters of an ad placement algorithm on a regular basis to maximize revenue in the current climate. Here the revenue at each epoch represents the different tasks to be optimized, which are optimized individually one after another. Although we could treat each optimization problem separately, they are clearly related, and with some care we may be able to use past performance to provide a "warm start" to each new optimization problem rather than start from scratch.

We may also consider the simultaneous optimization of performance across tasks. For example, a machine learning practitioner may wish to tune model hyperparameters to maximize the average predictive performance on several related datasets.[59] A naïve approach would formulate the problem as maximizing a single objective defined to be the average performance across tasks, with each evaluation entailing retraining the model for each dataset. However, this would be potentially wasteful, as we may be able to eliminate poorly performing hyperparameters with high confidence after training on a fraction of the datasets. A multitask approach would model each objective function separately (perhaps jointly) and consider evaluations of *single-task* performance to efficiently maximize the combined objective.

SWERSKY et al. described a particularly clever realization of this idea: selecting model hyperparameters via cross validation.[60] Here we recognize the predictive performance on each validation fold as being correlated due to shared training data across folds. If we can successfully share information across folds, we may potentially accelerate cross validation by iteratively selecting (hyperparameter, fold index) pairs rather than training proposed hyperparameters on every fold each time.

Formulation and approach

Let $\{f_i\}\colon \mathcal{X} \to \mathbb{R}$ be the set of objective functions we wish to consider, representing performance on the relevant tasks. As with multifidelity optimization, the key enabler of multitask optimization is a joint model $p(\{f_i\})$ over the tasks and a joint observation model $p(y \mid x, i, \phi)$ over evaluations thereof; this joint model allows us to share information between the tasks. This could, for example, take the form of a joint Gaussian process, as discussed previously.

Once this model has been chosen, we can turn to the problem of designing a multitask optimization policy. If each task is to be solved one at a time, a natural approach would be to design the utility function to ultimately evaluate performance on that task only. In this case, the problem devolves to single-objective optimization, and we may use any of the approaches discussed earlier in the book to derive a policy. The

56 Y. ZHANG et al. (2017). Information-Based Multi-Fidelity Bayesian Optimization. *Bayesian Optimization Workshop, NeurIPS 2017.*

57 S. TAKENO et al. (2020). Multi-Fidelity Bayesian Optimization with Max-value Entropy Search and Its Parallelization. *ICML 2020.*

58 J. SONG et al. (2019). A General Framework for Multi-Fidelity Bayesian Optimization with Gaussian Processes. *AISTATS 2019.*

simultaneous tasks

59 This could also be formulated as a scalarized version of a multiobjective optimization problem, discussed in the next section.

60 K. SWERSKY et al. (2013). Multi-Task Bayesian Optimization. *NeurIPS 2013.*

modeling task objectives and observations

joint GPs for modeling multiple functions: § 11.5, p. 264

sequential tasks

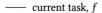 current task, f

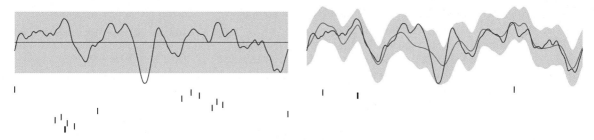

Figure 11.9: A demonstration of sequential multitask optimization. Left: a prior distribution over an objective function along with 13 observations selected by maximizing expected improvement, revealing the global maximum with the last evaluation. Right: the posterior distribution over the same objective conditioned on the observations of the two functions (now interpreted as related tasks) in Figure 11.8. The global maximum is now found after three observations due to the better informed prior.

only difference is that the objective function model is now informed from our past experience with other tasks; as a result, our initial optimization decisions can be more targeted.

This procedure is illustrated in Figure 11.9. Both panels illustrate the optimization of an objective function by sequentially maximizing expected improvement. The left panel begins with no information and locates the global optimum after 13 evaluations. The right panel begins the process instead with a *posterior* belief about the objective conditioned on the data obtained from the two functions in Figure 11.8, modeled as related tasks with cross-correlation 0.8. Due to the better informed initial belief, we now find the global optimum after only three evaluations.

simultaneous tasks

The case of simultaneous multitask optimization – where we may evaluate any task objective with each observation – requires somewhat more care. We must now design a utility function capturing our joint performance across the tasks and design each observation with respect to this utility. One simple option would be to select utility functions $\{u_i\}$ quantifying performance on each task separately and then take a weighted average:

$$u(\mathcal{D}) = \sum_i w_i u_i(\mathcal{D}).$$

This could be further adjusted for (perhaps task- and/or input-dependent) observation costs if needed. Now we may write the expected marginal gain in this combined utility as a weighted average of the expected marginal gain on each separate task. One-step lookahead would then maximize the weighted acquisition function

$$\alpha([x,i];\mathcal{D}) = \sum_i w_i \alpha_i([x,i];\mathcal{D})$$

over all possible observation location–task pairs $[x,i]$, where α_i is the one-step expected marginal gain in u_i. Note that observing a single task

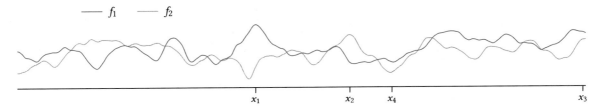

Figure 11.10: A simple multiobjective optimization example with two objectives $\{f_1, f_2\}$ on a one-dimensional domain. We compare four identified points: x_1, the global optimum of f_1, x_2, the global optimum of f_2, x_3, a compromise with relatively high values of both objectives, and x_4, a point with relatively low values of both objectives.

could in fact yield improvement in *all* utilities due to information sharing through the joint belief on task objectives.

11.7   MULTIOBJECTIVE OPTIMIZATION

Like multitask optimization, *multiobjective optimization* addresses the simultaneous optimization of multiple objectives $\{f_i\} \colon \mathcal{X} \to \mathbb{R}$. However, whereas in multitask optimization we usually seek to identify the global optimum of each function separately, in multiobjective optimization we seek to identify points *jointly* optimizing all of the objectives. Of course, this is not possible unequivocally unless all of the maxima happen to coincide, as we may need to sacrifice the value of one objective in order to increase another. Instead, we may consider the optimization of various *tradeoffs* between the objectives and rely on subjective preferences to determine which option is preferred in a given scenario. Multiobjective optimization may then be posed as the identification of one-or-more optimal tradeoffs among the objectives to support this analysis.

A classic example of multiobjective optimization can be found in finance, where we seek investment portfolios optimizing tradeoffs between *risk* (often captured by the standard deviation of return) and *reward* (often captured by the expected return). Generally, investments with higher risk yield higher reward, but the optimal investment strategy depends on the investor's risk tolerance – for example, when capital preservation is paramount, low-risk, low-reward investments are prudent. The set of investment portfolios maximizing reward for any given risk is known as the *Pareto frontier*,[61] which jointly span all rational solutions to the given problem. We generalize this concept below.

risk: standard deviation of return

reward: expected value of return

61 In modern portfolio theory the term "efficient frontier" is more common for the equivalent concept.

Pareto frontier

Pareto optimality

To illustrate the tradeoffs we may need to consider during multiobjective optimization, consider the two objectives in Figure 11.10. The first objective f_1 has its global maximum at x_1, which nearly coincides with the global *minimum* of the second objective f_2. The reverse is true in the other direction: the global maximum of the second objective, x_2,

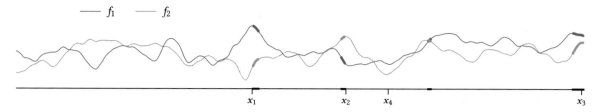

Figure 11.11: The objectives from Figure 11.10 with the Pareto optimal solutions highlighted. All points along the intervals marked on the horizontal axis are Pareto optimal, with the highlighted corresponding objective values forming the Pareto frontier (see margin). Points x_1, x_2, and x_3 are Pareto optimal; x_4 is not.

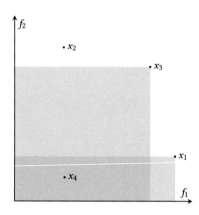

The regions dominated by points x_1 and x_3 in Figure 11.10 are shaded. x_4 is dominated by both, and x_2 by neither.

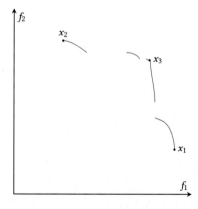

The Pareto frontier for the scenario in Figures 11.10–11.11. The four components correspond to the highlighted intervals in Figure 11.11.

62 K. M. MIETTINEN (1998). *Nonlinear Multiobjective Optimization.* Kluwer Academic Publishers.

achieves a relatively low value on the first objective. Neither point can be preferred over the other on any *objective* grounds, but a rational agent may have *subjective* preferences over these two locations depending on the relative importance of the two objectives. Some agents might even prefer a compromise location such as x_3 to either of these points, as it achieves relatively high – but suboptimal – values for both objectives.

It is clearly impossible to identify an unambiguously optimal location, even in this relatively simple example. We can, however, *eliminate* some locations as plainly subpar. For example, consider the point x_4 in Figure 11.10. Assuming preferences are nondecreasing with each objective, *no* rational agent would prefer x_4 to x_3 as the latter point achieves higher value for *both* objectives. We may formalize this intuition by defining a partial order on potential solutions consistent with this reasoning.

We will say that a point x *dominates* another point x', denoted $x' \prec x$, if no objective value is lower at x than at x' and if at least one objective value is higher at x than at x'. Assuming preferences are consistent with nondecreasing objective values, no agent could prefer a dominated point to any point dominating it. This concept is illustrated in the margin for the example from Figure 11.10: all points in the shaded regions are dominated, and in particular x_4 is dominated by both x_1 and x_3. On the other hand, none of x_1, x_2, or x_3 is dominated by any of the other points.

A point $x \in \mathcal{X}$ that is *not* dominated by any other point is called *Pareto optimal*, and the image of all Pareto optimal points is called the *Pareto frontier*. The Pareto frontier is a central concept in multiobjective optimization – it represents the set of all possible solutions to the problem consistent with weakly monotone preferences for the objectives. Figure 11.11 shows the Pareto optimal points for our example from Figure 11.10, which span four disconnected intervals. We may visualize the Pareto frontier by plotting the image of this set, as shown in the margin.

There are several approaches to multiobjective optimization that differ in terms of when exactly preferences are elicited.[62] So-called *a posteriori methods* seek to identify the entire Pareto frontier for a given problem, with preferences among possible solutions to be determined afterwards. In contrast, *a priori methods* assume that preferences are already predetermined, allowing us to seek a single Pareto optimal solution consistent with those preferences. Bayesian realizations of both types of approaches have been realized, as we discuss below.

Formalization of decision problem and modeling objectives

Nearly all Bayesian multiobjective optimization procedures model each decision as choosing a location $x \in \mathcal{X}$, where we make an observation of every objective function. We could also consider a setting analogous to multitask or multifidelity optimization where we observe only one objective at a time, but this idea has not been sufficiently explored. For the following discussion, we will write $\mathbf{y}$ for the vector-valued observation resulting from an observation at a given point x, with y_i being associated with objective f_i.

vector of observations at x, $\mathbf{y}$

As in the previous two sections, we build a joint model for the objectives $\{f_i\}$ and our observations of them via a prior process $p(\{f_i\})$ and an observation model $p(\mathbf{y} \mid x, \{\phi_i\})$. The models are usually taken to be independent Gaussian processes on each objective combined with standard observation models. *Joint* Gaussian processes could also be used when appropriate, but a direct comparison of independent versus dependent models did not demonstrate improvement when modeling correlations between objectives, perhaps due to an increased burden in estimating model hyperparameters.[63]

63 J. SVENSON and T. SANTNER (2016). Multiobjective Optimization of Expensive-to-evaluate Deterministic Computer Simulator Models. *Computational Statistics and Data Analysis* 94: 250–264.

Expected hypervolume improvement

The majority of Bayesian multiobjective optimization approaches are a posteriori methods, seeking to identify the entire Pareto frontier or a representative portion of it. Many algorithms represent one-step lookahead for some utility function evaluating progress on this task.

64 E. ZITZLER (1999). Evolutionary Algorithms for Multiobjective Optimization: Methods and Applications. Ph.D. thesis. Eidgenössische Technische Hochschule Zürich. [§ 3.1]

One popular utility for multiobjective optimization is the volume under an estimate of the Pareto frontier, also known as the $\mathcal{S}$ *metric.*[64] Namely, given observations of the objectives, we may build a natural statistical lower bound of the Pareto frontier by eliminating the outcomes dominated by the observations with high confidence. When observations are exact, we may simply enumerate the dominated regions and take their union; when observations are corrupted by noise, we may use a statistical lower bound of the underlying function values instead.[65] This procedure is illustrated in the margin for our running example, where we have made exact observations of the objectives at three mutually nondominating locations; see Figure 11.12. The upper-right boundary of the dominated region is a lower bound of the true Pareto frontier.

To evaluate progress on mapping out the Pareto frontier, we consider the volume of space dominated by the available observations and bounded below by an identified, clearly suboptimal reference point $\mathbf{r}$; see the shaded area in the margin. The reference point is necessary to ensure the dominated volume does not diverge to infinity. Assuming the reference point is chosen such that it will definitely be dominated, this utility is always positive and is maximized when the true Pareto fron-

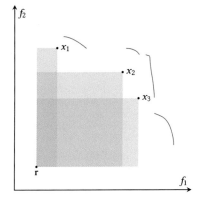

A lower bound of the Pareto frontier for our example given the data in Figure 11.12.

65 M. EMMERICH and B. NAUJOKS (2004). Metamodel Assisted Multiobjective Optimisation Strategies and Their Application in Airfoil Design. In: *Adaptive Computing in Design and Manufacture VI.*

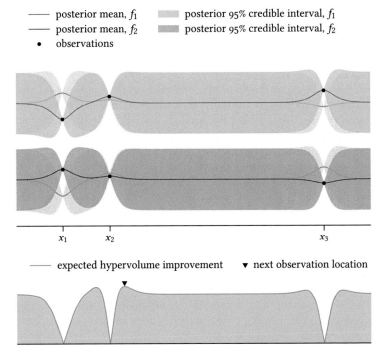

posterior mean, f_1 posterior 95% credible interval, f_1
posterior mean, f_2 posterior 95% credible interval, f_2
• observations

Figure 11.12: The posterior belief about our example objectives from Figure 11.10 given observations at the marked locations. The beliefs are separated vertically (by an arbitrary amount) for clarity, with the belief over the other function shown for reference.

—— expected hypervolume improvement   ▼ next observation location

Figure 11.13: The expected hypervolume improvement acquisition function for the above example.

66 M. FLEISCHER (2003). The Measure of Pareto Optima: Applications to Multi-Objective Metaheuristics. *EMO 2003*.

67 M. T. M. EMMERICH et al. (2006). Single- and Multiobjective Evolutionary Optimization Assisted by Gaussian Random Field Metamodels. *IEEE Transactions on Evolutionary Computation* 10(4):421–439.

68 W. PONWEISER et al. (2008). Multiobjective Optimization on a Limited Budget of Evaluations Using Model-Assisted S-Metric Selection. *PPSN X*.

69 K. YANG et al. (2019b). Multi-Objective Bayesian Global Optimization Using Expected Hypervolume Improvement Gradient. *Swarm and Evolutionary Computation* 44:945–956.

70 K. YANG et al. (2019a). Efficient Computation of Expected Hypervolume Improvement Using Box Decomposition Algorithms. *Journal of Global Optimization* 75(1):3–34.

tier is revealed by the observed data.[66] Therefore it provides a sensible measure of progress for a posteriori multiobjective optimization.

The one-step marginal gain in this utility is known as *expected hypervolume improvement* (EHVI)[67,68] and serves as a popular acquisition function. This score is shown in Figure 11.13 for our example; the optimal decision attempts to refine the central portion of the Pareto frontier, but many alternatives are almost as favorable due to the roughness of the current estimate. Computation of EHVI is involved, and its cost grows considerably with the number of objectives. The primary difficulty is enumerating and integrating with respect to the lower bound to the Pareto front, which can become a complex region in higher dimensions. However, efficient algorithms are available for computing EVHI[69] and its gradient.[70]

Information-theoretic a posteriori methods

Several popular information-theoretic policies for single-objective optimization have been adapted to a posteriori multiobjective optimization. The key idea behind these methods is to approximate the mutual information between a joint observation of the objectives and either the set of Pareto optimal points (in the domain), $\mathcal{X}^*$, or the Pareto frontier (in the codomain), $\mathcal{F}^*$. These approaches operate by maximizing the predictive form of mutual information (8.35) and largely follow the parallel single-objective cases in their approximation.

HERNÁNDEZ-LOBATO et al. proposed maximizing the mutual information between the observations $\mathbf{y}$ realized at a proposed observation location x and the set of Pareto optimal points $\mathcal{X}^*$:

$$\alpha_{\text{PESMO}}(x; \mathcal{D}) = H[\mathbf{y} \mid x, \mathcal{D}] - \mathbb{E}_{\mathcal{X}^*}\big[H[\mathbf{y} \mid x, \mathcal{D}, \mathcal{X}^*] \mid x, \mathcal{D}\big],$$

calling their policy *predictive entropy search for multiobjective optimization* (PESMO).[71] As in the single-objective case, for Gaussian process models with additive Gaussian noise, the first term of this expression can be computed exactly as the differential entropy of a multivariate normal distribution (A.16). However, the second term entails two computational barriers: computing an expectation with respect to $\mathcal{X}^*$ and conditioning our objective function belief on this set. The authors provide approximations for each of these tasks for Gaussian process models based on Gaussian expectation propagation; these are reminiscent of the procedure used in predictive entropy search.

BELAKARIA et al. meanwhile proposed maximizing the mutual information with the Pareto frontier $\mathcal{F}^*_*$

$$\alpha_{\text{MESMO}}(x; \mathcal{D}) = H[\mathbf{y} \mid x, \mathcal{D}] - \mathbb{E}_{\mathcal{F}^*}\big[H[\mathbf{y} \mid x, \mathcal{D}, \mathcal{F}^*] \mid x, \mathcal{D}\big].$$

The authors dubbed the resulting policy *max-value entropy search for multiobjective optimization* (MESMO).[72] This policy naturally shares many features with the PESMO policy. Again the chief difficulty is in addressing the expectation and conditioning with respect to $\mathcal{F}^*$ in the second term of the mutual information; however, both of these tasks are rendered somewhat easier by working in the codomain. To approximate the expectation with respect to $\mathcal{F}^*_*$ the authors propose a Monte Carlo approach where posterior samples of the objectives are generated efficiently using a sparse-spectrum approximation, which are fed into an off-the-shelf, exhaustive multiobjective optimization routine. Conditioning $\mathbf{y}$ on a realization of the Pareto frontier now entails appropriate truncation of its multivariate normal belief.

A priori methods and scalarization

When preferences regarding tradeoffs among the objective functions can be sufficiently established prior to optimization, perhaps with input from a domain expert, we may reduce multiobjective optimization to a *single* objective problem by explicitly maximizing the desired criterion. This is called *scalarization* and is a prominent a priori method. Reframing in terms of a single objective offers the obvious benefit of allowing us to appeal to the expansive methodology for that purpose we have built up throughout the course of this book.

Scalarization is an important component of some a posteriori multiobjective optimization methods as well. The idea is to construct a family of exhaustive parametric scalarizations of the objectives such that the solution to any such problem is Pareto optimal, and that by spanning the parameter range we may reveal the entire Pareto frontier one point at a time.

71 D. HERNÁNDEZ-LOBATO et al. (2016a). Predictive Entropy Search for Multi-Objective Bayesian Optimization. *ICML 2016*.

predictive entropy search: § 8.8, p. 180

72 S. BELAKARIA et al. (2019). Max-value Entropy Search for Multi-Objective Bayesian Optimization. *NeurIPS 2019*.

sparse spectrum approximation: § 8.7, p. 178

scalarization

a posteriori optimization via scalarization

Figure 11.14: A series of linear scalarizations of the example objectives from Figure 11.10. One end of the spectrum is f_1, and the other end is f_2.

vector of objective values at x, ϕ

scalarization function, g

Let ϕ denote the vector of objective function values at an arbitrary location x, defining $\phi_i = f_i(x)$. A *scalarization function* $g\colon x \mapsto g(\phi) \in \mathbb{R}$ maps locations in the domain to scalars determined by their objective values. We may interpret the output as defining preferences over locations in a natural manner: namely, if $g(\phi) > g(\phi')$, then the outcomes at x are preferred to those at x' in the scalarization. With this interpretation, a scalarization function allows us to recast multiobjective optimization as a single-objective problem by maximizing g with respect to x.

A scalarization function can in principle be arbitrary, and a priori multiobjective optimization can be framed in terms of maximizing any such function. However, several tunable scalarization functions have been described in the literature that may be used in a general context. A straightforward and intuitive example is *linear scalarization:*

$$g_{\text{LIN}}(x; \mathbf{w}) = \sum_i w_i\, \phi_i, \qquad (11.19)$$

where each weight w_i is nonnegative. A range of linear scalarizations for our running example is shown in Figure 11.14, here constructed to smoothly interpolate between the two objectives. The maximum of a linear scalarization is guaranteed to lie on the Pareto frontier; however, not every Pareto optimal point can be recovered in this manner unless the frontier is strictly concave. That is the case for our example, illustrated in the marginal figure. If we model each objective with a (perhaps joint) Gaussian process, then the induced belief about any linear scalarization is conveniently also a Gaussian process, so no further modeling would be required for the scalarization function itself.

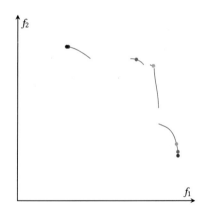

The marked points represent the maxima of the linear scalarizations in Figure 11.14.

Another choice that has seen some use in Bayesian optimization is *augmented Chebyshev* scalarization, which augments the linear scalarization (11.19) with an additional, nonlinear term:

$$g_{\text{AC}}(x; \mathbf{w}, \rho) = \min_i \big[w_i(\phi_i - r_i) \big] + \rho\, g_{\text{LIN}}(x; \mathbf{w}). \qquad (11.20)$$

Here $\mathbf{r}$ is a reference point as above and ρ is a small nonnegative constant; KNOWLES for example took $\rho = 0.05$.[73] The augmented Chebyshev scalarization function has the benefit that *all* points on the Pareto frontier can be realized by maximizing with respect to some corresponding setting of the weights, even if the frontier is nonconcave. GOLOVIN and ZHANG proposed a similar *hypervolume scalarization* related to the $\mathcal{S}$-metric.[74]

73 J. KNOWLES (2005). ParEGO: A Hybrid Algorithm with On-Line Landscape Approximation for Expensive Multiobjective Optimization Problems. *IEEE Transactions on Evolutionary Computation* 10(1):50–66.

74 D. GOLOVIN and Q. ZHANG (2020). Random Hypervolume Scalarizations for Provable Multi-Objective Black Box Optimization. *ICML 2020*.

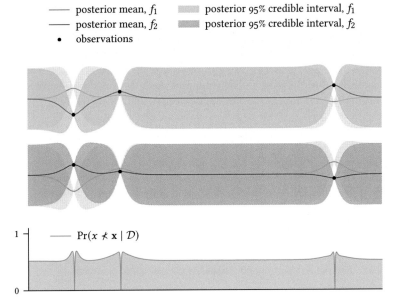

— posterior mean, f_1 posterior 95% credible interval, f_1
— posterior mean, f_2 posterior 95% credible interval, f_2
• observations

— $\Pr(x \not\succ \mathbf{x} \mid \mathcal{D})$

Figure 11.15: The probability of nondominance by the available data for our running example (above).

Several authors have derived Bayesian methods for a posteriori multiobjective optimization by solving a series of carefully constructed scalarized problems. KNOWLES for example proposed sampling random weights for the augmented Chebyshev scalarization (11.20) and optimizing the resulting objective, repeating this process until satisfied.[73] PARIA et al. proposed a similar approach incorporating a prior distribution over the parameters of a chosen scalarization function to allow the user to focus on an identified region of the Pareto frontier if desired.[75] The procedure then proceeds by repeatedly sampling from that distribution and maximizing the resulting objective. This is effectively the same as KNOWLES's approach, but the authors were able to establish theoretical regret bounds for their procedure. These results were improved by GOLOVIN and ZHANG, who derived (stronger) theoretical guarantees for a procedure based on repeatedly optimizing their proposed hypervolume scalarization.

75 B. PARIA et al. (2019). A Flexible Framework for Multi-Objective Bayesian Optimization Using Random Scalarizations. *UAI 2019*.

Other approaches

ZULUAGA et al. outlined an intriguing approach to a posteriori multiobjective optimization[76] wherein the problem was recast as an *active learning* problem.[77] Namely, the authors considered the binary classification problem of predicting whether a given observation location was (approximately) Pareto optimal or not, then designed observations to maximize expected performance on this task. Their algorithm is supported by theoretical bounds on performance and performed admirably compared with KNOWLES's algorithm discussed above.[73]

PICHENY proposed a spiritually similar approach also based on sequentially reducing a measure of uncertainty in the Pareto frontier.[78]

76 M. ZULUAGA et al. (2016). ε-PAL: An Active Learning Approach to the Multi-Objective Optimization Problem. *Journal of Machine Learning Research* 17(104):1–32.

77 B. SETTLES (2012). *Active Learning*. Morgan & Claypool.

78 V. PICHENY (2015). Multiobjective Optimization Using Gaussian Process Emulators via Stepwise Uncertainty Reduction. *Statistics and Computing* 25(6):1265–1280.

Given a dataset $\mathcal{D} = (\mathbf{x}, \mathbf{y})$, we consider the probability that a given point $x \in \mathcal{X}$ is *not* dominated by any point in the current dataset (that is, the probability x may lie on the Pareto frontier but not yet be discovered), $\Pr(x \not\prec \mathbf{x} \mid \mathcal{D})$. The integral of this score over the domain can be interpreted as a measure of uncertainty in the Pareto frontier as determined by the data, and negating this measure provides a plausible utility function for a posteriori multiobjective optimization:

$$u(\mathcal{D}) = -\int \Pr(x \not\prec \mathbf{x}) \, \mathrm{d}x.$$

This probability is plotted for our running example in Figure 11.15; here, there is a significant probability for many points to be nondominated by the rather sparse available data, indicating a significant degree of uncertainty in our understanding of the Pareto frontier. However, as the Pareto frontier is increasingly well determined by the data, this probability will vanish globally and the utility above will tend toward its maximal value of zero. After motivating this score, PICHENY proceeds to recommend designing observations via one-step lookahead.

11.8 GRADIENT OBSERVATIONS

Bayesian optimization is often described as a "derivative-free" approach to optimization, but this characterization is misleading. Although it is true that Bayesian optimization methods do not *require* the ability to observe derivatives, it is *certainly* not the case that we cannot make use of such observations when available. In fact, it is straightforward to condition a Gaussian process on derivative observations, even if corrupted by noise, and so from a modeling perspective we are already done.

Of course, ideally, our policy should also consider the acquisition of derivative information due to its influence on our belief and the utility of collected data, of which they now form a part. To do so is by now relatively simple. A fairly general scheme would assume that an observation at x yields a pair of measurements $(y, \mathbf{g})$ respectively related to $(\phi, \nabla\phi)$ via a joint observation model.[79] We can then compute the one-step expected marginal gain in utility from observing these values:

$$\alpha_1(x; \mathcal{D}) = \iint \left[u(\mathcal{D}_1) - u(\mathcal{D}) \right] p(y, \mathbf{g} \mid x, \mathcal{D}) \, \mathrm{d}y \, \mathrm{d}\mathbf{g}, \qquad (11.21)$$

where the updated dataset $\mathcal{D}_1$ will reflect the entire observation $(x, y, \mathbf{g})$. Induction on the horizon gives the optimal policy as usual.

Figure 11.16 compares derivative-aware and derivative-unaware versions of the knowledge gradient (7.4) (assuming exact observation) for an example scenario. The derivative-aware version dominates the derivative-unaware one, as the acquisition of more information naturally leads to a greater expected marginal gain in utility. When derivative information is unavailable, the optimal decision is to evaluate nearby the previously best-seen point, effectively to estimate the derivative via finite differencing; when derivative information is available, an observation at this

conditioning a GP on derivative observations: § 2.6, p. 32

79 This could be, for example, exact observation or additive Gaussian noise. Recall that for a GP on f, the joint distribution of $(\phi, \nabla\phi)$ is multivariate normal (2.28), so for these choices the predictive distribution of $(y, \mathbf{g})$ is jointly Gaussian and exact inference is tractable.

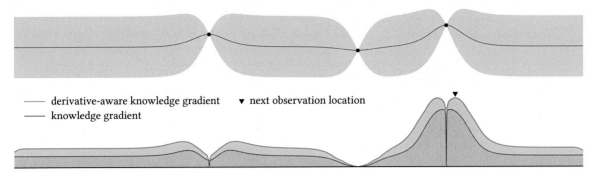

Figure 11.16: The knowledge gradient acquisition function for an example scenario reflecting the expected gain in global reward (6.5) provided exact observations of the objective function and its derivative. The vanilla knowledge gradient (7.4) based on an observation of the objective alone is shown for reference.

location yields effectively the same expected gain. However, we can fare even better in expectation by moving a bit farther astray, where the derivative information is less redundant.

When working with Gaussian process models in high dimension, it may not be wise to augment each observation of the objective with a full observation of the gradient due to the cubic scaling of inference. However, the scheme outlined above opens the door to consider the observation of *any* measurement related to the gradient. For example, we might condition on the value of a *directional* derivative, reducing the measurement to a scalar regardless of dimension and limiting computation. Such a scheme was promoted by wu et al., who considered the acquisition of a single coordinate of the gradient; this could be extended to non-axis-aligned directional derivatives without major complication.[80] We could also consider a "multifidelity" extension where we weigh various possible gradient observations (including none at all) in light of their expected utility and the cost of acquisition/inference.

scaling of Gaussian process inference: § 9.1, p. 201

80 J. wu et al. (2017). Bayesian Optimization with Gradients. *NeurIPS 2017*.

11.9 STOCHASTIC AND ROBUST OPTIMIZATION

In some applications, the performance of a given system configuration depends on stochastic exogenous factors. For example, consider optimizing the parameters of a mobile robot's gait to maximize some tradeoff of stability, efficiency, and speed. These objectives depend not only on the gait parameters, but also on the nature of the environment – such as the composition, slope, etc. of the surface to be traversed – which cannot be controlled by the robot at the time of performance and may vary over repeated sessions. In this scenario, we may seek to optimize some measure of performance accounting for uncertainty in the environment.

To model this and related scenarios, we may consider an objective function $g(x, \omega)$, where x represents a configuration we wish to optimize, and ω represents relevant parameters of the environment not under

partially controllable objective function, $g(x, \omega)$

environmental parameter, ω

special case: perturbed parameters

our control. In this context, ω is called an *environmental parameter* or *environmental variable*. A notable special case of this setup is where the environmental parameters represent a perturbation to the optimization parameters at the time of performance:

$$g(x, \omega) = h(x + \omega), \tag{11.22}$$

where h is an objective function to be optimized as usual. Such a model would allow us to consider scenarios where there may be instability or imprecision in the specification of control parameters.

The primary challenge when facing such an objective is in identifying a clear optimization goal in the face of parameters that cannot be controlled; once this has been properly formalized, the development of optimization policies is then usually relatively straightforward. Several possible approaches have been studied to this end, which vary somewhat in their motivation and details. One detail with strong influence on algorithm design is whether the environment and/or any perturbations to inputs can be controlled during optimization; if so, we can accelerate optimization through careful manipulation of the environment.

Stochastic optimization

In *stochastic optimization*,[81] we seek to optimize the *expected* performance of the system of interest (also known as the *integrated response*[82]) under an assumed distribution for the environmental parameters, $p(\omega)$:

$$f = \mathbb{E}_\omega[g] = \int g(x, \omega)\, p(\omega)\, d\omega. \tag{11.23}$$

Optimizing this objective presents a challenge: in general, the expectation with respect to ω cannot be evaluated directly but only estimated via repeated trials in different environments, and estimating the expected performance (11.23) with some degree of precision may require numerous evaluations of $g(x, \omega)$. However, when g itself is expensive to evaluate – for example, if every trial requires manual manipulation of a robot and its environment before we can measure performance – this may not be the most efficient approach, as we may waste significant resources shoring up our belief about suboptimal values.

Instead, when we can control the environment during optimization at will, we can gain some traction by designing a sequence of free parameter–environment pairs, potentially changing both configuration and environment in each iteration. The most direct way to design such an algorithm in our framework would be to model the environmental-conditional objective function g directly and define a utility function and policy with respect to this function, in light of the environmental-marginal objective f (11.23) and its induced Gaussian process distribution.

A Gaussian process model on g is particularly practical in this regard, as we may then use Bayesian quadrature to seamlessly estimate and quantify our uncertainty in the objective f (11.23) from observations.[83]

81 This is a heavily overloaded phrase, as it is used as an umbrella term for optimization involving any random elements. It is also used, for example, to describe optimization from noisy observations, to include methods such as stochastic gradient descent. As noisy observations are commonplace in Bayesian optimization, we reserve the phrase for stochastic environmental parameters only.

82 B. J. WILLIAMS et al. (2000). Sequential Design of Computer Experiments to Minimize Integrated Response Functions. *Statistica Sinica* 10(4):1133–1152.

83 If g has distribution $\mathcal{GP}(\mu, K)$, then f has distribution $\mathcal{GP}(m, C)$ with:

$$m = \int \mu(x, \omega)\, p(\omega)\, d\omega;$$

$$C = \iint K([x, \omega], [x', \omega'])\, p(\omega, \omega')\, d\omega\, d\omega'.$$

Bayesian quadrature: § 2.6, p. 33

This approach was explored in depth by TOSCANO-PALMERIN and FRAZIER, who also provided an excellent review of the related literature.[84]

Several algorithms have also been proposed for the special case of perturbed control parameters (11.22), where we seek to optimize an objective function h under a random perturbation of its input, whose distribution may depend on location:

$$f = \mathbb{E}_\omega[h] = \int h(x + \omega)\, p(\omega \mid x)\, d\omega. \qquad (11.24)$$

In effect, the goal is to identify relatively "stable" (or "wide") optima of the objective function; see the margin for an illustration. Once again, a Gaussian process belief on h induces a Gaussian process belief on the averaged objective (11.24),[85] which can aid in the construction of policies.

When the perturbations follow a multivariate Gaussian distribution, and when inputs are assumed to be perturbed during optimization (and not only at performance time), one simple approach is to estimate the expectation of an arbitrary acquisition function $\alpha(x; \mathcal{D})$ (defined with respect to the unperturbed objective h) with respect to the random perturbations,

$$\mathbb{E}_\omega[\alpha] = \int \alpha(x + \omega; \mathcal{D})\, p(\omega)\, d\omega,$$

via an unscented transform.[86] We may then maximize the expected acquisition function to realize an effective policy.

Under the assumption of unperturbed parameters during optimization, FRÖHLICH et al. described an adaptation of max-value entropy search for maximizing the expected objective (11.24).[87] OLIVEIRA et al. studied what is effectively the reversal of this problem: optimizing the *unperturbed* objective h (11.24) under the assumption of perturbed inputs during optimization. The authors proposed a variation of the Gaussian process upper confidence bound algorithm for this setting with theoretical guarantees on convergence.[88]

Robust optimization

Maximizing expected performance (11.23, 11.24) may not always be appropriate in all settings, as it is *risk neutral* by design. In the interest of risk aversion, in some scenarios we may instead seek parameters that ensure reasonable performance even in unfavorable environments. This is the goal of *robust optimization*. We can identify two families of approaches to robust optimization, differing according to whether we seek guarantees that are probabilistic (good performance in *most* environments) or adversarial (good performance in even the *worst* possible environment).

Probabilistic approaches focus on optimizing risk measures of performance such as the *value-at-risk* or *conditional value-at-risk*. In the former case, we seek to optimize a (lower) quantile of the distribution of $g(x, \omega)$, rather than its mean (11.23); see the figure in the margin:

$$\text{VAR}(x; \pi) = \inf\{\gamma \mid \Pr(g(x, \omega) \leq \gamma \mid x) \geq \pi\}.$$

84 S. TOSCANO-PALMERIN and P. I. FRAZIER (2018). Bayesian Optimization with Expensive Integrands. arXiv: 1803.08661 [stat.ML].

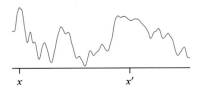

When stability to perturbation is critical, the relatively stable, but suboptimal, peak at x' might be preferred to the relatively narrow global optimum at x.

85 If h has distribution $\mathcal{GP}(\mu, K)$, then f has distribution $\mathcal{GP}(m, C)$ with:

$$m = \int \mu(x + \omega)\, p(\omega \mid x)\, d\omega;$$

$$C = \iint K(x + \omega, x' + \omega')$$
$$p(\omega, \omega' \mid x, x')\, d\omega\, d\omega'.$$

86 J. GARCÍA-BARCOS and R. MARTINEZ-CANTIN (2021). Robust Policy Search for Robot Navigation. *IEEE Robotics and Automation Letters* 6(2): 2389–2396.

The authors focused on expected improvement and also defined an "unscented incumbent" to approximate the maximum of (11.24).

87 L. P. FRÖHLICH et al. (2020). Noisy-Input Entropy Search for Efficient Robust Bayesian Optimization. *AISTATS 2020*.

88 R. OLIVEIRA et al. (2019). Bayesian Optimisation Under Uncertain Inputs. *AISTATS 2019*.

risk tolerance: § 6.1, p. 111

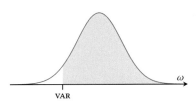

The value-at-risk (at the $\pi = 5\%$ level) for an example distribution of $g(x, \omega)$. The VAR is a pessimistic lower bound on performance holding with probability $1 - \pi$.

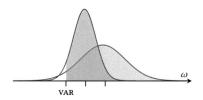

These distributions have the same value-at-risk at $\pi = 5\%$ (marked VAR); however, the wider distribution has greater *conditional* value-at-risk (the right-most of the unlabeled ticks), as its upper tail has a higher expectation than the narrower distribution's.

89 Q. P. NGUYEN et al. (2021b). Value-at-Risk Optimization with Gaussian Processes. *ICML 2021.*

90 Q. P. NGUYEN et al. (2021a). Optimizing Conditional Value-At-Risk of Black-Box Functions. *NeurIPS 2021.*

91 S. CAKMAK et al. (2020). Bayesian Optimization of Risk Measures. *NeurIPS 2020.*

92 BOGUNOVIC et al.'s main focus was actually the related problem of adversarial *perturbations*:

$$f(x) = \min_{\omega \in \Delta(x)} h(x + \omega);$$

however, they also extend their algorithm to robust objectives of the form given in (11.25).

reproducing kernel Hilbert spaces: § 10.2, p. 219

93 R. MARTINEZ-CANTIN et al. (2018). Practical Bayesian Optimization in the Presence of Outliers. *AISTATS 2018.*

94 See also § 11.11, p. 282 for related discussion.

95 I. BOGUNOVIC et al. (2020). Corruption-Tolerant Gaussian Process Bandit Optimization. *AISTATS 2020.*

We can interpret the value-at-risk as a pessimistic lower bound on performance with tunable failure probability π. Although a natural measure of robustness, the value-at-risk ignores the shape of the upper tail of the performance distribution entirely – any two distributions with equal π-quantiles are judged equal. The conditional value-at-risk measure accounts for differences in upper tail distributions by computing the expected performance in the favorable regime:

$$\text{CVAR}(x; \pi) = \mathbb{E}_\omega \big[g(x, \omega) \mid g(x; \omega) \geq \text{VAR}(x; \pi) \big].$$

Two performance distributions that cannot be distinguished by VAR but can be distinguished by their CVAR are illustrated in the marginal figure.

Optimizing both value-at-risk and conditional value-at-risk has received some attention in the literature, and optimization policies for this setting – under the assumption of a controllable environment during optimization – have been proposed based on upper confidence bounds,[89,90] Thompson sampling,[90] and the knowledge gradient.[91]

An alternative approach to robust optimization is to maximize some notion of *worst*-case performance. For example, we might consider an adversarial objective function of the form:

$$f(x) = \min_{\omega \in \Delta(x)} g(x, \omega), \tag{11.25}$$

where $\Delta(x)$ is a compact, possibly location-dependent subset of environments to consider. Note that value-at-risk is actually a special case of this construction, where $\Delta(x)$ is taken to be the upper tail of our belief over $g(x, \omega)$; however, we could also define such an adversarial objective without any reference to probability at all. BOGUNOVIC et al. for example considered robust optimization in this adversarial setting[92] and described a simple algorithm based on upper/lower confidence bounds with strong convergence guarantees.

KIRSCHNER et al. considered a related adversarial setting: *distributionally robust* optimization, where we seek to optimize effectively without perfect knowledge of the environment distribution. They considered an objective of the following form:

$$f(x) = \inf_{p \in \mathcal{P}} \int g(x, \omega) \, p(\omega) \, \mathrm{d}\omega,$$

where $\mathcal{P}$ is a space of possible probability measures over the environment to consider – thus we seek to maximize expected performance under the worst-case environment distribution. The authors proposed an algorithm based on upper confidence bounds and proved convergence guarantees under technical assumptions on g (bounded RKHS norm) and $\mathcal{P}$ (bounded maximum mean discrepancy from a reference distribution).

Finally, another type of robustness that has received some attention is robustness to extreme measurement errors (beyond additive Gaussian noise), including heavy-tailed noise such as Student-t errors (2.31)[93,94] and adversarial corruption.[95]

11.10 INCREMENTAL OPTIMIZATION OF SEQUENTIAL PROCEDURES

In some applications, the objective function is determined by a *sequence* of dependent steps eventually producing its final value. If we have access to this sequential process and can model its progression, we may be able to accelerate optimization via shrewd "early stopping": terminating evaluations still in progress when their final value can be forecasted with sufficient confidence.

Hyperparameter tuning presents one compelling example. Consider for example the optimization of neural network hyperparameters $\boldsymbol{\theta}$.[96] The objective function in this setting is usually defined to be the value of some loss function ℓ (for example, validation error) after the network has been trained with the chosen hyperparameters. However, this training is an *iterative* procedure: if the network is parameterized by a vector of weights $\mathbf{w}$, then the objective function might be defined by

$$f(\boldsymbol{\theta}) = \lim_{t\to\infty} \ell(\mathbf{w}_t; \boldsymbol{\theta}), \qquad (11.26)$$

the loss of the network after the weights have converged.[97] If we don't treat this objective function as a black box but take a peek inside, we may interpret it as the limiting value of the *learning curve* defined by the learning procedure's loss at each stage of training.

The iterative nature of this objective function offers the opportunity for innovation in policy design. Learning curves typically exhibit fairly regular behavior, with the loss in each step of training generally falling over time until settling on its final value. This suggests we may be able to faithfully *extrapolate* the final value of a learning curve from the early stages of training; a toy example is presented in the margin. When possible, we may then be able to speed up optimization by not always training to convergence with every setting of the hyperparameters we explore. With this motivation in mind, several sophisticated methods for extrapolating learning curves have been developed, including carefully crafted parametric models[98,99] and flexible Bayesian neural networks.[100]

Exploiting the ability to extrapolate sequential objectives requires that we expand our action space (step 1) to allow fine-grained control over evaluation. One compelling scheme was proposed by SWERSKY et al.,[98] who suggested maintaining a set of partial evaluations of the objective throughout optimization. In the context of our hyperparameter tuning example (11.26), we would maintain a set of thus-far investigated hyperparameters $\{\boldsymbol{\theta}_i\}$, each accompanied by a sequence (of variable length) of thus-far evaluated weights $\{\mathbf{w}_{t,i}\}$ and the associated losses $\{\ell_{t,i}\}$. Now, each action we design can either investigate a novel hyperparameter $\boldsymbol{\theta}$ or extend an existing partial evaluation by one step. The authors dubbed this scheme *freeze–thaw Bayesian optimization,* as after each action we "freeze" the current evaluation, saving enough state such that we can "thaw" it later for further investigation if desired.

Regardless of modeling details, this scheme offers the potential for considerable savings when optimizing sequential objective functions.

96 We will use $\boldsymbol{\theta}$ for the variable to be optimized here rather than x to be consistent with our previous discussion of Gaussian process hyperparameters in Chapter 3.

97 One could consider early stopping in the training procedure as well, but this simple example is useful for exposition.

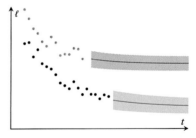

Learning curve extrapolation from initial training results. At this point, we may already wish to abandon the apparently inferior option.

98 K. SWERSKY et al. (2014). Freeze–Thaw Bayesian Optimization. arXiv: 1406.3896 [stat.ML].

99 T. DOMHAN et al. (2015). Speeding up Automatic Hyperparameter Optimization of Deep Neural Networks by Extrapolation of Learning Curves. *IJCAI 2015*.

100 A. KLEIN et al. (2017). Learning Curve Prediction with Bayesian Neural Networks. *ICLR 2017*.

freeze–thaw Bayesian optimization

101   L. LI et al. (2018b). Hyperband: A Novel Bandit-Based Approach to Hyperparameter Optimization. *Journal of Machine Learning Research* 18(185):1–52.

This idea of abandoning stragglers based on early progress is also the basis of the bandit-based *hyperband* algorithm.[101]

11.11   NON-GAUSSIAN OBSERVATION MODELS AND ACTIVE SEARCH

Throughout this book, we have focused almost exclusively on the additive Gaussian noise observation model. There are good reasons for this: it is a reasonably faithful model of many systems and offers exact inference with Gaussian process models of the objective function. However, the assumption of Gaussian noise is not always warranted and may be fundamentally incompatible with some scenarios.

Chapter 5: Decision Theory for Optimization, p. 87

Chapter 6: Utility Functions for Optimization, p. 109

GP inference with non-Gaussian observation models: § 2.8, p. 35

Fortunately, the decision-theoretic core of most Bayesian optimization approaches does not make any assumptions regarding our model of the objective function or our observations of it, and with some care the utility functions we developed for optimization can be adapted for virtually any scenario. Further, there are readily available pathways for incorporating non-Gaussian observation models into Gaussian process objective function models, so we do not need to abandon that rich model class in order to use alternatives.

Sequential optimization with non-Gaussian observation models

A decision-theoretic approach to optimization entails first selecting an objective function model $p(f)$ and observation model $p(y \mid x, \phi)$, which together are sufficient to derive the predictive distribution $p(y \mid x, \mathcal{D})$ relevant to every sequential decision made during optimization. After selecting a utility function $u(\mathcal{D})$, we may then follow the iterative procedure developed in Chapter 5 to derive a policy.

102   A. SHAH et al. (2014). Student-*t* Processes as Alternatives to Gaussian Processes. *AISTATS 2014*.

103   R. MARTINEZ-CANTIN et al. (2018). Practical Bayesian Optimization in the Presence of Outliers. *AISTATS 2018*.

104   We explored this possibility at length in § 2.8.

105   M. TESCH et al. (2013). Expensive Function Optimization with Stochastic Binary Outcomes. *ICML 2013*.

This abstract approach has been realized in several specific settings. For example, both Student-*t* processes[102] and the Student-*t* observation model[103] have been explored to develop Bayesian optimization routines that are robust to the presence of outliers.[104]

TESCH et al. explored the use of expected improvement for optimization from binary success/failure indicators, motivated by optimizing the *probability* of success of a robotic platform operating in an uncertain environment.[105] Here the utility function was taken to be this success probability maximized over the observed locations:

$$u(\mathcal{D}) = \max_{\mathbf{x}} \mathbb{E}[y \mid x, \mathcal{D}] = \max_{\mathbf{x}} \Pr(y = 1 \mid x, \mathcal{D}),$$

106   Note that the simple reward utility function (6.3) we have been working with can be written in this exact form if we assume any additive observation noise has zero mean.

107   N. HOULSBY et al. (2012). Collaborative Gaussian Processes for Preference Learning. *NeurIPS 2012*.

where for this expression we have assumed binary outcomes $y \in \{0, 1\}$ with $y = 1$ interpreted as indicating success.[106] The authors then derived a policy for this setting via one-step lookahead.

Another setting involving binary (or categorical) feedback is in optimizing human preferences, such as in A/B testing or user modeling. Here we might seek to optimize user preferences by repeatedly presenting a panel of options and asking for the most preferred item. HOULSBY et al. described a convenient reduction from preference learning to classification for Gaussian processes that allows the immediate use of standard policies such as expected improvement,[107,105] although more sophisticated policies have also been proposed specifically for this setting.[108]

108 See Appendix D, p. 329 for related references.

Active search

GARNETT et al. introduced *active search* as a simple model of scientific discovery in a *discrete* domain $\mathcal{X} = \{x_i\}$.[109] In active search, we assume that among these points is hidden a rare, valuable subset exhibiting desirable properties for the task at hand. Given access to an oracle that can – at significant cost – determine whether an identified point belongs to the sought after class, the problem of active search is to design a sequence of experiments seeking to maximize the number of discoveries in a given budget. A motivating application is drug discovery, where the domain would represent a list of candidate molecules to search for those rare examples exhibiting significant binding activity with a chosen biological target. As the space of candidates is expansive and the cost of even virtual screening is nontrivial, intelligent experimental design has the potential to greatly improve the rate of discovery.

109 R. GARNETT et al. (2012). Bayesian Optimal Active Search and Surveying. *ICML 2012*.

virtual screening: Appendix D, p. 314

To derive an active search policy in our framework, we must first model the observation process and determine a suitable utility function. The former requires consideration of the nuances of a given situation, but we may provide a barebones construction that is already sufficient to be of practical and theoretical interest. Given a discrete domain $\mathcal{X}$, we assume there is some identifiable subset $\mathcal{V} \subset \mathcal{X}$ of valuable points we wish to recover. We associate with each point $x \in \mathcal{X}$ a binary label $y = [x \in \mathcal{V}]$ indicating whether x is valuable ($y = 1$) or not ($y = 0$). A natural observation model is then to assume that selecting a point x for investigation reveals this binary label y in response.[110] Finally, we may define a natural utility function for active search by assuming that, all other things being held equal, we prefer a dataset containing more valuable points to one with fewer:

modeling observations

110 Other situations may call for other approaches; for example, if value is determined by thresholding a continuous measurement, we may wish to model that continuous observation process explicitly.

utility function

$$u(\mathcal{D}) = \sum_{x \in \mathcal{D}} y. \qquad (11.27)$$

This is simply the cumulative reward utility (6.7), which here can be interpreted as counting the number of valuable points discovered.[111]

111 The assumption of a discrete domain is to avoid repeatedly observing effectively the same point to trivially "max out" this score.

To proceed with the Bayesian decision-theoretic approach, we must build a model for the uncertain elements inherent to each decision. Here the primary object of interest is the predictive posterior distribution $\Pr(y = 1 \mid x, \mathcal{D})$, the posterior probability that a given point x is valuable. We may build this model in any number of ways, for example by combining a Gaussian process prior on a latent function with an appropriate choice of observation model.[112]

posterior predictive probability, $\Pr(y = 1 \mid x, \mathcal{D})$

112 C. E. RASMUSSEN and C. K. I. WILLIAMS (2006). *Gaussian Processes for Machine Learning*. MIT Press. [chapter 3]

Equipped with a predictive model, deriving the optimal policy is a simple exercise. To begin, the one-step marginal gain in utility (5.8) is

$$\alpha_1(x; \mathcal{D}) = \Pr(y = 1 \mid x, \mathcal{D});$$

113 R. GARNETT et al. (2012). Bayesian Optimal Active Search and Surveying. *ICML 2012*.

114 S. JIANG et al. (2017). Efficient Nonmyopic Active Search. *ICML 2017*.

115 R. GARNETT et al. (2015). Introducing the 'Active Search' Method for Iterative Virtual Screening. *Journal of Computer-Aided Molecular Design* 29(4):305–314.

cost of computing optimal policy: § 5.3, p. 99

moving beyond one-step lookahead: § 7.10, p. 150

batch rollout: § 5.3, p. 103

that is, the optimal one-step decision is to greedily maximize the probability of success. Although this is a simple (and somewhat obvious) policy that can perform well in practice, theoretical and empirical study on active search has established that massive gains can be had by adopting less myopic policies.

On the theoretical side, GARNETT et al. demonstrated by construction that the expected performance of *any* lookahead approximation can be exceeded by any arbitrary amount by extending the lookahead horizon even a single step.[113] This result was strengthened by JIANG et al., who showed – again by construction – that *no* policy that can be computed in time polynomial in $|\mathcal{X}|$ can approximate the performance of the optimal policy within any constant factor.[114] Thus the optimal active search policy is not only hard to compute, but also hard to approximate. These theoretical results, which rely on somewhat unnatural adversarial constructions, have been supported by empirical investigations on real-world data as well.[114,115] For example, GARNETT et al. demonstrated that simply using two-step instead of one-step lookahead can significantly accelerate virtual screening for drug discovery across a broad range of biological targets.[115]

This is perhaps a surprising state of affairs given the success of one-step lookahead – and the relative lack of less myopic alternatives – for traditional optimization. We can resolve this discrepancy by noting that utility functions used in that setting, such as the simple reward (6.3), inherently exhibit decreasing marginal gains as they are effectively bounded by the global maximum. Further, such a utility tends to remain relatively constant throughout optimization, punctuated by brief but significant increases when a new local maximum is discovered. On the other hand, for the cumulative reward (11.27), *every* observation has the potential to increase the utility by exactly one unit. As a result, every observation is on equal footing in terms of potential impact, and there is increased pressure to consider the entire search trajectory when designing each observation.

One thread of research on active search has focused on developing efficient, yet nonmyopic policies grounded in approximate dynamic programming, such as lookahead beyond one step.[113] JIANG et al. proposed one significantly less myopic alternative policy based on batch rollout.[114] The key observation is that we may construct the one-step optimal batch observation of size k by computing the posterior predictive probability $\Pr(y = 1 \mid x, \mathcal{D})$ for the unlabeled points, sorting, and taking the top k; this is a consequence of linearity of expectation and utility (11.27). With this, we may realize an efficient batch rollout policy for horizon τ by maximizing the acquisition function

$$\Pr(y = 1 \mid x, \mathcal{D}) + \mathbb{E}_y\left[\sideset{}{'}\sum_{\tau-1} \Pr(y' = 1 \mid x', \mathcal{D}_1) \mid x, \mathcal{D}\right]. \qquad (11.28)$$

Here the sum-with-prime notation $\sum'_{\tau-1}$ indicates the sum of the top-$(\tau-1)$ values over the unlabeled data – the expected utility of the optimal

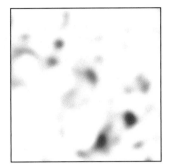 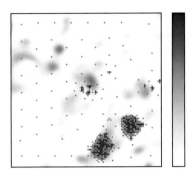

Figure 11.17: A demonstration of active search. Left: a $2d$ domain shaded according to the probability of a positive result. Right: 500 points chosen by a nonmyopic active search policy reflecting consideration of exploration versus exploitation. The darker observations were positive and the lighter ones were negative.

batch observation consuming the remaining budget.[116] In experiments, this policy showed interesting emergent behavior: it *underperforms* lookahead policies in the early stages of search due to significant investment in early exploration. However, this exploration pays off dramatically by revealing numerous promising regions that may be exploited later.

Figure 11.17 illustrates active search in a $2d$ domain, which for the purposes of this demonstration was discretized into a 100×100 grid. The example is constructed so that a small number of discrete regions yield valuable items, which must be efficiently uncovered for a successful search. The right-hand panel shows a sequence of 500 observations designed by iteratively maximizing (11.28); their distribution clearly reflects both exploration of the domain and exploitation of the most fruitful regions. The rate of discovery for the active search policy was approximately 3.8 times greater than would be expected from random search.

VANCHINATHAN et al. considered an expanded setting they dubbed *adaptive valuable item discovery* (AVID), for which active search is a special case. Here items may have nonnegative, *continuous* values and the cumulative reward utility (11.27) was augmented with a term encouraging diversity among the selected items.[117] The authors proposed an algorithm called GP-SELECT for this setting based on an acquisition function featuring two terms: a standard upper confidence bound score (8.25) and a term encouraging diversity related to *determinantal point processes*.[118] The authors were further able to establish theoretical regret bounds for this algorithm under standard assumptions on the complexity of the value function.

11.12   LOCAL OPTIMIZATION

Historically, the primary focus of Bayesian optimization research has been *global* optimization. However, when the domain is too enormous to search systematically,[119] or if we have prior knowledge regarding the most promising areas of the domain to search, we may prefer to perform *local* optimization, where we seek to optimize the objective only in the neighborhood of an initial "guess" $x_0 \in \mathcal{X}$.

Line search and *trust region* methods are two broad approaches to unconstrained local optimization in Euclidean domains $\mathcal{X} \subset \mathbb{R}^d$. The

116 The cost of computing this acquisition function is $\mathcal{O}(n^2 \log n)$, where $n = |\mathcal{X}|$; this is roughly the same order as the two-step expected marginal gain, $\mathcal{O}(n^2)$.

117 H. P. VANCHINATHAN et al. (2015). Discovering Valuable Items from Massive Data. *KDD 2015*.

118 A. KULESZA and B. TASKAR (2012). Determinantal Point Processes for Machine Learning. *Foundations and Trends in Machine Learning* 5(2–3):123–286.

119 For example, when faced with the curse of dimensionality; see § 3.5, p. 61, § 9.2, p. 208.

basic idea in both cases is to navigate a path $\{\mathbf{x}_0, \mathbf{x}_1, \dots\}$ through the domain – guided by the gradient of the objective function – hoping to generally progress "uphill" over time.

Starting from some arbitrary location $\mathbf{x} \in \mathcal{X}$, line search methods design the next step of the path $\mathbf{x} \to \mathbf{x}'$ through a two-stage process (pseudocode in margin).[120] First, we determine a *search direction* $\mathbf{d}$,[121] which restricts our choice to the one-dimensional subspace extending from $\mathbf{x}$ in the given direction: $\mathcal{L} = \{\mathbf{x} + \alpha\mathbf{d} \mid \alpha > 0\}$. Next, we explore the objective function along this subspace to choose a *step size* $\alpha > 0$ to take in this direction, which finally determines the next location: $\mathbf{x}' = \mathbf{x} + \alpha\mathbf{d}$.

Once a search direction has been chosen, classical methods for determining the step size boil down to searching along $\mathcal{L}$ for a point providing "sufficient progress" toward a local optimum. In the absence of noise, this notion of sufficiency is well-understood and can be captured by simple conditions on the objective function, such as the well-known *Armijo–Goldstein* and *Wolfe conditions*.[120] However, these conditions become difficult to assess in the presence of even a small amount of noise.

To overcome this barrier, several authors have developed Bayesian procedures for determining the step size informed by a probabilistic model of the objective function.[122] Notably, MAHSERECI and HENNIG proposed a Gaussian process model for the objective function (and thus, its directional derivative[123]) along $\mathcal{L}$,[120,124] which allows us to assess the *probability* that the Wolfe conditions are satisfied at a given location in light of noisy observations. The authors then proposed a lightweight and efficient line search procedure that explores along $\mathcal{L}$ guided by this probability and the expected improvement.

When we can effectively estimate the gradient of the objective function, we can often use an established procedure for *stochastic gradient ascent* to design effective search directions.[125] When this is not possible, the ability of Gaussian processes to infer the gradient from noisy observations of the objective function *alone* allows us to nonetheless build efficient Bayesian routines for "zeroth-order" local optimization.[123] This idea was pursued by MÜLLER et al., who proposed to alternate between efficiently estimating the gradient at the current location via Bayesian experimental design, then taking a step in the direction of the *expected* gradient.[126] NGUYEN et al. noted that the expected gradient is not necessarily the most *likely* direction of ascent and proposed maximizing the latter quantity directly to identify trustworthy search directions.[127]

Trust region methods operate by maintaining their namesake *trust region* throughout optimization, a subset of the domain on which a model of the objective function is trusted. In each iteration, we use the model to select the next observation location from this region, then adjust the trust region in light of the outcome (pseudocode in margin). Classical methods rely on very simple (for example, quadratic) models, but ERIKSSON et al. demonstrated success using Gaussian process models and Bayesian optimization policies instead.[128] The authors also showed how to use their Bayesian trust region routine in an outer *global* optimization procedure, with impressive results especially in high dimension.

Margin notes:

```
x ← x_0
repeat
    observe at x
    choose search direction d
    choose step size α
    x ← x + αd
until termination condition reached
```

120 For useful discussion in this context, see:

P. HENNIG et al. (2022). *Probabilistic Numerics: Computation as Machine Learning*. Cambridge University Press. [part IV]

121 When the search direction is the one of *steepest* ascent from $\mathbf{x}$ – that is, the gradient $\nabla f(\mathbf{x})$ – this procedure is known as *gradient ascent*.

122 For some early work in this direction, see:

J. MOCKUS (1989). *Bayesian Approach to Global Optimization: Theory and Applications*. Kluwer Academic Publishers. [chapter 7]

123 See § 2.6, p. 30.

124 M. MAHSERECI and P. HENNIG (2015). Probabilistic Line Searches for Stochastic Optimization. *NeurIPS 2015*.

125 For example, when optimizing a function of the form $f(\mathbf{x}) = \frac{1}{n}\sum_{i=1}^{n} f_i(\mathbf{x})$, we may estimate the gradient by only partially evaluating the sum (a "minibatch"). In some situations, the central limit theorem applies, and even evaluating the gradient for a random subset provides an unbiased estimate of the gradient corrupted by (approximately) Gaussian noise – perfect for conditioning a Gaussian process!

126 S. MÜLLER et al. (2021). Local Policy Search with Bayesian Optimization. *NeurIPS 2021*.

127 Q. NGUYEN et al. (2022). Local Bayesian Optimization via Maximizing Probability of Descent. arXiv: 2210.11662 [cs.LG].

```
x ← x_0
repeat
    observe at x
    update trust region T
    select next observation location x ∈ T
until termination condition reached
```

128 D. ERIKSSON et al. (2019). Scalable Global Optimization via Local Bayesian Optimization. *NeurIPS 2019*.

A BRIEF HISTORY OF BAYESIAN OPTIMIZATION

12

In this chapter we provide a historical survey of the ideas underpinning Bayesian optimization, including important mathematical precedents. We also document the progression of major ideas in Bayesian optimization, from its first appearance in 1962 to the present day. A major goal will be to identify the point of introduction of prominent Bayesian optimization policies, as well as notable instances of subsequent reintroduction when ideas were forgotten and later rediscovered and refined.

12.1 HISTORICAL PRECURSORS AND OPTIMAL DESIGN

The Bayesian approach to optimization is founded on a simple premise: experiments should be designed with purpose, both guided by our knowledge and aware of our ignorance. The optimization policies built on this principle can be understood as statistical manifestations of rational inquiry, where we design a sequence of experiments to systematically reveal the maximal value attained by the system of interest.

Statistical approaches to experimental design have a long history, with the earliest examples appearing over 200 years ago.[1,2] A landmark early contribution was SMITH's 1918 dissertation,[3] which considered experimental design for polynomial regression models to minimize a measure of predictive uncertainty. Shortly thereafter, FISHER published a hugely influential guide to statistical experimental design based on his experience analyzing crop experiments at Rothamsted Experimental Station,[4] which was instrumental in shaping modern statistical practice. These works served to establish the field of *optimal design,* an expansive subject which has now enjoyed a century of study. Numerous excellent references are available.[5,6]

Early work in optimal design did not consider the possibility of adaptively designing a *sequence* of experiments, an essential feature of Bayesian optimization. Instead, the focus was optimizing fixed designs to minimize some measure of uncertainty when performing inference with the resulting data. This paradigm is practical when experiments are extremely time consuming but can easily run in parallel, such as the agricultural experiments studied extensively by FISHER. The most common goals considered in classical optimal design are accurate estimation of model parameters and confident prediction at unseen locations; these goals are usually formulated in terms of optimizing some statistical criterion as a function of the design.[7] However, in 1941, HOTELLING notably studied experimental designs for estimating the location of the maximum of an unknown function in this nonadaptive setting.[8] This was perhaps the first rigorous treatment of batch optimization.

12.2 SEQUENTIAL ANALYSIS AND BAYESIAN EXPERIMENTAL DESIGN

Concentrated study of sequential experiments began during World War II with WALD, who pioneered the field of *sequential analysis.* The seminal

1 J. D. GERGONNE (1815). Application de la méthode des moindres quarrés à l'interpolation des suites. *Annales de Mathématiques pures et appliquées* 6:242–252.

2 C. S. PEIRCE (1876). Note on the Theory of the Economy of Research. In: *Report of the Superintendent of the United States Coast Survey Showing the Progress of the Work for the Fiscal Year Ending with June, 1876.*

3 K. SMITH (1918). On the Standard Deviations of Adjusted and Interpolated Values of an Observed Polynomial Function and Its Constants and the Guidance They Give towards a Proper Choice of the Distribution of Observations. *Biometrika* 12(1–2):1–85.

4 R. A. FISHER (1935). *The Design of Experiments.* Oliver and Boyd.

5 G. E. P. BOX et al. (2005). *Statistics for Experimenters: Design, Innovation, and Discovery.* John Wiley & Sons.

6 D. C. MONTGOMERY (2019). *Design and Analysis of Experiments.* John Wiley & Sons.

7 These criteria often have alphabetic names: A-optimality, D-optimality, V-optimality, etc.

8 H. HOTELLING (1941). Experimental Determination of the Maximum of a Function. *The Annals of Mathematical Statistics* 12(1):20–45.

9 A. WALD (1945). Sequential Tests of Statistical Hypotheses. *The Annals of Mathematical Statistics* 16(2):117–186.

10 A. WALD (1947). *Sequential Analysis.* John Wiley & Sons.

11 M. FRIEDMAN and L. J. SAVAGE (1947). Planning Experiments Seeking Maxima. In: *Selected Techniques of Statistical Analysis for Scientific and Industrial Research, and Production and Management Engineering.*

12 H. HOTELLING (1941). Experimental Determination of the Maximum of a Function. *The Annals of Mathematical Statistics* 12(1):20–45.

13 G. E. P. BOX and K. B. WILSON (1951). On the Experimental Attainment of Optimum Conditions. *Journal of the Royal Statistical Society Series B (Methodological)* 13(1):1–45.

14 G. E. P. BOX (1954). The Exploration and Exploitation of Response Surfaces: Some General Considerations and Examples. *Biometrics* 10(1):16–60.

15 G. E. P. BOX and P. V. YOULE (1954). The Exploration and Exploitation of Response Surfaces: An Example of the Link between the Fitted Surface and the Basic Mechanism of the System. *Biometrics* 11(3):287–323.

16 H. CHERNOFF (1959). Sequential Design of Experiments. *The Annals of Mathematical Statistics* 30(3):755–770.

17 H. CHERNOFF (1972). *Sequential Analysis and Optimal Design.* Society for Industrial and Applied Mathematics.

18 J. BATHER (1996). A Conversation with Herman Chernoff. *Statistical Science* 11(4):335–350.

result was a hypothesis testing procedure for sequentially gathered data that can terminate dynamically once the result is known with sufficient confidence. Such sequential tests can be significantly more data efficient than tests requiring an a priori fixed sample size. The potential benefit of WALD's work to the war effort was immediately recognized, and his research was classified and only published after the war.[9,10] The introduction of sequential analysis would kick off multiple parallel lines of investigation, leading to both Bayesian sequential experimental design and multi-armed bandits, and eventually all modern approaches to Bayesian optimization.

The success of sequential analysis led numerous researchers to investigate *sequential experimental design* in the following years. Sequential experimental design for optimization was proposed by FRIEDMAN and SAVAGE as early as 1947.[11] They argued that nonadaptive optimization procedures, as considered earlier by HOTELLING,[12] can be wasteful as many experiments may be squandered needlessly exploring suboptimal regions. Instead, FRIEDMAN and SAVAGE suggested sequential optimization could be significantly more efficient, as poor regions of the domain can be quickly discarded while more time is spent exploiting more promising areas. Their proposed algorithm was a simple procedure entailing successive axis-aligned line searches, optimizing each input variable in turn while holding the others fixed – what would now be known as *cyclic coordinate descent.*

BOX greatly expounded on these ideas, working for years alongside a chemist (WILSON) experimentally optimizing chemical processes as a function of environmental and process parameters, for example, optimizing product yield as a function of reactant concentrations.[13,14] BOX advocated the method of steepest ascent during early stages of optimization rather than the "one factor at a time" heuristic described by FRIEDMAN and SAVAGE, pointing out that the latter method is prone to becoming stuck in ridge-shaped features of the objective. BOX and YOULE also provided insightful commentary on how the process of optimization, and in particular geometric features of the objective function surface, may lead the experimenter to a greater fundamental understanding of underlying physical processes.[15]

In the following years, researchers developed general methods for sequential experimental design targeting a broad range of experimental goals. An early pioneer was CHERNOFF, a student of WALD's, who extended sequential analysis to the adaptive setting and provided asymptotically optimal procedures for sequential hypothesis testing.[16] He also wrote an survey of this early work,[17] and would eventually remark in an interview:[18]

> Although I regard myself as non-Bayesian, I feel in sequential problems it is rather dangerous to play around with non-Bayesian procedures.

Another important contribution around this time was the reintroduction of multi-armed bandits by ROBBINS, which would quickly explode into a massive body of literature. We will return to this line of work momentarily.

The Bayesian approach to sequential experimental design was formalized shortly after CHERNOFF's initial work. Authors such as RAIFFA and SCHLAIFER[19] and LINDLEY[20] promoted a general approach based on Bayesian decision theory, wherein the experimenter selects a utility function reflecting their experimental goals and a model for reasoning about experimental outcomes given data, then designs each experiment to maximize the expected utility of the collected data. This is precisely the procedure we outlined in Chapter 5. As we noted in our presentation, this framework yields theoretically *optimal* policies, but comes with an unwieldy computational burden.

19   H. RAIFFA and R. SCHLAIFER (1961). *Applied Statistical Decision Theory*. Division of Research, Graduate School of Business Administration, Harvard University.

20   D. V. LINDLEY (1972). *Bayesian Statistics, A Review*. Society for Industrial and Applied Mathematics.

12.3   THE RISE OF BAYESIAN OPTIMIZATION

By the early 1960s, the stage was set for Bayesian optimization, which could now be realized by appropriately adapting the now mature field of Bayesian experimental design.

KUSHNER was the first to seize the opportunity with a pair of papers on optimizing a one-dimensional objective observed with noise.[21,22] All of the major ideas in modern Bayesian optimization were already in place in this initial work, including a Gaussian process model of the objective function and appealing to Bayesian decision theory to derive optimization policies. After dismissing the optimal policy (with respect to the global reward utility (6.5)) as "notoriously difficult"[21] and "virtually impossible to compute,"[22] KUSHNER suggests two alternatives "on the basis of heuristic or intuitive considerations": maximizing an upper confidence bound (§ 7.8) and maximizing probability of improvement (§ 7.5), which share credit as the first Bayesian optimization policies to appear in the literature.[21] The probability of improvement approach seems to have won his favor, and KUSHNER later provided extensive practical advice for realizing this method, including careful discussion of how the improvement threshold could be managed interactively throughout optimization by a human expert in the loop.[22]

21   H. J. KUSHNER (1962). A Versatile Stochastic Model of a Function of Unknown and Time Varying Form. *Journal of Mathematical Analysis and Applications* 5(1):150–167.

22   H. J. KUSHNER (1964). A New Method of Locating the Maximum Point of an Arbitrary Multipeak Curve in the Presence of Noise. *Journal of Basic Engineering* 86(1):97–106.

A significant body of literature on Bayesian optimization emerged in the Soviet Union following KUSHNER's seminal work. Many of these authors notably explored the promise of one-step lookahead for effective policy design, proposing and studying both expected improvement and the knowledge gradient for the first time. ŠALTENIS[23] was the first to introduce expected improvement (§ 7.3) in 1971.[24] This work contains an explicit formula for expected improvement for arbitrary Gaussian process models and the results of an impressive empirical investigation on a Soviet mainframe computer with objective functions in dimensions up to 32. ŠALTENIS concludes with the following observation:

23   Also transliterated SHALTYANIS.

24   V. R. ŠALTENIS (1971). One Method of Multiextremum Optimization. *Avtomatika i Vychislitel'naya Tekhnika (Automatic Control and Computer Sciences)* 5(3):33–38.

The relatively large amounts of machine time spent in planning search and the complexity of the algorithm give us grounds to assume that the most effective sphere of application would be mul-

25 Often transliterated моčкus in early work.

26 J. MOCKUS (1972). Bayesian Methods of Search for an Extremum. *Avtomatika i Vychislitel'naya Tekhnika (Automatic Control and Computer Sciences)* 6(3):53–62.

27 J. MOCKUS (1974). On Bayesian Methods for Seeking the Extremum. *Optimization Techniques: IFIP Technical Conference.*

28 J. MOCKUS et al. (1978). The Application of Bayesian Methods for Seeking the Extrememum. In: *Towards Global Optimization 2.*

29 J. MOCKUS (1989). *Bayesian Approach to Global Optimization: Theory and Applications.* Kluwer Academic Publishers.

30 J. MOCKUS et al. (2010). *Bayesian Heuristic Approach to Discrete and Global Optimization: Algorithms, Visualization, Software, and Applications.* Kluwer Academic Publishers.

31 See equation 8 in citation 26 above.

32 J. MOCKUS (1972). Bayesian Methods of Search for an Extremum. *Avtomatika i Vychislitel'naya Tekhnika (Automatic Control and Computer Sciences)* 6(3):53–62. [equations 36–37]

33 M. SCHONLAU (1997). Computer Experiments and Global Optimization. Ph.D. thesis. University of Waterloo.

34 D. R. JONES et al. (1998). Efficient Global Optimization of Expensive Black-Box Functions. *Journal of Global Optimization* 13(4):455–492.

35 J. SACKS et al. (1989). Design and Analysis of Computer Experiments. *Statistical Science* 4(4): 409–435.

tiextremum target functions whose determination involves major computational difficulties.

This remains the target domain of Bayesian optimization today.

Another prominent early contributor was MOCKUS,[25] who wrote a series of papers on Bayesian optimization in the 1970s[26,27,28] and has written two books on the subject.[29,30] Like KUSHNER, MOCKUS begins his presentation in these papers by outlining the optimal policy for maximizing the global reward utility (6.5), but rejects it as computationally infeasible. As a practical alternative, MOCKUS instead promotes what he calls the "one-stage approach," that is, one-step lookahead.[26] As he had chosen the global reward utility, the resulting optimization policy is to maximize the knowledge gradient (§ 7.4).

This claim may give some readers pause, as MOCKUS's work is frequently cited as the origin of *expected improvement* instead. However, this is inaccurate for multiple reasons. Expected improvement had been introduced by ŠALTENIS in 1971, one year before MOCKUS's first contribution on Bayesian optimization. Indeed, MOCKUS was aware of and cited ŠALTENIS's work. Further, the acquisition function MOCKUS describes is defined with respect to the global reward utility underlying the knowledge gradient,[31] not the simple reward utility underlying expected improvement.

That said, the situation is slightly more subtle. MOCKUS also discusses two convenient choices of models on the unit interval for which the knowledge gradient happens to equal expected improvement: the Wiener process and the Ornstein–Uhlenbeck (OU) process. Both are rare examples of *Gauss–Markov processes,* whose Markovian property renders sequential inference particularly convenient, and the early work on Bayesian optimization was dominated by these models due to the extreme computational limitations at the time. MOCKUS also points out these models have a "special propert[y]";[32] namely, their Markovian nature ensures that the posterior mean is always maximized *at an observed location,* and thus the simple and global reward utilities coincide!

12.4   LATER REDISCOVERY AND DEVELOPMENT

The expected improvement and the knowledge gradient acquisition strategies were both reintroduced decades later when computational power had increased to the point that Bayesian optimization could be a practical approach for real problems.

SCHONLAU[33] and JONES et al.,[34] working together, proposed maximizing expected improvement for efficient global optimization in the context of the *design and analysis of computer experiments* (DACE).[35] Here the objective function represents the output of a computational routine and is assumed to be observed without noise. In addition to promoting expected improvement as a policy, JONES et al. also provided extensive detail for practical implementation, including an insightful discussion on model validation and a branch-and-bound strategy for maximizing the expected improvement acquisition function for a certain class of Gaussian process models. The knowledge gradient was picked up again and further developed by FRAZIER and POWELL,[36] who coined the name and studied the policy in the discrete and independent (bandit-like) setting, and SCOTT et al.,[37] who adopted the policy for continuous optimization.

Three years after reintroducing expected improvement, JONES wrote an extensive survey of then-current Bayesian optimization policies.[38] Despite the now-pervasive nature of expected improvement, it is striking that JONES actually promotes maximizing the probability of improvement as the most promising policy for Bayesian optimization throughout this survey. His concern with expected improvement was a potential lack of robustness if the objective function model is misspecified. His proposed alternative was maximizing the probability of improvement over a wide range of improvement targets and evaluating the objective function in parallel,[39] which he regarded as more robust when practical.

The concept of mutual information (§ 7.6) first appeared with SHANNON's introduction of information theory,[40] where it was called the *channel capacity* and served as a measure of the amount of information that could be transferred effectively over a noisy communication channel. LINDLEY later reinterpreted mutual information as the expected information gained by a proposed experiment and suggested maximizing this quantity as an effective means of general Bayesian experimental design.[41]

The application of this information-theoretic framework to Bayesian optimization was first proposed by VILLEMONTEIX et al.[42] and later independently by HENNIG and SCHULER,[43] the latter of whom coined the now-prominent term *entropy search*. Both of these initial investigations considered maximizing the mutual information between a measurement and the location of the global optimum x^* (§ 7.6), using the formulation in (7.14). HERNÁNDEZ-LOBATO et al. later proposed a different set of approximations based on the equivalent formulation in (7.15) under the name *predictive entropy search*, as the key quantity is the expected reduction in entropy for the predictive distribution.[60] Both HOFFMAN and GHAHRAMANI[44] and WANG and JEGELKA[45] later pursued maximizing the mutual information with the value of the global optimum f^* (§ 7.6). These developments occurred contemporaneously and independently.

Prior to these algorithms designed to reduce the *entropy* of the value of the global maximum, there were occasional efforts to minimize some other measure of dispersion in this quantity. For example, CALVIN studied an algorithm for optimization on the unit interval $\mathcal{X} = [0, 1]$ wherein the *variance* of $p(f^* \mid \mathcal{D})$ was greedily minimized via one-step lookahead.[46] Here the model was again the Wiener process, which has the remarkable property that the distribution of $p(f^* \mid \mathcal{D})$ (and its variance) is analytically tractable.[47] The Wiener and OU processes are among the *only* nontrivial Gaussian processes with this property.[48]

No history of Bayesian optimization would be complete without mentioning the role hyperparameter tuning has played in driving its recent development. With the advent of deep learning, the early 2010s

36 P. FRAZIER and W. POWELL (2007). The Knowledge Gradient Policy for Offline Learning with Independent Normal Rewards. *ADPRL 2007*.

37 W. SCOTT et al. (2011). The Correlated Knowledge Gradient for Simulation Optimization of Continuous Parameters Using Gaussian Process Regression. *SIAM Journal on Optimization* 21(3):996–1026.

38 D. R. JONES (2001). A Taxonomy of Global Optimization Methods Based on Response Surfaces. *Journal of Global Optimization* 21(4):345–383.

39 See § 7.5, p. 134 for a discussion of this proposal.

40 C. E. SHANNON (1948). A Mathematical Theory of Communication. *The Bell System Technical Journal* 27(3):379–423.

This was a central concept in § 10.3, p. 222 as well.

41 D. V. LINDLEY (1956). On a Measure of the Information Provided by an Experiment. *The Annals of Mathematical Statistics* 27(4):986–1005.

42 J. VILLEMONTEIX et al. (2009). An Informational Approach to the Global Optimization of Expensive-to-evaluate Functions. *Journal of Global Optimization* 44(4):509–534.

43 P. HENNIG and C. J. SCHULER (2012). Entropy Search for Information-Efficient Global Optimization. *Journal of Machine Learning Research* 13(Jun):1809–1837.

44 M. W. HOFFMAN and Z. GHAHRAMANI (2015). Output-Space Predictive Entropy Search for Flexible Global Optimization. *Bayesian Optimization Workshop, NeurIPS 2015*.

45 Z. WANG and S. JEGELKA (2017). Max-value Entropy Search for Efficient Bayesian Optimization. *ICML 2017*.

46 J. M. CALVIN (1993). Consistency of a Myopic Bayesian Algorithm for One-Dimensional Global Optimization. *Journal of Global Optimization* 3(2):223–232.

47 In fact, the *joint density* $p(x^*, f^* \mid \mathcal{D})$ is analytically tractable for the Wiener process with drift, which forms the posterior on each subinterval subdivided by the data:

L. A. SHEPP (1979). The Joint Density of the Maximum and Its Location for a Wiener Process with Drift. *Journal of Applied Probability* 16(2):423–427.

48 R. J. ADLER and J. E. TAYLOR (2007). *Random Fields and Geometry*. Springer–Verlag. [chapter 4, footnotes 1–2]

saw the rise of extraordinarily complex learning algorithms trained on extraordinarily large datasets. The great expense of training these models created unprecedented demand for efficient hyperparameter tuning to fuel the rapid development in the area. One could not ask for a more-perfect fit for Bayesian optimization!

Interest in Bayesian optimization for hyperparameter tuning was kicked off in earnest by SNOEK et al., who reported a dramatic improvement in performance when tuning a convolutional neural network via Bayesian optimization, even compared with carefully hand-tuned hyperparameters.[49] This served as a watershed moment for Bayesian optimization, leading to an explosion of interest from the machine learning community in the following years – although this history began in 1815, over half of the works cited in this book are from after 2012!

49 J. SNOEK et al. (2012). Practical Bayesian Optimization of Machine Learning Algorithms. *NeurIPS 2012*.

12.5   MULTI-ARMED BANDITS TO INFINITE-ARMED BANDITS

We have now covered the evolution of decision-theoretic Bayesian optimization policies from WALD's introduction of sequential analysis in 1945 to the state-of-the-art. Alongside these developments, a rich and expansive body of literature was forming on the multi-armed problem. A complete survey of this work would be out of this book's scope; however, we can point the interested reader to comprehensive surveys.[50,51] Both contain excellent bibliographic notes and combined serve as an indispensable guide to the literature on multi-armed bandits (§ 7.7). Our goal in the following will be to cover developments that directly influenced the evolution of Bayesian optimization.

50 D. A. BERRY and B. FRISTEDT (1985). *Bandit Problems: Sequential Allocation of Experiments*. Chapman & Hall.

51 T. LATTIMORE and C. SZEPESVÁRI (2020). *Bandit Algorithms*. Cambridge University Press.

THOMPSON was the first to seriously study the possibility of sequential experiments in the context of medical treatment;[52,53] this work predated WALD's work by a decade. THOMPSON considered a model scenario where there are two possible treatments a doctor may prescribe for a disease, but it is not clear which should be preferred. To determine the better treatment, we must undertake a clinical trial, assigning each treatment to several patients and assessing the outcome. Traditionally, a single preliminary experiment would be conducted, after which the apparently better-performing treatment would be adopted and the worse-performing treatment discarded. However, THOMPSON argued that one should *never* eliminate either treatment at any stage of investigation, even in the face of overwhelming evidence. Rather, he proposed a *perpetual* clinical trial modeled as what we now call a two-armed bandit: the possible treatments represent alternatives available to the clinician, and patient outcomes determine the rewards. We can now consider assigning treatments for a sequence of patients guided by our evolving knowledge, hoping to efficiently and confidently determine the optimal treatment.

52 W. R. THOMPSON (1933). On the Likelihood That One Unknown Probability Exceeds Another in View of the Evidence of Two Samples. *Biometrika* 25(3–4):285–294.

53 W. R. THOMPSON (1935). On the Theory of Apportionment. *American Journal of Mathematics* 57(2):450–456.

To conduct such a sequential clinical trial effectively, THOMPSON proposed maintaining a belief over which treatment is better in light of available evidence and always selecting the nominally better treatment according to its posterior probability of superiority. This is the eponymous Thompson sampling policy (§ 7.9), which elegantly addresses the exploration–exploitation dilemma. The more evidence we have in favor of one treatment, the more often we prescribe it, exploiting the apparently better choice. Meanwhile, we maintain a diminishing but nonzero probability of selecting the other treatment, forcing continual exploration until the better treatment becomes obvious. In the long term, we will eventually assign the correct treatment to new patients with probability approaching certainty.

THOMPSON's work was in retrospect groundbreaking, but its significance was perhaps not fully realized at the time. However, Thompson sampling for multi-armed bandits has recently enjoyed an explosion of attention due to impressive empirical performance[54,55] and strong theoretical guarantees (Chapter 10).[56,57,58] The first direct application of Thompson sampling to Bayesian optimization is due to SHAHRIARI et al.,[59] who adopted an efficient approximation first proposed by HERNÁNDEZ-LOBATO et al. in the context of entropy search.[60]

Although THOMPSON had introduced bandits in the early 1930s, concerted effort began with ROBBINS's landmark 1952 reintroduction and analysis of the problem.[61] This work introduced the modern formulation of multi-armed bandits presented in § 7.7, where an arbitrary, unknown reward distribution is associated with each arm and the agent seeks a policy to maximize the expected cumulative reward. ROBBINS explores this problem in the special case of a two-armed bandit with Bernoulli rewards, demonstrating that a simple adaptive policy ("switch on lose, stay on win") can achieve better performance than nonadaptive or random policies. He also presents a family of policies that can achieve asymptotically optimal behavior for any reward distributions. These policies are defined by a simple mechanism that explicitly forces continual but decreasingly frequent exploration of both arms according to a pregenerated schedule, effectively – if crudely – balancing exploration and exploitation.

The simple policies proposed by ROBBINS eventually achieve near-optimal cumulative reward, but they are not very *efficient* in the sense of achieving that behavior quickly. ROBBINS returned to this problem three decades later to further address the issue of efficiency.[62] LAI and ROBBINS introduced policies that dynamically trade off exploration and exploitation by maximizing an upper confidence bound on the reward distributions of the arms (§ 7.8), and demonstrated that these policies are both asymptotically optimal and efficient. AUER et al. later proved that bandit policies based on maximizing upper confidence bounds can provide strong guarantees not only asymptotically but also in the finite-budget case.[63] Interestingly, KUSHNER had proposed optimization policies based on maximizing an upper confidence bound of the objective function in the continuous case two decades earlier than LAI and ROBBINS's work,[21] although he did not prove any performance guarantees for this procedure and abandoned the idea in favor of maximizing probability of improvement. This optimization policy would be rediscovered several times, including by COX and JOHN[64] and by SRINIVAS et al.,[65] who established theoretical guarantees on the rate of convergence of this policy in the Gaussian process case, as discussed in § 10.4.

54 O. CHAPELLE and L. LI (2011). An Empirical Evaluation of Thompson Sampling. *NeurIPS 2011.*

55 O.-C. GRANMO (2010). Solving Two-Armed Bernoulli Bandit Problems Using a Bayesian Learning Automaton. *International Journal of Intelligent Computing and Cybernetics* 3(2): 207–234.

56 S. AGRAWAL and N. GOYAL (2012). Analysis of Thompson Sampling for the Multi-Armed Bandit Problem. *COLT 2012.*

57 D. RUSSO and B. VAN ROY (2014). Learning to Optimize via Posterior Sampling. *Mathematics of Operations Research* 39(4):1221–1243.

58 D. RUSSO and B. VAN ROY (2016). An Information-Theoretic Analysis of Thompson Sampling. *Journal of Machine Learning Research* 17(68):1–30.

59 B. SHAHRIARI et al. (2014). An Entropy Search Portfolio for Bayesian Optimization. arXiv: 1406.4625 [stat.ML].

60 J. M. HERNÁNDEZ-LOBATO et al. (2014). Predictive Entropy Search for Efficient Global Optimization of Black-Box Functions. *NeurIPS 2014.*

61 H. ROBBINS (1952). Some Aspects of the Sequential Design of Experiments. *Bulletin of the American Mathematical Society* 58(5):527–535.

62 T. L. LAI and H. ROBBINS (1985). Asymptotically Efficient Adaptive Allocation Rules. *Advances in Applied Mathematics* 6(1):4–22.

63 P. AUER et al. (2002). Finite-Time Analysis of the Multiarmed Bandit Problem. *Machine Learning* 47(2–3):235–256.

64 D. D. COX and S. JOHN (1992). A Statistical Method for Global Optimization. *SMC 1992.*

65 N. SRINIVAS et al. (2010). Gaussian Process Optimization in the Bandit Setting: No Regret and Experimental Design. *ICML 2010.*

12.6   WHAT'S NEXT?

The mathematical foundations of Bayesian optimization, as presented in this book and chronicled in this chapter, are by now well established. However, Bayesian optimization continues to deliver impressive performance on a wide variety of problems, and the field continues to develop at a rapid pace in light of this success. What big challenges remain on the horizon? We speculate on some potential opportunities below.

Gaussian process modeling in high dimension: § 3.5, p. 61

- Effective modeling of objective functions remains a challenge, especially in high dimension. Meanwhile, methods such as stochastic gradient descent routinely (locally) optimize objectives in millions of dimensions, and are "unreasonably effective" at doing so – all with very weak guidance. Can we bridge this gap, either by extending or refining approaches for Gaussian process modeling, or by exploring another model class?

moving beyond one-step lookahead: § 7.10, p. 150

- *Nonmyopic* policies that reach beyond one-step lookahead have shown impressive empirical performance in initial investigations. However, these policies have not yet been widely adopted, presumably due to their (sometimes significantly) greater computational cost compared to myopic alternatives. The continued development of *efficient,* yet nonmyopic policies remains a promising avenue of research.

66   B. SHAHRIARI et al. (2016). Taking the Human out of the Loop: A Review of Bayesian Optimization. *Proceedings of the IEEE* 104(1):148–175.

This is an excellent companion survey on Bayesian optimization for readers who have reached this point but still want more.

- A guiding philosophy in Bayesian optimization has been to "take the human out of the loop" and hand over complete control of experimental design to an algorithm.[66] This paradigm has demonstrated remarkable success on "black-box" problems, where the user has little understanding of the system being optimized. However, in settings such as scientific discovery, the user has a *deep* understanding of and intuition for the mechanisms driving the system of interest, and we should perhaps consider how to "bring them back into the loop." One could imagine an ecosystem of *cooperative* tools that enable Bayesian optimization algorithms to benefit from user knowledge while facilitating the presentation of experimental progress and evolving model beliefs back to the users.

utility functions: § 6, p. 109

- In the author's experience, many consumers of Bayesian optimization have experimental goals that are not perfectly captured by any of the common utility functions used in Bayesian optimization – for example, users may want to ensure adequate coverage of the domain or to find a *diverse* set of locations with high objective values. Although the space of Bayesian optimization policies is fairly crowded, there is still room for innovation. If the ecosytem of cooperative tools envisioned above were realized, we might consider tuning the utility function "on the fly" via interactive preference elicitation.

- Bayesian optimization is not a particularly user-friendly approach, as effective optimization requires careful modeling of the system of interest. However, model construction remains something of a "black art," even in the machine learning community, and thus considerable machine learning expertise can be required to get the most out of this approach. Can we build turnkey Bayesian optimization systems that achieve acceptable performance even in the absence of clear prior beliefs?

THE GAUSSIAN DISTRIBUTION

The *Gaussian* (or *normal*) distribution is a fundamental probability distribution in probabilistic modeling and inference. Gaussian distributions are frequently encountered in Bayesian optimization as they serve as the foundation of *Gaussian processes,* an infinite-dimensional extension appropriate for reasoning about unknown objective functions. In this chapter we provide a brief introduction to finite-dimensional Gaussian distributions and establish important properties referenced throughout this book. We will begin with the univariate (one-dimensional) case, then construct the multivariate (vector-valued) case via linear transformations of univariate Gaussians.

Gaussian processes: Chapters 2–4, p. 15

A.1 UNIVARIATE GAUSSIAN DISTRIBUTION

The univariate Gaussian distribution on a random variable $x \in \mathbb{R}$ has two scalar parameters corresponding to its first two moments: $\mu = \mathbb{E}[x]$ specifies the mean (also median and mode) and serves as a location parameter, and $\sigma^2 = \text{var}[x]$ specifies the variance and serves as a scale parameter.

mean, μ

variance, σ^2

Probability density function and degenerate case

When the variance is nonzero, the distribution has the probability density function

$$\mathcal{N}(x; \mu, \sigma^2 > 0) = Z^{-1} \exp\left(-\tfrac{1}{2}z^2\right), \tag{A.1}$$

where $Z = \sqrt{2\pi}\sigma$ is a normalization constant and z is the familiar z-score of x:

$$z = \frac{x - \mu}{\sigma}. \tag{A.2}$$

This PDF is illustrated in the margin. The probability density is rapidly decreasing with the magnitude of the z-score, with for example 99.7% of the density lying in the interval $|z| \leq 3$, or $x \in (\mu \pm 3\sigma)$.

A univariate Gaussian probability density function $\mathcal{N}(x; \mu, \sigma^2)$ as a function of the z-score.

In the degenerate case $\sigma^2 = 0$, the distribution collapses to a point mass at the mean and a probability density function does not exist. We can express this case with the Dirac delta distribution:

degenerate case, $\sigma^2 = 0$

$$\mathcal{N}(x; \mu, \sigma^2 = 0) = \delta(x - \mu). \tag{A.3}$$

Standard normal distribution

The special case of zero mean and unit variance is called the *standard normal* distribution and enjoys a privileged role. We notate its density with the compact notation $\phi(x) = \mathcal{N}(x; 0, 1^2)$. The cumulative density function of the standard normal cannot be expressed in terms of elementary functions, but is such an important quantity that it also merits its

standard normal PDF, ϕ

standard normal CDF, Φ

own special notation:

$$\Phi(y) = \Pr(x < y) = \int_{-\infty}^{y} \phi(x)\,dx.$$

expressing arbitrary PDFs and CDFs in terms of the standard normal

We can write the PDF and CDF of an arbitrary nondegenerate Gaussian distribution $\mathcal{N}(x; \mu, \sigma^2)$ in terms of the standard normal PDF and CDF by appropriately rescaling and translating arguments to their z-scores (A.1):

$$p(x) = \frac{1}{\sigma}\phi\Big(\frac{x-\mu}{\sigma}\Big); \qquad \Pr(x < y) = \Phi\Big(\frac{y-\mu}{\sigma}\Big),$$

where the multiplicative factor in the PDF guarantees normalization.

Affine transformations

The family of univariate Gaussian distributions is closed under affine transformations, which simply translate and rescale the distribution and adjust its moments accordingly. If x has distribution $\mathcal{N}(x; \mu, \sigma^2)$, then the transformation $\xi = ax + b$ has distribution

$$p(\xi) = \mathcal{N}(\xi; a\mu + b, a^2\sigma^2).$$

The above results allow us to interpret *any* univariate Gaussian distribution as a translated and scaled copy of the standard normal after applying the transformation $x \mapsto \mu + \sigma x$. This process is illustrated in the margin, where a standard normal distribution is transformed via the mapping $x \mapsto 1 + x/\sqrt{2}$, resulting in a new Gaussian distribution with increased mean $\mu = 1$ and decreased variance $\sigma^2 = 1/2$. The PDF is appropriately translated and rescaled.

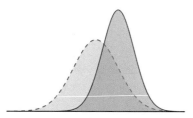

A standard normal PDF (dashed) and the PDF after applying the transformation $x \mapsto 1 + x/\sqrt{2}$ (solid).

A.2 MULTIVARIATE GAUSSIAN DISTRIBUTION

The multivariate Gaussian distribution extends the univariate case to an arbitrary random vector $\mathbf{x} \in \mathbb{R}^d$. We will provide an explicit construction of the multivariate Gaussian distribution as the result of applying an affine transformation to independent univariate standard normal random variables, extending the properties noted at the end of the previous section.

Standard multivariate normal and construction of general case

standard multivariate normal

First, we construct the *standard multivariate normal* distribution, represented by a random vector $\mathbf{z} \in \mathbb{R}^d$ whose entries are independent standard univariate normal random variables: $p(\mathbf{z}) = \prod_i \phi(z_i)$. It is clear from construction that the mean of this distribution is the zero vector and its covariance is the identity matrix:

$$\mathbb{E}[\mathbf{z}] = \mathbf{0}; \qquad \text{cov}[\mathbf{z}] = \mathbf{I}, \tag{A.4}$$

and we will denote its density with $p(\mathbf{z}) = \mathcal{N}(\mathbf{z}; \mathbf{0}, \mathbf{I})$.

As before, this will serve as the basis of the general multivariate case by considering arbitrary affine transformations of this "standard" example. Suppose $\mathbf{x} \in \mathbb{R}^d$ is a vector-valued random variable and $\mathbf{z} \in \mathbb{R}^k$, $k \le d$, is a k-dimensional standard multivariate normal vector. If we can write

$$\mathbf{x} = \boldsymbol{\mu} + \Lambda \mathbf{z} \qquad (\text{A.5})$$

for some vector $\boldsymbol{\mu} \in \mathbb{R}^d$ and $d \times k$ matrix Λ, then $\mathbf{x}$ has a multivariate normal distribution. We can compute its mean and covariance directly from (A.4–A.5):

$$\mathbb{E}[\mathbf{x}] = \boldsymbol{\mu}; \qquad \text{cov}[\mathbf{x}] = \Lambda \Lambda^\top = \Sigma.$$

This property completely characterizes the distribution. As in the univariate case, we can interpret every multivariate normal distribution as an affine transformation of a (possibly lower-dimensional) standard normal vector. We again parameterize this family by its first two moments: the mean vector $\boldsymbol{\mu}$ and the covariance matrix Σ. This covariance matrix is necessarily symmetric and *positive semidefinite,* which means all its eigenvalues are nonnegative. We can factor any such matrix as $\Sigma = \Lambda \Lambda^\top$ allowing us to recover the underlying transformation (A.5), although Λ need not be unique.

Probability density function and degenerate case

If Λ has full rank d, then the range of (A.5) is all of $\mathbb{R}^d$ and a probability density function exists. This condition further implies that the covariance matrix Σ is *positive definite;* that is, its eigenvalues are strictly positive, implying its determinant is positive and the matrix is invertible. The distribution has a probability density function in this case analogous to the univariate PDF (A.1):

$$\mathcal{N}(\mathbf{x}; \boldsymbol{\mu}, \Sigma) = Z^{-1} \exp\left(-\tfrac{1}{2}\Delta^2\right). \qquad (\text{A.6})$$

Here Z again represents a normalization constant:

$$Z = \sqrt{|2\pi\Sigma|} = (2\pi)^{\frac{d}{2}} |\Sigma|^{\frac{1}{2}}, \qquad (\text{A.7})$$

and Δ represents the *Mahalanobis distance,* a multivariate analog of the (absolute) z-score (A.2):

$$\Delta^2 = (\mathbf{x} - \boldsymbol{\mu})^\top \Sigma^{-1} (\mathbf{x} - \boldsymbol{\mu}). \qquad (\text{A.8})$$

It is easy to verify that these definitions are compatible with the univariate case when $d = 1$. Note in that case the condition of Σ being positive definite reduces to the previous condition for nondegeneracy, $\sigma^2 > 0$.

The dependence of the multivariate Gaussian density on $\mathbf{x}$ is entirely through the value of the Mahalanobis distance Δ. To gain some geometric insight into the probability density, we can set this value to a constant and compute isoprobability contours. In the case of the *standard* multivariate

Figure A.1: Isoprobability contours $\Delta = 1$ for the standard bivariate normal distribution (left), a distribution with diagonal covariance, scaling the probability along the axes (middle), and a distribution with nonzero off-diagonal covariance, tilting the probability (right). The standard normal contour is shown for reference on the latter two examples.

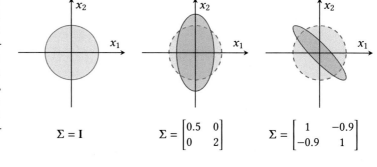

$$\Sigma = I \qquad \Sigma = \begin{bmatrix} 0.5 & 0 \\ 0 & 2 \end{bmatrix} \qquad \Sigma = \begin{bmatrix} 1 & -0.9 \\ -0.9 & 1 \end{bmatrix}$$

Probability density and circular isoprobability contours of a standard bivariate normal distribution.

degenerate case, $|\Sigma| = 0$

1 On this space, the PDF is similar to (A.6–A.8) but replaces the determinant with the pseudodeterminant and the inverse with the pseudoinverse. If $\Sigma = 0$, the distribution is a Dirac delta on μ.

distribution of affine transformation $Ax + b$

Gaussian distribution, the Mahalanobis distance reduces to the normal Euclidean distance, and the set of points satisfying $\Delta = c > 0$ is then a sphere of radius c centered at the origin – see the illustration in the margin.

We can now understand the geometry of the general case $\mathcal{N}(x; \mu, \Sigma)$ purely in terms of the affine transformation (A.5) translating and warping the spherical distribution of the standard normal. Taking this view, the action of multiplying by Λ warps the isoprobability contours into ellipsoids, which are then translated to the new center μ. The standard theory of linear maps then gives further insight: the principal axes of the ellipsoids are given by the eigenvectors of Λ, and their axis semilengths are given by the eigenvalues scaled by c. See Figure A.1 for an illustration.

The probability density function does not exist when Λ (and thus Σ) is rank-deficient, as the range of x would then be restricted to the lower-dimensional affine subspace $\{\mu + \Lambda z \mid z \in \mathbb{R}^d\}$ (A.5). However, it is still possible to define a probability density function in this degenerate case by restricting the support to this subspace.[1] This is analogous to the degenerate univariate case (A.3), where probability was restricted to the zero-dimensional subspace containing the mean only, $\{\mu\}$.

Affine transformations

The multivariate Gaussian distribution has a number of convenient mathematical properties, many of which follow immediately from the characterization in (A.5). First, it is obvious that any affine transformation of a multivariate normal distributed vector is also multivariate normal, as affine transformations are closed under composition. If $p(x) = \mathcal{N}(x; \mu, \Sigma)$, then $\xi = Ax + b$ has distribution

$$p(\xi) = \mathcal{N}(\xi; A\mu + b, A\Sigma A^\top). \tag{A.9}$$

Further, if we apply this result with the transformation

$$x \mapsto \begin{bmatrix} I \\ A \end{bmatrix} x + \begin{bmatrix} 0 \\ b \end{bmatrix} = \begin{bmatrix} x \\ \xi \end{bmatrix},$$

we can see that $\mathbf{x}$ and $\boldsymbol{\xi}$ in fact have a *joint* Gaussian distribution:

joint distribution with affine transformations

$$p(\mathbf{x}, \boldsymbol{\xi}) = \mathcal{N}\left(\begin{bmatrix} \mathbf{x} \\ \boldsymbol{\xi} \end{bmatrix}; \begin{bmatrix} \boldsymbol{\mu} \\ \mathbf{A}\boldsymbol{\mu} + \mathbf{b} \end{bmatrix}, \begin{bmatrix} \boldsymbol{\Sigma} & \boldsymbol{\Sigma}\mathbf{A}^\top \\ \mathbf{A}\boldsymbol{\Sigma} & \mathbf{A}\boldsymbol{\Sigma}\mathbf{A}^\top \end{bmatrix}\right). \qquad (\text{A.10})$$

Sampling

The characterization of the multivariate normal in terms of affine transformations of standard normal random variables (A.5) also suggests a simple algorithm for drawing samples from the distribution. Given an arbitrary multivariate normal distribution $\mathcal{N}(\mathbf{x}; \boldsymbol{\mu}, \boldsymbol{\Sigma})$, we first factor the covariance as $\boldsymbol{\Sigma} = \boldsymbol{\Lambda}\boldsymbol{\Lambda}^\top$ where $\boldsymbol{\Lambda}$ has size $d \times k$; when $\boldsymbol{\Sigma}$ is positive definite, the *Cholesky decomposition* is the canonical choice. We now sample a k-dimensional standard normal vector $\mathbf{z}$ by sampling each entry independently from a univariate standard normal; routines for this task are readily available. Finally, we transform this vector appropriately to provide a sample of $\mathbf{x}$: $\mathbf{z} \mapsto \boldsymbol{\mu} + \boldsymbol{\Lambda}\mathbf{z} = \mathbf{x}$. This procedure entails one-time $\mathcal{O}(d^3)$ work to compute $\boldsymbol{\Lambda}$ (which can be reused), followed by $\mathcal{O}(d^2)$ work to produce each sample.

Marginalization

Often we will have a vector $\mathbf{x}$ with a multivariate Gaussian distribution, but only be interested in reasoning about a subset of its entries. Suppose $p(\mathbf{x}) = \mathcal{N}(\mathbf{x}; \boldsymbol{\mu}, \boldsymbol{\Sigma})$, and partition the vector into two components:[2]

2 We can first permute $\mathbf{x}$ if required; as a linear transformation, this will simply permute the entries of $\boldsymbol{\mu}$ and the rows/columns of $\boldsymbol{\Sigma}$.

$$\mathbf{x} = \begin{bmatrix} \mathbf{x}_1 \\ \mathbf{x}_2 \end{bmatrix}. \qquad (\text{A.11})$$

We partition the mean vector and covariance matrix in the same way:

$$p(\mathbf{x}) = \mathcal{N}\left(\begin{bmatrix} \mathbf{x}_1 \\ \mathbf{x}_2 \end{bmatrix}; \begin{bmatrix} \boldsymbol{\mu}_1 \\ \boldsymbol{\mu}_2 \end{bmatrix}, \begin{bmatrix} \boldsymbol{\Sigma}_{11} & \boldsymbol{\Sigma}_{12} \\ \boldsymbol{\Sigma}_{21} & \boldsymbol{\Sigma}_{22} \end{bmatrix}\right). \qquad (\text{A.12})$$

Now writing the subvector $\mathbf{x}_1$ as $\mathbf{x}_1 = [\mathbf{I}, \mathbf{0}]\,\mathbf{x}$ and applying the affine property (A.9), we have:

$$p(\mathbf{x}_1) = \mathcal{N}(\mathbf{x}_1; \boldsymbol{\mu}_1, \boldsymbol{\Sigma}_{11}). \qquad (\text{A.13})$$

That is, to derive the marginal distribution of $\mathbf{x}_1$ we simply pick out the corresponding entries of $\boldsymbol{\mu}$ and $\boldsymbol{\Sigma}$.

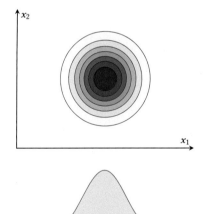

A bivariate Gaussian PDF $p(x_1, x_2)$ (top) and the Gaussian marginal $p(x_1)$ (bottom) (A.13).

Conditioning

Multivariate Gaussian distributions are also closed under conditioning on the values of given entries. Suppose again that $p(\mathbf{x}) = \mathcal{N}(\mathbf{x}; \boldsymbol{\mu}, \boldsymbol{\Sigma})$ and partition $\mathbf{x}$, $\boldsymbol{\mu}$, and $\boldsymbol{\Sigma}$ as before (A.11–A.12). Suppose now that we learn the exact value of the subvector $\mathbf{x}_2$. The posterior on the remaining entries $p(\mathbf{x}_1 \mid \mathbf{x}_2)$ remains Gaussian, with distribution

$$p(\mathbf{x}_1 \mid \mathbf{x}_2) = \mathcal{N}(\mathbf{x}_1; \boldsymbol{\mu}_{1|2}, \boldsymbol{\Sigma}_{11|2}).$$

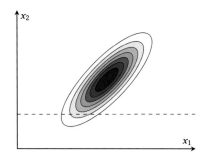

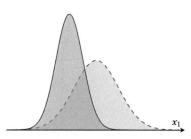

The PDFs of a bivariate Gaussian $p(x_1, x_2)$ (top) and the conditional distribution $p(x_1 \mid x_2)$ given the value of x_2 marked by the dashed line (bottom) (A.14). The prior marginal distribution $p(x_1)$ is shown for reference; the observation decreased both the mean and standard deviation.

independent case

The posterior mean and covariance take the form of updates to the prior moments in light of the revealed information:

$$\boldsymbol{\mu}_{1|2} = \boldsymbol{\mu}_1 + \Sigma_{12}\Sigma_{22}^{-1}(\mathbf{x}_2 - \boldsymbol{\mu}_2); \qquad \Sigma_{11|2} = \Sigma_{11} - \Sigma_{12}\Sigma_{22}^{-1}\Sigma_{21}. \quad (\text{A.14})$$

The mean is adjusted by an amount dependent on

1. the covariance between $\mathbf{x}_1$ and $\mathbf{x}_2$, Σ_{12},
2. the uncertainty in $\mathbf{x}_2$, Σ_{22}, and
3. the deviation of the observed values from the prior mean, $(\mathbf{x}_2 - \boldsymbol{\mu}_2)$.

Similarly, the uncertainty in $\mathbf{x}_1$, Σ_{11}, is reduced by an amount dependent on factors 1–2. Notably, the correction to the covariance matrix does *not* depend on the observed values. Note that if $\mathbf{x}_1$ and $\mathbf{x}_2$ are independent, then $\Sigma_{12} = \mathbf{0}$, and conditioning does not alter the distribution of $\mathbf{x}_1$.

Sums of normal vectors

Suppose $\mathbf{x}$ and $\mathbf{y}$ are d-dimensional random vectors with joint multivariate normal distribution

$$p(\mathbf{x}, \mathbf{y}) = \mathcal{N}\left(\begin{bmatrix}\mathbf{x}\\\mathbf{y}\end{bmatrix}; \begin{bmatrix}\boldsymbol{\mu}\\\boldsymbol{\nu}\end{bmatrix}, \begin{bmatrix}\Sigma & \mathbf{P}\\\mathbf{P} & \mathbf{T}\end{bmatrix}\right).$$

Then recognizing their sum $\mathbf{z} = \mathbf{x} + \mathbf{y} = [\mathbf{I}, \mathbf{I}][\mathbf{x}, \mathbf{y}]^\top$ as a linear transformation and applying (A.9), we have:

$$p(\mathbf{z}) = \mathcal{N}(\mathbf{z}; \boldsymbol{\mu} + \boldsymbol{\nu}, \Sigma + 2\mathbf{P} + \mathbf{T}).$$

When $\mathbf{x}$ and $\mathbf{y}$ are independent, $\mathbf{P} = \mathbf{0}$, and this simplifies to

$$p(\mathbf{z}) = \mathcal{N}(\mathbf{z}; \boldsymbol{\mu} + \boldsymbol{\nu}, \Sigma + \mathbf{T}), \quad (\text{A.15})$$

where the moments simply add.

Differential entropy

The differential entropy of a multivariate normal random variable $\mathbf{x}$ with distribution $p(\mathbf{x}) = \mathcal{N}(\mathbf{x}; \boldsymbol{\mu}, \Sigma)$, expressed in nats, is

$$H[\mathbf{x}] = \tfrac{1}{2}\log|2\pi e\Sigma|. \quad (\text{A.16})$$

In the univariate case $p(x) = \mathcal{N}(x; \mu, \sigma^2)$, this reduces to

$$H[x] = \tfrac{1}{2}\log 2\pi e\sigma^2. \quad (\text{A.17})$$

Sequences of normal random variables

If $\{\mathbf{x}_i\}$ is a sequence of normal random variables with means $\{\boldsymbol{\mu}_i\}$ and covariances $\{\Sigma_i\}$ converging respectively to finite limits $\boldsymbol{\mu}_i \to \boldsymbol{\mu}$ and $\Sigma_i \to \Sigma$, then the sequence converges in distribution to a normal random variable $\mathbf{x}$ with mean $\boldsymbol{\mu}$ and covariance Σ.

METHODS FOR APPROXIMATE BAYESIAN INFERENCE

B

In Bayesian optimization we occasionally face intractable posterior distributions that must be approximated before we can proceed. The *Laplace approximation* and *Gaussian expectation propagation* are two workhorses of approximate Bayesian inference, and at least one will suffice in most scenarios. Both result in Gaussian approximations to the posterior, especially convenient when working with Gaussian processes.

Approximate inference for GPS: § 2.8, p. 39

B.1 THE LAPLACE APPROXIMATION

Consider a vector-valued random variable $\mathbf{x} \in \mathbb{R}^d$ with arbitrary prior distribution $p(\mathbf{x})$. Suppose we obtain information $\mathcal{D}$, yielding an intractable posterior

$$p(\mathbf{x} \mid \mathcal{D}) = Z^{-1} p(\mathbf{x}) p(\mathcal{D} \mid \mathbf{x})$$

that we wish to approximate. The Laplace approximation is based on approximating the logarithm of the unnormalized posterior:

unnormalized log posterior, Ψ

$$\Psi(\mathbf{x}) = \log p(\mathbf{x}) + \log p(\mathcal{D} \mid \mathbf{x})$$

with a Taylor expansion around its maximum:

maximum a posteriori point, $\hat{\mathbf{x}}$

$$\hat{\mathbf{x}} = \arg\max_{\mathbf{x}} \Psi(\mathbf{x}).$$

Taking a second-order Taylor expansion around this point yields

$$\Psi(\mathbf{x}) \approx \Psi(\hat{\mathbf{x}}) - \tfrac{1}{2}(\mathbf{x} - \hat{\mathbf{x}})^\top \mathbf{H}(\mathbf{x} - \hat{\mathbf{x}}),$$

where $\mathbf{H}$ is the Hessian of the negative log posterior evaluated at $\hat{\mathbf{x}}$:

Hessian of negative log posterior, $\mathbf{H}$

$$\mathbf{H} = -\frac{\partial^2 \Psi}{\partial \mathbf{x} \, \partial \mathbf{x}^\top}(\hat{\mathbf{x}}).$$

Note the first-order term vanishes as we are expanding around a maximum. Exponentiating, we derive an approximation to the unnormalized posterior:

$$p(\mathbf{x} \mid \mathcal{D}) \propto \exp \Psi(\mathbf{x}) \approx \exp \Psi(\hat{\mathbf{x}}) \exp\!\big(-\tfrac{1}{2}(\mathbf{x} - \hat{\mathbf{x}})^\top \mathbf{H}(\mathbf{x} - \hat{\mathbf{x}})\big).$$

We recognize this as proportional to a Gaussian distribution, yielding a normal approximate posterior:

Laplace approximation to posterior

$$p(\mathbf{x} \mid \mathcal{D}) \approx q(\mathbf{x}) = \mathcal{N}(\mathbf{x}; \hat{\mathbf{x}}, \mathbf{H}^{-1}). \tag{B.1}$$

Through some accounting when normalizing (B.1), the Laplace approximation also gives an approximation to the normalizing constant Z:

Laplace approximation to normalizing constant, $\hat{Z}_{\mathrm{LA}}$

$$Z \approx \hat{Z}_{\mathrm{LA}} = (2\pi)^{\frac{d}{2}} |\mathbf{H}|^{-\frac{1}{2}} \exp \Psi(\hat{\mathbf{x}}). \tag{B.2}$$

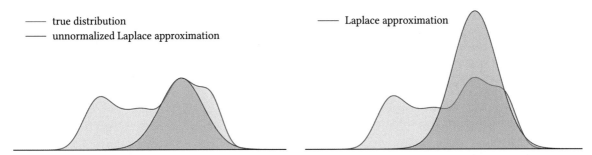

——— true distribution
——— unnormalized Laplace approximation

——— Laplace approximation

Figure B.1: A Laplace approximation to a one-dimensional posterior distribution. The left panel shows the Laplace approximation before normalization, and the right panel afterwards.

The Laplace approximation procedure is illustrated in Figure B.1, where we show the approximate posterior both before and after normalization. The posterior density is an excellent local approximation around the maximum but is not a great global fit as a significant fraction of the true posterior mass is ignored. However, the Laplace approximation is remarkably simple and general and is sometimes the only viable approximation scheme.

B.2   GAUSSIAN EXPECTATION PROPAGATION

Expectation propagation (EP) is a technique for approximate Bayesian inference that enjoys some use in Bayesian optimization. We will give a brief and incomplete introduction that should nonetheless suffice for common applications in this context. A complete introduction can be found in MINKA's thesis,[1] and CUNNINGHAM et al. provide in-depth advice regarding efficient and stable computation for the rank-one case we consider here.[2]

Consider a multivariate Gaussian random variable ξ with distribution

$$p(\xi) = \mathcal{N}(\xi; \mu_0, \Sigma_0).$$

Suppose we obtain information $\mathcal{D}$ about ξ in the form of a collection of *factors*, each of which specifies the likelihood of a scalar product $x = \mathbf{a}^\top \xi$ associated with that factor.[3] We consider the posterior distribution

$$p(\xi \mid \mathcal{D}) = Z^{-1} p(\xi) \prod_i t_i(x_i), \tag{B.3}$$

where ith factor t_i informs our belief about $x_i = \mathbf{a}_i^\top \xi$. Unfortunately, this posterior is intractable except the notable case when all factors are Gaussian.

Gaussian expectation propagation proceeds by replacing each of the factors with an unnormalized Gaussian distribution:

$$t_i(x_i) \approx \tilde{t}_i(x_i) = \tilde{Z}_i \, \mathcal{N}(x_i; \tilde{\mu}_i, \tilde{\sigma}_i^2).$$

1 T. P. MINKA (2001). A Family of Algorithms for Approximate Bayesian Inference. Ph.D. thesis. Massachusetts Institute of Technology.

2 J. P. CUNNINGHAM et al. (2011). Gaussian Probabilities and Expectation Propagation. arXiv: 1111.6832 [stat.ML].

3 These scalar products often simply pick out single entries of ξ, in which case we can slightly simplify notation. However, we sometimes require this more general formulation.

Here $(\tilde{Z}_i, \tilde{\mu}_i, \tilde{\sigma}_i^2)$ are called *site parameters* for the approximate factor $\tilde{t}_i$, which we may design to optimize the fit. We will consider this issue further shortly. Given arbitrary site parameters for each factor, the resulting approximation to (B.3) is

site parameters, $(\tilde{Z}, \tilde{\mu}, \tilde{\sigma}^2)$

Gaussian EP approximate posterior, $q(\xi)$

$$p(\xi \mid \mathcal{D}) \approx q(\xi) = \hat{Z}_{\text{EP}}^{-1} p(\xi) \prod_i \tilde{t}_i(x_i). \qquad \text{(B.4)}$$

As a product of Gaussians, the approximate posterior is also Gaussian:

$$q(\xi) = \mathcal{N}(\xi; \mu, \Sigma), \qquad \text{(B.5)}$$

4 The updated covariance incorporates only a series of rank-one updates, which can be applied using the Sherman–Morrison formula.

with parameters:[4]

Gaussian EP parameters, (μ, Σ)

$$\mu = \Sigma\Big(\Sigma_0^{-1}\mu_0 + \sum_i \frac{\tilde{\mu}_i}{\tilde{\sigma}_i^2}\mathbf{a}_i\Big); \qquad \Sigma = \Big(\Sigma_0^{-1} + \sum_i \frac{1}{\tilde{\sigma}_i^2}\mathbf{a}_i\mathbf{a}_i^\top\Big)^{-1}.$$

Gaussian EP also yields an approximation of the normalizing constant Z, if desired:

Gaussian EP approximation to normalizing constant, $\hat{Z}_{\text{EP}}$

$$Z \approx \hat{Z}_{\text{EP}} = \frac{\mathcal{N}(0; \mu, \Sigma)}{\mathcal{N}(0; \mu_0, \Sigma_0)} \prod_i \tilde{Z}_i \, \mathcal{N}(0; \tilde{\mu}_i, \tilde{\sigma}_i^2). \qquad \text{(B.6)}$$

What remains to be determined is an effective means of choosing the site parameters to maximize the approximation fidelity. One reasonable goal would be to minimize the Kullback–Leibler (KL) divergence between the true and approximate distributions; for our Gaussian approximation (B.5), this is achieved through moment matching.[2] Unfortunately, determining the moments of the true posterior (B.3) may be difficult, so expectation propagation instead matches the *marginal* moments for each of the $\{x_i\}$, approximately minimizing the KL divergence. This is accomplished through an iterative procedure where we repeatedly sweep over each of the approximate factors and refine its parameters until convergence.

setting site parameters

expectation propagation approximately minimizes KL divergence

We initialize all site parameters to $(\tilde{Z}, \tilde{\mu}, \tilde{\sigma}^2) = (1, 0, \infty)$; with these choices the approximate factors drop away, and our initial approximation is simply the prior: $(\mu, \Sigma) = (\mu_0, \Sigma_0)$. Now we perform a series of updates for each of the approximate factors in turn. These updates take a convenient general form, and we will drop factor index subscripts below to simplify notation.

site parameter initialization

Let $\tilde{t}(x) = \tilde{Z}\mathcal{N}(x; \tilde{\mu}, \tilde{\sigma}^2)$ be an arbitrary factor in our approximation (B.4). The idea behind expectation propagation is to drop this factor from the approximation entirely, forming the *cavity distribution*:

cavity distribution, $\bar{q}$

$$\bar{q}(\xi) = \frac{q(\xi)}{\tilde{t}(x)},$$

and replace it with the true factor $t(x)$, forming the *tilted distribution* $\bar{q}(\xi)\, t(x)$. The tilted distribution is closer to the true posterior (B.3) as the factor in question is no longer approximated. We now adjust the site

tilted distribution

Figure B.2: A Gaussian EP approximation to the distribution in Figure B.1.

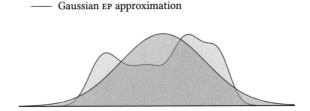

—— Gaussian EP approximation

parameters to minimize the KL divergence between the tilted distribution and the new approximation $q'(\xi) = \bar{q}(\xi)\,\tilde{t}'(x)$:

$$(\tilde{Z}, \tilde{\mu}, \tilde{\sigma}^2) = \arg\min D_{\mathrm{KL}}\big[\bar{q}(\xi)\,t(x) \,\|\, q'(\xi)\big]$$

by matching zeroth, first, and second moments.

Because Gaussian distributions are closed under marginalization, we can simplify this procedure by manipulating only *marginal* distributions for x rather than the full joint distribution.[5] The marginal belief about $x = \mathbf{a}^\top \xi$ in our current approximation (B.5) is:

$$q(x) = \mathcal{N}(x; \mu, \sigma^2); \qquad \mu = \mathbf{a}_i^\top \boldsymbol{\mu}; \qquad \sigma^2 = \mathbf{a}_i^\top \Sigma \mathbf{a}_i.$$

By dividing by the approximate factor $\tilde{t}(\xi)$, we arrive at the marginal cavity distribution, which is Gaussian:

$$\bar{q}(x) = \mathcal{N}(x; \bar{\mu}, \bar{\sigma}^2); \quad \bar{\mu} = \bar{\sigma}^2(\mu\sigma^{-2} - \tilde{\mu}\tilde{\sigma}^{-2}); \quad \bar{\sigma}^2 = (\sigma^{-2} - \tilde{\sigma}^{-2})^{-1}. \text{(B.7)}$$

Consider the zeroth moment of the marginal tilted distribution:

$$Z = \int t(x)\,\mathcal{N}(x; \bar{\mu}, \bar{\sigma}^2)\,\mathrm{d}x; \tag{B.8}$$

this quantity clearly depends on the cavity parameters $(\bar{\mu}, \bar{\sigma}^2)$. If we define

$$\alpha = \frac{\partial \log Z}{\partial \bar{\mu}}; \qquad \beta = \frac{\partial \log Z}{\partial \bar{\sigma}^2}; \tag{B.9}$$

and an auxiliary variable $\gamma = (\alpha^2 - 2\beta)^{-1}$, then we may achieve the desired moment matching by updating the site parameters to:[6]

$$\tilde{\mu} = \bar{\mu} + \alpha\gamma; \qquad \tilde{\sigma}^2 = \gamma - \bar{\sigma}^2; \qquad \tilde{Z} = Z\sqrt{2\pi}\sqrt{\bar{\sigma}^2 + \tilde{\sigma}^2}\,\exp\big(\tfrac{1}{2}\alpha^2\gamma\big). \tag{B.10}$$

This completes our update for the chosen factor; the full EP procedure repeatedly updates each factor in this manner until convergence. The result of Gaussian expectation propagation for the distribution from Figure B.1 is shown in Figure B.2. The fit is good and reflects the more global nature of the expectation propagation scheme achieved through moment matching rather than merely maximizing the posterior.

A convenient aspect of expectation propagation is that incorporating a new factor only requires computing the zeroth moment against an arbitrary normal distribution (B.8) and the partial derivatives in (B.9). We provide these computations for several useful factor types below.

5 M. SEEGER (2008). *Expectation Propagation for Exponential Families*. Technical report. University of California, Berkeley.

6 T. MINKA (2008). *EP: A Quick Reference*.

Figure B.3: A Gaussian EP approximation to a one-dimensional normal distribution truncated at a.

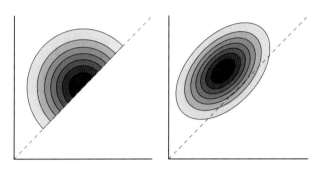

Figure B.4: A Gaussian EP approximation to a joint normal distribution conditioned on one coordinate being less than the other, corresponding to the dashed boundary. Contours of the tilted distribution are shown in the left panel, and contours of the approximate posterior in the right panel.

Truncating a variable

A common use of expectation propagation in Bayesian optimization is to approximately constrain a Gaussian random variable x to be less than a threshold a. We may capture this information by a single factor $t(x) = [x < a]$. In the context of expectation propagation, we must consider the normalizing constant of the tilted distribution, which is a truncated normal:

$$Z = \int [x < a]\, \mathcal{N}(x; \bar{\mu}, \bar{\sigma}^2)\, \mathrm{d}x = \Phi(z); \qquad z = \frac{a - \bar{\mu}}{\bar{\sigma}}. \tag{B.11}$$

The required quantities for an expectation propagation update are now (B.10):

$$\alpha = -\frac{\phi(z)}{\Phi(z)\bar{\sigma}}; \qquad \beta = \frac{z\alpha}{2\bar{\sigma}}; \qquad \gamma = -\frac{\bar{\sigma}}{\alpha}\left(\frac{\phi(z)}{\Phi(z)} + z\right)^{-1}. \tag{B.12}$$

A Gaussian EP approximation to a truncated normal distribution is illustrated in Figure (B.3). The fit is good, but not perfect: approximately 5% of its mass exceeds the threshold. This inaccuracy is the price of approximation.

We may also apply this approach to approximately condition our belief on ξ on one entry being dominated by another: $\xi_i < \xi_j$. Consider the vector $\mathbf{a}$ where $a_i = 1$, $a_j = -1$ and all other entries are zero. Then $x = \mathbf{a}^\top \xi = \xi_i - \xi_j$. The condition is now equivalent to $[x < 0]$, and we can proceed as outlined above. This approximation is illustrated for a bivariate normal in Figure B.4; again the fit appears reasonable.

conditioning on one variable being greater than another

Figure B.5: A Gaussian EP approximation to a one-dimensional normal distribution truncated at an unknown threshold a with the marked 95% credible interval.

Truncation at an uncertain threshold

A sometimes useful extension of the above is to consider truncation at an *uncertain* threshold a. Suppose we have a Gaussian belief about a:

$$p(a) = \mathcal{N}(a; \mu, \sigma^2).$$

Integrating the hard truncation factor $[x < a]$ against this belief yields the following "soft truncation" factor:

$$t(x) = \int [x < a]\, p(a)\, \mathrm{d}a = \Phi\left(\frac{\mu - x}{\sigma}\right). \tag{B.13}$$

We consider again the normalizing constant of the tilted distribution:

$$Z = \int \Phi\left(\frac{\mu - x}{\sigma}\right) \mathcal{N}(x; \bar{\mu}, \bar{\sigma}^2)\, \mathrm{d}x = \Phi(z); \qquad z = \frac{\mu - \bar{\mu}}{\sqrt{\sigma^2 + \bar{\sigma}^2}}.$$

Defining $s = \sqrt{\sigma^2 + \bar{\sigma}^2}$, we may compute:

$$\alpha = -\frac{\phi(z)}{\Phi(z)s}; \qquad \beta = \frac{z\alpha}{2s}; \qquad \gamma = -\frac{s}{\alpha}\left(\frac{\phi(z)}{\Phi(z)} + z\right)^{-1}.$$

The hard truncation formulas above may be interpreted as a special case of this result by setting $(\mu, \sigma^2) = (a, 0)$. This procedure is illustrated in Figure B.5, where we softly truncate a one-dimensional Gaussian distribution.

GRADIENTS

C

Under mild continuity assumptions, for Gaussian processes conditioned with exact inference, we may compute the gradient of both the log marginal likelihood with respect to model hyperparameters and of the posterior predictive moments with respect to observation location. The former aids in maximizing or sampling from the model posterior, and the latter in maximizing acquisition functions derived from the predictive distribution. In modern software these gradients are often computed via automatic differentiation, but we present their functional forms here to offer insight into their behavior.

We will consider a function $f : \mathbb{R}^d \to \mathbb{R}$ with distribution $\mathcal{GP}(f; m, K)$, observed with independent (but possibly hetereoskedastic) additive Gaussian noise:

$$p(y \mid x, \phi, \sigma_n) = \mathcal{N}(y; \phi, \sigma_n^2),$$

where the noise scale σ_n may optionally depend on x. We will notate the prior moment and noise scale functions with:

$$m(x; \theta); \qquad K(x, x'; \theta); \qquad \sigma_n(x; \theta),$$

and assume these are differentiable with respect to observation location and any parameters they may have. In a slight abuse of notation, we will use θ to indicate a vector collating the values of *all* hyperparameters of this model.

We will consider an arbitrary set of observations $\mathcal{D} = (\mathbf{x}, \mathbf{y})$. We will write the prior moments of $\boldsymbol{\phi} = f(\mathbf{x})$ and the noise covariance associated with these observations as:

$$\boldsymbol{\mu} = m(\mathbf{x}; \theta); \qquad \Sigma = K(\mathbf{x}, \mathbf{x}; \theta); \qquad \mathbf{N} = \operatorname{diag} \sigma_n^2(\mathbf{x}; \theta),$$

all of which have implicit dependence on the hyperparameters. It will also be useful to introduce notation for two repeating quantities:

$$\mathbf{V} = \operatorname{cov}[\mathbf{y} \mid \mathbf{x}, \theta] = \Sigma + \mathbf{N}; \qquad \boldsymbol{\alpha} = \mathbf{V}^{-1}(\mathbf{y} - \boldsymbol{\mu}).$$

C.1 GRADIENT OF LOG MARGINAL LIKELIHOOD

The log marginal likelihood of the data is (4.8):

$$\mathcal{L}(\theta) = \log p(\mathbf{y} \mid \mathbf{x}, \theta) = -\tfrac{1}{2}\left[\boldsymbol{\alpha}^\top(\mathbf{y} - \boldsymbol{\mu}) + \log |\mathbf{V}| + n \log 2\pi\right].$$

The partial derivatives with respect to mean function parameters have the form:

$$\frac{\partial \mathcal{L}}{\partial \theta} = \boldsymbol{\alpha}^\top \frac{\partial \boldsymbol{\mu}}{\partial \theta},$$

and partial derivatives with respect to covariance function and likelihood parameters (that is, the parameters of $\mathbf{V}$) take the form:

$$\frac{\partial \mathcal{L}}{\partial \theta} = \frac{1}{2}\left[\boldsymbol{\alpha}^\top \frac{\partial \mathbf{V}}{\partial \theta}\boldsymbol{\alpha} - \operatorname{tr}\left[\mathbf{V}^{-1}\frac{\partial \mathbf{V}}{\partial \theta}\right]\right].$$

C.2   GRADIENT OF PREDICTIVE DISTRIBUTION WITH RESPECT TO LOCATION

For a given observation location x, let us define the vectors

$$\mathbf{k} = K(\mathbf{x}, x); \qquad \boldsymbol{\beta} = \mathbf{V}^{-1}\mathbf{k}.$$

The posterior moments of $\phi = f(x)$ are (2.19):

$$\mu = m(x) + \boldsymbol{\alpha}^\top \mathbf{k}; \qquad \sigma^2 = K(x, x) - \boldsymbol{\beta}^\top \mathbf{k},$$

and the partial derivatives of these moments with respect to observation location are:

$$\frac{\partial \mu}{\partial x} = \frac{\partial m}{\partial x} - \boldsymbol{\alpha}^\top \frac{\partial \mathbf{k}}{\partial x}; \qquad \frac{\partial \sigma^2}{\partial x} = \frac{\partial K(x, x)}{\partial x} - 2\boldsymbol{\beta}^\top \frac{\partial \mathbf{k}}{\partial x}. \qquad \text{(C.1)}$$

The predictive distribution for a noisy observation y at x is (8.5):

$$p(y \mid x, \mathcal{D}, \sigma_n^2) = \mathcal{N}(y; \mu, s^2); \qquad s^2 = \sigma^2 + \sigma_n^2,$$

and the partial derivative of the predictive variance and standard deviation with respect to x are:

$$\frac{\partial s^2}{\partial x} = \frac{\partial \sigma^2}{\partial x} + \frac{\partial \sigma_n^2}{\partial x}; \qquad \frac{\partial s}{\partial x} = \frac{1}{2s} \frac{\partial s^2}{\partial x}.$$

C.3   GRADIENTS OF COMMON ACQUISITION FUNCTIONS

Gradient of noisy expected improvement

this picks up the discussion from § 8.2, p. 163

To aid in the optimization of expected improvement, we may also compute the gradient of g,[1] and thus the gradient of expected improvement with respect to the proposed observation location x. This will require several applications of the chain rule due to numerous dependencies among the variables involved.

First, we note that the $\{c_i\}$ values defining the intervals of dominance (8.15) depend on the vectors $\mathbf{a}$ and $\mathbf{b}$. In particular, for $2 \leq i \leq n$, c_i is the z-value where the $(i-1)$th and ith lines intersect, which occurs at

1 w. SCOTT et al. (2011). The Correlated Knowledge Gradient for Simulation Optimization of Continuous Parameters Using Gaussian Process Regression. *SIAM Journal on Optimization* 21(3):996–1026.

gradient of endpoints with respect to a, b

$$c_i = \frac{a_i - a_{i-1}}{b_{i-1} - b_i},$$

making the dependence explicit. For $2 \leq i \leq n$, we have:

$$\frac{\partial c_i}{\partial a_i} = \frac{1}{b_{i-1} - b_i}; \qquad \frac{\partial c_i}{\partial a_{i-1}} = -\frac{\partial c_i}{\partial a_i}; \qquad \frac{\partial c_i}{\partial b_i} = \frac{a_i - a_{i-1}}{(b_i - b_{i-1})^2}; \qquad \frac{\partial c_i}{\partial b_{i-1}} = -\frac{\partial c_i}{\partial b_i},$$

and at the fixed endpoints at infinity $i \in \{1, n+1\}$, we have

$$\frac{\partial c_i}{\partial \mathbf{a}} = \frac{\partial c_i}{\partial \mathbf{b}} = \mathbf{0}^\top.$$

gradient of g with respect to a and b

Now we may compute the gradient of $g(\mathbf{a}, \mathbf{b})$ with respect to its inputs, accounting for the implicit dependence of interval endpoints on these values:

$$\frac{\partial g}{\partial a_i} = \left[\Phi(c_{i+1}) - \Phi(c_i)\right]$$

$$+ \frac{\partial c_{i+1}}{\partial a_i}\left[a_i + b_i c_{i+1} - [i \le n](a_{i+1} + b_{i+1}c_{i+1})\right]\phi(c_{i+1})$$

$$- \frac{\partial c_i}{\partial a_i}\left[a_i + b_i c_i \quad - [i > 1](a_{i-1} + b_{i-1}c_i) \quad \right]\phi(c_i);$$

$$\frac{\partial g}{\partial b_i} = \left[\phi(c_i) - \phi(c_{i+1})\right]$$

$$+ \frac{\partial c_{i+1}}{\partial b_i}\left[a_i + b_i c_{i+1} - [i \le n](a_{i+1} + b_{i+1}c_{i+1})\right]\phi(c_{i+1})$$

$$- \frac{\partial c_i}{\partial b_i}\left[a_i + b_i c_i \quad - [i > 1](a_{i-1} + b_{i-1}c_i) \quad \right]\phi(c_i).$$

Here $[i > 1]$ and $[i \le n]$ represent the Iverson bracket. We will also require the gradient of the $\mathbf{a}$ and $\mathbf{b}$ vectors with respect to x:

gradient of $\mathbf{a}$ and $\mathbf{b}$ with respect to x

$$\frac{\partial \mathbf{a}}{\partial x} = \begin{bmatrix} \mathbf{0} \\ \frac{\partial \mu}{\partial x} \end{bmatrix}; \qquad \frac{\partial \mathbf{b}}{\partial x} = \frac{1}{s}\left[\frac{\partial K_{\mathcal{D}}(\mathbf{x}', x)}{\partial x} - \mathbf{b}\frac{\partial s}{\partial x}\right]. \qquad \text{(C.2)}$$

Note the dependence on the gradient of the predictive parameters. Finally, if we preprocess the inputs by identifying an appropriate transformation matrix $\mathbf{P}$ such that $g(\mathbf{a}, \mathbf{b}) = g(\mathbf{Pa}, \mathbf{Pb}) = g(\boldsymbol{\alpha}, \boldsymbol{\beta})$ (8.14), then the desired gradient of expected improvement is:

$$\frac{\partial \alpha_{\text{EI}}}{\partial x} = \frac{\partial g}{\partial \boldsymbol{\alpha}}\mathbf{P}\frac{\partial \mathbf{a}}{\partial x} + \frac{\partial g}{\partial \boldsymbol{\beta}}\mathbf{P}\frac{\partial \mathbf{b}}{\partial x}.$$

Gradient of noisy probability of improvement

We may compute the gradient of (8.23) via several applications of the chain rule, under the (mild) assumption that the endpoints ℓ and u correspond to *unique* lines (a_ℓ, b_ℓ) and (a_u, b_u).[2] Then we have

this picks up the discussion from § 8.3, p. 170

2 If not, probability of improvement is not differentiable as moving one of the lines at the shared intersection will alter the probability of improvement only in favorable directions.

$$\frac{\partial \alpha_{\text{PI}}}{\partial a_\ell} = -\frac{\phi(\ell)}{b_\ell}; \quad \frac{\partial \alpha_{\text{PI}}}{\partial b_\ell} = -\frac{\ell\phi(\ell)}{b_\ell}; \quad \frac{\partial \alpha_{\text{PI}}}{\partial a_u} = \frac{\phi(-u)}{b_u}; \quad \frac{\partial \alpha_{\text{PI}}}{\partial b_u} = \frac{u\phi(-u)}{b_u},$$

and we may compute the gradient with respect to the proposed observation location as

$$\frac{\partial \alpha_{\text{PI}}}{\partial x} = \frac{\partial \alpha_{\text{PI}}}{\partial \mathbf{a}}\frac{\partial \mathbf{a}}{\partial x} + \frac{\partial \alpha_{\text{PI}}}{\partial \mathbf{b}}\frac{\partial \mathbf{b}}{\partial x}.$$

The gradient with respect to $\mathbf{a}$ and $\mathbf{b}$ was computed previously (C.2).

Approximating gradient via Gauss–Hermite quadrature

We may also use numerical techniques to estimate the gradient of the acquisition function with respect to the proposed observation location:

this picks up the discussion from § 8.5, p. 172

$$\frac{\partial \alpha}{\partial x} = \frac{\partial}{\partial x}\int \Delta(x, y)\,\mathcal{N}(y; \mu, s^2)\,\mathrm{d}y. \qquad \text{(C.3)}$$

3 It is sufficient for example that both Δ and $\frac{\partial\Delta}{\partial x}$ be continuous in x and y, and that the moments of the predictive distribution of y be continuous with respect to x.

approximation with Gauss–Hermite quadrature

accounting for dependence of $\{y_i\}$ on predictive parameters

If we assume sufficient regularity,[3] then we may swap the order of expectation and differentiation:

$$\frac{\partial\alpha}{\partial x} = \int \frac{\partial}{\partial x}\Delta(x,y)\,\mathcal{N}(y;\mu,s^2)\,\mathrm{d}y,$$

reducing the computation of the gradient to Gaussian expectation.

Gauss–Hermite quadrature remains a natural choice, resulting in the approximation

$$\frac{\partial\alpha}{\partial x} \approx \sum_{i=1}^{n} \bar{w}_i \frac{\partial\Delta}{\partial x}(x,y_i), \tag{c.4}$$

which is simply the derivative of the estimator in (8.29). When using this estimate we must remember that the $\{y_i\}$ samples depend on x through the parameters of predictive distribution (8.29). Accounting for this dependence, the required gradient of the marginal gain at the ith integration node z_i is:

$$\frac{\partial\Delta}{\partial x}(x,y_i) = \left[\frac{\partial\Delta}{\partial x}\right]_y + \frac{\partial\Delta}{\partial y}\left[\frac{\partial\mu}{\partial x} + \frac{y_i-\mu}{s}\frac{\partial s}{\partial x}\right], \tag{c.5}$$

where $\left[\frac{\partial\Delta}{\partial x}\right]_y$ indicates the partial derivative of the updated utility when the observed value y is held constant.

Approximating the gradient of knowledge gradient

this picks up the discussion from § 8.6, p. 175

Special care is needed to estimate the gradient of the knowledge gradient using numerical techniques. Inspecting (c.4), we must compute the gradient of the marginal gain

$$\frac{\partial\Delta}{\partial x} = \frac{\partial}{\partial x}\max_{x'\in\mathcal{X}} \mu_{\mathcal{D}'}(x').$$

It is not clear how we can differentiate through the max operator in this expression. However, under mild assumptions we may appeal to the *envelope theorem* for arbitrary choice sets to proceed.[4] Consider a point x in the interior of the domain $\mathcal{X} \subset \mathbb{R}^d$, and fix an arbitrary associated observation value y.[5] Take any point maximizing the updated posterior mean:

$$x^* \in \arg\max_{x'\in\mathcal{X}} \mu_{\mathcal{D}'}(x');$$

4 P. MILGROM and I. SEGAL (2002). Envelope Theorems for Arbitrary Choice Sets. *Econometrica* 70(2):583–601.

5 We assume x is in the interior of $\mathcal{X}$ to avoid issues with defining differentiability on the boundary. We can avoid this assumption if the Gaussian process can be extended to all of $\mathbb{R}^d$. This is usually possible trivially unless the prior mean or covariance function of the Gaussian process is exotic.

6 Sufficient conditions are that the prior mean and covariance functions be differentiable.

this point need not be unique. Assuming the updated posterior mean is differentiable,[6] the envelope theorem states that the gradient of the global reward utility is equal to the gradient of the updated posterior mean evaluated at x^*:

$$\frac{\partial\Delta}{\partial x} = \frac{\partial}{\partial x}\mu_{\mathcal{D}'}(x^*).$$

For the knowledge gradient, and accounting for the dependence on x in the locations of the y samples (c.5), we may compute:

$$\frac{\partial\Delta}{\partial x}(x,y_i) = \frac{y_i-\mu}{s^3}\left[s\frac{\partial K_{\mathcal{D}}}{\partial x}(x,x_i^*) - \frac{\partial s}{\partial x}K_{\mathcal{D}}(x,x_i^*)\right],$$

where x_i^* maximizes the updated posterior mean corresponding to y_i. Combining this result with (C.4) yields a Gauss–Hermite approximation to the gradient of the acquisition function. This approach requires maximizing the updated posterior mean for each sample y_i. We may appeal to standard techniques for this task, making use of the gradient (C.1)

$$\frac{\partial \mu_{\mathcal{D}'}}{\partial x}.$$

Gradient of predictive entropy search acquisition function

The explicit formula (8.52) and results above allow us to compute – after investing considerable tedium – the gradient of the predictive entropy search approximation to the mutual information (8.41). We begin by differentiating that estimate:

this picks up the discussion from § 8.8, p. 187

$$\frac{\partial \alpha_{\mathrm{PES}}}{\partial x} = \frac{1}{s}\frac{\partial s}{\partial x} + \frac{1}{2n}\sum_{i=1}^{n}\frac{1}{s_{*_i}^2}\frac{\partial s_{*_i}^2}{\partial x}.$$

Given a fixed sample x^* and dropping the subscript, we may compute (8.39):

$$\frac{\partial s_*^2}{\partial x} = \frac{\partial \sigma_*^2}{\partial x} + \frac{\partial \sigma_n^2}{\partial x}.$$

We proceed by differentiating the approximate latent predictive variance (8.52):

$$\frac{\partial \sigma_*^2}{\partial x} = \frac{\partial \varsigma^2}{\partial x} - \frac{2\varsigma^2 - 2\rho}{\gamma}\left[\frac{\partial \varsigma^2}{\partial x} - \frac{\partial \rho}{\partial x}\right] + \frac{(\varsigma^2 - \rho)^2}{\gamma^2}\frac{\partial \gamma}{\partial x},$$

which depends on the derivatives of the expectation propagation update terms:

$$\frac{\partial \gamma}{\partial x} = \frac{1}{\alpha}\left[1 - \frac{\left(\Phi(z) - \phi(z)\right)^2}{\left(z\Phi(z) + \phi(z)\right)^2}\right]\left[\frac{\partial m}{\partial x} + z\frac{\partial \bar{\sigma}}{\partial x}\right] + \frac{2\gamma}{\bar{\sigma}}\frac{\partial \bar{\sigma}}{\partial x};$$

$$\frac{\partial \bar{\sigma}}{\partial x} = \frac{1}{2\bar{\sigma}}\left[\frac{\partial \varsigma^2}{\partial x} - 2\frac{\partial \rho}{\partial x}\right];$$

and the predictive parameters (8.51):

$$\frac{\partial m}{\partial x} = \frac{\partial \mu}{\partial x} + (\boldsymbol{\alpha}^*)^\top\frac{\partial \mathbf{k}}{\partial x};$$

$$\frac{\partial \varsigma^2}{\partial x} = \frac{\partial \sigma^2}{\partial x} - 2\mathbf{k}^\top\mathbf{V}_*^{-1}\frac{\partial \mathbf{k}}{\partial x}; \qquad \frac{\partial \rho}{\partial x} = \frac{\partial k_1}{\partial x} - \mathbf{k}_*^\top\mathbf{V}_*^{-1}\frac{\partial \mathbf{k}}{\partial x}.$$

Gradient of OPES acquisition function

To compute the gradient of the OPES approximation, we differentiate (8.63):

this picks up the discussion from § 8.9, p. 192

$$\frac{\partial \alpha_{\mathrm{OPES}}}{\partial x} = \frac{1}{s}\frac{\partial s}{\partial x} + \frac{1}{2}\sum_i\frac{w_i}{s_{*_i}^2}\frac{\partial s_{*_i}^2}{\partial x}.$$

Given a fixed sample f^* and dropping the subscript, we may compute (8.63):

$$\frac{\partial s_*^2}{\partial x} = \frac{\partial \sigma_*^2}{\partial x} + \frac{\partial \sigma_n^2}{\partial x}.$$

Finally, we differentiate (8.61):

$$\frac{\partial \sigma_*^2}{\partial x} = \sigma \frac{\phi(z)}{\Phi(z)} \left[\frac{\partial \mu}{\partial x} + z \frac{\partial \sigma}{\partial x} \right] \left[1 - 2 \frac{\phi(z)^2}{\Phi(z)^2} - 3z \frac{\phi(z)}{\Phi(z)} - z^2 \right]$$
$$+ \frac{\partial \sigma^2}{\partial x} \left[1 - z \frac{\phi(z)}{\Phi(z)} - \frac{\phi(z)^2}{\Phi(z)^2} \right].$$

D

ANNOTATED BIBLIOGRAPHY OF APPLICATIONS

Countless settings across science, engineering, and beyond involve free parameters that can be tuned at will to achieve some objective. However, in many cases the evaluation of a given parameter setting can be extremely costly, stymieing exhaustive exploration of the design space.

Of course, such a situation is a perfect use case for Bayesian optimization. Through careful modeling and intelligent policy design, Bayesian optimization algorithms can deliver impressive optimization performance even with small observation budgets. This capability has been demonstrated in hundreds of studies across a wide range of domains.

Here we provide a brief survey of some notable applications of Bayesian optimization. The selected references are not intended to be exhaustive (that would be impossible given the size of the source material!), but rather to be representative, diverse, and good starting points for further investigation.

CHEMISTRY AND MATERIALS SCIENCE

At a high level, the synthesis of everything from small molecules to bulk materials proceeds in the same manner: initial raw materials are combined and subjected to suitable conditions such that they transform into a final product. Although this seems like a simple recipe, we face massive challenges in its realization:

- We usually wish that the resulting products be *useful,* that is, that they exhibit desirable properties. In drug discovery, for example, we seek molecules exhibiting binding activity against an identified biological target. In other settings we might seek products exhibiting favorable optical, electronic, mechanical, thermal, and/or other properties.

- The space of possible products can be enormous and the sought after properties exceptionally rare. For example, there are an estimated 10^{60} pharmacologically active molecules, only a tiny fraction of which might exhibit binding activity against any given biological target.

- Determining the properties of a candidate molecule or material ultimately requires synthesis and characterization in a laboratory, which can be complicated, costly, and slow.

For these reasons, exploration of molecular or material spaces can devolve into a cumbersome trial-and-error search for "needles in a haystack."

Over the past few decades, the fields of *computational chemistry* and *computational materials science* have developed sophisticated techniques for estimating chemical and material properties from simulation. As accurate simulation often requires consideration of quantum mechanical interactions, these surrogates can still be quite costly, but are nonetheless cheaper and more easily parallelized than laboratory experiments. This has enabled computer-guided exploration of large molecular and materials spaces at relatively little cost, but in many cases exhaustive

computational chemistry, computational materials science

exploration remains untenable, and we must appeal to methods such as Bayesian optimization for guidance.

Virtual screening of molecular spaces

The ability to estimate molecular properties using computational methods has enabled so-called *virtual screening,* where early stages of discovery can be performed *in silico.* Bayesian optimization and active search can dramatically increase the rate of discovery in this setting.

One challenge here is constructing predictive models for the properties of molecules, which are complex structured objects. The field of *chemoinformatics* has developed a number of *molecular fingerprints* intended to serve as useful feature representations for molecules when predicting chemical properties. Traditionally, these fingerprints were developed based on chemical intuition; however, numerous *neural* fingerprints have emerged in recent years, designed via deep representation learning on huge molecular databases.[1]

chemoinformatics
molecular fingerprints

neural fingerprints

1 See § 8.11, p. 199 and § 9.2, p. 209 for related discussion.

GRAFF, DAVID E. et al. (2021). Accelerating High-Throughput Virtual Screening through Molecular Pool-Based Active Learning. *Chemical Science* 12(22):7866–7881.

HERNÁNDEZ-LOBATO, JOSÉ MIGUEL et al. (2017). Parallel and Distributed Thompson Sampling for Large-Scale Accelerated Exploration of Chemical Space. *Proceedings of the 34th International Conference on Machine Learning (ICML 2017).*

JIANG, SHALI et al. (2017). Efficient Nonmyopic Active Search. *Proceedings of the 34th International Conference on Machine Learning (ICML 2017).*

De novo design

A recent trend in molecular discovery has been to learn deep *generative* models for molecular structures and perform optimization in the (continuous) latent space of such a model. This enables *de novo* design, where the optimization routine can propose entirely novel structures for evaluation by feeding selected points in the latent space through the generational procedure.[1]

the question of sythesizability

Although appealing, a major complication with this scheme is identifying a synthetic route – if one even exists! – for proposed structures. This issue deserves careful consideration when designing a system that can effectively transition from virtual screening to the laboratory.

GAO, WENHAO et al. (2020). The Synthesizability of Molecules Proposed by Generative Models. *Journal of Chemical Information and Modeling* 60(12):5714–5723.

GÓMEZ-BOMBARELLI, RAFAEL et al. (2018). Automatic Chemical Design Using a Data-Driven Continuous Representation of Molecules. *ACS Central Science* 4(2):268–276.

GRIFFITHS, RYAN-RHYS et al. (2020). Constrained Bayesian Optimization for Automatic Chemical Design Using Variational Autoencoders. *Chemical Science* 11(2):577–586.

KOROVINA, KSENIA et al. (2020). ChemBO: Bayesian Optimization of Small Organic Molecules with Synthesizable Recommendations. *Proceedings of the 23rd International Conference on Artificial Intelligence and Statistics (AISTATS 2020).*

Reaction optimization

Not all applications of Bayesian optimization in chemistry take the form of optimizing chemical properties as a function of molecular structure. For example, even once a useful molecule has been identified, there may remain numerous parameters of its synthesis – reaction environment, processing parameters, etc. – that can be further optimized, seeking for example to reduce the cost and/or increase the yield of production.

SHIELDS, BENJAMIN J. et al. (2021). Bayesian Reaction Optimization as a Tool for Chemical Synthesis. *Nature* 590:89–96.

Conformational search

Conformational search seeks to identify the configuration(s) of a molecule with the lowest potential energy. Even for molecules of moderate size, the space of possible configurations can be enormous and the potential energy surface can exhibit numerous local minima. Interaction with other structures such as a surface (*adsorption*) can further complicate the computation of potential energy, rendering the search even more difficult.

adsorption

CARR, SHANE F. et al. (2017). Accelerating the Search for Global Minima on Potential Energy Surfaces Using Machine Learning. *Journal of Chemical Physics* 145(15):154106.

FANG, LINCAN et al. (2021). Efficient Amino Acid Conformer Search with Bayesian Optimization. *Journal of Chemical Theory and Computation* 17(3):1955–1966.

PACKWOOD, DANIEL (2017). *Bayesian Optimization for Materials Science.* Springer–Verlag.

We may also use related Bayesian methods to map out minimal-energy pathways between neighboring minima on a potential energy surface in order to understand the intermediate geometry of a molecule as it transforms from one energetically favorable state to another.

mapping minimal-energy pathways

KOISTINEN, OLLI-PEKKA et al. (2017). Nudged Elastic Band Calculations Accelerated with Gaussian Process Regression. *Journal of Chemical Physics* 147(15):152720.

Optimization of material properties and performance

Bayesian optimization has demonstrated remarkable success in accelerating materials design. As in molecular design, in many cases we can perform early screening *in silico,* using computational methods to approximate properties of interest. The literature in this space is vast, and the studies below are representative examples targeting a range of material types and properties.

ATTIA, PETER M. et al. (2020). Closed-Loop Optimization of Fast-Charging Protocols for Batteries with Machine Learning. *Nature* 578:397–402.

FUKAZAWA, TARO et al. (2019). Bayesian Optimization of Chemical Composition: A Comprehensive Framework and Its Application to $R\mathrm{Fe}_{12}$-Type Magnet Compounds. *Physical Review Materials* 3(5): 053807.

HAGHANIFAR, SAJAD et al. (2020). Discovering High-Performance Broadband and Broad Angle Antireflection Surfaces by Machine Learning. *Optica* 7(7):784–789.

HERBOL, HENRY C. et al. (2018). Efficient Search of Compositional Space for Hybrid Organic–Inorganic Perovskites via Bayesian Optimization. *npj Computational Materials* 4(51).

JU, SHENGHONG et al. (2017). Designing Nanostructures for Phonon Transport via Bayesian Optimization. *Physical Review X* 7:021024.

MIYAGAWA, SHINSUKE et al. (2021). Application of Bayesian Optimization for Improved Passivation Performance in $\mathrm{TiO}_x/\mathrm{SiO}_y/\mathrm{c}$-Si Heterostructure by Hydrogen Plasma Treatment. *Applied Physics Express* 14(2):025503.

NAKAMURA, KENSAKU et al. (2021). Multi-Objective Bayesian Optimization of Optical Glass Compositions. *Ceramics International* 47(11): 15819–15824.

NUGRAHA, ASEP SUGIH et al. (2020). Mesoporous Trimetallic PtPdAu Alloy Films toward Enhanced Electrocatalytic Activity in Methanol Oxidation: Unexpected Chemical Compositions Discovered by Bayesian Optimization. *Journal of Materials Chemistry A* 8(27): 13532–13540.

OSADA, KEIICHI et al. (2020). Adaptive Bayesian Optimization for Epitaxial Growth of Si Thin Films under Various Constraints. *Materials Today Communications* 25:1015382.

SEKO, ATSUTO et al. (2015). Prediction of Low-Thermal-Conductivity Compounds with First-Principles Anharmonic Lattice-Dynamics Calculations and Bayesian Optimization. *Physical Review Letters* 115(20):205901.

Structural search

A fundamental question in materials science is how the structure of a material gives rise to its material properties. However, predicting the likely structure of a material – for example by evaluating the potential energy of plausible structures and minimizing – can be extraordinarily difficult, as the number of possible configurations can be astronomical.

KIYOHARA, SHIN et al. (2016). Acceleration of Stable Interface Structure Searching Using a Kriging Approach. *Japanese Journal of Applied Physics* 55(4):045502.

OKAMOTO, YASUHARU (2017). Applying Bayesian Approach to Combinatorial Problem in Chemistry. *Journal of Physical Chemistry A* 121(17):3299–3304.

TODOROVIĆ, MILICA et al. (2019). Bayesian Inference of Atomistic Structure in Functional Materials. *npj Computational Materials* 5(35).

Software for Bayesian optimization in chemistry and materials science

HÄSE, FLORIAN et al. (2018). Phoenics: A Bayesian Optimizer for Chemistry. *ACS Central Science* 4(9):1134–1145.

UENO, TSUYOSHI et al. (2016). COMBO: An Efficient Bayesian Optimization Library for Materials Science. *Materials Discovery* 4:18–21.

PHYSICS

Modern physics is driven by experiments of massive scope, which have enabled the refinement of theories of the Universe on all scales. The complexity of these experiments – from data acquisition to the following analysis and inference – offers many opportunities for optimization, but the same complexity often renders optimization difficult due to large parameter spaces and/or the expense of evaluating a particular setting.

Experimental physics

Complex physical instruments such as particle accelerators offer the capability of extraordinarily fine tuning through careful setting of their control parameters. In some cases, these parameters can be altered on-the-fly during operation, resulting in a huge space of possible configurations. Bayesian optimization can help accelerate the tuning process.

DURIS, J. et al. (2020). Bayesian Optimization of a Free-Electron Laser. *Physical Review Letters* 124(12):124801.

ROUSSEL, RYAN et al. (2021). Multiobjective Bayesian Optimization for Online Accelerator Tuning. *Physical Review Accelerators and Beams* 24(6):062801.

SHALLOO, R. J. et al. (2020). Automation and Control of Laser Wakefield Accelerators Using Bayesian Optimization. *Nature Communications* 11:6355.

WIGLEY, P. B. et al. (2016). Fast Machine-Learning Online Optimization of Ultra-Cold-Atom Experiments. *Scientific Reports* 6:25890.

Inverse problems in physics

The goal of an *inverse problem* is to determine the free parameters of a generative model[2] from observations of its output. Inverse problems are pervasive in physics – many physical models feature parameters (physical constants) that cannot be determined from first principles. However, we can *infer* these parameters experimentally by comparing the predictions of the model with the behavior of relevant observations.

2 This model may not be probabilistic but rather a complex simulation procedure.

In this context, determining the predictions of the model given a setting of its parameters is called the *forward map*. The inverse problem is then the task of "inverting" this map: searching the parameter space for the settings in the greatest accord with observed data.

forward map

We can draw parallels here with Bayesian inference, where the forward map is characterized by the likelihood, which determines the distribution of observed data given the parameters. The Bayesian answer to the inverse problem is then encapsulated by the posterior distribution of the parameters given the data, which identifies the most plausible parameters in light of the observations.

Bayesian analog

For complex physical models, even the forward map can be exceptionally expensive to compute, making it difficult to completely explore its parameter space. For example, the forward map of a cosmological model may require simulating the evolution of an entire universe at a fine enough resolution to observe its large scale structure. Exhaustively traversing the space of cosmological parameters and comparing with observed structure would be infeasible, but progress may be possible with careful guidance. Bayesian optimization has proven useful to this end on a range of difficult inverse problems.

ILTEN, P. et al. (2017). Event Generator Tuning Using Bayesian Optimization. *Journal of Instrumentation* 12(4):P04028.

LECLERCQ, FLORENT (2018). Bayesian Optimization for Likelihood-Free Cosmological Inference. *Physical Review D* 98(6):063511.

ROGERS, KEIR K. et al. (2019). Bayesian Emulator Optimisation for Cosmology: Application to the Lyman-Alpha Forest. *Journal of Cosmology and Astroparticle Physics* 2019(2):031.

VARGAS-HERNÁNDEZ, R. A. et al. (2019). Bayesian Optimization for the Inverse Scattering Problem in Quantum Reaction Dynamics. *New Journal of Physics* 21(2):022001.

BIOLOGICAL SCIENCES AND ENGINEERING

Biological systems are extraordinarily complex. Obtaining experimental measurements to shed light on the behavior of these systems can be difficult, slow, and expensive, and the resulting data can be corrupted with significant noise. Efficient experimental design is thus critical to make progress, and Bayesian optimization is a natural tool to consider.

LI, YAN et al. (2018). A Knowledge Gradient Policy for Sequencing Experiments to Identify the Structure of RNA Molecules Using a Sparse

Additive Belief Model. *INFORMS Journal on Computing* 30(4):625–786.

LORENZ, ROMY et al. (2018). Dissociating frontoparietal brain networks with neuroadaptive Bayesian optimization. *Nature Communications* 9:1227.

NIKITIN, ARTYOM et al. (2019). Bayesian optimization for seed germination. *Plant Methods* 15:43.

Inverse problems in the biological sciences

Challenging inverse problems (see above) are pervasive in biology. Effective modeling of biological systems often requires complicated, nonlinear models with numerous free parameters. Bayesian optimization can help guide the search for the parameters offering the best explanation of observed data.

DOKOOHAKI, HAMZE et al. (2018). Use of Inverse Modelling and Bayesian Optimization for Investigating the τ Effect of Biochar on Soil Hydrological Properties. *Agricultural Water Management* 2018: 268–274.

THOMAS, MARCUS et al. (2018). A Method for Efficient Bayesian Optimization of Self-Assembly Systems from Scattering Data. *BMC Systems Biology* 12:65.

ULMASOV, DONIYOR et al. (2016). Bayesian Optimization with Dimension Scheduling: Application to Biological Systems. *Computer Aided Chemical Engineering* 38:1051–1056.

Gene and protein design

The tools of modern biology enable the custom design of genetic sequences and even entire proteins, which we can – at least theoretically – tailor as we see fit. It is natural to pose both gene and protein design in terms of optimizing some figure of merit over a space of alternatives. However, in either case we face an immediate combinatorial explosion in the number of possible genetic or amino acid sequences we might consider. Bayesian optimization has shown promise for overcoming this obstacle through careful experimental design. A running theme throughout recent efforts is the training of generative models for gene/protein sequences, after which we may optimize in the continuous latent space in order to sidestep the need for combinatorial optimization.[3]

3 See § 8.11, p. 199 and § 9.2, p. 209 for related discussion.

GONZÁLEZ, JAVIER et al. (2015). Bayesian Optimization for Synthetic Gene Design. *Bayesian Optimization: Scalability and Flexibility Workshop (BayesOpt 2015), Conference on Neural Information Processing Systems (NeurIPS 2015)*.

HIE, BRIAN L. et al. (2021). Adaptive Machine Learning for Protein Engineering. arXiv: 2106.05466 [q-bio.QM].

ROMERO, PHILIP A. et al. (2013). Navigating the Protein Fitness Landscape with Gaussian Processes. *Proceedings of the National Academy of Sciences* 110(3):E193–E201.

SINAI, SAM et al. (2020). A Primer on Model-Guided Exploration of Fitness Landscapes for Biological Sequence Design. arXiv: 2010.10614 [q-bio.QM].

YANG, KEVIN K. et al. (2019). Machine-Learning-Guided Directed Evolution for Protein Engineering. *Nature Methods* 16:687–694.

plant breeding

A related problem is faced in modern plant breeding, where the goal is to develop plant varieties with desirable characteristics: yield, drought or pest resistance, etc. Plant phenotyping is an inherently slow process, as we must wait for planted seeds to germinate and grow until sufficiently mature that traits can be measured. This slow turnover rate makes it impossible to fully explore the space of possible genotypes, the genetic information that (in combination with other factors including environment and management) gives rise to the phenotypes we seek to optimize. Modern plant breeding uses genetic sequencing to guide the breeding process by building models to predict phenotype from genotype and using these models in combination with large gene banks to inform the breeding process. A challenge in this approach is that the space of possible genotypes is huge, but Bayesian optimization can help accelerate the search.

TANAKA, RYOKEI et al. (2018). Bayesian Optimization for Genomic Selection: A Method for Discovering the Best Genotype among a Large Number of Candidates. *Theoretical and Applied Genetics* 131(1):93–105.

Biomedical engineering

Difficult optimization problems are pervasive in biomedical engineering due to the complexity of the systems involved and the often considerable cost of gathering data, whether through studies with human subjects, complicated laboratory testing, and/or nontrivial simulation.

COLOPY, GLEN WRIGHT et al. (2018). Bayesian Optimization of Personalized Models for Patient Vital-Sign Monitoring. *IEEE Journal of Biomedical and Health Informatics* 22(2):301–310.

GHASSEMI, MOHAMMAD et al. (2014). Global Optimization Approaches for Parameter Tuning in Biomedical Signal Processing: A Focus of Multi-scale Entropy. *Computing in Cardiology* 41(12–2):993–996.

KIM, GILHWAN et al. (2021). Using Bayesian Optimization to Identify Optimal Exoskeleton Parameters Targeting Propulsion Mechanics: A Simulation Study. bioRxiv: 2021.01.14.426703.

KIM, MYUNGHEE et al. (2017). Human-in-the-loop Bayesian Optimization of Wearable Device Parameters. *PLOS ONE* 12(9):e0184054.

OLOFSSON, SIMON et al. (2019). Bayesian Multiobjective Optimisation with Mixed Analytical and Black-Box Functions: Application to Tissue Engineering. *IEEE Transactions on Biomedical Engineering* 66(3): 727–739.

ROBOTICS

Robotics is fraught with difficult optimization problems. A robotic platform may have numerous tunable parameters influencing its behavior in a highly complex manner. Further, empirical evaluation can be difficult – real-world experiments must proceed in real time, and there may be a considerable setup time between experiments. However, in some cases we may be able to accelerate optimization by augmenting real-world evaluation with simulation in a multifidelity setup.

multifidelity optimization: § 11.5, p. 263

BANSAL, SOMIL et al. (2017). Goal-Driven Dynamics Learning via Bayesian Optimization. *Proceedings of the 56th Annual IEEE Conference on Decision and Control (CDC 2017)*.

CALANDRA, ROBERTO et al. (2016). Bayesian Optimization for Learning Gaits under Uncertainty: An Experimental Comparison on a Dynamic Bipedal Walker. *Annals of Mathematics and Artificial Intelligence* 76(1–2):5–23.

JUNGE, KAI et al. (2020). Improving Robotic Cooking Using Batch Bayesian Optimization. *IEEE Robotics and Automation Letters* 5(2):760–765.

MARCO, ALONSO et al. (2017). Virtual vs. Real: Trading off Simulations and Physical Experiments in Reinforcement Learning with Bayesian Optimization. *Proceedings of the 2017 IEEE International Conference on Robotics and Automation (ICRA 2017)*.

MARTINEZ-CANTIN, RUBEN et al. (2009). A Bayesian Exploration–Exploitation Approach for Optimal Online Sensing and Planning with a Visually Guided Mobile Robot. *Autonomous Robotics* 27(2):93–103.

RAI, AKSHARA et al. (n.d.). Using Simulation to Improve Sample-Efficiency of Bayesian Optimization for Bipedal Robots. *Journal of Machine Learning Research* 20(49).

Modeling for robotics

Modeling robot performance as a function of its parameters can be difficult due to nominally high-dimensional parameter spaces and the potential for context-dependent nonstationarity.

JAQUIER, NOÉMIE et al. (2019). Bayesian Optimization Meets Riemannian Manifolds in Robot Learning. *Proceedings of the 3rd Conference on Robot Learning (CORL 2019)*.

MARTINEZ-CANTIN, RUBEN (2017). Bayesian Optimization with Adaptive Kernels for Robot Control. *Proceedings of the 2017 IEEE International Conference on Robotics and Automation (ICRA 2017)*.

YUAN, KAI et al. (2019). Bayesian Optimization for Whole-Body Control of High-Degree-of-Freedom Robots through Reduction of Dimensionality. *IEEE Robotics and Automation Letters* 4(3):2268–2275.

Safe and robust optimization

robust optimization: § 11.9, p. 277

A complication faced in some robotic optimization settings is in ensuring that the evaluated parameters are both *robust* (that is, that performance is not overly sensitive to minor perturbations in the parameters) and *safe* (that is, that there is no chance of catastrophic failure in the robotic platform). We may address these concerns in the design of the optimization policy. For example, we might realize robustness by redefining the utility function in terms of the expected performance of perturbed parameters, and we might realize safety by incorporating appropriate constraints.

Chapter 6: Utility Functions for Optimization, p. 109
constrained optimization: § 11.2, p. 249

BERKENKAMP, FELIX et al. (2021). Bayesian Optimization with Safety Constraints: Safe and Automatic Parameter Tuning in Robotics. *Machine Learning* Special Issue on Robust Machine Learning.

GARCÍA-BARCOS, JAVIER et al. (2021). Robust Policy Search for Robot Navigation. *IEEE Robotics and Automation Letters* 6(2):2389–2396.

NOGUEIRA, JOSÉ et al. (2016). Unscented Bayesian Optimization for Safe Robot Grasping. *Proceedings of the 2016 IEEE/RSJ International Conference on Intelligent Robots and Systems (IROS 2016).*

Adversarial attacks

A specific safety issue to consider in robotic platforms incorporating deep neural networks is the possibility of adversarial attacks that may be able to alter the environment so as to induce unsafe behavior. Bayesian optimization has been applied to the efficient construction of adversarial attacks; this capability can in turn be used during the design phase seeking to build robotic controllers that are robust to such attack.

BOLOOR, ADITH et al. (2020). Attacking Vision-Based Perception in End-to-end Autonomous Driving Models. *Journal of Systems Architecture* 110:101766.

GHOSH, SHROMONA et al. (2018). Verifying Controllers against Adversarial Examples with Bayesian Optimization. *Proceedings of the 2018 IEEE International Conference on Robotics and Automation (ICRA 2018).*

REINFORCEMENT LEARNING

The main challenge in reinforcement learning is that agents can only evaluate decision policies through trial-and-error: by following a proposed policy and observing the resulting reward. When the system is complex, evaluating a given policy may be costly in terms of time or other resources, and when the space of potential policies is large, careful exploration is necessary.

Policy search is one approach to reinforcement learning that models the problem of policy design in terms of optimization. We enumerate a space of potential policies (for example, via parameterization) and seek to maximize the expected cumulative reward over the policy space. This abstraction allows the straightforward use of Bayesian optimization to construct a series of policies seeking to balance exploration and exploitation of the policy space. A recurring theme in this research is the careful use of simulators, when available, to help guide the search via techniques from multifidelity optimization.

multifidelity optimization: § 11.5, p. 263

Reinforcement learning is a central concept in robotics, and many of the papers cited in the previous section represent applications of policy search to particular robotic systems. The citations below concern reinforcement learning in a broader context.

FENG, QING et al. (2020). High-Dimensional Contextual Policy Search with Unknown Context Rewards Using Bayesian Optimization. *Advances in Neural Information Processing Systems 33 (NeurIPS 2020).*

LETHAM, BENJAMIN et al. (2019). Bayesian Optimization for Policy Search via Online–Offline Experimentation. *Journal of Machine Learning Research* 20(145):1–30.

WILSON, AARON et al. (2014). Using Trajectory Data to Improve Bayesian Optimization for Reinforcement Learning. *Journal of Machine Learning Research* 15(8):253–282.

Bayesian optimization has also proven useful for variations on the classical reinforcement learning problem, such as the multiagent setting or the so-called *inverse reinforcement learning* setting, where an agent must reconstruct an unknown reward function from observing demonstrations from other agents.

BALAKRISHNAN, SREEJITH et al. (2020). Efficient Exploration of Reward Functions in Inverse Reinforcement Learning via Bayesian Optimizaiton. *Advances in Neural Information Processing Systems 33 (NeurIPS 2020).*

DAI, ZHONGXIANG et al. (2020). R2-B2: Recursive Reasoning-Based Bayesian Optimization for No-Regret Learning in Games. *Proceedings of the 37th International Conference on Machine Learning (ICML 2020).*

IMANI, MAHDI et al. (2021). Scalable Inverse Reinforcement Learning through Multifidelity Bayesian Optimization. *IEEE Transactions on Neural Networks and Learning Systems.*

CIVIL ENGINEERING

The optimization of large-scale systems such as power, transportation, water distribution, and sensor networks can be difficult due to complex dynamics and the considerable expense of reconfiguration. Optimization can sometimes be aided via computer simulation, but the design spaces involved can nonetheless be huge, precluding exhaustive search.

BAHERI, ALI et al. (2017). Altitude Optimization of Airborne Wind Energy Systems: A Bayesian Optimization Approach. *Proceedings of the 2017 American Control Conference (ACC 2017)*.

CORNEJO-BUENO, L. et al. (2018). Bayesian Optimization of a Hybrid System for Robust Ocean Wave Features Prediction. *Neurocomputing* 275:818–828.

GARNETT, R. et al. (2010). Bayesian Optimization for Sensor Set Selection. *Proceedings of the 9th ACM/IEEE International Conference on Information Processing in Sensor Networks (IPSN 2010)*.

GRAMACY, ROBERT B. et al. (2016). Modeling an Augmented Lagrangian for Blackbox Constrained Optimization. *Technometrics* 58(1):1–11.

HICKISH, BOB et al. (2020). Investigating Bayesian Optimization for Rail Network Optimization. *International Journal of Rail Transporation* 8(4):307–323.

KOPSIAFTIS, GEORGE et al. (2019). Gaussian Process Regression Tuned by Bayesian Optimization for Seawater Intrusion Prediction. *Computational Intelligence and Neuroscience* 2019:2859429.

MARCHANT, ROMAN et al. (2012). Bayesian Optimisation for Intelligent Environmental Monitoring. *Proceedings of the 2012 IEEE/RSJ International Conference on Intelligent Robots and Systems (IROS 2012)*.

Structural engineering

The following study applied Bayesian optimization in a structural engineering setting: tuning the hyperparameters of a real-time predictive model for the typhoon-induced response of a ~1000 m real-world bridge.

ZHANG, YI-MING et al. (2021). Probabilistic Framework with Bayesian Optimization for Predicting Typhoon-Induced Dynamic Responses of a Long-Span Bridge. *Journal of Structural Engineering* 147(1): 04020297.

ELECTRICAL ENGINEERING

Over the past few decades, sophisticated tools have enabled the automation of many aspects of digital circuit design, even for extremely large circuits. However, the design of *analog* circuits remains largely a manual process. As circuits grow increasingly complex, the optimization of analog circuits (for example, to minimize power consumption subject to performance constraints) is becoming increasingly more difficult. Even computer simulation of complex analog circuits can entail significant cost, so careful experimental design is imperative for exploring the design space. Bayesian optimization has proven effective in this regard.

CHEN, PENG (2015). Bayesian Optimization for Broadband High-Efficiency Power Amplifier Designs. *IEEE Transactions on Microwave Theory and Techniques* 63(12):4263–4272.

FANG, YAORAN et al. (2018). A Bayesian Optimization and Partial Element Equivalent Circuit Approach to Coil Design in Inductive Power Transfer Systems. *Proceedings of the 2018 IEEE PELS Workshop on Emerging Technologies: Wireless Power Transfer (WOW 2018).*

LIU, MINGJIE et al. (2020). Closing the Design Loop: Bayesian Optimization Assisted Hierarchical Analog Layout Synthesis. *Proceedings of the 57th ACM/IEEE Design Automation Conference (DAC 2020).*

LYU, WENLONG et al. (2018). An Efficient Bayesian Optimization Approach for Automated Optimization of Analog Circuits. *IEEE Transactions on Circuits and Systems–I: Regular Papers* 65(6):1954–1967.

TORUN, HAKKI MERT et al. (2018). A Global Bayesian Optimization Algorithm and Its Application to Integrated System Design. *IEEE Transactions on Very Large Scale Integration (VLSI) Systems* 26(4): 792–802.

MECHANICAL ENGINEERING

The following study applied Bayesian optimization in a mechanical engineering setting: tuning the parameters of a welding process (via slow and expensive real-world experiments) to maximize weld quality.

STERLING, DILLON et al. (2015). Welding Parameter Optimization Based on Gaussian Process Regression Bayesian Optimization Algorithm. *Proceedings of the 2015 IEEE International Conference on Automation Science and Engineering (CASE 2015).*

Aerospace engineering

Nuances in airfoil design can have significant impact on aerodynamic performance, improvements in which can in turn lead to considerable cost savings from increased fuel efficiency. However, airfoil optimization is challenging due to the large design spaces involved and the nontrivial cost of evaluating a proposed configuration. Empirical measurement requires constructing an airfoil and testing its performance in a wind chamber. This process is too slow to explore the configuration space effectively, but we can *simulate* the process via computational fluid dynamics. These computational surrogates are still fairly costly due to the need to numerically solve nonlinear partial differential equations (the Navier–Stokes equations) at a sufficiently fine resolution, but they are nonetheless cheaper and more easily parallelized than experiments.[4]

Bayesian optimization can accelerate airfoil optimization via careful and cost-aware experimental design. One important idea here that can lead to significant computational savings is multifidelity modeling and optimization. It is relatively easy to control the cost–fidelity tradeoff in computational fluid dynamics simulations by altering its resolution

[4] There are many parallels with this situation and that faced in (computational) chemistry and materials science, where quantum-mechanical simulation also requires numerically solving a partial differential equation (the Schrödinger equation).

multifidelity optimization: § 11.5, p. 263

accordingly. This allows to rapidly explore the design space with cheap-but-rough simulations, then refine the most promising regions.

CHAITANYA, PARUCHURI et al. (2020). Bayesian Optimisation for Low-Noise Aerofoil Design with Aerodynamic Constraints. *International Journal of Aeroacoustics* 20(1–2):109–129.

FORRESTER ALEXANDER, I. J. et al. (2009). Recent Advances in Surrogate-Based Optimization. *Progress in Aerospace Sciences* 45(1–3):50–79.

HEBBAL, ALI et al. (2019). Multi-Objective Optimization Using Deep Gaussian Processes: Application to Aerospace Vehicle Design. *Proceedings of the 2019 AIAA Scitech Forum*.

LAM, REMI R. et al. (2018). Advances in Bayesian Optimization with Applications in Aerospace Engineering. *Proceedings of the 2018 AIAA Scitech Forum*.

PRIEM, RÉMY et al. (2020). An Efficient Application of Bayesian Optimization to an Industrial MDO Framework for Aircraft Design. *Proceedings of the 2020 AIAA Aviation Forum*.

REISENTHEL, PATRICK H. et al. (2011). A Numerical Experiment on Allocating Resources between Design of Experiment Samples and Surrogate-Based Optimization Infills. *Proceedings of the 2011 AIAA/ASME/ASCE/AHS/ ASC Structures, Structural Dynamics and Materials Conference*.

ZHENG, HONGYU et al. (2020). Multifidelity Kinematic Parameter Optimization of a Flapping Airfoil. *Physical Review E* 101(1):013107.

Automobile engineering

Bayesian optimization has also proven useful in automobile engineering. Automobile components and subsystems can have numerous tunable parameters affecting performance, and evaluating a given configuration can be complicated due to complex interactions among vehicle components. Bayesian optimization has shown success in this setting.

LIESSNER, ROMAN et al. (2019). Simultaneous Electric Powertrain Hardware and Energy Management Optimization of a Hybrid Electric Vehicle Using Deep Reinforcement Learning and Bayesian Optimization. *Proceedings of the 2019 IEEE Vehicle Power and Propulsion Conference (VPPC 2019)*.

NEUMANN-BROSIG, MATTHIAS et al. (2020). Data-Efficient Autotuning with Bayesian Optimization: An Industrial Control Study. *IEEE Transactions on Control Systems Technology* 28(3):730–740.

THOMAS, SINNU SUSAN et al. (2019). Designing MacPherson Suspension Architectures Using Bayesian Optimization. *Proceedings of the 28th Belgian Dutch Conference on Machine Learning (Benelearn 2019)*.

ALGORITHM CONFIGURATION, HYPERPARAMETER TUNING, AND AUTOML

Complex algorithms and software pipelines can have numerous parameters influencing their performance, and determining the optimal configuration for a given situation can require significant trial-and-error. Bayesian optimization has demonstrated remarkable success on a range of problems under the umbrella of *algorithm configuration.*

In the most general setting, we may simply model algorithm performance as a black box. A challenge here is dealing with high-dimensional parameter spaces that may have complex structure, such as conditional parameters that only become relevant depending on the settings of other parameters. This can pose a challenge for Gaussian process models, but alternatives such as random forests can perform admirably.

alternatives to GPs, including random forests: § 8.11, p. 196

DALIBARD, VALENTIN et al. (2017). BOAT: Building Auto-Tuners with Structured Bayesian Optimization. *Proceedings of the 26th International Conference on World Wide Web (WWW 2017).*

GONZALVEZ, JOAN et al. (2019). Financial Applications of Gaussian Processes and Bayesian Optimization. arXiv: 1903.04841 [q-fin.PM].

HOOS, HOLGER H. (2012). Programming by Optimization. *Communications of the ACM* 55(2):70–80.

HUTTER, FRANK et al. (2011). Sequential Model-Based Optimization for General Algorithm Configuration. *Proceedings of the 5th Learning and Intelligent Optimization Conference (LION 5).*

KUNJIR, MAYURESH (2019). Guided Bayesian Optimization to AutoTune Memory-Based Analytics. *Proceedings of the 35th IEEE International Conference on Data Engineering Workshops (ICDEW 2019).*

SŁOWIK, AGNIESZKA et al. (2019). Bayesian Optimisation for Heuristic Configuration in Automated Theorem Proving. *Proceedings of the 5th and 6th Vampire Workshops (Vampire 2019).*

VARGAS-HERNÁNDEZ, R. A. (2020). Bayesian Optimization for Calibrating and Selecting Hybrid-Density Functional Models. *Journal of Physical Chemistry A* 124(20):4053–4061.

Hyperparameter tuning of machine learning algorithms

The task of configuring machine learning algorithms in particular is known as *hyperparameter tuning.* Hyperparameter tuning is especially challenging in the era of deep learning, due to the often considerable cost of training and validating a proposed configuration. However, Bayesian optimization has proven effective at this task, and the results of a recent black-box optimization competition (run by TURNER et al. below) focusing on optimization problems from machine learning soundly established its superiority to alternatives such as random search.

QUITADAMO, ANDREW et al. (2017). Bayesian Hyperparameter Optimization for Machine Learning Based eQTL Analysis. *Proceedings of the 8th ACM International Conference on Bioinformatics, Computational Biology, and Health Informatics (BCB 2017).*

SNOEK, JASPER et al. (2012). Practical Bayesian Optimization of Machine Learning Algorithms. *Advances in Neural Information Processing Systems 25 (NeurIPS 2012).*

TURNER, RYAN et al. (2021). Bayesian Optimization Is Superior to Random Search for Machine Learning Hyperparameter Tuning: Analysis of the Black-Box Optimization Challenge 2020. *Proceedings of the NeurIPS 2020 Competition and Demonstration Track.*

YOGATAMA, DANI et al. (2015). Bayesian Optimization of Text Representations. *Proceedings of the 2015 Conference on Empirical Methods in Natural Language Processing (EMNLP 2015).*

tuning samplers, etc.

In addition to tuning machine learning algorithms to maximize predictive performance, Bayesian optimization can also tune the parameters of other algorithms for learning and inference such as Monte Carlo samplers.

HAMZE, FIRAS et al. (2013). Self-Avoiding Random Dynamics on Integer Complex Systems. ACM *Transactions on Modeling and Computer Simulation* 23(1):9.

MAHENDRAN, NIMALAN et al. (2010). Adaptive MCMC with Bayesian Optimization. *Proceedings of the 13th International Conference on Artificial Intelligence and Statistics (AISTATS 2010).*

One recent high-profile use of Bayesian optimization was in tuning the hyperparameters of DeepMind's AlphaGo agent. Bayesian optimization was able to improve AlphaGo's self-play win rate from one-half of games to nearly two-thirds, and the version tuned with Bayesian optimization was used in the final match against Lee Sedol.

CHEN, YUTIAN et al. (2018). Bayesian Optimization in AlphaGo. arXiv: 1812.06855 [cs.LG].

Automated machine learning

The goal of *automated machine learning* (autoML) is to develop automated procedures for machine learning tasks in order to boost efficiency and open the power of machine learning to a wider audience. Hyperparameter tuning is one particular instance of this overall vision, but we can also consider the automation of other aspects of machine learning.

Chapter 4: Model Assessment, Selection, and Averaging, p. 67

neural architecture search

In *model selection,* for example, we seek to tune not only the hyperparameters of a machine learning model but also the structure of the model itself. One notable special case is *neural architecture search,* the optimization of neural network architectures. Such problems are particularly difficult due to the discrete, structured nature of the search spaces involved. However, with careful modeling and acquisition strategies, Bayesian optimization becomes a feasible solution.

JIN, HAIFENG et al. (2019). Auto-Keras: An Efficient Neural Architecture Search System. *Proceedings of the 25th ACM SIGKDD International Conference on Knowledge Discovery and Data Mining (KDD 2019).*

KANDASAMY, KIRTHEVASAN et al. (2018). Neural Architecture Search with Bayesian Optimisation and Optimal Transport. *Advances in Neural Information Processing Systems 31 (NeurIPS 2018)*.

MALKOMES, GUSTAVO et al. (2016). Bayesian Optimization for Automated Model Selection. *Advances in Neural Information Processing Systems 29 (NeurIPS 2016)*.

WHITE, COLIN et al. (2021). BANANAS: Bayesian Optimization with Neural Architectures for Neural Architecture Search. *Proceedings of 35th AAAI Conference on Artificial Intelligence (AAAI 2021)*.

Researchers have even considered using Bayesian optimization for dynamic model selection during Bayesian optimization itself to realize fully autonomous and robust optimization routines.

MALKOMES, GUSTAVO et al. (2018). Automating Bayesian Optimization with Bayesian Optimization. *Advances in Neural Information Processing Systems 31 (NeurIPS 2018)*.

Optimization of entire machine learning pipelines

We may also consider the joint optimization of entire machine learning pipelines, starting from raw data and automatically constructing a bespoke machine learning system. The space of possible pipelines is absolutely enormous, as we must consider preprocessing steps such as feature selection and engineering in addition to model selection and hyperparameter tuning. Nonetheless, Bayesian optimization has proven up to the task.

Building a working autoML system of this scope entails a number of subtle design questions: the space of pipelines to consider, the allocation of training resources to proposed pipelines (which may vary enormously in their complexity), and the modeling of performance as a function of dataset and pipeline, to name a few. All of these questions have received careful consideration in the literature, and the following reference is an excellent entry point to that body of work.

FEURER, MATTHIAS et al. (2020). Auto-Sklearn 2.0: The Next Generation. arXiv: 2007.04074 [cs.LG].

ADAPTIVE HUMAN–COMPUTER INTERFACES

Adaptive human–computer interfaces seek to tailor themselves on-the-fly to suit the preferences of the user and/or the system provider. For example:

- a content provider may wish to learn user preferences to ensure recommended content is relevant,
- a website depending on ad revenue may wish to tune their interface and advertising placement algorithms to maximize ad revenue,

- a computer game may seek to adjust its difficulty dynamically to keep the player engaged, or
- a data-visualization system may seek to infer the user's goals in interacting with a dataset and customize the presentation of data accordingly.

The design of such a system can be challenging, as the space of possible user preferences and/or the space of possible algorithmic settings can be large, and the optimal configuration may change over time or depend on other context. Further, we may only assess the utility of a given interface configuration through user interaction, which is a slow, cumbersome, and noisy channel from which to glean information. Finally, we face the additional challenge that if we are not careful, the user may become annoyed and simply abandon the platform altogether! Nonetheless, Bayesian optimization has shown success in tuning adaptive interfaces and in related problems such as preference optimization, A/B testing, etc.

BROCHU, ERIC et al. (2010). A Bayesian Interactive Optimization Approach to Procedural Animation Design. *Proceedings of the 2010 ACM SIGGRAPH/Eurographics Symposium on Computer Animimation (SCA 2010)*.

BROCHU, ERIC et al. (2015). Active Preference Learning with Discrete Choice Data. *Advances in Neural Information Processing Systems 20 (NeurIPS 2007)*.

GONZÁLEZ, JAVIER et al. (2017). Preferential Bayesian Optimization. *Proceedings of the 34th International Conference on Machine Learning (ICML 2017)*.

KADNER, FLORIAN et al. (2021). AdaptiFont: Increasing Individuals' Reading Speed with a Generative Font Model and Bayesian Optimization. *Proceedings of the 2021 CHI Conference on Human Factors in Computing Systems (CHI 2021)*.

KHAJAH, MOHAMMAD M. et al. (2016). Designing Engaging Games Using Bayesian Optimization. *Proceedings of the 2016 CHI Conference on Human Factors in Computing Systems (CHI 2016)*.

LETHAM, BENJAMIN et al. (2019). Constrained Bayesian Optimization with Noisy Experiments. *Bayesian Analysis* 14(2):495–519.

MONADJEMI, SHAYAN et al. (2020). Active Visual Analytics: Assisted Data Discovery in Interactive Visualizations via Active Search. arXiv: 2010.08155 [cs.HC].

REFERENCES

ABBASI-YADKORI, YASIN (2012). Online Learning for Linearly Parameterized Control Problems. Ph.D. thesis. University of Alberta.

ACERBI, LUIGI (2018). Variational Bayesian Monte Carlo. *Advances in Neural Information Processing Systems 31 (NeurIPS 2018)*, pp. 8213–8223.

ACERBI, LUIGI and WEI JI MA (2017). Practical Bayesian Optimization for Model Fitting with Bayesian Adaptive Direct Search. *Advances in Neural Information Processing Systems 30 (NeurIPS 2017)*, pp. 1836–1846.

ADAMS, RYAN PRESCOTT, IAIN MURRAY, and DAVID J. C. MACKAY (2009). Tractable Nonparametric Bayesian Inference in Poisson Processes with Gaussian Process Intensities. *Proceedings of the 26th International Conference on Machine Learning (ICML 2009)*, pp. 9–16.

ADLER, ROBERT J. and JONATHAN E. TAYLOR (2007). *Random Fields and Geometry.* Springer Monographs in Mathematics. Springer–Verlag.

AGRAWAL, RAJEEV (1995). The Continuum-Armed Bandit Problem. *SIAM Journal on Control and Optimization* 33(6):1926–1951.

AGRAWAL, SHIPRA and NAVIN GOYAL (2012). Analysis of Thompson Sampling for the Multi-Armed Bandit Problem. *Proceedings of the 25th Annual Conference on Learning Theory (COLT 2012)*. Vol. 23. Proceedings of Machine Learning Research, pp. 39.1–39.26.

ÁLVAREZ, MAURICIO A., LORENZO ROSASCO, and NEIL D. LAWRENCE (2012). Kernels for Vector-Valued Functions: A Review. *Foundations and Trends in Machine Learning* 4(3):195–266.

ARCONES, MIGUEL A. (1992). On the arg max of a Gaussian Process. *Statistics & Probability Letters* 15(5):373–374.

AUER, PETER, NICOLÒ CESA-BIANCHI, and PAUL FISCHER (2002). Finite-Time Analysis of the Multiarmed Bandit Problem. *Machine Learning* 47(2–3):235–256.

BALANDAT, MAXIMILIAN, BRIAN KARRER, DANIEL R. JIANG, SAMUEL DAULTON, BENJAMIN LETHAM, ANDREW GORDON WILSON, et al. (2020). BoTorch: A Framework for Efficient Monte-Carlo Bayesian Optimization. *Advances in Neural Information Processing Systems 33 (NeurIPS 2020)*, pp. 21524–21538.

BAPTISTA, RICARDO and MATTHIAS POLOCZEK (2018). Bayesian Optimization of Combinatorial Structures. *Proceedings of the 35th International Conference on Machine Learning (ICML 2018)*. Vol. 80. Proceedings of Machine Learning Research, pp. 462–471.

BATHER, JOHN (1996). A Conversation with Herman Chernoff. *Statistical Science* 11(4):335–350.

BELAKARIA, SYRINE, ARYAN DESHWAL, and JANARDHAN RAO DOPPA (2019). Max-value Entropy Search for Multi-Objective Bayesian Optimization. *Advances in Neural Information Processing Systems 32 (NeurIPS 2019)*, pp. 7825–7835.

BELLMAN, RICHARD (1952). On the Theory of Dynamic Programming. *Proceedings of the National Academy of Sciences* 38(8):716–719.

BELLMAN, RICHARD (1957). *Dynamic Programming.* Princeton University Press.

BERGER, JAMES O. (1985). *Statistical Decision Theory and Bayesian Analysis.* 2nd ed. Springer Series in Statistics. Springer–Verlag.

BERGSTRA, JAMES, RÉMI BARDENET, YOSHUA BENGIO, and BALÁZS KÉGL (2011). Algorithms for Hyper-Parameter Optimization. *Advances in Neural Information Processing Systems 24 (NeurIPS 2011)*, pp. 2546–2554.

BERGSTRA, JAMES and YOSHUA BENGIO (2012). Random Search for Hyper-Parameter Optimization. *Journal of Machine Learning Research* 13:281–305.

BERKENKAMP, FELIX, ANGELA P. SCHOELLING, and ANDREAS KRAUSE (2019). No-Regret Bayesian Optimization with Unknown Hyperparameters. *Journal of Machine Learning Research* 20(50):1–24.

BERRY, DONALD A. and BERT FRISTEDT (1985). *Bandit Problems: Sequential Allocation of Experiments.* Monographs on Statistics and Applied Probability. Chapman & Hall.

BERTSEKAS, DIMITRI P. (2017). *Dynamic Programming and Optimal Control.* 4th ed. Vol. 1. Athena Scientific.

BOCHNER, S (1933). Monotone Funktionen, Stieltjessche Integrale und harmonische Analyse. *Mathematische Annalen* 108:378–410.

BOGUNOVIC, ILIJA, ANDREAS KRAUSE, and JONATHAN SCARLETT (2020). Corruption-Tolerant Gaussian Process Bandit Optimization. *Proceedings of the 23rd International Conference on Artificial Intelligence and Statistics (AISTATS 2020).* Vol. 108. Proceedings of Machine Learning Research, pp. 1071–1081.

BOGUNOVIC, ILIJA, JONATHAN SCARLETT, STEFANIE JEGELKA, and VOLKAN CEVHER (2018). Adversarially Robust Optimization with Gaussian Processes. *Advances in Neural Information Processing Systems 31 (NeurIPS 2018)*, pp. 5760–5770.

BOX, G. E. P. (1954). The Exploration and Exploitation of Response Surfaces: Some General Considerations and Examples. *Biometrics* 10(1):16–60.

BOX, GEORGE E. P., J. STUART HUNTER, and WILLIAM G. HUNTER (2005). *Statistics for Experimenters: Design, Innovation, and Discovery.* 2nd ed. Wiley Series in Probability and Statistics. John Wiley & Sons.

BOX, G. E. P. and K. B. WILSON (1951). On the Experimental Attainment of Optimum Conditions. *Journal of the Royal Statistical Society Series B (Methodological)* 13(1):1–45.

BOX, G. E. P. and P. V. YOULE (1954). The Exploration and Exploitation of Response Surfaces: An Example of the Link between the Fitted Surface and the Basic Mechanism of the System. *Biometrics* 11(3):287–323.

BREIMAN, LEO (2001). Random Forests. *Machine Learning* 45(1):5–32.

BRENT, RICHARD P. (1973). *Algorithms for Minimization without Derivatives.* Prentice–Hall Series in Automatic Computation. Prentice–Hall.

BROCHU, ERIC, VLAD M. CORA, and NANDO DE FREITAS (2010). A Tutorial on Bayesian Optimization of Expensive Cost Functions, with Application to Active User Modeling and Hierarchical Reinforcement Learning. arXiv: 1012.2599 [cs.LG].

BROOKS, STEVE, ANDREW GELMAN, GALIN L. JONES, and XIAO-LI MENG, eds. (2011). *Handbook of Markov Chain Monte Carlo.* Handbooks of Modern Statistical Methods. Chapman & Hall.

BUBECK, SÉBASTIEN and NICOLÒ CESA-BIANCHI (2012). Regret Analysis of Stochastic and Nonstochastic Multi-Armed Bandit Problems. *Foundations and Trends in Machine Learning* 5(1):1–122.

BUBECK, SÉBASTIEN, RÉMI MUNOS, and GILLES STOLTZ (2009). Pure Exploration in Multi-Armed Bandits Problems. *Proceedings of the 20th International Conference on Algorithmic Learning Theory (ALT 2009).* Vol. 5809. Lecture Notes in Computer Science. Springer–Verlag, pp. 23–37.

BULL, ADAM D. (2011). Convergence Rates of Efficient Global Optimization Algorithms. *Journal of Machine Learning Research* 12(88):2879–2904.

CAFLISCH, RUSSEL E. (1998). Monte Carlo and Quasi-Monte Carlo Methods. *Acta Numerica* 7:1–49.

CAI, XU, SELWYN GOMES, and JONATHAN SCARLETT (2021). Lenient Regret and Good-Action Identification in Gaussian Process Bandits. *Proceedings of the 38th International Conference on Machine Learning (ICML 2021)*. Vol. 139. Proceedings of Machine Learning Research, pp. 1183–1192.

CAKMAK, SAIT, RAUL ASTUDILLO, PETER FRAZIER, and ENLU ZHOU (2020). Bayesian Optimization of Risk Measures. *Advances in Neural Information Processing Systems 33 (NeurIPS 2020)*, pp. 18039–18049.

CALANDRA, ROBERTO, JAN PETERS, CARL EDWARD RASMUSSEN, and MARC PETER DEISENROTH (2016). Manifold Gaussian Processes for Regression. *Proceedings of the 2016 International Joint Conference on Neural Networks (IJCNN 2016)*, pp. 3338–3345.

CALVIN, J. and A. ŽILINSKAS (1999). On the Convergence of the P-Algorithm for One-Dimensional Global Optimization of Smooth Functions. *Journal of Optimization Theory and Applications* 102(3):479–495.

CALVIN, JAMES M. (1993). Consistency of a Myopic Bayesian Algorithm for One-Dimensional Global Optimization. *Journal of Global Optimization* 3(2):223–232.

CALVIN, JAMES M. (2000). Convergence Rate of the P-Algorithm for Optimization of Continuous Functions. In: *Approximation and Complexity in Numerical Optimization: Continuous and Discrete Problems*. Ed. by PANOS M. PARDALOS. Vol. 42. Nonconvex Optimization and Its Applications. Springer–Verlag, pp. 116–129.

CALVIN, JAMES M. and ANTANAS ŽILINSKAS (2001). On Convergence of a P-Algorithm Based on a Statistical Model of Continuously Differentiable Functions. *Journal of Global Optimization* 19(3):229–245.

CAMILLERI, ROMAIN, JULIAN KATZ-SAMUELS, and KEVIN JAMIESON (2021). High-Dimensional Experimental Design and Kernel Bandits. *Proceedings of the 38th International Conference on Machine Learning (ICML 2021)*. Vol. 139. Proceedings of Machine Learning Research, pp. 1227–1237.

CARTINHOUR, JACK (1989). One-Dimensional Marginal Density Functions of a Truncated Multivariate Normal Density Function. *Communications in Statistics – Theory and Methods* 19(1):197–203.

CHAPELLE, OLIVIER and LIHONG LI (2011). An Empirical Evaluation of Thompson Sampling. *Advances in Neural Information Processing Systems 24 (NeurIPS 2011)*, pp. 2249–2257.

CHERNOFF, HERMAN (1959). Sequential Design of Experiments. *The Annals of Mathematical Statistics* 30(3):755–770.

CHERNOFF, HERMAN (1972). *Sequential Analysis and Optimal Design*. CBMS–NSF Regional Conference Series in Applied Mathematics. Society for Industrial and Applied Mathematics.

CHEVALIER, CLÉMENT and DAVID GINSBOURGER (2013). Fast Computation of the Multi-Points Expected Improvement with Applications in Batch Selection. *Proceedings of the 7th Learning and Intelligent Optimization Conference (LION 7)*. Vol. 7997. Lecture Notes in Computer Science. Springer–Verlag, pp. 59–69.

CHOWDHURY, SAYAK RAY and ADITYA GOPALAN (2017). On Kernelized Multi-Armed Bandits. *Proceedings of the 34th International Conference on Machine Learning (ICML 2017)*. Vol. 70. Proceedings of Machine Learning Research, pp. 844–853.

CLARK, CHARLES E. (1961). The Greatest of a Finite Set of Random Variables. *Operations Research* 9(2):145–162.

CONTAL, EMILE, DAVID BUFFONI, ALEXANDRE ROBICQUET, and NICOLAS VAYATIS (2013). Parallel Gaussian Process Optimization with Upper Confidence Bound and Pure Exploration. *Proceedings of the 2013 European Conference on Machine Learning and Prin-

ciples and Practice of Knowledge Discovery in Databases (ECML PKDD 2013). Vol. 8188. Lecture Notes in Computer Science. Springer–Verlag, pp. 225–240.

COVER, THOMAS M. and JOY A. THOMAS (2006). *Elements of Information Theory*. 2nd ed. John Wiley & Sons.

COX, DENNIS D. and SUSAN JOHN (1992). A Statistical Method for Global Optimization. *Proceedings of the 1992 IEEE International Conference on Systems, Man, and Cybernetics (SMC 1992)*, pp. 1241–1246.

CUNNINGHAM, JOHN P., PHILIPP HENNIG, and SIMON LACOSTE-JULIEN (2011). Gaussian Probabilities and Expectation Propagation. arXiv: 1111.6832 [stat.ML].

CUTAJAR, KURT, MICHAEL A. OSBORNE, JOHN P. CUNNINGHAM, and MAURIZIO FILIPPONE (2016). Preconditioning Kernel Matrices. *Proceedings of the 33rd International Conference on Machine Learning (ICML 2016)*. Vol. 48. Proceedings of Machine Learning Research, pp. 2529–2538.

DAI, ZHENWEN, ANDREAS DAMIANOU, JAVIER GONZÁLEZ, and NEIL LAWRENCE (2016). Variational Auto-encoded Deep Gaussian Processes. *Proceedings of the 4th International Conference on Learning Representations (ICLR 2016)*. arXiv: 1511.06455 [cs.LG].

DAI, ZHONGXIANG, HAIBIN YU, BRYAN KIAN HSIANG LOW, and PATRICK JAILLET (2019). Bayesian Optimization Meets Bayesian Optimal Stopping. *Proceedings of the 36th International Conference on Machine Learning (ICML 2019)*. Vol. 97. Proceedings of Machine Learning Research, pp. 1496–1506.

DALIBARD, VALENTIN, MICHAEL SCHAARSCHMIDT, and EIKO YONEKI (2017). BOAT: Building Auto-Tuners with Structured Bayesian Optimization. *Proceedings of the 26th International Conference on World Wide Web (WWW 2017)*, pp. 479–488.

DANI, VARSHA, THOMAS P. HAYES, and SHAM M. KAKADE (2008). Stochastic Linear Optimization under Bandit Feedback. *Proceedings of the 21st Conference on Learning Theory (COLT 2008)*, pp. 355–366.

DAVIS, PHILIP J. and PHILIP RABINOWITZ (1984). *Methods of Numerical Integration*. 2nd ed. Computer Science and Applied Mathematics. Academic Press.

DE ATH, GEORGE, RICHARD M. EVERSON, ALMA A. RAHAT, and JONATHAN E. FIELDSEND (2021). Greed Is Good: Exploration and Exploitation Trade-offs in Bayesian Optimisation. *ACM Transactions on Evolutionary Learning and Optimization* 1(1):1–22.

DE ATH, GEORGE, JONATHAN E. FIELDSEND, and RICHARD M. EVERSON (2020). What Do You Mean? The Role of the Mean Function in Bayesian Optimization. *Proceedings of the 2020 Genetic and Evolutionary Computation Conference (GECCO 2020)*, pp. 1623–1631.

DE FREITAS, NANDO, ALEX J. SMOLA, and MASROUR ZOGHI (2012a). Regret Bounds for Deterministic Gaussian Process Bandits. arXiv: 1203.2177 [cs.LG].

DE FREITAS, NANDO, ALEX J. SMOLA, and MASROUR ZOHGI (2012b). Exponential Regret Bounds for Gaussian Process Bandits with Deterministic Observations. *Proceedings of the 29th International Conference on Machine Learning (ICML 2012)*, pp. 955–962.

DEGROOT, MORRIS H. (1970). *Optimal Statistical Decisions*. McGraw–Hill.

DESAUTELS, THOMAS, ANDREAS KRAUSE, and JOEL W. BURDICK (2014). Parallelizing Exploration–Exploitation Tradeoffs in Gaussian Process Bandit Optimization. *Journal of Machine Learning Research* 15(119):4053–4103.

DIACONIS, PERSI (1988). Bayesian Numerical Analysis. In: *Statistical Decision Theory and Related Topics IV*. Ed. by SHANTI S. GUPTA and JAMES O. BERGER. Vol. 1. Springer–Verlag, pp. 163–175.

DJOLONGA, JOSIP, ANDREAS KRAUSE, and VOLKAN CEVHER (2013). High-Dimensional Gaussian Process Bandits. *Advances in Neural Information Processing Systems 26 (NeurIPS 2013)*, pp. 1025–1033.

DOMHAN, TOBIAS, JOST TOBIAS SPRINGENBERG, and FRANK HUTTER (2015). Speeding up Automatic Hyperparameter Optimization of Deep Neural Networks by Extrapolation of Learning Curves. *Proceedings of the 24th International Conference on Artificial Intelligence (IJCAI 2015)*, pp. 3460–3468.

DUVENAUD, DAVID, JAMES ROBERT LLOYD, ROGER GROSSE, JOSHUA B. TENENBAUM, and ZOUBIN GHAHRAMANI (2013). Structure Discovery in Nonparametric Regression through Compositional Kernel Search. *Proceedings of the 30th International Conference on Machine Learning (ICML 2013)*. Vol. 28. Proceedings of Machine Learning Research, pp. 1166–1174.

EMMERICH, MICHAEL T. M., KYRIAKOS C. GIANNAKOGLOU, and BORIS NAUJOKS (2006). Single- and Multiobjective Evolutionary Optimization Assisted by Gaussian Random Field Metamodels. *IEEE Transactions on Evolutionary Computation* 10(4):421–439.

EMMERICH, MICHAEL and BORIS NAUJOKS (2004). Metamodel Assisted Multiobjective Optimisation Strategies and Their Application in Airfoil Design. In: *Adaptive Computing in Design and Manufacture VI*. Ed. by I. C. PARMEE. Springer–Verlag, pp. 249–260.

ERIKSSON, DAVID, MICHAEL PEARCE, JACOB R. GARDNER, RYAN TURNER, and MATTHIAS POLOCZEK (2019). Scalable Global Optimization via Local Bayesian Optimization. *Advances in Neural Information Processing Systems 32 (NeurIPS 2019)*, pp. 5496–5507.

FERNÁNDEZ-DELGADO, MANUEL, EVA CERNADAS, SENÉN BARRO, and DINANI AMORIM (2014). Do We Need Hundreds of Classifiers to Solve Real World Classification Problems? *Journal of Machine Learning Research* 15(90):3133–3181.

FEURER, MATTHIAS, JOST TOBIAS SPRINGENBERG, and FRANK HUTTER (2015). Initializing Bayesian Hyperparameter Optimization via Meta-Learning. *Proceedings of 29th AAAI Conference on Artificial Intelligence (AAAI 2015)*, pp. 1128–1135.

FISHER, RONALD A. (1935). *The Design of Experiments*. Oliver and Boyd.

FLEISCHER, M. (2003). The Measure of Pareto Optima: Applications to Multi-Objective Metaheuristics. *Proceedings of the 2nd International Conference on Evolutionary Multi-Criterion Optimization (EMO 2003)*. Vol. 2632. Lecture Notes in Computer Science. Springer–Verlag, pp. 519–533.

FORRESTER, ALEXANDER I. J., ANDY J. KEANE, and NEIL W. BRESSLOFF (2006). Design and Analysis of "Noisy" Computer Experiments. *AIAA Journal* 44(10):2331–2339.

FRAZIER, PETER and WARREN POWELL (2007). The Knowledge Gradient Policy for Offline Learning with Independent Normal Rewards. *Proceedings of the 2007 IEEE International Symposium on Approximate Dynamic Programming and Reinforcement Learning (ADPRL 2007)*, pp. 143–150.

FRAZIER, PETER, WARREN POWELL, and SAVAS DAYANIK (2009). The Knowledge-Gradient Policy for Correlated Normal Beliefs. *INFORMS Journal on Computing* 21(4):599–613.

FRIEDMAN, MILTON and L. J. SAVAGE (1947). Planning Experiments Seeking Maxima. In: *Selected Techniques of Statistical Analysis for Scientific and Industrial Research, and Production and Management Engineering*. Ed. by CHURCHILL EISENHART, MILLARD W. HARTAY, and W. ALLEN WALLIS. McGraw–Hill, pp. 363–372.

FRÖHLICH, LUKAS P., EDGAR D. KLENSKE, JULIA VINOGRADSKA, CHRISTIAN DANIEL, and MELANIE N. ZEILINGER (2020). Noisy-Input Entropy Search for Efficient Robust Bayesian Optimization. *Proceedings of the 23rd International Conference on Artificial*

Intelligence and Statistics (AISTATS 2020). Vol. 108. Proceedings of Machine Learning Research, pp. 2262–2272.

GARCÍA-BARCOS, JAVIER and RUBEN MARTINEZ-CANTIN (2021). Robust Policy Search for Robot Navigation. *IEEE Robotics and Automation Letters* 6(2):2389–2396.

GARDNER, JACOB R., CHUAN GUO, KILIAN Q. WEINBERGER, ROMAN GARNETT, and ROGER GROSSE (2017). Discovering and Exploiting Additive Structure for Bayesian Optimization. *Proceedings of the 20th International Conference on Artificial Intelligence and Statistics (AISTATS 2017)*. Vol. 54. Proceedings of Machine Learning Research, pp. 1311–1319.

GARDNER, JACOB R., MATT J. KUSNER, ZHIXIANG (EDDIE) XU, KILIAN Q. WEINBERGER, and JOHN P. CUNNINGHAM (2014). Bayesian Optimization with Inequality Constraints. *Proceedings of the 31st International Conference on Machine Learning (ICML 2014)*. Vol. 32. Proceedings of Machine Learning Research, pp. 937–945.

GARDNER, JACOB R., GEOFF PLEISS, DAVID BINDEL, KILIAN Q. WEINBERGER, and ANDREW GORDON WILSON (2018). GPyTorch: Blackbox Matrix–Matrix Gaussian Process Inference with GPU Acceleration. *Advances in Neural Information Processing Systems 31 (NeurIPS 2018)*, pp. 7576–7586.

GARNETT, ROMAN, THOMAS GÄRTNER, MARTIN VOGT, and JÜRGEN BAJORATH (2015). Introducing the 'Active Search' Method for Iterative Virtual Screening. *Journal of Computer-Aided Molecular Design* 29(4):305–314.

GARNETT, ROMAN, YAMUNA KRISHNAMURTHY, XUEHAN XIONG, JEFF SCHNEIDER, and RICHARD MANN (2012). Bayesian Optimal Active Search and Surveying. *Proceedings of the 29th International Conference on Machine Learning (ICML 2012)*, pp. 1239–1246.

GARNETT, ROMAN, MICHAEL A. OSBORNE, and PHILIPP HENNIG (2014). Active Learning of Linear Embeddings for Gaussian Processes. *Proceedings of the 30th Conference on Uncertainty in Artificial Intelligence (UAI 2014)*, pp. 230–239.

GARNETT, R., M. A. OSBORNE, and S. J. ROBERTS (2010). Bayesian Optimization for Sensor Set Selection. *Proceedings of the 9th ACM/IEEE International Conference on Information Processing in Sensor Networks (IPSN 2010)*, pp. 209–219.

GELBART, MICHAEL A., JASPER SNOEK, and RYAN P. ADAMS (2014). Bayesian Optimization with Unknown Constraints. *Proceedings of the 30th Conference on Uncertainty in Artificial Intelligence (UAI 2014)*, pp. 250–259.

GELMAN, ANDREW and AKI VEHTARI (2021). What Are the Most Important Statistical Ideas of the Past 50 Years? *Journal of the American Statistical Association* 116(536):2087–2097.

GERGONNE, JOSEPH DIEZ (1815). Application de la méthode des moindres quarrés à l'interpolation des suites. *Annales de Mathématiques pures et appliquées* 6:242–252.

GHOSAL, SUBHASHIS and ANINDYA ROY (2006). Posterior Consistency of Gaussian Process Prior for Nonparametric Binary Regression. *The Annals of Statistics* 34(5):2413–2429.

GIBBS, MARK N. (1997). Bayesian Gaussian Processes for Regression and Classification. Ph.D. thesis. University of Cambridge.

GILBOA, ELAD, YUNUS SAATÇI, and JOHN P. CUNNINGHAM (2013). Scaling Multidimensional Gaussian Processes Using Projected Additive Approximations. *Proceedings of the 30th International Conference on Machine Learning (ICML 2013)*. Vol. 28. Proceedings of Machine Learning Research, pp. 454–461.

GINSBOURGER, DAVID and RODOLPHE LE RICHE (2010). Towards Gaussian Process-Based Optimization with Finite Time Horizon. *Proceedings of the 9th International Workshop in Model-Oriented Design and Analysis (MODA 9)*. Contributions to Statistics. Springer–Verlag, pp. 89–96.

GINSBOURGER, DAVID, RODOLPHE LE RICHE, and LAURENT CARRARO (2010). Kriging is Well-Suited to Parallelize Optimization. In: *Computational Intelligence in Expensive Optimization Problems*. Ed. by YOEL YENNE and CHI-KEONG GO. Adaptation Learning and Optimization. Springer–Verlag, pp. 131–162.

GOLOVIN, DANIEL and QIUYI (RICHARD) ZHANG (2020). Random Hypervolume Scalarizations for Provable Multi-Objective Black Box Optimization. *Proceedings of the 37th International Conference on Machine Learning (ICML 2020)*. Vol. 119. Proceedings of Machine Learning Research, pp. 11096–11105.

GOLUB, GENE H. and CHARLES F. VAN LOAN (2013). *Matrix Computations*. 4th ed. Johns Hopkins Studies in the Mathematical Sciences. Johns Hopkins University Press.

GÓMEZ-BOMBARELLI, RAFAEL, JENNIFER N. WEI, DAVID DUVENAUD, JOSÉ MIGUEL HERNÁNDEZ-LOBATO, BENJAMÍN SÁNCHEZ-LENGELING, DENNIS SHEBERLA, et al. (2018). Automatic Chemical Design Using a Data-Driven Continuous Representation of Molecules. *ACS Central Science* 4(2):268–276.

GONZÁLEZ, JAVIER, ZHENWEN DAI, PHILIPP HENNIG, and NEIL LAWRENCE (2016a). Batch Bayesian Optimization via Local Penalization. *Proceedings of the 19th International Conference on Artificial Intelligence and Statistics (AISTATS 2016)*. Vol. 51. Proceedings of Machine Learning Research, pp. 648–657.

GONZÁLEZ, JAVIER, MICHAEL OSBORNE, and NEIL D. LAWRENCE (2016b). GLASSES: Relieving the Myopia of Bayesian Optimisation. *Proceedings of the 19th International Conference on Artificial Intelligence and Statistics (AISTATS 2016)*. Vol. 51. Proceedings of Machine Learning Research, pp. 790–799.

GRAMACY, ROBERT B. and HERBERT K. H. LEE (2011). Optimization under Unknown Constraints. In: *Bayesian Statistics 9*. Ed. by J. M. BERNARDO, M. J. BAYARRI, J. O. BERGER, A. P. DAWID, D. HECKERMAN, A. F. M. SMITH, et al. Oxford University Press, pp. 229–256.

GRANMO, OLE-CHRISTOFFER (2010). Solving Two-Armed Bernoulli Bandit Problems Using a Bayesian Learning Automaton. *International Journal of Intelligent Computing and Cybernetics* 3(2):207–234.

GRÜNEWÄLDER, STEFFEN, JEAN-YVES AUDIBERT, MANFRED OPPER, and JOHN SHAWE-TAYLOR (2010). Regret Bounds for Gaussian Process Bandit Problems. *Proceedings of the 13th International Conference on Artificial Intelligence and Statistics (AISTATS 2010)*. Vol. 9. Proceedings of Machine Learning Research, pp. 273–280.

HANSEN, NIKOLAUS (2016). The CMA Evolution Strategy: A Tutorial. arXiv: 1604.00772 [cs.LG].

HASTIE, TREVOR and ROBERT TIBSHIRANI (1986). Generalized Additive Models. *Statistical Science* 1(3):297–318.

HENNIG, PHILIPP, MICHAEL A. OSBORNE, and MARK GIROLAMI (2015). Probabilistic Numerics and Uncertainty in Computations. *Proceedings of the Royal Society A: Mathematical, Physical and Engineering Sciences* 471(2179):20150142.

HENNIG, PHILIPP, MICHAEL A. OSBORNE, and HANS KERSTING (2022). *Probabilistic Numerics: Computation as Machine Learning*. Cambridge University Press.

HENNIG, PHILIPP and CHRISTIAN J. SCHULER (2012). Entropy Search for Information-Efficient Global Optimization. *Journal of Machine Learning Research* 13(Jun):1809–1837.

HENSMAN, JAMES, ALEXANDER G. DE G. MATTHEWS, MAURIZIO FILIPPONE, and ZOUBIN GHAHRAMANI (2015). MCMC for Variationally Sparse Gaussian Processes. *Advances in Neural Information Processing Systems 28 (NeurIPS 2015)*, pp. 1648–1656.

HERNÁNDEZ-LOBATO, DANIEL, JOSÉ MIGUEL HERNÁNDEZ-LOBATO, AMAR SHAH, and RYAN P. ADAMS (2016a). Predictive Entropy Search for Multi-Objective Bayesian Optimization. *Proceedings of the 33rd International Conference on Machine Learning (ICML 2016)*. Vol. 48. Proceedings of Machine Learning Research, pp. 1492–1501.

HERNÁNDEZ-LOBATO, JOSÉ MIGUEL, MICHAEL A. GELBART, RYAN P. ADAMS, MATTHEW W. HOFFMAN, and ZOUBIN GHAHRAMANI (2016b). A General Framework for Constrained Bayesian Optimization Using Information-Based Search. *Journal of Machine Learning Research* 17:1–53.

HERNÁNDEZ-LOBATO, JOSÉ MIGUEL, MATTHEW W. HOFFMAN, and ZOUBIN GHAHRAMANI (2014). Predictive Entropy Search for Efficient Global Optimization of Black-Box Functions. *Advances in Neural Information Processing Systems 27 (NeurIPS 2014)*, pp. 918–926.

HERNÁNDEZ-LOBATO, JOSÉ MIGUEL, JAMES REQUEIMA, EDWARD O. PYZER-KNAPP, and ALÁN ASPURU-GUZIK (2017). Parallel and Distributed Thompson Sampling for Large-Scale Accelerated Exploration of Chemical Space. *Proceedings of the 34th International Conference on Machine Learning (ICML 2017)*. Vol. 70. Proceedings of Machine Learning Research, pp. 1470–1479.

HESTENES, MAGNUS R. and EDUARD STIEFEL (1952). Methods of Conjugate Gradients for Solving Linear Systems. *Journal of Research of the National Bureau of Standards* 49(6):409–436.

HIE, BRIAN L. and KEVIN K. YANG (2021). Adaptive Machine Learning for Protein Engineering. arXiv: 2106.05466 [q-bio.QM].

HOANG, TRONG NGHIA, QUANG MINH HOANG, RUOFEI OUYANG, and KIAN HSIANG LOW (2018). Decentralized High-Dimensional Bayesian Optimization with Factor Graphs. *Proceedings of 32nd AAAI Conference on Artificial Intelligence (AAAI 2018)*, pp. 3231–3238.

HOFFMAN, MATTHEW D. and ANDREW GELMAN (2014). The No-U-turn Sampler: Adaptively Setting Path Lengths in Hamiltonian Monte Carlo. *Journal of Machine Learning Research* 15(4):1593–1623.

HOFFMAN, MATTHEW W. and ZOUBIN GHAHRAMANI (2015). Output-Space Predictive Entropy Search for Flexible Global Optimization. *Bayesian Optimization: Scalability and Flexibility Workshop (BayesOpt 2015), Conference on Neural Information Processing Systems (NeurIPS 2015)*.

HOFFMAN, MATTHEW W. and BOBAK SHAHRIARI (2014). Modular Mechanisms for Bayesian Optimization. *Bayesian Optimization in Academia and Industry (BayesOpt 2014), Conference on Neural Information Processing Systems (NeurIPS 2014)*.

HOTELLING, HAROLD (1941). Experimental Determination of the Maximum of a Function. *The Annals of Mathematical Statistics* 12(1):20–45.

HOULSBY, NEIL, JOSÉ MIGUEL HERNÁNDEZ-LOBATO, FERENC HUSZÁR, and ZOUBIN GHAHRAMANI (2012). Collaborative Gaussian Processes for Preference Learning. *Advances in Neural Information Processing Systems 25 (NeurIPS 2012)*, pp. 2096–2104.

HUANG, D., T. T. ALLEN, W. I. NOTZ, and R. A. MILLER (2006a). Sequential Kriging Optimization Using Multiple-Fidelity Evaluations. *Structural and Multidisciplinary Optimization* 32(5):369–382.

HUANG, D., T. T. ALLEN, W. I. NOTZ, and N. ZENG (2006b). Global Optimization of Stochastic Black-Box Systems via Sequential Kriging Meta-Models. *Journal of Global Optimization* 34(3):441–466.

HUTTER, FRANK, HOLGER H. HOOS, and KEVIN LEYTON-BROWN (2011). Sequential Model-Based Optimization for General Algorithm Configuration. *Proceedings of the 5th Learning and Intelligent Optimization Conference (LION 5)*. Vol. 6683. Lecture Notes in Computer Science. Springer–Verlag, pp. 507–523.

HUTTER, FRANK, LIN XU, HOLGER H. HOOS, and KEVIN LEYTON-BROWN (2014). Algorithm Runtime Prediction: Methods & Evaluation. *Artificial Intelligence* 206:79–111.

INGERSOLL JR., JONATHAN E. (1987). *Theory of Financial Decision Making*. Rowman & Littlefield Studies in Financial Economics. Rowman & Littlefield.

IRWIN, JOHN J., KHANH G. TANG, JENNIFER YOUNG, CHINZORIG DANDARCHULUUN, BENJAMIN R. WONG, MUNKHZUL KHURELBAATAR, et al. (2020). ZINC20 – A Free Ultralarge-Scale Chemical Database for Ligand Discovery. *Journal of Chemical Information and Modeling* 60(12):6065–6073.

JANZ, DAVID, DAVID R. BURT, and JAVIER GONZÁLEZ (2020). Bandit Optimisation of Functions in the Matérn Kernel RKHS. *Proceedings of the 23rd International Conference on Artificial Intelligence and Statistics (AISTATS 2020)*. Vol. 108. Proceedings of Machine Learning Research, pp. 2486–2495.

JIANG, SHALI, HENRY CHAI, JAVIER GONZÁLEZ, and ROMAN GARNETT (2020a). BINOCULARS for Efficient, Nonmyopic Sequential Experimental Design. *Proceedings of the 37th International Conference on Machine Learning (ICML 2020)*. Vol. 119. Proceedings of Machine Learning Research, pp. 4794–4803.

JIANG, SHALI, DANIEL R. JIANG, MAXIMILIAN BALANDAT, BRIAN KARRER, JACOB R. GARDNER, and ROMAN GARNETT (2020b). Efficient Nonmyopic Bayesian Optimization via One-Shot Multi-Step Trees. *Advances in Neural Information Processing Systems 33 (NeurIPS 2020)*, pp. 18039–18049.

JIANG, SHALI, GUSTAVO MALKOMES, GEOFF CONVERSE, ALYSSA SHOFNER, BENJAMIN MOSELEY, and ROMAN GARNETT (2017). Efficient Nonmyopic Active Search. *Proceedings of the 34th International Conference on Machine Learning (ICML 2017)*. Vol. 70. Proceedings of Machine Learning Research, pp. 1714–1723.

JONES, D. R., C. D. PERTTUNEN, and B. E. STUCKMAN (1993). Lipschitzian Optimization without the Lipschitz Constant. *Journal of Optimization Theory and Application* 79(1):157–181.

JONES, DONALD R. (2001). A Taxonomy of Global Optimization Methods Based on Response Surfaces. *Journal of Global Optimization* 21(4):345–383.

JONES, DONALD R., MATTHIAS SCHONLAU, and WILLIAM J. WELCH (1998). Efficient Global Optimization of Expensive Black-Box Functions. *Journal of Global Optimization* 13(4):455–492.

JYLÄNKI, PASI, JARNO VANHATALO, and AKI VEHTARI (2011). Robust Gaussian Process Regression with a Student-t Likelihood. *Journal of Machine Learning Research* 12(99): 3227–3257.

KANAGAWA, MOTONOBU, PHILIPP HENNIG, DINO SEJDINOVIC, and BHARATH K. SRIPERUMBUDUR (2018). Gaussian Processes and Kernel Methods: A Review on Connections and Equivalences. arXiv: 1807.02582 [stat.ML].

KANDASAMY, KIRTHEVASAN, GAUTAM DASARATHY, JUNIER OLIVA, JEFF SCHNEIDER, and BARNABÁS PÓCZOS (2016). Gaussian Process Bandit Optimisation with Multi-Fidelity Evaluations. *Advances in Neural Information Processing Systems 29 (NeurIPS 2016)*, pp. 992–1000.

KANDASAMY, KIRTHEVASAN, GAUTAM DASARATHY, JEFF SCHNEIDER, and BARNABÁS PÓCZOS (2017). Multi-Fidelity Bayesian Optimisation with Continuous Approximations.

Proceedings of the 34th International Conference on Machine Learning (ICML 2017). Vol. 70. Proceedings of Machine Learning Research, pp. 1799–1808.

KANDASAMY, KIRTHEVASAN, AKSHAY KRISHNAMURTHY, JEFF SCHNEIDER, and BARNABÁS PÓCZOS (2018). Parallelised Bayesian Optimisation via Thompson Sampling. *Proceedings of the 21st International Conference on Artificial Intelligence and Statistics (AISTATS 2018).* Vol. 84. Proceedings of Machine Learning Research, pp. 133–142.

KANDASAMY, KIRTHEVASAN, JEFF SCHNEIDER, and BARNABÁS PÓCZOS (2015). High Dimensional Bayesian Optimisation and Bandits via Additive Models. *Proceedings of the 32nd International Conference on Machine Learning (ICML 2015).* Vol. 37. Proceedings of Machine Learning Research, pp. 295–304.

KATHURIA, TARUN, AMIT DESHPANDE, and PUSHMEET KOHLI (2016). Batched Gaussian Process Bandit Optimization via Determinantal Point Processes. *Advances in Neural Information Processing Systems 29 (NeurIPS 2016)*, pp. 4206–4214.

KIM, JEANKYUNG and DAVID POLLARD (1990). Cube Root Asymptotics. *The Annals of Statistics* 18(1):191–219.

KIM, JUNGTAEK and SEUNGJIN CHOI (2020). On Local Optimizers of Acquisition Functions in Bayesian Optimization. Lecture Notes in Computer Science 12458:675–690.

KIM, JUNGTAEK, MICHAEL MCCOURT, TACKGEUN YOU, SAEHOON KIM, and SEUNGJIN CHOI (2021). Bayesian Optimization with Approximate Set Kernels. *Machine Learning* 110(5):857–879.

KLEIN, AARON, SIMON BARTELS, STEFAN FALKNER, PHILIPP HENNIG, and FRANK HUTTER (2015). Towards Efficient Bayesian Optimization for Big Data. *Bayesian Optimization: Scalability and Flexibility Workshop (BayesOpt 2015), Conference on Neural Information Processing Systems (NeurIPS 2015).*

KLEIN, AARON, STEFAN FALKNER, JOST TOBIAS SPRINGENBERG, and FRANK HUTTER (2017). Learning Curve Prediction with Bayesian Neural Networks. *Proceedings of the 5th International Conference on Learning Representations (ICLR 2017).*

KNOWLES, JOSHUA (2005). ParEGO: A Hybrid Algorithm with On-Line Landscape Approximation for Expensive Multiobjective Optimization Problems. *IEEE Transactions on Evolutionary Computation* 10(1):50–66.

KO, CHUN-WA, JON LEE, and MAURICE QUEYRANNE (1995). An Exact Algorithm for Maximum Entropy Sampling. *Operations Research* 43(4):684–691.

KONISHI, SADANORI and GENSHIRO KITAGAWA (2008). *Information Criteria and Statistical Modeling.* Springer Series in Statistics. Springer–Verlag.

KSCHISCHANG, FRANK R., BRENDAN J. FREY, and HANS-ANDREA LEOLIGER (2001). Factor Graphs and the Sum–Product Algorithm. *IEEE Transactions on Information Theory* 47(2):498–519.

KULESZA, ALEX and BEN TASKAR (2012). Determinantal Point Processes for Machine Learning. *Foundations and Trends in Machine Learning* 5(2–3):123–286.

KUSHNER, HAROLD J. (1962). A Versatile Stochastic Model of a Function of Unknown and Time Varying Form. *Journal of Mathematical Analysis and Applications* 5(1):150–167.

KUSHNER, H. J. (1964). A New Method of Locating the Maximum Point of an Arbitrary Multipeak Curve in the Presence of Noise. *Journal of Basic Engineering* 86(1):97–106.

KUSS, MALTE (2006). Gaussian Process Models for Robust Regression, Classification, and Reinforcement Learning. Ph.D. thesis. Technische Universität Darmstadt.

LAI, T. L. and HERBERT ROBBINS (1985). Asymptotically Efficient Adaptive Allocation Rules. *Advances in Applied Mathematics* 6(1):4–22.

LAM, REMI R., KAREN E. WILCOX, and DAVID H. WOLPERT (2016). Bayesian Optimization with a Finite Budget: An Approximate Dynamic Programming Approach. *Advances in Neural Information Processing Systems 29 (NeurIPS 2016)*, pp. 883–891.

LANGE, KENNETH L., RODERICK J. A. LITTLE, and JEREMY M. G. TAYLOR (1989). Robust Statistical Modeling Using the *t* Distribution. *Journal of the American Statistical Association* 84(408):881–896.

LATTIMORE, TOR and CSABA SZEPESVÁRI (2020). *Bandit Algorithms.* Cambridge University Press.

LÁZARO-GREDILLA, MIGUEL, JOAQUIN QUIÑONERO-CANDELA, CARL EDWARD RASMUSSEN, and ANÍBAL R. FIGUEIRAS-VIDAL (2010). Sparse Spectrum Gaussian Process Regression. *Journal of Machine Learning Research* 11(Jun):1865–1881.

LETHAM, BENJAMIN, BRIAN KARRER, GUILHERME OTTONI, and EYTAN BAKSHY (2019). Constrained Bayesian Optimization with Noisy Experiments. *Bayesian Analysis* 14(2): 495–519.

LEVINA, ELIZAVETA and PETER J. BICKEL (2004). Maximum Likelihood Estimation of Intrinsic Dimension. *Advances in Neural Information Processing Systems 17 (NeurIPS 2004)*, pp. 777–784.

LÉVY, PAUL (1948). *Processus stochastiques et mouvement brownien.* Gauthier–Villars.

LI, CHUN-LIANG, KIRTHEVASAN KANDASAMY, BARNABÁS PÓCZOS, and JEFF SCHNEIDER (2016). High Dimensional Bayesian Optimization via Restricted Projection Pursuit Models. *Proceedings of the 19th International Conference on Artificial Intelligence and Statistics (AISTATS 2016)*. Vol. 51. Proceedings of Machine Learning Research, pp. 884–892.

LI, CHUNYUAN, HEERAD FARKHOOR, ROSANNE LIU, and JASON YOSINSKI (2018a). Measuring the Intrinsic Dimension of Objective Landscapes. *Proceedings of the 6th International Conference on Learning Representations (ICLR 2018)*. arXiv: 1804.08838 [cs.LG].

LI, LISHA, KEVIN JAMIESON, GIULIA DESALVO, AFSHIN ROSTAMIZADEH, and AMEET TALWALKAR (2018b). Hyperband: A Novel Bandit-Based Approach to Hyperparameter Optimization. *Journal of Machine Learning Research* 18(185):1–52.

LI, ZIHAN and JONATHAN SCARLETT (2021). Gaussian Process Bandit Optimization with Few Batches. arXiv: 2110.07788 [stat.ML].

LINDLEY, D. V. (1956). On a Measure of the Information Provided by an Experiment. *The Annals of Mathematical Statistics* 27(4):986–1005.

LINDLEY, D. V. (1972). *Bayesian Statistics, A Review.* CBMS–NSF Regional Conference Series in Applied Mathematics. Society for Industrial and Applied Mathematics.

LOCATELLI, M. (1997). Bayesian Algorithms for One-Dimensional Global Optimization. *Journal of Global Optimization* 10(1):57–76.

LÖWNER, KARL (1934). Über monotone Matrixfunktionen. *Mathematische Zeitschrift* 38: 177–216.

LUKIĆ, MILAN N. and JAY H. BEDER (2001). Stochastic Processes with Sample Paths in Reproducing Kernel Hilbert Spaces. *Transactions of the American Mathematical Society* 353(10):3945–3969.

LYU, YUEMING, YUAN YUAN, and IVOR W. TSANG (2019). Efficient Batch Black-Box Optimization with Deterministic Regret Bounds. arXiv: 1905.10041 [cs.LG].

MACKAY, DAVID J. C. (1998). Introduction to Gaussian Processes. In: *Neural Networks and Machine Learning.* Ed. by CHRISTOPHER M. BISHOP. Vol. 168. NATO ASI Series F: Computer and Systems Sciences. Springer–Verlag, pp. 133–165.

MACKAY, DAVID J. C. (2003). *Information Theory, Inference, and Learning Algorithms.* Cambridge University Press.

MAHSERECI, MAREN and PHILIPP HENNIG (2015). Probabilistic Line Searches for Stochastic Optimization. *Advances in Neural Information Processing Systems 28 (NeurIPS 2015)*, pp. 181–189.

MALKOMES, GUSTAVO and ROMAN GARNETT (2018). Automating Bayesian Optimization with Bayesian Optimization. *Advances in Neural Information Processing Systems 31 (NeurIPS 2018)*, pp. 5984–5994.

MALKOMES, GUSTAVO, CHIP SCHAFF, and ROMAN GARNETT (2016). Bayesian Optimization for Automated Model Selection. *Advances in Neural Information Processing Systems 29 (NeurIPS 2016)*, pp. 2900–2908.

MARAVAL, ALEXANDRE, MATTHIEU ZIMMER, ANTOINE GROSNIT, RASUL TUTUNOV, JUN WANG, and HAITHAM BOU AMMAR (2022). Sample-Efficient Optimisation with Probabilistic Transformer Surrogates. arXiv: 2205.13902 [cs.LG].

MARMIN, SÉBASTIEN, CLÉMENT CHEVALIER, and DAVID GINSBOURGER (2015). Differentiating the Multipoint Expected Improvement for Optimal Batch Design. *Proceedings of the 1st International Workshop on Machine Learning, Optimization, and Big Data (MOD 2015)*. Vol. 9432. Lecture Notes in Computer Science. Springer–Verlag, pp. 37–48.

MARSCHAK, JACOB and ROY RADNER (1972). *Economic Theory of Teams*. Yale University Press.

MARTINEZ-CANTIN, RUBEN, KEVIN TEE, and MICHAEL MCCOURT (2018). Practical Bayesian Optimization in the Presence of Outliers. *Proceedings of the 21st International Conference on Artificial Intelligence and Statistics (AISTATS 2018)*. Vol. 84. Proceedings of Machine Learning Research, pp. 1722–1731.

MASSART, PASCAL (2007). *Concentration Inequalities and Model Selection: Ecole d'Eté de Probabilités de Saint-Flour XXXIII – 2003*. Vol. 1896. Lecture Notes in Mathematics. Springer–Verlag.

MCCULLAGH, P. and J. A. NELDER (1989). *Generalized Linear Models*. 2nd ed. Monographs on Statistics and Applied Probability. Chapman & Hall.

MEINSHAUSEN, NICOLAI (2006). Quantile Regression Forests. *Journal of Machine Learning Research* 7(35):983–999.

MIETTINEN, KAISA M. (1998). *Nonlinear Multiobjective Optimization*. International Series in Operations Research & Management Science. Kluwer Academic Publishers.

MILGROM, PAUL and ILYA SEGAL (2002). Envelope Theorems for Arbitrary Choice Sets. *Econometrica* 70(2):583–601.

MINKA, THOMAS P. (2001). A Family of Algorithms for Approximate Bayesian Inference. Ph.D. thesis. Massachusetts Institute of Technology.

MINKA, THOMAS (2008). *EP: A Quick Reference*. URL: https://tminka.github.io/papers/ep/minka-ep-quickref.pdf.

MOCKUS, JONAS (1972). Bayesian Methods of Search for an Extremum. *Avtomatika i Vychislitel'naya Tekhnika (Automatic Control and Computer Sciences)* 6(3):53–62.

MOCKUS, JONAS (1974). On Bayesian Methods for Seeking the Extremum. *Optimization Techniques: IFIP Technical Conference*. Vol. 27. Lecture Notes in Computer Science. Springer–Verlag, pp. 400–404.

MOCKUS, JONAS (1989). *Bayesian Approach to Global Optimization: Theory and Applications*. Mathematics and Its Applications. Kluwer Academic Publishers.

MOCKUS, JONAS, WILLIAM EDDY, AUDRIS MOCKUS, LINAS MOCKUS, and GINTARAS REKLAITAS (2010). *Bayesian Heuristic Approach to Discrete and Global Optimization: Algorithms, Visualization, Software, and Applications*. Nonconvex Optimization and Its Applications. Kluwer Academic Publishers.

MOCKUS, J., V. TIEŠIS, and A. ŽILINSKAS (1978). The Application of Bayesian Methods for Seeking the Extrememum. In: *Towards Global Optimization 2*. Ed. by L. C. W. DIXON and G. P. SZEGÖ. North–Holland, pp. 117–129.

MØLLER, JESPER, ANNE RANDI SYVERSVEEN, and RASMUS PLENGE WAAGEPETERSEN (1998). Log Gaussian Cox Processes. *Scandinavian Journal of Statistics* 25(3):451–482.

MONTGOMERY, DOUGLAS C. (2019). *Design and Analysis of Experiments*. 10th ed. John Wiley & Sons.

MOORE, ANDREW W. and CHRISTOPHER G. ATKESON (1993). Memory-Based Reinforcement Learning: Efficient Computation with Prioritized Sweeping. *Advances in Neural Information Processing Systems 5 (NeurIPS 1992)*, pp. 263–270.

MORICONI, RICCARDO, MARC PETER DEISENROTH, and K. S. SESH KUMAR (2020). High-Dimensional Bayesian Optimization Using Low-Dimensional Feature Spaces. *Machine Learning* 109(9–10):1925–1943.

MOSS, HENRY B., DANIEL BECK, JAVIER GONZÁLEZ, DAVID S. LESLIE, and PAUL RAYSON (2020). BOSS: Bayesian Optimization over String Spaces. *Advances in Neural Information Processing Systems 33 (NeurIPS 2020)*, pp. 15476–15486.

MÜLLER, SARAH, ALEXANDER VON ROHR, and SEBASTIAN TRIMPE (2021). Local Policy Search with Bayesian Optimization. *Advances in Neural Information Processing Systems 34 (NeurIPS 2021)*, pp. 20708–20720.

MURRAY, IAIN (2016). Differentiation of the Cholesky decomposition. arXiv: 1602.07527 [stat.CO].

MURRAY, IAIN, RYAN PRESCOTT ADAMS, and DAVID J. C. MACKAY (2010). Elliptical Slice Sampling. *Proceedings of the 13th International Conference on Artificial Intelligence and Statistics (AISTATS 2010)*. Vol. 9. Proceedings of Machine Learning Research, pp. 541–548.

MUTNÝ, MOJMÍR and ANDREAS KRAUSE (2018). Efficient High Dimensional Bayesian Optimization with Additivity and Quadrature Fourier Features. *Advances in Neural Information Processing Systems 31 (NeurIPS 2018)*, pp. 9005–9016.

NEAL, RADFORD M. (1997). *Monte Carlo Implementation of Gaussian Process Models for Bayesian Regression and Classification*. Technical report (9702). Department of Statistics, University of Toronto.

NEAL, RADFORD M. (1998). Regression and Classification Using Gaussian Process Priors. In: *Bayesian Statistics 6*. Ed. by J. M. BERNARDO, J. O. BERGER, A. P. DAWID, and A. F. M. SMITH. Oxford University Press, pp. 475–490.

NGUYEN, QUAN, KAIWEN WU, JACOB R. GARDER, and ROMAN GARNETT (2022). Local Bayesian Optimization via Maximizing Probability of Descent. arXiv: 2210.11662 [cs.LG].

NGUYEN, QUOC PHONG, ZHONGXIANG DAI, BRYAN KIAN HSIANG LOW, and PATRICK JAILLET (2021a). Optimizing Conditional Value-At-Risk of Black-Box Functions. *Advances in Neural Information Processing Systems 34 (NeurIPS 2021)*.

NGUYEN, QUOC PHONG, ZHONGXIANG DAI, BRYAN KIAN HSIANG LOW, and PATRICK JAILLET (2021b). Value-at-Risk Optimization with Gaussian Processes. *Proceedings of the 38th International Conference on Machine Learning (ICML 2021)*. Vol. 139. Proceedings of Machine Learning Research, pp. 8063–8072.

NGUYEN, VU, SUNIL GUPTA, SANTU RANA, CHENG LI, and SVETHA VENKATESH (2017). Regret for Expected Improvement over the Best-Observed Value and Stopping Condition. *Proceedings of the 9th Asian Conference on Machine Learning (ACML 2017)*. Vol. 77. Proceedings of Machine Learning Research, pp. 279–294.

NICKISCH, HANNES and CARL EDWARD RASMUSSEN (2008). Appproximations for Binary Gaussian Process Classification. *Journal of Machine Learning Research* 9(Oct):2035–2078.

O'HAGAN, A. (1978). Curve Fitting and Optimal Design for Prediction. *Journal of the Royal Statistical Society Series B (Methodological)* 40(1):1–42.

O'HAGAN, A. (1991). Bayes–Hermite Quadrature. *Journal of Statistical Planning and Inference* 29(3):245–260.

O'HAGAN, ANTHONY and JONATHAN FORSTER (2004). *Kendall's Advanced Theory of Statistics.* 2nd ed. Vol. 2B: Bayesian Inference. Arnold.

OH, CHANGYONG, JAKUB M. TOMCZAK, EFSTRATIOS GAVVES, and MAX WELLING (2019). Combinatorial Bayesian Optimization Using the Graph Cartesian Product. *Advances in Neural Information Processing Systems 32 (NeurIPS 2019)*, pp. 2914–2924.

ØKSENDAL, BERNT (2013). *Stochastic Differential Equations: An Introduction with Applications.* 6th ed. Universitext. Springer–Verlag.

OLIVEIRA, RAFAEL, LIONEL OTT, and FABIO RAMOS (2019). Bayesian Optimisation Under Uncertain Inputs. *Proceedings of the 22nd International Conference on Artificial Intelligence and Statistics (AISTATS 2019)*. Vol. 89. Proceedings of Machine Learning Research, pp. 1177–1184.

OSBORNE, MICHAEL A., DAVID DUVENAUD, ROMAN GARNETT, CARL E. RASMUSSEN, STEPHEN J. ROBERTS, and ZOUBIN GHAHRAMANI (2012). Active Learning of Model Evidence Using Bayesian Quadrature. *Advances in Neural Information Processing Systems 25 (NeurIPS 2012)*, pp. 46–54.

OSBORNE, MICHAEL A., ROMAN GARNETT, and STEPHEN J. ROBERTS (2009). Gaussian Processes for Global Optimization. *Proceedings of the 3rd Learning and Intelligent Optimization Conference (LION 3)*.

PARIA, BISWAJIT, KIRTHEVASAN KANDASAMY, and BARNABÁS PÓCZOS (2019). A Flexible Framework for Multi-Objective Bayesian Optimization Using Random Scalarizations. *Proceedings of the 35th Conference on Uncertainty in Artificial Intelligence (UAI 2019)*. Vol. 115. Proceedings of Machine Learning Research, pp. 766–776.

PEIRCE, C. S. (1876). Note on the Theory of the Economy of Research. In: *Report of the Superintendent of the United States Coast Survey Showing the Progress of the Work for the Fiscal Year Ending with June, 1876.* Government Printing Office, pp. 197–201.

PICHENY, VICTOR (2014). A Stepwise Uncertainty Reduction Approach to Constrained Global Optimization. *Proceedings of the 17th International Conference on Artificial Intelligence and Statistics (AISTATS 2014)*. Vol. 33. Proceedings of Machine Learning Research, pp. 787–795.

PICHENY, VICTOR (2015). Multiobjective Optimization Using Gaussian Process Emulators via Stepwise Uncertainty Reduction. *Statistics and Computing* 25(6):1265–1280.

PICHENY, VICTOR, DAVID GINSBOURGER, YANN RICHET, and GREGORY CAPLIN (2013a). Quantile-Based Optimization of Noisy Computer Experiments with Tunable Precision. *Technometrics* 55(1):2–13.

PICHENY, VICTOR, TOBIAS WAGNER, and DAVID GINSBOURGER (2013b). A Benchmark of Kriging-Based Infill Criteria for Noisy Optimization. *Structural and Multidisciplinary Optimization* 48(3):607–626.

PLEISS, GEOFF, MARTIN JANKOWIAK, DAVID ERIKSSON, ANIL DAMLE, and JACOB R. GARDNER (2020). Fast Matrix Square Roots with Applications to Gaussian Processes and Bayesian Optimization. *Advances in Neural Information Processing Systems 33 (NeurIPS 2020)*, pp. 22268–22281.

POINCARÉ, HENRI (1912). *Calcul des probabilités*. 2nd ed. Gauthier–Villars.

PONWEISER, WOLFGANG, TOBIAS WAGNER, DIRK BIERMANN, and MARKUS VINCZE (2008). Multiobjective Optimization on a Limited Budget of Evaluations Using Model-Assisted *S*-Metric Selection. *Proceedings of the 10th International Confernce on Parallel Problem Solving from Nature (PPSN X)*. Vol. 5199. Lecture Notes in Computer Science. Springer–Verlag, pp. 784–794.

POWELL, WARREN B. (2011). *Approximate Dynamic Programming: Solving the Curses of Dimensionality*. 2nd ed. Wiley Series in Probability and Statistics. John Wiley & Sons.

PRONZATO, LUC (2017). Minimax and Maximin Space-Filling Designs: Some Properties and Methods for Construction. *Journal de la Société Française de Statistique* 158(1):7–36.

RAIFFA, HOWARD and ROBERT SCHLAIFER (1961). *Applied Statistical Decision Theory*. Division of Research, Graduate School of Business Administration, Harvard University.

RASMUSSEN, CARL EDWARD and ZOUBIN GHAHRAMANI (2002). Bayesian Monte Carlo. *Advances in Neural Information Processing Systems 15 (NeurIPS 2002)*, pp. 505–512.

RASMUSSEN, CARL EDWARD and CHRISTOPHER K. I. WILLIAMS (2006). *Gaussian Processes for Machine Learning*. Adaptive Computation and Machine Learning. MIT Press.

RIQUELME, CARLOS, GEORGE TUCKER, and JASPER SNOEK (2018). Deep Bayesian Bandits Showdown. *Proceedings of the 6th International Conference on Learning Representations (ICLR 2018)*. arXiv: 1802.09127 [cs.LG].

ROBBINS, HERBERT (1952). Some Aspects of the Sequential Design of Experiments. *Bulletin of the American Mathematical Society* 58(5):527–535.

ROLLAND, PAUL, JONATHAN SCARLETT, ILIJA BOGUNOVIC, and VOLKAN CEVHER (2018). High-Dimensional Bayesian Optimization via Additive Models with Overlapping Groups. *Proceedings of the 21st International Conference on Artificial Intelligence and Statistics (AISTATS 2018)*. Vol. 84. Proceedings of Machine Learning Research, pp. 298–307.

ROSS, ANDREW M. (2010). Computing Bounds on the Expected Maximum of Correlated Normal Variables. *Methodology and Computing in Applied Probability* 12(1):111–138.

RUDIN, WALTER (1976). *Principles of Mathematical Analysis*. 3rd ed. International Series in Pure and Applied Mathematics. McGraw–Hill.

RUE, HÅVARD, SARA MARTINO, and NICOLAS CHOPIN (2009). Approximate Bayesian Inference for Latent Gaussian Models by Using Integrated Nested Laplace Approximations. *Journal of the Royal Statistical Society Series B (Methodological)* 71(2):319–392.

RUSSO, DANIEL and BENJAMIN VAN ROY (2014). Learning to Optimize via Posterior Sampling. *Mathematics of Operations Research* 39(4):1221–1243.

RUSSO, DANIEL and BENJAMIN VAN ROY (2016). An Information-Theoretic Analysis of Thompson Sampling. *Journal of Machine Learning Research* 17(68):1–30.

SACKS, JEROME, WILLIAM J. WELCH, TOBY J. MITCHELL, and HENRY P. WYNN (1989). Design and Analysis of Computer Experiments. *Statistical Science* 4(4):409–435.

SALGIA, SUDEEP, SATTAR VAKILI, and QING ZHAO (2020). A Computationally Efficient Approach to Black-Box Optimization Using Gaussian Process Models. arXiv: 2010.13997 [stat.ML].

ŠALTENIS, VYDŪNAS R. (1971). One Method of Multiextremum Optimization. *Avtomatika i Vychislitel'naya Tekhnika (Automatic Control and Computer Sciences)* 5(3):33–38.

SANCHEZ, SUSAN M. and PAUL J. SANCHEZ (2005). Very Large Fractional Factorial and Central Composite Designs. *ACM Transactions on Modeling and Computer Simulation* 15(4): 362–377.

SCARLETT, JONATHAN (2018). Tight Regret Bounds for Bayesian Optimization in One Dimension. *Proceedings of the 35th International Conference on Machine Learning (ICML 2018)*. Vol. 80. Proceedings of Machine Learning Research, pp. 4500–4508.

SCARLETT, JONATHAN, ILIJA BOGUNOVIC, and VOLKAN CEVHER (2017). Lower Bounds on Regret for Noisy Gaussian Process Bandit Optimization. *Proceedings of the 2017 Conference on Learning Theory (COLT 2017)*. Vol. 65. Proceedings of Machine Learning Research, pp. 1723–1742.

SCARLETT, JONATHAN and VOLKAN CEVHAR (2021). An Introductory Guide to Fano's Inequality with Applications in Statistical Estimation. In: *Information-Theoretic Methods in Data Science*. Ed. by MIGUEL R. D. RODRIGUES and YONINA C. ELDAR. Cambridge University Press, pp. 487–528.

SCHONLAU, MATTHIAS (1997). Computer Experiments and Global Optimization. Ph.D. thesis. University of Waterloo.

SCHONLAU, MATTHIAS, WILLIAM J. WELCH, and DONALD R. JONES (1998). Global versus Local Search in Constrained Optimization of Computer Models. In: *New Developments and Applications in Experimental Design*. Vol. 34. Lecture Notes – Monograph Series. Institute of Mathematical Statistics, pp. 11–25.

SCOTT, WARREN, PETER FRAZIER, and WARREN POWELL (2011). The Correlated Knowledge Gradient for Simulation Optimization of Continuous Parameters Using Gaussian Process Regression. *SIAM Journal on Optimization* 21(3):996–1026.

SEEGER, MATTHIAS (2008). *Expectation Propagation for Exponential Families*. Technical report. University of California, Berkeley.

SETTLES, BURR (2012). *Active Learning*. Synthesis Lectures on Artificial Intelligence and Machine Learning. Morgan & Claypool.

SHAH, AMAR and ZOUBIN GHAHRAMANI (2015). Parallel Predictive Entropy Search for Batch Global Optimization of Expensive Objective Functions. *Advances in Neural Information Processing Systems 28 (NeurIPS 2015)*, pp. 3330–3338.

SHAH, AMAR, ANDREW GORDON WILSON, and ZOUBIN GHAHRAMANI (2014). Student-t Processes as Alternatives to Gaussian Processes. *Proceedings of the 17th International Conference on Artificial Intelligence and Statistics (AISTATS 2014)*. Vol. 33. Proceedings of Machine Learning Research, pp. 877–885.

SHAHRIARI, BOBAK, KEVIN SWERSKY, ZIYU WANG, RYAN P. ADAMS, and NANDO DE FREITAS (2016). Taking the Human out of the Loop: A Review of Bayesian Optimization. *Proceedings of the IEEE* 104(1):148–175.

SHAHRIARI, BOBAK, ZIYU WANG, MATTHEW W. HOFFMAN, ALEXANDRE BOUCHARD-CÔTÉ, and NANDO DE FREITAS (2014). An Entropy Search Portfolio for Bayesian Optimization. arXiv: 1406.4625 [stat.ML].

SHAMIR, OHAD (2013). On the Complexity of Bandit and Derivative-Free Stochastic Convex Optimization. *Proceedings of the 24th Annual Conference on Learning Theory (COLT 2013)*. Vol. 30. Proceedings of Machine Learning Research, pp. 3–24.

SHANNON, C. E. (1948). A Mathematical Theory of Communication. *The Bell System Technical Journal* 27(3):379–423.

SHAO, T. S., T. C. CHEN, and R. M. FRANK (1964). Tables of Zeros and Gaussian Weights of Certain Associated Laguerre Polynomials and the Related Generalized Hermite Polynomials. *Mathematics of Computation* 18(88):598–616.

SHEPP, L. A. (1979). The Joint Density of the Maximum and Its Location for a Wiener Process with Drift. *Journal of Applied Probability* 16(2):423–427.

SILVERMAN, B. W. (1986). *Density Estimation for Statistics and Data Analysis*. Monographs on Statistics and Applied Probability. Chapman & Hall.

SLEPIAN, DAVID (1962). The One-Sided Barrier Problem for Gaussian Noise. *The Bell System Technical Journal* 41(2):463–501.

SMITH, KIRSTINE (1918). On the Standard Deviations of Adjusted and Interpolated Values of an Observed *Polynomial Function* and Its Constants and the Guidance They Give towards a Proper Choice of the Distribution of Observations. *Biometrika* 12(1–2): 1–85.

SMOLA, ALEX J. and BERNHARD SCHÖLKOPF (2000). Sparse Greedy Matrix Approximation for Machine Learning. *Proceedings of the 17th International Conference on Machine Learning (ICML 2000)*, pp. 911–918.

SNELSON, EDWARD and ZOUBIN GHAHRAMANI (2005). Sparse Gaussian Processes Using Pseudo-inputs. *Advances in Neural Information Processing Systems 18 (NeurIPS 2005)*, pp. 1257–1264.

SNOEK, JASPER, HUGO LAROCHELLE, and RYAN P. ADAMS (2012). Practical Bayesian Optimization of Machine Learning Algorithms. *Advances in Neural Information Processing Systems 25 (NeurIPS 2012)*, pp. 2951–2959.

SNOEK, JASPER, OREN RIPPEL, KEVIN SWERSKY, RYAN KIROS, NADATHUR SATISH, NARAYANAN SUNDARAM, et al. (2015). Scalable Bayesian Optimization Using Deep Neural Networks. *Proceedings of the 32nd International Conference on Machine Learning (ICML 2015)*. Vol. 37. Proceedings of Machine Learning Research, pp. 2171–2180.

SNOEK, JASPER, KEVIN SWERSKY, RICHARD ZEMEL, and RYAN P. ADAMS (2014). Input Warping for Bayesian Optimization of Non-Stationary Functions. *Proceedings of the 31st International Conference on Machine Learning (ICML 2014)*. Vol. 32. Proceedings of Machine Learning Research, pp. 1674–1682.

SONG, JIALIN, YUXIN CHEN, and YISONG YUE (2019). A General Framework for Multi-Fidelity Bayesian Optimization with Gaussian Processes. *Proceedings of the 22nd International Conference on Artificial Intelligence and Statistics (AISTATS 2019)*. Vol. 89. Proceedings of Machine Learning Research, pp. 3158–3167.

SPRINGENBERG, JOST TOBIAS, AARON KLEIN, STEFAN FALKNER, and FRANK HUTTER (2016). Bayesian Optimization with Robust Bayesian Neural Networks. *Advances in Neural Information Processing Systems 29 (NeurIPS 2016)*, pp. 4134–4142.

SRINIVAS, NIRANJAN, ANDREAS KRAUSE, SHAM KAKADE, and MATTHIAS SEEGER (2010). Gaussian Process Optimization in the Bandit Setting: No Regret and Experimental Design. *Proceedings of the 27th International Conference on Machine Learning (ICML 2010)*, pp. 1015–1022.

STEIN, MICHAEL L. (1999). *Interpolation of Spatial Data: Some Theory for Kriging*. Springer Series in Statistics. Springer–Verlag.

STRELTSOV, SIMON and PIROOZ VAKILI (1999). A Non-Myopic Utility Function for Statistical Global Optimization Algorithms. *Journal of Global Optimization* 14(3):283–298.

SUTTON, RICHARD S. (1990). Integrated Architectures for Learning, Planning, and Reacting Based on Approximating Dynamic Programming. *Proceedings of the 7th International Conference on Machine Learning (ICML 1990)*, pp. 216–224.

SVENSON, JOSHUA and THOMAS SANTNER (2016). Multiobjective Optimization of Expensive-to-evaluate Deterministic Computer Simulator Models. *Computational Statistics and Data Analysis* 94:250–264.

SWERSKY, KEVIN, JASPER SNOEK, and RYAN P. ADAMS (2013). Multi-Task Bayesian Optimization. *Advances in Neural Information Processing Systems 26 (NeurIPS 2013)*, pp. 2004–2012.

SWERSKY, KEVIN, JASPER SNOEK, and RYAN P. ADAMS (2014). Freeze–Thaw Bayesian Optimization. arXiv: 1406.3896 [stat.ML].

TAKENO, SHION, HITOSHI FUKUOKA, YUHKI TSUKADA, TOSHIYUKI KOYAMA, MOTOKI SHIGA, ICHIRO TAKEUCHI, et al. (2020). Multi-Fidelity Bayesian Optimization with Max-value Entropy Search and Its Parallelization. *Proceedings of the 37th International Conference on Machine Learning (ICML 2020)*. Vol. 119. Proceedings of Machine Learning Research, pp. 9334–9345.

TALLIS, G. M. (1961). The Moment Generating Function of the Truncated Multi-Normal Distribution. *Journal of the Royal Statistical Society Series B (Methodological)* 23(1): 223–229.

TESCH, MATTHEW, JEFF SCHNEIDER, and HOWIE CHOSET (2013). Expensive Function Optimization with Stochastic Binary Outcomes. *Proceedings of the 30th International Conference on Machine Learning (ICML 2013)*. Vol. 28. Proceedings of Machine Learning Research, pp. 1283–1291.

THE UNIPROT CONSORTIUM (2021). UniProt: The Universal Protein Knowledgebase in 2021. *Nucleic Acids Research* 49(D1):D480–D489.

THOMPSON, WILLIAM R. (1933). On the Likelihood That One Unknown Probability Exceeds Another in View of the Evidence of Two Samples. *Biometrika* 25(3–4):285–294.

THOMPSON, WILLIAM R. (1935). On the Theory of Apportionment. *American Journal of Mathematics* 57(2):450–456.

TIAO, LOUIS C., AARON KLEIN, MATTHIAS SEEGER, EDWIN V. BONILLA, CÉDRIC ARCHAMBEAU, and FABIO RAMOS (2021). BORE: Bayesian Optimization by Density-Ratio Estimation. *Proceedings of the 38th International Conference on Machine Learning (ICML 2021)*. Vol. 139. Proceedings of Machine Learning Research, pp. 10289–10300.

TITSIAS, MICHALIS (2009). Variational Learning of Inducing Variables in Sparse Gaussian Processes. *Proceedings of the 12th International Conference on Artificial Intelligence and Statistics (AISTATS 2009)*. Vol. 5. Proceedings of Machine Learning Research, pp. 567–574.

TOSCANO-PALMERIN, SAUL and PETER I. FRAZIER (2018). Bayesian Optimization with Expensive Integrands. arXiv: 1803.08661 [stat.ML].

TURBAN, SEBASTIEN (2010). *Convolution of a Truncated Normal and a Centered Normal Variable.* Technical report. Columbia University.

TURNER, RYAN, DAVID ERIKSSON, MICHAEL MCCOURT, JUHA KIILI, EERO LAAKSONEN, ZHEN XU, et al. (2021). Bayesian Optimization Is Superior to Random Search for Machine Learning Hyperparameter Tuning: Analysis of the Black-Box Optimization Challenge 2020. *Proceedings of the NeurIPS 2020 Competition and Demonstration Track.* Vol. 133. Proceedings of Machine Learning Research, pp. 3–26.

ULRICH, KYLE, DAVID E. CARLSON, KAFUI DZIRASA, and LAWRENCE CARIN (2015). GP Kernels for Cross-Spectrum Analysis. *Advances in Neural Information Processing Systems 28 (NeurIPS 2015)*, pp. 1999–2007.

VAKILI, SATTAR, NACIME BOUZIANI, SEPEHR JALALI, ALBERTO BERNACCHIA, and DA-SHAN SHIU (2021a). Optimal Order Simple Regret for Gaussian Process Bandits. *Advances in Neural Information Processing Systems 34 (NeurIPS 2021)*.

VAKILI, SATTAR, KIA KHEZELI, and VICTOR PICHENY (2021b). On Information Gain and Regret Bounds in Gaussian Process Bandits. *Proceedings of the 24th International*

Conference on Artificial Intelligence and Statistics (AISTATS 2021). Vol. 130. Proceedings of Machine Learning Research, pp. 82–90.

VAKILI, SATTAR, JONATHAN SCARLETT, and TARA JAVIDI (2021c). Open Problem: Tight Online Confidence Intervals for RKHS Elements. *Proceedings of the 34th Annual Conference on Learning Theory (COLT 2021)*. Vol. 134. Proceedings of Machine Learning Research, pp. 4647–4652.

VALKO, MICHAL, NATHAN KORDA, RÉMI MUNOS, ILIAS FLAOUNAS, and NELLO CRISTIANINI (2013). Finite-Time Analysis of Kernelised Contextual Bandits. *Proceedings of the 29th Conference on Uncertainty in Artificial Intelligence (UAI 2013)*, pp. 654–663.

VAN DE CORPUT, J. G. (1935). Verteilungsfunktionen: Erste Mitteilung. *Proceedings of the Koninklijke Nederlandse Akademie van Wetenschappen* 38:813–821.

VAN DER VAART, AAD W. and JON A. WELLNER (1996). *Weak Convergence and Empirical Processes with Applications to Statistics*. Springer Series in Statistics. Springer–Verlag.

VANCHINATHAN, HASTAGIRI P., ANDREAS MARFURT, CHARLES-ANTOINE ROBELIN, DONALD KOSSMANN, and ANDREAS KRAUSE (2015). Discovering Valuable Items from Massive Data. *Proceedings of the 21st ACM SIGKDD International Conference on Knowledge Discovery and Data Mining (KDD 2015)*, pp. 1195–1204.

VAZQUEZ, EMMANUEL, JULIEN VILLEMONTEIX, MARYAN SIDORKIEWICZ, and ÉRIC WALTER (2008). Global Optimization Based on Noisy Evaluations: An Empirical Study of Two Statistical Approaches. *Proceedings of the 6th International Conference on Inverse Problems in Engineering: Theory and Practice (ICIPE 2008)*. Vol. 135. Journal of Physics: Conference Series, paper number 012100.

VEHTARI, AKI and JANNE OJANEN (2012). A Survey of Bayesian Predictive Methods for Model Assessment, Selection and Comparison. *Statistics Surveys* 6:142–228.

VILLEMONTEIX, JULIEN, EMMANUEL VAZQUEZ, and ERIC WALTER (2009). An Informational Approach to the Global Optimization of Expensive-to-evaluate Functions. *Journal of Global Optimization* 44(4):509–534.

VIVARELLI, FRANCESCO and CHRISTOPHER K. I WILLIAMS (1998). Discovering Hidden Features with Gaussian Process Regression. *Advances in Neural Information Processing Systems 11 (NeurIPS 1998)*, pp. 613–619.

VON NEUMANN, JOHN and OSKAR MORGENSTERN (1944). *Theory of Games and Economic Behavior*. Princeton University Press.

VONDRÁK, JAN (2005). Probabilistic Methods in Combinatorial and Stochastic Optimization. Ph.D. thesis. Massachusetts Institute of Technology.

WALD, A. (1945). Sequential Tests of Statistical Hypotheses. *The Annals of Mathematical Statistics* 16(2):117–186.

WALD, ABRAHAM (1947). *Sequential Analysis*. Wiley Mathematical Statistics Series. John Wiley & Sons.

WANG, JIALEI, SCOTT C. CLARK, ERIC LIU, and PETER I. FRAZIER (2020a). Parallel Bayesian Global Optimization of Expensive Functions. *Operations Research* 68(6):1850–1865.

WANG, ZEXIN, VINCENT Y. F. TAN, and JONATHAN SCARLETT (2020b). Tight Regret Bounds for Noisy Optimization of a Brownian Motion. arXiv: 2001.09327 [cs.LG].

WANG, ZI and STEFANIE JEGELKA (2017). Max-value Entropy Search for Efficient Bayesian Optimization. *Proceedings of the 34th International Conference on Machine Learning (ICML 2017)*. Vol. 70. Proceedings of Machine Learning Research, pp. 3627–3635.

WANG, ZI, BOLEI ZHOU, and STEFANIE JEGELKA (2016a). Optimization as Estimation with Gaussian Processes in Bandit Settings. *Proceedings of the 19th International Con-*

ference on Artificial Intelligence and Statistics (AISTATS 2016). Vol. 51. Proceedings of Machine Learning Research, pp. 1022–1031.

WANG, ZIYU and NANDO DE FREITAS (2014). Theoretical Analysis of Bayesian Optimization with Unknown Gaussian Process Hyper-Parameters. arXiv: 1406.7758 [stat.ML].

WANG, ZIYU, FRANK HUTTER, MASROUR ZOGHI, DAVID MATHESON, and NANDO DE FREITAS (2016b). Bayesian Optimization in a Billion Dimensions via Random Embeddings. *Journal of Artificial Intelligence Research* 55:361–387.

WENDLAND, HOLGER (2004). *Scattered Data Approximation.* Cambridge Monographs on Applied and Computational Mathematics. Cambridge University Press.

WHITTLE, PETER (1982). *Optimization over Time: Dynamic Programming and Stochastic Control.* Vol. 1. Wiley Series in Probability and Mathematical Statistics. John Wiley & Sons.

WHITTLE, P. (1988). Restless Bandits: Activity Allocation in a Changing World. *Journal of Applied Probability* 25(A):287–298.

WILLIAMS, BRIAN J., THOMAS J. SANTNER, and WILLIAM I. NOTZ (2000). Sequential Design of Computer Experiments to Minimize Integrated Response Functions. *Statistica Sinica* 10(4):1133–1152.

WILLIAMS, CHRISTOPHER K. I. and MATTHIAS SEEGER (2000). Using the Nyström Method to Speed up Kernel Machines. *Advances in Neural Information Processing Systems 13 (NeurIPS 2000),* pp. 682–688.

WILSON, ANDREW GORDON and RYAN PRESCOTT ADAMS (2013). Gaussian Process Kernels for Pattern Discovery and Extrapolation. *Proceedings of the 30th International Conference on Machine Learning (ICML 2013).* Vol. 28. Proceedings of Machine Learning Research, pp. 1067–1075.

WILSON, ANDREW GORDON, ZHITING HU, RUSLAN SALAKHUTDINOV, and ERIC P. XING (2016). Deep Kernel Learning. *Proceedings of the 19th International Conference on Artificial Intelligence and Statistics (AISTATS 2016).* Vol. 51. Proceedings of Machine Learning Research, pp. 370–378.

WILSON, JAMES T., FRANK HUTTER, and MARC PETER DEISENROTH (2018). Maximizing Acquisition Functions for Bayesian Optimization. *Advances in Neural Information Processing Systems 31 (NeurIPS 2018),* pp. 9884–9895.

WU, JIAN and PETER I. FRAZIER (2016). The Parallel Knowledge Gradient Method for Batch Bayesian Optimization. *Advances in Neural Information Processing Systems 29 (NeurIPS 2016),* pp. 3126–3134.

WU, JIAN and PETER I. FRAZIER (2019). Practical Two-Step Look-Ahead Bayesian Optimization. *Advances in Neural Information Processing Systems 32 (NeurIPS 2019),* pp. 9813–9823.

WU, JIAN, MATTHIAS POLOCZEK, ANDREW GORDON WILSON, and PETER I. FRAZIER (2017). Bayesian Optimization with Gradients. *Advances in Neural Information Processing Systems 30 (NeurIPS 2017),* pp. 5267–5278.

WU, JIAN, SAUL TOSCANO-PALMERIN, PETER I. FRAZIER, and ANDREW GORDON WILSON (2019). Practical Multi-Fidelity Bayesian Optimization for Hyperparameter Tuning. *Proceedings of the 35th Conference on Uncertainty in Artificial Intelligence (UAI 2019).* Vol. 115. Proceedings of Machine Learning Research, pp. 788–798.

YANG, KAIFENG, MICHAEL EMMERICH, ANDRÉ DEUTZ, and THOMAS BÄCK (2019a). Efficient Computation of Expected Hypervolume Improvement Using Box Decomposition Algorithms. *Journal of Global Optimization* 75(1):3–34.

YANG, KAIFENG, MICHAEL EMMERICH, ANDRÉ DEUTZ, and THOMAS BÄCK (2019b). Multi-Objective Bayesian Global Optimization Using Expected Hypervolume Improvement Gradient. *Swarm and Evolutionary Computation* 44:945–956.

YUE, XUBO and RAED AL KONTAR (2020). Why Non-Myopic Bayesian Optimization Is Promising and How Far Should We Look-ahead? A Study via Rollout. *Proceedings of the 23rd International Conference on Artificial Intelligence and Statistics (AISTATS 2020)*. Vol. 108. Proceedings of Machine Learning Research, pp. 2808–2818.

ZHANG, WEITONG, DONGRUO ZHOU, LIHONG LI, and QUANQUAN GU (2021). Neural Thompson Sampling. *Proceedings of the 9th International Conference on Learning Representations (ICLR 2021)*. arXiv: 2010.00827 [cs.LG].

ZHANG, YEHONG, TRONG NGHIA HOANG, BRYAN KIAN HSIANG LOW, and MOHAN KANKANHALLI (2017). Information-Based Multi-Fidelity Bayesian Optimization. *Bayesian Optimization for Science and Engineering Workshop (BayesOpt 2017), Conference on Neural Information Processing Systems (NeurIPS 2017)*.

ZHOU, DONGROU, LIHONG LI, and QUANQUAN GU (2020). Neural Contextual Bandits with UCB-Based Exploration. *Proceedings of the 37th International Conference on Machine Learning (ICML 2020)*. Vol. 119. Proceedings of Machine Learning Research, pp. 11492–11502.

ZIATDINOV, MAXIM A., AYANA GHOSH, and SERGEI V. KALININ (2021). Physics Makes the Difference: Bayesian Optimization and Active Learning via Augmented Gaussian Process. arXiv: 2108.10280 [physics.comp-ph].

ZILBERSTEIN, SCHLOMO (1996). Using Anytime Algorithms in Intelligent Systems. *AI Magazine* 17(3):73–83.

ŽILINSKAS, ANTANAS G. (1975). Single-Step Bayesian Search Method for an Extremum of Functions of a Single Variable. *Kibernetika (Cybernetics)* 11(1):160–166.

ZITZLER, ECKART (1999). Evolutionary Algorithms for Multiobjective Optimization: Methods and Applications. Ph.D. thesis. Eidgenössische Technische Hochschule Zürich.

ZULUAGA, MARCELA, ANDREAS KRAUSE, and MARKUS PÜSCHEL (2016). ε-PAL: An Active Learning Approach to the Multi-Objective Optimization Problem. *Journal of Machine Learning Research* 17(104):1–32.

INDEX

Primary references and definitions are indicated in bold.

Printed in the United States
by Baker & Taylor Publisher Services